HUMAN NATURE AND HISTORY

HUMAN NATURE AND HISTORY

A Study of the Development of Liberal Political Thought

VOLUME TWO

Robert Denoon Cumming

The University of Chicago Press
Chicago and London

FOR MY FATHER

Library of Congress Catalog Card Number 68–29058
THE UNIVERSITY OF CHICAGO PRESS, CHICAGO 60637
THE UNIVERSITY OF CHICAGO PRESS, LTD., LONDON W.C.1

Published 1969. Printed in the United States of America

Contents

VOLUME ONE

VOLUME TWO

PART IV

INDIVIDUALISM

PART V

UTILITARIANISM

PART VI

LIBERALISM

Part IV

Individualism

10

The Role of the Individual

Each individual should keep to what is his own.—Cicero

Self-Interest

The characteristic problems of modern political theory are not "political" problems. They are not problems of the state itself but problems of the relation between the individual and the state. Even to translate *polis* as "state" obscures the change which took place when the individual emerged as the theoretically significant unit of political behavior, for this change involved not only a changed conception of the individual's human nature but also a changed conception of his *political* relations to other men.

It is true that Mill will find that his principle of individuality is illustrated by "the whole stream of Greek history," as a "series of examples of how often events on which the whole destiny of subsequent civilization turned were dependent on the personal character for good or evil of some one individual."[1] But whatever may have been the role of the individual in Greek history, he does not play any decisive role in Plato's or Aristotle's political theory. Cicero's *Republic* is the earliest surviving political theory which is largely composed of examples of how much depends on the personal character for good or evil of some one individual.

The changed conception of human nature which is usually correlated with the emergence of the individual in modern political theory is the conception that "human nature is essentially selfish, and that the effective motives on which a statesman must rely are egoistic"—as Sabine puts it in his *History of Political Theory*. This individualistic assumption Sabine detects "behind nearly everything that Machiavelli said about political policy." This individualistic assumption Sabine considers an anticipation of Hobbes: "When completed by a systematic psychology to explain and justify it, this phase of Machiavelli becomes the political philosophy of Hobbes."[2]

The changed conception of the "state," to which Machiavelli's assumption of *Universal Egoism* logically leads as a conclusion, is (in Sabine's interpretation) that of an *Omnipotent Legislator:* "If human individuals are by nature radically egoistic, the state and the force behind the law must be the only power that holds society together; moral obligations must in the end be derived from law and government." Here again Sabine finds an anticipation of Hobbes: "In this respect also it was Hobbes who gave a systematic statement of what Machiavelli suggested."[3] Sabine goes on to interpret Hobbes' systematic statement as the correlation of two historical tendencies which "have been among the most pervasive in modern times"—the assumption that "self-interest" is "the dominant motive in life" and "the increase of legal power."[4] Machiavelli and Hobbes are therefore to be regarded as the founders of modern political theory.

Machiavelli's political theory is not, however, an unsystematic psychology. It is an assessment of historical episodes which are fitted, in his most comprehensive work, to a cyclical theory of history that derives from Polybius. Nor is Hobbes giving a systematic statement of what Machiavelli suggested. How could he, when he asserts that his systematic psychology "excludes history?"[5]

Machiavelli's historical approach and Hobbes' psychological approach impose different treatments of the individual, his selfish interest, and his relation to the state. Sabine's readiness to overlook these differences can be explained by his preoccupation with the pervasive tendencies of modern times. Self-interest takes the form in Locke, as in Machiavelli and in Hobbes, of the individual's effort to preserve himself. But this effort becomes in Locke an effort on the part of the individual to acquire as "his own" (*proprium*) something which will preserve him; the individual acquires "property" by "mixing" the labor of his body and the work of his hands," which are "properly his," with some portion of external nature.[6] Since the primary function of the state's legal power in Locke is to enforce the recognition by others of the property which the individual has already acquired, and since "what portion" he has "carved to himself" is "easily seen," any detailed investigation of the selfish motives that lay behind his acquisitive action becomes superfluous.[7] The differences between Hobbes' and Machiavelli's handling of self-interest then become correspondingly unimportant in retrospect.

In their theories, however, no portion of external nature is delimited and reserved to the individual as "his own," where he can act simply with reference to his self-interest and without reference to other men. The problem posed by his self-interest is not the easily solved problem of securing public recognition by others of what is "easily seen" to be already his. A very different problem of public recognition is posed in the theories of Hobbes and Machiavelli. The lineaments of this problem, are obscured when their theories are assimilated in retrospect to the later individualistic tradition that begins with Locke. But the problem can be recovered by considering its treatment in an earlier individualistic tradition which emerges from the humanistic tradition we have explored in Part III. There we have already found that Cicero's adjustment of the relation between the internal and external poses a problem of recognition.[8] In this first chapter on the individualistic tradition, I shall explore the implications of this tradition for Machiavelli's and Hobbes' conceptions of the individual; in the next chapter I shall explore the implications of this tradition for their conceptions of the relation between the individual and the state; in the third chapter, I shall follow out the way Hobbes' conception of the individual and of his relation to the state is transformed when the individual acquires property in Locke's and later theories.

The New Method

Part Two began with Machiavelli's proclamation of a new method:

> I know many have written on this problem, and I fear it may be thought presumptuous on my part to write about it too, especially since I shall depart completely from the methods of others. I am concerned to write something of practical relevance for those who can understand, so it seems to me more appropriate to go directly to the actual truth of the matter (*verità effettuale della cosa*), instead of accepting something imaginary. For many have imagined republics and principalities which have never been seen or known to exist in reality.[9]

In tracing the derivation of this practical criterion of relevance as an historical criterion, we neglected the specific problem of effectiveness that Machiavelli is raising and the tradition that he is repudiating. The problem is "How the prince should act and rule in relation to his subjects and friends." The many who have written on this problem are authors of *On the Rule of Princes,* and their tradition is usually labeled *The Mirror of Princes* genre.[10]

Before we take up the specific problem itself, let us follow our usual interpretative procedure of adopting a retrospective point of view. Machiavelli's proclamation betrays his conviction that the tradition he is up against is overwhelmingly homogeneous, but he seems to have Plato's *Republic* particularly in mind. Thus we should try to recover the homogeneity this tradition had for Machiavelli by tracing its development back to Plato—or rather to revivals of Plato, for we have found that these revivals are as far back as we need go in tracing the development of modern political thought.

Polybius' revival of Plato and Cicero's revival of Plato have already been examined in Parts II and III as contributing to the development of two divergent traditions in modern political theory—one the tradition to which Machiavelli belongs where political problems are fitted for treatment to the context of a theory of history, and the other the tradition to which Hobbes belongs where they are fitted to the context of a theory of human nature. When I separated these two traditions in Part I, I warned that the development of political theory is not unilinear, nor can any single line of development be pulled entirely away from other lines and drawn out straight. The individual as Machiavelli conceives him (as well as the individual as Hobbes conceives him) is partly a product of the humanistic tradition. And some of the differences between Machiavelli's and Hobbes' conceptions of the individual, his self-interest, and his relation to the state, can be traced back to divergent lines of development within the humanistic tradition.

The first task, however, in locating Machiavelli's place in the history of political thought, is to determine how the humanistic and historicist traditions were woven together for him. Though his cyclical theory of history derives from Polybius, the history itself is largely Livy's, and Livy's criteria of relevance were not themselves historical. "What history offers above all else," Livy explained, "are examples," from which "you may select for yourself and your state what to imitate."[11] The exploitation of history as a "storehouse" of examples, the freedom with which these examples can be selected without reference to the actual sequence of historical evolution—these are characteristics of the traditional way in which history was drawn within a humanistic context.[12] Machiavelli retains this exemplarist conception of history to the extent that his procedure is to select examples for imitation. In dealing with his version of this exemplarist conception, the line of development we need to trace is one which we shall eventually find some justification for labeling *esthetic*, in order to separate it from the various strands which we have previously unraveled in the composition of the humanistic tradition.

This rather puzzling label will have to be clarified by a close examination of texts. So far I have used the labels "literary" and "poetic" widely and loosely. In sorting out in Part I the relations between the study of politics and "other studies," I described Mill's moralism as primarily "literary" or "poetic."[13] I have similarly labeled the moralism of Petrarch, who has brought us to the threshold of the history of modern classicism.[14] In my original survey of this history, I tried to take into account the primarily *esthetic* character of modern classicism by sketching a rough parallel between the history of classicism as a succession of stages in the way classic works of art are perceived, and the history of classicism in political theory. The sketch obtained some initial plausibility from the way Machiavelli begins his *Discourses on Livy* by being "astonished and distressed" by the discrepancy between his contemporaries' concern to imitate ancient works of art and their failure to imitate "the splendid works of virtue which history exhibits."[15] In this chapter we shall see that traditional exemplarism retains a certain esthetic relevance for Machiavelli, in spite of his rejection of the ideal prince of the *Mirror of Princes* genre.

The context into which Machiavelli weaves the examples he selects is itself historicist. Remember his explanation of the contemporary failure to imitate ancient works of virtue:

> This failure is due to . . . our not having real knowledge of history. . . . Most of those who read history take pleasure only in the variety of the different events which history relates, without ever thinking of imitation, considering that to do so is not just difficult but even impossible—as though the heavens, the sun, the elements, and men had varied and in their motion,

their order, their force, were become different from what they were in antiquity.[16]

His contemporaries are impressed only by the variety of different events—by their irreducibility to any theory. They read history only as a literary diversion. This is in a sense the spirit in which Livy wrote his history. "One of the rewards," Livy declared, "on which I am counting for my labors is diversion from the evils which our age has too long witnessed."[17] Machiavelli absorbs from Livy nostalgia for the good old days of the Roman Republic. This nostalgia might have continued for Machiavelli, too, merely a diversion from the evils that his own age had so long witnessed, for what he read in Livy was embedded in an account of Rome's decline: "with the lowering of moral standards (*labente disciplina*), let him [the reader] follow the decay in men's conduct, then a progressive sinking until the final plunge, as he reaches our own days, in which neither our vices nor their reform can be put up with."[18] But when Machiavelli selects examples from Livy's history, he moves them into the historicist context of Polybius' cyclical theory. With the prospect this theory holds out of an upturn, Machiavelli's nostalgia can become a longing for effective reform, instead of remaining as defeatist and futile as Livy's.[19] With "real knowledge of history" there is a real prospect of Italy's "returning to its [Roman] starting point."

The "motion," and the "order" which have not become different from what they were in antiquity is a cyclical historical sequence. But it is not exactly the historical sequence of forms of governments which Machiavelli transcribes from Polybius. The humanistic tradition encroaches on Machiavelli's reconstruction of this historical sequence so that he views it as a sequence of "motion" and "force" in which *men* have not become different in the long run from what they were in Antiquity. Polybius had transformed the unpredictable operations of fortune into a theory of history which rendered them predictable. Hence it is easy for Machiavelli to retrieve, in the context of this theory, the moralistic antithesis which had been fundamental to the humanistic tradition—the antithesis between virtue and fortune.[20] We can detect his conflation of the two traditions in one of his versions of the cyclical theory: the first phase is "virtue," which has as its effect a relatively stable government or state; this stability has in turn as its effect "ennervation" and "enfeeblement" (i.e., the opposite of virtue), which finally has as its effect political instability, until virtue again takes hold of political events and is temporarily effective.[21]

Otium and Negotium

The composition of the humanistic tradition must next be reexamined with particular attention to its recurrent individualistic phase when the antithesis reemerges between virtue and fortune. When we came across this phase before, we sidestepped it because it seemed so obviously an apolitical phase in which the moral requirements of reflection were set forth as incompatible with the circumstances of the active political life. We concentrated upon the other recurrent phase, which was illustrated by Cicero's *Republic,* when this antithesis between *otium* and *negotium* was surmounted and moral requirements were satisfied by political activity and by the institutional arrangements it could maintain in effect.

We now need to reconsider the relation between these two phases. The original vehicle for the recurring vacillation between them was the *figure* of Socrates, as we learned from Scipio's brief scholarly controversy with Tubero.[22] Socrates, on the one hand, brought philosophy down from the heavens to earth; on the other hand, he partici pated after his death in Plato's metaphysical return to the heavens. The martyrdom and death of Socrates was the original moment of crisis which reversed the descending movement from the heavenly to the terrestrial and initiated the ascending movement from the terrestrial to the heavenly. This reversal took on general significance in Plato's *Phaedo,* where philosophy itself became the reflection on the life that is really death, and this process of reflection continued in the *Dream of Scipio,* Augustine's *Confessions,* and in Petrarch's confessions to Saint Augustine. Once the *Dream* became separated from the rest of Cicero's *Republic,* we were dealing with an individual who is never less alone than when disengaged from active political relations. By the beginning of the quattrocento, humanism regained its political implications in Florence, and became again (at least for rhetorical purposes) the Ciceronian tradition of political humanism.[23] Humanists, however, continued to vacillate, and by Machiavelli's generation humanism was again, in the Florentine Academy, a literary tradition of Neoplatonic withdrawal from politics to enjoy the *otium* of reflection on philosophical texts.

This movement of withdrawal, in Machiavelli's view, was leaving political problems behind unsolved. At the beginning of the *Discourses* he has another explanation of the political ineffectiveness of his contemporaries besides their lack of "real knowledge of history." It is "the feeble state in which the world has been brought by the "education" [or "religion"] of today, especially as a result of the ennervating influence of the presiding moral ideal of *ozio*.[24] The movement of inner withdrawal and upward ascent, Machiavelli is able to pull back from by bringing to bear the "real knowledge of history" which he obtains from Polybius and which introduces a "motion" and an "order" that are historical. He is able to detach ancient figures and episodes from the hierarchial ordering of human aspiration from which they had gained their Neoplatonic, Augustinian, and Petrarchian significance. But insofar as Machiavelli's political theory is individualistic, insofar as he would restore the ancient virtue these figures and eposides once exemplified, he was also helped (as had been previous political humanists of the Italian Renaissance) by Cicero's *On Duties* where the virtue of the individual is ordered towards his relation to other men. Thus we can also use this classic to disentangle the individualistic tradition to which Machiavelli belongs from the ascending movement to which it was largely assimiliated in the *Dream*, in later Antiquity, in the Middle Ages, and in the Florentine Academy.

Before we take up the detail of Cicero's treatment of virtue, let us assign *On Duties* to its place in the development of the individualistic tradition. At the beginning of Part III, I began tracing the recurrent vacillation of the humanistic tradition as a horizontal movement of alternating moral retrenchment and external political expansion. This alternation was a feature of the development of the Cynic tradition out of the Socratic tradition, and of the Stoic tradition out of the Cynic tradition and into the humanistic tradition. The original horizontal movement can now be disentangled from the later ascending movement by taking apart the Neoplatonic and Augustinian formula *ab exterioribus ad interiora, ab inferioribus ad superiora*.[25] Neoplatonism and Augustinianism are transcendental philosophies in that the movement from the external to the internal is assimilated to the movement from the lower to the higher. But Stoicism seems to have been originally an immanentist moral philosophy in which the movement from the lower to the higher remains within the confines of the movement from the external to the internal. The moral elevation achieved by the Stoic philosopher was the elevation of his mind (*altitudo mentis*). There was nothing higher in the universe. No higher insight into the nature of the universe was needed beyond the insight into human nature provided by the mind of the philosopher when he inwardly fortifies himself against the onslaughts of fortune—of external circumstances.

Morals and Politics

When I stress the moralistic character of the humanistic tradition, even in its recurrent phase of external political expansion, I am not merely anticipating Machiavelli's verdict, which identifies this tradition as an ineffective treatment of "How the prince should act and rule in relation to his subjects and friends." I am also commenting on the history of the humanistic tradition. In the last chapter we watched the humanistic tradition become a classical tradition in which classics are revived as texts to be reflected upon. The history of humanism is a succession of revivals. But the reviving betrays an unbalanced rhythm. Successive writers' political texts (e.g., Cicero's *Republic*) lose their influence and disappear, while their moral texts (e.g., Cicero's *On Duties*) survive and continue to influence later treatments of political as well as of moral problems. Thus modern times will usually assume that Stoicism is a distinctively moral tradition. But we need not wait until modern times for this assumption. In his *Laws* Cicero has his learned friend and publisher Atticus express surprise at being told that Stoics had ever written political treatises.[26] The *Republic* written by Zeno, the founder of Stoicism does not survive. The *Republic* written by Panaetius who imported Stoicism into Rome does not survive, but Cicero's *On Duties* reproduces Panaetius' moral treatise *On Duty*. Cicero's own *Republic* in turn does not survive indefinitely the fall of Rome and Augustine's refutation, but Cicero's *On Duties* does, even though it loses most of its political implications for the early Middle Ages, partly as a result of its having been recast in the form of St. Ambrose's *On the Duties of Priests*.[27]

This unbalanced rhythm consolidates an increasingly moralistic context for the later treatment of political problems. Concern with the solution of the individual's moral problems—and hence the study of ancient moral texts—continues and is even heightened by the fall of a state and the disappearance of "public things." The renewal of concern with public problems that accompanies the later rise and expansion of another state takes the obvious form of the revival of an earlier political theory. (I began with the obvious, offering as a textual illustration the revival of Plato's *Republic* that is Cicero's *Republic*.) But the renewal of concern with public problems can take another less obvious form—the expansion of the uninterrupted moral tradition into a treatment of political problems. (My textual illustration has been the political implications Stoicism acquires with Cicero's Stoic revision in his *Republic* of the political theory of Plato's *Republic*.) The third step is to deal with the unbalanced rhythm itself, as the increasing reinforcement of the movement *ab exterioribus ad interiora*. There is not only the cumulative shifting, which was traced in the previous chapter, away from political problems to the individual's moral problems, but also a cumulative shifting to an individualistic and moralistic treatment of political problems themselves. My textual illustration will be the further shift in Cicero's point of view that takes place between his *Republic* and his *On Duties*.

The conflation of Stoicism with Platonism in Cicero's *Republic* has already illustrated, when this *Republic* was compared with Plato's *Republic*, a certain shift to an individualistic and moralistic approach. What I found in Cicero's *Republic* was a theory of human nature in which the requirements for the treatment of political problems were construed as moral obligations binding on the individual. The further shift to be illustrated by *On Duties* is a further moralization of the criteria for political conduct.

Before presenting the textual evidence, I have offered a schematic presentation in the hope that the evidence will be more readily construed as evidence that the history of political theory is not the history of political theory. It is, rather, the history of political theory in its relation to "other studies." If, moreover, we are to deal eventually with the development of liberal political theory, the most relevant other study is moral theory. In Antiquity itself the continuity of the development of political theory can be traced less easily by reference to political theories (most of which are lost or fragmentary—e.g., Cicero's *Republic*) than by reference to their psychological and moral context. In retrospect at least, the continuous tradition is an individualistic moral theory, which under favorable public circumstances expands its scope (e.g., with "the easy flow" of Cicero's eloquence) to take in problems of political action.[28] It then becomes (e.g., in Cicero's *Republic*) a theory of virtue in which justice "looks outside of oneself." Under depressing public circumstances the theory contracts again into a theory of the individual's moral retrenchment where what one is left with as "one's own" is a virtue which is "silent and enclosed within oneself." The "fist" expands and contracts.[29]

Let us first consider the place in this tradition of *On Duties.* Let us start again with what seems to be obvious: *On Duties* is not a political theory in the sense that Cicero's *Republic* is. It is a moral theory. Cicero is addressing his son, Marcus, who was in Athens supposedly to study philosophy. Regretably the young man was finding less creditable pursuits more congenial. Because Cicero is out of politics, he is able to find time to assume the appropriate paternal role. Thus the immediate setting of *On Duties* is Cicero's moral responsibility for his son, or rather his son's moral responsibility to act like his father's son.[30] Cicero's *Republic* began with the tradition established by the individual statesman who had assumed responsibility for the Roman state.[31] The list, to which the reader was intended to add Cicero's name, probably began with Romulus as the prototype of Roman statesman. What it provided philosophically was a succession of living refutations of the refusal of a Socrates to participate in the politics of any actual state. *On Duties,* however, begins with the background of the tradition in moral philosophy which the son needs to place Cicero as a philosopher. Cicero is again entering a tradition. He announces that he is a follower of Socrates and Plato. But he imposes a different interpretation on the Socratic tradition than he did in the *Republic.* We shall be better prepared to gauge the shift that has taken place in Cicero's point of view since he wrote the *Republic* if we start again (as we did in interpreting Cicero's *Republic*) with this Socratic tradition. By now we realize that Cicero's shift itself is in some measure traditional.

Memorabilia

What survives as a tradition, or is revived as precedent, is largely a matter of what men want to be reminded of. "Mankind," Mill reminds us in expounding his principle of individuality, "can hardly be too often reminded that there was once a man called Socrates, between whom and the legal authorities and public opinion of his time there took place a memorable collision."[32] We were reminded of this collision in Cicero's *Republic*; we will be reminded of it again in *On Duties*. We need to realize how frequently these reminders occur and how difficult it is to separate the actual memorableness of the original collision from the *memorabilia* which would remind us. Their frequency is a function of the transformation of the humanistic tradition into an individualistic tradition.

"This man," Mill continues, "has been handed down to us by those who best knew both him and the age as the most virtuous man in it; while we know him as the head and prototype of all subsequent teachers of virtue." Socrates is an example for Mill of how the whole destiny of subsequent civilization was dependent on the character of some one individual. Furthermore, in Mill's reminder, as in many of the earlier reminders, there is hardly any more crucial evidence of Socrates' virtue than the collision itself. In Plato's *Crito* the political collision was somewhat deflected by Socrates' accepting the legal authority of the state and refusing to go into exile. The moral collision with public opinion remained, and it was shaped into a broader and blunter antithesis in the anecdotes told of Diogenes, the reputed founder of Cynicism, who challenged all authority because he "preferred liberty to all else."[33]

Cynicism may in fact have been the longest, most continuous philosophical tradition in Antiquity. "Even before Heracles . . . there were those who practiced this philosophy, for it seems to be in some fashion a universal philosophy and the most natural"—this was Julian the Apostate's retrospect on Cynicism.[34] Julian's apostacy contributed to the last of the classical renaissances of Antiquity. What Julian sought was a revival of the traditional Cynicism of Socrates and Diogenes, which he felt was very different from that of the "uncultured Cynics" of his own period, who could hardly be distinguished from "solitaries" (i.e., Christian monks). (Revivals of Cynicism were recurrent in Antiquity, until at last the moral duties of the solitary individual did, in fact, become virtually indistinguishable from the monastic "duties of priests.") Although the Cynicism that the Apostate would revive is "cultured," he explains that "it does not require any special study, only that we should listen to the Delphic God, when he enjoins, 'Know Thyself' and 'Alter the Currency.' "[35] Diogenes' father, a banker, had debased the currency. In other words, Diogenes was to achieve Socratic self-knowledge by discounting and driving out of circulation the conformist values which public opinion accepts as current, legal tender. Socrates had equipped himself with a mother who was a midwife so that he could undertake his philosophic mission of bringing men to self-knowledge. Diogenes' banker father was a further item of equipment which weaves an additional link to the perennial model of the philosopher.

In reviving the cultured Cynicism of Socrates and Diogenes, Julian the Apostate is conceiving culture as classical—as the imitation of a memorable ancient model. This conception of culture we traced back to the elucidation (which the founder of Stoicism received) of the original Delphic injunction to Socrates, "Know Thyself." Zeno was enjoined by Delphi to "Take on the Color of the Dead," which he construed as meaning "Study the Ancients."[36] The Apostate's qualification that no special study is required indicates that the process of imitation was primarily the recollection of a moral role. Stoicism was linked up with Cynicism by Zeno's searching for a man whom he could take as a Socratic model for the moral role which he had found by studying Xenophon's *Memorabilia*.[37] Xenophon's title itself probably belongs to what was, or was becoming, a traditional genre, and in the *Memorabilia* Socrates himself is presented as a student of the ancients. "I study," he explains, "the treasure the wise men of old have left us in their writings . . . and make excerpts."[38] Xenophon's Socrates is explaining the procedure of composing *memorabilia* which provide us with the exemplary figures and anecdotes I have been reciting.

Socrates' successor—the Cynic or the Stoic who "plays the Cynic"—entrenches himself in the inner fortress of his soul by resisting the influence of external circumstances on his thinking. These he assigns to the sphere of fortune. He thereby deprives us of any literal reference to his specific circumstances that would enable us to segregate him in his own period as a way of pinning down the implications of his thought. It is often impossible to date the exemplary anecdotes I have been reciting, or to punctuate the development of specific features of the Cynic tradition, by correlating the moments of specific entrenchment with such political misfortunes as the fall of a specific state. Taking on the color of the dead as a means to self-knowledge consecrates the typological at the expense of the topical: when an individual plays the cultured Cynic, he is finding his place in the past and debasing whatever happens to be publicly current in his own period. When he adopts an exemplary individual from another period as his model, his virtuous indifference to circumstances becomes virtuous resistance to the changes in circumstances that have taken place since the earlier period. His inner fortress is the consolidation at once of his individualism and his traditionalism, and the individualistic tradition which is consolidated will be able to outlast future changes in circumstances and assist the individual to emerge and play a role in modern thought.

EXILE

Because his father had debased the currency, Diogenes had to go into exile. He was reproached for his exile, as we might expect from the disparity between his behavior and that of the prototype Socrates. But Diogenes offers the counter-claim, "It was by my exile that I became a philosopher."[39] For once, a reference to external, political circumstances enjoys a certain philosophical cogency: the subject-matter of modern politcal philosophy, as it begins to take shape in the Hellenistic Period, is not the *polis* or its politics, but the relation between philosophy and politics. Successive exiles add to the tension of this relationship until finally the individual realizes he belongs, not to any state, but to a philosophical tradition of alienation from the state. The problem then of political philosophy, whenever it is revived, is the problem of the relation between the individual and the state.

Hobbes was not "the first of all who fled."[40] Exiles contribute a disproportionate number of the political philosophers whom we have to take into account in dealing with the origins of modern political thought: Polybius, Cicero, Augustine, Petrarch, Machiavelli, Hobbes, Locke. Even Mill will collide with public opinion, because of his ininvolvement with another man's wife, and eventually he will withdraw with her to the seclusion of Avignon, where Petrarch had been in exile with Laura.

Of course Augustine was only figuratively an exile. Life itself was an exile to him.[41] But then the founder of this tradition of exile, Diogenes, became a *figura* and led a legendary life. It does not matter. By now we have realized that the continuity of the emerging individualistic tradition is less obviously the continuity of external circumstances than a typological continuity in which external circumstances, including political relations (and even the exile's lack of political relations), are transformed to provide metaphorical renderings for the condition of an individual's soul. When the individual does return to politics, it is with a sense of his role as an individual, as well as with criteria of personal relevance. He arrives with an obligation to solve political problems as if they were metaphorical renderings of moral problems.

On Duties belongs to this tradition of exile and return. Cicero has been going into exile. Because he has changed his mind, he has to write his son *On Duties*. He is not going into exile after all. He has an obligation to return to politics, and so can no longer expect to talk things over with his son in Athens. *On Duties* is the "voice" of paternal admonition, which is journeying on to Greece, while Cicero returns to Rome.[42] Thus Cicero will still be preoccupied with politics in *On Duties*, but as an individual whom he will view in a different way than he did in the *Republic*, and in a different relation to the state.

In *On Duties* more than one phase is consolidated in the development of individualism into a classical tradition. It is a revival of Panaetius' theory of duty, which was itself a revival of earlier Greek theories.[43] Let us compare Cicero's final consolidation with the structure which we examined earlier as the outcome of the humanistic tradition: "All forms of knowledge which are relevant to human life [*ad humanitatem pertinent*] have a common bond and mutual interrelations holding them together."[44] This indifference towards differences of subject matters contributed to the formation of the humanistic context. But in my interpretation I tried to rescue humanism from the usual imputation, in histories of thought, of being the odds and ends of classicism—a ragbag. Confronted with its indifference towards differences of subject-matter, I sorted out in its composition various strands of argument. The modern historian prefers to correlate differences between successive philosophies with differences between successive circumstances. But humanism requires interpretation as a tradition: involved in its formation is virtuous indifference towards differences between circumstances as well as indifference towards differences between philosophies, except when a philosophy undermines virtue—as does Epicureanism—by exposing minds to the influence of circumstances.

The indifference of the individual finds its traditional political formulation in the alienation of the exile. But there is also a positive obligation that sustains his indifference towards all of the differences which the modern historian cherishes. It is summed up by the criterion of relevance which Cicero cites in *On Duties,* and which had been conveyed from Greek into Latin by Panaetius' friend, the poet Terence—"*homo sum nil humanum alienum puto.*"[45] This criterion can be interpreted as liberating the humanistic study of the ancients from the specific requirements of the particular subject-matters of the particular ancient philosophies which were absorbed by the tradition, as well as from the specific requirements of the particular times and countries when these philosophies were written.

The Individual as Personality

Liberation from all these requirements would not itself articulate a context. But from this undifferentiated background of humanistic culture a new differentiated structure emerges. The individual becomes responsible for his "*cultura animi.*" He is obliged (to anticipate Mill's later phrase) to engage in "self-culture" in order to obtain criteria of personal relevance. The "internal culture of the individual" can become an obligation (as we already know from Mill's own case) only when differences between individuals are acknowledged.[46] *On Duties* confers on these differences, and thereby on the individuality of the individual himself, a moral relevance which had not originally been accorded by the Stoic tradition:

> It is important to understand that each of us has been assigned by nature two roles [*personae*]. One of these is common to all men in that we all share in reason and in that preeminence by which we are superior to the animals and from which all rectitude [*honestum*] and propriety [*decorum*] derive, and the rational procedure for discovering what our duty is. The other role is assigned to each individual. . . . There are countless . . . differences between men's natures and characters but these differences are not blameworthy as such. Each individual should keep to what is his own, providing his particular characteristics are not vicious but really his own [*propria*]. In this way propriety . . . may be more readily maintained.[47]

This conception of propriety can be distinguished as the *esthetic* strand in the composition of the humanistic tradition. The label is warranted by the source Cicero attributes to the term:

> Its ordinary meaning can be determined from its use as a poetic criterion. Poets respect propriety when the actions and words of each of their individual characters are approprite to his role.[48]

Further warrant for the label is the analogy with physical perception with which Cicero clarifies the moral implications of propriety:

> As physical beauty—the appropriate structure of the body—affects our vision and gives us visual satisfaction, inasmuch as all the parts of the body gracefully harmonize (*consentiunt*), so analogically that propriety which is visibly displayed by our life (*elucet in vita*) affects the judgment of those with whom we live and elicits their approval, because of the order, the consistency, and self-control of our every word and action.[49]

The way this esthetic strand is woven in *On Duties* into the humanistic tradition will involve a certain reweaving of the strands we have already distinguished in Cicero's *Republic*—of the cosmological and rhetorical strands, as well as of the moral and the political strands. To trace this reweaving is to discover that the more modern adjustment in *On Duties* of the relation between the individual and the state is a more moralistic adjustment of the relation between politics and "other studies." Let us begin with the conception of *personality* which is involved in the definition of propriety. *Persona* originally referred to the "mask" worn by an actor; by extension it has come to mean "role" or "character."[50] When I dealt with the *dramatis personae* of Cicero's *Republic*, I considered the implications of the change in cast from Plato's *Republic*, and yet tried to bring out the extent to which their Roman "characters" had been formed by Greek culture, so that the Romans, who had no ancestral culture comparable to the legends of the Greeks, might acquire "ancestors" they could become "worthy of."[51] To this extent the Romans acquired not only their roles as Romans but even their sense of role, less from "nature" (as Panaetius has just alleged) than from their Greek culture (which Panaetius himself helped render relevant to Romans).

In his *Republic* Cicero was uncertain as to his appropriate role. He had inherited no ancestral role, and we regarded him as establishing the claims of a *homo novus* to play a role by advancing a Greek theory of human nature in which it was natural for a man to play a role. The *imagines* of real ancestors on the walls then became dispensable. The ideal models which had been the prototypes for human conduct in

Plato had been transcendental rather than human, but Cicero could adopt the theory of human nature which was the Stoic outcome of the Cynic search for a man, since this search had been prompted by the loss of the "political" role which the Greek πόλις had originally assigned to a man as a πολίτης, and the only role that was left to be played was the moral role assigned him as a man.[52]

In writing *On Duties* Cicero feels that he has lost his political role—the role his theory of human nature had assigned him in his *Republic*. But the novelty of the conception of man in *On Duties* is that man has a role, not only as a man to whom nothing human is alien, but also as a particular individual who is *personally* different from other men. Probably Panaetius as well as Cicero was convinced that there are "countless . . . differences between men's natures and characters" and that these differences are relevant to man's moral obligations, but it is Cicero who is so impressed with these individual differences that he has changed Panaetius' title *On Duty* to *On Duties*.

Moral Order

Since the continuity of the individualistic tradition in political theory is more readily traceable as a moral tradition, it will be necessary in this section to consider the way the introduction of *propriety* as an esthetic criterion alters the fabric of this moral tradition, before we can consider in the next section its political implications. To clarify the individual's distinctively individual role, Panaetius has introduced *propriety* as a second criterion of moral action which will supplement the traditional Stoic criterion of *rectitude*. Traditionally the wise man's actual actions were morally irrelevant to the extent that their consequences were beyond the scope of his intentions and could therefore be consigned to the external realm of fortune. But his moral scope is extended in *On Duties*: the individual's intentions reach their fulfillment in actual actions which exhibit their appropriateness to his moral nature as a particular individual. Furthermore, nature's assignment of an additional role to man is the assignment of an additional function to reason. Traditionally the *rectitude* of the wise man's intention was indistinguishable in its direction from his wisdom—his rational insight into the order of universal nature. But in *On Duties*, "knowledge of nature, is as it were, maimed and incomplete, if no actual actions are its consequences."[53] Thus the wise man becomes a man of action, and reason acquires the practical function of orienting his actions. The comparable order which they should exhibit is *propriety*.

This virtue in turn has a double function which illustrates a readjustment in the "order" that is at stake in a moral action, and therefore a corresponding reshuffling of the relations between Stoicism and the traditions that contribute to its formation and recurrent reformation—Cynicism and Platonism. The inner moral order, which was established in Stoicism by rational insight into the order of the universe, was the wise man's establishment of absolute control over his passions. But insofar as this inner moral order can be visibly expressed by the wise man's actions, his self-control has the further function, in the guise of *propriety*, of bringing him into relation with other men. This visibly expressed order is the *decorum* which the Cynics refused to display when they refused to conform to public opinion—much to the embarrassment of Stoics, when they tried to "play the Cynic." At any rate, when Zeno tried, he seems to have been embarrassed, and may have founded Stoicism because he was reluctant to get any closer to the Cynic movement than its "tail."[54]

The explicit importation of the moral virtue of *propriety* into the Stoic tradition is probably attributable to Panaetius. If its importation is a repudiation of Cynicism, it is also a revival of Plato's definition of self-control as "like a harmony," and as "a sort of order (κόσμος) and restraint of passions and desires."[55] Without acknowledging that it is Plato's, Cicero revises the definition. In his translation, *propriety* lends "some sort of visible order to one's life (*quasi quidam ornatus vitae*).[56] Plato was vague as to the sort of order that is in question because he was beginning an analysis which would become more definite only as he worked out the details of his tripartite analogy between the harmonious internal structure of the mind and the harmonious internal structure of the state. But Cicero, as we saw in his *Republic*, cannot follow Plato in this ensuing analysis, since Plato's tripartite analogy is incompatible with Cicero's Stoic dualism. In his *Republic*, Cicero revised Plato's definition so that self-control became a practical means whereby the statesman exercised external political control in establishing *concordia ordinum*.[57] Approximately the same readjustment occurs with Cicero's revision in *On Duties* of the implications of

Plato's definition. Such readjustments in the relation between the internal and the external have been pivotal in our interpretation of the development of political thought ever since we discovered that they determined for John Stuart Mill the relation between morals and politics.[58] Let us therefore be clear as to what is involved in Cicero's readjustment of Plato's adjustment. In Plato's *Republic*, the ring of Gyges was put on the finger of the ideally virtuous man, so that he might remain invisible to others. He was thereby restricted to harmonizing and ordering his actions by reference to what was really his own—the inner requirements of his own mind, regardless of whether or not his actions were recognized to be virtuous by others.[59] Although the *ornatus* of Cicero's *ornatus vitae* translates Plato's term for "order," this vague internal order of the individual's mind takes on more definite implications for Cicero only as it becomes externalized in the individual's "life" as the setting in which he orders his relations with other men.[60] Thus the requirements which had remained inner in Plato will be externalized in Cicero. At the same time (as I have already anticipated), their externalization will pull Plato's analysis of the mind back from the direction that will be taken by the transcendental movement of Neoplatonism.[61] This was the movement which we traced in the last chapter when we followed out the later history of Cicero's redefinition of Platonic self-control as instituting a *concordia ordinum* and arrived at the *tranquillitas ordinis* of Augustine's universe.[62] The order that prevails with Cicero's translation is not the ascending movement of a hierarchial cosmology, but an ordering of the actions of an individual whose mind animates his relations with other men.

Visible Order

This reorientation of the analysis of moral virtue, and the attendant reshuffling of the relation between Stoicism and Platonism, are both illustrated by the treatment in *On Duties* of the Stoic virtue of *rectitude*, even before the Platonic virtue of self-control is treated as *propriety*. At the beginning of the analysis in *On Duties*, Plato's four cardinal virtues are outlined as parts of *rectitude*. Thus the moral subject-matter of *On Duties* is initially Stoic. But Cicero's treatment of this subject-matter continues with a quotation from Plato: "Here, son Marcus, you perceive the very outline (*forma*) and as it were the appearance of *rectitude,* 'which could she be perceived with the eyes would attract,' as Plato says, 'an overwhelming love of wisdom.' "[63] Cicero has probably left his own mark as translator. The term "*forma*" has crept in. It may illustrate the esthetic transformation that the ideal form, as conceived by Plato, is undergoing in *On Duties.* This is a possibility we shall consider in a moment. But "forma" also refers to the "outline" Cicero has just given. This reference is a professorial touch which prepares us for the transformation of the Stoic and Platonic tradition into a literary tradition in which *On Duties* will become a textbook, in spite of (or is it because of?) Cicero's concern to prepare his son to meet not the requirements of philosophy so much as the obligations of real life.

If Marcus had not preferred other amorous attractions in Athens to philosophy, he might have perceived that his father's quotation is the conflation of Stoicism and Platonism. Cicero is distorting Stoicism by quoting Plato, but his quotation itself is a Stoic distortion of Plato. In the first place it was with reference, not to *rectitude,* but to wisdom itself that Plato had said in the *Phaedrus* that "it would attract an overwhelming love, if as clear an image of it were available to sight [as we have of beauty]."[64] Cicero's misquotation is dictated by the disappearance in traditional Stoicism of the distinction between moral *rectitude* and wisdom and by the conception of wisdom that went with the Stoic materialistic epistemology. Love of wisdom for Plato was a love of ideal forms as distinguished from visible forms, and his comparison between the love of wisdom and the love of beauty presupposes a contrast between the attraction of a beauty which is visible to the senses and the attraction of a transcendent ideal order which is not visible. This distinction would have become weakened by the materialistic Stoic epistemology, which discarded the Platonic theory of ideas and derived knowledge of nature not from ideal prototypes but from the senses. The weakening of this distinction helps account for Panaetius' "enthusiasm" for astronomy, to which Scipio alluded in the *Republic,* and for the ideal significance the visible astronomical order of the universe acquired in Scipio's dream.[65] In the *Phaedrus,* from which Cicero borrowed in the dream as well as here in *On Duties,* the eventual satisfaction of the love of wisdom was described as the return of the mind from the realm of the visible to the realm of ideas. Stoic materialism could also have stayed Panaetius' hand here in his borrowing from Plato; Panaetius discredited, along with the theory of ideal forms, the prospect of the mind's immortality, which Cicero entertains in the dream.

Panaetius nonetheless continued, according to Cicero, to "revere" Plato as the "Homer of philosophers."[66] The transcendental orientation of Plato's philosophy having been abandoned, Panaetius is left with the Plato who is a poet as well as a moralist. This poetic Plato will become an indispensable inspiration for the modern classical tradition. The classicism which in Petrarch and the Renaissance was almost indiscriminately moralistic and poetic, will later become almost indiscriminately moralistic and esthetic. When epistemological issues are sharpened in the seventeenth and eighteenth centuries, moral phenomena will be treated as perceptions, and moral perceptions as comparable to esthetic perceptions. The actual vision of an ideal order, for which Plato could only sigh in the *Phaedrus,* becomes available in *On Duties,* where this order is visible not only in the physical universe but also in human conduct:

> As this beauty is found in the Shape and Form of corporeal things, so also is there analogous to it a Beauty of another kind, an Order, a Symmetry and Comeliness in the moral world. . . . This moral beauty was known to the ancients by the name of *honestum.*[67]

Just as Machiavelli refers without historical discrimination to "ancient virtue," so Bishop Berkeley is here attributing to "the ancients" generally the Stoic conception of *rectitude,* which he is identifying with the *moral beauty* it came to display as the result of Panaetius' conception of *propriety* as an ordering principle for men's actions. The enduring influence of Panaetius' Platonizing Stoicism, as represented by Cicero's *On Duties,* is further suggested by the widespread use of the Latin term *decorum* (as well as of its translation *propriety*) in British moral and esthetic theory. Panaetius, with Plato's assistance, softens the moral austerity of Stoic rationalism, so that (in the phraseology of Cicero's translation from Plato) "the appearance of moral *rectitude*" can be perceived. Thus *decorum* in *On Duties "appareat cum specie quadam liberali"*—in the "bearing and manner that make a gentleman."[68] This liberalized Stoicism may not have succeeded in making Marcus a gentleman, but it will provide English youth with a certain polish (*quidam ornatus vitae*). He should not, according to

Locke, "have any system of ethics put into his hand, till he can read Tully's *Offices*, not as a school-boy to learn Latin, but as one that would be informed in the principles and precepts of virtue, for the conduct of his life."[69]

This moral tradition will culminate in the analysis of *propriety* undertaken by Adam Smith, who will follow Cicero as an historian of philosophy in assuming the homogeneity of the classical tradition. The criterion for moral conduct which Smith attributes to the Ancients generally (excepting the Epicureans, of course) is the one found in *On Duties*: "According to Plato, to Aristotle, and to Zeno, virtue consists of propriety of conduct."[70] Later we shall see that this theory of *propriety* will eventually be undermined by the change in the sense of what is the individual's *own* that accompanies the development of a utilitarian theory of *property* in Locke, Hume, and Smith.[71]

Political Order

We do not need to wait for modern times to locate the beginning of this utilitarian tradition. We need only go on from the discussion of the *honestum* in the first book of *On Duties* to the discussion of the *utile* in the second book. Although Panaetius departs in the first book from the Stoic tradition by emphasizing that what is morally right [*honestum*] is also esthetically attractive, in that it appears *appropriate* to others, this criterion of *propriety* still refers to the mind and character of the individual himself. Even though his moral scope has been extended, he should still "keep to what is *his own*."[72] It is his own inner moral self-control which is displayed publicly as *propriety*. But a supplementary analysis, which is absent from traditional Stoicism, then becomes possible of the perception by others of the moral character which his actions exhibit. This analysis, which is provided by the second book's discussion of the *utile* (i.e., of what is in the individual's self-interest), is a treatment of the problem of exercising control over others. "The chief function of virtue" in the second book is "to conciliate the minds of men and secure their support for one's interests."[73] The way in which such support can be secured is investigated in terms of "the various causes which induce men to subject themselves to the control and power of another man."[74] An investigation so conceived comes close to the problem of political control as it will be formulated in Machiavelli. His solution to this problem will be clearer once we have examined the way Cicero handles the esthetic criterion of *propriety*.

The problem of political control in Cicero's *Republic* was the problem of how the statesman, by exercising moral control over himself, also exercised political control over others. In *On Duties*, too, the Platonic conception of the harmonious order of a self-controlled mind is externalized in that the appropriateness of this order is displayed in actions and is recognizable by other men. In carrying out this externalization, Cicero takes advantage of the fact that *propriety* had been applied in the rhetorical tradition as a criterion of persuasiveness. It had been so applied to the construction of a speech in Aristotle's *Rhetoric*.[75] We are prepared for its rhetorical application in *On Duties* both by the way the *cosmos* became a universe of discourse in Cicero's major rhetorical work, and by the way in which self-control became a means of political control in Cicero's *Republic*, where he worked an allusion to the speaking "voice" into the Platonic phraseology of his comparison of class harmony with musical harmony.[76] The statesman in the *Republic* needed the virtue of eloquence so as "to reveal with easily flowing speech what is concealed in his mind and thus control the people."

This rhetorical revelation not only solved the problem of political control in Cicero's *Republic*, but also complicated it. Once the Platonic distinction between internal and external had been bridged, the relation between the statesman and the state had to be approached not only from the side of the statesman's moral and rhetorical role but also from the side of the state, which had to respond to his eloquence and recognize the moral role he was playing by according him glory.[77] It is this relation which has again to be explored from both sides in *On Duties*. Where the first book treats the problem of self-control in terms of the appropriateness to the individual's own moral character of the role he performs in relation to others, the second book treats the problem of controlling others in terms largely of the individual's "glory," which is the primary psychological inducement that operates when men "subject themselves to the control and authority of another man."[78] It is by cultivating rhetorically the persuasive effects of his *personality* that the individual can "conciliate the minds of men and secure their support."[79]

The second book's problem of exercising political control is attached to the first book's problem of exercising self-control by lending political implications to the traditional Socratic and Cynic moral recipe, "The short-cut to glory is to *really* be [morally] what is one's interest [politically] to *appear* to be to others."[80] The attachment illustrates Panaetius' characteristic transition beyond traditional Stoicism. Traditionally Stoic philosophers had restricted themselves to the private educational role of moral exhortation. Even the philosopher's playing this private role Panaetius describes in rhetorical fashion as the communication of what he has in mind to other men. What in traditional Stoicism had been concern with the integrity of the individual's moral character becomes in Panaetius concern with the part played by moral character in the process of communication. The philosopher should be careful, for example, "lest his conversation expose any defects in his moral character."[81]

Politics and Vision

Panaetius as a Greek could only play a private educational role in relation to Scipio, but his philosophy was the education of a Scipio for a public role. The prospect this philosophy held out of cultivating rhetorically the persuasive effects of one's "personality," Cicero must have found congenial. *On Duties* itself blends Cicero's own private and public roles: philosophical and moral considerations merge with rhetorical and political considerations; Panaetius' philosophy of duty is presented in the form of a moral exhortation which Cicero is addressing to his wayward son, yet this moral exhortation begins with Cicero's drawing his son's attention to his public orations, as well as to his earlier philosophical works. No previous philosopher or orator, Cicero points out to Marcus, had effectively played each other's role.[82]

Marcus' *personal* conduct did not display that sense of duty which was to be expected of his father's son. In the second book Cicero accordingly interrupts his exposition of Panaetius' philosophy of duty in order to address his son. But when he has repeated that "the crucial rule" for obtaining glory is that the individual should really be himself what he would appear to be to other men, it is to remind his son of their point of view:

> Whatever young man finds himself in the public gaze, either because he has inherited a reputation from his father (as you have, I think, my dear Marcus), or because of accidental circumstances, then the eyes of all men are turned towards him, his actions and his mode of life are a matter of knowledge, and he is, as it were, surrounded by a dazzling light, so that nothing he says or does can remain concealed.[83]

Cicero's appeal as a father to his son lends itself to comparison with the exhortation of Scipio's grandfather in the *Republic.* But reconsider first the tradition of luminaries that lies in the background of this exhortation. The search for "a man," which Diogenes had initiated unsuccessfully when he lit his lamp in a dark world, Cicero continued until he found in Scipio a luminous mind which qualified him for the role of the ideal statesman, who "should be assigned almost no other role and duty besides this single one, which includes all the others, of never relaxing his effort at self-improvement and self-examination, or urging others to imitate him, and of holding himself up—by means of the the luminousness of his mind and life—as a mirror for his fellow-citizens."[84] In Scipio's dream, his grandfather therefore exhorted him "to display to your fatherland the light of your mind, of your character, and of your wisdom."[85] The exhortation was reinforced by an analogy between this illuminating role in the state of the statesman (as an embodiment of the Platonic idea of the good) and the illuminating role in the universe of the sun (which had been the embodiment in Plato of the idea of the good).[86] The *cosmos* became a temple, and the religious mysticism of Macrobius' version of the dream will help set the tone of some medieval *Mirrors of Princes.* But Cicero in *On Duties* is transcribing Panaetius who rejected the mind's immortal destiny. And the shift of emphasis in the first book of *On Duties* to the *personal* characteristics of the statesman as a particular individual will encourage concentration by humanistic writers of *Mirrors of Princes* during the Renaissance on the particular qualifications of a prince for his position in the actual state, rather than on his divinely appointed destiny in the larger state of the medieval tradition—the universe.

The further shift of emphasis in the second book of *On Duties* enables us to place Machiavelli's *Prince* in relation to this humanistic tradition. The exhortation in the first book to display an exemplary moral character, although more sober than the mysticism of Scipio's dream, is still consistent with the moral point of view adopted in the dream. But Cicero is adopting a different point of view when he addresses his son in the second book. Not only does the path to virtue and glory no longer point to the heavens, but the source of illumination is also no longer initially the individual's own mind and moral character. It is the limelight of publicity that is focused on Marcus because of his position as his father's son. The initial visual situation is one in which "the eyes of all men are turned towards him," and this visual situation takes precedence over the wisdom that the individual's moral character will then bring to men.

According to Cicero, Panaetius was in agreement with Socrates as well as with the Stoic tradition in arguing that there could be no real conflict between what is *morally right* and what is in the individual's self-interest.[87] But Socrates in Plato's *Republic* had pursued this argument in terms of the requirements of the individual's own mind as his real self,[88] while Panaetius has treated *self-interest* in terms of the individual's relation to others and of their reactions to his actions. Thus Panaetius has to admit that self-interest does sometimes appear to conflict with what is *morally right*. Having discussed the question of what is *morally right* and then the question of *self-interest*, it was up to Panaetius to show that no real conflict can arise when these criteria are conjointly applied to determine how the individual should act. Panaetius, according to Cicero, announced that he would discuss this third question, and Cicero is "amazed that he never did so," despite the fact that "he was still alive thirty years after the publication of the previous books" in which he had discussed the previous questions.[89] I shall examine in the next chapter Cicero's not very convincing effort in the third book of *On Duties* to supply this discussion as he claims, "single-handedly."[90] What is pertinent now is that the inadequacy of Cicero's effort leaves in rather precarious balance the relationship between morally right self-control, as treated in the first book, and politically effective control, as treated in the second book.

Cicero's handling of this relationship between morals and politics in *On Duties* was an ambivalent and unstable bequest to the Middle Ages and the Renaissance. We have already found that his handling of this relationship in the *Republic* was an ambivalent and unstable bequest to later Antiquity. We found that when Augustine reads Cicero's *Republic*, he is able to subordinate political to moral considerations. On the one hand, Augustine retrieves the Platonic distinction, which Cicero had collapsed, between any real state and the ideal state. On the other hand, Augustine retrieves the traditional Stoic doctrine of moral integrity; he identifies the true statesman reflexively as the ruler who "prefers to rule his vicious desires to ruling nations."[91] Cicero's ambivalance can equally be overcome by repudiating this moral ideal. When Machiavelli appeals to the *"verità effettuale della cosa,"* he is rejecting the moral preferences of ideal statesman, as well as the Platonic state, in favor of the requirements of real statesmanship.

The Individual and Others

The political tradition which intervenes between Augustine's true statesman and Machiavelli's true statesman is the *Mirror of Princes* genre. In many of its exhortations, the visual situation remains pivotal whereby the eyes of all men are turned towards the prince. In the handling of this visual situation, the way the individual is related to others is still Ciceronian. Cicero in *On Duties* attempted to regain his first book's argument on behalf of what is right when in his second book he exhorted the individual really to be morally what he would appear to be politically to others. Similarly, the writers of *Mirrors of Princes* will usually view the ruler as really acting with reference to the private requirements of his own moral character, even though he is apparently acting politically in relation to others, and even though the writers' own point of view in exhorting the ruler is that of one of his subjects. In Machiavelli, however, other men are really present. They are acting themselves, as well as looking at the prince:

> The individual who is concerned to be moral on every occasion must necessarily be destroyed among so many who are not moral. Thus it is necessary for a prince, if he wishes to maintain his position, to learn how not to be moral, and to use or not to use this knowledge as circumstances may require.[92]

The prince must learn how not to be "moral" in the traditional sense we have been exploring. If he is to maintain his political position, he cannot maintain a private moral point of view but must learn how to act, not with reference to the requirements of his own moral character, but with reference to the requirements of external circumstances, and these include the point of view of other men. The problem he faces when he acts is posed by his political position itself:

> Dismissing those matters which concern only an imaginary prince, and discussing those that are real, I assert that all men—and particularly princes who are stationed at a greater height—have attributed to them certain characteristics which bring them praise or blame.[93]

To the extent that the prince's position renders his actions particularly visible, his particular problem of preserving himself is a quasi-rhetorical problem of preserving certain characteristics in the minds of his subjects. But the visibility of his actions is not, as it was in Cicero's exhortation to his son, the occasion for the revelation of his own moral character. His politically relevant moral characteristics are no longer his own, but those which others attribute to him by way of praise or blame.

This displacement of the point of view of the ruler towards himself by the point of view of his subjects towards him explains not only the way in which moral considerations are excluded in the *Prince* but also the respect in which they still remain relevant. The moral requirements the ruler was traditionally supposed to have in mind when he acts have been supplanted by the moral attributes he will have in the minds of his subjects as the result of their reactions to his actions. Cicero's "shortcut" of striving really to be morally what it is in your political interest to appear to be to others is a route which in Machiavelli is open only to imaginary rulers. Yet although Machiavelli is employing historical examples in order to discuss the public policies of real rulers, he is not disposing of all moral considerations and ushering his prince into the realm of realpolitik in quite the sense sometimes alleged by his interpreters. The prince, in Machiavelli's discussion of his relation to his subjects, inhabits the realm of the public imagination. The public image of the ruler—what he appears to be morally to others—is what a ruler really is politically, since he is likely to maintain his position and remain a ruler only so long as his subjects attribute to him certain moral characteristics rather than others. The moral appearance is a large portion of the political reality.

The Individual as Ruler

In assessing Machiavelli's break with the *Mirror of Princes* tradition, we have to take into account another important source (besides Cicero's *On Duties*) for the moral characteristics the prince displayed in this tradition. This source is the catalog of moral virtues in Aristotle's *Nicomachaean Ethics.* It perhaps had already been relied on by Panaetius as a source for his *On Duty.* Whether or not Cicero relied on it independently of Panaetius, his *On Duties* is the still available juncture at which we can examine the entry of these virtues into the humanistic political tradition. The importance of this source is a further illustration of the extent to which the approach to political problems in this tradition became individualistic. Just as Cicero's major contribution to the political tradition is his moral treatise *On Duties,* rather than his political treatise, the *Republic,* so Aristotle's *Ethics* is a much more influential source than his *Politics.* Once the ruler's moral character—the way in which he rules his different passions—is viewed in the Ciceronian fashion not merely as a matter of private self-control but as publicly mirrored by the way in which he rules his subjects, the moral virtues assigned the individual in Aristotle's *Ethics* can become the political virtues of the ruler.

Aristotle himself did not draw the distinction between private moral behavior and public political behavior in the antithetical fashion traditional with Cynicism and with Stoics who "played the Cynic." In Aristotle's *Ethics,* "complete moral virtue" involves "acting virtuously not merely by oneself but in relation to others." Aristotle argued that the virtue which is required in these two situations is "the same," and in pursuing this argument he endorsed the adage, "rule [i.e., a political position] reveals the man," explaining that "ruling brings the individual into relation to others and makes him a member of a community."[94] That rule reveals the ruler's moral character as a man is the specific implication of the *Mirror of Princes* analogy which we have selected for attention. But Aristotle himself did not carry this implication (or his catalog of moral virtues) directly over into his political theory, even though he assumed that to be morally a man, the individual must be politically a member of a community. For Aristotle did not focus his analysis of the political community on the relation to it of the ruler as an individual. It is this relationship that becomes the subject-matter of political theory in Cicero, the *Mirror of Princes* tradition, and in Machiavelli.

In analyzing this relationship differently from the tradition, Machiavelli discards as politically irrelevant most of the Aristotelian moral virtues which the *Mirror of Princes* tradition attributed to the ruler as an individual who is really ruling his own passions even when he is apparently ruling his subjects. These moral virtues retain some relevance in Machiavelli only insofar as they will be attributed to the ruler by his subjects as the result of the passions with which they react to his actions. Their retaining even this relevance renders Machiavelli's analysis almost a parody of the traditional Aristotelian ethical analysis of moral actions by reference to the particular passions which the individual is controlling when he acts. Machiavelli pulls the Aristotelian analysis inside out by analyzing the political actions of the ruler by reference to the particular passions of his subjects that he is attempting to control. For example, cruelty was traditionally the vice of the ruler who failed to control his anger; clemency, the virtue of the ruler who controlled his anger. But the issue in question when Machiavelli treats "Of Cruelty and Clemency" is "Whether it is Better to be Loved or Feared,"—love being the subjects' reaction to the ruler's clemency and fear being their reaction to his cruelty.[95]

Thus the result of the displacement of the reflexive point of the ruler towards himself by the public point of view of his subjects towards him is a psychological analysis in which their passions replace his passions. It is not simply because the individual is radically self-interested (in the pervasive modern sense that Sabine has stressed)[96] that he obtains a psychological significance in Machiavelli's *Prince* which he did not traditionally have. He is self-interested in a traditional sense which I have tried to pin down by considering the treatment of the *utile* in *On Duties*. The theoretically significant individual in *The Prince* is the ruler, and he obtains his theoretical significance as a consequence not of his moral characteristics as a private individual but, rather, as a consequence of the public role he plays as the individual of whom other men are particularly conscious. Their moral reactions to the prince are investigated in *The Prince*, in order to determine what a prince must really be. Thus Machiavelli's humble justification for addressing his *Prince* to a real prince is that it is "necessary to be one of the people to know the nature of princes."[97]

The Individual as Citizen

Machiavelli is considered the founder of modern political thought. But what do we mean by "modern political thought?" How is the political identified in modern thought? Roughly speaking, we assume a range of problems which are posed by the tendency of the modern mind to be self-interested, and of individuals therefore to compete with each other and engage in a struggle for power which has to be regulated in some political way. It is this assumption which I have illustrated by citing Sabine: "If human individuals are by nature radically egotistic, the state and the force behind the law must be the only power that holds society together. . . ." Sabine is commenting on Hobbes' "systematic statement of what Machiavelli suggested."[98] Thus what we mean by "modern political thought," and the sense in which Machiavelli is the founder of "modern political thought," can only be fully specified by comparing his accomplishment with that of the second founder, and both their accomplishments with ancient and medieval political thought.

Hobbes writes, not of *The Prince,* but *Of the Citizen*; he addresses, not the individual who happens to be a ruler or who might become a ruler, but the individual who is a subject. Hobbes' political theory is "a doctrine of subjection."[99]

We cannot, however, begin our comparison here, for Hobbes' *De Cive* is preceded deductively by a *De Homine* in which Hobbes is concerned with what the individual can know about himself not as a subject but as a man. Machiavelli observes men, but what his psychological observations provide is that knowledge of his subjects' passions which the individual ruler (or prospective ruler) needs to maintain (or to attain) his distinctive position as a ruler. Hobbes' *De Homine* in contrast is a psychological theory which provides any individual with that knowledge of his own passions which he needs to accept his distinctive position as a subject.[100]

This contrast between the way the two theorists envisage the political structure does not complete the comparison. The modernity of Machiavelli and Hobbes is not simply political. It is in part the problem of knowledge they both confront as a problem of the form knowledge must take to be politically relevant. Their different solutions implicate at one and the same time the structure of knowledge and the structure of the state. The problem takes shape from their denial of the assumption which had been traditional in the moralistic political thought of their predecessors—the assumption that men's political actions reveal their moral character. This denial reinforces, and is reinforced by, the distinction both draw between ruler and subject.

Since Hobbes holds Aristotle primarily responsible for this moralistic political tradition, it is worth noting the way Aristotle's moral and political theories are interrelated: Aristotle not only assumes in his moral theory that "rule reveals the man," but he also assumes in his political theory that men can act politically only if they have "knowledge of each others' moral characters."[101] Such mutual recognition is indispensable to the political process, since Aristotle defines "political" action as "ruling and being ruled in turn," and "political" virtue as requiring "knowledge of how to rule and to be ruled."[102] Thus the individual enters Aristotle's political theory neither as distinctively a ruler nor as distinctively a subject, and the knowledge sought by this theory is neither distinctively that of a ruler or that of a subject. The emergence of this distinction in modern political theory is illustrated by the fact that political theory itself takes the form in Machiavelli's *Prince* of the knowledge the individual needs to remain or become a prince, and in Hobbes' *De Homine* the form of knowledge the individual needs of himself as a man if he is to remain or become a citizen.

This fundamental distinction is obscured when Machiavelli and Hobbes are lumped together (in the way they are in Sabine's interpretation) as political theorists who are modern because they both make the "pervasive" assumption of "modern times" that the individual is self-interested. Antiquity was not unacquainted with this assumption. And at least as pervasive in modern times is the contrast between the two approaches to political problems that we have undertaken: the ruler or prospective ruler (or the ruling class or prospective ruling class) usually comes to the forefront in continental theories as the *historical* agent of political and social changes. But the characteristic problems of the British tradition are problems of representative government, which are formulated in terms of the *psychological* and *moral* traits of men in general.[103]

Self-consciousness

In his theory of human nature, Hobbes confronts a problem of knowledge which differs from Machiavelli's, even though he (like Machiavelli) denies that men's actions reveal their moral characters. He therefore identifies quite differently the moralistic political tradition. In the Introduction to the *Leviathan* Hobbes discounts this tradition, not as a tradition in which the prince was assumed to mirror his own soul when he ruled other men, but as a tradition in which the individual was assumed to be able to probe other men's souls. Hobbes protests, "The characters of man's heart, blotted and confounded as they are, with dissembling, lying, counterfeiting, and erroneous doctrines, are legible only to him that searcheth hearts."[104] Hobbes, like Machiavelli, is reviving the distinction which the moralistic political tradition had blurred between the inner moral sphere and the external sphere of action, but he is not leaving the inner moral sphere to God and relying with Machiavelli on observing the way men actually do act: "Though by men's actions we do discover their design sometimes; yet to do it without comparing them with our own, and distinguishing all circumstances, by which the case may come to be altered, is to decyphere without a key, and be for the most part deceived, by too much trust, or by too much diffidence; as he that reads, is himself a good or evil man." Thus the illegibility of other men's hearts locates a key for the reader. Hobbes is turning against the moralistic political tradition not only the epistemological prerogative that had been traditionally reserved to God, but also the epistemological prerogative that had been traditionally reserved to the individual—"*Nosce teipsum*, Read thy self." As Hobbes' use of the Socratic precept suggests, his theory of human nature "admitteth no other Demonstration" than that which his individual reader's own self-consciousness will provide: "for the similitude of the thoughts, and Passions of one man, to the thoughts, and Passions of another, whosoever looketh into himself, and considereth what he doth, when he does think, opine, reason, hope, feare, etc., and upon what grounds; he shall thereby read and know, what are the thoughts and Passions of all other men, upon the like occasions."[105]

The psychological phase of Machiavelli's political theory does not need this reflexive "demonstration" in order (as Sabine has suggested) to complete, "explain, and justify it."[106] Hobbes' "key" (the supplementary evidence which only the individual's own self-consciousness can yield) is superfluous in Machiavelli, where the ruler attains his psychological prominence as the individual whom others are particularly conscious of. Even though their reactions are unreliable as evidence of the moral character that lies behind his actions, they yet impose politically reliable requirements on his actions. In this respect Machiavelli's *Prince* might also still be regarded as a specimen of the *Mirror of Princes* genre; the visible actions of the ruler, if no longer mirroring his own mind, are still mirrored in the minds of his subjects.

In Hobbes, however, the significant psychological fact is that the mind of one individual never mirrors directly the visible actions of others: "All men are by nature provided of notable multiplying glasses—that is, their Passions and Selfe-love."[107] Hobbes' deductive analysis of their Passions and Selfe-love will provide the "prospective glasses" which are the necessary rectification. These optical analogies are not casually tossed off by Hobbes. Eight of the fifteen sections of his *De Homine* are taken up with problems of visual perception. Such problems are treated as reflections in mirrors, and the laws of refraction are established which explain optical illusions and determine the construction of prospective glasses.[108] This treatment is usually interpreted as Hobbes' unloading materials he had collected on optics in the inappropriate setting of his theory of human nature. But his analysis of the passions in the later sections of this *De Homine* is, in effect, an epistemological treatment of the psychological laws of refraction which both explain why it is illusory to appeal to what is *morally right*, and determine the construction of this explanation (the *Leviathan* itself) as a prospective glass.

Because the passions with which each individual reacts to others' actions are a self-magnifying distortion of the actual actions they perform, Hobbes' analysis of these passions is geared, not directly to these actions (as Machiavelli's analysis is geared to the prince's actual actions, because these are what others are conscious of), but to the individual's own self-consciousness. The different role of the individual in Machiavelli and Hobbes can accordingly be illustrated by differences in their treatment of the moral virtue which in the moralistic political tradition controlled the individual's consciousness of himself in his relation to other men. The differences will expose the ambivalence of this tradition.

Greatness of Mind

Greatness of mind (*magnitudo animi* or *magnanimitas*) is the superiority displayed by the individual who performs *great actions*. Since this superiority had been attributed both to individuals who remain patiently indifferent to changes in their fortune (e.g., Socrates) and to individuals who are impatient of dishonor (e.g., the angry Achilles, and the suicide Ajax), magnanimity was picked by Aristotle as a prime example of an ambivalent term.[109] In his own moral theory, Aristotle has no serious difficulty in resolving the ambivalence. He defines magnanimity as the morally superior individual's knowledge that the moral superiority displayed in his actions deserves recognition by others, yet one of the marks of his moral superiority is that he remains indifferent if it is not in fact recognized by others. Since Aristotle assumes that actions reveal moral character, no problem of knowledge—of the relation between what the individual really is and what he may appear to be—need be solved, and magnanimity has no distinct psychological function to perform. In fact it cannot "exist independently of the other virtues," each of which does have the distinct psychological function of enabling the individual to control in his actions certain specific passions with which he reacts to certain kinds of circumstances. Magnanimity can only be distinguished as an *"ornatus omnium virtutum."*[110] It is an "ordering of all the moral virtues" with respect to the enhancement they receive from a superior performance. To this extent we might stretch the translation and describe magnanimity as an "ornamental" virtue;[111] Aristotle rounds out his treatment of magnanimity with a portrait of the magnanimous individual, presumably because his superior performance involves some sense of self-portrayal. This sense of role is missing from Aristotle's more functional treatment of the other virtues.

But it is these other moral virtues which no longer have any specific psychological functions to fulfill in Machiavelli's political theory. The prince does not need specific dispositions built into his mind and character in order to control his reactions to particular circumstances. Rather, his character must remain in a certain fashion structureless. He must have "a mind disposed to turn in any direction as the winds of fortune and the variability of his circumstances require."[112] Why then does Machiavelli disconcert his interpreters by referring so frequently to the prince's *virtù*? Why does he also retain its humanistic antithesis, *fortuna,* as a general description of external circumstances, despite the care he takes to specify historically the particular circumstances to which leaders adapted their actions or failed to adapt their actions?[113]

Opportunism does have its place in Machiavelli's theory. But fortune is impetuous. External circumstances are always changing, and changing usually with their own momentum, so that the only way of effectively altering the direction of change, if it can in fact be altered, is by forceful action. Their momentum will elude the prince's control unless his action has an impact sufficient to survive some of these ensuing changes. Furthermore, the *greatness* of his actions does have a psychological dimension. While each of these actions must, of course, be performed with reference to the specific requirements of particular circumstances, all of these actions must also satisfy the general psychological requirement of maintaining his position in the minds of other men. Magnanimity thus becomes a functional political virtue in approximately the respect that it was merely an "ornamental" moral virtue in Aristotle. At the same time, what had been in Aristotle the specific and functional moral virtues become "ornamental" in Machiavelli; insofar as they can be publicly displayed, they become subsidiary to the general virtue of magnanimity.

Since it is obvious that this political virtue of magnanimity in Machiavelli is only a distant descendant of the moral virtue of magnanimity in Aristotle, we have to take the intervening tradition into account. In the *Mirror of Princes* tradition, magnanimity, like self-control, already enjoyed a general political significance, and the way it had acquired this significance can be illustrated by the use to which Cicero puts Panaetius' transition beyond traditional Stoicism. Self-control we remember, had acquired general moral significance in the Stoic tradition because the wise man was required to exercise absolute control over all his passions, regardless of the particular circumstances to which they were reactions, for whatever the particular circumstances were, they belonged to the domain of fortune. But the Stoic tradition acknowledged that there were specific passions—the fear of pain and of death—which were particularly difficult to resist.[114] Self-control thus requires reinforcement by courage in the sense of moral courage—"strength of mind [*robur animi*]," which requires in turn a heightened self-consciousness, in the form of the wise man's consciousness of his independence of and superiority to fortune—that is, to external circumstances as such. Just as Stoic self-control was an inner ordering of the individual's mind in conformity with his rational insight into the order of the universe, so this heightened consciousness of moral autonomy and superiority was not only an introspective virtue but also a cosmological virtue. It was "high-mindedness [*altitudo mentis*]"—the wise man's consciousness of the elevated place of mind in the universe; it was the *rerum externarum despicientia* that Scipio was exhorted in his dream to attain by looking down upon the lowly earth from his lofty position in the heavens.[115]

In Panaetius' liberalized Stoicism, we have already encountered two realignments in the structure of knowledge (that is, in knowledge as structured by the mind of the wise man). First of all, his "knowledge of nature" is considered "maimed and incomplete if no actual actions are its consequences."[116] Accordingly, the wise man, without relinquishing his superior place in the Stoic universe, takes his place among other men and plays an active role in relation to them. Secondly, he plays this role as an individual. These two realignments converge in the knowledge of human nature with which Panaetius defines the role of the individual. The knowledge itself merges three different philosophical traditions. The wise man displays (1) Stoic *strength* and *elevation of mind*; these attributes are identified with (2) Aristotelian *greatness of mind*; and this attribute in turn acquires broader relevance than it had in Aristotle from its identification as (3) the fulfillment of θυμός, which had been a general tendency of the mind in Plato.

This interweaving of three different philosophical traditions twists together several implications. Perhaps a certain pattern can be traced in the way the mind is being restructured. Let us begin by tracing the implications of Plato's analogical treatment of θυμός, since the analogy supplies some of the leverage Panaetius needs to get the wise man into active relation with other men. In Plato's *Republic*, the internal structures of the state and of the mind had been analogically tripartite. Plato's soldier-administrators, because they had to deal with other men, had a function to perform which was distinct from both the reflexive function of philosophers and from the workers' function of producing external goods. Using this analogy, Plato had distinguished θυμός (as a competitive and aggressive desire for power and recognition) both from *reason* (which had to be reflexively oriented in order to investigate the internal structure of the mind) and from *desires* (which were directed towards external goods). It is in his handling of θυμός that Plato comes closest to treating that coalescence of problems of self-interest, competition, and power, which in modern thought are usually identified as political.[117] These problems largely disappear whenever the Stoic tradition disparaged political activity. θυμός was depressed (as we observed in Cicero's *Republic*)[118] to the same level as the other desires, so that the moral problem became simply the problem of reason's overcoming reflexively all desires as reactions to external things. When Panaetius revives Plato's θυμός, he defines it (in Cicero's translation) as an *appetitio quaedam principatus*.[119] The characteristics of "rule" that the individual desires in this definition are the independence and superiority which were attained in the Stoic tradition by the strength and elevation of the wise man's mind. But since θυμός brings with it from Plato's *Republic* its analogical implications, these moral characteristics can be displayed by military and political activity, once Panaetius manages to overcome the Stoic disparagement of θυμός and to bridge the Stoic distinction between the internal sphere of the wise man's moral responsibility as an individual and the external sphere of political action. This is more readily managed when the fulfillment of Platonic θυμός is identified with Aristotelian *greatness of mind*.

Finally, Panaetius has to smooth over the patching and present the emerging pattern as Stoic. The virtues of *strength* and *elevation of mind* were attached in the Stoic tradition to the cardinal virtue of courage. Panaetius can incorporate Aristotelian *greatness of mind* within the Stoic tradition by associating it too with courage:

All courage or greatness of mind involves two things. On the one hand [and this is the traditional Stoic conception of strength and elevation of mind], it involves the contempt for external circumstances *(rerum externarum despicientia)*, for such a mind is convinced that there is nothing which a man should admire, seek, or pursue, except what is morally right and appropriate, and that a man should not yield to either passion or fortune. On the other hand [now the traditional conception is expanded], the consequence of the mind's being so disposed is that great actions are undertaken which are not only useful but are also exceptionally difficult and dangerous, both to the things we live by and to life itself. From the latter disposition derive all the luminousness and scope—I would even add, the usefulness *(utilitatem)*—of the virtue. The conviction itself, however, is the disposition which makes men great.[120]

Although the disposition behind the virtue is still an inner philosophical conviction, the individual must actually attain a political position if this disposition is to become effective in action:

> Those who have been endowed by nature with the qualifications required for ruling, ought without any hesitation to seek a political position, for there is no other way in which a state can be ruled or greatness of mind revealed.[121]

The traditional hesitation of the Stoics who "played the Cynic," no longer demonstrate their moral independence of, and superiority to, fortune—to external circumstances. It becomes evidence instead of their immoral yielding to "fear of toil and trouble and even of the humiliation of political rejection and defeat;" for "their lives are less exposed to the blows of fortune, . . . and when misfortune strikes they do not have so far to fall."[122] The Stoic philosopher's traditional problem of maintaining his lofty moral position in the universe is thus conflated with the statesman's problem of maintaining his precarious position in the state.

The Roman Mind

As a result of this conflation, philosophical highmindedness becomes encumbered with two issues of Cicero's own career. The first we encountered in his *Republic*, where Scipio had exemplified *greatness of mind*, as he doubtless also had to Panaetius. But Cicero was not what Africanus had been—a great military leader. When Cicero attempts in *On Duties* to determine the mind and character appropriate to a military leader or statesman who performs great actions, he cannot avoid a comparison between his qualifications for leadership with Pompey's and Caesar's.[123] He has to concede that *greatness of mind* has been at once a distinctively Roman and a distinctively military virtue:

> The Roman people itself is superior to all others in its greatness of mind. Indeed our ardor for military glory is evidenced by the fact that the statues of our heroes are usually dressed in military style.[124]

The virtue may have been Roman, but to specify what it was Cicero had coined the term *magnanimitas* as a translation of the Greek, *μεγαλοψυχία*.[125] As already noted, this virtue had been attributed by the Greeks to such military leaders as Achilles and Ajax, as well as to philosophers. Cicero's handling of the term in *On Duties* illustrates what I have described as the increasing moralization of the criteria of political leadership. It is plausible that Cicero would go beyond Panaetius (as Panaetius himself may have gone beyond previous Stoics) in transferring to the political leader the moral implications of the philosophical conception of greatness of mind. Cicero has to outmaneuver the military implications older Latin usage associated with the term "mind" itself. *Animus* meant aggressive military spirit. Thus what is at stake in Cicero's maneuver is the structure of the mind itself, as well as the nature of political power. *Animus* was hardly distinguishable in its meaning from physical courage. Polybius extolled "courage" as "the most crucial part of virtue in the affairs of state, and especially so at Rome." Courage here retained the meaning suitable for a history of the wars in which the Roman state had conquered the world. Cicero, however, is able to resort to the Platonic and Stoic traditions in which courage has become moral courage. This shift in the meaning of the term had in fact taken place during the course of Plato's *Republic*. Once Plato had controlled and tamed *θυμός* with music, it was no longer the aggressive military spirit his soldiers had needed initially in his *Republic*. They were converted into peaceable administrators.[126] Since Panaetius associated Aristotelian *greatness of mind*, as the fulfillment of Platonic *θυμός*, with the moral courage of the Stoic tradition, Cicero is well equipped philosophically for his effort to transform the traditional conception of the Roman "mind." The merging of the three traditions in Panaetius enables Cicero to become the exemplification of *greatness of mind* himself and to argue that the moral courage which is required of him as a statesman is superior to the merely physical courage of the military leader.[127]

In this argument a confrontation of his own character and that of Pompey the Great had originally been in question, and a comparison of his own political role, when he "saved" the state during his consulate by suppressing Catiline's conspiracy, with Pompey's military role as conqueror abroad. Cicero still recalls in *On Duties* a favorite line from his own poem which exalted his role as consul: "Arms should surrender to the toga, the soldier's laurels to political glory." Against this claim, he complains, "the unprincipled and the envious still inveigh."[128] These are the "popular leaders" who are attempting to inherit pieces of Caesar's role.

Catiline had been, in Cicero's view, an instrument of the ambitions of Caesar. The confrontation of Cicero's character with Caesar's posed for Cicero a second question of philosophical principle. When the highminded individual takes his place among other men, his consciousness of his superiority can become a political danger:

> What is disconcerting is that such elevation and greatness of mind develops all too readily into . . . an uncontrollable desire for superiority (*cupiditas principatus*). . . . The greater the mind of an individual, the greater his desire to rule (to be *princeps omnium*) and to rule alone.[129]

Panaetius may have been sensitive to this danger, since the tendency of the mind which *greatness of mind* fulfilled in his theory was the Platonic θυμός that the Stoic tradition had distrusted. But Cicero himself would have had every reason to hedge here and retrieve the traditional Stoic emphasis on the moral integrity of the philosopher:

> True and wise greatness of mind regards moral rightness . . . as residing in actions, not in glory, and prefers really to be superior [*principatus*] rather than merely to appear superior; for he can never be regarded great who relies on the support of the erratic and ignorant multitude.[130]

The appeal from political appearances to moral reality discloses (as it so often does in the history of political thought) at the heart of the moral reality a class distinction. But although the identification of Caesar as one of the *populares* disposes of his pretensions to *greatness*, Cicero continues with the confrontation:

> In fact, the loftier a mind is the more readily is it inclined to perform unjust actions out of a desire for glory. We are, to be sure on very slippery ground here, since it is hard to find a man who, when has endured toil and dangers [i.e., satisfied the moral requirements met by the traditional Stoic conception of *strength of mind*] does not desire glory [to which the Stoic was traditionally indifferent] as a reward for his actions.[131]

Glory

Probably it is the statesman Cicero, rather than the philosopher Panaetius, who is losing his footing here, as he feels the ground slipping from under him. In any case, Machiavelli and Hobbes do not construct their political theories on this slippery ground. Even though Cicero has exploited Panaetius' realignment of the structure of knowledge to state his own problem of recognition, it can hardly be dignified as a problem of knowledge. But in order to trace a neglected continuity in the history of political thought, let me in this concluding section pull one line of development tighter than the vagaries of this history warrant. For after the loose reshuffling of *On Duties,* we are better able to appreciate the tautness of Machiavelli's and Hobbes' theorics.

In raising their modern problem of knowledge, Machiavelli and Hobbes can be interpreted as readjusting the relation between the internal and the external, so as to remove in opposite ways the traditional ambivalence of *greatness of mind.* Machiavelli, as we have seen, rejects the private moral point of view and takes as the political reality the individual's moral appearance to others. The individual who becomes a prince must perform *great actions* to maintain the appearance of his superiority to other men. But the *greatness of mind* his actions reveal is less an attribute of his own mind than it is the glory he obtains in their minds as the result of these actions. Yet we have also seen that the general way Machiavelli pits *virtù* against *fortuna* throughout his political theory (despite the care with which he also specifies particular historical circumstances) indicates his continued debt to the humanistic tradition in which the virtuous individual triumphs over the influence of external circumstances as such.

Hobbes also remains indebted to this tradition. His earliest definition of magnanimity as "no more than glory, . . . but glory well grounded upon certain experience of power sufficient to attain his end in open manner,"[132] almost retains the traditional double reference to what the individual is himself conscious of and to the recognition of the significance of his actions by other men. In Machiavelli, where this second reference prevailed at the expense of the first, the struggle for power was psychological to the extent that it was a struggle in which the ruler had to maintain his political position in the minds of his subjects. But the first reference prevails in Hobbes at the expense of the second. Even "glory" itself he defines as a self-conscious sense of glory: it is "an *internal* gloriation or triumph of the mind," which "proceedeth from the imagination or conception of our own power above the power of him that contendeth with us."[133] What is psychologically at stake in this struggle for power is the moral stature that the individual is striving to maintain in his own mind.

Hobbes' definition of glory is not just a matter of psychological observation. Hobbes, like Machiavelli, is disposing of the traditional confusion whereby the political position of the ruler was credited to his moral superiority over other men. Thus Hobbes smuggles into a parenthesis a comment on the traditional theorist's consciousness of his own moral stature: "I know that Aristotle in the first book of his Politiques, for a foundation of his doctrine, maketh men by Nature, some more worthy to Command, meaning the wiser sort (such as he thought himself to be for his Philosophy)." The leveling of this distinction is the foundation of Hobbes' own doctrine. For Aristotle's foundation Hobbes is substituting the psychological assumption that individuals are naturally equal, or at least that each individual is so conscious of his own moral stature, because he is striving to maintain it, that he will not ordinarily accept another's claim to moral superiority. Thus Hobbes slides from men's external relations to each other, "If Nature . . . have made men equall, that equalitie is to be acknowledged," to the way self-consciousness renders this acknowledgement problematic, "or if Nature have made men unequall, yet . . . men . . . think themselves equall."[134]

Hobbes' political theory has to wait until the next chapter. At the moment we are only concerned with the way Hobbes allows self-consciousness to dislocate the traditional structure of the moralistic theory which political theory had become in the humanistic tradition. If individuals are equal, or at least if each individual is so self-conscious that he is not likely to acknowledge to himself another's superiority, then no individual's sense of his own superiority is likely to be so "well-grounded" that he can long remain confident of "attaining his ends in open manner." The virtue of magnanimity in this traditional sense is therefore "rarely found."[135] When Hobbes in the *Leviathan* offers his own definition of magnanimity, what he retains from the tradition is the fact that it is a kind of "contempt." But he undermines the superiority and independence this contempt traditionally involved (as *rerum externarum despicientia*), by rendering the *greatness* relative: magnanimity is "contempt of *little* helps and hindrances."[136] This relativity further undermines the independence of the individual in that his contempt is no longer a virtue—that is, it no longer carries a reference to actions which the individual is disposed to take entirely on his own initiative. The contempt in question is only a passion with which he reacts to the actions of other men. Hobbes' disparaging definition of magnanimity illustrates the restructuring of moral theory attendant upon his methodological resort to self-consciousness. The subject-matter of Hobbes' "Of Man" (as we noted in his Introduction to the *Leviathan*) are the individual's passions, not his actions. There is accordingly no place in Hobbes' for the "true and wise magnanimity" of the humanistic tradition, which "regards moral rightness as residing in actions, not in glory." Nor can the alternative "glory" perform in Hobbes the function it had in Machiavelli, where we found that the passions which were crucial were the reactions of *other* men to the individual's actions (e.g., their love, fear, and admiration as ingredients in the prince's glory). Crucial instead in Hobbes are the individual's *own* passions as reactions to other men's actions. Thus glory itself (in its new sense of an "internal gloriation or triumph of the mind") is not only a *universal* passion (in contrast with the "*rarely* found" magnanimity), but is also defined by Hobbes (in contrast with his definition of magnanimity as a kind of "contempt") as the passion with which an individual reacts to a contemptuous action on the part of another individual. Hobbes explains: "Every man looketh that his companion should value him at the same rate he sets upon himself; and upon all signs of contempt, or undervaluing, naturally endeavours . . . to extort a greater value from his contemners by dommage, and from others by example."[137]

Internal Gloriation

This endeavour to secure recognition from others is not the individual's direct reaction to their actions. The actions that he construes as "signs of contempt" are merely such "trifles as a word, a smile, a different opinion,"[138] and his passionate reactions are disproportionate because the rate he sets upon himself is the self-magnifying distortion which is required to maintain his "internal gloriation." The difficulty of settling the moral rating perhaps indicates a sense in which actions as such cannot be performed in an "open manner" in Hobbes' theory. My reactions to others' actions are indirect in that I am not conscious of the actions as actions (as I am in Cicero or even in Machiavelli). Not only does my self-consciousness intrude as a feature of my reactions in Hobbes, but I also construe actions as "signs" of what the agent's intentions are. Problems of how to act had traditionally been the subject-matter of moral theory, but they are assimilated in Hobbes to problems of knowledge.[139]

Thus the traditional humanistic treatment of virtuous action fractures in Machiavelli and Hobbes along a line of cleavage the beginnings of which can be traced in the development of the tradition itself. Its development was a succession of classical revivals which attempted to overcome the distinction which Cynics, and Stoics who "played the Cynic," had introduced between the private moral sphere of the individual's own mind and the public sphere of his political relations to other men. The particular virtue that survives and assumes general significance in Machiavelli is *greatness of mind,* but its significance is largely public and political; it is the glory that is the acknowledgment by other minds of the superiority an individual displays by *great actions.* In Hobbes, however, glory is the individual's private sense of his own moral superiority as compared with other men. Glory in this particular sense assumes general significance, for "virtue generally is . . . somewhat that is valued for eminence, and consisteth in comparison,"[140] but the individual cannot expect, in Hobbes' psychological theory, that others will make the same comparison that he does and acknowledge his superiority over them: "Who hath that eminency of virtue above others . . . shall never be agreed upon amongst men."[141]

Eminency of virtue in the *princeps,* Cicero envisaged as the solution to political problems. His eminence would lend structure to the state only if men acknowledged his superiority by bestowing glory on him, but the Romans never agreed in a *concordia ordinum* which would bestow glory on Cicero. The problem of recognition and agreement which Cicero's philosophy, as well as his career, ultimately left unsolved, is reformulated by Hobbes. In the next chapter we shall examine some of the comparisons of their leaders that the Romans made (to the detriment of Cicero), in the process of identifying the individual who exemplified the virtue of *greatness of mind,* for their comparisons contributed to the development of the humanistic tradition into an individualistic tradition of political thought. We shall see that the contract which determines the relation between one individual and another in Hobbes is an agreement which is quite different in its structure from the *consensus* Cicero sought as a *concordia ordinum*. The authority the sovereign in Hobbes obtains from this agreement is neither the moral authority *greatness of mind* displayed in the humanistic tradition, nor is it the public authority which *greatness of mind* obtains for the prince in Machiavelli.

Notes

1. A *System of Logic,* 8th ed. (London: Longmans, Green and Co., 1941), p. 615.

2. Georges Sabine, *A History of Political Theory*, 3rd ed. (New York: Holt, Rinehart and Winston, 1966), pp. 342–43.

3. *Ibid.*, p. 345.

4. *Ibid.*, p. 471.

5. Thomas Hobbes, *English Works*, ed. W. Molesworth, 11 vols. (London: John Bohn, 1839–45), 1: 471. (All my references to Hobbes' works, except to the *Leviathan*, are to this Molesworth edition.) Consider the license so wantonly taken by an historian of ideas when he offers the interpretation I have already cited: "These tendencies—the increase of legal power and the recognition of self-interest as the dominant motive in life have been among the most pervasive in modern times. That Hobbes made them the premises of his system and followed them through with relentless logic is the true measure of his philosophical insight and of his greatness as a political thinker." Despite the fact that Hobbes' system "excludes history," historical tendencies have been brought inside his "system," becoming its premises. Thus his "philosophical insight" becomes historical insight: "Individualism is the thoroughly modern element in Hobbes and the respect in which he caught most clearly the note of the coming age" (Sabine, *A History of Political Theory*, p. 471). But there is not a single statement in Hobbes that can be summed up as an effort to catch the note of the coming age. What are the credentials of an historican of political theory who so completely disregards the historical facts about a political theory? If I seem hard on Sabine, it should be remembered that even though his history was first published in 1937, it has not been superseded as the standard presentation in English of the history of political theory. In no other area in the history of theory or of philosophy has a single textbook been so widely used or survived so long. Sabine's disregard of textual evidence is, of course, quite characteristic of historians of political ideas (see vol. 1, pp. 114–16).

6. See p. 123, this vol.

7. See p. 124, this vol.

8. See vol. 1, pp. 257, 264.

9. *The Prince,* chap. 15.

10. See vol. 1, p. 249.

11. Livy, *Ab urbe condita Praefatio.*

12. See vol. 1, p. 239 and accompanying n. 9.

13. See vol. 1, pp. 45–48.

14. See vol. 1, pp. 327–31.

15. See vol. 1, p. 97.

16. *Discourses on Livy*, I, Introduction.

17. *Ab urbe condita Praef.*

18. *Ab urbe condita Praef.*

19. See vol. 1, p. 303.

20. As a result of this conflation of the two traditions, the *"ritirarla . . . verso il suo principio"* (*Discourses* II, chap. 1; see vol. 1, p. 96) is at once a regaining of an historical starting point and a reembodiment of an ideal normative principle. Accordingly the return can be either the historical effect of *fortune* or the moral effect of exemplary *virtue*. But even the historical effect of fortune is often repeatable as an exemplary episode. Thus Rome's capture by the Gauls in 390 B.C. was an accident; yet we are to "recognize that Rome had to be taken by the French in order to be reborn and that in being reborn she had to take on new life and new virtue and to renew the observance of religion and justice, both of which had begun to suffer corruption" (*ibid.*). In recalling that "as soon as Rome had been recaptured from the French, they renewed all the rites (*ordini*) of their ancient religion" (*ibid.*), Machiavelli is recalling Livy's report (5. 50) of Rome's renaissance after its capture by the Gauls, but he would also seem to have in mind the invasion of Italy by Charles VIII, as a possible occasion for renewal. On the other hand, tracing the effect of exemplary virtue (or of its absence) can involve some reference to historical sequence. Consider Machiavelli's historical interpretation of the display of virtue in the traditional form of moral solitude: "Such a return in republics to their principle is sometimes the result of the simple virtue of one man alone, . . . whose reputation and example are such that good men wish to imitate it. . . . But between the two Catos there was so great a distance, and they were so solitary, that their good examples could have no good effects" (*ibid.*).

21. I am merely paraphrasing Machiavelli who offers various versions of the cycle (see n. 24, below). The formulation of the humanistic antithesis between virtue and fortune that Machiavelli finds most relevant historically (*Discourses* II, chap. 1, "Whether Virtue or Fortune was the Primary Cause of the Empire which Rome Acquired") is that offered by Plutarch: "Virtue and Fortune, who have often engaged in many great contests, are now engaging each other in the present contest, which is the greatest of all; for in this they are striving for a decision regarding the supremacy of Rome, to determine whose work (ἔργον) it is and which of them created such a power" (*Moralia* 316C ["On the Fortune of the Romans"]). See vol. 1, p. 96 for the cyclical relation between the period of Rome's expansion in the second book of the *Discourses* and the periods covered in the first book and in the third book. See vol. 1, p. 92 for the character of the "contest" as a philosophical (or rhetorical) contest which is superimposed on a military contest. It should be observed that philosophy can take either side in the contest. On the one hand, the morally virtuous philosopher can discount an Alexander as the protégé of fortune (see vol. 1, p. 197); on the other hand, since the political function of virtue is to reconcile men and secure their unanimity, philosophy can ally itself with the unifier of the world, who becomes in this perspective a virtuous philosopher: "Fortune . . . declares that Alexander is her own characteristic work and hers alone. But some rejoinder must be made on behalf of philosophy, or rather on Alexander's behalf, . . . who was indeed a philosopher" (*Moralia* 326D ["On the Fortune or the Virtue of Alexander"]). See vol. 1, p. 198 for the claim that the unity of the world that Alexander achieved by his conquests was the philosophical insight of Zeno into the unity of the *cosmos* and the unanimity he sought.

22. See vol. 1, p. 289 for the controversy and chap. 7, nn. 28, 65, for the exemplarist conception of an historical figure.

23. See vol. 1, p. 272 and accompanying note 99.

24. *Discourses*, Introduction. Machiavelli attaches to the historical cycle not only the

humanistic antithesis between virtue and fortune, but also the humanistic antithesis between *otium* and *negotium*. See esp. the version of the cycle given in the *History of Florence* (V, chap. 1): "Countries generally move from order to disorder and then from disorder move back to order, for since nature does not allow things in the world to remain stable, when they come to their final perfection . . . they must decline. Likewise, when they have declined and because of their disorders have reached the very bottom, they necessarily move up, since they cannot go any lower. . . . Because virtue brings forth peace (*quiete*); peace, ennervation (*ozio*); ennervation, disorder; disorder, ruin; and likewise from ruin comes order; from order, virtue; from the last, glory and good fortune. Therefore the wise have observed that letters come after arms and that in countries and cities generals are born before philosophers. The reason for this is that after good and well ordered armies have produced victory, and their victory peace, the virtue of military courage cannot be corrupted with a more honorable ennervation (*onesto ozio*) than that of letters. . . . When the philosophers, Diogenes and Carneades, arrived in Rome, . . . Cato understood this, and when he saw that the young men of Rome began to follow them with admiration, he recognized the evil that such honorable ennervation might bring upon his country, and made a law that no philosophers should be admitted to Rome." For Carneades' performance, see chap. 7, n. 95. His expulsion was the paradigmatic episode that began the tradition of exiling philosophers from Rome. This tradition will be taken up in chap. 11 (see esp. n. 42 in chap. 11 for the identification of philosophers as subversive).

25. See vol. 1, p. 308.

26. *De Legibus* 3. 14.

27. See vol. 1, p. 331.

28. See vol. 1, p. 266.

29. See vol. 1, p. 203, 257, 266.

30. As Cicero phrases it, "most suited to your age and to my authority" (*De Officiis* 1. 4).

31. See vol. 1, pp. 188–89.

32. *On Liberty* (New York: Liberal Arts Press, 1956), p. 29.

33. Diogenes Laertius *Lives of the Philosophers* 6. 71.

34. Julian *Oratio* 6. 187D ("To the Uncultured Cynics"). In order to give some sense of the continuity of this individualistic tradition, I am beginning my interpretation with Julian the Apostate's fourth-century retrospect, just as I began my interpretation of the humanistic tradition with Lactantius' fourth-century retrospect (see vol. 1, p. 183).

35. Julian *Oratio* 7. 211C ("To the Cynic Heracleios").

36. See vol. 1, p. 200.

37. See vol. 1, p. 202.

38. *Memorabilia* 1. 6. 14.

39. Diogenes Laertius *Lives of Eminent Philosophers* 6. 49.

40. Thomas Hobbes, *The Life of Mr. Thomas Hobbes of Malmesbury*. Written by himself in a Latine Poem. And now Translated into English (London: Prited for A. C., 1680).

41. See vol. 1, pp. 307–8 and accompanying n. 76 on *peregrinatio*. Cicero himself was figuratively an exile as well as briefly an actual exile. For his inner migration, see the letter of May 46 B.C. in which he refers to himself as "an exile in his own country" insofar as it is no longer "constitutionally a republic." But he adds: "It's a great consolation to be without blame, especially considering the two things that sustain me—my knowledge of

the noblest arts (this no one can take from me so long as I live) and the glory of the greatest deeds (this cannot be taken from me even when I am dead)" (*Epistulae ad Familiares* 7. 3. 4). With these two pronouncements, Cicero ushers himself into the humanistic tradition.

42. *De Officiis* 3. 121.

43. I shall not ordinarily try to suggest whether a position taken in *On Duties* is to be attributed to Panaetius or only to Cicero. To distinguish their successive classical revivals is an immensely difficult scholarly task.

44. See vol. 1, p. 268.

45. *Off.* 1. 30.

46. See vol. 1, pp. 40–44.

47. *Off.* 1. 107, 109–110. Since *On Duties* is primarily a moral treatise, we are not concerned with the interpretation of its technical details. In starting out with the treatment of propriety, I have skipped over the treatment of the first three cardinal virtues as "parts of *rectitude*." In one sense propriety is only a "particular virtue" which occupies the traditional place of self-control among these cardinal virtues. But in another sense it is a "general virtue" (1. 96) which is "associated with every part of *rectitude*" (1. 95). Cicero's (or Panaetius') arrival at this extended and general sense of propriety is the restructuring of moral theory that does concern us, because it will render moral theory politically relevant. The restructured moral theory is not only an esthetic theory (i.e., a theory of perception), but as such also involves a shift from theory to practice. Cicero explains that propriety "can be separated from virtue only in theory, not in practice," for "the relation is so close that it is obvious—to perceive it no obscure (*recondita*) reasoning is required" (see n. 49, below).

48. *Off.* 1. 97. Cicero next indulges in drama criticism. He is drawing on the rhetorical tradition. We must realize that when Cicero draws on this tradition he is not restricted to political and legal rhetoric, even though he is expanding moral theory into a context for the treatment of political and legal problems. He is liberating from the technicalities of literary criticism certain rhetorical procedures which were designed to guide the judgment of the poet and critic. We cannot go into detail here. But we can observe the way the process of liberalization (1) brings poetic and political rhetoric into a closer relationship and thereby (2) brings morals and politics into a relationship which differs from that which we explored in Cicero's *Republic*. With respect to the first relationship, consider Cicero's assertion: "The poet is closely related to the orator . . . ; he is his ally and almost his counterpart; in one respect indeed he can be regarded as identical, for he sets no limits or boundaries to his prerogative, which would keep him from ranging at will with the same facility and fluency (*copia*) as the orator" (*De Or.* 1. 70–71). (For the facility and fluency with which the orator ranges at will, see nn. 75, 76, below.) The second relationship in *On Duties* depends on the extent to which an individual's moral action can be viewed more broadly as a political performance because it is viewed as a dramatic action which renders character visible to an audience. Thus the procedures of the dramatic poet, as analyzed in rhetorical theory, contribute to the delineation of the "roles"—the typological reenactments—which we discovered in the previous chapter were crucial to the formation of the humanistic tradition as an exemplarist tradition. Compare Cicero's demand: "Every individual should recognize his own ability and talent and render himself a critical judge of his moral strengths and defects, and not let actors show more practical sense. For they select not the plays which are best but those most suited to themselves. . . . Shall an actor concern himself with the selection of his role, and a wise man neglect to do so?" (*Off.* 1. 114).

49. *Off.* 1. 98. To be able to perceive this analogy between esthetic perception and moral judgment is to be able to perceive the "close" and "obvious" relation between propriety and virtue and to realize that "no obscure reasoning is required" to demonstrate

this relation (see n. 47, above). Clear reasoning itself takes the practical form in *On Duties* of perceiving such relations and analogies (see n. 60, below). The full significance for modern classicism of the analogy between esthetic perception and moral judgment will only be worked out when we reach Hume's and Adam Smith's theories of moral sentiments (see pp. 209, this vol. and chap. 14, n. 126).

50. In this chapter and the next I italicize *personality* (as I did *scholarly* in the previous chapter) by way of warning that its etymological sense should be retained. We are not confronted in Cicero with a "mask" that conceals, but with a "role" that expresses moral character. Compare the discussion of man's superiority to other animals here with Cicero's account in the *Laws* (1. 27) of the way "God has created and equipped [or "embellished"] man" (The Latin is *ornavit*—see n. 76, below). Cicero points out that what is termed "facial expression" (*vultus*) is not found in any other animal besides man and reveals his moral character." Cicero here perhaps feels a certain measure of Roman confidence, for he claims that "the Greeks had no term at all for *vultus*." Moral character, Cicero admits, can be revealed in other ways besides the expression of a face—by "the control of the voice [i.e., its different tones—see vol. 1, p. 267 and accompanying n. 83]" and by "the power of speech [see vol. 1, p. 271] which is the most effective means of establishing a community among men (*conciliatrix est humanae maxime societatis*)." But Cicero points out that "this topic has been adequately treated by Scipio." This portion of Cicero's *Republic* having been lost, I turned in chap. 8 to *On the Orator* (see pp. 265–67) for Cicero's conception of the rhetorical revelation of moral character. At this juncture *On the Orator, The Republic, The Laws, On Duties* (i.e., Cicero's rhetorical, political, legal, and moral problems) overlap, despite the fashion among most scholars to assign various Greek sources. There is even a considerable overlap in the connotations of Cicero's liberalized Latin terminology. *Ornatus*, which covers in *On the Orator* most of the problems of rhetoric as such, was often used interchangeably with *dignitas* (see *Rhetorica ad Herennium* 1. 10), which refers like *decorum* to *quid decet* ("what is appropriate"), but which carries more definite implications over into the moral and political sphere (see chap. 8, n. 44) and which is closer in its implications to the legal term *auctoritas*.

51. See vol. 1, p. 137

52. See vol. 1, p. 197.

53. *Off.* 1. 153.

54. See vol. 1, p. 201. "Indifference to public opinion (ἀδοξία), Cicero explains (*Off.* 1. 99), "is not just [Stoic] self-reliance but complete lack of principle (*non sum arrogantis est, sed etiam omnino dissoluti*)."

55. *Rep.* 430E.

56. *Off.* 1. 93.

57. See vol. 1, pp. 244–47.

58. See vol. 1, pp. 44–45.

59. See vol. 1, pp. 257.

60. "Life" is the setting throughout for Cicero's treatment of "duties." He specifies at the beginning (1. 7) that he is dealing with "the practical rules by which daily life in all its aspects can be regulated." This setting he identifies as the psychological context provided by man's distinctively human nature. "The crucial difference is that the animal, insofar as it is moved by the senses, responds to what is present at the moment, with very little perception of the past or future, whereas man, because he is endowed with reason, perceives effects and causes and understands their relation, makes comparisons and analogies, and associates the present with the future, so that he easily visualizes the course of life as a whole and makes the necessary preparations for leading it." (1. 11). This extended process of perception includes as its counterpart the process

of expression that finds its fulfillment in other men's perception of him. It is this two-sided process of perception and expression that I am singling out as the esthetic strand which is stretched and generalized in *On Duties* to compose a more concrete and more vital psychological context for the treatment of political problems. The political problems identifiable in this context as problems of *perception* and *expression* were treated in a more abstract and loftier fashion in Cicero's *Republic* as problems of *recognition* and *revelation* (see vol. 1, pp. 264–65). The difference in treatment that concerns us now is cosmological—a difference with respect to what is taken to be insight into a κόσμος. While acknowledging this difference, I shall bring out the continuity of treatment by continuing to refer to Cicero's problem of recognition.

61. See p. 10, this vol.

62. See vol. 1, pp. 313–15.

63. *Off.* 1. 15. In the preceding sentence Cicero has identified the "*rectitude* (*honestum*), which is the subject-matter of our investigation, as something which is honorable even though it is not always honored." Once again Cicero would seem to be turning to moral philosophy at the juncture where he would distinguish between the moral elite for which he is qualified and the senatorial aristocracy from which he is excluded as a *homo novus* (see vol. 1, pp. 190, 255).

64. *Phaedrus* 250D.

65. See vol. 1, pp. 288, 295. Weakening the Platonic distinction enables Cicero to construe more concretely (more literally) the Platonic analogy between the visual perception of physical beauty and the intellectual conception of a moral order: "Man is the only living thing that has a perception of order, of propriety, of control in words and actions. Thus no other living thing perceives beauty, charm, harmony; and nature and reason, extending this analogy from the realm of sight to that of the mind, discover that beauty, consistency, order are to be maintained even more in thought and action" (*Off.* 1. 14). We have already observed (n. 60, above) that man's perception of analogies is itself one of his distinctive traits. But when Marcus is invited to "perceive the very outline and as it were the appearance of *rectitude*," he is being invited to perceive an analogy which was not accessible to visual perception in Plato.

66. *Tusculanae Disputationes* 1. 79.

67. Berkeley, *Alciphron*, Dialogue III, 3.

68. *Off.* 1. 96.

69. John Locke, *Works*, 10 vols. (London: Thomas Tegg, 1832), 9: 176.

70. *The Theory of Moral Sentiments* (London: Henry G. Bohn, 1853), p. 315.

71. See chap. 12.

72. *Off.* 1. 110.

73. *Off.* 2. 17.

74. *Off.* 22.

75. *Rhetoric* 3. 1404B. Here as elsewhere I am neglecting Cicero's borrowings from the Aristotelian tradition (as well as from Isocrates) in order to follow out instead the expanding movement of his Platonizing of Stoicism—the movement which sweeps up his borrowings from other traditions. The primary rhetorical consideration for Aristotle is "persuasiveness" (*Rh.* 1. 1355B), and as the most "appropriate" means to this end, "clarity" of speech (*Rh.* 3. 1404B). Cicero is probably discounting both criteria in favor of "expressiveness" when he challenges: "No one ever exalted an orator whose speech made his meaning clear to his audience, but only despised one who was unable to accomplish this. Who then is the orator who arouses men? Whom do they gaze at in admiration when he

speaks? Whom do they applaud? Whom do they consider, as it were, a god among men?—The orator . . . whose style I term 'expressive' (*ornate*)" (*De Or.* 3. 52–53). With this shift in criteria, the Stoic criterion of "concision" (*brevitas*) has to be relinquished: "what is appropriate" in a speech is no longer determined by the specific requirements of a restricted subject-matter (see Diogenes Laertius 7. 59 for this Stoic criterion); "what is appropriate" to a speech is the impression the orator makes on his audience by the way he treats the subject-matter. It is a rhetorical theory of this relation beween the *personality* of the orator and the emotional responsiveness of his audience that is extended in *On Duties* to become a general moral theory of the relation between the individual and other men.

76. For the *cosmos* as a universe of discourse, see vol. 1, p. 317. For Cicero's allusion to the speaking voice, see vol. 1, pp. 244, 267, and accompanying n. 83. The best I can manage in the way of translation which respects some of the ordinarily neglected implications of *ornatus* (κόσμος) is the paraphrase, "the expression of an order." The usual translation in the rhetorical theory of modern Neoclassicism is "ornament" or "embellishment." But this translation reflects the modern tendency to confine rhetorical considerations to particular technical means of expression. A more sweeping translation is needed which retains the philosophical scope of the moral "order" exhibited by the mind of the orator. Since Cicero extends and generalizes the meaning of *ornatus*, the following Loeb translation makes little sense: "The most *ornate* speeches are those which take the widest range and which turn aside from the particular matter in dispute to engage in the explanation of the meaning of the general issue" (*De Or.* 3. 120). (I would translate instead "the most expressive speeches . . .") The explanation of the meaning of a general issue becomes philosophical with Cicero's refusal to sever rhetorical means of expression from the philosophical content which they are designed to express. Thus rhetoric becomes concerned with "a philosophy of life (*omni vivendi ratione*)" (*De Or.* 3. 122–23), which "includes the origin, the operation, and transformation of all things, all the virtues, all the duties, all the natural principles that relate to the practices, the minds, and the life of men," which "involves as well their customs, laws, and rights," which "controls the state, and treats everything whatsoever in an expressive and expansive manner (*ornate copiosoque*)" (*De Or.* 3. 76). The expansive manner finds its justification in this expansion of the subject-matter of rhetoric itself. Furthermore, here (as so often) Cicero's own characteristic *copia* as a rhetorician is illustrated by his having at his disposal a larger supply of technical terms than he needs to convey his treatment of this subject-matter. The criterion of expressive treatment is hardly distinguishable from the criterion of expansive treatment, and the process of expanding rhetoric's scope so that the orator can fully express himself is one in which "the orator is liberated [from the "technicalities" (*De Or.* 3. 148) of the traditional handbooks of rhetoric] to roam in so general and extended an area as to be without limits, and wherever he may take his stand, he finds himself on his own ground, and available to him all the resources and means of expression (*omnem apparatus ornatusque dicendi*)" (*De Or.* 3. 124–25). This liberation from "technicalities" is legitimated philosophically by Cicero's vulgarized version of Platonic recollection (see vol. 1, p. 190). "Nearly all the theory of those Greek technicians *(istorum artificum doctrina)*" Cicero explains, "is composed of rules (*praecepta*)." (For the way the Romans diminished the status of Greek *praecepta*, see chap. 7, n. 67.) Cicero does not claim that "theory is pointless, for in fact it provides *reminders*, so to speak, to the orator, as to the ideal norm which he must contemplate. But to my way of thinking," he adds, "all rules derive their force (*vis*), not from the fact that orators have gained their reputation for eloquence by following them, but because the theorists have observed and taken note of the performance of men who were naturally eloquent. This eloquence is not the product of theory, but the theory is the product of eloquence" (*De Or.* 1. 145–46). This reversal of the relation between scholarly "technicalities" and forceful oratory is linked with the reversal of the Platonic relation between theory and practice which we traced as a feature of the logic of Roman imperialism (see vol. 1, p. 206). Just as that reversal was the displacement

of the philosopher as a political theorist by the authoritative statesman, so the present reversal is the displacement of the rhetorical theorist by the forceful orator. (See vol. 1, p. 267 and accompanying n. 82 for *vis* as characteristic of Cicero's impressiveness as an orator.) The role that is played here by the *personality* of the orator exceeds any analytic theorizing about this role. In this connection, consider the comment A. E. Douglas offers, when tracing the sources for Cicero's rhetorical theory: "The stress he lays on the 'overall' stylistic impression produced by an orator as something not fully analyzable into component elements does not appear to be traceable beyond him to any other source" (*Brutus* [Oxford: Clarendon Press, 1966], p. xxxiii). We may perhaps compare the way the impression we receive of Socrates' personality exceeds Plato's actual portrayal (see chap. 7, n. 65).

77. See vol. 1, p. 265.

78. *Off.* 2. 22.

79. *Off.* 2. 17.

80. *Off.* 2. 43.

81. *Off.* 1. 134.

82. *Off.* 1. 1–4.

83. *Off.* 2. 44.

84. See vol. 1, p. 244.

85. See vol. 1, p. 294.

86. See vol. 1, p. 296.

87. *Off.* 2. 12. To bring out the way *honestum* is used as a criterion, I am offering "what is *morally right*" as an alternative translation to *rectitude*.

88. See vol. 1, p. 257.

89. *Off.* 3. 8.

90. *Off.* 3. 8.

91. See vol. 1, p. 316. Because the term *real* is ambiguous (see vol. 1, p. 238), I intrude the term *true* to carry through the comparison.

92. *The Prince*, chap. 15. Machiavelli's argument may possibly have been shaped by Cicero's admission, "Those we live with are not perfectly moral and ideally wise; in them it is enough if an appearance of virtue [*simulacra virtutis*] can be found" (*Off.* 15. 46). But Machiavelli would regard the political "appearance" as more autonomous. Cicero is merely relaxing the ideal standards of traditional Stoicism in favor of some more practical approximation to virtue; he is not admitting that those we live with are not moral at all. J. H. Whitfield is sensitive to Machiavelli's debt in *The Prince* to *On Duties*, but he seems to go too far in his attempt to make Machiavelli as moral as Cicero (*Machiavelli* [New York: Russell & Russell, 1965], pp. 69–71, 74, 103). To discover what Machiavelli means by other men not being "moral" (*buoni*), we need to take into account what "moral" had come to imply politically in the intervening and increasingly moralistic tradition that separates Machiavelli from Cicero. Machiavelli's argument then becomes in effect a retort to the frequently cited proverb. "*Rex eris si recte facies, si non facias, non eris* (You really will be ruler if you act morally; if you don't, you won't)." This traditional medieval subordination of political considerations to moral considerations is crystallized in the stereotype deriving "*rex a recte regendo.*" I am citing that storehouse of medieval stereotypes, Isidore's *Etymologia* (9. 13).

93. *The Prince*, chap. 15.

94. *Nicomachean Ethics* 5. 1130A.

95. *The Prince,* chap. 17. Machiavelli is taking exception to some strongly moralistic phase in the development of this *topos* (a phase which could be illustrated by Seneca's *On Clemency*). Cicero's utilitarian treatment (*Off.* 2. 23–31) is more realistic, though of course he resolves the problem in favor of love and winds up with a reference to his dialogue *On Friendship.* This reference is one possible explanation of Machiavelli's identifying the problem of this part of *The Prince* as the question of "the ruler's relation to his subjects and friends." In any case, friendship represents the moralistic consideration which Machiavelli would brush to one side. But it must not be thought that Machiavelli would condone distinguishing private life, where the individual can afford to be moral and friendly, from public life, where the individual must be Machiavellian. See Martin Fleisher, "Trust and Deceit in Machiavelli's Comedies," *Journal of the History of Ideas,* 27, no. 3 (July–September, 1966), pp. 365–80.

96. See p. 4, this vol.

97. *Prince,* Dedication.

98. See p. 4, this vol.

99. *Works,* 1, Author's Epistle to the Reader.

100. "The principles of the politics consist in knowledge of the motions of the mind" (*ibid.*, 74).

101. Aristotle, *Politics* 7. 1326B.

102. *Pol.* 2. 1261A, 1264B; 3. 1277B.

103. The original topological distinction I drew between the two traditions was extracted from Mill. The present topological refinement could perhaps be extracted from Mill: "The same laws will not suit the English, who place their habitual reliance in themselves, and the French, who place theirs in leaders" (suppressed passage from "Bentham," *Essays on Literature and Society,* ed. J. B. Schneewind [New York: Collier Books, 1965], p. 288.

104. *Leviathan*, Introduction, "Characters" here of course retains its etymological sense and refers to what is engraved in man's heart. For the pertinence of this literary metaphor, see both n. 139, below, and p. 194, this vol.

105. *Ibid.*

106. See p. 4, this vol.

107. *Leviathan,* pt. 2, chap. 18.

108. Secs. 2–9. Sec. 9 is entitled, "*De deoptris duplicatis sive de Telescopio et Microscopio.*"

109. *Posterior Analytics* 2. 97B.

110. Thomas Aquinas (*Summa Theologica* II^{a} II^{ae}. Qu. 121. Art. 4) is citing Aristotle (*Nic. Eth.* 4. 1124A). The Greek term here translated *ornatus* is *κόσμος*—i.e., the same term which Cicero translates *ornatus* when he takes over Plato's definition of self-control (see p. 22, this vol.).

111. My English translation, "the expression of an order," respects Cicero's attempt to circumvent the unclassical (even if Neoclassical) distinction between ornament and function, expression and content. At the same time, of course, my entire interpretation is an interpretation of the different ways the relations are "ordered" (adjusted) that compose the structure of a political theory. At the present stage of this interpretation I am analyzing the way the individual's relations with himself and others are "ordered" in Cicero's *On Duties* by concentrating on the two virtues of propriety and magnanimity which overlap each other insofar as each is an "expression" of an "ordering" of these relations.

112. *The Prince,* chap. 18. Cf. chap. 25 and *The Discourses,* bk. 3, chap. 9, which is entitled, "*Come conviene variare co' tempi, volendo sempre avere buona fortuna.*" I am not proposing a firm contrast between Machiavelli's endorsement of opportunism and Cicero's repudiation of opportunism. There is perhaps a more definite contrast between Machiavelli's or Cicero's opportunism and traditional Stoic inflexibility. Cicero was usually prepared to "move with the times (*temporibus adsentiendum*)," arguing that "undeviating persistence in a judgment has never been commended in the case of those exceptional men who govern [steer] the state" (*Fam.* 1. 9. 21). Cicero goes on to justify "tacking" before the wind. For the metaphor, see chap. 8, n. 44; for the use of this metaphor in defense of Cicero's Stoic withdrawal from politics, see chap. 9, n. 167; for the contrast between Cicero's opportunism and Stoic inflexibility, see p. 66, this vol. and accompanying n. 21.

113. In *The Prince,* chap. 25, Machiavelli explains that he is dealing first with "opposing fortune in general," and then "restricts" himself "to particular cases."

114. See, e.g., *Tusc.* 2. 43.

115. See vol. 1, p. 296.

116. See pp. 20–21, this vol.

117. See vol. 1, p. 226.

118. See vol. 1, p. 222.

119. *Off.* 1. 3.

120. *Off.* 1. 66–67.

121. *Off.* 1. 72.

122. *Off.* 1. 71, 73. For the traditional Stoic hesitation, see vol. 1, pp. 202–4.

123. *Off.* 1. 77–78.

124. *Off.* 1. 61.

125. *Off.* 1. 152. *Magnitudo animi* remained, however, the usual translation in Antiquity.

126. See vol. 1, p. 250.

127. *Off.* 1. 78–79.

128. *Off.* 1. 77–78.

129. *Off.* 1. 64.

130. *Off.* 1. 65.

131. *Off.* 1. 65.

132. *Works,* 4: 32.

133. *Ibid.,* p. 40.

134. *Leviathan,* chap. 15.

135. *Ibid.* Hobbes is referring to "a certain Noblenesse or Gallantnesse of courage;" the Latin text of the Leviathan translates "*Generositas.*" *Générosité* was Descartes' translation for *Magnanimitas* (*Les passions de l'ame,* 3eme Partie, art. 161).

136. *Leviathan,* chap. 6; italics added.

137. *Ibid.,* chap. 13; italics added.

138. *Ibid.*

139. We have here an instance of the large-scale reshuffling of the relations between moral theory and "other studies" (see vol. 1, p. 14). Problems of knowledge had been formulated and reformulated during Antiquity and the Middle Ages, but in Hobbes they acquire general relevance for the transition from the individual to his relation to other men: "Having spoken of the powers of the mind . . . considered in every man by himself, without relation to another, it will fall fitly . . . to speak of the effect of the same powers upon one another, which effects are also the signs, by which one taketh notice what another conceiveth and intendeth" (*Works,* 4: 70–71). It is true that in Aristotle's *Rhetoric* the passions had been treated in terms of their effects on men's judgments, that this treatment had influenced Stoic moral theory, and that with the encroachment of the rhetorical tradition on Stoic moral theory men's actions had come to be construed as "signs" of their conceptions and intentions (see, e.g., chap. 11, n. 38). But the problem of recognizing what another conceiveth and intendeth had never been extended and generalized as it is by Hobbes. Thus when he has pointed out that "countries as well as men . . . publicly profess their mutual fear and diffidence," he picks up as an explanation the traditional theological difficulty of distinguishing the wicked from the righteous, but he then arrives at a list of politically relevant actions all of which illustrate the problem of knowledge: "That men are evil by nature, follows not from this principle [i.e., from "their mutual fear and diffidence"]; for though the wicked were fewer than the righteous, yet because we cannot distinguish them, there is a necessity of suspecting, heeding, anticipating, subjugating, self-defending, ever incident to the most honest and fairest conditioned" (*Works,* 2: xv–xvi).

140. *Leviathan,* chap. 8.

141. *Works,* 4: 102.

11

The Individual and the State

I speak not of the men, but in the abstract of the Seat of Power.—Hobbes

Liberty and Authority

"The subject of this essay," Mill points out at the beginning of his *On Liberty,* "is the nature and limits of the power which can be legitimately exercised by society over the individual." This subject, he goes on to explain, "is so far from being new that, in a certain sense, it has divided mankind, almost in the remotest ages."[1] He finds that "the struggle between Liberty and Authority is the most conspicuous feature in the portions of history with which we are earliest familiar, particularly in that of Greece, Rome and England."

Mill recalls how this subject acquired scope for him while he was sight-seeing in Rome. He had "planned and written . . . a short essay in 1854; . . . mounting the steps of the Capitol, in January 1855, . . . the thought first arose of converting it into a volume."[2] What was on Mill's mind was not the prospect of renewing Rome's greatness, which had dazzled Petrarch and Machiavelli, but the threat of tyranny visualized against the backdrop of the decline and fall of the Roman Republic. Before we consider this ambivalence of Rome in the history of political thought, we must cut down the historical scope of Mill's subject. We have to introduce the qualification which we appended in the last chapter to his appraisal of "the whole stream of Greek history," as a series of examples of the decisive role of the individual.[3] Whatever may have been the most conspicuous feature of the history of Greece, the struggle between the liberty of the individual and the authority of the state is not a correspondingly conspicuous feature of Greek political theory, as we shall see that it is of the political theory of Rome and England.

The Greeks had no word for the authority of the state and therefore no word antithetical in its implications for the liberty of the individual. But when timorous Hobbes worries about the reception of his *Leviathan,* it is because he does not know "how the world will receive it, nor how it may reflect on those that shall seem to favor it; for in a way beset with those that contend, on one side for too great Liberty, and on the other side for too much Authority, 'tis hard to passe between the points of both unwounded."[4] The terms designating the two sides of this way also designate steps in Hobbes' deduction of his political theory. His *De Cive* is divided into two parts. The first part, where Hobbes constructs his theory of human nature, by abstracting the individual (as we saw in the previous chapter) from his political relations to other men, is entitled *Libertas;* the second part, where he brings the individual back into the state, is entitled *Imperium.*

Machiavelli's *Prince* begins, "All those states and empires which have had, and have, authority over men have been and are either republics or principates."[5] The term "liberty" is equally prominent in Machiavelli's *Discourses,* and later interpreters have often found the two works antithetical. But it was in fact left to the thinkers of the next century to develop the antithesis that finally receives a systematic formulation in Hobbes. The Monarchomachs raised the specific question of whether or not the power of a tyrant can legitimately be resisted by a "private citizen." In dealing with this question, the Huguenot author of *Vindiciae contra tyrannos*—perhaps the most influential of the sixteenth-century Monarchomach tracts in the struggle between liberty and authority that divided seventeenth-century England—recalled "the law of tyrannicide which honors the living with great and memorable recompenses, and the dead with worthy epitaphs and glorious statues, that have been their country's liberators from tyrants: as Harmodius and Aristogiton at Athens, Brutus and Cassius at Rome."[6] The examples of Harmodius and Aristogiton had been honored in Athenian folklore and propaganda, and liberators from a tyrant were in fact assigned certain rights by Athenian law. Such examples had therefore been entirely available for theoretical consideration by Plato and Aristotle; yet neither of them had dealt with the question of the right of the individual to resist a tyrant;

neither had found these examples deserving either of the honor the Monarchomachs accord them or of the execration of a Hobbes.

Despite the fact that Hobbes' political theory is conceived as an answer to the question the Monarchomachs had raised regarding the right of resistance, Hobbes usually prefers to deal with their classical sources. Indeed he assigns to all ancient philosophers without discrimination the Monarchomach's answer to the question which Plato and Aristotle did not even raise:

> At this day it [tyrannicide] is by many divines, and of old it was by all the philosophers—Plato, Aristotle, Cicero, Seneca, Plutarch, and the rest of the maintainers of the Greek and Roman anarchies—held not only lawful, but even worthy of the greatest praise. . . . And by reading of these Greek and Latine authors, men from their childhood have gotten a habit (under a false shew of Liberty) of favouring tumults, and of licentious controlling the actions of their Soveraigns; and again of controlling those controllers, with the effusion of so much blood; as I think I may truely say, there was never any thing so deerly bought, as these western parts have bought the learning of the Greek and Latine tongues.[7]

We have become so accustomed today to such expositions of Plato's political theory as Karl Popper's that we have come to regret that the price these Western parts have paid for its classical heritage is the prestige Plato has lent authoritarianism. We are therefore a little surprised at Hobbes' complaint that Plato made his contribution to modern bloodshed as an anarchist. Just as Plato's political theory might not lend itself to Popper's interpretation as an historicist theory were it not for the use to which Polybius had put it when he contributed to the development of modern historicism, so Plato's political theory might not lend support to either side of the modern struggle between liberty and authority were it not for the two different uses to which it had been put by Cicero, who contributed to the development of the humanistic political tradition by taking both sides in this struggle. In the *Republic* he was the partisan of *authority;* in *On Duties*—particularly in the third book—he became the partisan of *liberty*.[8]

In Cicero's *Republic* the initial debate pitted monarchist and aristocratic proponents of authority against democratic proponents of liberty. When Cicero resolved this debate largely in favor of the quasi-monarchical authority to be exercised by the *princeps* on behalf of the aristocratic class, he drew on Plato's *Statesman* and on the Stoic tradition.[9] In order to circumvent Roman political prejudice against monarchy, and to have his own role recognized as a *princeps* who was not an aristocrat, he exploited the moral implications of both Plato's conception of the ideal ruler as "king *or* statesman" and the Stoic conception of the absolute moral authority the wise man exercises over himself. The assimilation of political authority to moral authority continues in the *Mirror of Princes* genre and constitutes the moralistic political tradition to which Machiavelli assigns his predecessors when he rejects the way "many" have treated the problem of "how the prince should act and rule in relation to his subjects and friends."[10] But when Hobbes rejects tradition, he is, in effect, assigning "all the philosophers" to a different moralistic political tradition—a libertarian tradition which stresses the individual's moral right to resist the tyrant who has usurped authority. Cicero's *Republic* having disappeared, Hobbes is disposing of the only Ciceronian tradition with which he is familiar when he defends the principle of authority by attacking the monarchomach language of Roman politics:

It was the speech of the Roman people (to whom the name of king had been rendered odious, as well by the tyranny of the Tarquins, as by the genius and decretals of that city); it was the speech, I say, of the public, however pronounced from a private mouth (if yet Cato the Censor were no more than such: that all kings are to be reckoned amongst ravenous beasts.[11]

In Cicero's *Republic* the tyranny of Tarquin was only a subordinate episode in Cicero's effort to rehabilitate a moral contrast between the tyrant as a bestial lapse from human nature and the ideal statesman as its fulfillment so that his contemporaries would learn enough Greek moral philosophy to distinguish between a Caesar and a Cicero, and recognize in a Cicero "the man" whom Scipio and his fellow aristocrats had been "anxious to find."[12] But Cicero's own philosophical and political position has changed between the *Republic* and *On Duties* in a fashion which begins a new chapter in the history of political thought—the chapter Hobbes will attempt to bring to an end.

The Private Citizen

We saw in the last chapter that the statesman with the moral stature of a Stoic wise man has become more difficult to find in *On Duties:*

> He can never be regarded great who relies on the support of the erratic and ignorant multitude. In fact the loftier the mind the more readily is it inclined to perform unjust actions out of desire for glory. To be sure we are on very slippery ground here, for it is difficult to find a man who, when he has endured toils and dangers, does not desire glory as a reward for his actions.[13]

Caesar was a lofty mind who performed unjust actions out of desire for glory; Cicero is a man who has endured toils and dangers and who desires glory as a reward for his actions. Their confrontation in *On Duties* still involves the antithesis drawn in the *Republic* between the tyrant and the just ruler. But another antithesis emerges in *On Duties.* At the time when Cicero was writing the *Republic,* he could still envisage with some confidence the prospect of his regaining the political authority that would enable him to dispel the threat of Caesar's tyranny. What has happened in the meantime is brought out by the dramatic way Caesar's entry in the third book of *On Duties* scatters other problems:

> Why on earth compile examples of petty crimes, such as the forging of wills and fraudulent business transactions? Here you have a man whose desire it was to become king of the Roman people and the ruler of the whole world, and who satisfied this desire! Anyone who says that such a desire is morally right is out of his mind, for he is applauding the overthrow of law and liberty and considering their hideous monstrous destruction a glorious action.[14]

Confronted by the tyrant, Cicero is no longer primarily the defender of authority he had been in the *Republic.* In *On Duties* he becomes, and will remain in the history of political thought, the defender of liberty.

In other words, the shift in the focus of theoretical interest from the role of the individual ruler in Machiavelli to the role of the individual citizen in the Monarchomachs and Hobbes begins in Cicero's *On Duties.* Here even the glory of Cicero's spokesman in the *Republic* is no longer beyond comparison:

> Africanus, outstanding as he was as a man and as a general, rendered no greater service to the Republic by the destruction of Numantia than

Publius Nasica, a private citizen *(privatus),* rendered at the same time by assassinating Tiberius Gracchus.[15]

On Duties offers the justification for a private citizen's assuming this political role even without recognized political authority.

In the *Republic* Laelius' rallying to Scipio in his search with the suggestion, "You are perhaps looking for the wise man?" indicated that they were looking for an individual who would exercise that moral authority over himself that was traditionally associated with the Stoic philosopher.[16] This individual would thereby be qualified, Scipio went on to explain, to exercise political authority over others. But when Cicero deals in *On Duties* with the issues raised by the assassination of Caesar, the moral emphasis which he carries over from Stoicism into his political theory moves from the authority which the wise man exercises over himself to the liberty which he secures by the unwavering resistance of his mind to changing circumstances external to it. Just as the privileged position the Stoic wise man had attained in the universe by his self-control and magnanimity becomes in Panaetius and Cicero his privileged position among men that enables him to exercise political control over them, so his resistance to external control by fortune now becomes his resistance to political control. The traditional lineaments of the wise man which Cicero employed in the *Republic* in characterizing the just ruler, he now employs to characterize the private citizen who resists the tyrant. In this way a Stoic contrast between the morally responsible citizen and the tyrant supersedes the Stoic contrast of the *Republic* between the morally responsible ruler and the tyrant. There is a corresponding redefinition of magnanimity: "Those who are to be regarded courageous and great are . . . those who resist unjust actions."[17]

Ordinarily the outstanding individual's sense of his superiority would be qualified—according to the first definition of magnanimity in *On Duties*—by his respect for both philosophical and political authority: "The mind which has been well endowed by nature will never consent to obey anyone, except one who can teach it or guide it, or has a just and legal right to rule."[18] But the political qualification is removed when the wise man confronts the tyrant, who has no moral or legal right to rule. An uncompromising Stoicism can then be revived in which the magnanimous man regains his traditional philosophical posture of complete moral integrity.

VINDICIAE CONTRA TYRANNOS

Sometimes Cicero felt that he was a philosopher who had descended into the Platonic cave of Roman politics; he was "blinded" because he held too firmly to the vision of the ideal.[19] But in the long run Cicero too often occupied slippery ground in his political maneuvering (as well as in piecing together his eclectic philosophy) to secure recognition for integrity and refusal to compromise. Cicero was (to adapt Bismark's comment on Salisbury) a lathe which was painted with a little Stoicism so that it looked like iron. The Romans preferred to think of the tyrant as confronted by the less pliable Cato of Utica.

Sometimes Cicero felt that it was Cato who held too firmly to the vision of the ideal. He complained when Cato spoke in the Senate "as though he were living in Plato's ideal state rather than in the sewer that is Rome."[20] But when Cicero applied the criterion of *propriety,* with which Panaetius had introduced some flexibility into Stoicism, it was to admit that the inflexibility of the martyr was a role more appropriate to Cato than to himself.[21]

There had always been moments in Cicero's career when he did not insist on a leading role for himself. He would have been satisfied to find someone else to do the leading. "I have someone to run from," he once confessed ruefully, "no one to follow."[22] In most of his later philosophical writings he no longer continued to be quite the politically leading figure he had implied he was in his *Republic.* There were a few shouts of *Cicero et libertas* after Caesar's assassination, but what counts for our historical purposes is that his philosophical placing of the leading political figures of his day assigned them their roles in most of later political thought.[23]

In *On Ends* Cato of Utica is selected by Cicero for the role of defending the integrity of Stoic philosophy against his own facile and eclectic humanism. Cato had modeled himself on his great-grandfather, whom Cicero designates "the wisest of men." Cicero does not except the traditional designee. He disposes of Socrates by insisting on the Socratic identification of wisdom with virtue: "Socrates is admired only for what he said; Cato, for what he really did."[24] Unfortunately, for the relevance of the comparison, the elder Cato did not admire Socrates even for what he said. The elder Cato disposed of Socrates (according to Plutarch) as "a big talker who tried his best to become his country's tyrant by undermining its traditions." The elder Cato was sensitive to the threat that philosophy was to tradition. He not only exemplified traditional Roman virtue but also its "complete hostility to philosophy and Greek culture."[25] In modeling himself on his great-grandfather, the younger Cato illustrates the extent to which adherence to traditional Roman virtue became philosophical and Greek—a self-conscious literary pose. The younger Cato was a *perfectus Stoicus*.[26] Cicero recalls coming upon him in the library "surrounded by piles of books on Stoicism."[27] Cicero also recalls watching Cato demonstrate his Stoic indifference to public opinion by reading in the Senate while waiting for his colleagues to assemble.[28]

It was to describe Cato that Cicero first employed the term *greatness of mind*.[29] Cato's last stand for liberty was the greatness of a mind that was beyond the reach of the tyrant's usurped authority. In fact, "God himself could seek no nobler sight" than Cato's martyrdom.[30] The fact of his martyrdom removed "any doubt that virtue really exists."[31] Of this fact Cicero reminded Brutus, when he addressed to him *On Ends* and its sequel, the *Tusculan Disputations*. Brutus had both the philosophical qualifications and the family connections to continue Cato's struggle for liberty. He was the author of a treatise *On Virtue*, which he appropriately addressed to Cicero.[32] He inherited his political role as the lineal descendant of the assassin of Tarquin—typology having triumphed over the difficulty that the original Brutus had further displayed his devotion to liberty by slaying his sons while they were still youths. The descendant could also take over from Cato. Brutus was Cato's nephew. His own father had died when he was seven. He had been brought up by Cato and he divorced his wife to marry Cato's daughter, over the objections of her mother—Cato's half-sister—who had been Caesar's mistress. There was some suspicion that Brutus was Caesar's son. This family connection is chronologically implausible. Here typology would falter anyway, but a trio of father figures is probably more than even Freud could cope with.

Cicero and Brutus both composed eulogies of Cato's virtue which helped lay the foundations of the later Cato legend. Caesar himself showed the political antagonist he preferred by replying to Cicero's *Cato* in an *Anti-Cato* with conciliatory praise for Cicero as a literary stylist.[33] With respect to this preference, Brutus seems to have agreed with Caesar. He stressed—much to Cicero's annoyance—Cato's role, at the expense of Cicero's, in the one episode to which Cicero clung as exhibiting his own *greatness of mind*—the suppression of the Catilinarian conspiracy.[34]

Although Cicero's, Brutus' and other *Catones* have been lost, Sallust not only dramatizes the confrontation of Caesar and Cato in his version of this exemplary episode, but also employs some of the conflicting conceptions of *greatness of mind* which Cicero (following Panaetius) attempted to reconcile in *On Duties*. External circumstances and the requirements of other men supply, in Sallust's visualization, occasions for Caesar to exhibit his *greatness of mind,* while Cato achieves this virtue in the traditionally inflexible manner of the Stoic philosopher:

> Their greatness of mind and glory were comparable, but achieved in different ways. Caesar became great by generosity and munificence; Cato, by the integrity of his life. Caesar was esteemed for his humanity and benevolence; austerity lent dignity to Cato. Caesar achieved recognition by giving, relieving, and pardoning; Cato by granting nothing. In Caesar there was a refuge for the unfortunate; in Cato, annihilation for the vicious. In Caesar, his adaptability was admired; in Cato, his rigidity. To conclude, Caesar had applied himself to a life of energy and action; intent upon the interests of his friends, he neglected his own; he refused nothing to others that was worthy of acceptance, while for himself he desired great authority, the command of an army and a new war in which his virtue might be displayed. But Cato's ambition was that of self-control, propriety, and above all, of austerity . . . ; he preferred really to be virtuous than to appear so, and thus the less he courted glory, the more it pursued him.[35]

In the writings glorifying the emperor that culminate with the *On Clemency* which Seneca addressed to Nero, the first conception of *greatness of mind* largely prevails, but it is absorbed into the Hellenistic Stoic tradition of the just king, which Cicero in his *Republic* had helped render relevant to a Roman ruler. This tradition, which might be termed "imperial" or "authoritarian," is continued by the set pieces of moral exhortation and flattery which belong to the *Mirror of Princes* genre. The second conception of magnanimity survives as a "republican" or "libertarian" tradition.[36] Augustus tried to twist Stoic intransigence to his political purposes by wryly suggesting that his regime, now that it was established, would have been supported by Cato, since Cato had "resisted change."[37] But the cult of Cato's *personality* became instead a way of dignifying republican resistance to the emperor.[38] This cult is labeled by scholars "The Philosophical Opposition,"[39] for its history is marked by the periodic exiling of Stoic philosophers from Rome and by a succession of exemplary suicides which trace a line of apostolic descent that matches the succession of Cynic saints whose pedigree had earlier been traced back to the *princeps nostrorum martyrum*.[40] The extent to which this cult, like the cult of the emperor, was grafted onto the Hellenistic Stoic tradition[41] helps account for the uncertainty of scholars and (scholars should be readier to suppose) of the cultists themselves as to whether this cult was merely Stoic *patientia* (i.e., merely passive moral resistance designed to maintain the *personal* dignity of a member of the aristocracy) or could entail active political resistance to the emperor.[42]

Cicero had performed some of the grafting, and his expositions of Stoic moral intransigence can be read as a summons to arms against Caesar. Cicero had compared Cato with the Socrates of the *Phaedo*,[43] just as he had implied by his use in *The Dream of Scipio* of materials from the *Phaedo* a comparison between the death of Scipio at the hand of *populares* and the death of Socrates at the behest of the Athenian democracy.[44] In the Cato legend Socrates actually became Cato's own model in meeting his death. The point is belabored in Plutarch's biography, where it is reported that Cato had read the *Phaedo* through twice before committing suicide, both times, apparently, circumventing the prohibition against suicide by identifying his situation as Socratic.[45] Plutarch himself obtained materials for this biography from the book on Cato which had been written by another courageous suicide, Thrasea Paetus,[46] who celebrated Brutus' birthday each year and modeled his own last hours on the example of Socrates as well as of Cato.[47] Thrasea's contemporary Seneca attempted to reconcile the two traditions by combining Stoic reverence for the emperor's *political* authority with Stoic reverence for Cato's *moral* liberty. Although the Nero of Seneca's *On Clemency* was the magnanimous king of the one Stoic tradition, Seneca was able to enhance with his own martyrdom the other Stoic tradition in which the "great mind" was a private kingdom, beyond the reach of the tyrant's power.[48] *Le courage aussi est une patrie.*

Doctrines of moral resistance and moral liberty were revived by the Monarchomachs in the sixteenth century for their political implications. We are not certain who was the author of *Vindiciae contra tyrannos,* but his pseudonymn was Junius Brutus. The extent to which this Latin libertarian tradition (like the authoritarian tradition which we examined in Cicero's *Republic*) had assimilated Greek moral philosophy accounts for the fact that Hobbes' defense of political authority against contemporary Monarchomachs is an attack on "all the philosophers—Plato, Aristotle, Cicero, Seneca, Plutarch, and the rest of the maintainers of the Greek and Roman anarchies," for holding tyrannicide "not only lawful, but even worthy of the greatest praise."[49]

The Conservation of Motion

Hobbes undercuts this resistance movement by defining liberty in terms of physical motion:

> Liberty, or Freedome, signifieth properly the absence of opposition; (by opposition, I mean externall impediments of motion) and may be applyed no lesse to irrationall, and inanimate creatures, than to rationall. . . . But when the words "Free" and "Liberty" are applyed to any thing but bodies, they are abused; for that which is not subject to motion, is not subject to impediment.[50]

Once liberty applies only to bodies in motion, liberty loses its distinctive moral significance as the immobile resistance traditionally attainted by the lofty and great mind. Hobbes' restriction in the application of the term "liberty" to what is "subject to motion" is so drastic a cosmological adjustment that it will take the rest of this chapter to trace the implications for his theory of human nature.

What is "subject to motion" in Hobbes is subject to the fundamental law of motion—the Galilean law (later construed as the principle of inertia) whereby every body conserves its motion. Since Hobbes' universe is a *plenum,* resistance becomes an ordinary physical occurrence: "I define Resistence to be the endeavour [*conatus*] of one moved body, either wholly or in part contrary to the endeavour of another moved body which toucheth the same."[51] Unfortunately Hobbes' correlative definition of liberty as the absence of external impediments is usually dislodged today from this cosmological setting. It is viewed simply as the first clear and definite statement of that negative conception of liberty as freedom from interference which has remained characteristic of liberal political thought. Thus my double use of the term "resistance" to embrace at once moral and physical implications may seem a misleading pun.[52]

I am not punning. What is at stake here is not merely my interpretative procedure of determining a theorist's place in his tradition by beginning with his cosmological or scientific adjustment; the criteria of relevance that determine the deductive structure of Hobbes' own philosophy is also at stake. Interpreters today miss the force of Hobbes' argument that liberty applies "no less to inanimate creatures than to Rationall" when they sever his deduction at the juncture at which he makes his transition from inanimate creatures to rational creatures. Leo Strauss claims that "the moral attitude which underlies Hobbes' political philosophy is independent of the foundation of modern science" (sc., Galilean physics).[53] Richard Peters admits that what "excited" Hobbes about natural science was "the possibility of deducing consequences from the law of intertia in spheres to which it had not yet been applied—sensation, psychology and politics."[54] But Hobbes' excitement becomes irrelevant as soon as Peters finds that Hobbes' psychology is only "ostensibly a deduction from the theory of motion," that it is "in fact constructed with an eye much more on its political relevance than on its theoretical adequacy."[55] Indeed the most detailed portion of Hobbes' psychology is not (in Peter's view) even ostensibly a deduction from his theory of motion:

> Hobbes' detailed classification of the passions scarcely repays detailed attention. It looks very much like the account of the passions in Aristotle's *Rhetoric* served up in rather a piecemeal manner to provide a transition from physiology to politics.[56]

At this juncture Peters' and Strauss' otherwise quite different interpretations of Hobbes converge. When Strauss finds a moral instead of a scientific attitude underlying Hobbes' political philosophy, he too turns back to Aristotle's *Rhetoric:* "it would be difficult to find another classical work whose importance for Hobbes' political philosophy can be compared with the *Rhetoric.*"[57]

If it is the case that Hobbes has managed the transition which is crucial to his deduction by serving up in rather a piecemeal manner the account of the passions in the *Rhetoric,* then Hobbes is a wretched philosopher who did not know what he was up to, and there is little prospect of any part of his philosophy repaying detailed attention. Pause to consider the relevance Hobbes attaches to the passions themselves in his deduction. The political conclusion that Hobbes reaches in his deduction is that the state of nature is a state of war. This conclusion Hobbes identifies as an "inference made from the passions."[58] The passions equip this stretch of his deduction with premises; when he makes his transition to politics in the first paragraph of part II of the *Leviathan,* Hobbes recalls "that miserable condition of Warre, which is necessarily consequent (as hath been shewn) to the naturall passions of men."[59] Nor can we neglect, if we are going to pay any attention to Hobbes as a philosopher, the details of his classification of these passions. Specific passions play a special part in his deduction. In beginning the deduction, Hobbes has to "first put such principles down for a foundation as passion not mistrusting may not seek to displace."[60] Not mistrusting is itself a certain alignment of specific passions. Other specific passions gain in force as the deduction proceeds, for it is to be distinguished as a deduction from an ordinary "trayne of thoughts" which is "unguided, without designe, and inconstant, wherein there is no passionate thought, to govern and direct those that follow to it self, as the end and scope of some desire, or other passion."[61] As we are all aware, fear is the most relevant passionate thought which is to govern and direct those that follow in the deduction.

It is, moreover, the reader's own train of thought that concerns Hobbes. We shall see that the fear that enters the deduction is the reader's fear for himself. Recall from the Introduction to the *Leviathan* Hobbes' appeal to self-consciousness, "Read Thyself," and his explanation, "Whosoever looketh into himself . . . shall thereby read and know what are the thoughts and passions of all other men."[62] We are to read our own thoughts and passions in reading Hobbes' words.

Since knowledge is in question, it may be objected that the deduction of the *Leviathan* is not "mentall discourse" but distinctively logical in the sense that it is a "discourse in words," in which their meanings are held constant by defining the words. But definitions are needed for this purpose precisely because of the fluctuating influence of the passions: "In reasoning a man must take heed of words," for "though the nature of what we conceive be the same, yet the diversity of our reception of it . . . gives every thing a tincture of our different passions."[63] Particular heed must then be taken in defining the passions themselves. Their definition is hardly a casual affair that would be safe to leave to Aristotle by lifting pieces of his account of the passions from the *Rhetoric.*

Peters' attribution of a piecemeal performance to Hobbes is prompted by Peters' own conviction that a deductive relation between physics or physiology and morals or politics is impossible in principle. I am not concerned with this question of principle. The relation with which I *am* concerned in principle is the relation between philosophy and the history of philosophy. My procedure is to deal with the way a theorist adjusts the relation between politics and "other studies" as determining at once the structure of his political philosophy and his place within his tradition. I am therefore refusing to accept the division of interpretive labor that prevails today between the philosopher and the historian of ideas.[64] The philosopher today finds a previous philosopher philosophically relevant insofar as he is a predecessor—i.e., insofar as he can be interpreted as anticipating some contemporary philosophical issue. I have no quarrel with this retrospective point of view as such, but rather with the way in which the previous philosopher's relation to his own predecessors is viewed as philosophically irrelevant and of merely historical interest. There is no serious prospect today of conducting a convincing philosophical attack on this division of labor. I am therefore attacking it on historical grounds. I have tried to show that the traditional humanistic theory of human nature, despite its piecemeal character, does have a discernible structure, or at any rate that it acquires a structure which is discernible whenever a philosopher finds a place within the humanistic tradition. I am now trying to determine Hobbes' place within this tradition, by showing that he has a philosophically consistent interpretation of this tradition and that this interpretation is a portion of the deductive structure of his own philosophy.

Whatever might be said regarding Peters' or Strauss' philosophical convictions regarding Hobbes' deductive procedure, their interpretation of Hobbes' philosophy is faulty as history of philosophy—faulty not just in the interpretation of specific details but in the general assumption regarding the history of philosophy that lies behind their interpretation of these details. When the historian today turns back to a classical text, such as Aristotle's *Rhetoric,* in order to elucidate an early modern text, he too often remains the accomplice or victim of nineteenth-century neo-Hellenism and forgets to take into account the intervening Latin classical tradition. I am not disputing Strauss' observation, "It would be difficult to find another classical work whose importance for Hobbes' political philosophy can be compared with the *Rhetoric.*"[65] I am merely pointing out that Strauss apparently restricts the adjective "classical" to Greek works. We shall find every reason to suspect that Latin works were more important to Hobbes so far as his classification of the passions is concerned, and indeed may even have influenced his interpretation of Aristotle's *Rhetoric.*[66]

If Peters had not become discouraged by the detail of Hobbes' classification of the passions, he might have counted them and discovered that Hobbes lists forty-eight passions in the *Leviathan.* Since Aristotle only lists fourteen in his *Rhetoric,* it is somewhat difficult to see how Hobbes can be serving up Aristotle's account "in rather a piecemeal manner." It is also difficult to understand Peter's claim that Hobbes' classification "looks very much like the account of the passions in Aristotle's *Rhetoric.*" Let us risk pedantry by taking a quick look. I reproduce Aristotle's complete list of fourteen passions and the first fourteen passions on Hobbes' list, and since "very much like" is a comparative expression, I add a third complete list of the passions. It is from a Latin writer who can be regarded (in this portion of his philosophy) as belonging to the humanistic tradition I have been tracing.

Aristotle	
Anger	Mildness
Hate	Love
Fear	Confidence
Shame	Shamelessness
Benevolence	Malevolence
Pity	Indignation
Envy	Emulation

Aquinas		*Hobbes*	
(concupiscible)		(*conatus*)	
Love	Hate	Desire	Aversion
Desire	Aversion	Love	Hate
Pleasure	Pain	Pleasure	Pain
(irascible)		Contempt	
Hope	Despair	Hope	Despair
Fear	Daring	Fear	Courage
Anger		Anger	
		Diffidence	Confidence

Motion and Rest

Hobbes' classification does not look at all like Aristotle's. But it does look rather like Aquinas'.[67] Aristotle's *Rhetoric* was doubtless important to Hobbes. He may have "studied it afresh," as Strauss claims to have found out, each of the three times he composed a theory of human nature.[68] But Hobbes is much closer to the stale Aristotelian tradition when he classifies the passions in the *Leviathan*. There are, of course, differences between Hobbes' and Aquinas' classifications. Before we leap to the conclusion that Hobbes is serving up Aquinas in some manner that would not repay attention, let us see if there is any coherent explanation available for these differences.

The first difference is in starting point, and it should be decisive since Hobbes' procedure is deductive. Hobbes starts with Endeavour *(conatus)*. Peters supposes that "Hobbes took over the term from the physical scientists and generalized its application to bridge the gaps between physics, physiology, and psychology."[69] Eventually we shall see that the gaps were not there, so far as the application of the term *conatus* is concerned; the Stoics applied it in physiology and psychology as well as in physics. Implicit in Hobbes' own use of the term is, of course, the law of the conservation of motion. Galileo's application of this law to horizontal motion, Peters explains, was the "death-knell" of Aristotelian physics; it was the abandonment of the "traditional dichotomy between motion and rest."[70] What Peters does not notice is that the abandonment of this traditional dichotomy is also the death-knell of scholastic Aristotelian psychology, which was a part of physics long before Galileo and Hobbes. When Aquinas locates the subject-matter of the passions, he cites Aristotle, "A passion is a motion."[71] This is not a citation from Aristotle's *Rhetoric* or his *Ethics* (the works in which Aristotle himself actually treats the passions), but from his *Physics,* and this location determines in part Aquinas' treatment of the passions.

Since both Hobbes and Aquinas classify the passions generally as motions, I shall be able to account for the differences in Hobbes' classification as a reconstruction which is the deductive result of his applying the law of the conservation of motion whenever he encounters Aquinas assuming a dichotomy between motion and rest. We need not leave the sphere of physics at all; no special intervention on Hobbes' part is needed to bridge any gap between physics and psychology. All we have to do is repeatedly replace Aquinas' distinction between motion and rest with a distinction between two motions, and then explain what was apparent rest to Aquinas as the resistance of one motion to another.

Although both Aquinas and Hobbes classify the passions generally as motions, Aquinas classifies them specifically as motions of the appetitive power, which is "assimilable to motion," and therefore to be distinguished from the apprehensive power, which is "assimilable rather to rest."[72] In dealing with what was the relevant operation of the apprehensive power in Aquinas, Hobbes distinguishes instead two motions, the one resisting the other: the "external . . . object . . . presseth the organ, . . . which pressure continued inwards [Hobbes is applying the law of conservation of motion] to the Brain, and Heart, causeth there a resistence, or counter-pressure, or endeavour of the heart . . ."[73] Hobbes comments on this Endeavour as the starting point of his treatment of the passions:

> Although unstudied men, doe not conceive any motion at all to be there, where the thing moved is invisible . . . ; yet that doth not hinder, but that such motions are. . . . These small beginnings of motion, within the body of man . . . are commonly called Endeavour.[74]

In treating the passions, Aquinas assumes that the mind, the "subject" of these motions, is initially at rest, until it is moved by its "object."[75] In starting with Endeavour, Hobbes is assuming that the mind is initially in motion, and he comments on the scholastic starting point as soon as the motions of Endeavour become differentiated in his first two specific passions, Appetite (or Desire) and Aversion:

> These words Appetite and Aversion we have from the Latines; and they both of them signifie the motions, one of approaching, the other of retiring. So also do the Greek words for the same, which are ὁρμή and ἀφορμή. For nature it selfe does often presse upon men those truths, which afterwards, when they look for somewhat beyond Nature, they stumble at. For the schooles find in meere Appetite to go or move, no actuall motion at all.[76]

This difference of starting point is illustrated more specifically by Aquinas' reason for taking Love as his first passion. He locates Love as the "starting-point of motion *(principium motus),*" but love does not involve "any motion of the appetite tending towards the appetible object." Actual motion towards the object Aquinas distinguishes as the next passion, Desire. In defending the priority of Love over Desire (which will be the first specific passion on Hobbes' List), Aquinas argues that "whatever tends to an end" must be "related to that end."[77] The relationship in the case of Love, he identifies as the "appetitive subject's connaturalness [*connaturalitas*] with the thing to which it tends," as "proper to it according to its nature." As an example Aquinas offers the connaturalness of the heavy body for the center," where it would find its resting place.[78] Since this example reminds us that Aquinas' account of the passions is a portion of his physics, we can pertinently cite Hobbes' disdainful comment,

> The schooles say, heavy bodies fall downwards, out of an appetite to rest, and to conserve their nature in that place which is most proper for them.[79]

Hobbes is not merely rejecting the scholastic conception of the conservation of a *nature* in favor of the Galilean law of the conservation of *motion* when he rejects Love in favor of Desire as his first passion. If he has also alluded to earlier "truths" which were once pressed upon men by nature, but which afterwards the scholastics stumbled at, he is not reviving Aristotle's *Rhetoric* or any early Greek work. He is reviving the Stoic treatment of the passions in the sense that he is rejecting the scholastic conception of "connaturalness" in favor of the earlier conception from which it derived—the *conatus* which was the starting point of Stoic psychology, where the motion of the subject begins at birth instead of waiting (as in Aquinas) for a connatural object to solicit desire. Cicero explains the Stoic *conatus:*

> As soon as it is born (simul atque *natum* sit), for we should start here [sc., if we are to take what is *natural* for our starting point], any animate being feels an attraction to itself, an impulse to preserve itself *(ad se conservandum)*. . . . It would be impossible for the young to desire *(appetereunt)* anything unless they had self-consciousness and experienced self-love. Hence we must conclude that it is self-love which is the starting point *(principium)*.[80]

This self-conscious *conatus* as the starting point of Stoic psychology needs to be brought to the attention of those contemporary interpreters of Hobbes who not only assume that he "took over the term from physical scientists" and imported it into psychology, but who also justify their severing his psychology from his physics on the ground that Hobbes himself has done so in the *Leviathan*. We recall that Hobbes in his Introduction appealed, not to physics, but to self-consciousness as a reliable starting point for a treatment of the passions. Furthermore, later in the deduction of the *Leviathan* Hobbes will refer back to self-love, which is not a passion that is listed in his own classification of passions. Its identification with the self-conscious *conatus* of self-preservation has to be supplied from some Stoic source such as my citation from Cicero.

The Psychology of Resistance

So far we have overlooked Aquinas' distinction between concupiscible and irascible passions, which renders his classification a double classification. Since Hobbes eliminates the distinction, we are not surprised to find that it involves in Aquinas a distinction between motion and rest: "In the concupiscible passions is found something relating to motion and something relating to rest. But in the irascible passions nothing is found relating to rest, but only to motion."[81] Thus Aquinas cannot treat the irascible passions by distinguishing between motion and rest. He has instead to distinguish two motions—the motion of the specific concupiscible passion (i.e., Desire or Aversion) which the irascible passion presupposes, and the motion specific to the irascible passion itself. But Hobbes finds nothing in any passion which relates to rest, so that in Aquinas' own terms Hobbes not only must eliminate the distinction between concupiscible and irascible passions but must also treat all the passions as irascible passions. An example of this process of extension and generalization is the way Hobbes deals with Appetite (Desire), which in Aquinas is the concupiscible passion that involves a single motion towards the object, and Pleasure, which is the concupiscible passion that Aquinas distinguishes from Desire as arrival at and "rest in the object."[82] Hobbes distinguishes two motions:

> This Motion, which is called Appetite, and for the apparence of it Delight, and Pleasure, seemeth to be, a corroboration of vitall motion, and a help thereunto; and therefore such things as caused Delight, were not improperly called *Jucunda,* (a *Juvando,*) from helping or fortifying; and the contrary, *Molesta,* Offensive, from hindering, and troubling the motion vitall.[83]

This fabric of definitions provides further illustrations of the fact that Hobbes treats all the passions as Aquinas treated the irascible passions. In Aquinas what "Hope [as the first irascible passion] adds over and beyond Desire [as a concupiscible passion] is a certain endeavor *(conatus).*"[84] In Hobbes all the passions are deduced from *conatus.* Indeed, to carry the starting point of the deduction back into physics, all motions in Hobbes are deduced from *conatus* (i.e., from the law of the conservation of motion); and in a universe that is a *plenum,* all motions are hindered or helped by other motions.

Earlier I anticipated the reference to this law in Hobbes' clarification of "absence of opposition" in his definition of liberty: "By opposition I mean external impediments of motion." But up until now I have only tried to bring out the sense in which such a term as liberty cannot be "applied to anything but bodies, . . . for that which is not subject to motion is not subject to Impediment." I have neglected Hobbes' further contention that his definition of liberty "may be applied no lesse to . . . inanimate creatures than to rationall."—that is, no less to those bodies in motion which are the subject-matter of physics than to those bodies in motion which are the subject-matter of psychology. Perhaps it is worth observing that long before Hobbes applied the law of the conservation of motion in physics (or Galileo formulated this law), the irascible passions had been treated in psychology as hindered (impeded) motions, and had thereby been distinguished from the concupisible passions. Aquinas presents the distinction as follows:

> In natural corruptible things there is needed an inclination not only . . . to the avoiding of what is harmful [i.e., Aversion] but also to resist corruptive and opposed agencies which are a hindrance to the acquisition of what is proper. . . . For example, fire has a natural inclination, not only to rise from a lower place which is improper to it, towards a higher place which is proper, but also to resist whatever destroys or hinders its action . . . so the soul needs two appetitive powers; one through which the soul is simply inclined [i.e., with a single motion] to flee from what is harmful and another whereby an animate thing resists those attacks that hinder what is proper and inflict harm, and this is called the irrascible.[85]

In this sense that irascible passions are phenomena of resistance for Aquinas, all passions are phenomena of resistance for Hobbes.

The next passion on Hobbes' list (after Pleasure and its opposite Pain) is a particularly striking instance of resistance. Hobbes defines Contempt as "an immobility or contumacy of the Heart, in resisting the action of certain things, and proceeding from that the Heart is already moved otherwise, by other more potent objects. . . ."[86] This definition in effect explains the fact that the passion is an outright addition to Aquinas' list. So far, Hobbes has been defining passions which were motions proceeding in contrary directions: Desire-Aversion, Love-Hate, Pleasure-Pain. In the case of Contempt, there is no apparent motion in any direction, and Hobbes' deductive application of the law of the conservation of motion displays its effectiveness since it shows that in this instance of apparent rest, where Aquinas did not notice a passion was occurring, two motions are in reality resisting each other.

This passion of Contempt we have already encountered in Hobbes' definition of the virtue of Magnanimity. We shall better appreciate the significance of this definition if we take into account other traditional virtues which turn up earlier on Hobbes' list and which are also demoted to passions. Hobbes' substitutes Courage *(Fortitudo)* for Daring in Aquinas' classification of passions, and this demotion is reinforced by Hobbes' definition of Anger as "sudden courage" and of Confidence (the traditional virtue of *Fiducia*) as "Constant Hope." Polin has suggested that Hobbes' strategy here is to "si bien mêler et confondre, contre la doctrine expresse d'Aristote les virtus et les vices avec les passions qu'on ne saurait plus distinguer les uns des autres."[87] But there is method in this confusion—deductive method.[88] Hobbes is selecting virtues for demotion neither in a piecemeal manner nor in any manner which could be accounted for as antagonism towards "la doctrine expresse d'Aristote." The intervening tradition has to be considered. Confidence and Magnanimity are both virtues which had been classified by Aquinas as "parts of courage."[89] We should not be surprised by the prominence Courage gains in Hobbes from turning up as the first traditional virtue in his deduction of the passions and from the way its traditional parts still cluster around it. We already know that the result of applying deductively the law of the conservation of motion to a classification of the passions which permits the distinction between motion and rest is to reclassify all the passions as irascible passions. The prominence that Courage gains in Hobbes, in another sense it retains, because it was already in Aquinas the specific virtue which regulates all the operations of the irascible power.[90]

Of course when Hobbes replaces Daring with Courage and redefines Courage as "Feare . . . with hope of avoyding that Hurt by resistence,"[91] Courage loses the position it held in Aquinas at a higher level than the two passions which it regulates as a mean. Courage becomes instead a complex phenomenon of resistance: the motion of Fear away from the object is resisted by the motion of Hope towards the object, etc. But this demotion of Courage need not merely represent (as it does to Strauss) the intrusion of bourgeois moral prejudice into Hobbes' deduction.[92] Hobbes is not just trying to soften the traditional truculence of the aristocracy. It is also possible that Hobbes is treating moral phenomena as natural phenomena (as had that aristocrat Aquinas). To interpret Hobbes' treatment, we need only identify a further result of his applying deductively the law of the conservation of motion to a classification of the passions which involves the distinction between motion and rest. In treating Courage, Hobbes is dealing with a moral situation in which the mind is apparently at rest and which had been regarded as at rest by "unstudied men" including Aquinas. Courage, Aquinas claims, is not only the specific virtue of the irascible power, but is also a "general virtue," or "rather a condition of all virtue," since "stability and immobility is required for virtue."[93] Thus Hobbes' demotion of Courage is not an arbitrary pulling down of a particular piece of the moral structure of scholasticism;

with the application of the law of the conservation of motion, the whole structure is dismantled.

Horizontal Motion

Still another result of the application of the law is illustrated by the fate of the "part" of Courage with which we became familiar in the last chapter. The traditional virtue of Magnanimity is defined by Hobbes as "Contempt of little helps and hindrances."[94] Does this belittling definition implement Hobbes' disparagement of aristocratic virtue?[95] Maybe. But we are aware of the fact that Magnanimity was already Contempt in the Stoic tradition, which was impeccably aristocratic for much of its career. In this tradition, the immobility that Magnanimity entailed was *despicientia rerum externarum*. It was attached to Courage, which was itself "contempt of pain and death,"[96] but it brought out specifically the way the wise man maintained his own moral stature by "looking down," impassively from above, on the changes taking place in "external things" and finding these changes of little or no help or hindrance in comparison with the greatness and elevation he was thereby maintaining in his own mind.

Maintaining this moral stature presupposes as its context a hierarchical organic universe where each nature, and nature as a whole, conserves itself.[97] Needless to say, Hobbes' law of the conservation of motion plays havoc with this universe and so with the implications of the traditional definition of Magnanimity. In Hobbes' universe, what is conserved is not a nature but a motion, and relations are not internal relations within nature as a whole, but external relations between bodies in motion. Hobbes' conception of the moral significance of psychological resistance differs from that of Aquinas (who is heir to the Stoic or humanistic conception) not only because Aquinas' physics is a physics of motion and rest, but also because whatever is in motion in Aquinas comes to rest at a resting place, which (when an analogy is needed to the aspiring motions of the mind) is at a higher level than the level at which the motion started. Recall the comparison to the motion of fire which Aquinas employed in distinguishing the irascible power from the concupiscible:

> Fire has a natural inclination, not only to rise from a lower place, which is improper to it, towards a higher place, which is proper, but also to resist whatever destroys or hinders its action.

The resistance of the irascible power takes the form too of an upward movement, for its object is "something steep, because its tendency is to overcome and rise above [*supereemineat*] impediments."[98]

Galileo had applied the law of conservation to horizontal motions.[99] The effect of Hobbes' extending this law to the motions of the mind (or of his substituting this law for the Stoic principle of the conservation of a nature) is to level the traditionally hierarchical relation between motion and rest. Hobbes accordingly employs a comparison quite different from Aquinas'. Hobbes employs a "comparison of the life of man to a race . . . that we may thereby both see and remember almost all the passions."[100] Peters cites this comparison instead of exploring the more detailed classification of the *Leviathan*.[101] Perhaps one reason why interpreters like to discount Hobbes' scientific pretensions is that Hobbes' English prose style is too racy to be scientific.

Hobbes does not engage in stylistic exercises at the expense of either his philosophy, or of his characteristic philosophical effort to dismantle tradition. If there has been any point in my recalling the traditional physics of motion and rest, there may also be some point in now recalling the most famous traditional race. To distinguish what becomes in the tradition the irascible "part" of the soul, Plato analyzed in his *Republic* the phenomenon of impeded motion or resistance in the soul.[102] He used his resulting tripartite psychological analysis to set up a hierarchy of ways of life in order to deal with the question of which way is the most pleasant.[103] The acquisitive life he correlated with the case for the appetitive part of the soul; the competitive, status-striving, victory-loving life, with the case for the irascible part, and the philosophical life with the case for the rational part. In Plato's *Republic* the second of these three ways of life found its fulfillment in military, political, and athletic prowess. We remember how the irascible was discredited in Stoicism (and in Cicero's *Republic*), but recovered in Panaetius (and in Cicero's *On Duties*) its positive role as "a desire to be first *(cupiditas principatus)*."[104] The renaissance of this desire was associated with the philosophical dignity which the *princeps*—such a military and political leader as a Scipio—also recovered in Panaetius. Athletic prowess, however, never recovered for Panaetius, Cicero, or the Romans generally its original Greek prestige. But just as Greek lives were retained as models for Roman lives, lived under very different circumstances, so Greek metaphors and analogies were retained, even when they had lost for the Romans the support of any literal exemplification. Thus the hierarchical comparison of lives continued to find expression in a classification of those who attended the Olympic games. There were those who came to acquire money, those who actually entered the race "to win a garland," and those who came as spectators "seeking nothing for themselves."[105]

In Hobbes the irascible is no longer a "part" of the soul. The whole soul, as it were, has become irascible.[106] This is why when Hobbes compares the life of man to the horizontal motion of a race, we can see from the comparison almost all the passions.[107] All men enter the race. Any way of life is a race, for all life is "but a motion of limbs" (not just the athlete's) and happiness "consisteth not in the repose of a mind satisfied" (as the philosopher-spectator assumes) but is "a continuall progresse of the desire from one object to another."[108] But this is also why the "comparison of the life of man to a race . . . holdeth not in every point." The race in life is never over, until by dying we "foresake the course." There is no rest: "We must suppose . . . no other goal, nor other garland, but being foremost." The irascible is no longer "the desire to be first" in Panaetius' or Cicero's erect, hierarchical sense of being outstanding.

The "part" of the soul which Plato (and Stoic revivers of Plato) found fulfilled by political activity has become the whole soul in Hobbes. But even if Hobbes' psychology were only "ostensibly a deduction from the theory of motion"—even if it were "in fact constructed with an eye much more on its political relevance than on its theoretical adequacy"—we would still have to pay detailed attention to this psychology in order to determine what the political is, to which it is relevant, and how political relations between men are structured. The criteria of relevance to the political are determined in the course of an "inference made from the passions," and the passions in this inference have all become irascible in senses which have in fact taken us back to Hobbes' theory of motion.

After so much detail, it is perhaps safe to put my interpretation in terms of relations which are illustrated by grosser motions than the specific passions: Hobbes' deduction is an inference from irascible relations between individuals—that is, from relations in which one individual is impeded in his motions by another individual and is conscious of this other individual as an impediment. In the Aristotelian tradition, the morally and politically relevant situation is an appetitive situation: the individual himself (in the first sentence of the *Nichomachaean Ethics*) or as a member of a community (in the first sentence of Aristotle's *Politics*) desires something. For this single motion or relationship of Appetite *(Ad-petitio),* Hobbes' inference from the passions substitutes an irascible relationship of "Competition *(Competitio),*" which is structured by the fact that "two men desire the same thing, which neverthelesse they cannot both enjoy."[109] We have two individuals in motion, the motion produced by the desire of one of them impeding the other's hope of completing the motion produced by his desire.[110]

This is the same restructuring of relationships which we encountered at earlier stages of the deduction: when we dealt with Desire itself, it was two motions (where there was only a single motion in Aquinas); at a still earlier stage, when we dealt with sensation (which produced the motion of imagination and of Desire), we were already dealing with the product of two motions. At all these junctures we have encountered a relation of "resistence or counter-pressure," which Hobbes originally defined in physics as "the endeavour of one moved body either wholly or in part contrary to the endeavour of another moved body."

Shall we conclude that Hobbes put two bodies into contrary motion in his physics with an eye cocked toward the eventual relevance of this situation to a political theory in which the paradigm political relationship would be a contract between two individuals? When Peters argues that Hobbes' psychology is only "ostensibly a deduction from the theory of motion," and that it was "in fact constructed with an eye much more on its political relevance," what Peters is overlooking is the political relevance of Hobbes' deducing his psychology from his theory of motion. Putting all questions of scientific "excitement" to one side, nothing could be more damaging to Hobbes' political theory itself than for his psychology to be severed from his physics. Hobbes' psychology is politically relevant only to the extent to which he is able to abstract in this psychology from the political (in Hobbes' own sense of an artificial contractual relation between individuals) in order to arrive at a "natural" state of human relationships, "when there is no visible power to keep them in awe, and tye them by fear of punishment to the performance of their covenants."[111] The most reliable way of ensuring an entire abstraction from the political is by deducing psychology from physics.

The Individual as Ruler

Having reached Hobbes' political theory, we can at last reconsider our comparison with Machiavelli, whose procedure is not deductive and who never abstracts from the political. By examining this difference between their theories, we shall be able to revise the interpretation which provides them both with the same moral and political conclusions, deduced from the same psychological premise: "If human individuals are by nature radically egoistic, the state and the force behind the law must be the only power that holds society together; moral obligations must in the end be derived from law and government."[112] Thus Sabine arrives at the modern sovereign state and the concomitant *raison d'état* argument that the end of preserving this state justifies as means actions on the part of the statesman which would be immoral if performed by a private citizen.

Since Machiavelli never abstracts from the political, we were forced to anticipate his political conclusions in the last chapter. His investigation of the *greatness of soul,* which we found the prince should display, reaches its climax in the chapter titled "In What Way Princes Must Keep Faith," which is often selected as an illustration of the *raison d'état* argument:

> Men in general judge more by the eyes than by actual contact; for everyone can see but few can understand. Everyone sees what you appear to be, few recognize what you are, and those few will not dare to oppose themselves to the opinion of the many, who have the majesty of the state to defend them. And in the actions of men, and particularly of princes, from whose verdict there is no appeal, look to the end. If a prince conquer and maintain the state, the means will always be judged honorable and praised by all. For the common people are always taken in by appearances and the outcome of a course of action; and in the world the common people are everything. The few have no recourse when the many have rallied against them.[113]

The end that justifies the means here is not a higher end that justifies what would otherwise be an immoral course of action. The end is a *fait accompli*—an historical outcome which must actually be attained; only then in retrospect are the means justified. Since, moreover, the particular outcome to be attained may be the conquest as well as the defense of the state, the argument is as much the recommendation of a *coup d'état* as it is an endorsement of *raison d'état* policies to meet the threat of a *coup d'état*. Yet mention of a *coup d'état* may also be somewhat misleading, since Machiavelli is not merely recommending aggressive action as a means, when the end to be attained is political power, but is basing even this recommendation on the superior defensive position which the individual will enjoy as a consequence of his status as a ruler.

The reference to men in general with which Machiavelli has begun this argument may seem comparable to some psychological generalization that Hobbes could make in "Of Man." But Machiavelli promptly distinguishes between the "few" and the "many." The course of action the prince has employed as a means can be justified in retrospect because it is with reference to its visible outcome that the "many" pass judgment on him. When the prince initiated this course of action, moral considerations were politically irrelevant, to the extent that only the "few" had the actual contact with him that enabled them to anticipate the eventual outcome. By thus distinguishing between people and times, Machiavelli renders inconsequential the comforting assumption that the politician cannot fool all of the people all of the time.

Machiavelli's distinction between people and times is a rudimentary socio-historical distinction, but Sabine overlooks its methodological implications when he redesigns Machiavelli's theory:

> Not very appropriately, it must be confessed, he reproduced at the beginning of the *Discourses* almost word for word the theory of the constitutional cycle from the sixth book of Polybius' *Histories*. The balance which he had in mind, however, was not political but social or economic—an equilibrium of competing interests held in check by a powerful sovereign. In this respect also a systematic statement of Machiavelli's philosophy needed the conception of sovereign power which Bodin and Hobbes added to it.[114]

Bemused by "pervasive" tendencies,[115] Sabine is reading into Machiavelli the later doctrine of "competing interests," which will derive much of its cogency from the utilitarian identification of self-interest as an economic motive. In Machiavelli, however, the competition is not economic, but a political struggle for power. And the consequences of the struggle cannot be stated systematically in the form of a deduction; they have to be traced historically. Machiavelli obtains an historical analysis of this struggle from Polybius' theory of the constitutional cycle and of the check-and-balance mechanism. The "one" ruler in Machiavelli competes politically with the "few"—that is, the nobles whom Machiavelli characterizes as a class by "their great desire to dominate others." The "many" or "common people" he characterizes as "desiring only not to be dominated and to live in liberty."[116] Given this class distribution of psychological motives, the ruler (or the legislator) need not (as Sabine has suggested he must) exercise sovereign power; he can rely on the people as a class to help preserve the balance. Because of their desire for liberty, they will operate as a check on the nobles who desire power.

Machiavelli's analysis, I pointed out earlier, is not exclusively historicist.[117] The check-and-balance mechanism does not function as mechanically as in Polybius. Machiavelli also draws on the humanistic tradition—for example, when he instructs the ruler to act decisively, as in the passage I have cited from *The Prince*. In this passage the people are not visualized as coming directly to the ruler's support, nor is he visualized as coming directly to their defense. It is the majesty of the state itself which elicits their support of him and defends them. In acting decisively, the prince is relying less on a *raison d'état* policy than on the image of the state—its *maiestas* in their minds. Although *maiestas* was traditionally a juridical attribute of the sovereign, we do not find in Machiavelli a juridical conception of sovereignty, but rather a conception of the position of the ruler in society. This conception does not need (as Sabine says it does) "the conception of sovereign power which . . . Hobbes added to it." Hobbes' conception is juridical; it belongs to a different theory; and it cannot be added to Machiavelli's, where the "state and the force behind the law" do not compose (as Sabine suggests they do) "the only power that holds society together." The state itself in Machiavelli is almost indistinguishable from those decisive actions which display the ruler's *greatness of soul*. To this extent the political position that the ruler succeeds in attaining, is not just a *fait accompli*, but is a demonstration of his *virtù*.

The Individual as Citizen

"From such reasoning as this," Hobbes protests, "successful wickedness hath obtained the name of Virtue; and some that in all other things have disallowed the violation of Faith; yet have allowed it, when it is for the getting of a Kingdome."[118] One may conjecture that Hobbes is here protesting against the reasoning I have just cited from Machiavelli's chapter "In What Way Princes Must Keep Faith." But Hobbes never mentions Machiavelli, and Hobbes' phraseology here resembles more closely the reasoning that Cicero puts in Julius Caesar's mouth in *On Duties*: "If what is right may ever be violated, it is for the getting of a kingdom; in all other things keep faith."[119]

The possibility that Hobbes and Machiavelli are mutually indebted to *On Duties* is less important, as a clue to interpreting their differences, than the shift of focus within Cicero's work from the duties of the ruler to those of the private citizen. The premise of the reasoning against which Hobbes is protesting (even though he may have attributed it to Machiavelli), is supplied by Hobbes' own psychology, and the conception of political power involved is Hobbes' own conception of absolute power: "reason . . . dictateth to every man his own good, and particularly then when it conduceth to such benefit as shall put a man in a condition to neglect not only the dispraise and revilings, but also the power of other men."[120] The problem of the prince's keeping faith in Machiavelli is *not* posed by the psychological egoism of every man but by the prince's particular position in the state, and Machiavelli does *not* conclude that this position enables the prince "to neglect not only the dispraise and revilings but also the power of other men." Rather the prince's attaining and maintaining his position depends in considerable measure on his ability to secure the approval of the "many" as a feature of a continuing struggle for power.

In Hobbes, however, the problem of keeping faith is not the problem of whether or not the prince should keep faith, but the problem of the individual subject's keeping faith with the other individual subjects with whom he is under an implicit contract to maintain a government that is already established, however it may have been established as a matter of historical fact. Hobbes is not protesting against history when he protests against successful wickedness obtaining the name of virtue. He is arguing that the ruler's *de facto* status should not be construed by the subject as merely a *fait accompli*—that is, not as merely an historical fact in Machiavelli's sense of the outcome of actions to which moral obligations were initially irrelevant. The distinction basic to Hobbes' political theory is not Machiavelli's *historical* distinction in the *Prince* between the moment the prince employs a course of action as a means, which can pass unnoticed by men in general, and the moment its outcome is reached, when they will react. Hobbes' distinction is a *psychological* distinction between two moments in a deduction. The two moments are instanced by his *De Homine* and his *De Cive*. In the *Leviathan* the transition from "The first Part, Of Man" to "The second Part, Of Common-wealth" is described in the first sentence of the second part:

> The final Cause, End, or Designe of men (who naturally love Liberty and Dominion over others) in the introduction of that restraint upon themselves (in which we see them live in Common-wealths,) is the foresight of their own preservation . . . ; that is to say, of getting themselves out from that miserable condition of Warre, which is necessarily consequent (as hath been shewn) to the naturall Passions of men, when there is no visible Power to keep them in awe, . . .[121]

At the first moment individuals are reacting to each other's actions as men (i.e., their reactions are determined by their "natural passions"), and at the second moment they are reacting to each other's actions as citizens, when there is an artificial, "visible power to keep them in awe."

We see men living in states: so far Machiavelli's and Hobbes' theories coincide. But as soon as they analyze what we see with respect to the foresight it illustrates, we encounter differently structured theories. In Machiavelli the individual attains "visible power" by becoming a ruler; other men then become conscious of them, and in acting to preserve himself and maintain his position, he must foresee their reactions as well as other consequences of his actions.[122] Thus his foresight is historical. But Hobbes' political theory is a "doctrine of subjection."[123] The doctrine articulates the foresight of the individual subject's—the foresight that is implicit in his situation as a subject—by requiring him to abstract from his consciousness of the "visible power" that actually operates as an artificial impediment to his actions, and to deduce the necessary consequences of any weakening of this power. Thus his foresight takes the form of a psychological deduction of these consequences.

In Machiavelli we see men living in states under the actual sociohistorical circumstances of class warfare. Under these circumstances the power of the ruler cannot be absolute, but he can rely on the reactions of the class which desires liberty and fears domination to operate as a check on the class which desires to dominate. But Hobbes dismisses such historical evidence as evidence that subjects have never actually acknowledged the power which his deduction shows their rulers should have:

> The greatest objection is that of the Practise; when men ask, where, and when, such Power has by Subjects been acknowledged. But one may ask them again, when, or where has there been a Kingdome long free from Sedition and Civill Warre. . . . But howsoever, an argument from the Practise of men that have not sifted to the bottom . . . is invalid.[124]

Hobbes is not commenting in the *Leviathan* on the socio-historical circumstances of the English Civil War, however often his interpreters may bring these circumstances to our attention. He is going beneath the surface of history and sifting to the bottom by a psychological deduction in which he concludes that the necessary consequence of men's natural reactions to each other's actions would be an even more "miserable condition of Warre" of "every man against every man" than any historical circumstances might illustrate. This deduction does not allocate the desire for liberty and the desire for dominion to two different social classes; every individual naturally loves "Liberty" for himself and "Dominion over others." Thus Hobbes' analysis can remain a psychological deduction. He does not need to consider social classes in their historically changing relations.

Revenge

In order to remove the "external impediments" to his liberty of movement which others may present, the individual in Hobbes may attempt "to master the persons of all men he can, so long, till he sees no other power great enough to endanger him." But what the individual sees is not necessarily the end of his desire for dominion. Because men are self-conscious, they can "take pleasure in contemplating their own power in the acts of conquest which they pursue farther than their security requires."[125] Even though not every individual will undertake such acts of conquest, every individual does have a sense of his own glory; as we found in the last chapter: "every man looketh that his companion should value him at the same rate he sets upon himselfe." He therefore reacts to actions which he construes as "signs of contempt," even when these are "trifles" (inasmuch as his own physical security is not in danger), and undertakes acts of revenge.[126]

Here let me break down the gross motions of the individual into the motions of one of the passions prominently involved, so that I can complete my interpretation of Hobbes' interpreters. In dealing with Revengefulness, Hobbes is probably indebted to Aristotle's account of Anger in the *Rhetoric,* but Hobbes' debt only makes more obvious his own originality, which Strauss and Peters did not discover when they discovered the debt. Hobbes' Anger we have already encountered. It turns up earlier in his deduction of the passions than Revengefulness. Anger is defined, we recall, as "sudden courage," and Courage as "fear of hurt from the object . . . with Hope of avoiding that hurt by resistence."[127] Hobbes does not want his Anger confused with Anger in the Aristotelian tradition. He explains that Anger "hath been commonly defined to be grief proceeding from an opinion of contempt; which is confuted by the often experience we have of being moved to anger by things inanimate . . . and consequently incapable of condemning us."[128] For we can be angry "at whatever things are impediments to our progress, whenever we are proceeding towards whatever end we have set before us." Thus Hobbes' definition places Anger in the setting of his physics of resistance.

Hobbes' definition of Revengefulness illustrates the additional complexity men's motions acquire at a later stage in Hobbes' deduction of the passions. Hobbes' Anger is not Aristotle's Anger nor is Hobbes' Revengefulness Aristotle's Anger, even though Aristotle defined Anger as involving "desire for revenge,"[129] and even though the translator of Homer, like Aristotle, uses the great-souled Achilles as an example of this desire. Hobbes defines Revengefulness in the *Leviathan* as "Desire by doing hurt to another, to make him condemn some fact of his own."[130] The relation between these two individuals is clarified by the more elaborate definition in *The Elements of Law:*

> Revengefulness is that passion which ariseth from an expectation or imagination of making him that hath hurt us, find his own action hurtful to himself, and to acknowledge the same; and this is the height of revenge. For though it be not hard, by returning evil for evil, to make one's adversary displeased with his own fact; yet to make him acknowledge the same, is so difficult, that many a man had rather die than do it. Revenge aimeth not at the death, but at the captivity or subjection of an enemy; which was well expressed in the exclamation of Tiberius Caesar, concern-

ing one, that to frustrate his revenge, had killed himself in prison: 'Hath he escaped me?' . . . Revenge aimeth at triumph, which over the dead is not.[131]

To what Aristotle's Anger involved—the desire for revenge which is an individual's reaction to a contemptuous action on the part of another individual—Hobbes has added, as an ingredient in the self-consciousness of the revengeful individual, an anticipation of the other individual's reflexive reaction to the action of revenge. Thus the psychological relation between individuals assumed by Aristotle's definition is complicated in a fashion which illustrates the structure of Hobbes' theory. Each individual in Hobbes is not only self-conscious —and thereby capable of following through Hobbes' deduction—but also conscious of other individuals as self-conscious—and thereby capable of entering at the conclusion of the deduction into mutual contractual relationship with them.

Insofar as the war of every man against every man culminates for every man in the "internal gloriation or triumph of the mind" which is at stake in his actions of revenge, no merely external checks (such as the class structure can provide in Machiavelli) could operate as ultimately effective restraints in men's struggle for power. The political control exercised by the ruler must be viewed by subjects not simply as the actions of another man (as it is in Machiavelli), but as representing their own mutual "restraint upon themselves." This is why Hobbes rejects a moralistic political tradition which is different (or differently interpreted) from the moralistic political tradition which Machiavelli rejects. What Machiavelli wants to reject is the confusion of the ruler's political control with the moral self-control which had been the traditional qualification for exercising political control. Hobbes wants to reject this confusion too, but as a failure on the part of the Monarchomachs to exercise moral self-control—in Hobbes' own words, as a

licentious controlling of the actions of their Soverains and again of controlling these controllers, with the effusion of so much blood, as I think I may truly say, there was never anything so deerly bought, as these Western tongues have bought the learning of the Greek and Latine tongues.[132]

Political Control

Hobbes' rejection of the moralistic political tradition is a readjustment in the relation between the subject's moral self-control and the ruler's political control. But the readjustment is not, as Sabine has suggested, the derivation of moral obligations from law and government. Hobbes affirms that they do "oblige *in foro interno*," even though they do not always oblige "*in foro externo*, that is, to the putting them in act."[133] In Hobbes, as in the moralistic political tradition, to make the transition from the psychology of morals to politics is to move out from within. But in making this move Hobbes breaks with tradition: law and government derive from moral obligations in Hobbes, inasmuch as the only external circumstances under which the individual can be expected to meet his moral obligations, by exercising self-control in his overt actions, are circumstances under which he is confident that other individuals will be politically controlled in their overt actions. Such mutual confidence is epistemologically impossible so long as their actions are determined solely by their "natural passions" (as they are in the first part of the *Leviathan*), since these begin "within the body of Man before they appear . . . in visible actions."[134] Lacking the knowledge of each other's moral characters (which the moralistic political tradition had taken for granted), no individual can trust another individual to keep faith. From this "diffidence of one another, there is no way for any man to secure himselfe, so reasonable, as Anticipation;"[135] men therefore "study how to preoccupate each other."[136] Mutual confidence is only epistemologically possible as mutual fear of a "visible power," which supplies (in the second part of the *Leviathan*) an external beginning for the respective actions of different individuals, and to this extent removes their mutual fear of each other.

Because the sovereign performs this psychological function, "Soveraignty" can be regarded as "an Artificiall Soul . . . giving life and motion to the whole body" of the state, just as the natural soul [sc., the heart, as the seat of the passions] gives life and motion to the body of an individual man.[137]

In a certain sense, the state for Hobbes (as for Machiavelli in *The Prince*), is hardly more than the status of the ruler in the minds of his subjects. But his status is artificial in Hobbes in that it is the deductive consequence of his subjects' foresight, not of the ruler's own foresight as in Machiavelli. The ruler in Hobbes could be a silly goose, if we take rather too literally the episode from Roman history to which Hobbes alludes in explaining why he has spoken of the "Civill Power" as absolute: "I speak not of the men, but (in the Abstract) of the Seat of Power, (like to those simple and unpartiall creatures in the Roman Capitol, that with their noyse defended those within it, not because they were they, but there)."[138]

The ruler in Machiavelli is still a man, and the psychological control he exercises over his subjects can still take the form of *greatness of soul.* But the soul that animates the *Leviathan* in Hobbes is an artificial mechanism that is needed to implement the "restraint" subjects exercise "upon themselves" when they accept the obligations of the contract. Their readiness to exercise this restraint is envisaged by Hobbes not as the historical consequence of the *great actions* the sovereign performs, but as the deductive consequence of Hobbes' psychological analysis, which is addressed to the self-consciousness of each of them as an individual. Just as the individual undergoes an external transformation in Machiavelli when he becomes a prince, since he is then no longer a private citizen but must act as someone whom others are particularly conscious of, so the self each individual is conscious of is reflexively transformed as he follows through Hobbes' deduction. What is at stake in this transformation can be detected more readily now we have discovered that desire for liberty from domination and desire for domination over others had alike been attributes of the great-souled in the humanistic tradition.[139] For Hobbes' deduction not only assigns both desires to every individual, but also demonstrates that these desires must be overcome by the passion that *greatness of soul* was traditionally associated with courage in overcoming—the fear of pain and death.[140]

Conceived as this psychological process of transformation, Hobbes' deduction is not only an "inference made from the passions" but also an inference wherein a "passionate thought" is inferred in order "to govern and direct those that follow to itself." To exercise this control over the thought of the individual, and to exercise it in the form of self-control, "the passion to be reckoned on" must be reflexive in its operation; it is the individual's fear as fear for himself.[141] When individuals succumb, in the course of this inference, to this fear of pain and death, they will "suffer the rude and cumbersome points of their present greatnesse to be taken off."[142] They will be restrained from undertaking the *great actions* which had been identified in the humanistic tradition as "exceptionally difficult and dangerous both to the things we live by and to life itself," and they will no longer speak in political theory "the speech of the Roman people."[143]

Notes

1. *On Liberty* (New York: Liberal Arts Press, 1956), p. 3.

2. *Autobiography* (New York: Columbia University Press, 1960), p. 170.

3. See p. 3, this vol.

4. *Leviathan,* Preface.

5. *The Prince,* chap. 1. This straightforward appeal to history eliminates the cosmological context of a theory of human nature in which the problem of authority had traditionally been treated (see vol. 1, p. 259). But we shall now have to reconsider the traditional cosmology as background for Hobbes before we can return to the comparison of Hobbes with Machiavelli.

6. *A Defence of Liberty Against Tyrants, with an Historical Introduction by Harold J. Laski* (Gloucester, Mass.: Peter Smith, 1963), p. 192. Laski argues that the Reformation "was the real starting point of democratic ideas" (p. 1). This familiar claim I am not attempting to assess. It may seem that I should weigh the comparative influence of the secular tradition I am tracing and the religious tradition that stems from the Reformation. But the development of this second tradition is ordinarily traced in a fashion which cannot easily be synchronized with the kind of history I am trying to present. Observe how Laski follows up his claim: "It [the Reformation] was the *real* starting point of democratic ideas; but, therein, it builded better, or, at least, differently than it knew. . . . The significance of Luther lies in the fact that, *all unconsciously,* he made the Reformation one of the great turning points in the history of political ideas" (italics added). I am not undertaking to uncover real starting points and developments as distinguished from what the thinkers involved were conscious of. I am only dealing with textual evidence. Furthermore, even in handling the textual evidence which a document like the *Vindiciae* jumbles together, there are special difficulties which are more cumbersome than those ordinarily posed by the composition of the classical tradition. Consider the following specimen: "As the Holy Scripture compares the king to a shepherd, so does it also resemble the tyrant to a roaring lion, to whom notwithstanding, the fox is oftentimes coupled. For a tyrant, as says Cicero, is culpable in effect of the greatest injustice that may be imagined, and yet he carries it so cunningly, that when he most deceives, it is then that he makes greatest appearance to deal sincerely. And therefore does he artificially counterfeit religion and devotion, wherein saith Aristotle 'he expresses one of the most absolute subtleties that tyrants can possibly practice: he does so compose his countenance to piety, by that means to terrify the people from conspiring against him; whom they may well imagine to be especially favoured of God, expressing in all appearance so reverently to serve Him' " (p. 188). With the conjunction of the lion with the fox, the author moves, without any sense of discrepancy or transition, from his Biblical source to classical sources. But Cicero compared the lion and fox and denounced deception (*De Officiis* 1. 13. 41) without referring to a tyrant, and the citation from Aristotle (*Politics* 5. 1314b–1315a) is considerably distorted and inflated. We might postulate some use of the expanded interpretation of this passage which was available in the *Commentary on the Politics,* begun by Aquinas and completed by Peter of Auvergne. But presiding over this selection of classical texts, and determining in some measure their interpretation, is Machiavelli identified as the ideologist for tyranny. In chap. 18 of *The Prince,* Machiavelli had utilized this selection of texts, and the phraseology that has crept in between the citation from Cicero and the citation from Aristotle in the *Vindiciae* probably derives from this chapter. Laski stresses, of course, the Machiavellianism of the period: "The sixteenth century is pre-eminently a century of raison d'état. The poison of Machiavelli was in its blood, and . . . a cynical utilitarianism is its predominant temper. . . . It is to

the credit of the Monarchomachs that they moved the question of the right of resistance to higher ground. . . . They were compelled to show . . . the inadequacy of any basis other than ethical for political institutions." (p. 27) Laski does not clarify the nature of this philosophical compulsion, or how the movement to a higher philosophical ground is related to the forward historical movement of modern social and economic development in which the Monarchomachs were caught up. Perhaps Laski says "compelled" because he interprets the Monarchmachs as caught up "all unconsciously" in the first movement as in the second. Perhaps their religiosity precluded in his view their realizing the secular philosophical implications of their thought, as it did their realizing the secular political implications. A first step in examining these secular implications might be to take into account the help Cicero provided the Monarchomachs in moving the question of resistance to the higher ground. In this chapter we shall see that Cicero intended *On Duties* to demonstrate the inadequacy of any basis other than ethical for political institutions.

7. Thomas Hobbes, *English Works,* ed. W. Molesworth, 11 vols. (London: John Bohn, 1839–45), 2: 153; *Leviathan,* pt. II, chap. 21.

8. We are concerned, it should be remembered, not merely with this particular antithesis as used to restructure the humanistic tradition so that it becomes the individualistic tradition culminating in Mill's liberalism; we are further concerned with the use of antitheses as such, culminating in Mill's principle of antagonism (see vol. 1, p. 50). For Cicero's use of antitheses, see vol. 1, pp. 224–25, and accompanying nn. 93, 94. Having concentrated in chap. 10 on the role that the individual assumes in the individualistic tradition, I am now bringing this individual into relation to the state by exploring some of the other antitheses that lend structure to this relationship—most fundamentally the antithesis between liberty and authority, but also the antitheses between individualistic virtue and the social virtues (see n. 35, below), between freedom of speech and the adulation of authority (see nn. 36, 38, below), between *otium* and *negotium* (see n. 47, below). With respect to Cicero's influence on the later use of these antitheses, consider Richard McKeon's comment: "The character of Cicero, as well as his ideas, has entered into the discussions that have determined major turns of doctrine and policy, but, what is more important, the distinctions which underlay the discussion, whether it eventuated in Cicero's conclusion or in opposition to it, have been influenced significantly by Cicero's formulation of problems and oppositions" (*Brutus* [Chicago: University of Chicago Press, 1950], p. 1). I would only add that there are major turns of doctrine and policy in Cicero's own discussion (at least as we view it in retrospect), and that his tergiversation has helped later thinkers around their turns of doctrine and policy. Cicero's procedure of reaching conclusions which seem in opposition to conclusions which he had previously reached is not inconsistent either with his conception of the methodological requirements of philosophical doctrine (see chap. 8, n. 95) or with his conception of the practical exigencies of political policy (see chap. 10, n. 112).

9. See vol. 1, pp. 209–13. Since I am only concerned with Cicero's handling and rehandling of the antithesis between liberty and authority and related antitheses, I am disregarding other Roman uses of *libertas*. A rapid survey can be found in Arnaldo Momigliano's "Review and Discussion" (*Journal of Roman Studies* 41 [1951]: 146–53) of Ch. Wirszubski's *Libertas as a Political Idea at Rome during the Late Republic and Early Principate* (Cambridge: Cambridge University Press, 1950). Momigliano brings out the "two different . . . interpretations" which have been offered: "According to one [e.g. Mommsen's] *Libertas* is a juridical notion," which "sums up the rights of a Roman 'civis'." According to the realists, however, *"Libertas* is a vague word which usually conceals egoistic interest." Momigliano cites Syme (*The Roman Revolution* [Oxford: Clarendon Press, 1939], p. 59: " 'Liberty and the Laws are high-sounding words. They will often be rendered, on a cool estimate, as privilege and vested interests'. . . . *Libertas* . . . is a convenient term of political fraud' " (*ibid.* p. 155). For Syme's cool estimate of Cicero's high-sounding words as fraudulent, see vol. 1, p. 302.) McKeon's point (see n. 8,

above) might be illustrated by noting that Syme's disposal of Cicero's words relies on a version of the antithesis, which is so characteristic of Cicero, between *verba* and *res*. In any case some of the issues that oppose the juridical and the realistic interpretations of *libertas* are comparable to those posed by the opposed interpretations of the opposition between *otium* and *dignitas* (see vol. 1, p. 254, and accompanying n. 44). In both disputes the relevance of Greek philosophy is in question. "Wirszubski," Momigliano complains, "has missed the full implications of the fall of the Roman Republical Government. When many of the rights usually connected with Roman *Libertas* were lost, some people rediscovered what the Greek philosophers had noticed before, that loss of political rights involves almost unexpectedly a much more serious offence to elementary moral values" (p. 148). I do not see what Roman experience Momigliano's "almost unexpectedly" is describing. The Romans he seems to have in mind were fully primed by Greek philosophy, and I do not know what evidence he has that they were ever intellectually surprised by events. He refers to Cicero's *On Duties,* but Cicero had studied Greek philosophy (and rhetoric) long before he thought of political rights as lost, and I would not describe *On Duties* as a rediscovery. It is a rather obvious readjustment in the way that Cicero had moralized about politics throughout his career. See n. 23, below, for evidence of Cicero's intellectual preparation to cope with a tyrant.

10. See p. 5, this vol.

11. *English Works,* 2: i.

12. See vol. 1, p. 243.

13. See p. 44, this vol.

14. *Off.* 3. 83.

15. *Off.* 1. 76. *"Privatus"* means without (official) political authority. Cicero's search for an exemplary precedent becomes a fudging of the issues, when he moves on from the comparison of the two Scipios to his own consulate. Cicero did have political authority as consul, but he exceeded it when he executed the conspirators without trial.

16. See vol. 1, p. 243.

17. *Off.* 1. 65.

18. *Off.* 1. 13.

19. *Epistulae ad Atticum* 2. 19. 1.

20. *Att.* 2. 1. 8.

21. *Off.* 1. 112. More is at stake in this posing of rigidity against flexibility than just opposed political positions or even than just the opposed political poses *appropriate* to the different *personalities* of Cato and Cicero. The fundamental opposition is between the Stoic conception of virtue and the more relaxed conceptions of other schools. Expounding the Stoic conception of *greatness of mind,* Seneca argues that just as "a carpenter's rule with which straight lines are measured cannot be flexible," so virtue is straight [*recta*], unbendable," and "rigid" (*Epistulae* 71. 18–20). Conversely, "the evil which is involved in torture and in those other things which we rate as hardships" is that "the mind sags, bends, and gives way." But "nothing of this sort can happen to the wise man; he stands upright *(rectus)* under any weight" (*Ep.* 71. 26). When this moral inflexibility becomes political, Stoic philosophy can be interpreted as *intempestiva sapientia* (Tacitus *Hist.* 3. 81). See n. 42, below for Seneca's refusal to accept the political implications of Stoic moral inflexibility.

22. *Att.* 8. 7. 1.

23. Most of the *topoi* which Cicero employs in placing these figures were already well established in the rhetorical tradition. During the war between Caesar and Pompey, Cicero explains to Atticus that he does not want "to surrender entirely to his mood of

depression," and so is "diverting" himself with "certain theses" which "are applicable to the present situation and give some exercises in the subject." Cicero lists the following theses in Greek: "Whether one should remain in one's country, even under tyranny. Whether any means may be legitimately employed to overthrow a tyranny, even if they endanger the existence of the state itself. Whether precautions should be taken lest he who overthrows the tyranny take over himself. Whether one ought to come to one's country's help when under a tyranny, by making the most of one's opportunities and by argument rather than by war. Whether one is fulfilling one's political obligations, if one withdraws to some other place and remains inactive, when there is a tyranny, or whether one ought to risk everything for liberty. Whether one ought to invade one's own country and attack one's native town, when it is under a tyranny. Whether one should join the loyalists, even if one does not approve of war as a means of overthrowing tyranny. Whether one ought in politics to share the dangers of one's benefactors and friends, even if one does not agree with their general policy. Whether someone who has served his country well, and has therefore been envied and maltreated, should deliberately take risks for that country, or may rather worry about himself and his family and avoid struggling against those in power" (*Att.* 9. 4). During the period I am covering in this section, such theses continued to provide ammunition for rhetorical exercises, without their applicability to present situations usually being made clear. Juvenal sneers at "countless scholars killing savage tyrants" (*Satura* 7. 151).

24. *De Amicitia* 2. 10.

25. *Cato Major* 22 (350).

26. For the full citation, see n. 33, below.

27. *De Finibus* 3. 7.

28. *Fin* 3. 7.

29. *Pro Murena* 60. In this chapter I shall use both the derivative *magnaminity* and the translation *greatness of mind* (or *greatness of soul*). No difference in meaning is intended.

30. Seneca *De Providentia* 2. 9.

31. *Tusculanae Disputationes* 5. 4. Cf. the way Cicero addresses Cato himself: "What could please me more than to discuss the virtues with the authoritative example *(auctore)* of all the virtues." Demonstration by authoritative exemplification (see chap. 7, nn. 22, 28) is a traditional procedure which can perhaps be traced back to that phase in the development of Stoicism when the wise man who had been merely an ideal norm became incarnate in a succession of individuals (see Diogenes Laertius *Lives of the Philosophers* 7. 91).

32. Cicero's own virtue, according to Brutus, "could be compared with that of any among our forefathers" (*Ad Brutum* 1. 4a. 2). Coming from someone with the authority of Brutus' ancestry, the comparison would have been most persuasive for a *homo novus*. But the ambivalence of Stoic virtue is evidenced by the scholarly conjecture that Brutus' *On Virtue* was a political manifesto, for this conjecture has been met with the counterclaim that *On Virtue* was precisely the opposite. Brutus did not initially join the Republican resistance; instead he accepted a governorship from Caesar. If Brutus did not advocate resistance in *On Virtue* but quietism, Cicero would seem in his *Brutus* to be commending the opposite conception of virtue when he reminds Brutus (331) of his ancestral role—that of a tyrannicide. (For this interpretation, see G. L. Hendrickson, "Brutus' *De Virtute*," *American Journal of Philology,* 60 [1939]: 401–13.) Although Brutus finally did play his ancestral role, he continued to display (in the ensuing tradition of interpreting his role) considerable ambivalence towards his virtue. The prevailing interpretation we are familiar with from Plutarch (*Brutus* 52 [1008–9]), where Brutus feels that he has

nothing to lose from his martyrdom: "He regarded himself as happier than his conquerors, . . . since he was leaving behind him such a *name for virtue* as those who had conquered him with all their wealth and power could never have." (No calculation of the resources of the two armies is implied here, but only the traditional Stoic opposition of virtue to both wealth and power.) The opposite interpretation managed to survive in Dio, where Brutus feels he has lost everything: "Ah wretched virtue, thou wert then but a name!/ Yet thee I followed as a thing substantial,/ Whilst of truth thou art but Fortune's slave." (I am citing Hendrickson's translation, p. 402).

33. Caesar reported that "reading it [Cicero's *Cato*] over and over had increased his flow of language" (*Att.* 13. 46). In the *Brutus* (254) Cicero has Brutus emphasize that Cicero is the "founder of fluency" (*copia*), so that "the only victory which conquered Greece won over us has been snatched from her." I have already suggested (see chap. 10, nn. 75, 76) the relation between Cicero's Platonizing expansion of the Stoic moral tradition into a political tradition and his fluent, forceful, and expressive style. What I am repeatedly trying to stress (see nn. 21, 23, above, and nn. 35, 38, below) is that we have here not just an adjustment in the relation between philosophy and rhetoric but a new style of philosophy. Philosophical oppositions do not remain an abstract scheme in Cicero but are exemplified by the political positions and rhetorical poses of individuals. Thus there may be some significance to be attached to the fact that Cicero's rejoinder to Brutus' quietist conception of virtue takes the form in the *Brutus* of a history of Roman rhetoric. It is this history of rhetoric which will come lamentably to an end, unless Brutus plays his ancestral role. At the same time it is clear that the climactic figure in this history is Cicero. Cicero makes this even clearer by following up the *Brutus* with the *Orator,* which is a defense (also addressed to Brutus) of Cicero's rhetorical style. But since the grounds of opposition shift in Cicero (see n. 8, above), no simple correlations survive, and several complications have to be conceded: (1) Cicero's "fluency" extends to his treatment of problems of style itself. With their liberation from the "technicalities" of traditional rhetoric (see chap. 10, n. 76), different styles can become appropriate to different parts of a speech, to different *personalities,* as well as to different audiences and to different political occasions. (2) Cicero's "fluency" in the case of his own style is compatible with a flexible reconciliation of opposed styles (including what was technically the distinctively "fluent" style) and can encompass a mixture of styles (see vol. 1, chap. 8, note 95). (3) Brutus' philosophical position was close to Cicero's (*Att.* 13. 25; *Academica* 1. 12) —i.e., a Platonizing dilution of Stoicism, but *brevitas* (the opposite of *copia*) was characteristic of Brutus' rhetoric as well as of Cato's. Even so, Cicero attempts to associate Brutus' style with their shared philosophical approach when he sets up the following opposition with Cato's strictly philosophical rhetoric: "I have often observed, Brutus, that your uncle Cato when speaking in the Senate would handle weighty topics which derived from philosophy and were incompatible with the usual procedure in the courts and the assembly, but that his oratory succeeded in making such topics acceptable even to the people. And this is a more remarkable accomplishment in his case than it would be in yours or mine, since we make more use of that philosophy [i.e., the Platonic] which has fathered oratorical fluency (*copiam*) and which asserts doctrines not very different from popular opinion, whereas Cato—in my judgment a model Stoic (*perfectus Stoicus*)—holds doctrines that are unacceptable to ordinary men, and retains the conviction of his school that oratorical ornament is not to be sought or expansiveness of exposition" (*Paradoxa Stoicorum* 1). (4) The political implications of the opposition of styles are further weakened by Cicero's acknowledging Caesar's "pure and luminous *brevitas*" (*Brutus* 262). Since this compliment is paid Caesar in a dialogue in which Brutus is being reminded of his inheritable role as a tyrannicide, Cicero would seem to be drawing the same distinction between *verba* and *res* that Caesar draws when he responds to Cicero's *Cato* with an *Anti-Cato* in which he praises Cicero's style without reference to the substantive issues. We have seen in chap. 9 that this distinction is a step in the transformation of classical humanism from the predominantly moral and political tradition it had been in Cicero's *De Re Publica* into the predominantly literary performance it becomes

under the Empire and remains during the early Italian Renaissance (see also chap. 8. n. 100).

34. *Att.* 12. 21. 1.

35. *Bellum Catilinae* 14. This comparison is misread if taken too literally as a character sketch of Caesar and Cato. It is rather a comparison of two opposed authoritative exemplifications of *greatness of mind.* Comparison and exemplification, we are by now well aware, were philosophical and rhetorical procedures integral to the development of the classical tradition as a typological tradition and which received explicit justification with Cicero's esthetic theory of style as the expression of moral character. Sallust's comparison is highly stylized in its phrasing and illustrates the extent to which theoretical oppositions and technical distinctions that had been elaborated by Greek philosophers and rhetoricians became exemplified in the practical roles played by Roman *personalities.* What Sallust would have us recognize are Caesar's and Cato's moral characters, but in a fashion that is heightened by our recollecting the traditional issues of moral theory embedded in their antagonism. In tracing the development of the classical tradition, I have had to neglect the more sophisticated procedures of exemplification and confrontation which were employed by Plato in his handling of characters in his dialogues, by Thucydides in his speeches, and by Greek rhetoricians; for their procedures will exercise little direct influence on modern political thought. What is important for our purposes is the eventual reversal in the development of the classical tradition whereby the issues and distinctions that had been exemplified in practice by the Romans will reemerge as distinctively theoretical issues and technical distinctions in modern philosophy. We have seen (vol. 1, pp. 190, 269) how Plato's theory of recollection helped shape Cicero's formulation of his *personal* problem of recognition. It can almost be said that this *personal* problem becomes in effect a technical epistemological problem in Hobbes (see pp. 45–48, this vol., and accompanying n. 139). Although Sallust is focusing on the *personalities* of Caesar and Cato, the distinction between the two types of greatness of mind they exemplify will become a technical distinction in modern moral philosophy. When Hume undertakes to expand "the catalogue of virtues" (see p. 165, this vol.) he recalls Sallust's comparison: "The characters of Caesar and Cato, as drawn by Sallust, are both of them virtuous, . . . but in a different way: Nor are the sentiments entirely the same, which arise from them. The one produces love; the other esteem; The one is amiable; the other awful" (*A Treatise of Human Nature,* bk. 3, pt. 3, sec. 4). Hume's method is itself comparative and emerges from the classical tradition which he regards as composed of a succession of comparisons; see pp. 157, 196, this vol. (For the respect in which his theory of sentiments supplements and alters the traditional theory of virtue, see pp. 165, 197, this vol.) Sullust's and Hume's distinction between "the amiable and respectable virtues" is central in Adam Smith's *Theory of Moral Sentiments.* The "two different sets of virtues" which he distinguishes are "the soft, the gentle, the amiable virtues, the virtues of candid condescension and indulgent humanity," and "the great, the awful and respectable . . . virtues of self-denial, of self-government" (pt. 1, sec. 1, chap. 5). Hume himself extends the ancient distinction between the particular *personalities* of Cato and Caesar so that it becomes a general distinction between the ancient moral character and the modern moral character: "Among the ancients, the heroes in philosophy [Hume has just drawn attention to our admiration for the "magnaminity" of Socrates and of the Stoic Epictetus], as well as those in war and patriotism [e.g., Brutus and Cato; for the original conjunction of the heroes in philosophy with those in war and patriotism, see p. 38, this vol.], have a grandeur and force of sentiment, which astonishes our narrow souls. . . . They in their turn . . . would have had equal reason to consider as romantic and incredible, the degree of humanity, clemency, order, tranquility, and other social virtues, to which, in the administration of government, we have attained in modern times [these were the virtues attained in ancient times by the Caesars who were identified as good administrators of the Empire]. . . . Such is the compensation which nature, or rather education, has made in the distribution of virtues in those different ages" (*An Enquiry into the Principles of Morals,*

sec. 7). A later age will update this ancient distinction between ancient and modern so that it becomes a distinction between ancient individualistic virtue and those modern social virtues which are fostered by a commercial society. Thus one of John Stuart Mill's applications of his principle of antagonism opposes the moral tendencies of democracy in America with the reading of the classics, which should be revived for their moral as well as their literary examples: "Not only do those literatures [the Greek and Roman] furnish examples of high finish and perfection in workmanship, to correct the slovenly habits of modern hasty writing, but they exhibit . . . precisely that order of virtues in which a commercial society is apt to be deficient [in Mill's mind modern journalism links up, as the vehicle of public opinion, with the leveling, socializing tendencies of commercial society; pp. 287, 299, this vol.]; and they altogether show human nature on a grander scale–with less benevolence but more patriotism, less sentiment, but more self-control; if a lower average of virtue, more striking individual examples of it; fewer small goodnesses but more greatness and appreciation of greatness; more which tends to exalt the imagination and inspire high conceptions of the capabilities of human nature" (for the full citation see p. 307, this vol.). These successive citations illustrate not only the extent to which the distinction between ancient and modern moral character was originally an ancient distinction but also the extent to which ancient moral thought has been regarded, from Hobbes to Mill, as a relatively homogeneous tradition which is assimilated to what I have identified as humanistic individualism.

36. Cicero's handling of the relation between liberty and authority focused on problems of the *res publica* (see vol. 1, p. 252). But when the focus shifts under the Empire to *verba* (see vol. 1, p. 186), a new antithesis emerges which involves in some measure a revival of Cynic "freedom of speech" (παρρησία). By the time of Tacitus the relevant opposition between liberty and authority is between *libertas* and *adulatio* (sycophancy): "If Tacitus is the first to make '*adulatio*' the centre of his analysis of tyranny, the problem of freedom of speech inevitably concerned most of the writers of the imperial age. . . . Precisely because *libertas* was no longer a clear juridical concept, these writers are not concerned with formal rights to speak in assemblies, but with *the opposite of 'adulatio'* " (Momigliano, in his "Review and Discussion" of Wirszubski, p. 149; italics added). The problem of liberty in this form (and Tacitus' presentation of this problem) will be revived in the seventeenth and eighteenth centuries. (The rubric Hume affixes to his *Treatise* is Tacitus' exclamation, "Rara temporum felicitas, ubi sentire, quae velis, et quae sentias, dicere licet," though the tyranny over literature that Hume fears is clerical rather than political.) Machiavelli does not envisage the problem of liberty in this form; he is closer to the problem as stated earlier by Cicero, Livy, Seneca, and Plutarch. Where Momigliano suggests that "the process which leads from *Libertas* to Liberty [in its modern sense] is a continuous one" (p. 146), my topological interpretation emphasizes that the process of development cannot be pulled out straight. Livy and Tacitus (to restrict the illustration to historians) belong to different periods in the development of modern classicism, as well as to different periods in Roman history. Consider the "curve in the assessment of the ancient Romans" drawn by J. H. Whitfield, who explains that "it is necessary before we evaluate Machiavelli to place him somewhere on its path, and not right at the end of it along with ourselves." He elaborates: "The enthusiasm of the humanists is for the Roman republic, . . . and it was in Livy that virtues of the Roman republic were admired, and accepted. Livy is the Roman historian for the fifteenth century, and the interest in him, and the editions of him, far outweigh the interest in what was known of Tacitus' text. . . . We are, with Machiavelli, before the emergence of the absolute monarchies of Europe, . . . and it is only after that phenomenon that the preoccupation with Tacitus instead of Livy . . . will come" (*Machiavelli* [New York: Russell & Russell, 1965], pp. 111–12).

37. Macrobius *Saturnalia* 2. 4. 18. Augustus composed a *Reply to Brutus' Cato* (Suetonius *Augustus* 85. 1). Compare Seneca: "Nobody ever saw Cato change when the state changed; he remained the same under all circumstances" (*Ep.* 104. 30). Cato's resistance

to change is, of course, Stoic moral rigidity and then by extension political rigidity (see n. 21).

38. See p. 19, this vol. for the conception of *personality* which Cicero obtains by applying the rhetorical and poetic criterion of propriety *(decorum)* to the problem of exhibiting moral character. See the accompanying n. 50 for the relation between *decorum* and *dignitas* and for the relevance of "facial expression" *(vultus)* to the exhibition of moral character. Cato's *personality* belongs to the same rhetorical and poetic tradition. "If it were up to me to express Cato's character *(Cato exprimendus)*," Seneca explains, when he borrows a metaphorical description from Virgil, "I would attribute to him this facial expression *(vultum)* and attitude *(habitum)*." The theory of expression instanced by this borrowing is itself borrowed from Posidonius and it was probably intended (like Cicero's esthetic theory of expression) to supplement the traditional theory of moral virtue: "Posidonius holds that the laying down of precepts is not enough. . . . He says that it is useful to exhibit each particular virtue, and this he calls ethology *(ethologian)*, while others call it characterization. It supplies the signs and evidence which distinguish each virtue and voice. . . . One procedure [traditional moral theory] supplies the precepts for virtue; the other procedure [this rhetorical supplement], its exemplification [*exemplar*]. Present and extol . . . these exhibitions or, to employ a term from commerce, these samples [*iconismos*], and men will imitate them" (*Ep.* 95. 65–70). (For Cicero's theory of expression and the relation between *praecepta* and *exempla* that constitutes a classical tradition for imitation, see p. 26, this vol. and the references in the accompanying n. 76.) What Seneca borrows from Virgil in order to exhibit Cato's "expression and attitude" during the Civil War is a description of a pedigree horse. What is usually exhibited, when *libertas* is opposed to *adulatio,* is the expression and attitude of a philosopher with a Socratic (or Cynic) pedigree. Professors of philosophy were viewed as subversive because their traditional attitude could be construed as the exact opposite of *adulatio*. Thus one sign of Thrasea's subversiveness (see n. 47) was that he wore "the sullen expression of a professor" (Suetonius *Nero* 37. 1).

39. For the label, "The Philosophical Opposition," see Gaston Bossier, *L'opposition sous les Cesars*, 3d. ed. (Paris: Hachette, 1892).

40. Socrates as Salutati would identify him (*De Fato* 2.8) had he died in the true faith. I am citing Eugenio Garin, *Italian Humanism* (Oxford: Basil Blackwell, 1965), p. 28.

41. In the Stoic tradition, the question of resistance was a moral rather than a political question. The formulation of the question can perhaps be traced back to a political metaphor Aristotle employs in his moral theory. Aristotle distinguished between mere "endurance" (*καρτερία—patientia*) and "restraint" (ἐγκράτεια—sometimes translated *continentia*), explaining that "endurance merely implies successful resistance, whereas restraint implies [etymologically in Greek] 'ruling over,' the difference being between avoiding defeat and achieving victory" (*Nichomachean Ethics* 7. 1150a). The metaphors of victory and defeat remain commonplaces in the Stoic tradition. But with the Stoic requirement of absolute "rule" to suppress the passions, Aristotle's distinction between "successful resistance . . . avoiding defeat" and "victory" becomes blurred. (In n. 93 an Aristotelian revival of the distinction will be considered.) Brutus composed a *De Patientia;* see n. 32, above, for the sense in which Brutus' (external) defeat was a (internal) victory over his (external) victors. The doctrine of moral resistance was consolidated by Seneca. See Gerda Busch, "*Fortunae resistere* in der Moral des Philosophen Seneca," *Antike und Abendland,* 10: 131–54.

42. Since the question of resistance raised issues in the relation between moral philosophy and political practice, we find a range of scholarly interpretations similar to those we encountered in the interpretation of *cum dignitate otium* (see vol. 1, p. 254) and accompanying n. 44). Some of these issues are reviewed by J. M. C. Toynbee, "Dictators and Philosophers in the First Century A. D.", *Greece and Rome* 38–39 (June, 1944): 44–58.

Bossier had described the philosophical opposition as "pas tout à fait politique dans son principe, mais plutôt morale," but D. R. Dudley (*A History of Cynicism* [London: Methuen, 1937], p. 128) emphasized that it represented "a resurgence of the old Roman aristocratic spirit which found its true embodiment in Cato." Toynbee rallies to Bossier's interpretation, insisting that the cult did not "involve political republicanism, that is, anti-imperial conspiracy" (p. 45) and did not constitute "any real political danger to the Principate as such" (p. 47). She distinguishes instead between Stoics who supported "enlightened monarchy" and "Cynic extremists" who were against "all forms of settled and established government" (p. 53). (On the fluctuating relations between the two movements, see vol. 1, p. 202, but after Seneca the distinction between Stoicism and Cynicism becomes increasingly difficult to maintain.) The issues of interpretation in Seneca are not only similar, but also overlap those we encountered in the interpretation of *cum dignitate otium.* On the one hand, Seneca rebuts the accusation that moral philosophy has subversive political implications by stressing the merely moral implications of the philosopher's *otium.* The accusation is that "those who have dedicated themselves loyally to philosophy are intransigent and refractory, contemptuous of magistrates and kings and of those who administer the state [the characteristics the Stoic displays in resisting external fortune have been transposed so that they become characteristics of his attitude towards other men]." Seneca's rebuttal is that "philosophers are readier to show their gratitude to their rulers than any other people—and properly so, for rulers bestow no greater privilege than making it possible for philosophers to enjoy peaceful leisure" (*Ep.* 73. 1–2). Thus the "philosopher will acknowledge the great debt he owes to the ruler whose administration and foresight enable him to enjoy full leisure *(otium),* the use of his own time, and tranquillity *(quies)* undisturbed by public responsibilities" (*Ep.* 73. 10). On the other hand, abstention from politics could also be construed as a subversive political gesture, especially when it seems to be implemented by an instransigent and refractory attitude. Seneca cautions, "the philosopher should not disturb public manners nor solicit popular attention by any unusual mode of life" (*Ep.* 14. 14). Thus the philosopher's abstention from politics to enjoy private leisure and tranquility should itself be a private, not a public gesture. The philosopher avoids "the powerful who could harm him, but he is careful not to seem to avoid him, for it is essential to security, not to seek security openly—what one avoids, one is condemning" (14. 7–8).

43. Despite having cited and dismissed the *Phaedo* as "ancient history and Greek at that," Cicero goes on to find that the same divine authorization for his death and "departure" which was granted Socrates was "extended to Cato and unnamed others: "ut tunc Socrati, nunc Catoni, saepe multis" (*Tusc.* 1. 74). The "departures of famous men" (like their exiles) was a fashionable rhetorical genre. See F. A. Marx, *"Tacitus und die Literatur der exitus illustrium virorum," Philologus,* 92 (1937): 83–103.

44. See vol. 1, p. 289.

45. *Cato Minor* 68 (792); 70 (793). Cato's reading imposed a Stoic interpretation on the *Phaedo:* "After supper the discussion turned to the Stoic paradoxes—that the moral man alone enjoys liberty while the immoral are all slaves" (67 [792]). In this setting Cato's suicide becomes an act of (inner) moral liberation, correlated with the (external) political liberation that fortune rendered impossible. Various manipulations of the concept of virtuous liberty are illustrated by the following selections from Seneca: "Fortune, you have gotten nowhere by opposing all my efforts. Up until now I have fought not for my own but for my country's liberty; I did not struggle so persistently for myself but to live among men who enjoyed liberty. Now since human affairs are hopeless, let Cato be withdrawn to a safe place" (*Ep.* 24 7–8). "Cato knows the route of departure, his arm [i.e., his suicide] will open up the road to liberation. . . . Liberty which he could not secure for his country, he secures for Cato" (*De Providentia* 2. 10). "At one and the same moment were extinguished what it would be irreverent to sunder: Cato who did not survive liberty; liberty which did not survive Cato" (*De constantia Sapientis* 2. 2). Cato is, however, irreverently sundered from liberty in the quietistic argument against the

philosopher's having participated in the Civil War: "What are you up to, Marcus Cato? Liberty is no longer at stake; it was long since destroyed. The present issue is whether Caesar or Pompey takes over the state. Why take sides? It's not your problem—the selection of a tyrant. What difference can it make to you who conquers" (*Ep.* 14. 13).

46. Thrasea's having written this biography of Cato was itself a treasonable act and Thrasea's own biographer will be condemned in turn.

47. Thrasea introduces one improvement on his model. Unlike Socrates, Thrasea was able to pour a libation, his own blood—to Jove the liberator. If Thrasea's suicide illustrates the general theme of liberation, the accusations against Thrasea (as reported in Tacitus *Annales* 16. 22) illustrate other themes I have been sorting out. (1) Confrontation: "Formerly Caesar was confronted by Cato; today Nero there is talk of you and Thrasea in a city avid for discord." (2) Attitude and expression: "Thrasea has his followers or rather his hangers-on who may not as yet emulate his intransigent opinions, but they imitate already his attitude and expression—austere and sullen—to reproach you [Nero] for your enjoyment of life" *(ibid.)*. (3) Abstention: "Thrasea has evaded the usual oath; . . . he did not offer a sacrifice for the health of the emperor or for the emperor's heavenly voice; . . . he has not entered the *curia;* . . . he has spent his time on the private cases of his clients. The journal of the Roman people is read in the provinces and in the armies with extra attention, to find out what Thrasea has *not* done." Thus abstention from political activity has become a significant form of political activity. I am now concluding my main account of the development of the humanistic tradition at the juncture where the antithesis has been crossed with which I began this account—the antithesis between *otium* (the abstention from political activity that liberates the mind of the philosopher) and *negotium* (the political activity that liberates Rome from her enemies—see vol. 1, p. 197).

48. Some of the confrontations of martyrs with emperors were collected in *On the Courage of Philosophers,* by Timothy of Pergamum, who is cited by Clement of Alexandria (*Stromateis* 4. 56. 2). The Cynic-Stoic tradition of solitude was continued as the Christian tradition of monasticism (see p. 14, this vol.) Thus the Greek verb "to philosophize" acquired a reference, which the medieval *philosophus* will retain, to the exercises of Christian ascetics. The consolidation of the classical tradition for Christian purposes is also marked by these ascetics becoming "athletes," "contestants," "militants"—i.e., by their falling heir to the metaphors with which I began my account of the formation of this tradition when I dealt with Polybius' debt to Platonic philosophy (see vol. 1, pp. 87–92). For Christian use of these metaphors, see Ramsey MacMullen, *Enemies of the Roman Order* [Cambridge: Harvard University Press, 1966], p. 315, and Victor C. Pfitzner, *Paul and the Agon Motif* [Leiden: E. J. Brill, 1967].

49. For the full citation, see p. 62, this vol. Plutarch as well as Cicero is responsible for the appearance of Plato's name on this list. Plutarch consolidated the humanistic tradition of resistance by writing *Parallel Lives* of Dion and Brutus. The initial justification for the comparison is that they both belong to the Platonic school: "Dion was an immediate follower of Plato's while Brutus was raised on the doctrine of Plato," so that "both set out from one athletic school to engage in the greatest of contests" (Dion 1 [958]). The consolidated tradition will continue intact until the nineteenth century. James Mill will select Sir James Mackintosh as the foremost antagonist of the Utilitarians, not only in political philosophy (see vol. 1, chap. 1, n. 20, for James Mill's *Essay on Government* as an attack on Mackintosh), but also in ethical philosophy (see chap. 15, n. 8, for James Mill's *Fragment on Mackintosh.* The following portion of Mackintosh's *The Progress of Ethical Philosophy chiefly during The Seventeenth and Eighteenth Centuries* is worth anticipating: "The pure school of Plato sent forth Marcus Brutus, the signal humanity of whose life was both necessary and sufficient to prove that his daring breach of venerable rules flowed only from that dire necessity which left no other means of upholding the most sacred principles" (3rd. ed. [Edinburgh: Adam and Charles Black, 1862]

p. 34). In the next sentence Mackintosh introduces Cicero: "The Roman orator, though in speculative questions he embraced that mitigated doubt which allowed most ease and freedom to his genius, yet in those moral writings where his heart was most deeply interested, followed the severest sect of philosophy, and became almost a Stoic." These references to Brutus and Cicero are placed in the setting of what I have been characterizing (see esp. n. 35, above) as a tradition in which Greek philosophical theory is authoritatively exemplified by the greatness of Roman minds: "The influence of the Grecian systems was tried by their effect on a body of men of the utmost originality, energy, and variety of character. . . . If any conclusion may be hazarded from this trial of systems, the greatest which history has recorded, we must not refuse our decided . . . preference to that noble school [i.e., the Stoic] which preserved great souls untainted at the court of dissolute and ferocious tyrants" (*ibid.*, pp. 34, 36). Hobbes in contrast had taken advantage of the ambivalence of this philosophical tradition (see vol. 1, p. 203) by identifying it as Cynic: "There walked in old Greece a certain phantasm, for superficial gravity, though full within of fraud and filth, a little like philosophy; which unwary men, thinking to be it, adhered to the professors of it." Hobbes also reminds us that Antiquity was aware of the subversive threat posed by these philosophers; he recalls the "diverse cities, from which they have been often by public edicts banished" (*English Works,* 1: ix).

50. *Leviathan,* pt. 2, chap. 21. The title of this chapter, "Of the Liberty of Subjects" retains the focus discussed above, p. 34, this vol.

51. *English Works,* 1: 211.

52. The thrust of Hobbes' definition of liberty (especially when we take into account his reference to "all living creatures, whilest they are imprisoned, or restrained, with walls, or chayns") may be directed against Epictetus'. When threatened, "I shall put you in chains," Epictetus retorts: "It is only my leg that you are putting in chains. My freedom of choice, not even Zeus can conquer." When threatened, "I shall put you in prison," Epictetus retorts, "Only my wretched body." Epictetus then summarizes "these reflections as those a philosopher should practice," and goes on to cite Thrasea (Epictetus, *Diatribes* 1. 23–27).

53. *The Political Philosophy of Hobbes* (Chicago: The University of Chicago Press, 1952), p. 5.

54. *Hobbes* (London: Penguin Books, 1956), p. 25.

55. *Ibid.,* p. 138.

56. *Ibid.,* p. 144.

57. Strauss, *The Political Philosophy of Hobbes,* p. 35.

58. *Leviathan,* pt. 1, chap. 13. Cf. "The principles of the politics consist in knowledge of the motions of the mind" (*De Corpore* I, vi, 7 *English Works* 1: 74).

59. *Ibid.,* pt. 2, chap. 1.

60. *English Works* 2: Epistle Dedicatory. Note that when Hobbes does turn from deduction to "experience," he explains that it is because he envisages "some man . . . not trusting to this inference made from the passions" (*Leviathan,* pt. 1, chap. 13).

61. *Leviathan,* pt. 1, chap. 3.

62. For the full citation, see p. 36, this vol.

63. *Leviathan,* pt. 1, chap. 4.

64. See vol. 1, pp. 7, 10, 53.

65. Strauss, *The Political Philosophy of Hobbes,* p. 35.

66. Perhaps a second general assumption gets in the way of acknowledging the significance of a period in the history of philosophy which is marked (as I have tried to

suggest in this chapter and in the previous chapter) by the encroachment of rhetorical considerations in the handling of the individual's relation to other men. This is the general assumption that rhetoric lacks the philosophical relevance of such "other studies" as morals and politics. An originally rhetorical treatment of the passions would therefore hardly be expected to repay detailed attention. But as historians of philosophy we should listen in the way that Hobbes himself did to "the seditious roarings of a troubled nation" (*Leviathan,* pt. 1, chap. 8). Hobbes explains, "For men . . . studying Greek and Latin, became acquainted with the democratical principles of Aristotle and Cicero, and from the love of their eloquence fell in love with their politics . . . till it grew into the rebellion we now talk of" (*Behemoth, English Works,* 6: 218). Hobbes' fuller explanation, as I have indicated, takes men's passions into account: "The authors of sedition . . . call right and wrong, good and bad, according to their passions, or according to the authorities or such as they admire as Aristotle, Cicero, Seneca, and others of like authority, who have given the names of right and wrong, as their passions have dictated or have followed the authority of other men, as we do theirs" (*Elements of Laws* [*English Works,* 4: 211]). This is not the sort of explanation of a civil war that we would be tempted to offer today, and interpreters of Hobbes have not tried to cope with this explanation. They instead cling to those arguments of Hobbes which have remained the stock in trade of political philosophy today.

67. Aristotle's list I have derived from the *Rhetoric* 2. 2–9 (1378a–1387b); Aquinas' list, from the *Summa Theologica* 1ª 2ªᵉ q. 22–48. (All my citations from Aquinas are from the *Summa Theologica.*) In the sixteenth and seventeenth centuries this portion of the *Summa* became segregated as a *Tractatus de passionibus.* I suspect that Hobbes' treatment of the passions in the *Leviathan* is in fact based on Franciscus Suarez' commentary on Aquinas' treatment (*Tractatus quinque ad Primam Secundae D. Thomae* [Mainz, 1629]). But I am undertaking a direct comparison of Hobbes with Aquinas in order to bring out the continuity of the humanistic tradition. I am neglecting too the relation between Hobbes' and Descartes' treatments of the passions as well as the interesting differences between Hobbes' treatment of them in the *Leviathan* and in his other works.

68. Strauss, *The Political Philosophy of Hobbes,* p. 41

69. Peters, *Hobbes,* p. 91. Cf. Peters' complaint that Hobbes' "transition from mechanics to physiology was accomplished by a generalized use of the notion of 'endeavour' —a good illustration of Hobbes' tendency to tear terms out of technical contexts and to use them to bridge gaps in his speculative scheme" (p. 99). We shall see that Hobbes did not have to do any tearing or bridging, since he was operating within the context of the humanistic tradition. He did not presuppose, in the way that his philosophical interpreters do today, the existence of distinct and separate sciences. In the next chapter I shall begin tracing the process of distinction and separation.

70. Peters, *Hobbes,* p. 90.

71. 1ª 2ªᵉ, q. 22, art. 1.

72. 1ª, q. 81, art. 1.

73. *Levithan,* pt. 1, chap. 1 ("Of Sense"). In chap. 2 ("Of Imagination") Hobbes identifies the imagination as "decaying sense." This identification presupposes the law of the conservation of motion: "When a Body is once in motion, it moveth (unless something els hinder it) eternally." In other words the original motion of a particular sensation decays as other motions impede it. This scientific deduction Hobbes sharply distinguishes from rhetorical resort to mental imagery whose confusion the deduction itself explains. The distinction does not, however, preclude Hobbes' own vivid use of imagery: "Sallust's character of Catiline (than whom there never was a greater artist in raising seditions) is this: that he had great eloquence, and little wisdom. . . . Now eloquence is twofold. The one is an elegant and clear expression of the conceptions of

the mind, . . . and riseth partly . . . from an understanding of words taken in their own proper and definite signification. The other is a commotion of the passions of the mind . . . and derives from a metaphorical use of words fitted to the passions. . . . The art of that is logic, of this rhetoric; the end of that is truth, of this victory. Each hath its use" (*De Cive,* xii, 12 (*English Works* 2: 162–62). This distinction can be applied to Hobbes' own use of words. On the one hand, I am urging against Peters and Strauss that a better case than they allow can be made for Hobbes' reliance on a deductive method, however unreliable they may regard such a method. On the other hand, Hobbes' own rhetorical use of imagery is deliberately tendentious. As the parenthesis following Catiline's name indicates, he does select his particular examples and their attendant imagery in a way which is fitted to the passions of his humanistic reader and with an eye (in Peters' phrase) to their political relevance. Thus. in "Of Imagination" he is concerned with the illusion of *greatness of mind* when he offers the example of "when a man imagins himselfe a Hercules or an Alexander." And when he turns to dream imagery, he cites the example of the tyrannicide who notoriously benefited from a ruler's clemency and betrayed his friendship: "We read of Marcus Brutus (one that had his life given him by Julius Caesar, and was also his favorite, and notwithstanding murthered him) how . . . hee saw a fearfull apparition, which is commonly related by Historians as a Vision: but considering the circumstances, one may easily judge to have been but a short Dream." Hobbes is not, however, the first to consider the circumstances and distinguish between vision and dream. We read (and Hobbes read) of Marcus Brutus' dream in Plutarch, where the story is already embedded in an Epicurean mechanistic explanation of dreams. Brutus as a Stoic could have accepted the experience as vision which was an accurate premonition of the future, but "as soon as it was light, he sought out Cassius," who supplied him with the Epicurean explanation of visions as dreams. The political partners thus seem to have become philosophical opponents in the tradition. Cassius' explanation includes a rudimentary application to the imagination of the principle of the conservation of motion: "The mind of man is ever occupied and that continual moving is nothing but imagination" (Plutarch, *Brutus* 37 (1001); I am citing Sir Thomas North's translation). I offer this minor illustration of the way that Hobbes operates within the context of the humanistic tradition in order to suggest that my case for Hobbes' reliance on deductive method takes into account his awareness of the extent to which humanistic tradition already incorporated ostensibly scientific arguments. I am making fuller use of the illustration provided by Aquinas.

74. *Ibid.,* chap. 6.

75. 1^{a}, q. 80. art. 2.

76. *Leviathan,* Pt. 1, chap. 6.

77. 1^{a} 2^{ae} q. 25, art. 2; q. 26, art. 1; q. 27, art. 4, *ad secundum.*

78. 1^{a} 2^{ae}, q. 26, art. 1.

79. *Leviathan,* Pt. 1, chap. 2.

80. *De Finibus* 3. 16.

81. 1^{a} 2^{ae}, q. 25, art. 1.

82. 1^{a} 2^{ae}, q. 25, art. 2; cf. q. 26, art. 2.

83. *Leviathan,* pt. 1, chap. 6.

84. 1^{a} 2^{ae}, q. 25, art. 1.

85. 1^{a}, q. 81, art. 2.

86. *Leviathan,* pt. 1, chap. 6.

87. Raymond Polin, *Politique et philosophie chez Thomas Hobbes* (Paris: Presses Universitaires, 1953), p. 165.

88. It is at this juncture that Hobbes is most anxious to straighten out what he

regards as the confusion of the tradition. "The names of Vertues and Vices" he considers notable instances of "inconstant names" which "can never be true grounds of any ratiocination."

89. 2ª 2ªᵉ, q. 29, art. 5, art. 6 *ad secundum.*

90. 1ª 2ªᵉ, p. 61, art. 2; 2ª 2ªᵉ, q. 128, art. 1, *ad primum.*

91. *Leviathan,* pt. 1, chap. 6.

92. Strauss, p. 113.

93. 2ª 2ªᵉ, q. 123, art. 2. In distinguishing the parts of *fortitudo,* Aquinas relies on the Aristotelian distinction between passive resistance and a more aggressive virtue (see n. 41, above). In conformity with the Stoic emphasis, Aquinas concludes that courage is primarily a virtue of passive resistance: "Sustinere, et immobiliter in periculis sistere, principalior est actus fortitudinis, quam aggredi pericula" (2ª 2ªᵉ, q. 123, art. 6). Observe how mechanistic his argument is: ". . . quia sustinere videtur aliquis ab aliquo fortiori invadente; qui autem aggreditur, invadit per modum fortioris. Difficilius autem est pugnare cum fortiori quam cum debiliori." The virtues, like the passions, did not need to wait until the inspiration of Galileo before they could become forces in motion. In Hobbes, Aquinas' distinction here between the primary sense of courage and the secondary sense becomes meaningless, since it is distinction between rest (immobile resistance) and motion. But Aquinas makes an alternative distinction available to Hobbes by distinguishing courage in its secondary sense as involving a "sudden motion." Thus when Hobbes defines Anger as "sudden courage," its suddenness is not his own mechanistic innovation in the philosophical tradition.

94. See p. 46.

95. One might have expected some such suggestion from Strauss. But in fact he claims that Hobbes' theory of magnanimity in the *Leviathan* "is not only not indispensable but even diametrically opposed to its fundamental purpose" (*The Political Philosophy of Hobbes,* p. 55) This theory Strauss assumes "Hobbes momentarily adopted . . . under the strength of the impression made by Descartes' *Passions de l'ame,*" inasmuch as Hobbes' own system of morals corresponds better to Descartes' deepest intention than does the morality of *Les passions de l'âme*" (*Hobbes,* p. 56). I cite these pieces of Strauss' interpretation only in order to illustrate the kind of jugglery that can pass for the history of ideas once the impressive efforts of two philosophers to be methodical are discounted in favor of their deeper intentions.

96. Observe the process of extension and generalization that backs up this definition: " 'Virtue' is derived from man *(viro);* and the distinctive virtue of a man is courage, which has two important functions, contempt of pain and death" (*Tusc.* 2. 43). Modern philosophers since Hume have been concerned with the place of reason in ethics (see vol. 1, p. 70, and this present vol., p. 189). Thus the fundamental problem in interpreting Hobbes has come to be deciding whether or not his ethics is merely prudential. But my topological concern is with the place of the individual in politics and with his relocation by Hobbes. Here the relevant virtue is not prudence but *greatness of mind* in its affiliation with courage, which had been the distinctively Roman virtue (p. 42, this vol.), which had become for the Romans the distinctively human virtue and which will become for the Christians a distinctively Christian virtue (see n. 48 above). Unless this process of extension and generalization is taken into account, Hobbes' timorousness remains merely a matter of the temperment of a particular individual threatened at birth by the Spanish Armada and during his life by the Civil War.

97. In the Stoic organic universe, "there are many obstacles and impediments for partial entities and movements, but none for the whole" (Chrysippos as cited by Plutarch ["On the Contradictions of the Stoics" 1056e]). The moral implications of this citation are explicitly brought out by Marcus Aurelius: "There is nothing that hinders

you from always doing and saying whatever conforms to the nature of which you are a part" (*Meditationes* 2. 9). The political implications are brought out by the formula, also attributed to Chrysippos, for Stoic hesitation over participating in politics: "the wise man will take part in politics, if nothing impedes" (Diogenes Laertius *Lives of the Philosophers* 7. 121). But for Hobbes all motions are impeded motions (in the sense that even when the motion of one body is "helped"—accelerated—by the motion of another body, it will not continue moving in its original direction), and his political theory is a specification of impediments, from which it follows that the prudent man will remain a private citizen and not claim the moral authority to exercise political authority.

98. I have been interpreting Hobbes as analyzing all the passions (including the traditional concupiscible passions) in the way that Aquinas analyzed only the irascible passions (i.e., as phenomena of resistance which involve two motions), and I have given as an illustration the fact that the motion which Hope (the first and fundamental irascible passion in Aquinas) "adds" over and beyond the motion of Desire (the first and fundamental passion involving actual movement in Aquinas) is "a certain *conatum* (i.e., the endeavor from which all motions are deduced in Hobbes). But Hope in Aquinas "adds" something more—"quemdam conatum et quamdam *elevationem* animi ad consequendum bonum arduum" (1^{a} 2^{ae}, q. 25, art. 1). Thus I am now qualifying my earlier interpretation: Hobbes does not analyze all the passions in the way that Aquinas analyzed the irascible passions; while retaining and generalizing the motion of *conatus* (or reviving the Stoic conception of *conatus*, Hobbes eliminates what Aquinas visualizes as its characteristic upward movement. (In the Aquinas' treatment of Fear, the opposite of Hope, what is added is a downward movement—"a certain *depressio animi*.")

99. In formulating the law, Galileo visualized a body in motion along a perfectly smooth (unimpeded) horizontal plane.

100. *English Works* 4: 52–53.

101. Peters, *Hobbes,* pp. 152–53.

102. *Republic* 437B, 439B–440A.

103. *Republic* 581B–D.

104. See p. 44, this vol.

105. *Tusc.* 5. 9.

106. Are we therefore to conclude with Peters that Hobbes' psychology is "in fact constructed with an eye much more on its political relevance than on its theoretical adequacy?" We should not reach this conclusion too promptly. The irascible power in Aquinas is already markedly pugnacious in its operations. It is identified as "*propugnatrix et defensatrix concupiscibilis*" (1^{a}, q. 81, art. 2). But there is no evidence that Aquinas had an eye on the political relevance of its operations, and in any case his political theory is not an Hobbesian *bellum omnium contra omnes.*

107. One detail of the comparison—the identification of Envy with the endeavor "to supplant or overthrow"—suggests that Hobbes may be showing his disdain for the Stoic conception of life as governed by the rules of the game: "When someone runs a race . . . he should make every effort he can to win, but he ought never to trip up *(supplantare)* a competitor, or to push him aside *(depellere)* with his hand; thus in life it is not unfair for anyone to strive for whatever he needs for his own use, but he has no right to take it away from another man" (*Off.* 3. 42). In Hobbes' *plenum* there is no room to exercise this option (see p. 127, this vol.).

108. *Leviathan,* Intro.; pt. 1, chap. 11. The Latin for "in the repose of a mind satisfied" is "*tranquillitate sive requie animi*" (*Latin Works,* ed. W. Molesworth, 5 vols. [London; John Bohn, 1839–45], 3: 77). *Tranquillitas* is one of Cicero's translations for ἀπάθεια and retains a comparably general significance in Aquinas as an effect of self-control *(temperantia).* This effect of self-control is, of course, undermined by Hobbes' eliminating in his physics the antithesis between rest and motion: "There is no such thing as

perpetuall Tranquillity of mind, while we live here; because Life it selfe is but Motion" (*Leviathan,* pt. 1, chap. 6). The elimination of the antithesis similarly undermines the traditional controversy between *otium* and *negotium* as alternative ways of life: "Negotium, bonum: etenim vitae motus est. . . . Otium torquet. Natura neque locum neque tempus vacuum esse patitur" (Latin Works 2: 100).

109. For the full citation, see p. 125, this vol.

110. The problem posed by the relation between these two individuals in motion can be rendered in the mechanistic terms of two things in motion: "Because the power of one man resisteth and hindreth the effects of the power of another, power simply is no more, but the excess of the power of one man above that of another" (*English Works* 4: 38).

111. *Leviathan,* pt. 2, chap. 17.

112. See p. 4, this vol.

113. *Prince,* chap. 18.

114. Georges Sabine, *A History of Political Theory,* 3rd ed. (New York: Holt, Rinehart and Winston, 1966), p. 344.

115. See p. 4, this vol.

116. *Discourses,* bk. 1, chap. 5.

117. See p. 7, this vol.

118. *Leviathan,* pt. 1, chap. 15.

119. *Off.* 3. 82. Caesar is quoting Euripides *Phoenissae* v. 524.

120. *Leviathan,* pt. 1, chap. 15.

121. *Ibid.* pt. 2, chap. 17.

122. See pp. 33, 39, this vol.

123. See p. 34, this vol.

124. *Leviathan,* pt. 2, chap. 20.

125. *Leviathan,* pt. 1, chap. 13.

126. *Ibid.* See p. 47, this vol.

127. See p. 81, this vol.

128. *English Works* 4: 42–43.

129. *Rhetoric* 2. 2 (1378a).

130. *Leviathan* pt. 1, chap. 6.

131. *English Works* 4: 43.

132. Cf. Tactius' appraisal: "To overthrow authority, they uphold liberty; when authority is overturned, they will attack liberty" (*Annales* 16. 22). But the issue is sharpened by Hobbes' distinction "between the ethics of subjects and the ethics of sovereigns" (*English Works,* 6: 219). We have seen (p. 35, this vol.) that this distinction is unclassical. It alters Hobbes' treatment of courage as well as of self-control: "Fortitude is a royal virtue; and though it be necessary in such private men as shall be soldiers, yet, for other men, the less they dare, the better it is both for the commonwealth and for themselves" *(ibid.).*

133. *Leviathan,* pt. 1, chap. 15.

134. *Ibid.,* chap. 6.

135. *Ibid.,* chap. 13.

136. *English Works,* 4: 84.

137. *Leviathan,* Intro.

138. *Leviathan,* Dedicatory Letter. In speaking in the abstract of the seat of power, Hobbes is speaking of "a Feigned or Artificiall person" (*Leviathan,* pt. 1, chap. 16). Although he cites Cicero's use of the term *persona,* Hobbes' conception of the ruler as acting on behalf of the citizens as their representative draws on the juridical and theological tradition rather than on the classical humanistic tradition. This is one of the junctures at which it is impossible to trace the development of modern political thought without attention to its mediaeval inheritance (see vol. 1, chap. 9, n. 95).

139. Hobbes' image for the state is taken from Job, "where God having set forth the great power of Leviathan, calleth him King of the Proud (*Leviathan,* pt. 2, chap. 28). Hobbes here may be availing himself of the difficulty of distinguishing (from the Christian point of view) pagan *greatness of soul* from pride. But Hobbes' state has to be a humbling *Leviathan* because he identifies the humanistic tradition as a tradition in which great actions were performed and which encourages their continued performance: "The more eminent actions and apothegms both of the Greeks and Romans have been indebted for their eulogies not so much to the reason, as to the greatness of them" (*De Cive,* Epistle Dedicatory [*English Works* 2: iii]; cf. Hume's and Mill's identification of the humanistic tradition, n. 35 above). These great actions Hobbes identifies in turn as libertarian. See one of his explanations of "how came the people to be so corrupted" as to engage in the civil war: "There were an exceeding great number of men of the better sort, that had been so educated, as that in their youth having read the books written by famous men of the ancient Grecian and Roman commonwealths concerning their polities and great actions; in which books the popular government was extolled by that glorious name of liberty, and monarchy disgraced by the name of tyranny" (*Behemoth* [*English Works* 6: 168]).

140. See p. 39, this vol. Pain was traditionally a problem of resistance. Aquinas defines the *"causa doloris"* as *"potestas cui non potest resisti"* and cites Augustine's Stoic definitions: "In animo dolorem facit voluntas resistens potestati maiori, in corpore dolorem facit sensus resistens corpori potentiori" (1^{a} 2^{ae}, q. 37, art. 4).

141. *Leviathan,* pt. 1, chap. 14.

142. *Ibid.,* pt. 2, chap. 29. Hobbes is here making a transition from men as the "Makers" to the design of the institutional structure which they should make: "For men, as they become at last weary of irregular justling and hewing one another, and desire with all their hearts to conforme themselves into one firme and lasting edifice; so for want, both of the art of making fit Lawes, and to square their actions by, and also of humility, and patience, to suffer the rude and combersome points of their present greatness to be taken off, they cannot without the help of a very able Architect, be compiled, into any other than a crasie building." Hobbes is elaborating his doctrine of absolute sovereignty in opposition not only to the individualistic tradition of *greatness of mind,* but also to the institutional tradition of mixed government (see vol. 1, pp. 110–11 and accompanying n. 65, for the importance the classical model of mixed government has in modern political thought). The conjunction of this classical conception of the individual with this classical conception of government is not an idiosyncrasy of Hobbes' but a continuing tradition. Cf. Hume's comment on the classical background of the Civil War: "A familiar acquaintance with the previous remains of antiquity excited in every generous breast a passion for a limited constitution, and begat an emulation of those manly virtues [see n. 96, above], which the Greek and Roman authors, by such animating examples [see n. 35, above], as well as pathetic expressions [see n. 38, above], recommend to us" (*History of England* in 8 vols. [Edinburgh: Lackington, Allen, 1805], p. 21).

143. See pp. 41, 63, this vol.

12

The Individual and His Property

Every man hath a property in his own person.—Locke

Other Studies

Hobbes was "the first to see clearly," from James Mill's point of view, that the treatment of political problems must be deduced from a theory of human nature.[1] This methodological conviction the son inherited from his father, but John Stuart Mill found himself unable to carry through the deduction, at any rate in the form of the political ethology which in his system was to take the place of traditional political theory. He did, however, succeed in deducing a *political* theory. When his hope of deducing a political ethology waned, Mill deduced a political economy, which was modeled on Adam Smith's *Wealth of Nations*.[2]

I have argued that a political theory cannot be identified succinctly with the treatment of political problems; it is also a context (or some portion of a context) that determines both what problems are to be gathered together for treatment as *political* and the relevance of "other studies" to their treatment, as well as the relevance of their previous treatment by other theorists.[3] These questions regarding the location of the *political* have to be reformulated, now that we face the emergence in the eighteenth century of two different kinds of *political* theory. We cannot continue simply to trace the shifting relations between the individual and the state, and between the moral and the political. We must take into account shifting relations between the moral, the political, and the economic. The shifting, moreover, is not merely a matter of economic problems intruding into areas previously occupied by moral and political theories. The structure of moral and political theories, and the relations between them—and ultimately the structure of knowledge itself—are altered by the intrusion.

These alterations are, in the long run, easily overlooked. For one thing, our attention can be distracted by the emergence of the new methodological principle which presides over the structure of knowledge in Mill. He leaves the question open as to what "other . . . sciences, similar to political economy, may admit of being carved out of the general body of the social science." He leaves this question open because he feels no methodological obligation to anticipate what other sciences are in the offing. Instead he is endorsing in principle the emergence of "distinct and separate" sciences, whatever the specific subject-matters these sciences may turn out to be sciences of. The principle exalts in general the methodological requirement that "different species of social fact . . . must be studied apart."[4]

Since the time Mill first endorsed this methodological principle of "distinct and separate" sciences, its repeated application by later theorists has so undermined the relations between these sciences, that it no longer solicits attention as a principle to be explicitly avowed and vindicated. Mill's "the social science" is now so carved up into the proliferating research studies which we identify as the social sciences that there is no longer any "general body" within which one distinct and separate social science can be located by reference to its relations to what it is distinguished and separated from; and these relations are now so disembodied that Mill's principle of "distinct and separate" sciences has itself lost the pristine force it enjoyed so long as there was a "general body" to be carved up. In short, the relations between one social research study and "other studies" can no longer be investigated as if they composed some coherent, overall structure of knowledge.

What can be investigated, however, is the fracturing of a structure that once existed. Granted that the pieces of the structure that have come apart from each other cannot now be fitted together again in their present form, we can yet work back from some particular piece to the original structure it came apart from. If the effort to move from particular subject-matter to overall structure lacks plausibility today, it becomes plausible to go back to the tradition where the problems treated as moral, political, and economic were still discernibly related within the general context of some theory of human nature. What we shall recover within this context are not just relations between the particular subject-matters which have since become separated, but also the relation (at a higher level) between the emergence of Mill's methodological principle that presides over their separation, and the emergence of political economy. For we shall see that it is this particular subject-matter which proved difficult to incorporate in the traditional context of a theory of human nature. Thus I shall argue that the methodological principle of "distinct and separate" sciences did not in fact initially emerge as neutral with respect to "the different species of social fact . . . studied."[5] In the dislocation of the original structure of a theory of human nature, one particular species of social fact was preeminently involved—economic fact.

I am not denying what we have recognized ever since we encountered the "great existing fact" of democracy in America—theories are not bent out of shape by facts. Facts are pliable, and theories are indispensable to specifying the location of the facts. The principle of "distinct and separate" sciences emerged from a process in which the different species of social facts were forced apart by differences between the way economic facts were specified for study and the way moral and political facts had traditionally been specified.

In the previous chapter, I criticized anachronistic interpretations of Hobbes that reflect the present-day distinction and separation of sciences. I tried to restore the continuity of Hobbes' deduction as operating within the traditional context of a theory of nature and of human nature. What in Hobbes is a continuous deduction, takes methodologically slacker forms in Locke, Hume, and Smith. In Locke the motive of self-interest continues to lend the individual, as it did in Hobbes, a privileged role; it also continues to lend (at the higher methodological level) a theory of individual human nature a correspondingly privileged place as a context for the treatment of moral, political, and economic problems.[6] In the context of this theory,.the emergence of political economy involves a succession of changes in the specification of what the individual is interested in when he is interested in himself. Self-interest becomes increasingly an acquisitive—that is, a specifically economic motive. This process of specification (when it is viewed as contributing to the development of liberalism) is usually regarded as culminating in Smith's "system of natural liberty,"[7] whereby each individual is to be left free to consult his distinct interest and to function in the economic sphere separately from other individuals, but it equally culminates methodologically in Smith's political economy as the analysis of this system which Smith initially offers as one portion of his overall theory of human nature, but which he eventually presents as a distinct and separate science.

To establish these correlations between the structure of human relations and the structure of knowledge, we shall have to interpret the procedure of distinguishing and separating (1) as a method for determining the relations between subject-matters, (2) as a method for treating the problems posed by any subject-matter, (3) as a method for treating the problems posed in a theory of human nature, and (4) as a method for treating specifically economic problems. We are already engaged in the first interpretation; in the next section it will become an interpretation of Locke's procedure in particular, and in the three sections that follow we shall undertake the three remaining interpretations of Locke's procedure.

Limits

Locke's methodological contribution to the development of political theory is missed in the conventional interpretation in which his treatment of political problems is compared with Hobbes' by contrasting his confidence in human nature with Hobbes' pessimism. Methodologically more fundamental is the fact that Locke does not deduce his treatment of political problems from a theory of human nature or of the physical universe. Locke's editor, Peter Laslett, stresses this difference in order to dampen the conventional enthusiasm for the comparison with Hobbes: "Locke did not write . . . with Thomas Hobbes in hand or in mind, either to refute him or to adopt his doctrine without confessing it. Locke did not write as a philosopher, applying to politics the implications of his view of reality as a whole."[8]

The way Locke did write, in contrast to Hobbes, remains pertinent (in Laslett's interpretation) to any attempt to trace the development of liberalism: "It is of importance to see in Locke, the recognized point of departure for liberalism, the liberal dilemma already present, the dilemma of maintaining a political doctrine without subscribing to a total, holistic view of the world."[9] Already present? Complacency is more characteristic of Locke than prodding by the horns of any dilemma. Not until we reach Mill himself will we encounter a thinker who combines a political doctrine, which he concedes is limited in its scope, with an unfulfilled methodological aspiration to achieve a total system of knowledge.

In tracing the development of liberalism, I am not taking as characteristically "philosophical" commitment to any "view of reality as a whole." Rather I am concerned with different conceptions (in my adaptation of Mill's phraseology) of "philosophical method as applied to politics,"[10] insofar as its application determines the structure of knowledge as a whole and within this structure the particular relations prevailing between the investigation of the political and "other studies." Locke has been recognized, Laslett is reminding us, as a *substantive* point of departure for liberalism, inasmuch as he defends liberty and the rights of the individual. Locke not only undertakes this defense in his *Treatises* without reference to his *Essay on Human Understanding*, but also defends such an undertaking with the claim that the "great provinces of the intellectual world" are "wholly separate and distinct from one another."[11] With this strong sense of subject-matter, Locke dismantles (we shall see) the sweeping analogies that operated in the humanistic tradition, largely unrestrained and unclarified by reference to differences of subject-matter. He thus provides a *methodological* point of departure from which we can come within sight of Mill's principle of "distinct and separate" sciences.

Since Locke severs the relations between these different provinces and treats each separately, the immediate issue to be faced is my commitment to interpret a theorist by reference to the place he assigns one study in relation to "other studies" as also determining his place within a tradition in relation to other theorists. Is it feasible to outflank Locke's limits in order to compare his conception of philosophical method with Hobbes'? If the "great provinces of the intellectual world" are for Locke "wholly separate and distinct from one another," how can Locke's provincial undertakings be compared with Hobbes' system of knowledge, where the problems of physics, psychology, and politics come up for treatment as successive steps in a continuous deduction? The answer is at hand: division into the separate and distinct is a principle of limitation which is itself as characteristic a procedure in Locke as continuity of deduction is in Hobbes, so that what I shall be able to compare is Locke's separating a problem from other problems in order to treat it within its limits, where Hobbes' treatment of the same problem follows deductively from his treatment of some prior problem. Locke's respect for limits need not be taken to imply that he does not write "as a philosopher." Preoccupation with limits is itself methodologically pervasive in Locke: if it takes the form in the *Human Understanding* of a discovery of the limited "extent of human knowledge,"[12] it takes the form in the *Second Treatise* of a discovery of the limited "extent . . . of Civil Government."[13] John Stuart Mill's defense of liberty will similarly involve an emphasis on the limitations of human knowledge, and the problem of the relation between liberty and authority (the problem which we broached in the previous chapter) will itself be formulated by Mill as a problem of "the limits of the power which can be legitimately exercised by society over the individual."[14]

Meddling

In urging against Laslett that Locke writes "as a philosopher," I am proposing that Locke's procedure determines in the same way the relation he assumes between sciences and his formulation of problems within any particular science. Thus our comparison of Locke with Hobbes can be pinned down by turning from the provinces—the different sciences whose subject-matters are for Locke "objects of the understanding"[15] in the broad sense—to his treatment of "ideas," which are the "immediate objects" of the understanding.[16] In identifying "ideas" as the "immediate objects" of the understanding, Locke is at once specifying the facts he will study in the *Essay* and separating its subject-matter from that of physics. He is not going to deal with the relationship between ideas and whatever physical motions may be involved in their production. He is refusing (as he himself puts it) to "meddle with the physical consideration of the mind."[17] He is refusing, in effect, to do what Hobbes has done when he went behind appearances in "Of Man" to reach, as his deductive starting point, the thing in motion which is the external cause of sensation. Locke instead reaches his own starting point analytically, by limiting his treatment initially to "appearances" which are "uncompounded"—that is, to ideas which are separate and distinct ("simple" and "unmixed").[18]

Only later can he reach the problems posed by "complex ideas," which are "made by the mind out of simple ones."[19]

I am beginning the comparison with Hobbes here, for although Mill and his father endorse Hobbes' attempt to deduce the treatment of political problems from a theory of human nature, neither of them adopted Hobbes' theory of human nature, or even his deductive procedure for constructing this theory. They thought of themselves as belonging to "the school of Locke."[20] When Mill endorsed the *Essay on Human Understanding* as "the beginning and foundation of the modern analytic psychology,"[21] he was endorsing its analytic method. James Mill's theory of human nature, John Mill describes as "an attempt to reach the simplest elements which by their combination generates the manifold complexity of our mental states. . . ." The character of this attempt, James Mill had "concisely expressed," his son goes on to point out, "by naming his work on *Analysis of the Phenomena of the Human Mind*."[22] James Mill's own Introduction identifies these phenomena by citing Locke's *Essay,* and he delimits these phenomena in his first chapter by citing Locke's "I shall not at present meddle with the physical consideration of the mind."[23]

Refusing to "meddle," putting problems to one side as "beside my present purpose," or as not "my business here,"[24] is one form taken by the sense of limits that Locke contributes to the analytic tradition, where disclaimers are as frequent as claims—and usually more impressive. "Meddle" is Locke's term for stigmatizing the procedure of philosophers who operate without any respect for limits, trying to do too many things at once. The term itself perhaps suggests the extent to which a "muddle" will become in the analytic tradition the characteristic guise assumed by philosophical problems, as they have been previously treated, so that analytic philosophy in contrast becomes limited (entirely or primarily or initially) to "clearing ground a little, and removing some of the rubbish that lies in the way to knowledge."[25] Even when Locke deals with political problems, he can be said to write "as a philosopher"—that is, as an analytic philosopher; for his *Treatises* are a denunciation of Filmer for "hudling several Suppositions together," and making "such a *medly* and confusion that it is impossible to show his Mistake without examining the several Senses wherein his Words may be taken."[26]

Laslett fails to find any pervasive method:

Two Treatises is not written on the "plain historical method" of the *Essay*. If it were, we might expect that it would insist on the limitations of our social and political understanding, for that is the chief enterprise in the *Essay*, to portray the character of our knowledge by showing up its limits.[27]

Such an expectation would be anachronistic, reflecting a later reduction of the methodological problems of an analytic philosophy to epistemological problems.[28] Although the *Treatises* compose a separate subject-matter from the *Essay*, their method is analytic in the sense that problems are separated and distinguished which previous philosophers had treated together, so that the methodological prohibition in the *Essay* against "meddling" becomes the complaint of the *Treatises* about Filmer's "hudling . . . medly and confusion."

Furthermore, this analytic method takes on substantive moral and political implications. Locke is complacent about his own "unmeddling temper."[29] This moral attitude takes one political form with his doctrine of toleration. It takes another political form with his analysis of a mixed government—the structure to which I am recurrently appealing to exhibit the pliability with which institutions as political and social facts can be adapted to the structure of a theory. Locke reconstructs the traditional analysis with his most famous contribution to liberal political thought—his doctrine of the separation of powers. He argues that "it may be too great a temptation to humane fraility, apt to grasp at Power, for the same Persons who have the Power of making laws to have also in their hands the power to execute them,"[30] but since he respects the separation of subject-matters between his *Treatises* and his *Essay*, he does not cast this argument in the form of a psychological analysis of the individual's tendency to grasp at power, such as we found in Hobbes. The separation of powers, as well as the other limits which Locke sets up in defense of liberty and the rights of the individual, indicate the substantive implications that his attack on meddling portends for the relation between the individual and other men. Finally, Locke's own relations with the other philosophers are congruent with his unmeddling temper. His shrinking from controversy is one way in which he writes "as a philosopher," and lends a cogency, which is more than a matter of Locke's temperament, to Laslett's appraisal "Locke did not write . . . with Thomas Hobbes . . . in mind."

Mixed Considerations

Let us, however, pursue the comparison, if only in the hope of being able to explain why Locke was not the controversialist that Hobbes was and therefore did not write with him in mind. Hobbes' treatment of the individual's relation to other men, and of his tendency to grasp at power, took primarily the form of an analysis of the passions. These Hobbes identified as motions and deduced from "Endeavour"—"small beginnings of Motion, within the body of man, before they appear . . . in visible actions."[31] Locke's analysis of the passions differs in several ways from Hobbes. He begins the analysis by reasserting the epistemological limitations of the *Essay*—that is, by again refusing to go behind appearances in the way that Hobbes did. It is not, he announces, "my business here to inquire any farther than into the bare ideas of our passions."[32] Thus he is again specifying his subject-matter in the *Essay* in a way that forces it apart from the subject-matter of physics. Instead of identifying the passions as motions, he identifies them as "modes of pleasure and pain."[33] These two passions are privileged in his epistemology; they are simple and unmixed ideas, the mind being "wholly passive" at the moment of their "reception."[34] Hobbes' different epistemology imposed a different structure on his treatment of pleasure and pain: having identified pleasure as "the appearance or sense of good," he had to go behind this appearance to the "motion of Endeavour which consisteth in Appetite," and this Appetite was already a complex motion—" a corroboration of vitall motion and a help thereunto."[35] The human mind in Hobbes could never be (in Locke's phrase) "wholly passive," for "Endeavour" itself was an active tendency to continue in motion, and in a physical universe which is a *plenum*, any actual motion (such as Appetite) was complex in that it involved a reaction to the motion (or motions) of a contiguous body (or bodies).

Locke himself concedes that "the necessity of such a motion" would follow deductively from "the supposition that the world is full." But since Locke is not meddling with physical considerations in the *Essay*, he is not concerned with the question of "whether bodies do so exist that the motion of one body cannot really be without the motion of another," or with the question of whether the world is really full. His analysis is limited to "the idea" of a vacuum, "which it is plain men have when they inquire and dispute whether there be a vacuum or no." Thus he asks "whether a man cannot have the idea of the motion of one single body alone, without any other succeeding immediately into its place?" And he concludes that "the idea of motion in one body" does not involve "the idea of motion in another."[36] There is then no epistemological reason why bodies should impede each other, and resistance become the universal physical phenomenon that it was for Hobbes. It is not necessary for an individual body to be meddlesome in Locke's universe, any more than it is for an individual mind—as Locke's unmeddling temper demonstrates. Where in Hobbes the motions of individual bodies and of individual minds encounter other motions as impediments, Locke is setting up limits.

Thus another difference between Locke's analysis of the passions and Hobbes' is that Locke considers the individual separately from other men. When Locke explicitly raises the question, "What passions all men have," his answer indicates that he is visualizing the passions of one single mind alone, in the same way that he visualizes "the motion of one single body alone" when he entertains the idea of empty space. The passions which he accepts as universal are those "terminated purely in pain and pleasure." Thus he dismisses as "not to be found in all men," the passions of envy and anger, which are not "caused by pain and pleasure *simply* in themselves, but having in them some *mixed* considerations of ourselves and others," inasmuch as they involve men's "valuing their merits or intending revenge."[37] If I am attributing a certain philosophical cogency to Locke's unmeddling temperament, it is because individual minds in Locke are ultimately as separate and distinct as bodies, just as the province of the *Essay*, where the mind of the individual is being treated, is separate and distinct from the province of physics in which bodies are treated. Hobbes treated any actual motion in physics as involving the motions of two (or more) bodies, and when he reached the mind in his deduction he included passions which involved (in Locke's phrase) "some mixed considerations" of the individual himself and others, for Hobbes' social world was a *plenum* in which the individual continued in motion by resisting other motions—that is, by reacting psychologically to the actions of other men. The individual in Hobbes necessarily valued his merits and he intended revenge whenever the actions of other men did not represent the same evaluation as his own. This reaction was a feature in Hobbes of a complex passion which is universal: "Every man looketh that his companion should value him at the same rate as he sets upon himself; and upon all signs of contempt, or undervaluing, naturally endeavours . . . to extort a greater value from his condemners."[38] What Locke cannot find in "all men," Hobbes found in "every man." The psychological facts could hardly be settled without some attention to the way they are specified for treatment, since individuals are forced apart by Locke's method in much the way that psychological facts are forced apart from the physical facts from which they were deduced by Hobbes.

PROPERTY

Since the analysis of the passions in Locke's *Essay* does not involve any "mixed considerations" of ourselves and others, it does not enjoy the political relevance of Hobbes' analysis of the passions. But since the problems of human understanding and political problems are assigned by Locke for treatment to separate provinces, the separation of these provinces has itself to be justified from the side of his political theory, as well as from the side of his psychological theory. In Locke's *Treatises* (as in Hobbes') political arrangements are the eventual outcome of the individual's endeavor to preserve himself, but Locke's treatment of this endeavor in his political theory does not take the form of an analysis of the passions. Hobbes' treatment did take this form, for once Hobbes had located "Endeavour" as the "small beginnings of motion within the body of man, before they appear in . . . visible actions," his methodological resort to self-consciousness took the form of going behind these appearances in order to deduce from "Endeavour" the more complicated motions of the passions. In his political theory Locke does not pick up the individual's endeavor to preserve himself until the juncture where it takes the form of the action of separating and distinguishing some portion of external nature as his own:

> Every Man has a *Property* in his own *Person*; this no body has any Right to but himself. The *Labour* of his Body and the *Work* of his hands . . . are properly his. Whatsoever then he removes out of the State that Nature hath provided and left it in, he hath mixed his *Labour* with, and joined to it something that is his own, and thereby makes it his *Property*.[39]

The sequence here in Locke's political theory is comparable to the sequence which Locke follows in treating the operations of the understanding in the *Essay*. There he begins with ideas which are "simple" and "unmixed," because they are passively received, and goes on to "complex" ideas which are a mixture, "made by the mind out of simple ones." In treating property, Locke is similarly beginning with something simple—the property which the individual has in his own person which nobody has any right to but himself—and going on to the individual's making something else his property by mixing his labor with it. But the two sequences from simple to complex are themselves (I must stress again) separate and distinct. In the *Essay* it is the mind which makes complex ideas; in the *Second Treatise* the action of making is physical. Locke (unlike Hobbes in the *Leviathan*) finds no epistemological reason in his political theory to enter the human mind and analyze endeavor before it becomes a physical action. The practical consequence of the physical action is entirely visible. That "Portion" which the individual has "carved to himself" (i.e., separated and distinguished as his own) is "easily seen."[40] Thus, although Locke's starting point (like Hobbes') is the individual's endeavor to preserve himself, Locke largely assimilates this endeavor to the overt physical action it entails so that *labor* takes on something of the general significance which endeavor had in Hobbes.

In Locke's political theory, at the juncture where the individual's labor has been mixed with some portion of physical nature, no "mixed considerations" of the individual with others occur any more than they occurred in his analysis of the passions in the *Essay*. Not only does the individual have in Locke's political theory a property in his own person which nobody has any right to but himself, but also no one else need be present when the mixture with external nature is achieved—for example, when the individual is "nourished by the Acorns he pickt up under an Oak or by the Apples he gathered from the Trees in the Wood," and thereby "appropriated them to himself," transforming them into his property.[41] Locke is visualizing the action of one single individual alone under the oak or apple tree, just as he visualized "the motion of one single body alone" in developing his idea of empty space.

In Hobbes' state of nature, "there is no Own, that is no Propriety"—not even in one's own person, because "every man has a Right to every thing, even to one another's body."[42] When Hobbes analyzes the acquisitive situation he does not select the moment the individual performs the act of appropriation (as Locke does). Instead, the most relevant fact for Hobbes is the presence of a second individual. He is not analyzing Ap-petite, which emerged earlier in his deduction of the passions, but Com-petition, which, he explains, "maketh men invade for gain."[43] Thus the endeavor of each of these two individuals to preserve himself is promptly diverted from the thing he desires to the other individual:

> If any two men desire the same thing, which nevertheless they cannot both enjoy, they become enemies; and in the way to their end . . . endeavour to destroy or subdue one another.[44]

Where Locke deals with the transformation of the relation between one individual and the thing he appropriates (the transformation whereby he "makes it his property"), Hobbes deals with the transformation of the relation between two individuals. "Competition" is only the first of the "three principall causes of quarrell," which Hobbes finds "in the nature of man." When the two men who desire the same thing become enemies, their competition for this thing is transformed into "Diffidence *of one another*"—the second principal cause of quarrel.[45] The alternative Hobbes leaves open, as to whether they "endeavour to destroy *or subdue* one another," allows for the way the operation of the third cause, "Glory," may further transform their relationship.[46] If the one individual were simply diffident of the other, he would simply destroy the other, and in this way eliminate the cause of his diffidence, so that he could turn back at last to enjoy in security the thing for which they were initially competing. But his sense of his own glory can only be fully satisfied if he subdues and dominates his enemy. There can be no triumph over the dead, since self-consciousness can only triumph over self-consciousness.[47]

For the purposes of the comparison with Locke, these "three principall causes of quarrell" can perhaps be regarded as a sequence, so that the different direction taken in Hobbes by the individual's endeavor to preserve himself will illustrate differences in the methodological orientation of the two political theories. In Hobbes the mind of the individual (during that evanescent moment each desires something before entering the relation of competition with the other individual) would be first directed (Gain) towards the *object* he desires (as in Locke), but then diverted (Diffidence) towards the *actions* of the other individual who also desires this object, until finally each of the two individuals become conscious of *himself* (Glory) in relation to the other individual. Hobbes, of course, does not assume that the passions of different individuals must actually follow this sequence of three moments. That the sequence is methodologically determined is suggested by the way Hobbes' original admission of differences between the passions of different individuals is itself oriented towards the reflexive function performed by each individual's self-consciousness in obtaining knowledge of these passions. When in the Introduction to the *Leviathan* the traditional humanist injunction "Know Thyself" became Know Thy Passions, Hobbes conceded that "the *objects* of the passions which are the things desired, feared, hoped, etc.," are not "the same in all men," and that "though by men's *actions* we do discover their design sometimes, yet to do it without comparing them with our own . . . is to decypher without a key."[48] Thus Hobbes must finally appeal to the *self-consciousness* that is involved in our reactions to objects and actions, if these reactions themselves—the passions—are to become a subject for knowledge.

Independence

We have watched the individual's endeavor to preserve himself take a different direction in Locke. It becomes an endeavor to subdue and dominate external nature, not other men. But the lack of relationship to other men can be brought out by a further contrast with Hobbes. In their natural condition men are, according to Hobbes, free and equal.[49] Their competitive relationship, which we have just examined, is a result of their freedom and equality—or of their self-conscious sense of equality, for "if nature . . . have made men equal then that equality is to be acknowledged, or if nature hath made men unequal, yet . . . men . . . think themselves equal."[50] According to Locke, men in their natural condition are "free, equal, and *independent*."[51] It is not a matter of their *thinking* themselves independent, for property is a physical relationship to external nature, and it is within the limits provided by this physical relationship that each individual can equally find room or space (as it were) to exercise his freedom independently of other men.[52]

This physical relationship, moreover, provides the theorist (at a higher level) with a subject-matter for delimitation, for the distinctively physical character of this relationship helps keep Locke's political theory separate from his theory of *Human Understanding*. A correlation, we note, is beginning to emerge between the development within political theory of the subject-matter which will eventually be preempted by economic theory, and the development of the methodological principle of "distinct and separate" sciences.

In Hobbes no comparable subject-matter can emerge, for there is room or space available in the state of nature: "There is no Own, that is no Propriety." Men's freedom and equality, in a social world that is a *plenum*, do not permit their mutual independence of each other's endeavors, but necessitate their mutual resistance to each other's endeavors. I admit that my comparison neglects the fact that Locke's treatment of property is not a step in a deduction, so that when I refer to the availability of physical space, the reference cannot be followed back into physics. Locke does argue in the *Essay* from the idea of empty space. But he does not pretend that his argument is scientific. He is arguing about "ideas" and his argument is, he admits, "spun out of my own coarse thoughts."[53] We should respect their coarseness in the *Treatises*, too. The physical situation that Locke is thinking of as the state of nature is not a situation which could be deduced from the laws of physics, but is the physical situation when "All the world was America."[54] Indeed, in securing contemporary application for this economic portion of his political theory, Locke argues that America is still a large part of the world:

> No Man's Labour could subdue or appropriate all [sc. in the state of nature]. . . . His Neighbor . . . would still have *room*. . . . Men were in more danger to be lost by wandering from their Company in the then vast Wilderness of the Earth than to be straitened for want of room to plant in. And the same measure may be allowed still . . . as *full* as the World seems. . . . Let him plant in some in-land, vacant places of America.[55]

We do not need to wait for Laski (or for Mill's generalization regarding democracy in America) to find in America *The Philosophy of a Business Civilization*.[56]

If Locke's empiricism compels us to abandon reference to the space of physics in favor of this coarser reference to the American experience, we can take advantage of the fact that Hobbes briefly drops his deductive procedure to cope with those who, "not trusting to this inference made from the passions, desire perhaps to have the same confirmed by experience." When Hobbes then cites America, what he finds relevant are not its great open spaces, but the social relations that prevail:

> The savage people in many places of America, except the government of small Families, the concord whereof dependeth on natural lust, have no government at all; and live at this day in that brutish manner [which his deduction has demonstrated would be the consequence of having no government at all].[57]

Liberty and Dominion

Now that the difference between Locke and Hobbes has been brought home to us, we realize the family and the household are social units whose relevance we have not yet had to consider in tracing the development of political thought. Nevertheless, in separating the individual's economic sphere from the political sphere of the state, Locke is restoring a traditional distinction between *Dominium* (economic authority) and *Imperium* (political authority), for he is convinced that "the great mistakes of late about government" (as committed, for instance, by Filmer) have "arisen from confounding these distinct powers with one another."[58] Economic authority had originally been vested by Aristotle in the "master" (δεσπότης, *dominus*) of a "household" (οἶκος, *domus*). This domain had included other men as slaves.[59] Thus when Hobbes emphasizes that in the state of nature, "every man has a right to everything, even to another's body," the right in question, even though he considers it deducible from his physics, takes the form of a traditional right to enslave another man. In other words Hobbes thinks in terms of social relations in treating the traditional subject-matter of *economic* theory, as in dealing with the brutishness of family life in America. (The comparison finds its justification in that social relations in America approximate those of the state of nature.)

Locke, however, distinguishes and separates the individual's relation to his property from his relation to other men, by resorting not only to the vacant places of America, but also to a Stoic commonplace.[60] What had been an *economic* relation to other men in Aristotle, became in the Stoic tradition a relation to what is one's own (οἰκεῖος), which developed from the endeavor to preserve oneself but expanded to include one's relation to other men.[61] This reflexive relation survives in Locke to the extent that "Man, by being Master of himself and Proprietor of his own Person and the actions or Labour of it" has "in himself the great Foundation of Property."[62] But this reflexive relation is transcended, insofar as this labor is exercised on some portion of external nature.

One feature of this readjustment in the relation between the internal and the external is a difference between Locke's and Hobbes' use of juridical terminology. As it loses its psychological implications and obtains physical reference instead, Locke's terminology becomes legalistic. At the level of subject-matter, the individual acquires by his physical action something as his own which is distinct and separate from what other individuals have; at the higher level of Locke's theory as a structure of knowledge, the term "individual," as well as what is "his own," acquires a more literal (i.e., distinct, separate, and limited) sense. The individual is thereby further qualified for his role as a person who owns property, both "person" and "property" being construed as strictly legal entities. Consider the similarly legalistic way in which Locke analyzes the individual's exercise of other forms of power besides economic power. Locke argues for the separation of political powers on the ground that "humane frailty" is "apt to grasp at power." But (as we have already observed) he does not analyze this tendency to grasp in the psychological fashion that Hobbes analyzed the passions. Locke deals instead with the quasi-external power that is grasped, which is a legal entity.

Locke's literalness is a readjustment of the relation between the internal and the external that weakens the analogies of self-rule and self-mastery which sustained the traditional assimilation of external political and economic relations to psychological relations within the mind. The traditional reflexive procedure survived in Hobbes to the extent that the state was an "Artificial Man," the "matter thereof" as well as the "artificer" being "man," so that the artificer could be viewed as exercising his art upon himself. At the same time, the construction of this "Artificial Man" was taken by Hobbes to "resemble that *Fiat* or the 'Let us make man' pronounced by God in the Creation."[63] Like the knowledge of "man's heart,"[64] on which it was to be based, this exercise of creative power that had been reserved to God in the theological tradition became in Hobbes available to man in a reflexive form. In other words, Hobbes could issue an invitation to man not only to secure knowledge of his own heart in the form of knowledge of his own passions, but also to employ this reflexive knowledge for the purpose of the reflexive action of constructing the state—"Let us make man."[65]

God's pronouncements and His creative power remain relevant in Locke. But God (like America) patiently succumbs to the different structure imposed by Locke's method. The mandate men receive from God in Locke is not (as it is in Hobbes) to act reflexively and reform themselves, but to "be Fruitful and Multiply and Replenish the Earth and subdue it, and have Dominion over the Fish of the Sea, and over the Fowl of the Air, and over every living thing that moveth upon the Earth." This "grant of God" did not, as Filmer supposed, give Adam (and hence rulers) the right to exercise dominion over "every living thing" (including other men as slaves), so that economic power becomes confused with political power, which thereby becomes unlimited. In his own exegesis of the phrases "dominion" and "every living thing," Locke employs his characteristic procedure of separating and distinguishing. This "grant of God" gave Adam (and hence men) the right to exercise "dominion," merely in the sense of economic power, over the earth and all irrational creatures.[66]

This divine pronouncement of the Creator is perhaps more relevant to the structure of Locke's universe, and hence to his state of nature, than any psychological or epistemological considerations that carry over from the *Human Understanding*. In Hobbes' state of nature, God's power remained "invisible." Theological considerations comparable to those raised by Locke in the *First Treatise* could be postponed by Hobbes until after his treatment "Of Man," except insofar as they took the form, susceptible of reflexive analysis, of man's "fear" of "invisible agents."[67] From this fear, it followed that God, as well as men, must be represented by the "visible power" of an earthly sovereign.[68] Locke faces no comparable epistemological problem in his state of nature. Not only is the reflexive moment when the individual was "master of himself" transcended in his exercise of dominion over some "portion" of external nature which he has "carved to himself"—not only is this portion, because external, "easily seen"—but God himself exercises his power less relevantly as the political ruler of the universe than as the "Lord" (*Dominus*) who is its economic "Master." The creation yields visible evidence that it is his domain, so that Locke's labor theory of property holds of the Creator, who has a "visible claim to us as his Workmanship."[69] Limits are thereby set to the independence (the self-dependence) which can be implemented in the vacant places of America, and in a way that displays the autonomy of Stoic self-mastery. It is God's providential concern as a property owner to preserve his creation, and not simply (as in Hobbes) the human foresight of the individual concerned to preserve himself, which is the setting for Locke's treatment in the *Second Treatise* of the state of nature:

> Though Man in that State have an uncontrollable Liberty to dispose of his person or possessions, yet he has not Liberty to destroy himself, or so much as any Creature in his Possession, but where some nobler use than its bare Preservation calls for it. . . . For Men being all the Workmanship of one Omnipotent and infinitely wise Maker All the Servants of one Sovereign Master, sent into the World by his order, and about his business—they are his Property whose Workmanship they are, made to last during his, not anothers Pleasure.[70]

This theological setting, in which limits are set to man's liberty and independence, Locke retains when he moves on from the problem of the individual's preserving himself by acquiring property to the problem of his preserving this property.[71] The individual remains within a structure of obligation and again comes up against limits:

> The same Law of Nature that does by this means give us Property does also bound that Property too. "God has given us all things richly," . . . But how far has He given it us? To enjoy. As much as any one can make use of to any advantage of life before it spoils, so much he may by his labour fix a Property in. . . . Nothing was made by God for Man to spoil or destroy.[72]

The psychological sphere of the self that was originally to be preserved has been left behind with the acquisition of physical property. Psychological criteria lose all relevance when the problem of preserving property obtains its final solution with the introduction of physical property in a preservable form:

> It is plain that Men have agreed to a disproportionate and unequal Possession of the Earth, they having, by a tacit and voluntary consent, found out a way how a man may fairly possess more land than he himself can use

the product of, by receiving in exchange for the overplus, Gold and Silver which may be hoarded up without injury to any one, these metalls not spoileing or decaying in the hands of the possessor.[73]

Since Locke has left the psychological sphere behind, he is able to adopt a legalistic solution which would have been psychologically paradoxical—an agreement or consent that is at once tacit and voluntary.

There is perhaps a certain incongruity in a philosophy which is dedicated to the setting of limits—for example, to knowledge and to political power—relaxing limits previously set by natural law to the acquisition of property. Here we may have an instance where the argument cannot have been spun out of Locke's thoughts, however coarse. The cunning of historical reason or class bias may have woven a strand, or rather have loosened a strand that had originally been woven. In any case, the original fabric can be examined by considering Locke's doctrine of natural law.

The Law of Nature

If Laslett is right that "Locke did not write . . . with Thomas Hobbes in hand or mind," the possibility is worth considering that the differences we have dealt with between Locke and Hobbes are due less to Locke's explicit rejection of Hobbes' deduction than to the different way in which Locke undermines the traditional theory of human nature. This context Locke himself originally adopted. Many of the problems that he separates in his *Essay on Human Understanding*, on the one hand, and in his *Two Treatises of Government*, on the other hand, he had muddled some twenty years before when he wrote his exposition of the law of nature.

In this exposition, Locke equates "the law of nature" with "the rule of morals." He begins with a God who "shows Himself to us as present everywhere, exhibiting Himself to the eyes of men . . . in the regular course of nature." Locke next insists that "man alone" cannot have "come into the world subject to no regulation, without a purpose, without a law, without a model for his life." Locke finds this "model" in "the morally right which the ancient philosophers and especially the Stoics sought with so much determination."[74] By now we are aware that this modern merging, in a theory of human nature, of the perspectives of ancient philosophers in general with the Stoic moral tradition identifies the humanistic tradition, which in fact emerged from the Stoic tradition as a result of successive revivals of ancient philosophers.

In his *Law of Nature* Locke may have Hobbes in mind when he attacks the assumption that "each individual's self-interest (*privata utilitas*) is the basis of the law of nature."[75] But the announced antagonist is Carneades, for Locke is attacking the individualistic position which had been attributed to Carneades in Cicero's *Republic* and is upholding the Ciceronian conception of "natural justice," whereby the individual can be expected to sacrifice his own interest and act in the interest of others.[76] The sequel to his attack is a criticism of economic individualism:

> Nature has provided a certain supply of goods for the use and convenience of men, distributing these in a definite way and in a fixed quantity. . . . Whenever the desire or the need of property increases among men, there is no resulting extension of the world's limits. . . . All . . . the goods of this life are given in common. Thus when any individual grabs for himself as much as he can, he takes away from the other what he is adding to his own pile. It is impossible for anyone to acquire wealth except at someone else's loss.[77]

In the *Second Treatise*, there is a change in the "model." God, we have already anticipated, shows Himself to the eyes of men as a property-owner, and property-owning is the "model" He has established for their lives. The fact that Locke's labor theory of property undercut the criticism of economic individualism in his lectures, may be one reason for Locke's repeated refusals to publish his *Law of Nature* when he was urged by friends to do so in order to escape the charge of "Hobbism," which the individualism of his published writings incurred. When the individual acquires wealth in the *Second Treatise*, it is no longer at someone else's loss. Locke is able to deny that it is "robbery" for the individual "to assume to himself what belonged to all in common." For the total supply of goods available is no longer fixed by nature's initial distribution, but is now the consequence of the individual's own labor:

> Nor is it so strange, as perhaps before consideration it may appear, that the property of labour should be able to overbalance the community of

land; for it is labour indeed that put the difference of value on everything . . . He who appropriates land to himself by his labour does not lessen but increases the common stock of mankind.[78]

On further consideration, Locke has found that there is no incompatibility between the individual's appropriating something to himself out of self-interest and his acting in the interests of others.

"Property," Locke boasts, "I have nowhere found more clearly explained than in a book entitled, *Two Treatises of Government*."[79] But although his explanation of property in these treatises represents a definite break with the position taken in the *Law of Nature*, it is more difficult to assess Locke's originality as over against the treatment of property that is a feature of the discussion of the *utile* (self-interest) in Cicero's *On Duties*. Here (as in Locke's *Law of Nature*), "To take something away from another and gain from his loss is . . . against nature, for if each individual grabs for himself the property of others and takes whatever he can for his own gain, the relation between men, their fellowship, is overturned." At the same time however (as in the *Second Treatise*), it is "not against nature for the individual to acquire for himself rather than for another what is useful in life, even though nature does not allow us to increase our resources and accumulate wealth by robbing others."[80]

The political implications of Locke's theory of property are also not entirely novel. In the investigation of what is morally right in the first book of *On Duties* (as in the defense of natural justice in his *Republic*), Cicero handles the individual's political relations to other men as relations which are internal to their human nature in the sense that the state is the outcome of their psychological tendency to "herd together." But he introduces a supplementary argument in the second book: "Although men naturally tend to herd together, it was because they desired greater security for their possessions that they sought the protection of cities [sc., city-walls]."[81] The individual now brings his external possessions with him, and the city state is no longer merely their intrinsic psychological relationship but has its external walls. States, in the second book of *On Duties* (as in Locke's *Second Treatise*), "were established in order that individuals should keep what is their own,"[82] and "one of the primary functions of government is to see that each individual keeps his own and private citizens suffer no loss of property at the hands of public authority."[83] In his discussion of "propriety" in the first book, Cicero employed the formula *suum quisque teneat* with the meaning "each individual should keep [to] his own [*personality*],"[84] playing the role in relation to others that is "appropriate" to his own moral character; but in the second book, Cicero re-employs this formula with the meaning "each individual should keep his own [property]." The reference to inner moral character has been replaced by an external reference.

Cicero's manipulation of this formula remained within the scope of the traditional definition of justice as distributing to each individual his own. In interpreting this distribution in his *Republic,* Cicero drew on Plato's *Republic,* where the just distribution was fundamentally a distribution of functions to be performed within the soul; but in Cicero's *Republic,* "natural justice" (the account to which Locke is in some debt for his *Law of Nature*) was a rhetorical virtue which was not "silent and enclosed in oneself," but "looked outside oneself"—towards other men.[85] The resulting ambivalent treatment of the individual's relation to others recurred with the shift from the first book of *On Duties,* which is written from the reflexive point of view of the individual's own character, to the second book where the individual views his character from the point of view of others. A second ambivalent relationship is introduced in *On Duties* when Cicero distinguishes what is the individual's own as at once his inner moral character and his external property. The ambivalence of the first relationship (Cicero's treatment of the individual's moral character in terms of his relation to other men) was resolved in opposite ways by Machiavelli and Hobbes. Locke's identification of what is the individual's own with his property may seem a comparable resolution of the ambivalence of the second relationship in Cicero: the humanistic individual retained his place in Machiavelli's theory, insofar as the prince had to preserve his political standing in the minds of his subjects; the humanistic individual retained his place in Hobbes' theory insofar as he endeavored to preserve his moral stature in his own mind; this humanistic individual would now retain his place in Locke's theory from his endeavor to preserve his "estate." But despite Locke's contempt for the "medly and confusion" in Filmer, despite the vaunted clarity of his own explanation of property, Locke exploits rather than definitely resolves the ambivalence in Cicero's treatment of what is the individual's own.[86] "By Property," Locke announces, "I must be understood . . . to mean that Property which men have in their Persons as well as Goods."[87] Property thus includes their "lives" and "liberties" as well as their "estates."[88]

What is clear, however, is that Locke is breaking with the humanistic tradition at the juncture at which it had remained relevant in Hobbes, who still treated the individual in terms of his relation to other men. Cicero had distinguished the individual's relation to other men, who are "animate," from his relation to external things which are "inanimate,"[89] and had developed a labor theory of the value of property to the extent of asserting that most of the inanimate things which are useful "are produced by the labor of men and would not be available to us were it not for their labor and skill—would not in fact be useful to us were it not for the intervention of other men."[90] The necessity of their intervention brings Cicero's treatment of the utility of property within the scope of his psychological treatment of the relationship between the individual and other men. The individual's utilitarian problem, even with respect to inanimate things, is itself animate; it is to utilize his "virtue" rhetorically in order to "conciliate the minds of men and acquire their support in obtaining what is useful to him."[91]

The acquisition of property in Locke's *Second Treatise* slips outside of this rhetorically woven, psychological context. The individual, instead of relying as in Cicero on the labor of other men, whose minds he must accordingly conciliate, appropriates by the labor of his body some external thing, which thereby becomes his property "without the assignation or consent of anybody."[92] He only enters into political relations with other men when he faces the problem of preserving the property which he has already acquired. Even then he can remain silent. He does not need to conciliate the minds of other men. Locke visualizes analytically one single mind alone, as well as "one single body alone." No rhetorical procedure is built (as it was in Cicero) into the structure of Locke's theory; *consensus* is no longer the rhetorical achievement of a speaker that it was for Cicero.[93] It can take the legalistic form of a "tacit agreement" implicit in men's physical activities—their use of money or other forms of property.[94]

Locke therefore does not need a theory of human nature to provide a psychological analysis of the process of arriving at this agreement.

Locke may still attach the individual's act of self-preservation (as Cicero and Hobbes did) to the traditional psychological tendency of self-preservation, but Locke's utilitarian shift of emphasis is a shift to the physical action of labor and to the physical property which is its consequence. This shift enables him to bypass the questions he had faced in his Ciceronian defense in his lectures of natural justice against the utilitarianism of Carneades and Hobbes. "It would be besides my present purpose," Locke explains in the *Two Treatises*, "to enter into the particulars of the law of nature."[95] What is left of a theory of human nature, once political and economic problems have slipped outside its scope, are the primarily epistemological problems of the *Human Understanding*.

This Avidity Alone

In his *Treatise*, David Hume reconstructs a theory of human nature. Since the theory is not individualistic, it has to be postponed until Part V, where we shall see that it involves a rhetorical reweaving of the psychological context which Locke had discarded. But Hume incorporates in the theory a treatment of the property relationship, and this treatment can be anticipated now as continuing the adjustment I have traced in Locke in the relation between political and economic problems.

Hume relocates political problems by manipulating the distinction between internal and external which had been employed in the traditional humanistic classification of goods: "the internal satisfaction of our minds, the external advantages of our body, and the enjoyment of such possessions as we have acquired by our industry and good fortune."[96] Working his way through this classification, Hume reduces the traditional problem of justice—securing to each his own—to the problem of securing to each his own property. The problem of psychological insecurity Hume discounts by making the traditional humanistic assumption. "We are perfectly secure in the enjoyment of . . . the internal satisfactions of our minds." Hume accordingly denies (as Locke had) the general relevance of the particular passions which in Hobbes rendered men psychologically as well as physically insecure. "Envy and revenge," Hume insists, "operate only by intervals, and are directed against particular persons, whom we consider as our superiors or enemies."[97] When Hume asserts with respect to the goods of the body, "They may be ravished from us, but can be of no advantage to him who deprives us of them,"[98] he is discounting Hobbes' problem of physical security. The problem of justice that still remains is the problem of the security of property:

> The principal disturbance in society arises from those goods which we call external, and from their looseness and easy transition from one person to another; they must seek a remedy, by putting these goods as far as possible, on the same footing with the fix'd and constant advantages of the mind or body. This can be done after no other manner, than by a convention enter'd into by all the members of the society to bestow stability on the possession of those external goods, and leave every one in the peaceable enjoyment of what he may acquire by his own fortune and industry.[99]

In Hobbes, the love of gain was associated with only one of the "three principall causes of quarrell."[100] But in Hume, "this avidity alone, of acquiring goods and possessions for ourselves and our nearest friends, is insatiable, perpetual, and directly destructive of society."[101] The fact that this threat to society is not presented by Hume (as it was by Hobbes) as the outcome of a psychological deduction, illustrates a readjustment which has taken place in the relation between internal and external, and which we shall see in the next chapter alters the individual's relation to other men. In Hume, external goods are "expos'd to the violence of others,"[102] but to explain their violence, a psychological deduction would be insufficient. The explanation must embrace "the concurrence of certain qualities of the human mind with the situation of external objects"—"their easy change, conjoined to their scarcity."[103] Hobbes mentioned only in passing the fact that "the same thing" which two individuals desire "they cannot both enjoy."[104] But Hume takes time to sketch the poet's "idle fiction" of a "Golden Age" in order to point up the fact that "the selfishness of men is animated by the few possessions we have, in proportion to our wants."[105]

Adam Smith reduces, even more completely than had Hume and Locke, political problems to problems of securing property. The "object of justice" and the "foundation of civil government" for Smith is "security from injury," but "till there be property there can be no government, the very end of which is to secure wealth and to defend the rich from the poor." He explains:

> Men who have no property can injure one another only in their persons or reputation. But when one man kills, wounds, beats, or defames another, though he to whom the injury is done suffers, he who does it receives no benefit. It is otherwise with injuries to property. The benefit of the person who does the injury is often equal to the loss of him who suffers it.[106]

In Smith, as in Hume and Locke, there accompanies this dismissal of problems of physical and psychological security, a shift of psychological emphasis away from the passions which in Hobbes rendered men physically and psychologically insecure:

> Envy, malice, or resentment are the only passions which can prompt one man to injure another in his person or reputation. But the greater part of men are not very frequently under the influence of those passions, and the very worst men are so only occasionally. . . . Men may live together in society with some tolerable degree of security, though there is no civil magistrate to protect them from the injustice of those passions.[107]

Tradition and Transition

Some of the methodological implications of this increasing encroachment of economic considerations in Locke, Hume, and Smith can finally be brought out by the development of Smith's thought to its culmination in *The Wealth of Nations.* Many of the materials of Smith's *Moral Sentiments* as well as of his *Wealth of Nations* were at one time different portions of a continuous series of lectures which he had begun giving at Glasgow in 1751 as the occupant of a chair in Moral Philosophy. After the publication of the *Moral Sentiments* in 1759, the surviving lectures became lectures on Jurisprudence. Two of the "great objects of law," Smith identifies as "Justice" and "Police." I have already noted the encroachment of economic considerations in Smith's handling of "the object of Justice." His comments on "Police" betray a further dislocation of the traditional subject-matter of political theory: "The name is French, and is originally derived from the Greek *πολιτεία,* which properly signified the policy of civil government, but now it only means the regulation of the inferior parts of government, viz—cleanliness, security, and cheapness or plenty."[108]

The first two topics Smith disdains: "The proper method of carrying dirt from the streets, and the execution of justice, so far as it regards regulations for preventing crimes or the method of keeping a city guard, though useful, are too mean to be considered in a general discourse of this kind." Furthermore, security of property need not be dealt with directly since it is one of the beneficial consequences of plenty: "Nobody will be so mad as to expose himself upon the highway, when he can make better bread in an honest and industrious manner."[109] Thus "the establishment of commerce and manufactures . . . is the best police for preventing crimes."[110] Smith accordingly devotes his attention to "Plenty" as the remaining "part of government." "Plenty" is no longer what it had been in Hume's *Treatise*—an "idle fiction" of the Golden Age. It has become an actual social achievement.

"Being in a commercial town," the *Times* of London sneered, Smith had "converted the chair of Moral Philosophy into a professorship of trade and finance."[111] The final disruption of the moral and political tradition had occurred when Smith expanded his treatment of "Plenty" in his lectures, eventually publishing it separately in 1776 as *The Wealth of Nations*. For he then discarded the heading "Police."[112] Economic problems could no longer remain confined within traditional political theory. In *The Wealth of Nations*, "the most proper way of securing wealth and abundance" was no longer one of the "great objects of law." It was not even one of "the inferior parts of government," since it was no longer subject to political regulation:

> The sovereign is completely discharged from a duty, in the attempting to perform which he must always be exposed to innumerable delusions, and for the proper performance of which no human wisdom or knowledge could ever be sufficient; the duty of superintending the industry of private people, and of directing it towards the employments most suitable to the interest of society.[113]

Something is happening to the traditional structure of knowledge and wisdom when reference to "the interest of society" passes beyond the scope of the ruler's, or indeed of any individual's, competence to discern. In the next chapter I shall trace the way this reference develops in Hume and Smith into a new context for the treatment of political and economic problems. This new context is distinctively social, in contrast with Hobbes' and Locke's individualism.

Notes

1. See vol. 1, p. 73.

2. See vol. 1, p. 60 and accompanying n. 24. See also chap. 13, n. 14.

3. See vol. 1, pp. 23–24.

4. *A System of Logic* (London: Longmans, Green), pp. 590, 587. See vol. 1, p. 15.

5. The methodological principle becomes neutral in Mill because he distinguishes sharply between method and its application to any subject-matter (see p. 280, this vol.) and regards political economy as merely one subject-matter among others.

6. I am following the terminological convention of using "self-interest" in expounding Locke and Hobbes as well as in translating Cicero's *utile*. But the concept of self-interest belongs strictly speaking to ultilitarianism. In Cicero, Hobbes, and Locke, it is more accurate to refer to "self-love" (see p. 78, this vol.) or to the tendency on the part of the individual to preserve himself (see nn. 71, 93, below).

7. *The Wealth of Nations*, 2 vols. (London: J. M. Dent, 1910), 2: 180.

8. John Locke, *Two Treatises of Government*, ed. Peter Laslett (New York: Mentor, 1965), p. x.

9. *Ibid.*, p. 103.

10. See vol. 1, p. 26.

11. *Essay on Human Understanding* (London: Ward, Lock, n.d.), p. 608. Locke is likewise cavalier regarding the wholeness of his undertaking in *On Human Understanding* itself: it was "written by incoherent parcels; and, after long intervals of neglect, resumed again" (p. x). As for the *Two Treatises*: "Reader, Thou hast here the Beginning and End of a Discourse concerning Government; what Fate has otherwise disposed of the Papers that should have filled up the middle, and were more than all the rest, 'tis not worth while to tell thee. . . . There will be no great miss of those which are lost, and my Reader, may be satisfied without them" (p. 171). Locke's preoccupation sometimes seems to be limited to the elaboration of a particular argument—as in the case of his modern heirs (see vol. 1, p. 66 and accompanying n. 46).

12. *Ibid.*, pp. 1, 439.

13. *Two Treatises*, p. 305.

14. *On Liberty* (New York: Liberal Arts, 1956) pp. 21–25, 3.

15. *On Human Understanding*, p. 608.

16. *Ibid.*, p. 6.

17. *Ibid.*, p. 1; cf. p. 202.

18. *Ibid.*, p. 70.

19. *Ibid.*, p. 108.

20. The continuity of this tradition to which Mill assigns himself and his father is illustrated by his identifying it as "the school of Locke and of Bentham" ("Coleridge," reprinted in *Mill's Essays on Literature and Society*, ed. J. B. Schneewind [New York: Collier Books, 1965], p. 302).

21. "Professor Sedgwick's Discourse," reprinted in *Dissertations and Discussions*, 3 vols. (London: Longmans Green Reader and Dyer, 1867) 1: 114.

22. John Stuart Mill's Preface to the *Analysis of the Phenomena of the Human Mind,* 2 vols. (London: Longmans Green Reader and Dyer, 1869), 1: x. Besides (1) its analytic method, there are two further characteristics of what James Mill attempts which he expresses by his title: (2) His phenomenalism—for analytic psychology in the Lockean tradition included what we would today distinguish as epistemology: "As to the fundamental difference of opinion respecting the sources of our knowledge . . . , the question lies . . . deep in the recesses of psychology. . . . The truth on this much-debated question lies with the school of Locke and of Bentham. The nature and laws of things in themselves, or of the hidden causes of the phenomena which are the objects of experience, appear to us radically inaccessible to the human faculties" ("Coleridge," p. 302). (3) In this school, accordingly, an analysis of the phenomena of the human mind assumed a privileged place as an analysis of the structure of knowledge. In other words, this Lockean tradition is the restriction of the theory of human nature to a theory of the human mind, construed as a primarily epistemological theory of the human understanding. See p. 155, this vol., and chap. 3, n. 52.

23. *Analysis,* 1: 2.

24. *On Human Understanding,* pp. 1, 2; *Two Treatises,* pp. 95, 161. In *On Human Understanding* Locke is concerned (1) to have his reader accept the limited extent of human knowledge: "This inquiry into the nature of the understanding . . . may be of use to prevail with the *busy* mind of man to be more cautious in meddling with things exceeding its comprehension, to stop when it is at the utmost extent of its tether, and to sit down in a *quiet* ignorance of those things which, upon examination, are found to be beyond the reach of our capacities" (p. 2; the italics which I have added bring out Locke's apparent play with the traditional *negotium/otium* antithesis). He is concerned (2) to have his reader accept the limited extent of this inquiry itself: "This therefore being my purpose, to inquire into the original, certainty, and extent of human knowledge, . . . I shall not at present meddle with the physical consideration of the mind" (p. 1). In conducting his limited inquiries, he is concerned (3) to avoid becoming enmeshed in such comprehensive and controversial traditional topics as the law of nature: "It would be besides my present purpose, to enter here into the particulars of the Law of Nature" (I am citing Locke from Laslett's Introduction to the *Two Treatises,* p. 95; see n. 95, below).

25. *On Human Understanding,* p. xii.

26. *Two Treatises,* p. 190; italics added. For the full citation see chap. 3, n. 46.

27. Introduction to the *Two Treatises,* p. 96. Laslett goes on to claim: "*Two Treatises* . . . cannot be said to represent his account of the implications for conduct, for politics, of the doctrines of the *Essay*. It was written for an entirely different purpose and in an entirely different state of mind" (p. 97). While we should respect Locke's different purposes (see n. 24, above), his different inquiries are not "entirely different." His pervasive preoccupation with limits takes a similar form in the *Two Treatises* and in the *Essay on Human Understanding*. In the setting afforded by its "True Original," the "Extent" of "Civil Government" is determined by its purpose or "End" (I am pressing the phraseology in Locke's subtitle to the *Second Treatise: An Essay Concerning the True Original, Extent, and End of Civil Government*), just as in the setting afforded by Locke's theory of the origin of ideas, the limited extent of men's understanding is shown to be sufficient for their purposes: "How short soever their knowledge may come of an universal or perfect comprehension of whatsoever is, it yet secures their great concernments that they have light enough to lead them to the knowledge of their Maker, and the sight of their own duties. . . . We shall not have much reason to complain of the narrowness of our minds, if we will but employ them about what may be of use to us. . . . It will be no excuse to an idle and untoward servant, who would not attend his business by candlelight, to plead that he had not broad sunshine. The candle that is set up in us shines bright enough for all our purposes. . . . Our business here is not to know all things, but those which concern our conduct" (*On Human Understanding,* pp. 3–4).

28. If Laslett rejects the assumption that Locke's "political thinking was related to his philosophy as the part to the whole" (p. 103), it is partly because he himself assumes that "philosophy as such" is concern with "the problem of knowledge" (p. 31). I have suggested (see n. 22, above) that Locke may be at the beginning of this process of restriction, but it is not fully consummated in Locke himself.

29. Cited by Laslett in his Introduction to *Two Treatises,* p. 54.

30. *Two Treatises,* p. 410. Locke does not, however, keep in separate hands all the powers that he distinguishes. See Laslett's Introduction, pp. 132–33.

31. See p. 76, this vol.

32. *On Human Understanding,* p. 161.

33. *Ibid.,* p. 160.

34. *Ibid.,* pp. 80, 108.

35. *Leviathan,* pt. 1, chap. 6; see p. 79, this vol.

36. *On Human Understanding,* p. 77.

37. *Ibid.,* p. 162; italics added.

38. See p. 47.

39. *Two Treatises,* pp. 328–29; italics added.

40. *Ibid.,* p. 344. Visual experience is also decisive in Locke's epistemology (see nn. 27, 52) and in his theology (see p. 131, this vol.) Locke draws an explicit analogy between the domain of the understanding and the domain of action with respect to the limitations of what we receive and what we can make: "the dominion of man in this little world of his own understanding, being much-what the same as it is in the great world of visible things, wherein his power, however managed by art and skill, reaches no farther than to compound and divide the materials that are made to his hand but can do nothing towards the making of the least particle of new matter, or destroying one atom of what is already in being" (*On Human Understanding,* p. 71). Not only does Locke find this analogy between a simple idea and a Newtonian atom, but he also finds that there is "no idea which we receive more constantly from sensation than solidity" (*ibid.,* p. 76; see p. 199, this vol.) For "dominion" as the economic authority an individual exercises over his property, see p. 128, this vol.

41. *Two Treatises,* pp. 329–30.

42. *Leviathan,* pt. 1, chaps. 14, 15. *Propriety* here means *property*

43. *Ibid.,* chap. 13; see p. 85, this vol.

44. *Ibid.,* chap. 13. The sentence preceding my citation reads: "From . . . equality of ability ariseth equality of hope in the attaining of our ends (acquirendi spes)." Note that this hope of acquiring does not qualify as one of the "three principall causes of quarrell," for Hope can be defined without reference to a second individual. Just as the first principal cause is instead "Competition" between individuals, so the second principal cause is not simply Fear, but "Diffidence of one another," which is explained in the Latin version of the Leviathan as "mutual fear." For the relevance in Hobbes of passions which involve the individual in relations with a second individual, see p. 85, this vol.

45. *Ibid.,* chap. 13. This "Diffidence of one another" presupposes the simpler "Diffidence of ourselves" which we encounter at an earlier stage in the deduction of the passions (*Leviathan,* pt. 1, chap. 6) and "mutual fear" presupposes the simpler fear for ourselves (see p. 75, this vol.) in much the same way that Revengefulness presupposes the simpler passion of Anger (see p. 92, this vol.).

46. *Ibid.,* italics added.

47. See pp. 92–93, this vol.

48. See p. 36, this vol.

49. *Leviathan*, pt. 1, chaps. 13, 14.

50. See p. 46, this vol.

51. *Two Treatises*, p. 374; italics added.

52. In describing the way the individual acquires private property Locke employs, as Laslett notes, "the language of agrarian enclosure" (*Two Treatises*, p. 330). For example, "He by his Labour does, as it were, inclose it from the Common" (p. 332). But Locke employs comparable language in describing the way the individual acquires knowledge: "Methinks the understanding is not much unlike a closet wholly shut from light, with only some little opening left to let in external visible resemblances or ideas of things without: would the pictures coming into such a dark room but stay there, and lie so orderly as to be found upon occasion, it would resemble the understanding of a man in reference to all objects of sight, and the ideas of them" (*On Human Understanding*, p. 107). This epistemological conception of the privacy of the process of acquiring knowledge underpins Locke's defense of the individual's intellectual independence, which can be compared with the economic and political independence the individual acquires by acquiring property. In spite of the fact that these acquisitive activities are assigned by Locke to separate and distinct provinces, his description of the process of acquiring knowledge is riddled with metaphors commending the acquisition of economic independence: "Perhaps we should make greater progress in the discovery of rational and contemplative knowledge, if we . . . made use rather of our own thoughts than other men's to find it: for, I think, we may as rationally hope to see with other men's eyes as to know by other men's understandings. . . . In the sciences every one has so much as he really knows and comprehends; what he believes only, and takes upon trust, are but shreds; which . . . make no considerable addition to his stock who gathers them. Such borrowed wealth . . . will be but leaves and dust when it comes to use" (*On Human Understanding*, p. 55). Thus "he who has raised himself above the alms-basket" is not content to live lazily on scraps of begged opinions," but "sets his own thoughts on work" (*ibid.*, p. ix). Compare the three criteria for the awarding of property: it is intended for "the use of the Industrious and Rational (and Labour was to be his title to it)" (*Two Treatises*, p. 333). Just as intellectual independence is to be tolerated by others, so the economic independence that is acquired in the form of property is to be respected: others "ought not to meddle with what was already improved by another's Labour" (*ibid.*).

The failure to acquire intellectual independence, like the failure to acquire property (see n. 59, below), deprives the individual of political independence. Thus the acceptance of ideas as "innate principles" (rather than as acquired, which they are for Locke) "eased the lazy from the pains of search, and stopped the inquiry of the doubtful; . . . and it was of no small advantage to those who affected to be masters and teachers, to make this the principle of principles—that principles must not be questioned; for, having once established this tenet, . . . it put their followers upon a necessity of receiving some doctrines as such; which was to take them off from the use of their own reason and judgment; . . . in which posture of blind credulity, they might be more easily governed by, and made useful to, some sort of men who had the skill and office to principle and guide them. Nor is it a small power it gives one man over another, to have the authority to be the dictator of principles, and teacher of unquestionable truths" (*On Human Understanding*, pp. 55–56).

53. *On Human Understanding*, p. xi.

54. *Two Treatises*, p. 243.

55. *Ibid.*, pp. 334–35; italics added.

56. See vol. 1, p. 2.

57. *Leviathan*, pt. 1, chap. 13.

58. *Two Treatises,* p. 427.

59. *Politics* 1. 2 (1253b–1255a). I shall italicize *economic* when its etymological meaning is pertinent. But its etymology is ambivalent. If the reference of οἰκεῖος in the Aristotelian tradition is to what pertains to an external institution, the home or household, and hence to the relation between master and slave, the reference in the Platonizing Stoic tradition is to what is the individual's own. For Plato's own usage, see vol. 1, p. 257; for Platonizing Stoic usage, see vol. 1, p. 291, where Scipio's appeal to what is really the individual's own provides a justification for Philus' analogical retort to Laelius' literal use of the term "home"; for Stoic usage, see n. 93, below. The institution of slavery (and Aristotle's treatment of it) seems to have been of negligible importance in the development of ancient political thought, and this indifference towards slavery as an institution persisted in the modern classical tradition. "Slavery" may be the first word of Locke's *Two Treatises,* but he is not challenging the economic institution, which he supplies with its traditional rationale (*Two Treatises,* pp. 325–26, 366). The term "slavery" instead carries political implications for Locke; it is tossed out at the beginning of *Two Treatises* as a taunt at Filmer for confounding political with *economic* relations. Aristotle had criticized Plato for failing to distinguish political from *economic* relations, but Locke's usage suggests that he probably obtained Aristotle's distinction from Filmer's criticism of Aristotle and Aristotle's modern expositors (Sir Robert Filmer, *Patriarcha,* reprinted as a supplement to Locke's *Two Treatises of Government,* ed. Thomas Cook [New York: Hafner, 1947], pp. 261–65).
Furthermore, although Locke criticizes Filmer for confounding political with *economic* relations, his own positive political theory makes more significant use of classical *economic* thought than of classical political thought. He reconstructs (in effect at least) the Aristotelian definition of a slave as a man who is an article of property, by defining him as a man who has "no property at all" (*Two Treatises,* p. 431), in the sense presumably that he does not have property even in his own person. Here the Stoic reference becomes relevant for Locke. But he also argues that men who are "in the State of Slavery" are "not capable of any property" (presumably in its external sense), so that they "cannot in that state be considered as any part of Civil Society; the chief end whereof is the preservation of Property" (*ibid.,* p. 366). Here "property" can be taken in both senses, for the end of *economic* preservation is the end both of the master/slave relation in the Aristotelian household and of the Stoic individual's endeavor. It is not worthwhile, however, to pursue the interpretation of Locke by sorting out the two traditions: his specific formulations are too strongly influenced by seventeenth century controversies. But I shall deal with the ambivalence of the term "property" again when I suggest Locke's possible reliance on Cicero's *De Officiis,* where the two traditions are already ambivalently conflated. (see p. 134, this vol.).

60. I do not intend a contrast between America and Stoicism. Locke regards both as providing evidence for the character of the state of nature.

61. See no. 59, above and p. 160, this vol.

62. *Two Treatises,* pp. 340–41.

63. *Leviathan,* Intro.

64. See p. 36, this vol.

65. *Leviathan,* Intro.

66. *Two Treatises,* pp. 191–92.

67. *Leviathan,* pt. 1, chap. 12.

68. See p. 94, this vol.

69. *Two Treatises,* p. 215.

70. *Ibid.,* p. 311.

71. The case for property is both theological and philosophical. On the one hand, "God . . . made Man, and planted in him . . . a strong desire of Self-preservation, and furnished the World with things fit for Food and Rayment and other Necessaries of Life, Subservient to his design, that Man should live and abide for some time upon the Face of the Earth, and not that so curious and wonderful a piece of Workmanship by its own Negligence, or want of Necessaries, should perish again" (*Two Treatises*, p. 242). On the other hand, "Natural reason" also "tells us that men, being once born, have a right to their preservation, and consequently to meat and drink and such other things as nature affords for their subsistence" (*ibid.*, p. 327).

72. *Two Treatises*, p. 332. Indestructibility was already a criterion for Locke's Newtonian atom (see n. 40, above).

73. *Ibid.*, p. 344.

74. *Essays on the Law of Nature*, ed. W. von Leyden (Oxford: Clarendon Press, 1954), p. 109.

75. *Ibid.*, p. 204.

76. Locke could have obtained the argument either from Lactantius (*Institutiones Divinae* 5. 16. 3; see vol. 1, p. 258) or from Grotius' reproduction of Lactantius' reproduction of Cicero's argument (*De Jure Belli ac Pacis Proleg.*, par. 5).

77. *Law of Nature*, p. 211.

78. *Two Treatises*, p. 338.

79. I am citing from Laslett's Introduction to the *Two Treatises*, p. 15.

80. *De Officiis* 3. 22. I am not claiming that Locke's treatment of property necessarily derived directly from the *De Officiis*. Cicero's treatment there had been absorbed into the humanistic tradition. Although there are no references to Cicero in Laslett's handling of the sources for the *Two Treatises*, Laslett does comment elsewhere: "Tully was Locke's favourite Latin author, perhaps his favourite author altogether. There are 29 entries under Cicero in this catalogue" (John Harrison and Peter Laslett, *The Library of John Locke* [Oxford: Oxford University Press, 1965], p. 21). In contrast, "Locke made almost no references to the Hobbesian texts in all the vast volume of notes and citations which fill his great series of notebooks" (*ibid.*, p. 22). See p. 25, this vol. for Locke's attitude towards the *De Officiis*.

81. *Off.* 2. 73.

82. *Ibid.* Locke's statement "The great and chief end . . . of Men's uniting into Commonwealths, and putting themselves under Government, is the Preservation of their Property" (*Two Treatises*, p. 395) could pass as a translation of Cicero's statement that "Hanc . . . ob causam maxime, ut sua tenerentur, res publicae civitatesque constitutae sunt" (*Off.* 2. 73). Cicero makes this statement in denouncing a speech endorsing the equal distribution of property. Locke is likewise concerned to justify "inequality of private possessions" (*Two Treatises*, p. 344). See also Cicero's pronouncement "the distinctive function (*proprium*) . . . of the state or city is to secure to every man the free and undisturbed use of his property" (*Off.* 2. 78–79).

83. *Off.* 2. 73. Contrast too our larger "home which is not shut in by the walls we build" vol. 1, p. 290).

84. See p. 18, this vol.

85. See vol. 1, p. 257.

86. It seems possible that Locke may be aware of this ambivalence when he substitutes the term "property" for the term "propriety" in his original text. Laslett is unable to offer any specific explanation for the substitution (*Two Treatises*, p. 232).

87. *Two Treatises*, p. 430.

88. *Ibid.*, p. 395.

89. *Off.* 2. 11.

90. *Off.* 2. 12.

91. *Off.* 2. 17.

92. *Two Treatises*, p. 330.

93. The term *consensus* can refer to the unanimous agreement indicated by applause. For Cicero's conception of the part speaking can play in securing this *consensus*, see vol. 1, p. 266. I am now stressing Cicero's use of the term *conciliare*. As a rhetorical term it refers to one of the aims a speaker attempts to achieve with his speech, but *conciliatio* is also a teleological term which refers to the internal psychological tendency towards a cohesion that "preserves" the relations which are intrinsic to some whole (see p. 82, this vol.) as "its own" (*conciliatio* translates *οἰκείωσις*), whether this whole be a self, a family, or a community (see p. 160, this vol., and accompanying n. 42). Without pretending that Locke is specifically indebted to any particular classical texts, I am attempting to pin down textually what Laslett describes as "the main theme" of the *Two Treatises*—"the development of the implications" of the "doctrine of natural political virtue" (p. 130), which "lays it down that all individuals . . . , even when alone, will have some tendency to allow for the existence, the desires, actions and needs of other men." (p. 122). Laslett identifies this tendency as "almost the Aristotelian *nisus*" (*ibid.*). But it is more obviously Stoic, and Locke is not really developing its implications. Rather, his analytic parceling of problems, and of mankind into individuals enjoying their private properties, is the loosening of the relational implications which we have explored in chap. 10 as composing the rhetorically woven, psychological context which Cicero developed in the *De Officiis*. In the next two chapters we shall watch Hume revive these relational implications.

94. There is no textual warrant for Laslett's phrase "natural political virtue," but he points out that the implications of this doctrine are "defined, checked and safeguarded by the concept of trust" (*Two Treatises*, p. 130). Here too, Locke may be indebted to the *De Officiis*, where "the foundation of justice is trust (*fides*), that is truthfulness and fidelity to promises and agreements" (1. 23). There is, however, in Locke a certain tightening of implications which is associated with his legalistic use of *trust* and similar terms. My interpretation of Locke as well as of Hobbes (see chap. 11, n. 138) suffers from my having to neglect the development of juridical language for the treatment of political problems. This development is not strictly a feature of the humanistic tradition and is of little relevance to the interpretation of liberalism as typified by John Stuart Mill.

95. See n. 24, above. The methodological character of Locke's reluctance is brought out by his reply, when he was urged to publish his exposition of the *Law of Nature*: "I know not how you would still have me, beside my purpose, and against all rules of method, run out into a discourse of the divine law" (I am citing Locke from W. von Leyden's Introduction, p. 76).

96. *A Treatise of Human Nature*, ed. L. A. Selby-Bigge (Oxford: Clarendon Press, 1888), p. 487. One form taken by the "utilitatum comparatio" in the second book of the *De Officiis* is the comparison of "corporis commoda cum externis" (2. 88). The triple classification Hume could have obtained from Cicero's criticism of the Stoic preoccupation with mental integrity in the fourth book of the *De Finibus* (see p. 211, this vol.)

97. *Treatise*, p. 491.

98. *Ibid.*, p. 487.

99. *Ibid.*, p. 489.

100. See p. 125, this vol.

101. *Treatise*, pp. 491–92.

102. *Ibid.*, p. 487.

103. *Ibid.*, p. 494.

104. See p. 125, this vol.

105. *Treatise*, pp. 493–95.

106. *Wealth of Nations*, 2: 199.

107. *Ibid.*

108. *Lectures on Justice, Police, Revenue, and Arms*, ed. Edwin Cannan (Oxford: Clarendon Press, 1896), p. 154.

109. *Ibid.*, p. 156.

110. *Ibid.*, p. 155.

111. Smith's obituary in *The Times* for July 24, 1790. I am citing from C. R. Fay, *Adam Smith* (Cambridge: Cambridge University Press, 1956), p. 34.

112. William R. Scott has published the manuscript where the separation initially took place: "The lectures which Adam Smith gave at Glasgow after the publication of the *Theory of Moral Sentiments* were on Jurisprudence. . . . The manuscript which is printed below was intended to be an economic treatise and nothing else. It begins with a chapter, headed the second, entitled 'The Nature and Causes of Public Opulence.' It is evident that the unwritten first chapter would have corresponded to the Introduction to the *Wealth of Nations*, and would have provided the plan of the work" (*Adam Smith as Student and Professor* [Glasgow: Glasgow University Publications, n. 46, 1937], p. 317).

113. *Wealth of Nations*, 2: 180.

Part V

Utilitarianism

13

The Individual and Society

Here is a kind of ATTRACTION, which in the mental world will be found to have as extraordinary effects as in the natural.—Hume

Motives and Consequences

The principle of utility, Mill recalls in his *Autobiography,* "burst upon" him in his youth "with all the force of novelty" when he came across it in "the first pages of Bentham" which he read. His father had put into his hands "Bentham's principal speculations," as presented "by Dumont in the Traité de Legislation." And Mill regards "the reading of this book" as having been "one of the turning points in my mental history." For Bentham "put into scientific form the application of the happiness principle to the morality of actions, by analyzing the various classes and orders of their consequences."[1]

Since we shall ultimately be concerned with utilitarianism as Mill interprets it in relation to his own liberalism, we are beginning with Bentham's impact on Mill.[2] Here priority must be given to the scientific way Bentham had applied the happiness principle to the morality of actions. Even after the crisis of Mill's break with Benthamite utilitarianism, he will continue to commend Bentham for having "introduced into morals and politics those . . . modes of investigation which are essential to the idea of science."[3] In the Introduction we found that Mill was convinced that the "backward state of the Moral Sciences [i.e, the psychological sciences which include for Mill not only moral theory (ethology) but also political theory (political ethology) and political economy] can only be remedied by applying to them the methods of Physical Science, duly extended and generalised."[4] But we anticipated that there were differences between Mill's idea of science and his utilitarian predecessors' idea of science, and that the differences could be illustrated by their different extensions and generalizations of the Newtonian model.[5] Our *initial* task then, in this opening chapter on the utilitarians, is to consider the way the elaboration of the Newtonian theory of the structure of the universe led to a restructuring of the individualistic theory of human nature as a psychological context for the treatment of moral, political, economic, and legislative problems.

Mill distinguishes utilitarianism from the individualistic tradition in two different ways—ways that we are prepared to deal with since we have already recognized that this tradition takes two different forms. There is first the individualistic tradition as it has emerged from the humanistic tradition. The individualism of this tradition Mill identifies as "dogmatism" which Bentham exposed as the individual "imposing" his "sentiments upon others under cover of sounding expressions which convey no reason for the sentiment, but set up the sentiment as its own reason."[6] Thus our *next* task will be to consider in chapter 14 how the humanistic tradition could come to be viewed by Bentham and Mill as dogmatic and sentimental, in contrast with their own scientific method.

When defenders of the humanistic tradition attacked utilitarianism in turn, they usually identified it with a second individualistic tradition—the tradition which had begun with Hobbes and Locke. Thus Mill protests that one of Bentham's antagonists "confounds the Happiness theory of Morals with the theory of Motives sometimes called the Selfish System, and attacks the later as Bentham's under the name of the former." But Mill denies that Bentham ever dreamt of "defining morality to be the self-interest of the agent."[7] Utilitarianism is a "morality of consequences."[8] When Bentham had "put into scientific form the application of the happiness principle to the morality of actions," it was (we have already seen) "by analyzing the various classes and orders of their consequences." In this analysis, moreover, Bentham was not simply concerned with the consequences for the individual himself. Bentham's " 'greatest happiness principle' was the greatest happiness of mankind."[9] In distinguishing utilitarianism from the individualistic tradition, we shall have to consider changes in the structure attributed to a moral action as well as changes in the structure attributed to the universe.

In distinguishing his own position in morals from Bentham's utilitarianism, Mill further alters the structure to be attributed to a moral action. Mill will eventually reject most of Bentham's utilitarian doctrines, even though he will continue to endorse Bentham's method: "It is not his opinions . . . but his method that constituted the novelty and the value of what he did—a value beyond all price, even though we should reject the whole, as we unquestionably must a large part of the opinions themselves."[10] The opinions that Mill will reject are mainly those resulting from Bentham's application of the principle of utility to morals. He will criticize Bentham for neglecting the agent's motive—"the relation of an act to a certain state of mind as its cause"—and for "confounding the principle of utility with the principle of specific consequences," so that moral appraisal of an action is based on "a calculation solely of the consequences to which that very action, if practised generally, would itself lead." Those of Bentham's opinions which Mill will continue to accept are mainly those resulting from Bentham's application of the principle of utility to legislation. Mill regards it as "fortunate that Mr. Bentham devoted a much larger share of his time and labor to the subject of legislation, than to that of morals; for the mode in which he understood and applied the principle of utility appears to me far more conducive to the attainment of true and valuable results in the former, than in the latter of these two branches of inquiry." While motive is an "important element in the moral relations" of an action, its consequences, "supposing it to be generally practised," assume their importance with respect to "the bearings of an action" which concern the legislator.[11] Thus our *final* task will be to consider in chapter 15 Bentham's program for legislative reform as an adjustment in the relevant relations of an action.

The criteria of relevance which are at stake in these adjustments involve the relationships between different studies: the theory of human nature in its relation to Newtonian physics in this chapter; moral theory in relation to the theory of the sentiments in chapter 14; moral theory in relation to Bentham's theory of legislation in chapter 15.

The political relevance of Mill's distinction between the agent's motives and the social consequences of his action could presumably have been more easily ascertained had Mill succeeded in constructing the political ethology which he projected in his "Logic of the Moral Sciences." But perhaps his distinction receives a relevant illustration in the political theory that Mill did succeed in constructing. "In political economy," he points out, "we shift our point of view, and consider not individual acts, and the motives by which they are determined, but national and universal results."[12] This adjustment in the relations of an action may help to clarify the very similar adjustment which Mill accepts with respect to Bentham's theory of legislation but disavows for a moral theory.

Although we shall continue in the next three chapters to employ our usual procedure of determining a theorist's place in relation to his predecessors by reference to the place each finds for one study in relation to "other studies," this does not imply that the history of utilitarianism follows a line of development which can be pulled out straight, as we move from predecessor to successor. Mill may credit his full conversion to utilitarianism to his first reading Bentham; Bentham himself credits his own conversion to utilitarianism to his first reading the third book of Hume's *Treatise Of Human Nature.* He recalls his discovery there "that the foundations of all *virtue* are laid in *utility,*" and how he then "felt as if scales had fallen from my eyes."[13] Yet Mill neglects Hume's *Treatise.* An omniverous reader, he never read what is usually respected today as the most notable philosophical work ever written in English.

Furthermore, Mill himself furnishes hardly more than bits and pieces of comment for tracing the development of utilitarianism. Because he thinks of distinct and separate adjustments as relevant to "distinct and separate" sciences, he also thinks in terms of distinct and separate predecessors. He thinks of Hobbes as the relevant predecessor when it is a question of providing utilitarianism with a precedent for deducing a political theory from a theory of human nature; he thinks of Locke as the relevant predecessor in analytic psychology; he thinks of Smith as the relevant predecessor in political economy; he thinks of Bentham as the relevant predecessor in the theory of legislation, just as he thinks of his own contributions as an ethology to supplement analytic psychology and a political ethology to supplement political economy and the theory of legislation.[14] Our interpretative procedure has been to explore a context as yielding the criteria of relevance which preside over the relations between political theory and "other studies," and to explore this context only in so far as it is implicit in a specific text.[15] Thus it would not be feasible to trace the development of utilitarianism as a succession of adjustments in the relations between different theorists and the different studies they promoted, if they had not all commented on a theorist who had brought these studies together in a single text which offers unmistakable allusions both to Locke and Hobbes and to the humanistic tradition. Mill neglected *Hume's Treatise Of Human Nature*, but we cannot.

The Association of Ideas

In the Introduction to the *Treatise* Hume asserts:

> All the sciences have a relation . . . to human nature. . . . There is no question of importance, whose decision is not compriz'd in the science of man. . . . In pretending therefore to explain the principles of human nature, we in effect propose a compleat system of the sciences.[16]

Hume would seem, moreover, to be locating this undertaking in relation to Locke's. When Hume announces that he will "march up directly to the capital or center of these sciences, to human nature itself, . . . instead of taking now and then a castle or village on the frontier," he is probably disparaging Locke's provincial strategy of attacking only epistemological problems in his *Essay on Human Understanding*. For when Hume has himself dealt with the nature "Of the Understanding" in the first book of his *Treatise*, he goes on in the second book to an analysis "Of the Passions," and instead of reserving political and economic problems for a separate treatise (as Locke had), he includes them in his third book, "Of Morals."

Since the first book of the *Treatise* lends itself to a comparison with Locke's *Essay on Human Understanding*, let us see if we can find any substantive differences which can be correlated with the different methodological conviction which inspires Hume's *Treatise* as a whole —"all the sciences have a relation . . . to human nature." In the previous chapter we found a certain correlation between the way Locke treats the understanding (by distinguishing simple from complex ideas and treating each simple idea separately) and his general methodological conviction (which is illustrated by his separating *The Essay on Human Understanding* from his treatment of political and economic problems) that "the great provinces of the intellectual world" are "wholly separate and distinct from one another."[17]

The first section of Hume's "Of the Understanding" deals with the problem "Of the Origin of our Ideas." This problem remained at the focus of Locke's entire *Essay*, since its main argument was that ideas are not innate. (His political treatises, even though separate, followed a parallel line of argument: the subtitle *An Essay Concerning the Original, Extent, and End of Civil Government*, could be adapted to an *Essay on Human Understanding*, where the limited extent and purpose of our knowledge were also determined by reference to its origin.) The origin of our ideas is so differently treated in Hume's first chapter that we can see that his focus is shifting to a different problem: Locke's "ideas" are redefined by Hume to become "ideas" and "impressions," so that Locke's problem of the origin of ideas becomes the problem of the relation of ideas to impressions.[18] Complex ideas, which Locke was able to reach only after spending ten chapters on simple ideas, Hume deals with in his opening pages, where the problem of the relation between ideas and impressions becomes conjoined with the problem of the relation between ideas. This problem in turn is differently formulated by Hume: "Were ideas entirely loose and unconnected, chance alone wou'd join them; and 'tis impossible the same simple idea should fall regularly into complex ones . . . without some bond of union among them, some associating quality, by which one idea naturally introduces another."[19] Hume's formulation deprives the mind of the active initiative which it eventually displayed in Locke by combining simple ideas into complex ideas. The mind becomes (to use Locke's terminology of Hume) as "wholly passive" in combining ideas as it was originally "in the reception of all its simple ideas."[20] Hume is stressing the mind's passivity by regarding the associative operation as analogous to the motion of a falling body. Hume is, of course, visualizing this motion as explained by Newton's theory of gravitation: "Here is a kind of ATTRACTION, which in the mental world will be found to have as extraordinary effects as in the natural, and to shew itself in as many and as various forms."[21]

We have become familiar with the way the relations instituted by such analogies not only provide a theory with its credentials "as a scientific theory,"[22] but also locate a subject-matter and determine the method requisite for its treatment. Hume's Newtonian analogy replaces Locke's problem of the origin of our ideas with the problem (which gives Hume's fourth section its title) "Of the Connexion or Association of Ideas."[23] Hume's own comment on the *Treatise* as a whole is that "If anything can entitle the author to so glorious a name as that of an 'inventor,' it is the use he makes of the principle of the association of ideas, which enters into most of his philosophy."[24] Note that Hume does not claim to have invented the principle itself. The principle had turned up belatedly in Locke's *Human Understanding*. It only found its place in the last section which Locke added to "Of Ideas" in the fourth edition, and Locke had used it only to explain the aberrations of the human mind—that is, those "connexions" of ideas which are "wrong" because they are "wholly owing to chance or custom."[25] Regularities indicated to Locke that "Some of our ideas have a natural correspondence and connexion with one another,"[26] but Hume protests, "In no single instance" is "the ultimate connexion . . . discoverable."[27] Having thus eliminated Locke's natural connexion between ideas, Hume is left (in Locke's own terms) with "chance" and "custom." Or rather, since regularity of connexion cannot be explained by "chance," Hume is left with "custom"—that is, with relations between ideas which have become established as associations as a consequence of their having occurred repeatedly.[28]

The analogy to Newtonian gravitation not only reinforces Hume's selection of the problem of the association of ideas as his central epistemological problem but also illustrates his conception of philosophical method. Locke's method of distinguishing and separating rendered simple ideas more fundamental than the relations between them: "All relation terminates in, and is ultimately founded on . . . simple ideas, so that all that we have in our thoughts themselves . . . is nothing but some simple ideas, or collections of simple ideas, compared one with another."[29] But since Hume denies that the mind has any ideas of things as they are in themselves, there is nothing for the mind to discover in its dealings with ideas besides the relations between ideas, and comparison therefore accordingly acquires unique methodological force: "Reason or science is nothing but the comparison of ideas, and the discovery of their relations." Methodologically the fundamental relation is resemblance, as "a relation without which no philosophical relation can exist, since no objects will admit of comparison but what have some degree of resemblance."[30]

Resemblance

We have obtained from Hume's first book some guidance with respect to his philosophical method; it is a comparative method for discovering relations, in contrast with Locke's analytic method for distinguishing and separating. We can now go on to the second book of the *Treatise* and to the question of its relation to the first. We find that Hume's analysis "Of the Passions" is also associationist and is reinforced by the resemblance he finds to the motion of bodies in the Newtonian system: "Nature has bestow'd a kind of attraction on certain impressions and ideas, by which one of them, upon its appearance, naturally introduces its correlative."[31] This resemblance he would not have been able to establish, if he had distinguished and separated, as Locke did, "the motion of one single body alone;"[32] the resemblance holds instead with such "operations of external bodies" as "the communication of their motion [i.e., from one body to another] . . . their attraction and mutual cohesion."[33] Similarly, what Hume is analyzing in Book Two are not the passions of one individual alone, but "sympathy or the communication of the passions" from one individual to another."[34] In fact, "no quality of human nature is more remarkable, both in itself and in its consequences, than the propensity we have to sympathize with others and to receive by communication their inclinations and sentiments."[35] The process of communication Hume analyzes as dependent on the principle of association and in particular on that of the resemblance between men:

> 'Tis evident, that the idea, or rather impression of ourselves is always intimately present with us . . . Whatever object therefore is related to ourselves must be conceived with a like vivacity of conception. . . . Now 'tis obvious, that nature has preserv'd a great resemblance among all human creatures, and that we never remark any passion or principle in others, of which, in some degree or other, we may not find a parallel in ourselves. . . . This resemblance must very much contribute to make us enter into the sentiments of others.[36]

Hume accordingly concludes that "what is principally remarkable in this whole affair is the strong confirmation these phenomena give to the foregoing system concerning the understanding, and consequently to the present one concerning the passions; since these are analogous to each other." In Hume's system concerning the understanding, "all ideas are borrow'd from impressions;" in the present system of sympathy, ideas in my mind of another's passions "are converted into the very impressions they represent."[37] But the associative process is also going on at the higher level of the operations of Hume's own mind, and we can transpose the terminology with which Hume has described the lower order operations and use it to describe his method. He has obtained strong confirmation by the comparison of the systems of the first and second books and the discovery that they are themselves analogous (as each is analogous to the Newtonian system); the relations that hold within each system (and, in particular, the relation of resemblance) resembles the relations that hold within the other system, so that the first book "naturally introduces" as a "correlative" system the analysis of the second book, and the two books themselves compose a mutually cohesive system.[38]

Finally we reach the third book, where Hume deals with the origin of society. We would anticipate that this problem cannot remain focal for Hume, for we have seen in the earlier books that the problem of the origin of our ideas and of the origin of our passions did not remain focal. Strictly speaking, the origin of society is not even a problem for Hume; just as we cannot step outside the range of the relations between our ideas and impressions and find things as they are in themselves, so we cannot step outside social relations and find individuals as they are in themselves. Man's "very first state and situation may justly be esteemed social."[39] Hume's starting point, once again, is a relational situation of "mutual cohesion." The *relata* cannot be separated from each other. Instead of starting with an individual preserving himself, as Hobbes and Locke had, Hume starts with a union between individuals that is preserved. "The first and original principle of human society" is "no other than that natural appetite betwixt the sexes, which unites them together, and preserves their union, till a new tye takes place in their concern for their common offspring. This new concern becomes also a principle of union betwixt the parents and offspring."[40]

The establishment of this triadic relationship is Hume's reconstruction of the individualistic theory of human nature so that it becomes a social context.[41] In carrying out this reconstruction Hume is reviving the starting point adopted by the Stoic tradition, but with an interpretation that differs from Hobbes' and Locke's. The Stoic tendency towards self-preservation (οἰκείωσις) we encountered in Hobbes in the form of self-love; it became in Locke an *economic* principle of appropriation. In the Stoic tradition this principle extended its operation (in the fashion which has inspired Hume here) to the love with which the individual is attracted to his mate and to his offspring as "his own."[42] But it also operated as an internal principle of attraction and cohesion which preserves the universe as a whole.[43] Just as Hobbes had refurbished the Stoic principle of self-preservation by deducing its operation from the Galilean principle of the conservation of motion, so the Stoic principle is refurbished by Hume's analogy to the attraction of bodies in the Newtonian universe:

> The cohesion of the parts of matter arises from natural and necessary principles . . . We must allow that human society is founded on *like* principles . . . for is it more certain, that two flat pieces of marble will unite together, than that two young savages of different sexes will copulate?[44]

Nothing could be more certain than copulation in Hume's universe, where relations are taken to be fundamental, or at any rate a *coniunctionis adpetitus.*[45] To emphasize with Locke or Hobbes the individual's endeavor to preserve himself is therefore from Hume's point of view to oversimplify human motivation. The more relevant psychological fact is social—"confined generosity"—that is, sympathy which is restricted in its exercise to those closely related to us (in particular, the members of our family).[46]

Of course, even to refer to the self as a distinct and separate object is to indulge in another oversimplification. Even before we reach the analysis of social relations in the third book, we discover that the self is a relational system—"that succession of related ideas and impressions of which we have an intimate memory and consciousness."[47] As relational systems, selves are not entirely separate and distinct from each other; individuals of different sexes gravitate together as the consequence of, and at the same time as, different impressions, ideas, and passions gravitate together to compose these selves as minds. Accordingly Hume cannot treat (as Locke did) the origin of society in a treatise which is distinct and separate from his treatment of the understanding and of the passions.

Principles of Motion

The comprehensiveness of Hume's theory of human nature, as contrasted with Locke's more limited theory of the human understanding, encourages a confrontation with Hobbes. Since man's very first situation is esteemed social by Hume, it cannot be deduced from a prior treatment of individual human nature, as it was in Hobbes. Once again we note that a philosophical method structures the relations between the parts of a *philosophy* in a way which can be correlated with the way it structures *physical* relations between things, *psychological* relations within the individual's mind and his *social* relations with other men. The methodological structure of Hobbes' philosophy is a linear deduction: the *same* principles of motion which operate in the natural world apply to the structure of the mind and of society; the motion which is fundamental to this deduction is inertial, rectilinear motion. The deduction itself is individualistic in that its cogency depends on the individual's becoming self-conscious—conscious of his endeavor to move in the direction of his own self preservation as the motion which is fundamental to the explanation of his passions. He therefore becomes conscious of other individuals as simply resisting his motion. In other words, he must abstract from and defer for later treatment ordinary social experiences, which are motions complicated by a considerable measure of political association and restraint. Because his deductive method is so abstract, Hobbes can anticipate himself encountering resistance from other men to his individualistic conclusion: "It may seem strange to some man that has not well weighed these things, that Nature should thus dissociate and render men apt to invade and destroy one another."[48]

To abstract from ordinary social experiences is precisely what Hume refuses to do. What Hume is proposing in the *Treatise* is to "glean up our experiments . . . from a cautious observation of human life, and take them as they appear in the common course of the world;" for if these experiments "are judiciously collected and compared, we may hope to establish on them a science."[49] This science is not established by laying down principles as premises. Its establishment depends on a "long chain of reasoning," which "will acquire new force as it advances."[50] "New force" is not a prospect which could be entertained of a deduction. But the methodological structure of Hume's philosophy is not deductive but analogical, deriving from repeated comparisons. The *Treatise* (according to its subtitle) is *An Attempt to Introduce the Experimental Method of Reasoning into Moral Subjects.* The principles of association which Hume is introducing into the analysis of mental relations and social relations are not the same as but are "like" the principles which explain gravitational attraction.[51] Resemblance itself is the fundamental principle of association; as such it is not only a principle of "union or cohesion among our simple ideas" and among individual men, but it also holds as a "philosophical relation" between the parts of Hume's philosophy.[52]

The links in Hume's long chain of reasoning are resembling relations, but the chain does not constitute a static structure; it is the movement of the mind which composes, out of the experiences it collects and compares, one relational system after another.[53] This movement of the mind is not the rectilinear movement of self-conscious endeavor which we have traced in Hobbes. It is characteristically "oblique and indirect." Despite its sophistication, Hume's reasoning can be compared, with respect to its obliquity, with the movement of the minds of the "two young savages" from their original union to their "new concern for their common offspring," which "becomes also a principle of union betwixt the parents and offspring." Their concern is not simply a continuation of their original desire for each other; it is a new concern, a new principle of union.[54] Similarly Hume's reasoning acquires new force as it advances from relation to relation, because these relations themselves are only the effects of the propensity of our minds to advance in particular ways from one idea or impression to another, and the propensity is strengthened as the resembling relations, which are the effects of these transitions, are repeated, further confirming our preceding experiences of resembling relations. The "effects" of the principles of association show themselves in "many" and "various forms," until they no longer seem as "extraordinary" as they were at the beginning of the first book. Finally in the third book a subject-matter is recomposed, out of our collection and comparison of experiences, which approximates more fully the complex relations of ordinary social experiences, and which therefore engages our understanding and passions more fully than the subjects of the understanding and the passions which had been segregated for analysis in the preceding books.[55]

Sympathy

Having taken into account the differences between Hume's theory of human nature and Hobbes', we can consider the resulting differences in their treatments of political problems. Hobbes' political theory was a deduction designed to induce men to consult their self-interest and exercise "restraint upon themselves."[56] Hume concedes that "self-interest is the original motive to the establishment of justice."[57] This motive is activated when men "observe that it is impossible to live in society without restraining themselves by certain general rules."[58] But when they do so, they are observing a situation which is already social; whereas in Hobbes it is compliance with the rules he deduces which is the creation of a social situation. Indeed we have seen the sense in which the problem of the origin of society is a pseudo-problem for Hume. Social regulations are for him only a more mutually cohesive form of social relations, and the problem of men's original motive for establishing these regulations similarly recedes into the background once Hume finds a difficulty with the application of Hobbes' deductive procedure. The difficulty itself is distinctively social: "When society has become numerous," men cannot "so readily perceive that disorder and confusion follow upon every breach of these rules, as in a more narrow and contracted society."[59] They accordingly do not usually exercise foresight in the direct manner Hobbes' deduction would illustrate:

> If we consider the ordinary course of human actions, we shall find that the mind restrains not itself by any general and universal rules, but acts on most occasions as it is determin'd by present motive and inclination. . . . This is the reason why men . . . prefer any trivial advantage that is present to the maintenance of order in society, which so much depends on the observance of justice. . . . The consequences of every breach of the social union seem to lie very remote, and are not able to counter-balance any immediate advantage that may be reaped from this breach."[60]

Recognition of the necessity of maintaining the order of society does not emerge (as it did in Hobbes) from a linear deduction, but from a process of comparison in which one observation is balanced against another. The necessity is recognized insofar as men become observers who (like Hume at the higher level of his theory) judiciously collect and compare their experiences. When men act, their action may be determined by its present motive and inclination, without benefit of any comparison. But we are not always acting. Not only do we sometimes suffer injustice ourselves; but we are also sometimes observers of the injustice suffered by others, and we then sympathize with their sufferings and may become sensitive in our judgments to the fact that the public interest has been violated, even "when the injustice is so distant from us, as no way to affect our interest." Repeated, these sympathetic reactions eventually become customary, and indirectly and obliquely a restraining influence on our own actions. To this extent we are less likely when we act to be influenced simply by a present motive and inclination and more likely to be influenced as well by the effects of having observed and compared other situations. We are further restrained by the reactions of others to our actions, for "we naturally sympathize with others in the sentiments they entertain of us."[61] We thereby become involved in further processes of comparison.

In dealing with the establishment of social regulations, Locke and Hobbes envisaged a situation where individuals were free and equal, and their analysis of this situation was individualistic in that any individual played essentially the same self-interested role. Even though two individuals were brought together in Hobbes, each desired the same thing as the other, each became fearful of the other, each gloried over the other.[62] But the process of comparison in Hume is envisaged as an irreducibly relational (i.e., social) situation in that the individuals present are playing different roles in relation to each other, so that their relations cannot be analyzed with reference to any single action, by any single individual, at any single moment (as in Locke), or even by reference to the actions and reactions of two individuals to each other (as in Hobbes), but only as the eventual consequences of an individual's observing and comparing the repeated actions of two (or more) individuals. It is a situation in which the individual whom Hobbes conceived to act out of self-interest cannot be counted upon to exercise the self-restraint required for the preservation of the social union. He instead is visualized as acting unjustly, but his action itself is visualized by reference to its consequences for a second individual who is suffering the injustice, but then a third individual has to be brought into the situation to observe these consequences and share the feelings of the sufferer. This third party is not directly involved in the action. He is present, as it were, only obliquely.[63] But he is the morally crucial individual who is visualized as likely later to act justly, to the extent that he observes the resemblance between (and thus compares) the situation in which he is now acting and the original situation, and is restrained by the consequences, not only of the earlier operation of his own sympathy for the second individual, but also by the earlier and repeated operation of the sympathies of other third parties who observe his actions and whose sympathetic reactions he in turn sympathizes with.

Justice

As a result of repeated operations of sympathy, justice evolves in Hume into the virtue, which it had been in the humanistic tradition, of acting in the interest of others, or in the public interest. Defending the *Treatise* in a letter to Francis Hutcheson (a leading eighteenth-century exponent of the humanistic tradition), Hume pleads that he had taken "his Catalogue of Virtues" from Cicero's *On Duties*. This work, Hume claims, "I had in my Eye in all my Reasonings."[64] But the operation of sympathy in Hume in fact undermines the traditional humanistic conception of virtue. Hume's verdict, "Reason is, and ought only to be the slave of the passions," has been interpreted as illustrating what is "truly distinctive and central in Hume's teaching: his reversal of the roles hitherto ascribed to Reason and to Feeling respectively."[65] The operation of sympathy can then be interpreted as extending the effects of this reversal to his treatment of the individual's relation to others: the social community is no longer what it hitherto had been, a rational structure; it is held together instead by the sympathetic "communication of sentiments and passions."[66] The sentimental dimension of Hume's analysis I shall examine in the next chapter. But the operation of sympathy in Hume also undermines the traditional humanistic conception of virtue and society in the fundamental way that I am now examining. Hume reverses the sequence which had traditionally been followed in cataloging the virtues. Cicero began *On Duties* with the individual and reflexive virtue of wisdom; Hume begins instead with the social virtue of justice and postpones all of the virtues of the individual. What is central in Hume's teaching is not just a reversal of the traditional roles Reason and Feeling play in the formation of the individual and of society, but a reversal as well of the traditional roles played morally by the individual and by society. If moral restraint is no longer rational self-restraint in Hume, it is not even self-restraint, but social restraint.

This reversal in the relation between the individual and others has restructured the analysis of justice itself. In *On Duties* the individual is assumed to retain the initiative. He acts *appropriately* to his own moral character as an individual, even when he expects other men to imitate his example.[67] But in Hume's social analysis, "the actions of each of us have reference to those of the other, and are perform'd upon the supposition that something is to be perform'd on the other part."[68] The expectation that others will imitate my example initially supplies the individual with his self-interested motive for acting justly, so that his action can only be visualized in relation to theirs:

> 'Tis only upon the supposition that others are to imitate my example that I can be induc'd to embrace that virtue; since nothing but this combination can render justice advantageous, or afford me any motives to conform my self to its rules. . . . I should be the cully of my integrity, if I alone shou'd impose on myself a severe restraint amidst the licentiousness of others.[69]

The individual in the humanistic tradition maintained his *firmitas* —the moral integrity and stability of his mind—by resisting the disturbing influence of *res externae* as *res alienae*.[70] In Hume's analysis of human nature, however, the mind "naturally seeks after foreign objects."[71] They are the external things which the individual seeks as his property in the third book; they are also other men, whose resemblance to him in the second book activates the operation of his sympathy. In either case, human nature is expanding its scope. When in the previous chapter we watched Hume take into consideration "the concurrence of certain qualities of the human mind with the situation of external objects,"[72] it may have seemed that Hume was relocating the problem of justice at the "frontier" of his theory of human nature, and that he was abandoning his march to the "center" of the sciences. But it is the theory of human nature itself which has been reconstructed as a relational context in which what is central is the concurrence of certain qualities of the human mind with the situation of external objects. Their "easy transition from one person to another" then introduces these external objects into another relational situation.[73]

Reconstruction was already under way in the second book, where Hume began his account of the passions not with Hobbes' self-interested endeavor, but with pride and humility, and where pride was no longer simply Hobbesian self-glorification. Hume argued that although pride and humility "have the qualities of our mind and body, that is self, for their natural and more immediate cause, we find by experience that there are many other objects which produce these affections, and that the primary one is in some measure obscured and lost by the multiplicity of foreign and extrinsic."[74] When Hume therefore passes on to the relations which are the effects of this associative process, he discovers that "the relation which is esteemed the closest and which of all others produces most commonly the passion of pride is that of Property."[75]

The Man of Action and of Virtue

When I dealt with the property relation in the previous chapter, I was following out a line of development whereby self-interest became increasingly identified as an acquisitive motive. We are now recognizing a further change in the structure of the traditional theory of human nature. This change too is involved in the increasing encroachment of economic considerations. When Hume in the *Treatise* reduces the problem of securing justice to the problem of securing property, he relied on the reflexive distinction, which had been pivotal to the traditional theory of human nature, between the security of the internal goods of the mind and the insecurity of the external goods of fortune.[76] But we have now seen that the reduction presupposes an associationist theory of human nature which this reflexive distinction cannot easily survive. Once the reference to the self (the object of the first pair of Hume's passions—pride and humility) has in some measure become obscured and lost amid the multiplicity of foreign and extrinsic objects, the reflexive distinction between internal and external goods is itself in some measure obscured. In the humanistic tradition the mind maintained its unity, clarity, and strength, by maintaining this distinction. But if the mind, as analyzed by Hume in terms of the process of association, "naturally seeks after foreign objects," it is because these "may produce a lively sensation and agitate the spirits." It is "on the appearance of such an object" in Hume that "the heart is elevated, and the whole man acquires a vigour which he cannot command in his solitary and calm moments."[77] The aloof self-elevation which was the traditional posture of the Stoic mind in the humanistic tradition can no longer be sustained. The individual is "altogether insufficient to support himself," so that "when you loosen all the holds he has on external objects, he immediately drops down into the deepest melancholy and despair."[78] But if we cannot "support" ourselves except by holding onto "external objects," we can hardly remain "perfectly secure in the internal satisfaction of our minds."[79] Thus it is not surprising that Hume in his mature work, the *Enquiry Concerning the Principles of Morals,* abandons the traditional humanistic distinction, which he had employed in the *Treatise,* between the security of the goods of the mind and the insecurity of the external goods of fortune.

One word of caution. This change is not any simple abandonment of traditional moral individualism. Rather, the initiative and integrity which the individual traditionally exercised in the moral sphere, and which we have watched him lose, is to a certain extent transferred to him in the economic sphere. Although this new sphere of activity was opened up in Locke by the individual's own labor, Locke still attached the act of labor to the traditional Stoic effort on the part of the individual to preserve himself.[80] And what might also have been expected to be the most novel portion of Hume's theory of human nature he too couches in traditional humanistic language. In his essay on "The Stoic" (which Hume published after the *Treatise* and before the *Enquiry*) it is the point of view of "the man of action and virtue" that is presented. To the traditional moral "indolence" of "The Epicurean," which leaves man on the same level as the animals, Hume opposes the traditional Stoic emphasis on man's privileged status in the universe. But the virtue with which Hume's Stoic raises himself aloft is not just the traditional self-control with which he resists the influence of *res externae* that belong to the sphere of fortune; it is a self-control which is analogous to the control he has already achieved over external things:

> There is this obvious and material difference in the conduct of nature with regard to man and other animals, that having endowed the former with a sublime celestial spirit, and having given him an affinity with superior beings, she allows not such noble faculties to lie lethargic or idle; but urges him by necessity to employ on every emergence his utmost art and industry. . . . Every thing is sold to skill and labour, and where nature furnishes the materials, they are still rude and unfinished, till industry, ever active and intelligent, refines them from their brute state, and fits them for human use and convenience. . . . Thy kind parent, nature, having given thee art and intelligence, has filled the whole globe with materials to employ these talents: Harken to her voice, which so plainly tells thee, that thou, thyself shouldest also be the object of thy industry, and that by art and attention alone thou canst acquire that ability which will raise thee to thy of the holders of mischievous power, be removed.[53]

We should not be put off by the stilted mannerism of the essay, which might suggest that the magniloquent Stoic posing for this portrait has no affinity at all to the Hume who recommends in the *Treatise* that "we . . . glean up our experiments . . . from a cautious observation of human life." In his youth Hume had entertained a Stoic conception of the task of philosophy; he had recognized that "his peace of mind" was "not sufficiently confirmed by philosophy to withstand the blows of fortune," because "this Greatness and Elevation of soul is to be found only in study and contemplation," which alone can teach us to look down on human accidents."[82] He had later discovered his mistake, and his discovery anticipates his later focus on the concurrence of qualities of the human mind with the situation of external objects:

> Having read many Books of Morality, such as Cicero, Seneca, and Plutarch, . . . I was continually fortifying myself with Reflections against Death, and Poverty, and Shame, and Pain, and all the other Calamities of Life. These no doubt are exceedingly useful, when joined with an active Life, because the Occasion being presented along with the Reflection, works it into the Soul, and makes it take a deep Impression; but in Solitude they serve to little other Purpose, than to waste the Spirits, the Force of the Mind meeting with no Resistance, but wasting itself in the air, like our Arm when it misses its Aim.[83]

The juncture with the active life had in fact been sought in these books of morality. (Hume's misconception can perhaps be explained by the way the later humanists whom he also read often preferred to seek solitude to study and reflect on these books.) But when Hume "resolved to seek out a more active scene of life,"[84] he did not, as had Cicero and Seneca, at once engage in political activity. He became instead a clerk in the countinghouse of a Bristol merchant.

Just as the Stoic conception of the moral role of the individual had broadened, during periods of political expansion in the ancient world, into the humanistic conception of the political role of the individual, so during the economic expansion of the eighteenth century, the humanistic tradition contributed to the formation of a conception of the economic role of the individual, which is fitted to a theory in which human nature itself expands its relations to external things.

Adam Smith (I earlier anticipated) follows Cicero, as an historian of philosophy, in assuming the fundamental homogeneity of the tradition which I have labeled "humanistic," and attributes to the entire tradition the criterion for moral conduct which is found in Cicero's *On Duties:* "According to Plato, to Aristotle, and to Zeno, virtue consists in the propriety of conduct."[85] In this humanistic tradition the sphere of propriety was the scope of what was within the individual's own control as distinguished from the external sphere of fortune. But in Smith the "self-command" which is instanced by "the practice of frugality, industry, and application, though directed to no other purpose than the acquisition of fortune . . . is approved of . . . as much under the aspect of propriety as under that of utility"[86]—that is, as much in traditional moral terms as in the utilitarian terms which we might have thought would be more congenial to the founder of political economy.

The Uncertainty of Merit

If we compare the "Origin of Justice and Property" in the *Treatise* with Hume's later discussion in the *Enquiry,* we observe a further restructuring of Hume's theory of human nature. In the *Treatise* Hume turns back to "men in their savage and solitary condition" and supposes that they would be "sensible of the misery of that state," and "foreseeing the advantages that wou'd result from society" would "enter into a convention for the stability of possession and for mutual restraint and forebearance."[87] In the *Enquiry*, Hume emphasizes instead the social consequences of tampering with the present distribution:

> We shall suppose that a creature possessed of reason, but unacquainted with human nature, deliberates with himself what rules of justice or property would best promote public interest, and establish peace and security among mankind. His most obvious thought would be to assign the largest possessions to the most extensive virtue, and give every one the power of doing good, proportioned to his inclination. . . . But were mankind to execute such a law, so great is the uncertainty of merit, both from its natural obscurity, and from the self-conceit of each individual, that no determinate rule of conduct would ever result from it, and the total dissolution of society must be the immediate consequence.[88]

The political significance of this new emphasis on social consequences is underscored by Hume's adding that the "civil magistrate very justly puts . . . on the same footing as common robbers" those "sublime theorists" who are so unacquainted with human nature as to moralize that " 'saints alone inherit the earth.' "[89]

The fact that the "fanatics" whom Hume has specifically in mind were the Levellers, permits a different contrast with Hobbes from that which we undertook in interpreting the *Treatise*. Hobbes' argument in the *Leviathan* was directed against Monarchomachs, whose fanaticism threatened to undermine the political structure of society. The fanaticism of the Levellers, against whom Hume's argument in the *Enquiry* is directed, threatened the economic structure of society. But Hume now regards the unequal distribution of property as itself indispensable to maintaining political authority. Thus he caps the economic argument against the Levellers, "Render possessions ever so equal, men's different degrees of art, care, and industry, will immediately break that equality," with the political argument, "Perfect equality of possessions, destroying all subordination, weakens extremely the authority of magistracy, and must reduce all power nearly to a level, as well as property."[90]

Even more definitely than Hume, Smith finds political authority not only needed to maintain, but also maintained by, the unequal distribution of property. In dealing in the *Wealth of Nations* with the "causes . . . which naturally introduce subordination" and "give some men superiority," he utilizes the traditional humanistic classification of goods, and of mental goods into the cardinal virtues of "prudence, justice, fortitude, and moderation of mind." But like Hobbes and Hume, Smith in effect rejects—with the argument from the uncertainty of merit—the humanistic conception of propriety whereby rule reveals the man, so that political authority can be the extension over others of the moral authority that the virtuous individual visibly exercises over himself:

> The qualifications of the mind . . . are . . . invisible qualities; always disputable and generally disputed. No society . . . has ever found it convenient to settle the rules of precedency of rank and subordination according to those invisible qualities; but according to something that is more plain and palpable.[91]

"Birth" and "fortune" are the visible qualities which are "the two great sources of personal distinction and . . . therefore the principal causes which naturally establish authority and subordination among men," but "the authority of riches" is more fundamental: "antiquity of family means everywhere the antiquity either of wealth, or of that greatness which is commonly either founded upon wealth, or accompanied with it."[92] The problem of securing justice—of securing to each his own—was eased when it became in Locke the problem of securing property: "What Portion a Man carved to himself, was easily seen."[93] But the problem of establishing political authority was still a separate problem in Locke and remained a separate problem in Hume's *Treatise*. In the *Enquiry* and in Smith the solution to this problem has in turn been eased by the visibility of property.

Plenty

The shift whereby the uncertainty of merit renders traditional moral considerations less politically relevant than economic considerations is an adjustment which alters the individual's relations to other men. This relationship tends to slip in Hume's and Smith's later writings outside the scope of their own earlier analysis of the motives which lie behind an individual's actions, and to become more closely attached to the consequences for society of his actions. In the *Treatise*, the "stability of possession," merely left "everyone in the peaceable enjoyment of what he may acquire by his fortune and industry."[94] But in the *Enquiry* Hume asks, "Who sees not . . . that whatever is produced by man's art or industry, ought for ever to be secured to him, in order to give encouragement to such useful habits and accomplishments?"[95] The beneficial social consequences of stability of possession are now so obvious that the detailed argument of the *Treatise* can be abbreviated in the *Enquiry:*

> Few enjoyments are given us from the open and liberal hand of nature; but by art, labour, and industry, we can extract them in great abundance. Hence the ideas of property become necessary in all civil society; hence justice derives its usefulness to the public; and hence alone arises its merits and moral obligation. These conclusions are so natural and obvious that they have not escaped even the poets in their descriptions of the felicity attending the golden age.[96]

Hume had already furnished in the *Treatise* the poets' description of this age of abundance. The point there of this otherwise "idle fiction" was that "justice derives its origin" partly from "the scanty provision nature has made for his [man's] wants." For "when there is such a plenty of anything [e.g., of air and water] as satisfies all the desires of men, . . . the distinction of property is entirely lost, and everything remains in common."[97] But in the *Enquiry* Hume's emphasis has moved on from the "few enjoyments" which are "given us from the open and liberal hand of nature," to the "great abundance" that can be extracted "by art, labour, and industry."[98]

This shift in point of view began in Locke. In his lectures as Censor of Moral Philosophy, Locke had assumed that "nature has provided a certain supply of goods . . . distributing these in a . . . fixed quantity," so that "whenever the desire or the need of property increases among men, there is no resulting extension of the world's limits." Because "it is impossible for anyone to acquire wealth except at someone else's loss," Locke had moralized that the individual must restrain his acquisitive self-interest.[99] But in the *Second Treatise* Locke left the motives of the individual behind, fastened on the social consequences of his actions, and reached the different conclusion that "he who appropriates land to himself by his labour increases the common stock of mankind."[100]

Hume referred in his *Treatise* to the "scanty provision" nature has made for man's wants, in order to clarify the concurrent operation of self-interest as the original motive to the establishment of justice: "The selfishness of men is animated by the few possessions we have, in proportion to our wants; and 'tis to restrain this selfishness that men have been oblig'd to distinguish betwixt their own goods and those of others."[101] But the discussion of justice in the *Enquiry* no longer begins from the point of view of the individual and of the operation of his self-interest. The shift to the "great abundance" that can be extracted "by art, labour, industry," brings the individual into relation to other men in terms, not of his wants and motives, but of the social consequences of his economic activity. "Who sees not . . .?" Hume has asked. These social consequences are publicly visible. The conclusions that Hume reaches in the *Enquiry* are accordingly more "natural and obvious" than those of the *Treatise*. He concluded in the *Treatise* that "*self*-interest is the *original* motive to the establishment of justice," but the corresponding conclusion in the *Enquiry* is that "*public* utility is the *sole* origin of justice."[102]

The Invisible Hand

An even sharper break with the individualistic tradition takes place when Smith's thought arrives at its culmination in the *Wealth of Nations*. Political economy (as we observed in the previous chapter) can no longer be confined within traditional political theory. Thus the link to a theory of human nature can also be cut. This link still survived in the Glasgow Lectures, even after Smith had excised the bulk of this theory for publication in the *Theory of Moral Sentiments*. In the Glasgow Lectures, Smith began his treatment of "Plenty" with an analysis "Of the Natural Wants of Mankind," since "all the arts are subservient" to these wants.[103] When Cannan discovered a student's transcript of these lectures, he was pleased at the thought that the analysis of these wants was "the theory of consumption" which is lacking in *The Wealth of Nations*.[104] But his pleasure was perhaps anachronistic: Smith was not anticipating the later economic theory of consumption; his analysis was a remnant of the theory of human motivation, which had been the traditional context for the treatment of economic problems but which Smith finally discards when his treatment of "Plenty" becomes *The Wealth of Nations*.

In beginning this later work with the division of labor, Smith offers what can be taken as justification for moving past the traditional starting-point:

> When the division of labour has been once thoroughly established, it is but a *very small part of man's* wants which the produce of his own labour can supply. He supplies the far greater part of them by exchanging that surplus part of the produce of his own labour, which is over and above his own consumption, for such parts of the produce of other men's labour as he has occasion for. Every man thus lives by exchanging, or becomes in some measure a merchant.[105]

The individual assumes here the economic role, not of a laborer as in Locke, but of a merchant, and the significant item of property that the individual acquires is not something which preserves him, but a commodity which he can exchange with other men.

The shift of point of view from the wants and motives that lie behind the individual's economic activity to its social consequences is more drastic in Smith than in Locke or even than in Hume. Smith is not dealing in *The Wealth of Nations*, as Locke did in the *Second Treatise*, with the individual's own labor, or with individual's own property that is the effect of his labor, but with "the effects of the division of labour in the general business of society."[106] Smith does not consider these effects, in the way that Hume did, as the effects of the "different degrees of man's art, care, and industry."[107] Smith considers them as effects of the division of labor as a social system of exchange. In fact Smith explains the "difference of natural talents in different men" as "not so much the cause as the effect of the division of labour."[108] And the division of labor itself is "not originally the effect of any human wisdom, which foresees and intends that general opulence to which it gives occasion."[109] The individual in his economic activities "intends only his own gain," but in a society structured by the division of labor, he is "led by an invisible hand to promote an end which is no part of his intention."[110] An analysis of the way this social structure promotes this end can therefore disregard the individual's intentions; *The Wealth of Nations* can be severed from the theory of human nature which Smith had elaborated in the *Moral Sentiments*.

In dealing with political problems in his lectures, Smith himself, we have noted, still treats wealth as a visible source of political power and does not resort to the invisible hand, as he does in dealing with economic problems in *The Wealth of Nations.* To this extent he still continues the political tradition which began when Machiavelli upheld visible power and rejected the moralistic approach of the humanistic tradition by posing the challenge (in Hume's phrase) of the "uncertainty of merit." Even though other men in Machiavelli generally lack knowledge of the prince's motives as an individual, his visible actions can still be assessed. His position makes him a public figure, and he must foresee the way in which the actions he performs to obtain or maintain this position will be viewed by his rivals and by his supporters.

If we originally missed the significance of Machiavelli's appeal to what "men in general" see,[111] it was because our attention was distracted by the socio-historical approach of later theorists who explain political rivalry in economic terms. Some of the terminology used in such explanations was first systematized by Smith's analysis of society as an economic structure. Although Smith himself does not resort to the invisible hand in dealing with political problems, as he does in dealing with economic problems, in many later social theories the visible exercise of political power becomes a largely meaningless ritual, except insofar as invisible economic hands can be detected leading individuals to promote social consequences which are no part of their intentions. An historian of political theory is then tempted, when he looks back to interpret the new route Machiavelli opened up for modern political theory, to overlook the visibility the prince's lofty position still conferred on his actions, as it had in the tradition of humanistic individualism,[112] and to flatten (as Sabine did) Machiavelli's vivid descriptions of these actions into abstract generalizations regarding "competing interests."[113] We ourselves, when we began the interpretation of Machiavelli's new route, slid past the first phrase of the *Discourses,* as if it were a merely conventional literary flourish:

> Although the envious nature of men makes the discovery of new methods and systems as dangerous as the exploration of unknown seas and lands . . . , I have resolved to open a new route.[114]

But we came to realize the extent to which the struggle for visible power in Machiavelli took such forms as envy, which rendered the individual's visibility dangerous, whether he was a political actor or a political theorist.

Hobbes too still belongs to the humanistic individualistic tradition, not only to the extent that he argues on behalf of the "visible power" of the ruler,[115] but also because he addresses this argument to the individual's self-consciousness. But we discovered in the previous chapter that two motives which the individual is conscious of in Hobbes—envy and the desire for revenge—lose their general significance in Locke: they are "not . . . found in all men."[116] In Hume's *Treatise* these motives operate only by intervals," and are only "directed against particular persons;" the "avidity alone of acquiring goods and possessions . . . is insatiable, perpetual and directly destructive of society."[117] In Hume's *Enquiry* and in Smith's *Wealth of Nations,* this acquisitive motive indirectly becomes socially beneficial. But the individual who intends his own gain recedes into the background.[118] An individualistic theory of human nature cannot embrace the consequences of the operation of an invisible hand, since they are no part of the individual's own intention. "In political economy," as I have anticipated Mill will point out, "we shift our point of view, and consider not individual acts, and the motives by which they are determined, but national and universal results."[119] To this extent the political theorist becomes a social theorist; his theory no longer expounds, as Machiavelli's and Hobbes' theories had, the foresight of an individual, whether conceived (as it is by Machiavelli) as historical foresight or conceived (as it is by Hobbes) as deductive foresight.

What happens then to these individual acts and their motives which have been left behind? The question is relevant because the treatment of political problems in terms of the foresight of the individual had traditionally been their assimilation to the moral treatment of the actions of the individual. In Part IV we were preoccupied with the ambiguity of the term *political*: in the first two chapters of Part IV we were preoccupied with the implications the term acquired when political problems became problems of the relation between the individual and the state; in the final chapter of Part IV we were preoccupied with the way the term's range of reference tended to shift when *economic* considerations encroached in the treatment of political problems. In the present chapter we have become concerned with the way a *social* context replaces an individualistic context for the treatment of political and economic problems.[120] We have therefore so far largely neglected Hume's and Smith's treatment of *moral* problems. We shall see in the next chapter that they both continue to accommodate the traditional treatment, but by an adjustment in the structure of the traditional theory of human nature whereby the motives of the individual come to be identified as passions or sentiments, and moral theory itself becomes a theory of the moral sentiments.

Notes

1. *Autobiography* (New York: Columbia University Press, 1924), pp. 45–46.

2. It is futile to attempt to identify utilitarianism with the adoption of the happiness principle itself. The thinkers who adopt it are too miscellaneous. (For the futility of the attempt, see David Baumgardt's survey, *Bentham and the Ethics of Today* [Princeton: Princeton University Press, 1952], pp. 33–63.) A tradition can only be defined precisely by reference to the place some theorist occupies within the tradition. Since I am focusing on the place Mill assigns Bentham, I do not pretend to be offering an accurate or adequate interpretation of utilitarianism in Bentham's own terms. See chap. 16, n. 109.

3. "Bentham," *Mill's Essays on Literature and Society*, ed. J. B. Schneewind (New York: Collier Books, 1965), p. 247.

4. See vol. 1, p. 12.

5. Compare Élie Halévy: "Utilitarianism . . . can be defined as nothing but an attempt to apply the principles of Newton to the affairs of politics and morals" (*The Growth of Philosophical Radicalism* [New York: A. M. Kelley, 1949], p. 6). But see n. 33, below.

6. *Autobiography*, p. 46.

7. "Dr. Whewell on Moral Philosophy," *Mill's Ethical Writings*, ed. J. B. Schneewind (New York: Collier Books, 1965), pp. 192. For the sustained opposition between the humanistic and the utilitarian tradition, see chap. 15, n. 8.

8. "Dr. Whewell on Moral Philosophy," p. 187.

9. *Ibid.*, 192.

10. "Bentham," pp. 247–48.

11. "Remarks on Bentham's Philosophy," *Mill's Ethical Writings*, pp. 48, 50. Mill will continue the utilitarian emphasis on consequences, but he will include among these consequences the "tendency" of any act whatever . . . to fix and perpetuate the state . . . of mind in which itself has originated." He will argue that if the motive "be not taken into account by the moralist as a cause, neither probably will it be taken into account as a consequence." Thus his complaint against Bentham and the utilitarians is that "when they came to discuss particular questions of ethics," they "have commonly, in the superior stress which they laid upon the specific consequences of a class of acts, rejected all contemplation of the action in its general bearings upon the entire moral being of the agent, or have, to say the least, thrown those considerations so far into the background as to be almost out of sight" (*ibid.*, p. 50). For Mill's complaint see pp. 293–94, this vol. For the conception of a self that is implicit in the agent's having an "entire moral being," see p. 386, this vol.

12. *Collected Works of John Stuart Mill* (Toronto: Toronto University Press, 1965), 2: 43.

13. *A Fragment on Government,* ed. F. C. Montague (London: Oxford University Press, 1951), p. 154.

14. For the places assigned Hobbes and Locke, see pp. 113, 119, this vol. For the place assigned Smith, note Mill's explanation in his preface to his *Principles of Political Economy* that its "design . . . is different from that of any treatise on Political Economy which has been produced in England since the work of Adam Smith (*Collected Works,* 2: xci).

15. See vol. 1, 119, 123.

16. David Hume, *A Treatise Of Human Nature,* ed. L. A. Selby-Bigge (Oxford: Clarendon Press, 1888), pp. xix–xx. See n. 41 below.

17. See p. 117, this vol.

18. *Treatise,* p. 1.

19. *Ibid.,* p. 10. See n. 53, below.

20. See p. 121, this vol., and n. 48, below.

21. *Treatise,* pp. 12–13. For the full citation, see n. 70, below.

22. See vol. 1, p. 9. I am thus beginning my comparison of Hume and Locke with what I originally distinguished by reference to Mill as the scientific adjustment. Since Mill assigned priority to this adjustment over his other adjustments, I have continued to consider it first (see vol. 1, p. 94 and my interpretation of Hobbes in the present vol., p. 71). But of course Hume himself begins with this adjustment when he resorts to the Newtonian analogy here in the *Treatise.* Locke, in contrast, not only refuses to "meddle with the physical consideration of the mind" (see p. 119, this vol.), but also distinguishes and separates his treatment of the mind from Newtonian science: "In an age that produces such masters as the great Huygenius, and the incomparable Mr. Newton, with some other of that strain, it is ambition enough to be employed as an under-labourer in clearing ground a little, and removing some of the rubbish that lies in the way to knowledge" (*Essay on Human Understanding* [London: Ward, Lock, n.d.], p. xii). The contrast reflects differences in the structure which Hume and Locke assign to knowledge (see n. 33, below).

23. *Treatise,* p. 10; see n. 73, below.

24. *An Abstract of A Treatise Of Human Nature,* reprinted as a supplement to *An Inquiry Concerning Human Understanding* (New York: Liberal Arts, 1955), p. 198.

25. Locke, *On Human Understanding,* p. 316.

26. *Ibid.*

27. *Treatise,* p. 400.

28. See n. 63, below.

29. *On Human Understanding,* p. 285.

30. *Treatise,* pp. 466, 14. Cf. p. 73: "All kinds of reasoning consist in nothing but a comparison, and a discovery of those relations . . . which two or more objects bear to each other."

31. *Ibid.,* p. 289. See n. 53, below.

32. See p. 122, this vol.

33. *Treatise,* p. 399. Historians of ideas frequently generalize regarding the dominance of the Newtonian model in eighteenth century moral and political philosophy, but without sufficient attention to the selective and varied interpretations of the model which are

implicit in the different uses to which it is put by different philosophers. The variations illustrate the extent to which its relevance to moral and political philosophy is relative to the structure each of these different philosophers assigns to knowledge. In the Introduction (vol. 1, p. 14) we anticipated that Mill's interpretation of the Newtonian model would differ from his father's; in the present volume, we shall see that the differences between Bentham's and Hume's interpretations (see p. 236), as well as between the two Mills' interpretations (see pp. 339–42) reflect differences in their conceptions of this structure.

34. *Treatise,* p. 398.

35. *Ibid.,* p. 316.

36. *Ibid.,* pp. 317–18.

37. *Treatise,* p. 319.

38. Hume's system provides the clearest illustration since Plato of the methodological point I made in vol. 1, p. 53, regarding the function analogies can play in the construction of political theories. If we were ruthlessly to rip away the analogies which sustain the relations between Hume's political thought and other parts of his system, there would be little left that could be identified as his political thought. We have already (p. 137, this vol.) followed out his reduction of the problems of society to economic problems (i.e., to problems of stabilizing property relations). Even the problem of stabilizing the fundamental social unit, the family (see n. 42, below), is reduced to an economic problem by Hume's analogical generalization and extension of the concept of property (see n. 63, below).

39. *Treatise,* p. 493.

40. *Ibid.,* p. 486.

41. It would not have been possible for me to propose the correlations offered in the present and in the previous chapter (see pp. 116, 138) if Hume's theory of human nature had not taken the relational form of "a compleat system of the sciences." Since the history of the British tradition from Locke on, with the exception of Hume's *Treatise,* is the history, by and large, of the development of "distinct and separate" sciences, the notion of "a compleat system'" may have become discredited. But its philosophical standing today is not my concern. My argument in Hume's case (as in Hobbes' case; see p. 73, this vol.) is historical: Hume cannot be circumvented in tracing the development of the British tradition (as he is when Mill refers to "the school of Locke and Bentham"; see chap. 12, n. 20), inasmuch as the transformation of the individualistic theory of human nature into a social context involved historically other adjustments in the structure of knowledge besides the introduction of a reference to social consequences. These are adjustments which are most readily discerned in Hume.

42. The doctrine of οἰκείωσις is "der Ausgangspunkt wie der feste Grund der stoischen Ethik" (Max Pohlenz, *Grundfragen der stoischen Philosophie* [Göttingen: Vandenhoeck & Ruprecht, 1940], p. 11). In Parts II and III, Polybius' and Cicero's different treatments of the origin of government, the decline of the state, and "the return to the starting point" were shown to derive different "principles" from the same Platonic materials. Polybius fitted these materials to a theory of social history; Cicero, to a theory of human nature. But this theory of human nature was ambivalent. Its ambivalence could now be reexplored in the form of the difference between the individualistic theory of human nature that emerges in Hobbes and Locke and the theory of human nature that emerges as a social context in Hume, for the divergence involves different interpretations of the "principle" the Stoics had taken as their "starting point." Let me cite, more fully than I did in interpreting Hobbes (p. 78, this vol.), Cato's presentation of the Stoic starting point: "As soon as it is born, for we should start here, any animate being feels an attachment and attraction to itself, which is a tendency to preserve itself and to feel drawn towards those things which would preserve it [the starting point which is taken as a principle by Locke] and alienated from those things which threaten destruction [the starting point which is taken

as a principle by Hobbes] . . . . Hence we must conclude that it is self-love which is the starting point (*principium*)" (*De Finibus* 3. 16–17). This tendency towards the preservation of what one is was generalized (apparently by Chrysippos) so that it extended to what is "one's own" and thus to one's offspring: "Furthermore, the Stoics consider it relevant to understand that parents naturally love their children, and here we find [as Hume finds] the origin of human society. . . . From this affection develops the feeling of mutual attraction which naturally brings men together" (*Fin.* 3. 62–63). Cf. the summary in the *De Officiis* 1. 11: "First of all, nature has endowed every animate being with a tendency to preserve itself, and so to avoid what seems harmful to life and body [Hobbes' starting point] and to secure what is needed for life—food, shelter, and other necessities [Locke's starting point]. Another common tendency is sexual desire (*coniunctionis adpetitus*) with the propagation of offspring as its purpose and some degree of concern with them [the origin of society for Hume]." The passage continues with "the crucial difference" between man and other animate beings which is his capacity to perceive relations (for this continuation, see chap. 10, n. 60). This perception is crucial to human nature in Hume. It is also a feature of Plutarch's treatment of οἰκείωσις as involving "the perception and recognition of what is like oneself" (*Stoicorum Veterum Fragmenta* 2. 721)—a treatment which lends itself to the development of a psychology of sympathy based on the resemblances between men. (For the moral implications of the resulting theory of universal human nature, see Cicero's claim, cited p. 330, this vol.). In Hume's revival of the Stoic starting point, successive relations are emphasized. This is not inconsistent with the Stoics having started with the individual. In Seneca's presentation of οἰκείωσις, "The animate being is first attached to itself, for there must be something to which other things are related" (*Epistulae* 121. 17).

43. In the context of the Stoic organic universe, the individual's attachments expanded, as he came to perceive relations as relations which were internal to himself, until a *consensus naturae* was finally reached. The principle of cohesion whereby like attracted like, so that the entire universe was held together, was identified as συμπάθεια.

44. *Treatise*, pp. 401–2; italics added.

45. See n. 12, above. Cf. both the traditional *Ad-petitio* and Hobbes' *Competitio* (p. 85, this vol.)

46. Hume offers the alternatives: "Men being naturally selfish, or endow'd only with a confin'd generosity" (*Treatise*, p. 519), but the second alternative is, as in Stoicism, an expansion of the first: "In the original frame of our mind, our strongest attention is confin'd to ourselves; our next is extended to our relations and acquaintance" (*ibid.*, p. 488).

47. *Ibid.*, p. 277.

48. *Leviathan*, pt. 1, chap. 13. The recurrence of the problem of resistance at the higher level of the progress of the deduction is illustrated by the way Hobbes describes encountering intellectual difficulties as stumbling over an impediment (see pp. 77, this vol.). In Hume the mind operates passively (characteristically it is "convey'd" [*Treatise*, p. 338]). It takes the route of least resistance by altering its direction (see n. 54, below). The association of ideas, which determines the route followed, is merely "a gentle force, which commonly prevails" (*ibid.*, p. 10). We have recognized (p. 79, this vol.) the sense in which for Hobbes all passions were movements in which the individual's endeavor is impeded, and therefore to be described as irascible passions had traditionally been described. But Hume's description of the passions is itself gentler, even in those instances where the individual's self-reference is in question: "The passage is smooth and open from the consideration of any person related to us to that of ourself. . . . But when the affections are once directed to ourself, the fancy passes not with the same facility from that object to any other person" (*ibid.*, p. 340).

49. *Treatise*, p. xxiii. See p. 193, this vol., for the way self-consciousness loses in Hume the methodological primacy it enjoyed in Hobbes.

50. *Ibid.*, p. 455.

51. See the citation p. 160, this vol.

52. *Treatise*, p. 14.

53. The construction of "a compleat system of sciences" involves in Hume a double transformation of knowledge. The first is the reduction of the science of nature to the more fundamental science of human nature (this "skeptical" reduction will be traced in the next chapter), and the second is the recognition, in this science of human nature, that the mind moves in a manner analogous to the movement of bodies in the Newtonian science of nature: [1] "We can never penetrate so far into the essence and construction of bodies, as to perceive the principle, on which their mutual influence depends [i.e, the Newtonian principle of gratitation]. 'Tis their constant union alone, with which we are acquainted. . . . If objects had not an uniform and regular conjunction with each other, we shou'd never arrive at any idea of cause and effect; [2] and even after all, the necessity, which enters into that idea, is nothing but a determination of the mind to pass from one object to its usual attendant, and infer the existence of one from the other" (*Treatise*, p. 400). Cf. p. 266: "We wou'd not willingly stop before we are acquainted with that energy in the cause, by which it operates on its effect; that tie, which connects them together; and that efficacious quality, on which the tie depends. . . . [1] We learn that this connexion, tie, or energy lies merely in ourselves, [2] and is nothing by that determination of the mind, which is acquir'd by custom [see n. 63, below], and causes us to make a transition from an object to its usual attendant." In these two citations Hume is dealing with the causal relation, but "all relations are nothing but a propensity to pass from one idea to another" (*ibid.*, p. 309).

54. Hume's theory of human nature is as mechanistic as Hobbes'. But since what Hume finds relevant in the theory of nature is not the principle of inertia, but the principle of gravitation, he characteristically envisages not one force resisting another force (as did Hobbes), but some alteration in the direction in which a force has previously been exercised. He will accordingly formulate the problem of regulating social relations in the following way: "No affection of the human mind has both a sufficient force, and a proper direction to counter-balance the love of gain. . . . There is no passion, therefore, capable of controlling the interested affection, but the very affection itself, by an alteration of its direction" (*ibid.*, p. 492). The regulations established are themselves "artificial, and seek their end in an oblique and indirect manner" (*ibid.*, p. 497); the moralist and the politician who regulate our conduct likewise "give a new direction" to our "natural passions and teach us that we can better satisfy our appetites in an oblique and artificial manner, than by their headlong and impetuous motion" (*ibid.*, 521). Political regulations are equally artificial in Hobbes, but there is nothing oblique about the structure they impose upon human movements. They are envisaged rather as their rectification (see p. 37, this vol.).

55. *Treatise*, pp. 455–56. Hume uses the terms "effects" and "consequences" interchangably. I use "effects" when I wish to stress the mechanistic character of his theory.

56. See p. 90, this vol.

57. *Treatise*, p. 499. In his more complete formulation, it is "from the selfishness and confin'd generosity of men . . . that justice derives its origin (*ibid.*, p. 495; cf. n. 46, above).

58. *Ibid.*, p. 533.

59. *Ibid.*, p. 499.

60. *Ibid.*, pp. 531, 535,

61. *Ibid.*, p. 499.

62. See pp. 125–26, this vol.

63. See n. 54, above. The contrast with Locke can be spelled out by taking as the paradigm case his analysis of the situation in which the individual acquires property (see p. 124). No one else was present besides the individual, and a single action on his part was sufficient to establish the property relation. But in Hume "this relation . . . is a species of cause and effect" (*Treatise,* p. 506), and in the least complicated illustration of the causal relation, we "suppose two objects to be presented to us, of which the one is the cause and the other the effect," and then find "that from the simple consideration of *one, or both* these objects we shall never perceive the tie, by which they are united" (*ibid.*, p. 162; italics added). A third conclusion follows besides the two previously indicated (see n. 53, above): [1] "this connexion, tie, or energy lies merely in ourselves, and [2] is nothing but that determination of the mind . . . which causes us to make a transition from an object to its usual attendant"; and [3] this determination is "acquired by custom." Thus we are to conclude in the case of property that [1] "'tis not the external and corporeal relation which forms the essence of property" (as in Locke), but "some internal relation," and that [2] "this external relation causes nothing in external objects, and has only an influence on the mind, by giving us a sense of duty in abstaining from that object" (*ibid.*, p. 527), and that [3] property is "stable possession" and could only be established by repeated comparisons of the relevant relations. In other words, the analysis required for the property relation is triadic, as in the cases of the performance of a just action or of the formation of family relations. It should be recognized, moreover, that the relations involved in the case of the performance of a just action can be compared with those involved in the case of property, and with those involved in the case of the family, because a just action is an action which (as the traditional definition indicates) renders to each individual what is due him as *his own,* and because a wife and offspring are forms of *property.* Thus Hume offers the following explanation of chastity: "Whoever considers the length and feebleness of human infancy, with the concern which both sexes naturally have for their offspring, will easily perceive, that there must be an union of male and female for the education of the young, and that this union must be of considerable duration. But in order to induce the men to impose on themselves this restraint, and undergo chearfully all the fatigues and expences, to which it subjects them, they must believe, that the children are their own, and that their natural instinct is not directed to a wrong object. . . . Now if we examine the structure of the human body, we shall find, that this security is very difficult to be attain'd; [Remember that the problem of justice for Hume is the problem of *securing* to the individual his own (external) property.] . . . and that since, in the copulation of the sexes, the principle of generation goes from the man to the woman, an error may easily take place on the side of the former, tho' it be utterly impossible with regard to the latter." Hence Hume reaches anatomically the *"a priori"* conclusion: "Men are induc'd to labour for the maintenance and education of their children, by the persuasion that they are really their own; and therefore 'tis reasonable, and even necessary, to give them some security in this particular" (*ibid.*, pp. 570–71).

64. *Letters of David Hume,* ed. J. Y. T. Grieg, 2 vols. (Oxford: Clarendon Press, 1932), 1:34.

65. Norman Kemp Smith, *The Philosophy of David Hume* (London: Macmillan, 1941), p. 8.

66. *Treatise,* p. 592.

67. See p. 27, this vol.

68. *Treatise,* p. 490.

69. *Ibid.*, pp. 498, 535.

70. See pp. 40, 82, this vol., for Stoic resistance to *res externae.* Their disturbing influence (in the form of passions) is illustrated by the following conventional formulation: "Every disturbance must be absent from the mind [vacandum autem omni est animi perturbatione (for the void thus created from Hume's point of view, see p. 169, this vol.)] . . .

so that there may be present that peace and security of mind which provide both moral stability (*constantia*) and moral stature (*dignitas*)" (*De Officiis* 1. 69). Compare also the difficulty one has in Hume (as we shall see in the next section) in maintaining one's moral stature: "Man is altogether insufficient to support himself; and . . . when you loosen all the holds, which he has of external objects, he immediately drops down in the deepest melancholy and despair" (*Treatise*, p. 352). Even though Hume's treatment of the problem of moral stability represents a break with the tradition, the problem itself remains for him the central moral problem. We have seen that it was already central in elucidations of Roman *gravitas* (see chap. 7, n. 40) in terms of Stoic *magnaminitas*. Cicero in particular inflated the statesman's problem of maintaining his precarious position in the state by conflating it with the Stoic philosopher's traditional problem of maintaining, by his *magnaminitas* and *fortitudo*, his lofty moral position in the universe. (See p. 42, this vol. for Cicero's argument that "when misfortune strikes philosophers do not have so far to fall.") The problem of stability recovered its moral generality in Aquinas (see p. 81, this vol.). In this chapter we are observing the revision its treatment undergoes in the psychological setting of Hume's theory of the association of ideas, and in the broader social context of his theory of human nature. In the next chapter we shall observe the analogous revision its treatment undergoes in the setting of a universe where falling bodies subscribe to the Newtonian theory of gravitation (see p. 200). Despite the *prima facie* implausibility of an idea falling, the analogy is asserted by Hume: "'Tis impossible the same ideas should fall regularly into complex ones . . . without some bond of union among them, some associating quality, by which one idea naturally introduces another. . . . The principles of union or cohesion among our simple ideas . . . in the imagination supply the place of that inseparable connexion, by which they are united in our memory. Here is a kind of ATTRACTION, which in the mental world will be found to have as extraordinary effects as in the natural . . ." (*Treatise*, pp. 10, 12–13).

71. *Ibid.*, p. 353.

72. *Ibid.*, p. 494. See p. 138, this vol.

73. Just as the crucial feature of the Newtonian universe in Hume's view is relational —the "communication" of motion from one body to another, "their attraction and mutual cohesion" (see p. 158, this vol.); just as the crucial problem of the understanding is relational—the association of ideas; just as the crucial problem of the passions is relational— "the propensity we have to sympathize with others and to receive by communication their inclinations and sentiments'"; so Hume is concerned less with the original acquisition of property (with which Locke was concerned, as he was with the way we originally acquire ideas) than with the relational problem of the "easy transition" of external goods (and once this problem is settled) with the problem posed by a too "rigid stability"—i.e., the relational problem "Of the Transference of Property" (pp. 514–16) from one person to another.

74. *Ibid.*, p. 303.

75. *Ibid.*, p. 309.

76. See p. 137.

77. *Treatise*, p. 353.

78. See n. 70, above.

79. See p. 137, this vol.

80. See p. 123, this vol.

81. David Hume, *The Philosophical Works*, ed. T. H. Green and T. H. Grose, 4 vols. (London: Longmans, Green, 1882), 3: 203.

82. *Letters*, 1: 10.

83. *Ibid.*, 14.

84. *Ibid.*, 17.

85. *The Theory of Moral Sentiments* (London: Henry G. Bohn, 1853), p. 395.

86. *Ibid.*, p. 272.

87. *Treatise*, pp. 502–3.

88. *An Enquiry Concerning the Principles of Morals*, ed. L. A. Selby-Bigge (Oxford: Clarendon Press, 1902), pp. 192–93.

89. *Ibid.*, p. 193.

90. *Ibid.*, p. 194.

91. *Wealth of Nations*, 2: 200.

92. *Ibid.*, pp. 202, 201.

93. See p. 124, this vol.

94. *Treatise*, p. 489.

95. *Principles of Morals*, p. 195.

96. *Ibid.*, p. 188.

97. *Treatise*, p. 495. See p. 000, this vol.

98. *Principles of Morals*, p. 188.

99. See p. 133, this vol.

100. See p. 134, this vol.

101. *Treatise*, p. 493. See p. 138, this vol.

102. See p. 163, this vol., *Principles of Morals*, p. 183; in both citations italics are added.

103. *Lectures On Justice, Police, Revenue and Arms*, ed. Edwin Cannan (Oxford: Clarendon Press, 1896), p. 157.

104. *Ibid.*, p. xxvii.

105. *Wealth of Nations*, 1: 19–20; italics added. This is perhaps the explanation which Cannan could not find when he commented, "It is not easy to explain why the first two sections were omitted from *The Wealth of Nations* (*Lectures*, p. xxvii). These were the sections entitled in the Glasgow Lectures, "Of the Natural Wants of Mankind," and "That all the Arts are Subservient to the Natural Wants of Mankind."

106. *Wealth of Nations*, 1: 4.

107. *Principles of Morals*, p. 194; see p. 171, this vol.

108. *Wealth of Nations*, 1: 14.

109. *Ibid.*, p. 12.

110. *Ibid.*, p. 400.

111. See p. 86, this vol.

112. See p. 18, this vol., for my initial identification of this tradition as "esthetic."

113. For the full citation, see p. 87, this vol.

114. For the full citation, see vol. 1, pp. 96–97.

115. For Hobbes' conception of "visible power," see p. 94, this vol.

116. See p. 122, this vol.

117. See p. 138, this vol.

118. The metaphor is Mill's. See n. 11, above.

119. See p. 154, this vol.

120. The social context whose development has been traced in this chapter is an expanded theory of human nature, even though an emphasis on unintended social consequences distinguishes it from the individualistic theory of human nature. Thus this social context is not to be confused with the Continental socio-historical context which was discussed in Part I (see p. 65). It is true that unintended social consequences are the most obvious point of transition from the first context to the second. But although they will receive in Hegel and Marx a socio-historical explanation (see chap. 3, n. 43), they are drawn back in Smith's *Moral Sentiments* into the context of his theory of human nature. In dealing with "The Influence of Fortune upon the Sentiments of Mankind," he begins by reasserting the humanistic distinction between virtue and fortune: "Whatever praise or blame can be due to any action, must belong, either, first, to the intention or affection of the heart, from which it proceeds; or, secondly, to the external action or movement of the body, which this affection gives occasion to; or, lastly, to the good or bad consequences, which actually, and in fact, proceed from it. . . . That the two last of these three circumstances cannot be the foundation of any praise or blame, is abundantly evident. . . . The consequences which actually, and in fact, happen to proceed from any action, are, if possible, still more indifferent either to praise or blame, than even the external movement of the body. As they depend, not upon the agent, but upon fortune, they cannot be the proper foundation for any sentiment, of which his character and conduct are the objects" (*Moral Sentiments*, pp. 133–34). But Smith then goes on to concede, "Scarce, in any one instance, perhaps, will our sentiments be found, after examination, to be entirely regulated by this rule, which we all acknowledge ought entirely to regulate them" (*ibid.*, p. 134). He then explains this irregularity. It is this explanation which draws unintended consequences back into the context of his theory of human nature: "Nor is that irregularity of sentiments altogether without its utility, by which the merit of an unsuccessful attempt to serve, and much more that of mere good inclinations and kind wishes, appears to be imperfect. Man was made for action, and to promote by the exertion of his faculties such changes in the external circumstances . . . as may seem most favorable to the happiness of all. . . . He is made to know, that the praise of good intentions, without the merit of good offices, will be but of little avail to excite either the loudest acclamations of the world, or even the highest degree of self-applause" (*ibid.*, pp. 153–54).

It is also true that a fuller account of the formation of a social context in Hume and Smith would take into consideration continental contributions—most notably Montesquieu's. For Hume's relation to Montesquieu, see vol. 1, p. 69, and accompanying n. 55. A student's recollection of Smith's lectures on justice (see p. 220, this vol.) describes him as having "followed the plan that seems to be suggested by Montesquieu, endeavouring to trace the gradual progress of jurisprudence . . . from the rudest to the most refined ages" ("An Account of the Life and Writings of Adam Smith," *The Theory of the Moral Sentiments* [London: Henry G. Bohn, 1853], p. xvii; for this report, see chap. 14, n. 118). In a third volume, *The Verdict of History*, I intend to study first the development of social thought during the eighteenth century, up until the link with the theory of human nature is broken in Smith's *Wealth of Nations*: I shall then trace the reconstruction of this social context as a socio-historical context. Montesquieu's, Hume's, and Smith's contributions to this line of development is sometimes identified as a conservative tradition, in contrast with the liberal tradition whose development we are now tracing. But the two traditions cannot be laid side by side, since even what is meant by tradition is differently defined in their two different contexts.

A full study of the development of this second tradition is, in any case, not directly relevant to the interpretation of Mill's liberalism. In the long run Mill makes little significant use (as we shall see in chap. 18 and in the Conclusion) of any theory of social history. In fact he blurs the differences between a social context and a socio-historical context. In his letter to Comte (January 28, 1843) in which he indicates that he has had to postpone the publication of his *Logic* because of the readjustments suggested by his better understanding of Comte's theory of social history (see chap. 3, n. 21), he attempts to cement still further an intellectual alliance with Comte by extolling his Scotch predecessors as virtually French thinkers: "Le véritable esprit scientifique est très rare chez nous, et si quelques-uns le possèdent jusqu'a un certain point, ils l'ont, le plus souvent, puisé dans les livres français; sauf peut-être les écossais, chez qui l'éducation publique a un caractère plus français qu'anglais, ce qui explique le mérite éminent des penseurs écossais depuis Kaimes [*sic*] et Ferguson jusqu'a mon père qui mort en 1836, fut le dernier survivant de cette grande école" (*Collected Works*, 13: 566). In his reply (February 27, 1843) Comte is indulgent towards Mill's "filiation écossaise." In his letter of October 5, 1844, Mill reasserts his lineage, but at least seems to realize that his father should be omitted from the list: "Je trouve qu'il y a une analogie réelle dans la tournure de l'esprit écossais et de l'esprit français. Vous n'avez certainement pu méconnaître à quel point les Hume, les Ferguson, les Adam Smith, les Millar, les Brown, les Reid, même les Chalmers ressemblent intellectuellement à des français" (*ibid.*, p. 638). By this time Comte is as much indebted to Mill for financial aid as Mill is to Comte for intellectual aid, and in his reply of October 21, 1844, Comte is "très disposé à croire que l'installation britannique du positivisme devra s'opére essentiellement par l'élaboration écossaise." (For Comte's two letters in reply, see *Lettres inédites de John Stuart Mill à Auguste Comte, publiées avec les réponses de Comte*, ed. L. Levy-Bruhl [Paris: F. Alcan, 1899], pp. 155–65, 359–69.)

14

Reason and Sentiment

The Moderns have not treated Morals as well as the Antients merely from their Reasoning turn, which carried them away from Sentiment.—Hume

VIRTUE AND FORTUNE

When the principle of utility "burst upon" Mill in his youth, the point of greatest impact was Bentham's exposure of traditional "reasoning in morals and legislation."[1] A fundamental feature of this reasoning in morals was a distinction between virtue as really one's own and external goods as belonging to the sphere of fortune.[2] The undermining of this traditional distinction Bentham himself credited to economic progress, as assessed in *The Wealth of Nations.* Recalling the Stoic plaint that wealth belongs "not to the owner but to fortune," he retorted:

> It is slippery and unsteady; which is, in plain English, the varnish being stripped off, it is liable to be lost. But . . . as is well observed by Adam Smith, in England at least, . . . for one man who has lost what he had, you have a good thousand who have not only kept it, but added to it.[3]

Those humanists who cannot make Smith's social calculation, Bentham dismisses as "blindfold travellers in the paths of commonplace." They are blindfold because they are "wholly heedless . . . of the changes which time has introduced into the value and security of wealth," so that what "in ancient days was with great propriety associated with uncertainty and mutability, might now be made to represent possession in its maximum of security."[4] A fortune is no longer a matter of fortune.

The preceding two chapters have suggested that "the changes which time had introduced into the value and security of wealth" were more than economic changes. Also involved were intellectual changes in the conception of what was valuable, such as Hume's readjustment of the relation between virtue and external goods, and the concomitant reduction of the virtue of justice to securing to each his own property.[5]

Another intellectual change is the triumph of Bentham's "plain English" over the Latin language:

> Worst of all, it [wealth] is not ours—it is not in our possession but in the temerity of Fortune. 'Non in nostra potestate, sed in Fortunae temeritate.' In this beautiful union of rhetoric with poetry—in this dance of Fortune between the two *tates,* lies the strength of the argument; which strength, . . . in the process of being decanted out of Latin into English, mostly evaporates.[6]

This intellectual change is crucial; Latin arguments so far have still retained considerable strength when decanted into English. Bentham's confidence in "plain English" may seem to echo Locke's confidence in his "coarse thoughts,"[7] as well as to be prophetic of the confidence in ordinary English which later analytic philosophers will profess when they undertake to evaporate the strength of traditional arguments. Mill does in fact admit that Bentham's method derives in some measure from Locke's analytic method.[8] But Locke did not denounce traditional reasoning as such; he singled out Filmer. What has to be taken into account in this and the next chapter is the general scope of Bentham's denunciation, for what the youthful Mill will exult over on first reading Bentham is the fact that "all previous moralists are superseded,"[9] Bentham initiated "nothing less than a revolution in philosophy."[10]

Revolutions in philosophy are always reappraisals of the philosophical tradition. Mill's exultation gains its unbridled sweep from Bentham's reappraisal of traditional "modes of reasoning" as "dogmatism in disguise, imposing its sentiments upon others under cover of sounding expressions which convey no reason for the sentiment, but set up the sentiment as its own reason."[11] The dogmatism in question Bentham himself describes as an attempt to prevail "upon the reader to accept of the author's sentiment or opinion as a reason for itself," in order to avoid "the obligation of appealing to any external standard."[12] The author's procedure thus exhibits the same reflexive structure as traditional moral virtue in its opposition to external fortune.

The reader who accepts the sentiment or opinion is accepting at the same time the "ipse-dixit principle" which provides tradition with its warrant.[13]

Morals and Rhetoric

In the next chapter we shall take up Bentham's and Mill's conception of intellectual progress as the stripping off of varnish, the removal of blindfolds, in order to expose the reflexive and merely subjective character of traditional reasoning as opposed to the "external standard" of utility. We shall then deal with the adjustment in the relation between internal and external the exposure would bring about. But this procedure of exposure presupposes a reappraisal of the traditional procedure as blindfolding, varnishing, disguising. We must accordingly first consider in the present chapter how the tradition could lend itself to being identified as a disguise, and more specifically as a "cover of sounding expressions which convey no reason for the sentiment, but set up the sentiment as its own reason." A revolution that supersedes all previous moralists might seem to obliterate earlier revolutions which we have taken the trouble to investigate as background for interpreting Mill. But Bentham's and the youthful Mill's delineation of the tradition they are revolting against betrays the lineaments of two earlier revolutions, which can largely be credited to Cicero and Hume.

"Nothing is more usual in philosophy," Hume points out in the *Treatise,* "than to talk of the combat of passion and reason, to give the preference to reason, and to assert that men are only so far virtuous as they conform themselves to its dictates." Thus "if any other motive or principle challenge the direction of his conduct, he ought to oppose it, 'till it be entirely subdu'd [the Stoic position], or at least brought to a conformity with that superior principle [the Platonic and Aristotelian position]." On this way of thinking, Hume adds, "the greatest part of moral philosophy, ancient and modern, seems to be founded."[14] We have already examined the way the greatest part of ancient moral philosophy (in the form that it was inherited by modern moral philosophy) was structured around the opposition between reason and the passions. Cicero reconciled Stoicism with Platonism (and Aristotelianism) as positions which alike gave the preference to reason, in opposition to

Epicurean utilitarianism, which surrendered to the passions, leaving the individual at the mercy of external circumstances controlled by fortune. Hume and Bentham are indebted to Cicero for this reconstruction of the moral tradition as a tradition committed to the rational control the individual must maintain in opposition at once to external circumstances and to utilitarianism.[15] This reconstruction survives Bentham's dismissal of "Ciceronian trash."[16] and his turning the opposition around, so that utilitarianism becomes rational control as opposed to the sentimentalism of Stoicism, Platonism, and all other schools of philosophy.[17]

Bentham's delineation of the opposition between utilitarianism and the moral tradition further takes for granted the methodological relevance which the passions had gained as moral sentiments in the eighteenth century.[18] In the *Treatise* Hume lumped ancient and modern philosophy together. In the *Enquiry Concerning the Principles of Morals*, Hume draws a distinction: "The ancient philosophers, though they often affirm, that virtue is nothing but conformity to reason, yet, in general seem to consider morals as deriving their existence from taste and sentiment."[19] In contrast, "the Moderns" can be criticized for not having "treated Morals so well as the Antients, merely from their Reasoning turn, which carried them away from Sentiment."[20] Here the substantive argument that was fitted in the *Treatise* to the opposition between reason and passion, between virtue and fortune, is displaced by a methodological argument with respect to the way morals should be treated. Hume is criticizing as rationalistic the procedure of Hobbes, Locke, and other moderns, and he is commending the ancient procedure, which he identifies as a sentimental treatment of morals.

This shift in Hume's appraisal from a substantive to a methodological issue involves a readjustment in the relation between internal and external and between moral philosophy and "other studies." What is at issue in *The Principles of Morals* is not the ambivalence Cicero had introduced in his treatment of the relation between morals and politics (between moral self-control and external political control)—the ambivalence which we saw in chapters 10 and 11 was resolved in different ways by Machiavelli and Hobbes. Nor is the issue the ambivalence Cicero had introduced in the relation between morals and economics (between moral self-control, as the control of what is distinctively one's own, and the external domain of fortune)—the ambivalence we have seen in chapters 12 and 13 was exploited by Locke but largely disappeared with the erosion of the distinction in Hume. We shall now see that the treatment of morals which Hume identifies as sentimental is the rhetorical strand in the composition of the humanistic tradition.

In this tradition the orator was a "vir bonus dicendi peritus."[21] Cicero always regarded the orator (as he did the statesman) primarily as "the moral man"—as the individual whose reason controlled his passions. (All three were, of course, the same individual in the case of Cicero.) But when this individual became "proficient in speaking," he risked a certain ambivalence in his relation to other men which is comparable to the other ambivalent relations we have already explored as Cicero's bequest. As a moral individual he had to maintain his virtue by suppressing the passions as movements of his mind which would disturb the stability of his self-control, but as an orator he had to move the minds of other men, in order to conciliate them.[22] As a moral philosopher, moreover, Cicero had continued the task of conciliation at a higher level. His reconciliation of Stoicism with Platonism (and Aristotelianism) was the transformation of the Stoic moral tradition into a humanistic tradition—that is, into a treatment of moral problems which was sentimental in the sense that it was designed to move men's minds, which was something, he felt, Stoicism had failed to do.[23] Thus the moral tradition can be denounced by Bentham as "an attempt to teach morals by declamation,"[24] though the real measure of Cicero's accomplishment is that Bentham would include along with Cicero in this denunciation the Stoics and Plato.[25]

Hume's contribution here must be considered too. Bentham may reject as rhetorical sentimentalism not only the moral tradition but also Hume's concessions in his own moral theory to rhetoric, sentiment and tradition, but Bentham thereby retains not only Hume's identification of the moral tradition as a rhetorical and sentimental tradition but also Hume's identification of rhetoric as a sentimental method, and of tradition itself as a deposit of moral sentiments.

In the next section, we shall have to trace the emergence of the moral sentiments as the subject-matter of Hume's moral theory before we can deal with his antithesis between ancient sentimentalism and modern rationalism and with the way he resolves in his own moral theory the ambivalence introduced by Cicero in the relation between morals and rhetoric. We shall then have to reexamine the differences we have already discerned between the *Treatise* and *The Principles of Morals,* for it is only with the shift from the substantive opposition between reason and the passions to the methodological opposition between reason and the sentiments that Hume's moral theory becomes a full-fledged rhetorical theory whose construction entails the reconstruction of the humanistic tradition as an explicitly rhetorical tradition.

The Agent and the Spectator

"In resolving the controversy . . . concerning the general foundation of morals—whether they be derived from reason or sentiment"—it is "a very simple method" that Hume proposes to follow in *The Principles of Morals:* "We shall analyze . . . personal merit; we shall consider every attribute of the mind which renders a man an object either of esteem and affection, or of hatred and contempt."[26] The simplicity of Hume's method is the result of its conformity with the social procedure by which personal merit is in fact acquired: "By our continual and earnest pursuit of a character, a name, a reputation in the world, we bring our deportment and conduct frequently in review, and consider how they appear in the eyes of those who approach and regard us."[27] The theorist can similarly compile the "catalogue" of the "mental qualities which form personal merit" by "entering into his own breast for a moment" in order "to consider whether or not he should desire to have this or that quality ascribed to him, and whether such or such imputation would proceed from a friend or an enemy."[28]

This very simple method works because Hume assumes that "the minds of men are mirrors to each other" and "reflect each others' emotions."[29] No individual's mind remains privileged, as it did in the humanistic tradition, where the example displayed to others for imitation, as in a mirror, is the superior individual's mind. Nor is the process of reflection finally distorted, as it was in Hobbes, by the magnifying glass of the individual's endeavor to become superior to others and to become conscious of himself as superior.[30] To this extent Hobbes retained the individualistic reflexive approach of the humanistic tradition. The magnifying glass of self-interest (especially when it took the form of "internal gloriation") disturbed the kind of balance (which is maintained by the comparative structure of Hume's analysis) between the passions of "esteem" and "contempt," "affection" and "hatred." In

Hobbes' lopsided analysis, the hostile reactions of hatred and contempt were more prevalent than affection and esteem. In Hume, Hobbes' "internal gloriation" becames "vanity." Hume does not overlook the distorting influence of "vanity," but its satisfaction depends on the reactions of other men, so it must be regarded "a social passion" and a "bond of union among men," rather than a merely selfish passion.[31]

Since the subjective distortion could not be eliminated in Hobbes, his only methodological resort was to appeal to the individual—"Read Thyself."[32] Hobbes used this metaphor because his appeal to individual self-knowledge was also an appeal from the erudition of the humanistic tradition as a literary tradition. Hume enters his own breast too, but only for a moment, and there is no inconsistency in his entry there in order to compile a catalog of virtues and yet finding this catalog already available in Cicero's *On Duties*.[33] Just as the individual in Hume arrives at an evaluation of himself by accepting the evaluations of other men, so Hume as a theorist accepts the values established and cataloged by tradition.

Hume has to accept tradition because he is an empiricist. To have an experience is for Hume to perceive something—to make an observation; to repeat an experience is to observe the resemblance between the experiences; the comparison of repeated observations establishes the customary associations which Hume as a theorist is himself observing, whether these associations compose property rights or the catalog of the virtues. By comparing ourselves these two processes of association, we can get at the structure of Hume's theory as a structure of comparisons. Having defined an individual's property as "some object related to him,"[34] Hume analyzes this relation as a social relationship established by a convention to bestow stability on the possession of external goods.[35] This convention "acquires force . . . by our repeated experience of the inconveniences of transgressing it," and "this experience" in turn "assures us still more that the sense of interest has become common to all our fellows, and gives us a confidence of the future regularity of their conduct."[36] The convention to bestow stability on the possession of external goods thus itself acquires stability as a social convention. The experiences involved are the individual's repeated observations of the resemblances (or other relations) between his experiences and his fellows.

Repeated observations, their social reinforcement and increasing stabilization similarly establish the catalog of virtues. At the lowest level repeated observation and comparison of another man's actions are required: in attributing a virtue to a man "we are never to consider any single action, . . . but only the quality and character from which the action proceeds," since "these alone are durable enough to affect our sentiments concerning the person."[37] When we turn from the single person to analyze our sentiments toward him we find that these have been determined not only by our observation of his actions and comparison of our observations, but also by our comparison of these observations with our previous observations of other men's actions. Indeed we have drawn on these previous observations in arriving at some conception of the virtue we are attributing to him. To go on to compile a complete catalog of these virtues, we have only "to consider every attribute of the mind which renders a man an object of esteem or affection."[38]

There is a further resemblance to be observed between the process of establishing this catalog and the process of establishing property rights. When "a convention" is established "to bestow stability on the possession of external goods, . . . every one knows what he may safely possess and the passions [sc., to possess external goods] are restrained in their partial and contradictory movements."[39] These movements must likewise be restrained in order to stabilize our moral judgments:

> Our situation, with regard both to persons and things, is in continual fluctuation. . . . Besides, every particular man has a peculiar position with regard to others; and 'tis impossible we cou'd ever converse together on any reasonable terms, were each of us to consider characters and persons, only as they appear from his peculiar point of view. In order, therefore to prevent those continual *contradictions,* and arrive at a more *stable* judgment of things, we fix on some *steady* and *general* points of view; and always in our thoughts, place ourselves in them, whatever may be our present situation.[40]

A More Stable Judgment

The experience which Hume picks as a crucial illustration of this process of stabilizing our observations suggests the extent to which his catalog of virtues emerges from the humanistic tradition as the steadiest and most general point of view:

Our servant, if diligent and faithful, may excite stronger sentiments of love and kindness than Marcus Brutus, as represented in history; but we say not upon that account that the former character is more laudable than the later. We know, that were we to approach equally near to that renown'd patriot, he wou'd command a much higher degree of affection and admiration. Such corrections are common with regard to all the senses; and indeed 'twere impossible we cou'd ever make use of language, or communicate our sentiments to one another, did we not correct the momentary appearances of things, and overlook our present situation.[41]

What Hume has in effect added to the humanistic tradition is an analysis of the process of observation, comparison, and correction by which it was established[42]—through the repeated experiences of individuals, each of whom had corrected his momentary impressions of things and overlooked his present situation by observing the resemblance between it and some comparable situation which had already been transformed into an exemplary situation through repetition. (Hume has also added a comparison of this process of observing "persons" with a process of observing "things," and I shall make further use of the comparison in the next section.) But we must remember what Hume has subtracted from the humanistic tradition—the self-control which the individual exercised in correcting and surmounting his momentary impressions of things (e.g., when Brutus as a Stoic triumphs over his fear of pain and of death). Thus although this analysis enables Hume to accommodate the traditional humanistic virtues (and such exemplary representatives of these virtues as Brutus), it at the same time undermines the traditional humanistic conception of virtue, as we saw in the preceding chapter was the case with the virtue of justice.[43] Hume's analysis precludes any individualistic analysis of moral action such as Cicero's where the individual, by his self-control, retains the initiative even when his actions bring him into relation to other men. Hume's analysis embodies a theory of social control—of the associative and sympathetic way in which the individual reacts to others' actions and they to his. Thus when Hume complains that "the Ancient philosophers" often define virtue as "nothing but conformity to reason," he views this definition as their answer to the question of the respective influence to be accorded reason and the passions on moral actions, and he refutes this definition by proving "that reason alone can never be a motive to any action of the will."[44] But the refutation also marks Hume's passage to a question which cannot be answered by reference to the motives of the individual alone. The question of the respective influence of reason and sentiment on the formation of moral judgments (and ultimately, therefore, on the catalog of moral virtues) is a question which Hume resolves by introducing a spectator as well as an agent:

> The hypothesis which we embrace is plain. It maintains that morality is determined by sentiment. It defines virtue to be 'whatever mental action or quality gives to a spectator the pleasing sentiment of approbation.'[45]

With this redefinition of virtue, what is theoretically relevant is no longer the agent alone but the spectator observing the agent and the entire system of social control which is built into the process of observation. In the light of this redefinition, Hume can commend "the ancient philosophers" for having "in general" considered "morals as deriving their existence from taste and sentiment."[46] This commendation is more fundamental in Hume's eyes than his original complaint about the humanistic definition, since what is now at stake is the very existence of morals.

The shift from self-control to social control we watched take place in the case of the virtue of justice. But we have now traced the way moral phenomena generally derive their existence from the process of observing, comparing, correcting, and thereby stabilizing observations until they are built up into the traditional catalog of the moral virtues. At last we reach the higher level where a science of human nature emerges from this process. When Hume applies the method of "gleaning up experiments in this science from a cautious observation of human life," the experiments in question are merely experiences of the process of observation, judgment, and comparison. The experiences need only be "judiciously collected and compared."[47] In short, Hume's theory is continuous with these experiences, and it is this continuity which renders it inherently traditional.

Stability and Solidity

The later utilitarians regarded Hume as in some sense the founder of utilitarianism, and they were distressed by his traditionalism and sentimentalism. But they had an explanation for his lapse: he rejected the rationalism of the moderns (e.g., of Hobbes and Locke) and succumbed to tradition and sentiment because of what Mill stigmatizes as Hume's "absolute skepticism in speculation."[48] Before we can appreciate the moral relevance of this charge, we have to turn back from Hume's analysis of moral experience in terms of the spectator's perception of "persons" to his analysis of experience in terms of the observer's perception of "things."

Hume's skepticism involves a loss of confidence in the reasoning turn of the moderns even before he reaches the moral sentiments. When he develops his "Sceptical System" at the end of the first book of the *Treatise,* he takes as "the fundamental principle" of "the modern philosophy" the assertion that "colours, sounds, tastes, smells, heat and cold" are "nothing but impressions in the mind derived from the operations of external objects, and without any resemblance to the qualities of the objects."[49] But he argues that skepticism cannot halt at this assertion. Once secondary qualities are denied to be qualities of physical objects themselves, the objectivity of their primary qualities can no longer be demonstrated.

The fact that "solidity" is the primary quality which Hume selects for attention in this argument suggests that the modern philosopher he has particularly in mind is Locke. The epistemological implications that carry over from the skepticism of the first book of the *Treatise* to his later treatment of the moral sentiments may emerge more clearly if we renew our earlier comparison between the atomism implicit in Locke's *Essay* and his individualism in the *Two Treatises.* Solidity is indispensable to Locke's atomistic conception of "one single body alone."[50] If we grant Locke's conviction that his thoughts are "coarse," we can also recognize some correlation between his conception of the individual who acquires property in the *Treatises,* to the exclusion of other men, and his conception of "a solid substance" as taking up space "so to possess it that it excludes all other solid substances."[51]

Hume agrees that to perceive a physical object as solid is to perceive that it is impenetrable by another physical object, but he argues that when we observe the distinction between these two objects we are relying on such subjective impressions as color, so that if color is merely a subjective impression, solidity cannot be attributed to the physical object itself. This argument of course indicates that the problem of solidity cannot be treated by reference to any single physical object alone but only by reference to its relation to another physical object, as this relation is established in the mind of the observer.[52] Thus Hume's skepticism takes for him the more relevant form of discovering that the ostensibly objective relationship which Locke had presupposed (the principle of causality) is a subjective relationship (the effect of the operation of the principle of association). With this discovery, a further reaction takes place in the mind of the observer:

> We desire to know the ultimate and operating principle, as something which resides in the external object. . . . This is our aim in all our studies and reflections: And how must we be disappointed when we learn that this connexion, tie, or energy lies merely in ourselves.[53]

This disappointment entails an admission of the "weakness" of our faculties, and Hume's skepticism collapses into "melancholy" and "despair."[54] The comparison with Locke can be carried through by considering the ground on which Locke singled out the idea of solidity:

> There is no idea which we receive more constantly from sensation than solidity. Whether we move or rest, in what posture soever we are, we always feel something under us that supports us, and hinders our farther sinking downwards.[55]

Hume is less secure. Just as the individual external object loses its traditional solidity to the principle of association, which establishes its relation to other external objects and relocates this relation in the mind of the observer, so the individual mind loses its traditional integrity and stability to the principles of association and sympathy, which establish its relation to external objects and to other minds and relocate these relations as effects of processes of observation and comparison. In other words, there is a resemblance between the epistemological predicament of the skeptic (in the first book of the *Treatise*) and the moral predicament of the individual (in the second book of the *Treatise*) who finds himself "altogether insufficient to support himself," so that "when you loosen all the holds he has on external objects, he immediately drops down into the deepest melancholy and despair."[56]

Does observing this resemblance seem to push the comparison too far? Hume himself comes to my rescue. He points out that such "ideas" as "descent" are "methods of thinking and of expressing ourselves" which "are not of so little consequence as they may appear at first sight." It is "as if our ideas acquire a kind of gravity from their objects."[57] The resemblance of all forms of relationship to gravitation is pervasive in Hume and is relevant to all processes of stabilization and consolidation, including processes of observation and comparison.

We have seen how the individual's experience of resemblance and other relations becomes reinforced and stabilized in Hume by becoming, through the mechanism of sympathy, a social experience. This mechanism is reversible in its operation. Hume's skepticism is a "system" just as much as his analysis of association or of sympathy. It, too, is a phase in his analysis of his system of human nature as a whole, but it is a phase in which relations are loosened, instead of becoming mutually cohesive. Skepticism is not a social experience: other men cannot share sympathetically in the skeptic's disappointment, melancholy, and despair; he experiences a loosening of his relations to other men at the same time that he experiences the loosening of the relations between his mind and external objects. His epistemological predicament is compounded by the moral predicament which it resembles: "Such is my weakness, that I feel all my opinions loosen and fall of themselves, when unsupported by the approbation of others."[58]

Anatomy and Painting

Hume's skepticism is not, however, the "absolute skepticism" which a loss of confidence in reason necessarily represents to Mill as a rationalist. No form of philosophical skepticism is ever absolute. Philosophical skepticism is the discounting or dismissal of previous criteria of relevance in favor of other criteria which relocate the subject-matter of philosophy. Hume's skeptical reduction of the primary qualities of objects to secondary qualities—to subjective impressions in the mind—implements the methodological requirement that "we ought always to correct the first judgment, derived from the nature of the object, by another judgment derived from the nature of the understanding."[59] Hume is systematically achieving this correction when he establishes a science of human nature as "the only foundation for the other sciences,"[60] including physical science, and begins with the nature of the understanding in the first book of the *Treatise*.

A comparable methodological adjustment is carried out in the third book by Hume's redefinition of virtue in the fashion we have traced as the derivation from the sentiments of both morals and the humanistic tradition in moral theory. When our diligent and faithful servant excites stronger sentiments of love and kindness than Marcus Brutus, but we say not upon that account that the former character is more laudable than the latter, what we say represents our correction of our first judgment of the object by a second judgment derived from our experience of the process of making moral judgments. This moral experience Hume compares with perceptual experience:

> Such corrections are common with regard to all the senses; and indeed 'twere impossible we cou'd ever make use of language, or communicate our sentiments to one another, did we not correct the momentary appearances of things, and overlook our present situation.[61]

Hume further compares the two processes of observation and judgment by carrying over into morals the distinction between the primary and secondary qualities of objects:

> Vice and virtue . . . may be compar'd to sounds, colours, heat and cold, which, according to modern philosophy, are not qualities in objects, but perceptions in the mind: And this discovery in morals, like that other in physics, is to be regarded as a considerable advancement of the speculative sciences.[62]

This skeptical discovery in morals Hume credits to Francis Hutcheson. And before Hume published this third book he sent the manuscript to Hutcheson, drawing his attention to the passage I have just cited and asking, "Is not this laid a little too strong?"[63] Hume is seeking advice from the respected and influential Hutcheson on passages which might be defective in a "Point of Prudence." Another purpose which Hume may have had in mind is to canvas the issues which divided him from Hutcheson over the methodological implications of this discovery. Hutcheson in his lectures on morals "displayed a fervent and persuasive eloquence which was irresistible,"[64] and he must have urged (in a previous letter to Hume which has been lost) more rhetorical fervor on Hume, for Hume's reply is a defense of his own coldly theoretical analysis:

> What affected me most in your Remarks is your observing that there wants a certain Warmth in the Cause of Virtue, which, you think, all good Men

wou'd relish, and cou'd not displease amidst abstract Enquirys. I must Own this has not happen'd by Chance. . . . There are different ways of examining the Mind as well the Body. One may consider it either as an Anatomist or as a Painter; either to discover its most secret Springs & Principles or to describe the Grace and Beauty of its Actions. I imagine it impossible to conjoin these two Views. Where you pull off the Skin, and display all the minute Parts, there appears something trivial, even in the noblest Attitudes and most vigorous Actions. . . . Any Warm Sentiment of Morals, I am afraid, wou'd have the Air of Declamation amidst abstract Reasonings.[65]

Hume is answering a humanist, and the analogical distinction he is drawing is a commonplace which he has perhaps been prompted to use by Cicero's criticism as a rhetorician of the Stoic dialectical analysis as "laying bare the bones" in a manner "too minute" to "move men's minds."[66] Whatever may have been Hutcheson's reply, Hume added to his manuscript, before publishing the third book, a paragraph in which he does briefly display rhetorical warmth in the cause of virtue. But he then repeats what had been his answer to Hutcheson's criticism, "Such reflexions require a work a-part, very different from the genius of the present."[67] And he brings out the difference between his own moral theory and a rhetorical performance by incorporating in his conclusion to the third book his letter's analogous distinction between anatomy and painting.

Philosophical Principles

This analogy, however, does not remain for Hume the afterthought it is in the *Treatise*. It turns up in the first section of the *Enquiry Concerning Human Understanding*. The different implications it takes on there raise again the question which we faced at the end of the last chapter of the differences between the *Treatise* and the *Enquiries*. But since the *Enquiry Concerning Human Understanding* abbreviates and reorganizes materials from the first book of the *Treatise*, we also face this question as a question of the relation between the epistemological skepticism of the first book and the esthetic sentimentalism of the third book. These two attitudes, moreover, are lumped together in the youthful Mill's contemptuous utilitarian verdict:

Hume possessed powers of a very high order; but regard for truth formed no part of his character. He reasoned with surprising acuteness; but the object of his reasonings was, not to attain truth, but to shew that it is unattainable. His mind, too, was completely enslaved by a taste for literature.[68]

The question of the relation between the third book and the rest of the *Treatise* (as well as the overlapping question of the relation between the *Treatise* and the *Enquiries*) is also posed by Bentham's interpretation of the *Treatise,* even though he had been converted to utilitarianism by reading the third book:

> I would not wish to send the Reader to any other than this [sc., the third book of the *Treatise*], which if I recollect aright, stands clear of the objections that have of late been urged, with so much vehemence, against the work in general. As to the two first, the Author himself, I am inclined to think, is not ill disposed, at present, to join with those who are of the opinion, that they might, without any great loss to the science of Human Nature, be dispensed with. . . . But, after all retrenchments, there will still remain enough to have laid mankind under indelible obligations. That the foundations of all virtue are laid in utility is there demonstrated. . . .[69]

But what *was* the author's own opinion? The "objections" that Bentham is acknowledging had been advanced by James Beattie in his attack on Hume's *Sophistry and Scepticism*. Bentham's reference to the author's own disposition is a reference to Hume's public disavowal of the *Treatise*. The second edition (1777) of Hume's works did not include the *Treatise,* and appeared with the advertisement, "Henceforth the Author desires that the following Pieces may alone be regarded as containing his philosophical sentiments and principles."[70] Hume himself described this advertisement as "a complete Answer to . . . that bigoted silly fellow Beattie."[71] (Perhaps it is one reason why John Stuart Mill never bothered to read the *Treatise.*) In the twentieth century, philosophers are possibly less bigoted and silly, and the *Treatise* has become accepted as perhaps the greatest philosophical work ever written in English, quite eclipsing the *Enquiries,* so that the question of the differences between it and the *Enquiries* has come up for considerable commentary.

If Hume had merely disavowed the *Treatise,* the only other disconcerting fact would be our preference today for the *Treatise*. But in 1754 Hume had insisted that "the philosophical principles are the same" in the *Enquiries* as in the *Treatise*.[72] This insistence has seemed to commentators a denial that there are any significant differences. But it does point up one significant difference: the later Hume is concerned more explicitly with his own philosophical principles. Thus "Of Morals" (the title of book III of the *Treatise*) has become an *Enquiry Concerning the Principles of Morals.* If we compare the section titles of Part III of Book III (i.e., the part of the *Treatise* that we have been examining in this chapter) with the corresponding portions of *The Principles of Morals,* we find that the materials which Hume originally assembled in Part III under the first section title "Of the Origin of the Natural Virtues and Vices" are reassembled in *The Principles of Morals* under the section title "Why Utility Pleases." The new title brings out the principle that is at stake in Hume's analysis. The titles of the second and third sections of Part III Book III, of the *Treatise,* refer to traditional substantive moral topics—"Of Greatness of Mind," and "Of Goodness and Benevolence"; in *The Principles of Morals,* these titles are replaced by titles which bring out the distinctions which Hume himself employs in treating these topics: "Of Qualities useful to ourselves, Of Qualities immediately agreeable to Ourselves," "Of Qualities immediately Agreeable to others." Similarly the "Of Natural Abilities" (the title of the fourth section of Part III) is replaced by the title, "Some Verbal Disputes," which brings out the kind of issue Hume finds at stake in treating the topic of natural abilities.

Heightened preoccupation with philosophical principles is also a feature of the *Enquiry Concerning Human Understanding,* which is Hume's new version of the first book of the *Treatise.* It is instanced by the title of the first section, "Of the Different Species of Philosophy." The first section of the *Treatise* began brusquely with a substantive distinction: "All the perceptions of the human mind resolve themselves into two distinct kinds which I shall call impressions and ideas."[73] We reach this substantive distinction in the second section of the *Enquiry* (which bears the same title—"Of the Origin of Ideas"—as the first section of the *Treatise*). One point about this distinction which Hume emphasizes (in the second section of the *Enquiry*) is the fact that "all ideas, especially abstract ones, are naturally faint and obscure," so that the "mind has but a slender hold of them," whereas "all impressions are strong and vivid."[74] But this fact has already received methodological illustration in the first section to which Hume has transferred the analogical distinction between the abstract, anatomizing species of philosophy, which cannot "easily retain any influence over our conduct and behavior," and the pictorial species, which "enters more into common life," and "moulds the heart and affections."[75] Thus the methodological consideration of philosophical principles becomes the first portion of Hume's subject-matter in the *Enquiries*.

That this relocation is not entirely incompatible with the methodological program of the *Treatise* is indicated by the way Hume's method developed in the *Treatise* from the procedures of observation, judgment, and comparison which are characteristic of "common life." To this extent, the first *Enquiry* begins (as the transference of the analogical distinction suggests) where the *Treatise* ended. Hume's skepticism in the first book of the *Treatise* was a transitional moment, and by the time Hume reached the end of the *Treatise*, he assumed that the relevance of his anatomizing method was no longer problematic, and that Hutcheson's misgiving could be brushed off with the analogical distinction between anatomy and painting. But when the *Treatise* falls "deadborn from the press,"[76] the relevance of Hume's anatomizing method becomes problematic, a gap opens up between it and the pictorial method that "enters more into common life," and this pictorial method becomes dignified as an alternative species of philosophy.

Egotisms

So far I have been trying to explain Hume's insistence that the principles in the *Enquiries* are the same as in the *Treatise*. This insistence has sometimes been reconciled with his eventual disavowal of the *Treatise*, by relying on his comment that "his want of success" in publishing the *Treatise* had "proceeded more from the manner than from the matter."[77] The *Enquiries* are interpreted as representing merely a change in manner (i.e., in literary style) which Hume undertook "simply in order to make his doctrines intelligible to an audience dominated by the ideal of elegance."[78] Since Hume's disavowal of the *Treatise* seems more drastic than this interpretation would allow, Hume's description of the disavowal as "a complete Answer to . . . that bigoted silly fellow Beattie" has to be discounted as the "posthumous utterance of a splentic invalid."[79]

Hume was undoubtedly bitter over the fact that Beattie's attack on his sophistry and skepticism had not fallen deadborn from the press but had instead gone through five editions by the time Hume penned the advertisement. But even if we make every possible allowance for invalidism, spleen, and posthumousness, how could a complete answer to an attack on Hume's skepticism, amount to nothing more than a change of style? After all, this change the bigoted silly fellow himself had already granted:

> The style of the *Treatise Of Human Nature* is so obscure and uninteresting, that if the author had not in his *Essays* republished the capital doctrines of that work in a more elegant and sprightly manner, a confutation of them would have been altogether unnecessary; their uncouth and gloomy aspect would have deterred most people from courting their acquaintance.[80]

That something more than a change in style is at stake is perhaps hinted by the fact that Beattie's characterization of Hume's style in the *Treatise* approximates Hume's own characterization of the egocentric predicament in which he finds himself as a result of his skepticism:

> I am first affrighted and confounded with that forlorn solitude in which I am plac'd in my philosophy, and fancy myself some strange uncouth monster, who not being able to mingle and unite in society, has been expell'd all human commerce, and left utterly abandon'd and disconsolate.[81]

In the *Enquiries* Hume no longer goes in for this gloomy posturing. There is less probing of his own motives, less flaunting of his own aspirations. These self-centered characteristics of the *Treatise* had met with sarcasm in the first full length review which it had received: "This work abounds throughout with Egotisms; the Author would scarcely use that Form of Speech more frequently if he had written his own Memoirs."[82]

The disappearance of egotisms in the *Enquiries* is not just the change in Hume's style that Beattie and later commentators on Hume have seized upon, but a change in the structure of his theory of human nature. It is a shift of focus from the individual himself and the motives that lie behind his actions to their practical social consequences. This shift I traced in the previous chapter when I compared Hume's attitude towards economic activity in the *Treatise* with that in the *Enquiry Concerning the Principles of Morals*. We did not then suspect that the shift coincides with a change in Hume's attitude towards the activity of a philosopher. In the *Treatise,* "careless and inattention alone" provide the philosopher with a "remedy" for his skepticism, though they do not succeed in eliminating his egotisms:

I dine, I play a game of backgammon, I converse, and am merry with my friends; and when after three or four hours' amusement, I wou'd return to these speculations, they appear so cold, and strain'd and ridiculous, that I cannot find in my heart to enter into them any further.[83]

In the *Enquiry Concerning Human Understanding,* less frivolous, less personal, and more public remedies are available: "The great subverter of . . . the excessive principles of scepticism, is action, and employment, and the occupations of common life." The skeptical arguments of the *Treatise* can themselves be abbreviated in the *Enquiry:*

These arguments might be displayed at greater length, if any durable good or benefit to society could ever be expected to result from them. For here is the chief and most confounding objection to excessive scepticism, that no durable good can ever result from it, while it remains in its full force and vigour.[84]

In the last chapter we saw that this shift to practical social consequences enabled Hume to arrive promptly at conclusions which are "natural and obvious" in comparison with his procedure in the *Treatise,* where the process of establishing the corresponding conclusions by observation and comparison is long and drawn out.[85] A concomitant of this shift is Hume's stylistic attempt to present these conclusions in an "easy and obvious manner."[86] But this "easy and obvious manner" of presentation is feasible because the "matter" to be presented are conclusions which are readily publicizable as of durable benefit to the public. If, on the one hand, egotisms have disappeared from Hume's style, and his skeptical arguments have been abbreviated, it is not only because he is no longer a "solitary Scotchman,"[87] but also because his philosophy no longer places the individual in a forlorn solitude. It now disparages extreme skepticism as a form of egoism. If, on the other hand, Hume has become attentive to his style, it is not only because he has become urbane, but also because society, as a frame of reference, has acquired a more significant place in his philosophy.

Manner and Matter

I have admitted that the falling of the *Treatise* "deadborn from the press," must have played a part in these changes in Hume's philosophy. But I am arguing that the changes are not just stylistic and that insofar as they are stylistic, they are determined by his philosophy itself. In the first section of the *Enquiry Concerning Human Understanding,* Hume himself admits that one of the ways in which "abstruse thought and profound researches" are "punished" is by the "cold reception" they "meet with when communicated."[88] The cold reception of the *Treatise* has been an addition to the "experiments" in "the science of human nature" that Hume had undertaken in the *Treatise* to "glean up . . . from a cautious observation of human life."[89] In this science (stylistic) "manner" cannot be as entirely disassociated from (substantive) "matter" as it can be for us, since we are not dominated by an ideal of "elegance" and do not regard style as a scientific or philosophical consideration. The substantive conclusion that Hume reaches in the *Treatise* by "displaying so carefully" skeptical arguments is "that belief is more properly an act of the sensitive than of the cogitative part of our natures, and depends on some peculiar manner of conception, which 'tis impossible for mere ideas and reflections to destroy."[90] This "manner of conception" is the "matter" of the *Treatise.* The contrast between the (stylistic) manner of the *Treatise* and the (stylistic) manner of *The Principles of Morals* is tied up with a somewhat different analysis of the manner of conception. The contrast of the *Treatise* between the cogitative and the sensitive faculties becomes in *The Principles* a sharper contrast between the operation of reason and taste: "The one discovers objects, as they really stand in nature, without addition or diminution; the other has a productive faculty, and gilding and staining all natural objects with colours borrowed from internal sentiment, raises in a manner a new creation."[91]

Perhaps because Hume has severed this second *Enquiry* from the *Enquiry Concerning Human Understanding,* he no longer carries over the skeptical implications of the first book of the *Treatise,* where the prospect of discovering objects as they really stand in nature was undermined by the distinction drawn by "modern philosophy" between such subjective perceptions as color, which are "excluded from any real existence,"[92] and the objects themselves. It is true that Hume is still comparing sentiments with colors, but he no longer pulls off the skin. He seems instead to be taking advantage of the technical reference the expression *colores* had to the way in which the rhetorician's manner of presenting his case to an audience "colors" the objective facts. At any rate, not only does ordinary perception become a productive faculty—a painter who gilds or stains natural objects—but the argument of the third book of the *Treatise* that moral qualities are subjective now also takes the form of comparing moral perceptions not with the observer's ordinary perceptions of natural objects, but with his esthetic perceptions of an art object:

> Attend to Palladio and Perrault, while they explain all the parts and proportions of a pillar. . . . 'Till . . . a spectator appear, there is nothing but a figure of such particular dimensions and proportions. From his sentiments alone arise its elegance and beauty. Again, attend to Cicero, while he paints the crimes of a Verres or a Catiline; you must acknowledge that the moral turpitude results, in the same manner, from the contemplation of the whole, when presented to a being whose organs have such a particular structure and formation.[93]

Just as the process of scientific observation in the *Treatise* was continuous with the ordinary observer's perceptions and judgments of natural objects and other men, so the process of scientific observation in the *Principles* is continuous with the esthetic perception of an art object or with an audience's response to a speech. Thus Hume is ready to face in the *Enquiries* the artistic problem of the rhetorician which had been disparaged in the *Treatise*. In the introduction to the *Treatise* he conveyed his "hope for success" in the guise of an analogy to military conquests. The analogy dramatized his confidence in his initiative as an individual thinker: "Instead of taking now and then a castle or village on the frontier," he proposed "to march up directly to the capital or center [of the sciences], to human nature itself, which being once masters of, we may everywhere else hope for an easy victory."[94] Equally belligerent was his disdain of the rhetorical manner and of the reactions of an audience to the rhetorician's art:

> 'Tis not reason, which carries the prize, but eloquence; and no man needs ever despair of gaining proselytes to the most extravagant hypothesis, who has art enough to represent it in any favorable colours. The victory is not gained by the men at arms, who manage the pike and the sword; but by the trumpeters, drummers, and musicians of the army.[95]

When Hume brings forward, in the introductory section of the *Enquiry Concerning Human Understanding*, the analogical distinction which he had employed in his reply to the eloquent Hutcheson, and which he had incorporated in the ending of the *Treatise*, it acquires different implications in its new setting. In the *Treatise* Hume insisted that the "anatomist ought never to emulate the painter, nor in his accurate dissections and portraitures of the smaller parts of the human body, pretend to give his figures any graceful and engaging attitude or expression." For an artistic treatment of moral subjects was "a work a-part, very different" from the philosophical attempt of the *Treatise* to introduce the scientific method of reasoning into these subjects. The analogy is no longer an afterthought in the *Enquiries,* for the confident philosopher of the *Treatise* has become "the mere philosopher."[96] And a rhetorical or artistic treatment of moral problems has itself acquired philosophical standing:

> Moral philosophy, or the science of human nature, may be treated after two different manners. . . . The one considers man chiefly as *born for action,* and as influenced in his measures by taste and sentiment; pursuing one object, and avoiding another, according to the value which these objects seem to possess, and according to the light in which they present themselves. As virtue, of all objects, is allowed to be the most valuable, this species of philosophers paint her in the most amiable colours; borrowing all helps from poetry and eloquence, and treating their subject in an easy and obvious manner, and such as is best fitted to please the imagination, and engage the affections. . . . The other species of philosophers consider man in the light of a *reasonable,* rather than an active being. . . . They regard human nature as a subject of speculation; and with a narrow scrutiny examine it, in order to find those principles which regulate our understanding, excite our sentiments, and make us approve or blame any particular object, action, or behaviour.[97]

At the same time, the methodological risks of this second species of philosophy have become alarming:

> It is easy for a profound philosopher to commit a mistake in his subtle reasonings; and one mistake is the necessary parent of another, while he pushes on his consequences, and is not deterred from embracing any conclusion, by its unusual appearance, or its contradiction to popular opinion. But a philosopher, who purposes only to represent the common sense of mankind in more beautiful and more engaging colours, if by accident he falls into error, goes no farther; but renewing his appeal to common sense, and the natural sentiments of the mind, returns into the right path, and secures himself from any dangerous illusions. The fame of Cicero flourishes at present; but that of Aristotle is utterly decayed.[98]

The conviction that "we are born for action" had been Cicero's—

"nos agendum esse natos."[99] And it is a conviction with methodological as well as substantive implications. Hume, as an anatomist in the *Treatise,* was primarily concerned with substantive arguments, and the crucial substantive moral argument had been resolved, he pleaded with Hutcheson, by Cicero:

> You are a great admirer of Cicero as well as I am. Please to review the fourth book *De Finibus Bonorum et Malorum:* where you find him prove against the Stoics, that if there be no other goods but virtue, 'tis impossible there can be any virtue, because the mind would then want all motives to begin its actions upon; and 'tis on the goodness or badness of the motives that the virtue of the actions depends. This proves, that to every virtuous action there must be a motive or impelling passion distinct from the virtue, and that virtue can never be the sole motive to any action. You do not assent to this: though I think there is no proposition more certain or important.[100]

A possible methodological implication of this proposition is that an abstract theory of virtue that pulls off the skin and lays bare the bones is not sufficient to secure the actual practice of virtue. A different manner, a more rhetorical treatment of virtue is needed, as Cicero had exclaimed: "A Stoic ever arouse warmth of feeling? He's much more likely to extinguish it. . . . How meager are their propositions about the force of virtue! . . . They may gain assent but they do not move the mind. The matter (*res*) may be certain, and it is important, but they do not treat it in the manner it deserves, but too analytically (*minutius*)."[101]

Hume may have had this passage in mind when he defended his third book against Hutcheson's complaint "that there wants a certain Warmth in the Cause of Virtue," but he was then more concerned with substantive arguments.[102] Since writing the third book, however, he has come to realize that so sharp a distinction as he had drawn between substantive arguments and a rhetorical presentation was not quite compatible with his (and Cicero's) substantive argument that for "every virtuous action there must be a motive or impelling passion distinct from the virtue." If so, virtuous action deserves rhetorical treatment.

Analysis and Sympathy

When Hume writes his *Enquiries* he is no longer afraid that "any warm Sentiment of Morals . . . would have the Air of Declamation amidst abstract Reasonings." Now that he has become aware of the dangers of abstract reasonings, he attempts to "unite the boundaries" of the two "species of philosophy."[103] Their unification is achieved, however, at the expense of the unity of the theory of human nature which he had elaborated in the *Treatise.*

In the second book of the *Treatise,* Hume had analyzed the sympathetic way the individual enters into the feelings of others' minds, and this analysis had provided in the third book a portion of his explanation of the entry of individuals into association with each other in society. Although Hume in the third book reached the conclusion that "self-interest is the original motive to the establishment of justice," he also employed the principle of sympathy in order to manage a transition from the self-interested point of view of the individual to the larger interests of society: "We have no extensive concern for society but from sympathy; and consequently 'tis that principle which takes us so far out of ourselves as to give us the same pleasure or uneasiness in the character of others, as if they had a tendency to our advantage or loss."[104] Hume in this way reached the supplementary conclusion that "sympathy with public interest is the source of the moral approbation which attends that virtue [sc. justice]."[105]

The more "natural and obvious" conclusions which Hume reaches in the *Principles of Morals* are that "public utility is the *sole* origin of Justice and that reflections on the beneficial consequences of this virtue are the *sole* foundations of its merit."[106] Hume is heightening his utilitarian emphasis on consequences, but he is no longer abstracting the self-interested individual as his starting point. He therefore no longer faces the same difficulty in taking this individual out of himself. Hume still employs sympathy as a principle, but in urging against Hobbes and Locke that "everything which contributes to the happiness of society recommends itself *directly* to our approbation and good will."[107] Sympathy is no longer a mechanism whose operation is to be disclosed by analyzing the process of observation and comparison that composes human experience; it has become itself an experience:

> It is needless to push our researches so far as to ask why we have . . . a fellow-feeling with others. It is sufficient that this is experienced to be a principle in human nature.[108]

Hume can accordingly dispense with the analysis, which he had given in the second book of the *Treatise,* of sympathy as a mechanism which operates in a fashion which resembles the operation of the principle of association, as analyzed in the first book. Thus he is weakening the links in what he had described, at the beginning of the third book, as "a long chain of reasoning" in which the difficulty of preserving "to the end the evidence of the first propositions" will be partly overcome by the fact that his "reasoning concerning morals will corroborate whatever has been said concerning the understanding and the passions."[109]

In chapter 12 we found that problems which were originally fitted in Locke's *Lectures* to the context of a theory of human nature he later sorted out into his *Essay on Human Understanding* and into his *Two Treatises of Government.*[110] Implicit in Hume's *Treatise Of Human Nature* is a criticism of Locke for failing to advance beyond the human understanding—the castle on the frontier—to a complete theory of human nature.[111] Nevertheless, the problems which Hume himself originally took up in sequence in the three books of the *Treatise,* he too later sorted out and treated separately in the *Enquiry Concerning Human Understanding,* in the *Dissertation of the Passions,* and in the *Enquiry Concerning the Principles of Morals.* Now that the sensitive faculty, "with colours borrowed from internal sentiment, raises in a manner a new creation," what had been the third book of the *Treatise* has become a new and distinct subject-matter. At the same time the long chain of reasoning has slackened which had once held Hume's theory of human nature together as a context for treating all problems. Its weakness at what had been the central link (the second book of the *Treatise* where Hume had analyzed the mechanism of sympathy) is suggested by his deferring the publication of the *Dissertation* until 1757, after he had published the two *Enquiries* in 1748 and 1751.

Utility and Sympathy

When Adam Smith undertakes a theory of human nature in the avowed form of a *Theory of Moral Sentiments,* he rescues the mechanism of sympathy which Hume had discarded, expands the scope of its operation, and criticizes Hume for too exclusive reliance on the principle of utility. Hume's theory, Smith points out, "places virtue in utility and accounts for the pleasure with which the spectator surveys the utility of any quality from sympathy with the happiness of those who are affected by it."[112] But Smith protests that "the approbation of virtue would then be a sentiment of the same kind with that by which we approve of a convenient and well-contrived building." We are thus left with "no other reason for praising a man than that for which we commend a chest of drawers." Whenever a man is praised, "the sentiment of approbation always involves in it" what Smith terms "a sense of propriety," which he argues is "quite distinct from the perception of utility," for while the latter involves reference to the consequences of an action for those affected by it, the former arises from our sympathy with "the motives of the agent."[113]

The development of the utilitarian tradition we first traced as a shift in the focus of the theorist to the social consequences of an action. When a distinct reference to the agent's motives is sought by Smith in criticism of Hume, the point of view of the humanistic tradition is being revived; Smith's conception of virtue as "propriety" is an extension and generalization of Cicero's conception, although Smith attributes this conception to Plato, Aristotle, and Zeno alike.

Smith's distinction between motives and consequences alters not only the treatment (in Mill's phrase) of the "moral relations" of an action within Smith's theory of human nature but also the relation between this theory and "other studies." Smith's detaching his *Wealth of Nations* from the context of this theory we previously interpreted as prompted by his becoming preoccupied with unintended social consequences in his treatment of economic problems. But we should be more sensitive to the fact that there are two sides to a distinction and that it cuts both ways. If Smith is ready to sever *The Wealth of Nations* from his theory of human nature, it is also because he has remained preoccupied in this theory with human motivation. Since we are now confronted with two "distinct and separate" theories, we have to trace two lines of development in Smith's thought. There is the development already traced of his treatment of economic problems to its culmination in his separation of the science of political economy. There is a concomitant development in his theory of human nature itself, which suffered an even more obvious shortcoming than Hume's theory, even though Smith undertook his own theory partly in criticism of the too restricted operation of sympathy in Hume. Smith had originally planned to include economic problems in a work entitled *Theory of Moral Sentiments.* But since Smith (in contrast with Hume) analyzes the moral sentiments primarily in terms of men's propensity to sympathize with each other's motives, he could no longer continue to confine economic problems in this analysis (as Hume could in his) once their treatment became attached to unintended social consequences.

As the starting point for tracing these consequences in *The Wealth of Nations,* Smith takes the division of labor as a system of exchange. He admits that this system is "the necessary, though very slow and gradual consequence of a propensity in human nature . . . to truck, barter, and exchange one thing for another." But the division of labor as a system is an unintended consequence of this psychological propensity, "which has in view no such extensive utility."[114] Thus Smith can delimit the subject-matter of *The Wealth of Nations* by arguing that it "belongs not to the present subject to inquire whether this propensity be one of those original principles in human nature of which no further account can be given; or whether, as seems more probable, it be the necessary consequence of the faculties of reason and speech."[115]

This delimiting of his subject-matter marks the specific juncture where Smith has severed *The Wealth of Nations* from the theory of human nature which he elaborated in the form of a theory of moral sentiments.[116] But it also does not belong to the subject of Smith's published *Theory of Moral Sentiments* to inquire into the psychological origin of the division of labor. What we do find in the published theory is a general suggestion of the fundamentally rhetorical character of human nature:

> The desire of being believed, the desire of persuading, of leading and directing other people . . . is perhaps the instinct upon which is founded the faculty of speech, the characteristical faculty of human nature. No other animal possesses this faculty, and we cannot discover in any other animal any desire to lead and direct the judgment and conduct of its fellows.[117]

This general suggestion as to the psychological origin of language was once relevant in Smith to explaining the psychological origin of the division of labor, but the explanation no longer belongs in *The Wealth of Nations,* once it has been severed from the psychological theory of the *Moral Sentiments.* The explanation can, however, be recovered, if we go back to Smith's *Glasgow Lectures* which once included an earlier version of the psychological theory published in the *Moral Sentiments* as well as an earlier version of the economic theory published in *The Wealth of Nations.*[118] In the student's transcript we still find this explanation:

> The real foundation of it [this disposition to barter which is the cause of the division of labor] is that principle to persuade which so much prevails in human nature. When any arguments are offered to persuade, it is always expected that they should have their effect. If a person asserts anything about the moon, though it should not be true, he will feel a kind of uneasiness in being contradicted, and would be very glad that the person he is endeavouring to persuade should be of the same way of thinking with himself. We ought then mainly to cultivate the power of persuasion, and indeed we do so without intending it.[119]

This explanation of economic exchange as fundamentally rhetorical in its motivation brings together modes of behavior which seem to us as remote from each other as Smith thought assertions about the moon would seem from ordinary practical concern. And one reason they seem remote from each other to us, is that we have been so much influenced by the drastically altered view of economic exchange that Smith introduced when he founded political economy as an analysis of unintended social consequences that left human motives out of account.[120]

Theory and Observation

When we first traced the development of Smith's theory of human nature to the point where he severed his political economy, we were preoccupied with the ambiguities of the terms "political" and "economic." We slighted the ambiguities of the term "theory," which has at last come forward in his title *Theory of Moral Sentiments.* We assumed the term must mean simply a scientific theory. There is no earlier quite so striking instance of the use of this term in English.[121] It might seem worth holding a triple celebration on behalf of Adam Smith—as the founder of the first social science, as the first professor to contribute notably to scientific theory, and as the first noteworthy theorist to exalt the term "theory" to a place in a title. But we had better discover what it is that we are celebrating as a scientific theory and as social science. Smith's use of the term "theory" does imply a scientific theory, if by this we mean a commitment to observation. Yet we have already discovered in Hume's case that observation need not be conceived as a distinctively scientific procedure. The analogy to the esthetic perception of a spectator became more relevant when Hume published an *Enquiry Concerning the Principles of Morals* which was separate from his *Enquiry Concerning Human Understanding.*

Hume's influence, however, is insufficient to account for Smith's usage. Observational behavior derives an esthetic character in Smith from the fact that the role of the spectator in his theory is woven out of the rhetorical strand which we have distinguished in the composition of the humanistic tradition. Language itself confronts the theorist of the moral sentiments with a problem of observation: "It is impossible by language to express . . . the invisible features of all the different modifications of the passions as they show themselves within." The reflexive method, which Hobbes still retained from the humanistic moral tradition, when he analyzed the passions, has lost its efficacy in Smith's theory. But it is possible to treat these internal modifications as they show themselves externally:

> There is no other way of marking and distinguishing them but by describing the effects which they produce without, the alterations which they occasion in the countenance, in the air and external behavior, the resolutions they suggest, the actions they prompt to. It is thus that Cicero, in the first book of his Offices, endeavours to direct us to the practice of the four cardinal virtues.[122]

Smith's method of marking and distinguishing the moral sentiments in his *Theory* is by describing the effects which they produce without, the alterations which they occasion in the countenance, in the air and external behavior, the resolutions they suggest, the actions they prompt to.

It is true that Smith does not merely describe the operation of the moral sentiments but also explains their operation by resorting to the mechanism of sympathy. He does acknowledge a distinction between offering this theoretical explanation and Cicero's endeavor to direct us to the practice of virtue. "To examine," Smith concedes, "from what contrivance or mechanism" (i.e., sympathy) the moral sentiments "arise is a mere matter of philosophical curiosity." The question "though of the greatest importance in speculation, is of none in practice."[123] Smith's *Theory of Moral Sentiments,* as an analysis of human behavior from the "theoretical" point of view of the scientific observer, is to be distinguished from the practical point of view from which the "question concerning the nature of virtue" is to be resolved, and this question we have seen Smith resolves by accepting the ancient (or rather Ciceronian) conception of "propriety."

Nevertheless Smith's *Theory of Moral Sentiments* is not merely a modern scientific theory, designed to supplement the ancient practice of virtue. It is also the transformation into a modern scientific method of an ancient rhetorical method. This transformation can be understood in the context of the *Theory of Moral Sentiments* insofar as it can be interpreted as a general theory of human motivation. The operation of sympathy explains the role of the theorist as a scientific observer as well as the role the moral spectator plays within the theory. Indeed the scientific observer plays essentially the same rhetorical role as the moral spectator—he leads and directs the judgment and conduct of other men.[124] The role he plays can only be fully appreciated by recalling the humanistic tradition in much the way that we did when we discovered that Cicero's specifically rhetorical problem of recognition became extended and generalized in Hobbes as an epistemological problem. Smith similarly found in Cicero a rhetorical solution to his epistemological problem of observation. The solution is relevant because Cicero's rhetorical endeavor to direct men to the practice of virtue was an endeavor to persuade them to accept his direction as a leader, in order to achieve an harmonious state, and this specifically rhetorical endeavor is extended and generalized in Smith's theory by becoming a universal human motive—"the desire of being believed, the desire of persuading, of leading and directing other people." Any individual desires "that the person he is endeavouring to persuade should be of the same way of thinking with himself," and the eventual consequence of this operation of sympathy is that a measure of social harmony is achieved.

Social Harmony

Interpreters of Smith have devoted most of their attention to the social harmony an invisible hand achieves in a society structured by the division of labor. They have perhaps overworked their identification of the invisible hand with a Calvinistic Providence. In any case they have overlooked the more visible hand of Cicero. The economic consequences of the division of labor and the psychological motivation for social harmony compose two social systems which are analyzed separately by Smith in *The Wealth of Nations* and the *Moral Sentiments*. But the two social systems were once in Smith's thought—and once before in the history of thought—inseparable phases of the same social system. It is Plato's *Republic,* not Calvinist theology, which is the original source both for Smith's division of labor in the *Wealth of Nations* and for the social harmony which Smith analyzes in the *Moral Sentiments* as "a certain correspondence of sentiments and opinions which like so many musical instruments coincide and keep time with one another."[125] But it was Cicero who transformed Plato's conception of a harmonious, rationally controlled, virtuous society, by introducing an allusion to speech into Plato's musical analogy.[126] Smith's linking of reason with speech, and of virtue with propriety, revives Cicero's transformation of the Platonic conceptions of reason and virtue, and his transformation of the moral tradition into a fundamentally rhetorical tradition. Cicero, we recall, sought to reconcile "reason" *(ratio),* as the Platonic reflexive procedure the individual employs in clarifying his own thoughts, with "speech" *(oratio),* as the rhetorical procedure for communicating these thoughts to other men. This reconciliation was necessary if the political leader was to achieve as a "public thing" the political harmony which had been in Plato only an ideal rendering of the inner harmony achieved by the self-controlled individual. The emphasis in the Platonic treatment of virtue on inner harmony, therefore, became in Cicero's *On Duties* an emphasis on the persuasive, publicly observable effects of virtue, and its "primary effect" was to "conciliate the minds of men."[127] This political harmony which was the orator's specific achievement in Cicero can be extended and generalized as social harmony in Smith, since he is extending and generalizing the orator's performance to all men in order to explain the origin of language.

When the humanistic tradition, as a rhetorical and political tradition, is thus transformed into a rhetorical theory of social structure, little material is left over for the treatment of specifically political problems.[128] A "gap" in fact is left, where Smith's treatment of political problems should have come, as soon as his original theory of man's rhetorical nature disintegrates on the one hand (in the *Moral Sentiments*) into a psychological analysis of moral motivation, and on the other hand (in *The Wealth of Nations*) into an analysis of the unintended social consequences of man's economic activity. At the end of the *Moral Sentiments,* Smith promises a "theory of jurisprudence," which would supply "an account of the general principles of law and government." This theory would have recast his lectures on Justice, just as *The Wealth of Nations* recast his lectures on Plenty.[129] But when Smith left for London, in 1773, taking with him the manuscript of *The Wealth of Nations,* he made Hume his literary executor with the instruction that his lectures did not merit publication and were to be destroyed if he died. In 1785 he was still dissatisfied with his theory of jurisprudence, and on his deathbed in 1790 he repeated to friends the instruction he had given Hume. It was carried out.

This "gap" is closed in Bentham's theory of jurisprudence. Bentham consolidates a theory of human nature in which the *Principles of Morals and Legislation* are psychologically the same. In the next chapter we shall see how this consolidation assimilates moral and political problems to problems of legislation. This assimilation is a further illustration of the way political problems in the utilitarian tradition tend to slip outside the scope of an analysis of the motives which lie behind an individual's actions, and to become attached instead to the social consequences of his actions. This line of development is continuous with the partial assimilation already traced of moral and political theory to economic problems, for Bentham will disregard Smith's theory of human nature in the *Moral Sentiments* in favor of the utilitarian theory of human nature which he finds implicit in Smith's *Wealth of Nations.*[130] In this theory of human nature, sentiments and motives can be disregarded, not only on the grounds that actions alone have consequences directly affecting other members of society and directly accessible to legislative control, but also on the ground that actions and their consequences are alone directly accessible to scientific observation. But Bentham's conception of scientific method is quite different, we shall see, from Hume's and Smith's.

Notes

1. *Autobiography* (New York: Columbia University Press, 1924), p. 46.
2. See p. 137, this vol.
3. Jeremy Bentham, *Deontology or The Science of Morality,* arranged and ed. John

Bowring, 2 vols. (London: Longman, Rees, Orme, Browne, Greene, and Longman, 1834), 1: 49–50. The *Deontology* is Bentham's only published work that is strictly a moral theory. (This fact itself illustrates the extent of his preoccupation with social consequences rather than simply with individual actions.) I select citations which seem to bear the stamp of Bentham's style.

4. *Ibid.*

5. See p. 137, this vol.

6. *Deontology,* 1: 50–51. Bentham is quoting the *Oxford Compendium* as "the text-book and authority of that famous university" (*ibid.,* 1:38). But the quotations are often from Cicero or adapted from Cicero (see e.g., the quotations from *De Officiis, Deontology,* pp. 54–55).

7. See p. 127, this vol.

8. See chap. 12, nn. 20, 22.

9. *Autobiography,* p. 46.

10. "Bentham," *Mill's Essays on Literature and Society,* ed. J. B. Schneewind (New York: Collier Books, 1965), p. 253.

11. See p. 152, this vol.

12. *The Principles of Morals and Legislation* (New York: Hafner, 1948), p. 17. The footnote to this description embodies the same reappraisal of tradition as the youthful Mill encountered in Dumont's version of Bentham (see p. 151, this vol.). Even after his crisis, Mill remained impressed with Bentham's reappraisal; materials from this footnote compose by far the longest citation in Mill's "Bentham" (pp. 250–51).

13. Bentham admits the variety of traditional moral theories, but he claims that they "may all be reduced" to this one principle (*ibid.; cf. Deontology,* 1: 323). They "are but one and the same method, couched in different forms of words" (*Morals and Legislation,* p. 19). With an irony that may well be Bentham's own, Bowring claims for "the appellative of *ipse-dixitism* . . . an antique and high authority,—it is the principle recognized (so Cicero informs us) by the disciples of Pythagoras. Ipse (*he,* the master, Pythagoras), ipse dixit,—he has said it; the master has said that it is so; therefore, say the disciples of the illustrious sage, therefore so it is" (*Deontology,* 1: 323).

14. *Treatise Of Human Nature,* ed. L. A. Selby-Bigge (Oxford: The Clarendon Press, 1888), p. 413

15. For instances of the way this opposition holds for Cicero at both these levels, see vol. 1, pp. 185, 299. For Cicero's manipulation of oppositions in general, see vol. 1, p. 225, and accompanying n. 95. For the influence of his oppositions, see chap. 11, n. 8.

16. *Deontology,* 1: 300. "I was not thirteen," Bentham is quoted by Bowring as recalling, "when the abominations of Cicero shocked me." The youngster had been set "the task of rendering into English . . . The Tusculan Questions" (*ibid.,* pp. 227, 300–301).

17. Should it seem unhistorical to regard this humanistic tradition as constituting *the* tradition in moral philosophy, remember that Cicero did not consider Epicureanism capable of constituting an historical tradition, inasmuch as it cannot provide any *exempla virtutis* (see chap. 7, n. 20). Bentham himself views Epicurus as an isolated figure: "Epicure, il est vrai, a seul parmi les anciens le mérite d'avoir connu la véritable source de la morale" (I am citing Bentham from David Baumgardt, *Bentham and The Ethics of Today* [Princeton: Princeton University Press, 1952], p. 334.)

18. In the eighteenth century the term *sentiment* (and thus the reference of my term *sentimental*) still reflects French and Latin usage (see the rubric for the*Treatise,* cited chap. 11, n. 36). Hume does distinguish between a passion and the accompanying judgment (see, e.g., the *Treatise,* p. 416). A passion he usually treats as a motive for performing

a particular action or for making a particular judgment (see his expression "a motive or impelling passion"—(see p. 211, this vol.), but he usually treats a sentiment as a motive which impels us to make a particular judgment. Adam Smith cites Malebranche—"our passions . . . all justify themselves; that is, suggest to us opinions which justify them" (*The Early Writings of Adam Smith* [New York: Augustus M. Kelley, 1967], p. 47), and he often blurs the distinction by treating the passions in Stoic fashion as judgments. In Bentham and Mill *sentiment* usually means feeling, but they employ the term in this sense in settings where the feeling in question is felt to justify the holding of some opinion.

19. *Enquiry Concerning the Principles of Morals,* ed. L. A. Selby-Bigge (Oxford: Clarendon Press, 1902), p. 170.

20. Manuscript memorandum cited by E. C. Mossner, *The Life of David Hume* (Austin: University of Texas Press, 1941), p. 76.

21. I am citing this commonplace from Alain Michel, *Les rapports de la rhétorique et de la philosophie dans l'oeuvre de Cicéron (*Paris: Presses Universitaires, 1960), p. 11.

22. Bentham recognizes that the rhetorician's "object being to put others in a passion, his course is to appear to be in a passion himself" (*Deontology,* 1: 36). The moral ambivalence of this rhetorical predicament was stressed in Stoicism (see chap. 9, n. 76).

23. See p. 211, this vol. See also vol. 1, p. 267, for Cicero's rhetorical effort to move men's minds, and accompanying n. 82, for the failure of the Stoics to do so.

24. *Deontology,* 2: 73.

25. Bentham's contempt for Socrates and Plato, Mill found most "distressing" ("Bentham," p. 256). See p. 305, this vol.

26. *Principles of Morals,* pp. 170, 173–74.

27. *Ibid.,* p. 276.

28. *Ibid.,* p. 174.

29. *Treatise,* p. 365.

30. See p. 48, this vol.

31. *Treatise,* p. 491. The balanced character of the comparative structure of Hume's analysis is Neoclassical (see n. 42, below). For illustrations of counter-balancing moves in Hume's analysis, see chap. 15, n. 55. With respect to the esthetic application of his conception of balance, see his insistence; "There is no rule in painting or statuary more indispensable than that of balancing the figures, and placing them with the greatest exactness on their proper centre of gravity. A figure, which is not justly balanced, is ugly; because it conveys the disagreeable ideas of fall, harm, and pain" (*Principles of Morals,* p. 245). For the classical problem of stability, see chap. 13, n. 70.

32. See this vol., p. 36.

33. See this vol., p. 165.

34. *Treatise,* p. 491.

35. See this vol., p. 138.

36. *Treatise,* p. 490.

37. *Ibid.,* p. 375.

38. *Principles of Morals,* p. 209.

39. *Treatise,* p. 489.

40. *Ibid.,* pp. 581–82; italics Hume's.

41. *Ibid.*, p. 582.

42. The addition of this analysis would justify identifying Hume's 18th-century classicism as "Neoclassicism." Compare Bronson's answer to the question, "When was Neoclassicism?" (chap. 4, n. 76).

43. See p. 165, this vol.

44. *Treatise*, p. 413.

45. *Principles of Morals*, p. 289.

46. See p. 191, this vol.

47. *Treatise*, p. xxiii.

48. See p. 235, this vol.

49. *Treatise*, p. 226.

50. See p. 122, this vol.

51. *Essay on Human Understanding* (London: Ward, Lock, n.d.), p. 76.

52. For this triadic relation, see pp. 164–65, this vol.

53. *Treatise*, pp. 266–67. See chap. 14, n. 53.

54. *Ibid.*, p. 264.

55. *On Human Understanding*, p. 76.

56. See p. 168, this vol.

57. *Treatise*, pp. 434–35.

58. *Ibid.*, pp. 264–65.

59. *Ibid.*, pp. 181–82.

60. *Ibid.*, p. xx.

61. See p. 196, this vol.

62. *Treatise*, p. 469.

63. David Hume, *Philosophical Works*, ed. T. H. Green and T. H. Grose, 4 vols. (London: Longmans, Green, 1882), 3: 31–32.

64. I am citing from *The Letters of David Hume*, ed. J. Y. T. Greig, 2 vols. (Oxford: Clarendon Press, 1932), 1: 32.

65. *Philosophical Works*, 3: 27–28.

66. *De Finibus* 4. 6; see p. 211, this vol.

67. *Treatise*, p. 620.

68. Review of Brodie's *History of the British Empire*, *Westminster Review* 2 (Oct., 1824): 346.

69. *Fragment on Government*, ed. F. C. Montague (London: Oxford University Press, 1951), pp. 153–54.

70. *Philosophical Works*, 3: 38.

71. *Letters*, 1: 301.

72. *Philosophical Works*, 3: 36.

73. *Treatise*, p. 1.

74. *Enquiry Concerning The Human Understanding*, ed. L. A. Selby-Bigge (Oxford: Clarendon Press, 1902), pp. 21–22.

75. *Ibid.,* p. 7.

76. "My Own Life" (I am citing from *Philosophical Works,* 3:2).

77. *Ibid.,* p. 3.

78. John Passmore, *Hume's Intentions* (Cambridge: Cambridge University Press, 1952), p. 16.

79. Grose's comment (*Philosophical Works,* p. 39).

80. I am citing Beattie from Passmore, pp. 15–16.

81. *Treatise,* p. 264.

82. This review in the *History of the Works of the Learned* (1739). I am citing from Mossner, *The Life of David Hume,* p. 121.

83. *Treatise,* p. 269.

84. *Human Understanding,* p. 159.

85. See pp. 173–74, this vol.

86. For the full citation, see p. 210, this vol.

87. "The *Treatise* from beginning to end," Grose identifies as "the work of a solitary Scotchman" (*Philosophical Works,* 3: 40).

88. *Human Understanding,* p. 9.

89. See p. 161, this vol.

90. *Treatise,* p. 184.

91. *Principles of Morals,* p. 294.

92. *Treatise,* p. 228.

93. *Principles of Morals,* p. 292.

94. See p. 155, this vol.

95. *Treatise,* p. xviii.

96. *Human Understanding,* p. 4.

97. *Ibid.,* p. 5; italics added. Note that the last sentence lists the topics of the three books of the *Treatise.*

98. *Ibid.,* p. 7.

99. *Fin.* 5. 58.

100. *Philosophical Works,* pp. 29–30. Compare *Fin.* 4. 48.

101. *Fin.* 4. 7. See n. 23, above. See chap 7, n. 23 for Cicero's misgiving regarding the coldness of the Stoic treatment of virtue.

102. See p. 201, this vol. To defend the *Treatise* against a humanist, Hume appealed to Cicero for a substantive argument. But one of the more obvious changes in manner in the *Principles of Morals* is the wealth of humanistic erudition that Hume displays. In "My Own Life" he recalls, "I very soon recovered from the blow [the fact that the *Treatise* had fallen "deadborn from the press"] and prosecuted with great ardor my studies." These included "the Greek language, which I had too much neglected in my early youth" (*Philosophical Works,* 3: 2–3). But although Hume cites Greek writers in the *Principles,* there is not the slightest evidence that he was influenced by any of their substantive arguments. Hume belongs to the Latin humanistic tradition. Thus when he cites from Plato's *Republic* (*Principles,* p. 207), it is to justify the Ciceronian equation of the *utile* with the *honestum,* and the justification is confirmed by citations from later writers. No philoso-

pher today would cite Plato in their company. See my general claim that "when any writer from the Renaissance to the eighteenth century cites a classical Greek text (e.g., Plato) he will usually interpret it in the way some Latin writer, or Greek writer of the Hellenistic or Roman period . . . had already interpreted it" (Vol. 1, p. 112).

103. *Human Understanding,* p. 16.

104. *Treatise,* p. 579.

105. *Ibid.,* pp. 499–500.

106. *Principles of Morals,* p. 183. See p. 174, this vol.

107. *Ibid.,* p. 219; italics added.

108. *Ibid.* In *A Dissertation on the Passions* (Hume's later revision of the second book of the *Treatise*), he does not begin with Pride, as the passion whose object is self, and he does not rely on sympathy as a mechanism for explaining the experience of fellow-feeling.

109. *Treatise,* p. 455.

110. See this vol., p. 132.

111. See this vol., p. 155.

112. *The Theory of Moral Sentiments* (London: Henry G. Bohn, 1853), p. 480.

113. *Ibid.,* pp. 271, 103. In Hume's *Treatise* only the third book constituted a theory of moral sentiments. With Smith's expansion of the scope of the operation of sympathy, the theory of moral sentiments absorbs the treatment of the passions, which Hume had completed in his second book. The mechanism of sympathy Hume first introduced in order to give an account "Of the Love of Fame" (sec. 11 of pt. 1 of the second book). The first sentence of this section makes the following transition: "But beside these *original* causes of pride and humility [e.g., property and riches, which were treated in the preceding section] there is a *secondary* one in the opinions of others . . . In order to account for this phaenomenon 'twill be necessary to take some compass, and first explain the nature of sympathy" (*Treatise,* p. 316; italics added). Hume has begun with pride (and humility), inasmuch as "the idea, or rather impression of ourselves is always intimately present with us;" in his explanation of sympathy, he is moving on to "whatever object . . . is related to ourselves" (p. 317), and arriving at the "great resemblance among all human creatures" as a result of which "we never remark any passion or principle in others, of which, in some degree or other, we may not find a parallel in ourselves" (p. 318). But sympathy is introduced in the first sentence of Smith's *Theory of Moral Sentiments,* and all the passions (the "selfish" and "unsocial," as well as the "social passions") are treated (pp. 44–60) in a social setting: "To a man who from his birth was a stranger to society, the objects of his passions, the external bodies which either pleased or hurt him, would occupy his whole attention. The passions themselves, the desires or aversions, the joys or sorrows, which those objects excited . . . could scarce ever be the objects of his thoughts" (p. 162). The moral sentiments are themselves social phenomena and Smith's *Theory* as a whole is "An Analysis of the Principles by which Men Naturally Judge Concerning the Conduct and Character *First* of their Neighbors, and *Afterwards* of Themselves" (Smith's subtitle; italics added). In Hume's *A Dissertation On the Passions,* men's "strong love of fame" is explained as an effort "to fix and confirm their favourable opinions of themselves." They are assumed by Hume (in contrast with Smith) to have reached these opinions by themselves, so that "the favourable suffrages of the world are regarded only . . . as confirmations" (*Essays and Treatises,* 2 vols. [London: J. Jones, 1822], 2: 184–85). For a further illustration of this contrast between Hume and Smith, see n. 125, below.

114. *The Wealth of Nations,* 2 vols. (London: J. M. Dent, 1910), 1: 12.

115. *Ibid.*

116. See pp. 174, 177, this vol.

117. *Moral Sentiments,* p. 495.

118. According to a student's report (see n. 119, below), Smith's Glasgow Lectures on Moral Philosophy were "divided into four parts. The first contained Natural Theology. . . . The second comprehended Ethics, strictly so called, and consisted chiefly of the doctrines which he afterwards published in his Theory of Moral Sentiments. In the third part, he treated at more length of that branch of morality which relates to *justice* [see p. 220, this vol.]. . . . This important branch of his labours he also intended to give to the public; but this intention . . . , he did not live to fulfil. In the last part of his lectures, he examined those political regulations which are founded, not upon the principle of *justice*, but that of expediency, and which are calculated to increase the riches, the power, and the prosperity of a State. . . . What he delivered on these subjects contained the substance of the work he afterwards published under the title of An Inquiry into the Nature and Causes of the Wealth of Nations" (John Millar's report cited by Dugald Stewart in his "Account of the Life and Writings of Adam Smith," *Moral Sentiments,* p. xvii). The student's transcript edited by Cannan (see next note) reproduces a later version of these lectures when the second part had been extracted for publication in the *Moral Sentiments,* but the fourth part as well as the third part was still covered, since Smith had not yet published *The Wealth of Nations.*

119. *Lectures on Justice, Police, Revenue and Arms,* ed. Edwin Cannan (Oxford: Clarendon Press, 1896), p. 171. The second clause of the last sentence—"indeed we do so without intending it"—anticipates the consideration present to Smith's mind when he severs *The Wealth of Nations* from his *Lectures.* The first clause of the last sentence—"We ought then mainly to cultivate the power of persuasion"—reminds us that if Smith reached the climax of his academic career at Glasgow as a professor of moral philosophy who taught economics (see p. 140 this vol.), he began as a professor of logic who taught rhetoric. The way this earlier shift in criteria of relevance altered the relations between logic and rhetoric and between rhetoric and "other studies," as well as the character of rhetoric itself, is brought out by Millar's summary of his lectures: "In the Professorship of Logic to which Mr. Smith was appointed on his first introduction into this University, he soon saw the necessity of departing widely from the plan that had been followed by his predecessors, and of directing the attention to his pupils to studies of a more interesting and useful nature than the logic and the metaphysics of the schools. Accordingly, after exhibiting a general view of the powers of the mind, and explaining so much of the ancient logic as was requisite to gratify curiosity with respect to an artificial method of reasoning, which had once occupied the universal attention of the learned, he dedicated all the rest of his time to the delivery of a system of rhetoric and belles lettres. The best method of explaining and illustrating the various powers of the human mind, the most useful part of metaphysics, arises from an examination of the several ways of *communicating our thoughts by speech,* and from an attention to the principles of those literary compositions which contribute to persuasion or entertainment. By these arts, *everything that we perceive or feel, every operation of our minds,* is expressed and delineated in such a manner, that it may be clearly distinguished and remembered" '(John Millar's report cited from Dugald Stewart by John M. Lothian in his introduction to Adam Smith's *Lectures on Rhetoric and Belles Lettres* [London: Thomas Nelson, 1963], p. xvi; italics added). Note the methodological claims entered on behalf of rhetoric, the comprehensiveness of its scope as a theory of the human mind, and the fact that it is conceived as a theory of literary expression (see chap. 10, nn. 75, 76).

120. Thus Cannan was excited by discovering the *Lectures on Justice,* because of their obvious relevance to *The Wealth of Nations,* but he was relatively indifferent to the supposed disappearance of Smith's lectures on rhetoric, for he failed to realize that the passage I have cited from the *Lectures on Justice* suggested an originally close relation between rhetorical and economic behavior as analyzed by Smith.

121. The immediate source of Smith's title is probably Levesque de Pouilly, *Théorie*

des sentimens agréables, which is a Platonizing mixture of humanistic esthetics with Newtonian mechanics.

122. *Moral Sentiments,* p. 484. The problem of observation, and the solution available in a theory of literary expression in which the feelings expressed are those of an observer (or auditor—see n. 126, below) had already been worked out in Smith's *Lectures on Rhetoric and Belles Lettres*: "That way of expressing any quality of an object which does it by describing the several parts that constitute the quality we want to express, may be called the direct method. When, again, we do it by describing the effects this quality produces on those who behold it, this may be called the indirect method. The latter in most cases is by far the best. We see accordingly Shakespeare's descriptions are greatly more animated than those of Spenser. Shakespeare, as he wrote in dialogues, had it always in his power to make the persons of the dialogue relate the effects any object had upon them. . . . Pindar, Homer, and Milton never attempt to describe music directly; they always do it by describing the effects it produced on some other creatures. . . . The describing or expressing internal, invisible objects is a matter of far greater difficulty. . . . Whatever difficulty there is in expressing the external objects that are the objects of our senses, there must be far greater in describing the internal ones, which pass within the mind itself. . . . Internal objects, as passions and affections, can be well described only by their effects" (pp. 63, 64, 71).

123. *Moral Sentiments,* p. 462.

124. The rhetorical character of the scientific observer's performance is demonstrated by Smith's essay on "The Principles which Lead and Direct Philosophical Enquiries Illustrated by the History of Astronomy" (reprinted in *The Early Writings of Adam Smith*). The principles in question are the sentiments of Wonder, Surprise, and Admiration. Hume's conception of the function of the imagination in constituting belief is incorporated by Smith within a larger theory of the operation of these sentiments: "When two objects, however unlike, have often been observed to follow each other, and have constantly presented themselves to the senses in that order, they come to be so connected together in the fancy, that the idea of the one seems, of its own accord, to call up and introduce that of the other. If the objects are still observed to succeed each other as before, this connection, or, as it has been called, this association of their ideas, becomes stricter and stricter. . . . There is no break, no stop, no gap, no interval. . . . But if this customary connection be interrupted, if one or more objects appear in an order quite different from that to which the imagination has been accustomed, . . . we are at first surprised by the unexpectedness of the new appearance, and when that momentary emotion is over, we still wonder how it came to occur in that place. . . . Philosophy is the science of the connecting principles of nature. . . . Philosophy, by representing the invisible chains which bind together all these disjointed objects, endeavours to introduce order . . . , to allay this tumult of the imagination, and to restore it, when it surveys the great revolutions of the universe, to that tone of tranquility and composure, which is both most agreeable in itself, and most suitable to its nature. Philosophy, therefore, may be regarded as one of those arts which address themselves to the imagination. . . . Let us examine, therefore, all the different systems of nature, which . . . have successively been adopted . . . ; and . . . let us . . . content ourselves with inquiring how far each of them was fitted to sooth the imagination, and to render the theatre of nature a more coherent, and therefore a more magnificent spectacle. . . . According as they have failed or succeeded in this, they have constantly failed or succeeded in gaining reputation and renown to their authors; and this will be found to be the clew that is most capable of conducting us through all the laybrinths of philosophical history" (*The Early Writings,* pp. 39–40, 45–46). The climax of this history is our admiration for Newton's system, which offers so magnificent a spectacle that it "now prevails over all opposition and has advanced to the acquisition of the most universal empire that was ever established in philosophy" (*ibid.,* p. 108).

This essay was a juvenile work. According to Smith's literary executors it was a part of "a plan he once had formed" which "long since he found necessary to abandon as far too extensive (*ibid.*, p. 29). Perhaps Smith originally planned a theory of human nature (in the guise of a theory of sentiments) which would have been sufficiently extensive to have included a theory of nature as a spectacle (or rather a psychological account of the way the spectator responds to theories of nature with sentiments of Wonder, Surprise, and Admiration), as well as the political and economic subject-matters which were later disconnected from the published *Theory of Moral Sentiments*. Smith's considerable debt to Hume permits me to put the suggestion in the form of a postulated reorganization of the materials of Hume's *Treatise*. We have already noted (see n. 113, above) that Smith's published *Theory of Moral Sentiments* (as compared with Hume's theory of moral sentiments which is confined to the third book of the *Treatise*) swallows Hume's theory of the passions (the second book of the *Treatise*). The more extensive theory of sentiments which I am suggesting Smith originally planned would have encompassed even the epistemological problems of Hume's theory of belief (the first book of the *Treatise*); for Smith would have taken as more fundamental to the operation of the imagination the rhetorical "desire of being believed, the desire of persuading, of leading and directing other people" (p. 215, this vol.), and this desire would have yielded an explanation, for example, of why and how Newton established a "universal empire" over the human imagination. The "connecting principles" of this planned theory of sentiments would be the sentiments which "Lead and Direct Philosophical Enquiries"—i.e., Wonder, Surprise, and Admiration. In this planned theory there would be "no break, no stop, no gap, no interval" between Smith's astronomical illustrations of these principles and his literary illustrations of these and other sentiments in his theory of rhetoric and belles lettres, since he construes astronomy in his "History of Astronomy" as "one of the arts which address themselves to the imagination." Further, there would be no "gap" between both sets of illustrations and Smith's psychological explanation of the division of labor, since the "real foundation" of the disposition to barter "is that principle to persuade which so much prevails in human nature" (see p. 216, this vol.). That the planner of a theory so fitted rhetorically to sooth our imagination should have founded instead the dismal science of economics is a remarkable confirmation of his doctrine of unintended consequences.

125. *Moral Sentiments,* p. 497. For the Platonic analogy between musical harmony and unanimity, see vol. 1, pp. 245, 250, 280. Drawn into the Newtonian context of Hume's *Treatise,* the analogy becomes mechanistic: "As in strings equally wound up, the motion of one communicates itself to the rest; so all the affections readily pass from one person to another, and beget correspondent movements in every human creature" (*Treatise,* p. 576). Hume is expounding "the nature and force of sympathy." Consistent with the change in Hume's conception of sympathy (see pp. 212–13, this vol.), the *mechanistic* analogy of the *Treatise* becomes an *esthetic* analogy in *The Principles of Morals*: When an individual uses moral "language," Hume views him as expressing "sentiments, in which he expects all his audience are to concur with him. . . . He must move some universal principle of the human frame, and touch a string to which all mankind have an accord and symphony" (p. 272). Sympathy now, instead of requiring a mechanistic analysis involving "strings," the communication of motion, and "correspondent movements," is simply a single string which is touched. Note too that while the movements in Hume's *Treatise* merely correspond or are "parallel" (see n. 113, above), the "musical instruments" in Smith "*coincide* and keep time with each other" (italics added). Nevertheless the individualistic tradition intervening between Plato and Smith has exercised its influence. The individual in Smith is literally an individual and the relation between the individual and other men falls short of Platonic unanimity: "Though they will never be unisons, they may be concords, and this is all that is wanted or required "for the harmony of society" (*Moral Sentiments,* p. 23).

126. See vol. 1, p. 267 and accompanying n. 83. When I go behind Smith's obvious debt to Hume's theory of sympathy to the humanistic tradition, I am doing what Smith's contemporaries and near contemporaries would have done in interpreting Smith. In fact

Dugald Stewart feels that he has to defend Smith's theory of sympathy against "a charge of plagiarism." Dr. Gillies had concluded, according to Stewart, that "the general idea which runs through Mr. Smith's Theory, was obviously borrowed from . . . Polybius" (*Moral Sentiments,* pp. xxxi–xxxiii), though the real issue for Dr. Gillies was Smith's transformation of the classical theory of sympathy, which was a rationalistic theory, into a sentimental theory (*ibid.,* p. xxxii—compare p. 165, this vol.). Dugald Stewart neglects to mention Smith's much more obvious (to us) debt to Hume's theory of sympathy.

In going behind Smith's debt to Hume's theory of sympathy to the humanistic tradition, my concern is not to detect "echoes" (see chap. 4, n. 5) in order to arrive at an accurate history of ideas (see vol. 1, p. 7), but is a methodological attempt to trace adjustments in the relation between one study and "other studies." In spite of Hume's occasional use of the musical analogy (see n. 125, above), he more characteristically brings out the esthetic character of moral experience (as the product of the operation of sympathy) by comparing it with visual experience (recall his analogies to painting, even in the case of Cicero's speeches against Verres and Catiline—pp. 209–10, this vol.). For Hume thinks of language as primarily descriptive, and when he does introduce an auditor who is affected by the description (as in the case of these speeches), he thinks of him as a spectator. Smith, however, thinks of language as spoken and brings out the esthetic character of moral experience (as the product of the operation of sympathy) by comparing it with musical experience, and even though he introduces the spectator whom he has inherited from Hume, he often thinks of him as an auditor. Take as an example the following explanation of the self-command which is induced in the sufferer by the presence of spectators: "To see the emotions of their hearts in every respect beat time to his own . . . constitutes his sole consolation. But he can only hope to obtain this by lowering his passion to that pitch, in which the spectators are capable of going along with him. He must flatten . . . the sharpness of natural tone, in order to reduce it to harmony and concord with the emotions of those who are about him" (*Moral Sentiments,* p. 23).

A basis for this analogical extension of musical harmony to the relation between the individual and other men (compare vol. 1, p. 250) is Smith's theory of music. Smith prefers music to the visual arts: "Music, by arranging, and as it were bending to its own time and measure, whatever sentiments and passions it expresses, not only assembles and groups, as well as Statuary and Painting, the different beauties of Nature which it imitates, but it clothes them, besides, with a new and exquisite beauty of its own; it clothes them with melody and harmony." The assembling and grouping are in the case of music not only enhanced in this way by the harmony of the music itself but the analogy of the *Moral Sentiments* between musical harmony and the operation of sympathy also finds a justification in the fact that "the sentiments and passions which Music can best imitate are those which unite and bind men together in society." These are "all Musical Passions; their natural tones are all clear distinct, and almost melodious; and they naturally express themselves in a language which is distinguished by pauses at regular, and almost equal, intervals; and which, upon that account, can more easily be adapted to the regular returns of the correspondent periods of a tune." This theory of music Smith inserts into the humanistic tradition by adapting its crucial precedent for adjusting the relation between esthetics and morals—the precedent that Cicero had already adapted: "What Plato said of Virtue [Plato in fact said it of wisdom, but Smith is adapting Cicero's adaptation of Plato—see p. 23, this vol.], that it was of all beauties the brightest, may with some sort of truth be said of the proper and natural objects of musical imitation. They are either the sentiments and passions, in the exercise of which consist both the glory and the happiness of human life, or they are those from which it derives its most delicious pleasures, and most enlivening joys; or, at the worst and the lowest, they are those by which it calls upon our indulgence and compassionate assistance to its unavoidable weaknesses, its distresses, and its misfortunes" ("Of the Nature of that Imitation which takes place in what are called The Imitative Arts," reprinted in *Early Writings,* pp. 155–56).

One other step in interpretation could be taken at the juncture where Smith argues that the moral sentiments "which Music can best imitate are those which unite and bind men together in society," because these are "all Musical Passions," which "naturally express themselves in a language which is distinguished by pauses at regular, and almost equal, intervals." We could interpret Smith's use of language to express moral sentiments in the *Moral Sentiments*. At this juncture we would be passing from an interpretation of the differences between Smith's and Hume's theories of sympathy as *contexts* determining their different treatments of esthetic problems, to an interpretation of the differences of *texture* (see chap. 8, n. 95) between Smith's rhythmic prose and Hume's more pictorial style. The critical reader needs only the encouragement here which Dugald Stewart offers: "It may gratify the curiosity of some readers to know, that when Mr. Smith was employed in composition, he generally walked up and down his apartment, dictating to a secretary. All Mr. Hume's works (I have been assured) were written with his own hand. A critical reader may, I think, perceive in the different styles of these two classical writers, the effects of their different modes of study" ("Account of the Life and Writings of Adam Smith," *The Theory of Moral Sentiments* [London: Henry G. Bohn, 1853], p. lxiii).

127. See p. 25, this vol. Smith (like Machiavelli, Hobbes, Locke, Hume—see p. 135, this vol.) is taking advantage of an ambivalence latent in the humanistic tradition. *Consensus* can refer to the end the orator would achieve by conciliating the minds of men, but *conciliatio* (as a translation for the Stoic οἰκείωσις) can also refer to the *consensus* which already exists teleologically among men. See chap. 12, n. 93.

128. This transformation could be assessed in terms of the overarching theory of sentiments that I have postulated as the theory of human nature which Smith originally planned (see n. 124, above). As a structure of knowledge, this theory is political; its architectonic is the pervasive metaphor of political leadership (compare chap. 7, n. 29)—i.e., its "connecting principles" are sentiments which "lead and direct" the operations of the human imagination. A treatment of political problems would therefore have introduced "no gap" in this theory. Smith's metaphorical extension and generalization of the political conception of leadership and direction (as well as his use of "self-command" for moral self-control—see p. 170, this vol.) derive from the conception of the ἡγεμονικόν—the ruling principle which in Stoicism presides over the universe and the state, as well as over the two domains which are more literally our own (οἰκεῖος), the household (οἶκος) and the mind (see chap. 12, n. 59). I am not, however, considering here Smith's extensive use of Stoic materials in the construction of his philosophy. Although these materials are scattered throughout the earlier editions of the *Moral Sentiments*, most of them are finally pulled together in a review "Of Systems of Moral Philosophy" (Part VII of the last edition). To this extent their treatment is to be assigned to the historical dimension of Smith's thought and is relevant to the development of an historical approach (e.g., in Millar and Ferguson and their continental heirs) rather than to the development of liberal political thought. I am also deferring to *The Verdict of History* (see chap. 13, n. 116) any examination of the sense in which Smith's "History of Astronomy," (which Comte finds more significant than *The Wealth of Nations*) is a history.

129. See n. 118, above. "Gap" recalls Smith's own criterion for the construction of a philosophical system (see n. 124, above).

130. The evidence for this interpretation is Bentham's *Defence of Usury; shewing the impolicy of the present legal restraints of the terms of pecuniary bargains in letters to a friend to which is added a letter to Adam Smith* (reprinted in Bentham's *Economic Writings*, ed. Werner Stark, 3 vols. [New York: Burt Franklin, 1952], 1: 124–207. In the letter to Adam Smith, Bentham attacks Smith's endorsement of usury laws. (This target illustrates the coalescence of economic and legal considerations in Bentham; usury laws were a peripheral problem in *The Wealth of Nations*.) Smith's endorsement, Bentham assumes, is inconsistent with the utilitarian theory of human nature that is implicit in

The Wealth of Nations. In *The Verdict of History* I shall show that *The Wealth of Nations* presupposes the theory of human nature presented in the *Moral Sentiments,* not the utilitarian theory of human nature which has usually been read into it. Since I am not presenting Bentham's utilitarian interpretation here, let me offer an anecdote which suggests that some shift in criteria of relevance separates Smith from the utilitarians. One of Bentham's allies, Romilly, happened to be in Edinburgh the day Smith died and was inclined to complain that so little attention was being paid to the death of Scotland's greatest figure. But then he reflected, "One ought not perhaps to be very much surprised that the public does not do justice to the works of Adam Smith since he did not do justice to them himself, but always considered his *Theory of Moral Sentiments* a much superior work to his *Wealth of Nations*" (I am citing from John Rae, Life of Adam Smith [London: Macmillan, 1895], p. 435).

15

Morals and Legislation

The season of fiction is over.—Bentham

Analysis and Tradition

Mill identifies Bentham's scientific method as "a sifting and anatomizing method"—as a way of "breaking every question into pieces before attempting to solve it." By employing this analytic method, Bentham has "for the first time, introduced precision of thought into moral and political philosophy." And "this is nothing less than a revolution in philosophy," since philosophers from now on will have to "join a precise issue in every dispute."[1]

Unfortunately for us, precision seems unnecessary to Mill with respect to the topological questions we would want to raise regarding this revolution. What place, we would ask, does Bentham's moral and political philosophy then come to occupy in relation to "other studies," what scientific adjustment is involved in its relocation, and how does its relocation affect the place Bentham occupies in relation to his predecessors? Mill does not pretend that Bentham's "sifting and anatomizing" was entirely original, yet he refuses to deal with the question of "the precise amount of originality of this process, considered as a logical conception—its degree of connection with the methods of physical science, or with the previous labors of Bacon, Hobbes or Locke."[2]

Mere precision can hardly account for a revolution as final as Bentham's. Precision would seem to be a matter of more or less, like the confusion it is intended to alleviate. Mill does include Locke in his list of presumptive predecessors for Bentham, and we remember that Locke found Filmer confused. Yet there is a difference. In analyzing Filmer's confusions, Locke deliberately resorted to traditional distinctions, whereas Mill regards Bentham as reconstructing "all philosophy *ab initio* without reference to the opinions of his predecessors."[3] In fact Bentham does refer fairly frequently to their opinions. To appreciate the initiative that Mill credits to Bentham, we have to take into account the fact that Bentham was revolting against tradition as such. From the utilitarian point of view, an appeal to tradition is a way of maintaining confusion, just as analysis is the opposed way of attaining precision. The utilitarian is not exposing, as Locke did, this or that opinion which happens to be traditional; when the utilitarian pits reason against sentiment (as we saw he does in the previous chapter), his procedure is inherently revolutionary, for he is opposing, exposing, and superseding tradition as inherently confused.

Later we shall see that this opposition between utilitarianism and traditionalism is geared to opposed renderings of the structure of a moral experience. Utilitarian analysis is forward-looking. Utilitarian analysis is a reconstruction of moral experience which undermines tradition because the point of view of tradition is retrospective. Traditionalists accept already established moral sentiments as "ultimate facts" which cannot be explained by analysis. *Qua* traditionalists, they are "contemners of analysis."[4] Let us consider one example of this methodological opposition between utilitarianism and traditionalism. Mill draws our attention to the way Professor Adam Sedgwick commends Bishop Butler "for not being more explanatory" in making the traditionalist claim, "However much men may have disputed about the nature of virtue, . . . in general there is an universally acknowledged standard of it"—"that which all ages and all countries have made a profession of." Mill also sites Sedgwick's commendation: "Here everything . . . remains indefinite. . . . The author knew well that the things he had to deal with were indefinite, and that he could not fetter them in the language of a formal definition, without violating their nature. But how small has been the number of moral writers who have understood the real value of this forbearance!"[5]

The utilitarian does not understand and forbear. He violates the indefinite and indefinable. What to the traditionalist is inexplicable and unanalyzable, is to the utilitarian a confusion which is to be explained by analysis, so that a "precise issue" may be joined "in every dispute." Utilitarianism constitutes a revolution in philosophy, less because Bentham had for the first time introduced precision of thought into philosophy, than because the way he sought to achieve precision imposed on nearly every dispute a structure in which utilitarians were locked in fundamental methodological opposition to the traditionalists.[6]

Most of Mill's expositions of utilitarianism are in fact exposures of traditionalism. His first important exposition is the attack on Professor Sedgwick. His second important exposition is "Dr. Whewell on Moral Philosophy." If Mill's generalization regarding the finality and scope of Bentham's revolution in philosophy is unqualified, so is his generalization regarding Dr. Whewell's traditionalism: "The tendency of his efforts, is to shape the *whole* of philosophy . . . into a form adapted to serve as a support and a justification of *any* opinions which happen to be established."[7] Mill's expository procedure he has taken over from his father who published (the same year as Mill's Sedgwick article) *A Fragment on Mackintosh.*[8] This was James Mill's only extended exposition of utilitarianism. The title and procedure were modeled on *A Fragment on Government,* Bentham's first political work in which he exposed the confusions of Blackstone's traditionalist conception of the British Constitution. Let us turn to this prototype for utilitarian analysis.

Analysis and Chemistry

In identifying Bentham's analytic method as scientific, Mill may not examine "its degree of connection with the methods of physical science." But Bentham himself stresses the connection. "Any work of mine," he announces with regard to the *Fragment,* "on the subject of legislation or any other branch of moral science is an attempt to extend the experimental method of reasoning from the physical branch to the moral."[9] The year before Bentham published the *Fragment,* the claims of chemistry to be an experimental science were vindicated; Priestly had analyzed the "all vivifying and subtle element of the air." This analysis launches Bentham's own analysis, for it not only seems to Bentham "striking" evidence that "in the natural world, in particular, everything teems with discovery and improvement," but also encourages his introduction of a correspondingly analytic method into the mental world. "If it be of importance or use to us to know the principles of the element we breathe," Bentham urges, "surely it is not of much less importance nor of much less use to comprehend the principles and endeavour at the improvement of those laws by which we breathe it in security."[10]

Mill may not face the question as to the degree of connection between Bentham's analytic method and chemistry, but he does face the further question which is raised by Bentham's extending and generalizing this method to moral subjects—the question of the relation between theory and practice.[11] Mill distinguishes and separates this question from the question of Bentham's method, doubtless in order to bring out the precise issue. He also selects a different predecessor to illustrate the opposition here between Bentham's revolution in philosopsy and traditionalism.[12] "If Bentham had merely continued the work of Hume," Mill concedes, "he would scarcely have been heard of in philosophy." However, Mill goes on to point out, "there was a wide field left vacant for him by Hume, and which he has occupied to an unprecedented extent—the field of practical abuses." This field became Bentham's "peculiar province." He carried "the warfare against absurdity," which Hume's skepticism had initiated, "into things practical." Finding "the practice of the law an Augean stable," Bentham "turned the river into it which is mining and sweeping away mound after mound of its rubbish."[13]

In the previous chapter our attention was restricted to the theoretical implications of Hume's skepticism. Mill's confrontation of Hume with Bentham adds its practical implications. Hume was "the prince of *dilettanti,* from whose writings one will hardly learn that there is such a thing as truth, far less that it is attainable; but only that the *pro* and *con* of everything may be argued with infinite ingenuity, and furnishes a fine intellectual exercise." If Hume left a wide field vacant for Bentham, it was because (according to Mill) "this absolute skepticism in speculation very naturally brought him round to Toryism in practice; for if no faith can be had in the operations of human intellect, and one side of every question is about as likely as another to be true, a man will commonly be inclined to prefer that order of things which, being no more wrong than every other, he has hitherto found compatible with his private comforts."[14] This passage from skepticism to traditionalism may be very natural in a utilitarian theory of the operation of self-interest. But it involves a drastic oversimplification of the relation between theory and practice as treated by Hume. We can examine this treatment by going behind Mill's "very naturally" to Hume's own theory of human nature. There we can try to locate the differences between his theory and Bentham's which are pertinent to the opposition between Hume's traditionalism and Bentham's utilitarianism.

Let us retrace our steps by beginning with Bentham's and Hume's *scientific* adjustment. In a sense Bentham does continue the work Hume had begun. In the *Fragment* Bentham recalls how he had been converted to utilitarianism by reading Hume's *Treatise Of Human Nature*. Indeed when Bentham announces with regard to the *Fragment* itself, "Any work of mine . . . on the subject of legislation or any other branch of moral science is an attempt to extend the experimental method of reasoning from the physical branch to the moral," his announcement is probably reminiscent of the subtitle to Hume's *Treatise—An Attempt to Introduce the Experimental Method of Reasoning into Moral Subjects.*

Nevertheless this attempt takes different forms in Bentham and Hume. In Bentham a certain relation between theory and practice is already a feature of the development of scientific theory, in that scientific progress itself includes technological progress. "In the natural world," as we have seen, "everything teems with discovery and improvement." Visualizing scientific progress as incorporating this technological component facilitates correlating scientific progress, not just with progress in the science of legislation, but directly with legislative reform: "Correspondent to discovery and improvement in the natural world is reformation in the moral." What Hume borrowed in his theory of human nature from the modern advance in physical science was the skeptical distinction between primary and secondary qualities. But his transition from skepticism to traditionalism was not as simple as Mill would have us suppose. Rather, Hume restricted the practical implications of his skepticism as a theorist:

> Vice and virtue . . . may be compar'd to sounds, colours, heat and cold, which according to modern philosophy, are not qualities in objects, but perceptions in the mind: And this discovery in morals, like that other in physics, is to be regarded as a considerable advancement of the speculative sciences; though, like that too, it has little or no influence on practice.[15]

The qualities of experience, whether perceptual or moral, which become secondary in a theoretical analysis remain primary (so to speak) in practice.

Furthermore, if the theoretical analysis of human nature be carried so far as to become the reduction of moral experience to manifestations of self-interest, Hume feels a further misgiving, which he conveys by comparing this analysis with chemistry. Bentham will be enthused by the comparison, but Hume is not very impressed by the attempt of "an epicurean or a Hobbist . . . by a philosophical chymistry, to . . . explain every affection to be self-love, twisted and moulded, by a particular turn of imagination into a variety of appearances." Hume accepts the twisting, the moulding, and the variety of appearances. Their moral coloring retains its relevance in practice, regardless of the results attained by an anatomizing analysis:

> The natural sentiments arising from the general appearances of things, are not easily destroyed by subtile reflections concerning the minute origin of these appearances. Does not the lively, cheerful colour of a countenance inspire me with complacency and pleasure; even though I learn from philosophy, that all difference of complexion arises from the most minute differences of thickness in the most minute parts of the skin; by means of which a superficies is qualified to reflect one of the original colours of light, and absorb the others?[16]

Anatomy and Medicine

We have approached the question of the relation between theory and practice as a question which is raised by what Bentham follows Hume in attempting to do, and by what Mill will follow Bentham in attempting to do—to extend a scientific method of reasoning to moral subjects. But we have to be careful lest Mill's interpretation distort our comparison of Bentham's and Hume's theories of human nature. The question is raised by Mill in the context, not of a theory of human nature, but of a logic.[17] This is why he assumes that Bentham's method too is to be "considered as a logical conception." When he identifies it as an "anatomizing method," he is identifying it with the merely logical process "of breaking every question into pieces before attempting to solve it."

Bentham himself identifies his method not merely as a logical process but also as a psychological process. His logic is "a logic of the will,"[18] and the demonstration to be obtained by applying this logic, he defines as a "quiescent feel of the mind."[19] His refusal to distinguish, as Hume does, between practice and theory thus takes the form of conceiving both in the same psychological terms:

> *Practice,* in proportion as *attention* and *exertion* are regarded as necessary to due *performance,* is termed art: knowledge, in proportion as *attention* and *exertion* are regarded as necessary to *attainment,* is termed science. . . .
>
> In the very nature of the case, they will be found so combined as to be inseparable. Man cannot do anything well, but in proportion as he *knows* how to *do* it: he cannot . . . know anything but in proportion as he has practised the *art* of learning it. . . .
>
> Only by attention to the end . . . can improvement in any shape be made. Only with reference to use—understood always as the attainment of happiness . . . has knowledge . . . any claim to attention: only with reference to practice has knowledge any use: only by its subservience to art is science of any use.[20]

What Mill describes as Bentham's "anatomizing method" is the attention and exertion of an agent—whether he be engaged in a practical art or in theorizing—which are prompted by his interest in attaining happiness.[21]

Similarly when Hume confronted the practical problem of applying his psychological theory, he confronted it as a problem for this theory; that is, he applied his psychological theory to the problem of the relation between a psychological theory and its practical application. Having begun by comparing this theory, as an analysis of men's minds, to an anatomical dissection of their bodies, he introduced a further analogy to painting in order to acknowledge the psychological fact of the discrepancy between this analysis and its practical application. Hume's artist, we recall, could not directly apply anatomical knowledge: there is something hideous, or at least minute, in the analytic view of things which the anatomist presents, so that it is psychologically necessary for the painter to disguise the anatomist's dissections if his painting is to arouse the sympathetic response of the spectator.[22]

Bentham's theory of legislation is also fitted to the context of an analysis of the operations of men's minds,[23] and Bentham draws the same analogy with anatomy. (It is this analogy between mind and body which becomes a dead metaphor when Mill deprives Bentham's anatomizing method" of its reference to mental conduct and visualizes it as the merely logical process of "breaking every question into pieces before attempting to solve it.") But the problem of application in Bentham is analogous not to the problem of fine art faced by Hume's painter, but to the problem of a practical art: "The science of law . . . is to the art of legislation, what the science of anatomy is to the art of medicine."[24] Thus when the Benthamite legislator applies in practice his knowledge of "anatomy," he does not encounter the esthetic problem of Hume's rhetorical "artist," who has to disguise the "anatomical" analysis. But this does not mean that the legislator can directly apply in practice his science of legislation. A prior practical problem intervenes, which the doctor does not face. It is posed by the previous manipulation of men's minds by rhetorical artists (for example, by a Hume). Bentham has therefore to distinguish, as Hume did, between a rational analysis of human nature and a sentimental, pictorial rendering of human nature. But Bentham (in contrast with Hume) applies his analysis to the sentimental pictures in order to dissolve, as it were chemically, the moral coloring suffused by the rhetorical artifices of moralists and politicians over associations previously established by the operation of their self-interest, whether these associations compose the traditional conception of virtue or the traditional conception of political relations between men. The removal of the artificial coloring exposes the operation of self-interest in establishing and disguising these associations. Only then can the principle of utility be applied positively to the rational reconstruction of these associations—to the educational reconstruction of men's minds and to the legislative reconstruction of society.

Sympathy and Utility

No single statement is adequate to the differences between Hume's and Bentham's handling of the relation between theory and practice. To try to state the differences more definitely is to be thrown back on the differences between their theories of human nature. And these are differences (1) in the "moral relations" of an action (that is, in the relations which each takes to be relevant in determining the morality of an action), and (2) in the relations between the individual and other men, as well as (3) in the relation between theory and practice. Yet these differences are similarly articulated throughout in a fashion which is suggested by Mill's contrast between Bentham and his predecessors:

> Whatever originality there was in the method, . . . in the rigidity with which he adhered to it, there was the greatest.[25]

> The eminently consistent and systematic character of his intellect prevented him from ever swerving [from] . . . the uniform and unflinching application of his own greatest-happiness principle. . . . In the writings of no philosopher, probably, are to be detected so few contradictions—so few instances of even momentary deviation from the principles he himself has laid down.[26]

At each juncture where we attempt to track the differences down between Bentham and Hume, we reenter a differently structured theory; the differences illustrate the way the prince of *dilettanti* arrives at his practical problem by flinching and swerving away from the practical problem which Bentham confronts directly.

In Bentham's theory of human nature the performance of any action is to be explained ultimately by the operation of self-interest. But the moral relation of an action which Bentham finds most relevant is its relation to its social consequences.[27] Although the principle of utility has its place in Hume's theory of human nature, the morally more relevant phase of the individual's experience (and this is the swerve that Hume introduces at the level of the individual's *experience*) is less the moment when he is acting with reference to the consequences that he is selfishly interested in, than the esthetic moment when he is a sympathetic spectator who is reacting both to other men's actions (by inferring their motives for these actions and attributing to them virtues or vices) and to their reactions to his actions (with which they infer his motives and attribute virtues or vices to him). The process of reaction is reinforced by the rhetorical artistry of moralists and politicians, so that the individual's esthetic reactions become a stronger practical restraint on his actions. Insofar as the individual eventually becomes unable, when he acts, to analyze and isolate his selfish interests, his inability is itself in the public interest. For to the extent that he does consult his selfish interests, he is likely to take into account only the immediate consequences of his actions, and neglect his more remote selfish interest in what is also in the public interest. Thus he is more likely to act in conformity with the public interest insofar as he acts disinterestedly, his actions being less the result of his analysis of their consequences, than the unanalyzed results of his having previously participated sympathetically as a spectator in the reactions of other men.[28]

These previously established results Bentham's analysis can remove as an artificial coloring because he rejects the principle of sympathy which in Hume both explains and justifies an artistic rendering of human nature.[29] In adopting the single principle of utility, Bentham is following a linear deduction. Hume, in contrast, flinched and swerved, as Bentham acknowledged in recalling his conversion to the principle of utility on reading the third book of the *Treatise*:

> That the foundations of all virtue are laid in utility is there demonstrated, after a few exceptions made . . . ; but I see not . . . what need there was for the exceptions . . . I learnt to see that utility was the test and measure of all virtue.[30]

From Bentham's point of view, Hume's resort to sympathy is a matter of justifying "exceptions" to the uniform, unswerving application of the principle of utility.[31] But sympathy in Hume is a principle which is needed to supplement the principle of utility. Hume's obliquity (and this is the swerving that takes place at the level of his *theory* of experience) is his adjustment, balancing, and reconciliation of two principles.[32] His method is not a linear deduction but a succession of comparisons.[33] Sympathy is the principle that explains the process of comparison with which the spectator shares the experiences of other men; and the explanation justifies (at a higher level) Hume's treatment of moral experiences in an artistic manner to which other men will be responsive in practice. Hume's pictorial esthetics is not a matter of coloring up theory for the purpose of applying it in practice. To the extent that individuals are merely self-interested, it is impossible to elaborate any theory of their human nature. In fact:

> 'Tis impossible we cou'd ever converse together on any reasonable terms, were each of us to consider characters and persons, only as they appear from his peculiar point of view. In order, therefore, to . . . arrive at a more stable judgment of things, we fix on some steady and general points of view; and

always, in our thoughts, place ourselves in them, whatever may be our present situation.[34]

In other words, the operation of sympathy, during the phases of the individual's experience when he is a disinterested spectator comparing experiences (rather than an agent who is interested in the immediate consequences of the action he is performing), not only renders his experience an esthetic and social experience, but thereby also lends it that general scope, continuity, and stability that is necessary if a subject-matter is to be established for the theorist to treat. It is the establishment of this subject-matter which I have traced as the establishment of a "catalogue of virtues" in the humanistic tradition.[53]

Now we reach finally the problem of applying theory to practice in Hume and Bentham. Hume's theory of sympathy provides an explanation of men's actions which is not directly applicable in *practice* (and this is Hume's third swerve). Just as Hume's spectator, when he observes and compares the actions of other men, refers these actions back to the passions or sentiments that were their motives, so Hume as a theorist is offering a retrospective explanation of the actions he is observing and comparing (or accepting the evaluation of from the humanistic tradition). The mind of the individual when he acts is likely to be oriented toward the future consequences he can expect from performing his action, but Hume's explanation of this action is oriented toward previous phases of the agent's experience, when he was a spectator sympathetically contemplating the actions and sufferings of others. For it was then that the associations were established which now extend their influence to the way in which he acts, even though their influence is hardly, if at all, present to his mind when he acts.

When Bentham discards the principle of sympathy in favor of the single principle of utility, he is reorienting the operations of men's minds—as well as his theory of these operations—toward the future consequences of their actions. Indeed if Bentham, in contrast with the prince of *dilettanti,* seems unflinching and unswerving, it is partly because the structure of his theory conforms to the stance of an agent embarking on a course of action. The esthetic attitude of a spectator loses its relevance; virtue becomes foresight; and Bentham protests against Hume that "utility is the test and measure of all virtue." The availability of a universal test renders irrelevant the influence of past sentiments on actions, or rather exposes this influence (and thus the humanistic tradition) as deflecting and confusing the testing procedure. Virtue is no longer what had been already cataloged by successive spectators in the humanistic tradition; virtue as foresight is what can be tested in practice by arriving at the consequences of actions.

These consequences are testable insofar as they are precisely measured, and they are precisely measurable insofar as they are reducible to calculable units of pleasure and pain: The utilitarian "is but an arithmetician whose numbers are pains and pleasures. His science is that of addition, subtraction, multiplication, and division."[36] The principle of sympathy is to be discarded, not only as irrelevant to the testing procedure, but also because it is useless as a measure and therefore as a principle. It is fundamentally confusing in that it is an uncalculating feeling, which is "the negation of all principle" in the etymological sense of that term; for it yields no "starting point" for moral and political calculations.[37] Until the individual's participation in the pleasures and pains of other men has been analyzed into his own feelings of pleasure and pain, precise units of pleasure and pain are not available for addition and subtraction, and he cannot be entered himself as a precise unit in the calculations of the legislator, who should take each individual as a starting point and count him as one in computing the greatest happiness of the greatest number.[38]

Authority and Liberty

Just as the question of the originality of Bentham's utilitarian moral theory is complicated by his debt to the third book of Hume's *Treatise,* where Bentham found demonstrated that "the foundations of all virtue are laid in utility," so the question of the originality of Bentham's political theory is complicated by the debt he admits to Hume's criticism in the third book of the contract theory:

> I well remember, no sooner had I read that part of the work which touches on this subject [sc. of the contract], than I felt as if scales had fallen from my eyes. I then, for the first time, learnt to call the cause of the people, the cause of virtue.[39]

Hume's criticism of the contract is a protest against a theory which is a rationalistic fiction in that it does not take into account the disparity between theory and practice: "Would these reasoners look abroad in the world they would meet with nothing that in the least corresponds to their ideas." Considering man as a reasonable being, they evolve too "refined and philosophical a system,"[40] for their theory implies that political relations between men have in practice been formed in the rational, deliberate, and legalistic fashion in which they as theorists evolve a theory of these relations. Hume would accordingly criticize any similar attempt to apply theory directly to practice, such as Bentham's legislative program for the rational and deliberate reformation of political relations.

I have pretty much neglected the doctrine of the contract which bulks so large in most histories of political theory. Doctrines with so long a history, I have argued, remain opaque unless the different contexts are examined which have determined their implications.[41] Consider the three phases now before us in the history of the doctrine of the contract. Even though Bentham endorses Hume's rejection of the contract, it embodies (e.g., in Locke's version) a rational appeal which is comparable to Bentham's appeal to the self-interest of the individual, in that both theorists assume that the individual's mind is fully formed independently of his association with other men—or, at any rate, that he is able to abstract from this association and assess the advantageous consequences which accrue to him as an individual from this association. Thus when Bentham endorses Hume's rejection of the contract, it is on approximately the same grounds that he rejects Hume's principle of sympathy, which provided the grounds on which Hume rejected the contract. Instead of the impossibly rational and deliberate calculation of practical consequences which Hume had discerned in a contract theory, Bentham discerns an irrational and retrospective point of view which impedes the application of theory to practice. By sentimentalizing previously established political relationships, the contract leaves men politically inert: it is "a recipe of sovereign efficacy for reconciling the accidental necessity of resistance with the general duty of submission." But Bentham's "stomach revolted" against this "opiate;"[42] previously established political relationships become irrelevant once his theory of human nature has turned men around toward the consequences they can expect from their actions.

Bentham identifies this opiate as an opiate of the people. The moment the scales had fallen from his eyes was the moment when he "for the first time, learnt to call the cause of the people the cause of virtue."[43] When their happiness—the greatest happiness of the greatest number—becomes the test of virtue, the fictitious moral relationship, consecrated by the contract, can be dissolved, so that their consent to be governed has to be secured by appealing to the consequences they can expect from the actions of their government. The problems of government will therefore be solved as soon as legislative reforms have extended the franchise and introduced regular elections. Membership in the government will then no longer remain the already established and sanctified prerogative of a particular group in society. The members of the government will be induced to identify their interests in governing with those of the people, and to apply to their actions the test of the greatest happiness of the greatest number.

The scales may have fallen from Bentham's eyes on reading Hume's criticism of the contract, but what Bentham saw when he looked forward to these legislative reforms was not what Hume had seen when he looked abroad in the world. Hume had not learned in politics that the cause of the people was the cause of virtue, any more than he had learned in morals that the foundations of all virtue was laid in utility.[44] In Hume's theory of human nature, what any individual is likely to be immediately interested in politically is the liberty which would allow him to pursue other selfish interests. To his interest in liberty is opposed, however, his more remote interest in maintaining the authority of government. As a result, "in all governments, there is a perpetual intestine struggle, open or secret, between Authority and Liberty; and neither of them can ever absolutely prevail in the contest."[45] Recognizing that men cannot overcome "their violent propension to prefer contiguous to remote," Hume finds the "origin of civil government" in the psychological necessity of establishing the distinction between governors and governed that the radicals will attempt to weaken by their reforms. Although, Hume points out, "men cannot change their natures," they can "change their situation, and render the observance of justice the immediate interest of some particular persons and its violation their more remote." These particular persons —the members of the government—"being satisfied with their present condition and their part in society, have an immediate interest in every execution of justice, which is so necessary to the upholding of society." They are therefore, "not only induced to observe those rules [of justice] in their own conduct, but also to constrain others to a like regularity."[46]

Here again Hume does not rely merely on the operation of selfish interest in order to explain the establishment of government and assure its stability:

> Nothing appears more surprising to those who consider human affairs with a philosophical eye, than the easiness with which the many are governed by the few, and the implicit submission with which men resign their own sentiments and passions to those of their rulers. When we inquire by what means this wonder is effected, we shall find, that as force is always on the side of the governed, the governors have nothing to support them but opinion. It is therefore on opinion only that government is founded.[47]

Those who govern must accordingly strengthen this foundation of government. As political artists they paint in moral colors the objects of political pursuit and avoidance. The governed then become sympathetic spectators of the actions of the government, losing sight of their own immediate interests.

Hume's theory of human nature further enables him to reconcile not only the principle of liberty and the principle of authority but also to reconcile what Bentham criticizes contract theorists for reconciling—"the accidental necessity of resistance with the general duty of submission." The reconciliation turns on the distinction which Hume draws, when he looks abroad in the world, between rationalistic theory and actual practice. Although Hume rejects the contract theory as a theory—as "the philosophical or speculative system of principles" adopted by the party of liberty (sc., the Whigs)—he salvages a practical principle:

> Those political writers [e.g., Locke] who have recourse to [an] . . . original contract, as the source of our allegiance to government intended to establish a principle, which is perfectly just and reasonable; tho' the reasoning, upon which they endeavour'd to establish it, was fallacious and sophistical. They wou'd prove, that our submission to government admits of exception, and that an egregious tyranny in the rulers is sufficient to free the subjects from all ties of allegiance.[48]

Their reasoning was fallacious, for if one were "to chuse a period of time, when the people's consent was the least regarded in public transactions, it would be precisely on the establishment of a new government." Only "in a settled constitution," where submission to the government is already firmly established by tradition, are "their inclinations often consulted."[49] Any drastic reform tends to unsettle the government, and to render it difficult to consult the inclinations of the people. "An established government" for Hume "has an infinite advantage, by that very circumstance, of its being established."[50]

At the same time Hume similarly discounts, as a philosophical or speculative system, the doctrine of passive obedience propounded by the party of authority (sc., the Tories):

> 'Tis certain, that if we remount to the first origin of every nation, we shall find there scarce is any race of kings, or form of commonwealth that is not primarily founded on usurpation and rebellion, and whose title is not at first worse than doubtful and uncertain.[51]

But here, as always in Hume, what is fundamental is not the original experience (as in Locke), but the comparison of repeated experiences. From the doctrine of passive obedience Hume is able to salvage the practical principle which prevails when tradition, "operating gradually on the minds of men, reconciles them to any authority, and makes it seem just and reasonable."[52] It then becomes "certain, that in the ordinary course of human affairs nothing can be more pernicious and criminal" than to resist this authority.[53]

Factions and Fictions

Balanced reconciliation is the outcome of the comparative procedure which Hume employs at all levels of his philosophy, and which culminates at the highest level in his comparison of the two species of philosophy and in his attempt to "unite" their "boundaries."[54] We have watched him compare and reconcile the principles of utility and of sympathy, the principles of liberty and of authority, and the practical principles at stake in the theoretical controversies between the party of liberty and the party of authority. Since the reconciliation is achieved in each instance by distinguishing between theory and practice, and by appealing from theory to practice, we are not surprised to find Hume observing a tendency in practical politics toward the coalition of parties, and anticipating that "this tendency to a coalition affords the most agreeable prospect of future happiness."[55]

But we cannot fully appreciate Hume's conciliatory method unless we take into account his admission that certain differences are irreconcilable.[56] There is one partisan group which he attacks as motivated by selfish interests which cannot be reconciled with the public interest. This is the clerical faction.[57] Incurring the obligation of a promise (to which Hume regards the contract theorist as assimilating the obligation of allegiance to government) is "one of the most mysterious and incomprehensible operations of the mind that can possibly be imagined, and may even be compared to transubstantiation, or holy orders, where a certain form of words, along with a certain intention in the mind, changes entirely the nature of an external object, and even of a human creature." But a difference remains between the fiction of a promise and these clerical fictions:

> Though these mysteries be so far alike, it is very remarkable that they differ widely in other particulars, and that this difference may be regarded as a strong proof of the difference of their origin. As the obligation of promises is an invention for the public interest, it is warped into as many different forms as that interest requires and even rushes into direct contradictions rather than lose sight of its object. But as those other monstrous doctrines are merely priestly inventions, and have no public interest in view, they are less disturb'd in their progress by new obstacles; and it must be own'd, that, after the first absurdity they follow more directly the current of reason and good sense.[58]

In Hume's theory of human nature, "the heart of man is made to reconcile contradictions,"[59] and the process of reconciliation proceeds by comparison, and therefore in an "indirect" and "oblique" manner.[60] But in the context of Bentham's deductive theory, contradictions cannot be reconciled; they must be removed. Bentham does not discriminate between mysteries. His criticism of fictions is an unqualified attack on all factions for disguising their interests with artifices of mystification. A legal fiction, such as the contract, is a "wilful falsehood, having for its object the stealing of legislative power, by and for hands which durst not, or could not, openly claim it; and but for the delusion thus produced could not exercise it."[61] Wherever Bentham encounters political and legal terminology or arguments that are warped, he detects a fiction or a fallacy to be exposed, and in either case he exposes partisanship at work behind the scene, distorting its "sinister interests" so that they will assume a disguise which makes them appear reconcilable with the general interest. To find the only word that will suit his purpose, the partisan "is obliged to soar into the region of vagueness, until he arrive at a word whose extensiveness of import enables him to confound thought by confounding language."[62] This "aerial mode of reasoning," is rejected by any theorist who is "desirous of contributing to the welfare of the community." He adopts instead a method of "close reasoning,"[63] for since he is calculating interests as units of pleasure and of pain, his process of calculation can find expression in terminology which is precise in its reference:

> By indication of the relation which the import of a word bears to the fundamental ideas of pain and pleasure, a distinct and fixed meaning . . . is given to a numerous tribe of words, of which . . . the meaning has been floating in the clouds.[64]

Thus Bentham contributes to the welfare of the community by applying the same anatomizing procedure to language that he applies to this community itself; to calculate its welfare as the greatest happiness of the greatest number, the meanings of words must be distinguished by reference to computable units of pleasure and pain, just as the community itself must be dissolved into individuals, each of whom is to be counted as one.[65] In Hume, language provides evidence of the practical limitations of any theoretical analysis of social relationships: just as the meaning of words are gradually established by repetition and by tradition without individuals deliberating over their obligations to respect the meanings of these words, so the obligations of society come to be established and respected without deliberation.[66] Hume's own theory (as we have seen in the case of the catalog of the virtues) is continuous with the process by which these meanings have been established.[67] Society for Hume, like language, is not a rational construction, and so cannot be reconstructed rationally. But in Bentham the rational reconstruction of society requires the rational reconstruction of language.

On the one hand, Bentham's analysis is a sponge which wipes away the highly colored fictions and fallacies of political artists; on the other hand, his analysis substitutes a terminology which is "neutral" and colorless.[68] "Sponge" is too weak a metaphor to convey Bentham's full sense of accomplishment. He felt himself confronted with the Herculean task of flushing out an "Augean stable."[69] He had to liquidate the "vague generalities" of the humanistic tradition in moral and political theory—all the "Ciceronian trash" and the "moral unintelligibles" produced by Plato, "the master-manufacturer of nonsense."[70]

Bentham does not, however, visualize so sweeping a linguistic reform as a merely personal accomplishment. In the autobiographical footnote which I have already cited, he is giving a "short-sketch" of the "wanderings" of his "raw but well-intentioned mind," until the moment when at last the "scales fell from his eyes" on reading Hume. But Bentham's justification for this sketch is the claim that the "history of one mind is the history of many." We have seen that "everything teems with discovery and improvement," and that Bentham is only extending the range of discovery and improvement from the natural sciences to the science and art of legislation. Everywhere intellectual progress is removing scales from men's eyes. With respect to the contract and other fictions, Bentham concedes, "there was once a time, perhaps, when they had their use." To this extent Bentham has an historical criterion of relevance.[71] But the political contract can now be rejected: "the season of fiction is over." For the progressive diffusion of knowledge is itself altering the political structure of society:

> In point of political discernment, the universal spread of learning has raised mankind in a manner to a level with each other, . . . nor is any man now so far elevated above his fellows as that he should be indulged in the dangerous licence of cheating them for their good.[72]

This indulgence will be withheld when fictions and fallacies can no longer be employed with impunity in parliamentary debates: "In the course of time, . . . any legislator anywhere who is so far off his guard as through craft or simplicity to let drop any of these irrelevant and at one time deceptive arguments instead of Order! Order! a voice shall be heard . . . crying aloud, Stale! Stale!"[73]

Staleness is an historical criterion which Hume could not have endorsed. In Hume the influence of fictions is not seasonal, and it is not eliminated by scientific progress. The artificial colors produced by the moral and political artist, abetting the mind's own artistry, do not disappear from human experience as the result of the theorist's anatomizing the sentimental process by which they are stimulated, any more than such secondary qualities as colors have disappeared from human experience as the result of Newton's analysis in the *Optics*. Indeed the theorist himself, however far he may push his analysis of human nature, still remains a specimen of human nature, and therefore unavoidably subject to stimulation. Rather than anticipating with Bentham the progressive elevation of all men to the same level of rational discernment as the theorist, Hume finds that the sentimental reactions of the theorist, when he turns from his theoretical speculations to cope with practical problems, are as irrational as those of the man in the street:

> The abstruse philosophy being founded on a turn of mind which cannot enter into business and action, vanishes when the philosopher leaves the shade, and comes into the open day; nor can its principles easily retain any influence over our conduct and behavior. The feelings of our heart, the agitation of our passions, the vehemence of our affections, dissipate all its conclusions, and reduce the profound philosopher to a mere plebian.[74]

We have seen that Bentham's philosophy is founded on a turn of mind which enters into business and action.[75] In his view, to continue to employ such devices of mystification as the contract is a reactionary effort to so confuse and debilitate the minds of men as to induce their passive submission to intellectual authority, and thereby to political authority, [76] so that they will (in Hume's phrase) "resign their own sentiments and passions to those of their rulers,"[77] Bentham's linguistic reform, in contrast, is the liberation of the mind's active initiative:

> In the whole field of language, there being no hard words, there shall be no absolutely dark spots, nothing that shall have the effect of casting a damp upon the mind by presenting to it the idea of its ignorance and hence of its weakness.[78]

It is not just a question of what the hard words are about, or of the subject-matter with respect to which Bentham is bringing enlightenment—as it might seem from Mill's restricting Bentham's accomplishment largely to the field of legislation.[79] Bentham's accomplishment has to be restored to its context—the theory of human nature in which he analyzes the operations of the mind in order to enlighten these operations in practice. When the mind stumbles over hard words it loses confidence in all of its operations. Bentham's linguistic reform will leave no words "that do not contribute their share towards the production of so desirable an effect as that of substituting the exhilarating perception of mental strength to the humiliating consciousness of ignorance and weakness."[80]

Youthful Propagandism

In 1824 the utilitarians founded the *Westminster Review* in order to promote that "spread of learning" which, in Bentham's view, was raising "mankind to a level with each other." Our final effort to trace the utilitarian adjustment in the relation between theory and practice must be an effort to appreciate the relevance journalism assumed, in the context of the utilitarian theory of human nature, as an instrument of political reform. For John Stuart Mill soon became "the most frequent" contributor, though he was only eighteen in 1824.[81] It is true that the mature Mill will consign these contributions themselves to "oblivion,"[82] but he will remain preoccupied, as a liberal, with the operations of the individual's mind—in this instance with the contributor's. He will preserve for his contemporaries and for posterity an autobiographical account of his journalistic activity in the chapter entitled, "Youthful Propagandism—Westminster Review."

The chapter title is something of an anachronism; it betrays his mature conception of his youthful journalism. At the time Mill was writing for the *Westminster Review,* he did not view this activity as merely propaganda. The *Review* was diffusing the scientific knowledge which rendered the diffusion of political power inevitable.

A second distinction must be anticipated if we are not to confuse the youthful utilitarian with the mature liberal for whom the youthful utilitarian was a propagandist. The conception of historical change which is implicit in the prospect of raising mankind to a level with each other is not the historicist conception that will animate the conception of journalism the mature Mill will adopt (as we shall see later) when he has learned from the Saint-Simonians and Comte that history "exhibits a determinate course, a certain order of development."[83] The first phrase of the first article of the first issue of the *Westminster Review* did greet historical change, "*Tempora mutantur.*" However it was historical change conceived in a fashion which guaranteed a utilitarian review its political leverage. "*Tempora mu-*

tantur" was flung out with the explanation that "Man is compounded of a fixed and a flowing quantity," and that "Nature always makes him the same, and events always make him different." But this first article winds up as a declaration of faith in human nature as prevailing over all other factors, including historical events:

> The sameness is in all cases much greater than the diversity; the essentials of humanity are mightier than climate, education, habit, society, government, and events; they are untouched by these causes, in all their combinations, and continually limit their results.[84]

The utilitarian assumes that the increasing diffusion of scientific knowledge of the essential characteristics of human nature would increasingly undermine the "accumulated influence of past generations over the present." Here, for purposes of contrast, I am borrowing Mill's later phrase expounding Comte, who will assume (in opposition to the utilitarians) that "as society proceeds in its development, its phenomena are determined more and more, not by the simple tendencies of human nature, but by the accumulated influence of past generations over the present."[85]

The effectiveness the youthful propagandist credited to journalism, as a means of undermining this stale accumulation, is brought out by the experiment he invites us to perform in an article defending the liberty of the press:

> Once remove it, and not only are all existing abuses perpetuated, but *all* which, in the course of successive ages, it has overthrown revive *in a moment,* along with that ignorance and imbecility against which it is the *only* safeguard. Conceive the horrors of an oriental despotism—from this and worse we are protected *only* by the press. Convey next the imagination, not to any living example of prosperity and good government, but to the *furthest limit* of happiness which is compatible with human nature; and behold that which may be attained if the restrictions under which the press still groans, merely for the security of the holders of mischevous power, be removed.[86]

Mill may seem to be relying on the Comtean procedure of viewing the history of humanity as "a comprehensive whole," but the sudden sweep of his experiment indicates that it is not the history of humanity which he is viewing comprehensively, but humanity itself—the essential characteristics of human nature. Influences are not cumulative for the youthful utilitarian: ignorance, imbecility, and despotism could revive in a moment. And they can equally be undermined in a moment; the only limit to the happiness held out as a prospect by Mill's experiment is compatibility with human nature. Mill believes (to repeat the phraseology already cited from the first article of the first issue) that "the essentials of humanity are mightier . . . than events," that they are "untouched" by all influences.

Mill's youthful commitment to journalism as a way of undermining the "accumulated influence of past generations over the present" cannot be understood until we recognize the extent to which moral and political problems, as posed by the utilitarian theory of human nature, find their practical solution in journalism. Mill himself suggests the range of his commitment: "From the winter of 1821, when I first read Bentham, and especially from the commencement of the Westminster Review, I had what might truly be called an object in life; to be a reformer of the world."[87] We are now ready to deal with Mill's climactic "especially." In the light of the utilitarian theory of human nature, we have interpreted the impression made on Mill by "the first pages of Bentham" which he read—the pages where he encountered the principle of utility scientifically applied to expose traditional "modes of reasoning in morals and legislation . . . as dogmatism in disguise, imposing its sentiments upon others under cover of sounding expressions which convey no reason for the sentiment, but set up the sentiment as its own reason."[88] We have seen that the Benthamite position is the opposition of reason to sentiment and the exposure of an authoritative tradition as dogmatism in disguise. We have seen that this structure of opposition is an adjustment of "the moral relations" of an action, and (at a higher level) the relation between theory and practice. The congruence in Bentham of scientific theory with political practice (in contrast with the discrepancy between theory and practice in Hume) we now need to reconsider as the congruence of scientific theory with journalistic activity.

The fundamental adjustment introduced by utilitarianism in "the moral relations" of an action is an adjustment in the relation between internal and external. And the fundamental opposition, in the structure of oppositions in which the utilitarians were locked with traditionalists, is the opposition between internal sentiments and an "external standard." Remember Mill's appraisal on first reading Bentham: "All previous moralists were superseded."[89] They could be superseded with one fell swoop, since their theories "may all be reduced" to the one dogmatic principle of ipse-dixitism:

> One account may serve for all of them. They consist all of them in so many contrivances for avoiding the obligation of appealing to any external standard, and for prevailing upon the reader to accept of the author's sentiment or opinion as a reason for itself. The phrases different, but the principle the same.[90]

The adoption of an "external standard" completes the utilitarian adjustment whereby the motives of the individual lose their moral relevance to the social consequences of his actions.[91] Hume and Smith did take consequences into account in their moral theories,[92] but the spectator's moral reactions to the consequences which he could observe were inferences with respect to what the individual's motives must have been for the action.[93] Bentham would suspend "the search after motive," since it is "one of the prominent causes of men's bewilderment in the investigation of questions of morals." The search is "the chase of an inaccessible, wandering will-o'-the-wisp, . . . an entity buried in inapproachable darkness."[94] In suspending this search, the utilitarian is insisting on "the uncertainty of merit"[95]—the epistemological issue which originally prompted the utilitarian shift from the motives of the individual to the social consequences of his actions. In Bentham's uniform and unflinching utilitarianism the uncertainty of merit is finally eliminated. The reference to consequences brings with it a mode of reasoning in morals which lends itself to legislative enactment; the principle can be applied by laws in a fashion which respects the requirements of the deduction, since laws can control actions by regulating rigidly, uniformly and unflinchingly their consequences. But the principle of utility is also a uniquely scientific principle in that it is an "external standard." Consequences can be observed; an individual's action can be controlled not just by legislation but also by exposing its consequences to rigid, uniform and unflinching publicity.

Periodical Literature

"It was my father's opinions," John Mill points out, "which gave the distinguishing character to the Benthamic or utilitarian propagandism."[96] I am quoting the mature Mill who regards his father's opinions (as well as his own youthful opinions) as propaganda. He therefore fails to bring out the sense in which the distinguishing character of utilitarian propagandism was not merely a set of opinions but also a method for controlling opinions. James Mill's journalistic method is displayed in an article on "Periodical Literature," which he wrote for the first issue of the *Westminster*,[97] which his son continued in the second issue, and which, in effect launched the new review, by opposing and exposing the modes of reasoning employed by the already established journals.[98]

Some sense of the mightiness of events, some attention to the way one event succeeds and tends to influence another, may seem to us entailed in the enterprise of publishing periodically, but James Mill analyzes "the tendencies of periodical literature" with reference not to any historical events or influences, but to the simple irrational tendency of man, in the utilitarian theory of human nature, to seek an immediate pleasure at the expense of a greater, but more remote pleasure:

> A periodical production must sell immediately. . . . Every motive, therefore, which prompts to the production of anything periodical, prompts to the study of immediate effect, of unpostponed popularity. . . . It [a periodical production] must aim at that immediate applause which is bestowed only for immediate pleasure; for gratification administered to the mind in its present state. . . . But what is the class most instrumental in setting the fashion, which exercises the greatest control over the opinions of other men? . . . The people in power compose it.

He then clinches the relation between political opinions and political power:

> The favourite opinions of people in power are the opinions which favour their own power. . . . To these opinions periodical literature is under a sort of necessity . . . of serving as a pander.[99]

The necessity of pandering that James Mill is exposing is psychological. The "characteristic malady" of periodical literature is that it is "opposed" to "beneficent progress"[100] because men find it psychologically difficult to look beyond the present to the future. The sequence in which present and future are being placed by James Mill is a perennial psychological sequence, not a cumulative historical sequence of unrepeatable periods.

Just as the opposition of journalism to beneficent progress illustrates the irrational tendency of men to seek an immediate pleasure at the expense of a greater but more remote pleasure (or at the risk of a more remote pain), so James Mill's exposure of periodical literature illustrates one way that this tendency can be rationally overcome. "The great difficulty of insuring the practice of morality," James Mill acknowledges, "consists in the want of a motive always present and powerful enough to counteract the instant motive." The solution is suggested to James Mill by "the fable of Momus," who "found grievous fault that a window had not been placed in the breast of every man." This fault would be remedied insofar as any man had "the knowledge that he had the eyes upon him of all those, the good opinion of whom it was his interest to preserve, that no immoral act of his would escape their observation." Religion, James Mill admits, with its doctrine of "a high and constant observer," has sometimes been regarded as supplying a moral sanction which can counteract the instant motive. But the motives supplied by religion are "feeble," since "the pains and pleasures" on which their operation depends are "distant, vague, or uncertain."[101] Journalism can operate more promptly, more definitely, and with greater certainty.

In Adam Smith's *Moral Sentiments* "The Divine Judge" himself had conceded his distance from mankind and had therefore "made man . . . the immediate judge of mankind," appointing "him his vicegerent upon earth to superintend the behavior of his brethren."[102] This appointment involved a further delegation of moral authority besides the divine: Smith, following Hume, was denying that the individual himself was equipped with an authoritative moral sense. Humanists like Hutcheson had extracted from the humanistic tradition support for the doctrine of a moral sense, but Hume and Smith had deprived the individual of his traditional moral authority by deriving his moral sentiments from his reactions to other men's actions and from their reactions to his actions,[103] and by interpreting the humanistic tradition as a rhetorical tradition in which the regulation of the individual's actions by other men's reactions had eventually become stabilized.

Bentham's liquidation of the humanistic tradition involves a further adjustment in "the moral relations" of an action. Like Hume and Smith, Bentham repudiates the doctrine of an authoritative moral sense—that is, the reflexive doctrine, as Bentham construes it, "that the opinion of the actor is the true rule of action."[104] The doctrine represents to Bentham an effort on the part of the individual to exercise moral authority over other men.[105] The reflexive conviction of the actor that his opinion is the true rule of action thus becomes "dogmatism"—the attempt on the part of the individual "to impose his sentiments on other men."[106] But it is also discreditable as "dogmatism is disguise," since it remains a reflexive procedure and as such a contrivance "for avoiding the obligation of appealing to any external standard."[107]

Tradition and Transition

With the adoption of an "external standard" as "the true rule of action," a further adjustment supervenes; the process of observation and judgment can itself become externalized. The man who was "the immediate judge of mankind" in Smith was an "impartial spectator" who remained hidden "within the breast."[108] But in Bentham and James Mill any observer who is hidden cannot be objective and impartial. It is psychologically necessary that he become dogmatic and capricious. However, the process of observation which is presided over by the principle of utility as an "external standard" is susceptible of external embodiment in a *Panopticon* or *Inspection-House*. "By the gradual adoption and diversified application" of this "simple idea in architecture," Bentham explains, enlightenment can be obtained, for it represents "a new mode of obtaining power of mind over mind, in a quantity hitherto without example."[109]

The simple idea is the location of an observer at the center and the observed at the circumference, whether the construction is a prison, workhouse, factory, or school. We can thereby, Bentham assures us, "see a new scene of things spread itself over the face of civilized society—morals reformed, health preserved, industry reinvigorated, instruction diffused, public burthens lightened, economy seated as it were upon a rock."[110]

Bentham's *Panopticon* was never constructed, unfortunately for the future of mankind, who had to wait over a century and a half for television. But the *Westminster Review* was also an external embodiment of the process of observation. Indeed, if the sentiments and motives of the individual are irrelevant, because unobservable, if the most relevant relation of an action is to its public consequences, then the most relevant judge of these consequences is public opinion. Its judgments are the appropriate "moral sanction."[111] Since consequences are still in question, the operation of the moral sanction can be assimilated to the legal model, as the use of the term "sanction" itself implies. The "directions" of public opinion become "a sort of factitious law."[112] The moral sanction, like the legal sanction, is public control, in contrast with the private, unobservable, and therefore capricious, and hence despotic authority exercised by the moral sense of an agent, or by the moral sentiments of the spectator. Here again we see that Bentham's program for the future cannot be restricted, as Mill would restrict it, to the field of legislation. When Bentham looks forward to "the reign of utility" as the final epoch in the history of the human mind, he anticipates a readjustment in the relation between morals and legislation:

> Under its auspices [i.e., the auspices of the principle of utility] the work of the legislator will be lightened, and the moralist will assume many of the legislator's functions. The great court of public opinion will take charge of the decision of many questions which are now in the keeping of penal judicature.[113]

James Mill is utilizing the appropriate moral sanction when in the first issue of the *Westminster Review* he exposes the moral sanction exercised by already established journals. Their moral sanction is aristocratic in its substantive, practical content, in that they approve of actions which are advantageous for the aristocracy, though not for the rest of the community. At the same time, this aristocratic moral sanction is irrational and unscientific in the way it has to be exercised: the procedure these journals employ for judging whether or not an action is good is by an introspective appeal to some "inner standard"—to moral sense, conscience, or motive. The moral sanction as exercised by James Mill is at once democratic and scientific: because his judgments refer to consequences which are good for the public in general, his journalism is democratic in its substantive, practical content; because this reference is accessible to general public observation, his journalism is a distinctively scientific method for diffusing enlightenment. Though Bentham's *Panopticon* was never constructed, the *Westminster Review* institutionalized the same democratic and scientific principle of public exposure:

> It were to be wished that no such thing as secrecy existed—that every man's house were made of glass. There would be the less reason to desire windows to his breast. . . . The more men live in public, the more amenable they are to the moral sanction. The greater dependence men are in to the public, . . . the clearer the evidence comes out, the more it has of certainty in its results. The liberty of the press throws all men into the public presence. . . . Under such influence, it were strange if men grew not every day more virtuous. . . . A whole kingdom, the great globe itself, will become a gymnasium, in which every man exercises himself before the eyes of every other man. Every gesture, every turn of limb or feature, in those whose motions have a visible influence on the general happiness, will be noticed and marked down. The constitution of the human mind being opened by degrees, the labyrinth is explored, a clue is found out for it. That clue is the influence of interest. . . . It is put into the hands of every man. The designs by which short-sighted iniquity would mask its projects are every day laid open. There will be no moral enigmas by and by.[114]

This vision of journalistic exposure provided the youthful propagandist with the prospect of becoming "a reformer of the world."

However, the moment arrived when the propagandist could no longer look forward to this prospect. He found he was a moral enigma to himself.[115] In the course of struggling with this moral enigma he became a liberal.

Notes

1. "Bentham," *Mill's Essays on Literature and Society,* ed. J. B. Schneewind (New York: Collier Books, 1965), pp. 248, 253.

2. *Ibid.,* p. 248. For the respects in which Locke and Hobbes were identified as predecessors of utilitarianism, see pp. 113, 119, this vol. Francis Bacon was the perennial predecessor for an intellectual revolution. He offered the distinct advantage that he could be viewed as a predecessor in relation to whom the successor could present himself as a Newton. See Bentham's proclamation: "What Bacon was to the physical world, Helvetius was to the moral. The moral world has therefore had its Bacon, but its Newton is yet to come" (Bentham MS quoted by David Baumgardt, *Bentham and the Ethics of Today* [Princeton: Princeton University Press, 1952], p. 62). (I shall often cite Bentham from

secondary sources, which sometimes make unpublished material available and are in any case more attractive to consult than the cumbersome and unreliable Bowring edition.) Compare Hume's schedule: " 'Tis no astonishing reflection to consider, that the application of experimental philosophy to moral subjects should come after that to natural at the distance of above a whole century; since we find in fact, that there was about the same interval betwixt the origins of these sciences; and that reckoning from Thales to Socrates, the space of time is nearly equal to that betwixt my Lord Bacon and some late philosophers in England, who have begun to put the science of man on a new footing" (*A Treatise Of Human Nature,* ed. L. A. Selby-Bigge [Oxford: Clarendon Press, 1888], pp. xx–xxi). Mill in turn will regard Bacon's experimental method as superseded by Newton's deductive method, which Mill takes as his own model.

3. "Bentham," p. 255.

4. "Professor Sedgwick's Discourse on the Studies of the University of Cambridge," (*Mill's Ethical Writings,* ed. J. B. Schneewind [New York: Collier Books, 1965], pp. 79, 104. The opposition between the retrospective point of view of the traditionalist and the forward-looking point of view of the utilitarian was epitomized by the two slogans, "the wisdom of ancestors and the march of intellect," which Mill points out "are bandied from mouth to mouth; each phrase originally an expression of respect and homage, each ultimately usurped by the partisans of the opposite catch-word, and in the bitterness of their spirit, turned into the sarcastic gibe of hatred and insult" ("The Spirit of the Age," *Mill's Essays on Literature and Society,* p. 28). This appraisal reflects Mill's conciliatory point of view as a liberal.

5. "Professor Sedgwick's Discourse," p. 93.

6. I am focusing on this structure of opposition because it will be transformed when Mill becomes a liberal and adopts the conciliatory "principle of antagonism" (see vol. 1, pp. 48–51). He will discover that to reconstruct all philosophy *ab initio,* is to neglect "the whole unanalysed experience of the human race" ("Bentham," p. 256). Experience was relevant for the utilitarian only insofar as it was experimental—a process of testing by a precise analysis. "Unanalysed experience" can acquire relevance for Mill because he distinguishes between analysis as a method and the subject-matter to which it may be applied: "His [Bentham's] peculiar method, admirably calculated to make clear thinkers, and sure ones to the extent of their materials, has not equal efficacy for making those materials complete. It is a security for accuracy, but not for comprehensiveness" (*ibid.,* p. 254). Note that precision as a criterion for analysis undergoes considerable restriction, once comprehensiveness of materials emerges as an additional criterion. See pp. 278–80, this vol. for the fashion in which Mill reserves methodological considerations for treatment in a logic independently of their application to any subject-matter (e.g., psychology), whereas Bentham conceives his method as at once a logical and a psychological process.

7. "Dr. Whewell on Moral Philosophy," *Mill's Ethical Writings,* p. 173; italics added. Whewell, like Sedgwick, was a Cambridge professor—Cambridge and Oxford being of course instruments of the establishment for perpetuating tradition.

8. *A Fragment on Mackintosh* was a large fragment—431 pages of counterattack. Sir James Mackintosh had attacked utilitarianism in his *Dissertation on the Progress of Ethical Philosophy chiefly during the Seventeenth and Eighteenth Centuries.* The *Dissertation* illustrates the continuity the traditionalist maintained with the humanistic tradition, even when he was interpreting in the nineteenth century the progress of ethical philosophy during the seventeenth and eighteenth centuries. (See chap. 11, n. 49, where we found Mackintosh seeking inspiration from the humanistic tradition.) The *Dissertation* was originally composed for the eighth edition of the *Encyclopaedia Britannica,* but was published separately in 1836 with a preface by Professor Whewell (a further illustration of the continuity of traditionalism) in which he leapt to the "defence of

Mackintosh" against James Mill's "captiousness and petulance, fierceness and menace, personal contumely and angry buffoonery" (I am citing from the 3rd edition [Edinburgh: Adam and Charles Black, 1862]), p. xlii).

9. I am citing Bentham from Baumgardt, p. 24.

10. *A Fragment on Government,* ed. F. C. Montague (London: Oxford University Press, 1899), pp. 93–94. Discovering an analogy between a psychological analysis and a chemical analysis is also one difference between James Mill's *Analysis of the Phenomena of the Human Mind* and Locke's analytic method. (For James Mill's debt to Locke, see p. 119, this vol. and accompanying n. 22.) John Mill gives the following description of his father's method: "Not only is the order in which the more complex mental phenomena follow or accompany one another, reducible, by an analysis similar in kind to the Newtonian, to a comparatively small number of laws of succession among simpler facts, connected as cause and effect; but the phenomena themselves can mostly be shown, by analyses resembling those of chemistry, to be made up of simpler phenomena" (James Mill's *Analysis of the Phenomena of the Human Mind,* 2 vols. [London: Longmans Green Reader and Dyer, 1869], 1: viii). James Mill does not himself distinguish Newtonian analysis from chemical analysis. The distinction is introduced from John Mill's own methodology (see vol. 1, p. 15). John Mill, moreover, is less confident of the extent to which an analytic method can be applied in psychology. "He [James Mill] has occasionally gone further in the pursuit of simplification, and in the reduction of the more recondite mental phenomena to the more elementary, than I am able to follow him" (*ibid.,* 1: xx). John Mill, like his father, does gain confidence in the applicability of an analytic, reductive method from the analogy to a chemical analysis: "The generation of a complex feeling from simple ones, being a sort of chemical union, not a mechanical juxtaposition, it is quite to be expected that the compound will be to appearance unlike the elements" (*Mill's Ethical Writings,* p. 258). But John Mill does not gain quite the same confidence. He concedes to sentiments or feelings a certain esthetic and moral status with respect to the way they appear. When, for example, he deals with the feelings of the poet (see chap. 16, n. 90), he will respect our feeling that they are irreducibly different: "The distinction between poetry [which for Mill is a matter of feeling] and what is not poetry ["matter of fact or science"] is felt to be fundamental. Where everyone feels a difference, a difference there must be. All other appearances may be fallacious, but the appearance of a difference is itself a real difference." ("What is Poetry?" *Mill's Essays on Literature and Society,* pp. 103–104) Mill may belong, as he insists, to the phenomenalist "school of Locke and Bentham" (see chap. 12, n. 22), but he is more respectful towards the phenomena as it appears than his utilitarian predecessors. Hume and Smith also respected the appearances (see p. 237, this vol. and n. 16, below), but Mill's poetic esthetics differ from their pictorial esthetics (see pp. 298–99, this vol.).

11. For my claim that this question is not a scientific question, see vol. 1, pp. 13–16 and accompanying n. 34.

12. For Mill's selective use of predecessors, see p. 154, this vol.

13. "Bentham," pp. 244–45, 269.

14. *Ibid.,* p. 288.

15. See p. 201, this vol.

16. *Enquiry Concerning the Principles of Morals,* ed. L. A. Selby-Bigge (Oxford: Clarendon Press, 1902), pp. 296–97. Smith's even more pronounced emphasis on the esthetic character of experience (i.e. on appearances as perceived) renders the method of chemistry even less susceptible of extension and generalization: "Why has the chemical philosophy in all ages crept along in obscurity, and been so disregarded by the generality of mankind, while other systems, less useful, and not more agreeable to experience, have possessed universal admiration for whole centuries together? The connecting principles

of the chemical philosophy are such as the generality of mankind know nothing about, have rarely seen, and have never been acquainted with; and which to them, therefore, are incapable of smoothing the passage of the imagination betwixt any two seemingly disjointed objects" ("The Principles which Lead and Direct Philosophical Enquiries, Illustrated by The History of Astronomy," *The Early Writings of Adam Smith* [New York: Augustus M. Kelley, 1967], p. 46).

17. See p. 278, this vol.

18. *The Principles of Morals and Legislation* (New York: Hafner, 1948), p. xxxi.

19. I am citing from Mary Mack, *Jeremy Bentham, An Odyssey of Ideas* (New York: Columbia University Press, 1963), p. 268.

20. *Ibid.*, p. 263.

21. This reduction of science to the exercise of attention and to exertion takes place in the context of Bentham's logic of will: "Interest appeals to the *will,* argument to the understanding. What can argument do against interest? The understanding is but the servant—the very slave to the will" (Mack, *Jeremy Bentham,* p. 166).

22. See pp. 202–205, this vol., where I try to show that Hume's relocation of the analogical distinction in the *Enquiries* represented a higher-level reapplication of his psychological theory to the problem of its practical application.

23. The theory of legislation can be fitted to this context inasmuch as law is an expression of will.

24. *Morals and Legislation,* p. xxxi. Mrs. Mack comments: "This medical analogy is the key to Bentham's new science. He pursued it always, in dozens of nuances" (*Jeremy Bentham,* p. 264). The methodological point I am trying to illustrate is the one already reemphasized with regard to Hume (see chap. 13, n. 38).

25. "Bentham," p. 248.

26. "Remarks on Bentham's Philosophy," *Mill's Ethical Writings,* p. 48. Mill's metaphors embody his conception of Bentham's method as the same "Geometrical or Abstract Method" of deduction which had been employed by Hobbes (*Logic* [London: Longmans, Green, 1941], pp. 578–80). Bentham himself regarded his method as experimental and repudiated the deductive method, which he identified as the traditional method of Blackstone. "Why," complains Mrs. Mack, "has the mistaken association with geometry, begun by J. S. Mill, never been questioned?" (*Jeremy Bentham,* p. 270) She suggests that it was James Mill who "had the rationalist, reductionist, deductive, and 'geometric' mind that his son John attributed to Bentham" (*ibid.*). But in fact Mill's attribution of a geometrical deductive method to Bentham satisfies the exigencies of Mill's own conception of the opposition between his predecessors' method and their antagonists' method as the opposition which he proposes to surmount with his own distinctively Newtonian method. Since I am more concerned with Mill's interpretation of utilitarianism than with utilitarianism itself, I shall retain Mill's conception of Bentham's method as a linear deduction which is the same as Hobbes'. But see chap. 17, n. 92.

27. "A man's motives affect nobody until they give birth to action; and it is with the action and not with the motive, that individuals and societies have any concern" (*Deontology,* arranged and ed. by John Bowring, 2 vols. [London: Longman, Rees, Orme, Browne, Green, 1834], 2: 156). Compare James Mill: "All the value of acts consists in the consequences of the acts; . . . if the acts are detached from their consequences they are unmeaning contractions of muscles" (*A Fragment on Mackintosh* [London: Longmans, Green, Reader, and Dyer, 1870], p. 231). See n. 36, below.

28. See pp. 163–64, this vol.

29. James Mill similarly rejects the confusion in Hume and in the humanistic tradi-

tion of morals with esthetics. He does so by insisting on the moral irrelevance of the attitude of the spectator: "It has been said, that there is a beauty, and a deformity, in moral and immoral acts. . . . But is it in this way only that we are concerned in moral acts? Do we value them for nothing, but as we value a picture, or a piece of music, for the pleasure of looking at them, or hearing them? Every body knows the contrary. Acts are objects of importance to us, on account of their consequences, and nothing else. This constitutes a *radical distinction* between them and the things called beautiful. . . . It is only an abuse of language to call them beautiful or ugly" (*A Fragment on Mackintosh,* pp. 262–63; italics added).

30. *Fragment,* pp. 154–55.

31. James Mill similarly accused Hume of "wonderful inconsistency" (*A Fragment on Mackintosh,* p. 264).

32. For the obliquity of Hume's analysis, see p. 162, this vol. and accompanying n. 54.

33. For Hume's comparative method, see pp. 157–63, this vol.

34. See p. 195, this vol.

35. See pp. 165, 194, this vol.

36. *Deontology,* 2: 19. This juncture where rational analysis becomes calculation is a crucial point of opposition between the utilitarians and their antagonists: "In the great controversy about the foundations of right and wrong among the reproaches cast by the *Sentimentalists* upon their adversaries the Utilitarians, [is the charge that they] are mean and frivolous enough to have recourse to calculation" (I am citing Bentham from Mack, *Jeremy Bentham,* p. 248). Compare James Mill: "Morality . . . depends . . . upon calculation. A man cannot act without . . . looking at the consequences of his act. If he looks imperfectly at them; that is, takes not the necessary pains to ascertain the evil, which the act may do to others, and nevertheless performs it, he is criminal with regard to all the consequences which he might have foreseen. . . . Where there is no calculation, therefore, there is no morality; in fact, there is nothing rational, any more than moral. To act, without regard to consequences, is the property of an irrational nature. But to act without calculation is to act without a regard to consequences" (*A Fragment on Mackintosh,* pp. 162–64).

37. *Morals and Legislation,* p. 16. Bentham explains: "By the principle of sympathy and antipathy, I mean that principle which approves or disapproves of certain actions, not on account of their tending to augment the happiness, nor yet on account of their tending to diminish the happiness of the party whose interest is in question, but merely because a man finds himself disposed to approve or disapprove of them: holding up that approbation or disapprobation as a sufficient reason for itself, and disclaiming the necessity of looking out for an extrinsic ground" (*ibid.,* pp. 15–16). See p. 255 this vol., for the requirement that a principle point "out some external consideration, as a means of warranting and guiding the internal sentiments of approbation and disapprobation" (*ibid.,* p. 16). Whenever the legislator rewards or punishes without reference to the Greatest-Happiness Principle, the internal sentiments of sympathy or antipathy remain unwarranted and unguided, and their alleged principle is mere *ipse-dixitism* (*Deontology,* 1: 323; see p. 190, this vol, and accompanying n. 13). Bentham also employs "the principle of caprice" as "the appellative . . . for the designation of that branch of the ipse-dixit principle which applies to the civil branch of law" (*Deontology,* 1: 323).

38. Sympathy is a "phantastic principle" inasmuch as it operates on the imagination (*Morals and Legislation,* p. 13). In rejecting sympathy as a principle, Bentham is rejecting (as does James Mill; see n. 29) the confusion in the rhetorical tradition of morals with esthetics. Bentham satirizes "the sounding expressions" (see p. 189, this vol.) of legal rhetoric: "Were the inquiry diligently made, it would be found that the goddess

of harmony has exercised more influence, however latent, over the dispensations of Themis, than her most diligent historiographers . . . seem to have been aware of. Every one knows, how, by the ministry of Orpheus, it was she who first collected the sons of men beneath the shadow of the sceptre. . . . Every one knows, that measured numbers were the language of the infancy of law: none seem to have observed with what imperious sway they have governed her maturer age. In English jurisprudence in particular, the connexion betwixt law and music, however less perceived than in Spartan legislation, is not perhaps less real nor less close. The music of the Office, though not of the same kind, is not less musical in its kind, than the music of the Theatre; that which hardens the heart, than that which softens it:—sostenutos as long, cadences as sonorous. . . . Search indictments, pleadings, proceedings in chancery, conveyances, whatever trespasses you may find against truth or common sense, you will find none against the laws of harmony" (*ibid.*, pp. 14–15). Bentham is of course recalling the function Plato attributes to music in Spartan education and to musical harmony in the education of the citizens of his own ideal state (see vol. 1, p. 250). For Bentham's satire of "the sounding expressions" of moral rhetoric, see p. 189, this vol.

39. *A Fragment on Government,* p. 154.

40. *Philosophical Works,* ed. T. H. Green and T. H. Grose, 4 vols. (London: Longmans, Green, 1882), 3: 446.

41. See vol. 1, pp. 24, 58.

42. *A Fragment on Government,* p. 154.

43. I am not making any attempt to trace the development of Bentham's thought. Mill was largely indifferent to the way Bentham's thought had developed, as was indeed Bentham himself even though he stresses this moment when the scales had fallen from his eyes (see p. 368, this vol.). Any convincingly detailed attempt to reconstruct the actual development of Bentham's thought has to wait upon the projected reediting of his works.

44. Just as Hume repudiates the analytic procedure of dissolving virtue into the calculation of interests, so he repudiates the analytic procedure of dissolving government into the calculation of interests: "Dissolve these ties [of authority and precedent], you break all the bonds of civil society, and leave every man at liberty to consult his private interest, by those expedients which his appetite, disguised under the appearance of reason, shall dictate to him" (*Philosophical Works,* 3: 466).

45. *Philosophical Works,* 3: 116.

46. *Treatise,* p. 537.

47. *Philosophical Works,* 3: 109–10.

48. *Treatise,* p. 549.

49. *Philosophical Works,* 3: 450.

50. For Hume's explanation of this advantage, see the setting for my citation: "It is not with forms of government as with other artificial contrivances, where an old engine may be rejected, if we can discover another more accurate and commodious. . . . An established government has an infinite advantage, by that very circumstance, of its being established; the bulk of mankind being governed by authority, not reason, and never attributing authority to any thing that has not the recommendation of antiquity. To tamper, therefore, in this affair, to try experiments merely upon the credit of supposed argument and philosophy, can never be the part of a wise magistrate, who will bear a reverence to what carries the marks of age; and though he may attempt some improvements for the public good, yet will he adjust his innovations as much as possible to the ancient fabric, and preserve entire the chief pillars and supports of the constitution" (*Philosophical Works,* 3: 480). In editions H to P, the paragraph began: "Of all mankind

there are none so pernicious as political projectors, if they have power; nor so ridiculous, if they want it." Perhaps Hume discarded this sentence because it was balanced merely in style, not as an argument (see n. 55, below).

51. *Treatise,* p. 556.

52. *Ibid.*

53. *Ibid.,* p. 553.

54. See p. 212, this vol.

55. *Philosophical Works,* 3: 464. This essay "On the Coalition of Parties" completes the process of reconciliation begun in the two preceding essays—"Of the Original Contract" and "On Passive Obedience." Another instance of "this tendency to a coalition" that Hume commends is the operation of the English constitution, which Hume conceives as "the most perfect example of that mixed government which philosophers had eulogized since the days of Polybius and Cicero" (Corinne Weston, *English Constitutional Theory and the House of Lords,* 1556–1832 [New York: Columbia University Press, 1965], p. 174). But we face here the paradox that Hume because of his traditionalism breaks with the traditional reduction of the problems of government to problems of "the character and conduct of the governors" (*Philosophical Works,* p. 98; for the reduction see chap. 8, nn. 31, 61). Hume would be "sorry to think, that human affairs admit of no greater stability than what they receive from the casual humours and characters of particular men." Tradition, from Hume's point of view, is a process whereby human affairs become stabilized, and the process incorporates a check-and-balance operation: our "original inclination" (to satisfy an immediate selfish interest) is "checked and restrained by a subsequent judgment or observation" (*ibid.,* p. 455), until eventually we "arrive at a more stable judgment of things" (see p. 241, this vol.). Philosophical reflections continue this process of stabilization (p. 195, this vol.); they are "nothing but the reflections of common life methodized and corrected" (*Enquiry Concerning the Human Understanding,* ed. L. A. Selby-Bigge [Oxford: Clarendon Press, 1902], p. 162). Since Hume's method of correction is to observe counterbalancing and concurring factors (see chap. 13, n. 54), Hume's philosophy itself displays a tendency to a coalition. (This tendency can be counted on, and stability and concurrence can be achieved, because Hume construes Resemblance as a more fundamental relation than Contrast or Contrariety—*ibid.,* p. 24; see also p. 158, this vol.) Thus Hume's commendation of the tendency to a political coalition is still another illustration of the way a philosophical *theory* can impose its own methodological structure on the operations of institutions (see vol. 1, p. 51). But because Hume's philosophical theory is *practical* in its orientation, he himself regards its counterbalancing method as a means toward the practical end of a political coalition. In other words, granted that "this tendency to a coalition [of parties] affords the most agreeable prospect of future happiness," it "ought to be . . . promoted by every lover of his country," and Hume loves his country: "There is not a more effectual method of promoting so good an end, than to prevent all unreasonable insult and triumph of the one party over the other, to encourage *moderate* opinions, to find the proper *medium* in all disputes, to persuade each that its antagonist may possibly be sometimes in the right, and to keep a *balance* in the praise and blame which we bestow on either side" (*Philosophical Works,* 3: 464; italics added).

56. "The only dangerous parties are such as entertain opposite views with regard to the essentials of government, the succession of the crown, or the more considerable privileges belonging to the several members of the constitution; where there is no room for any compromise or accomodation, and where the controversy may appear so momentous as to justify even an opposition by arms to the pretensions of antagonists" (*Philosophical Works,* 3: 464). Irreconcilable opposition can be allowed no place in an analysis guided by the rhetorical criterion of conciliation.

57. Interpreters of Hume throw the Neoclassical structure of his philosophy (see chap. 14, n. 31) off balance when they are sensitive to the thrust of his anti-clericalism while neglecting his esthetic criteria as mere elegance (see p. 205, this vol.). It would not be entirely farfetched to suggest that the process of conciliation in Hume is anchored to a repudiation of selfish interest, as manifested by the clerical faction and its doctrine of the original contract, in much the same way that the process of conciliation in Cicero is anchored to the repudiation of selfish interest, as manifested by the popular faction which he would discredit as Epicurean in doctrine (see chap. 7, n. 95; chap. 8, n. 44). Cicero demonstrated the psychological irreconcilability of the popular faction by attributing to it the distinctive motivation of *ira,* as condemned by Stoicism (see vol. 1, pp. 212, 252, 299). Hume similarly demonstrates the psychological irreconcilability of the clergy: "Few men can bear contradiction with patience; but the clergy too often proceed even to a degree of fury on this head. . . . The *Odium Theologicum* . . . is noted even to a proverb, and means that degree of rancour which is the most furious and implacable. Revenge is a natural passion to mankind; but seems to reign with the greatest force in priests and women. . . . Thus many of the vices of human nature are . . . inflamed in that profession; and . . . all wise governments will be on their guard against the attempts of a society, who will for ever combine into one faction, and while it acts as a society, will for ever be actuated by ambition, pride, revenge, and a persecuting spirit" (*Philosophical Works,* 3: 246–47). I am not pretending to trace here a discernible influence; I am merely trying to bring out a certain similarity of structure between Cicero's and Hume's philosophy.

58. *Treatise,* pp. 524–25.

59. *Philosophical Works,* 3: 139.

60. See p. 248, this vol. and accompanying n. 54.

61. I am citing Bentham from C. K. Ogden, *Bentham's Theory of Fictions* (London: Kegan Paul, 1932), p. xviii.

62. Bentham, *Handbook of Political Fallacies* (New York: Harper), pp. 150, 188.

63. *Ibid.,* pp. 188–89.

64. I am citing Bentham from Ogden, p. xxviii.

65. "The general end of government . . . is the happiness of the community: the happiness of the community is made up of the several happinesses . . . of the several individual members of which that body is composed. These happinesses are all reducible into such and such pains or evils averted and such or such pleasures or advantages procured or secured" (I am citing Bentham from Mack, p. 174).

66. *Treatise,* p. 490.

67. See pp. 193–95, this vol.

68. *Handbook,* p. 139.

69. See p. 235, this vol. The comparison was originally Bentham's own.

70. *Deontology,* 1: 42; Mack, p. 110.

71. Bentham's criteria are not, however, *historicist* in the sense of presupposing a theory of history (see chap. 1, n. 22). Bentham outlines a "history of morality" in which he distinguishes three periods, "dynasties that have ruled over human actions." The first is the period "of Force" when "this *vis* . . . took the name of courage or *virtus*"—"a quality far more animal than moral." Next comes the "reign of Fraud," and Bentham explains that "its influence, like that of force, is usurpation; but it comes with fallacies, instead of open violence. . . . It takes hold of the terrors of the mind and makes

them subservient to its real, but often concealed despotism." Finally will come "the reign of Justice, the reign of utility" (*Deontology,* 2: 48). These ostensibly historical distinctions between periods are all reducible to psychological and moral distinctions deriving from Bentham's theory of human nature (see vol. 1, p. 69). Bentham's periodization is hardly more than a reevaluation of the humanistic tradition as an authoritative and rhetorical tradition; the concealed despotism that he is exposing is ipse-dixitism—"dogmatism in disguise, imposing its sentiments upon others under cover of sounding expressions" (see p. 189, this vol.). Indeed the distinction Bentham draws between courage as physical force and rhetorically exercised moral force, we have already encountered as a feature of Cicero's theory of human nature (see chap. 8, n. 82, and p. 43, this vol.), granted that Bentham wants to stress that rhetorically exercised moral force is "like" physical force since "its influence . . . is usurpation" and that it is fraudulent, operating "with fallacies, instead of open violence." Of course Bentham's humanistic antagonist did not reduce courage to physical force *(vis)*; he preferred Cicero's "happy dirivation of *Virtus* from *Vir*" as giving "a beauty and force" to the expression "which cannot be preserved in our language" (Mackintosh, *Dissertation on the Progress of Ethical Philosophy,* p. 250). For this derivation see chap. 11, n. 96; for the esthetic character of rhetorically exercised moral force in Cicero, see chap. 8, n. 29, as well as his analysis of the process of moral perception (pp. 18–26, this vol.).

72. *Fragment on Government,* p. 155.

73. *Handbook,* p. 259. See n. 81, below.

74. *The Principles of Morals,* p. 7. One remedy for avoiding a complete surrender to plebian sentiments is to resort to rhetorical and sentimental writers in the humanistic tradition: "Where any real, affecting incident happens; when passion is awakened, fancy agitated, example draws, and council urges; the philosopher is lost in the man, and he seeks in vain for that persuasion which before seemed so firm and unshaken. What remedy for this inconvenience? Assist yourself by a frequent perusal of the entertaining moralists: Have recourse to the learning of Plutarch, the imagination of Lucian, the eloquence of Cicero, the wit of Seneca, the gaiety of Montaigne, the sublimity of Shaftesbury. Moral precepts, so couched, strike deep, and fortify the mind against the illusions of passion" *(Philosophical Works,* 3: 229–30). Note that this remedy was not offered in the *Treatise.* Its availability now illustrates the change that has taken place in Hume's theory of human nature (see chap. 14, n. 102, and pp. 204–205.).

75. Thus one fallacy Bentham exposes is the drawing of a distinction between theory and practice in order to argue against some reform that it "is good in theory; but, alas, bad in practice" (*Handbook,* p. 199.

76. Hume therefore rejects the tradition of "philosophical opposition" in favor of the "authoritarian" tradition (see pp. 68–69, this vol.) in which the philosopher submits to authority in the fashion endorsed by Seneca (see chap. 11, n. 42). Ordinarily "the zeal of *patriots* is . . . much less requisite than the patience and submission of *philosophers* [for *patientia* as the moral concomitant of political submission, see chap. 11, nn. 32, 41]. The virtue and good intentions of Cato and Brutus are highly laudable; but to what purpose did their zeal serve? Only to hasten the fatal period of the Roman government, and render its convulsions and dying agonies more violent and painful" (*Philosophical Works,* 3: 109). Like Seneca, Hume distinguishes between the moral and the political situation, but Hume's distinction is a utilitarian distinction between intended and unintended consequences. Thus Hume defends his moral theory to Hutcheson as follows: "I desire you to consider if there be any quality that is virtuous, without having a tendency either to the public good or to the good of the person who possesses it. . . . I desire you would only consider the *tendencies* of qualities, not their actual operations, which depend on chance. Brutus riveted the chains of Rome faster by his opposition; but the natural tendency of his noble dispositions—his public spirit

and magnanimity—was to establish her liberty" (*Ibid.*, 29). Brutus can therefore continue to play an exemplary role in Hume's moral theory (see p. 196, this vol.), which he is denied in Hume's political theory.

77. See p. 246, this vol.

78. I am citing Bentham from Ogden, pp. cxxxvii–cxxxviii,

79. See p. 153, this vol.

80. I am citing Bentham from Ogden, p. cxxxviii. Although I am retaining the enlightenment metaphor, I have neglected Bentham's considerable debt to thinkers of the French Enlightenment—Helvetius in particular (see chap. 13, n. 120).

81. *Autobiography*, p. 68. Mill contributed thirteen articles. Even more characteristic of the Benthamite effort at analysis was the *Parliamentary History and Review*, which exposed "the fallacies of the speakers" (*Autobiography*, p. 82) along the lines proposed by Bentham's *Handbook of Political Fallacies*. This review was edited by the editor of the *Handbook*, but it lasted only three years (1825–28).

82. *Ibid.*, p. 83; see also p. 128.

83. See vol. 1, p. 22.

84. *Westminster Review*, 1 (January, 1824): 1. The youthful propagandist had the same attitude towards history. His protégé and closest ally, John Roebuck, recalled: "I learned [from Mill] that there was a *Science of Government*. . . . That the true experience on which the conclusions respecting Government rested, was not derived simply or chiefly from the faulty chronicles called the History of Nations, but depended upon principles of our nature which are invariable" (letter to Daniel O'Connell, cited by Joseph Hamburger, *Intellectuals in Politics: John Stuart Mill and the Philosophic Radicals* [New Haven: Yale University Press, 1965], p. 11).

85. See vol. 1, p. 22.

86. *Westminster Review*, 3 (April, 1825), reprinted in *Prefaces to Liberty*, ed. Bernard Wishy (Boston: Beacon Press, 1959), p. 147; italics added.

87. *Autobiography*, p. 93. Mill recalls his first reading Bentham, as "one of the turning points in my mental history" (*ibid.*, p. 45), and places this recollection near the beginning of the third chapter of his *Autobiography* (p. 45); the fourth chapter makes the transition of the "especially" and covers "Youthful Propagandism—The Westminster Review." The retrospect I have cited in the text sets the stage for the fifth chapter, covering "A Crisis In My Mental History." In chap. 18 we shall be concerned with the organization of Mill's *Autobiography* as illustrating the way he structured his mental history.

88. See p. 189, this vol.

89. See p. 189, this vol. See n. 94, below, for the opposition between the internal and the external as construed by Mackintosh.

90. *Morals and Legislation*, p. 17.

91. See n. 27, above, and p. 242, this vol.

92. The traditionalist attack on the utilitarians was not a repudiation of the principle of utility itself (see chap. 13, n. 2). Rather, it was an attack on Bentham for assuming "that because the principle of utility forms a necessary part of every moral theory, it ought therefore to be the chief motive of human conduct." In other words, the issue was topological: "The later moralists who adopt the principle of utility have so *misplaced* it, that in their hands it has as great a tendency as any theoretical error can have to lessen the intrinsic pleasure of virtue, and to unfit our habitual feelings for being the most

effectual inducements to good conduct. This is the natural tendency of a discipline which brings utility too closely and frequently into contact with action" (*Dissertation on the Progress of Ethical Philosophy,* pp. 244, 256). To this extent Mackintosh is contemning analysis (see p. 233, this vol., but see also n. 94, below).

93. " 'Tis evident, that when we praise any actions, we regard only the motives that produced them, and consider the actions as signs or indications of certain principles in the mind and temper. The external performance has no merit. We must look within to find the moral quality. This we cannot do directly; and therefore fix our attention on actions, as on external signs" (David Hume, *A Treatise Of Human Nature,* ed. L. A. Selby-Bigge [Oxford: Clarendon Press, 1888], p. 477). Compare Mackintosh: "The *direct* object of Ethics is only mental disposition. It considers action *indirectly* as the signs by which such dispositions are manifested" (*Dissertation on the Progress of Ethical Philosophy,* p. 258). The identification of actions as signs of inward dispositions is usually one of the marks of the influence of the rhetorical tradition on the moral tradition (see chap. 10, n. 139).

94. *Deontology,* pp. 125–26. When Mackintosh attacked Bentham for assuming "that because the principle of utility forms a necessary part of every moral theory, it ought therefore to be the chief motive of human conduct" (see n. 92, above), he was adjusting the relation between the internal and the external in a different way from Bentham, and therefore faced a different problem of observation: "Virtue has often outward advantages, and always inward delights; but the second, though constant, strong, inaccessible, and inviolable, are not easily considered by the common observer as apart from the virtue with which they are blended. They are so subtile and evanescent as to escape the distinct contemplation of all but the very few who meditate on the acts of mind. [To this extent, Mackintosh endorses analysis (contrast n. 92, above), but it is a contemplative meditative performance, and does not involve the experimental "exertion" characteristic of utilitarian analysis (see p. 238, this vol.).] The outward advantages, on the other hand, cold, uncertain, dependent, and precarious as they are, yet stand out to the sense and to the memory, may be handled and counted, and are perfectly on a level with the general apprehension. Hence they have become the almost exclusive theme of all moralists who profess to follow reason. There is room for suspecting that a very general illusion prevails on this subject" (*Dissertation on the Progress of Ethical Philosophy,* p. 251).

95. Although the issue was explicitly posed by Hume (see p. 171, this vol.), he failed to resolve the uncertainty to the satisfaction of the utilitarian: "How should Hume be safe from error, who makes 'a sense of virtue'—a 'feeling' referable to no results, the groundwork of good conduct?" (*Deontology,* 2: 70). Certainty for the traditionalist is not to be obtained by reference to observable and calculable results: "The outward advantages" are "cold, uncertain, dependent, and precarious," even though they "may be . . . counted" (see n. 94, above). According to the traditionalist, a further uncertainty is introduced when the principle of utility becomes inculcated: "The frequent appeal to utility as the standard of action tends to introduce an uncertainty with respect to the conduct of other men, which would render all intercourse insupportable" (*Dissertation on the Progress of Ethical Philosophy,* p. 256).

96. *Autobiography,* p. 72.

97. Considering the Benthamite commitment to publicity, and James Mill's role as the publicist for Benthamism, it seems a little ironical that Bentham kept a secret from James Mill when he "announced to him 'the money [for publishing a review] is found.' " John Mill must be echoing his father's complaint when he recalls: "Not only no desire was shewn for his advice, but such a mere *secret de la comédie* as where the money was to come from, was not confided to him" (*The Early Draft of John Stuart Mill's Autobiography,* ed. Jack Stillinger [Urbana: University of Illinois Press, 1961], p. 90).

98. See Mill's account of his father's article: "As it had been a favourite portion of the scheme formerly talked of [the scheme for a radical review] that part of the work should be devoted to reviewing the other Reviews, this article of my father's was to be a general criticism of the Edinburgh Review from its commencement. Before writing it he made me read through all the volumes of the Review, or as much of each as seemed of any importance, . . . and make notes for him of the articles which I thought he would wish to examine. . . . This paper of my father's was the chief cause of the sensation which the Westminster Review produced at its first appearance, and is, both in conception and in execution, one of the most striking of all his writings" (*Autobiography,* pp. 64–65).

99. *Westminster Review,* 1 (Jan., 1824): 207–8.

100. *Ibid.,* 208.

101. *Liberty of the Press,* reprinted from the Supplement to the Encyclopaedia Britannica (London: J. Innes, n.d.), pp. 10–11. James Mill worked on this article in 1821.

102. *Moral Sentiments* (London: Henry G. Bohn, 1953), p. 185.

103. See pp. 165, 197, this vol.

104. *Deontology,* 1: 70. Bentham is referring to Shaftesbury's version of the doctrine of moral sense. But Bentham seems to attribute the same version of this doctrine to Hume.

105. Bentham's interpretation is not entirely arbitrary. The humanistic tradition lends itself to this interpretation both as a tradition in which the individual extends over other men the authority he exercises reflexively over himself (see pp. 62–65, this vol., and accompanying references to vol. 1), and as a tradition which was constituted a tradition by assigning individuals authoritative roles as predecessors (see chap. 7, nn. 28, 29, and chap. 11, n. 31).

106. This was Hume's offense as a moral theorist: "He occupies a pulpit whence he deals out his moral dogmas, and speaks as if he were the representative of higher virtues than the man to whom he is speaking" (*Deontology,* 2. 250).

107. See p. 255, this vol.

108. *Moral Sentiments,* p. 185.

109. *The Works of Jeremy Bentham,* ed. John Bowring, 11 vols. (Edinburgh: William Tate, 1843), 4: 66, 39.

110. *Ibid.,* p. 66.

111. "The moral or popular sanction is that which is commonly called public opinion; it is the received decision of society on conduct" (*Deontology,* 1: 90).

112. *Ibid.,* 2:3.

113. *Ibid.,* 1: 48–49.

114. *Ibid.,* pp. 100–101. The gymnasium the whole world would become is probably Plato's. Plato had argued that in an ideal state the women must strip for exercise (*Republic* 457A). Plato defended their exposure on utilitarian grounds, and his defense provided a succinct version of the utilitarian formula—a version which is cited, for example, by Hume (see chap. 14, n. 102).

115. See p. 376, this vol.

Part VI

Liberalism

16

Public Opinion

Our mental light . . . has . . . lost in intensity, at least a part of what it has gained in diffusion.—Antiquus

1776

Our undertaking in this study, it sometimes seems today, may not be *philosophia* but *necrophilia:*

> It is one of the assumptions of intellectual life in our country [sc., Great Britain] that there should be amongst us men whom we think of as political philosophers. Philosophers themselves and sensitive to philosophic change, they are to concern themselves with political and social relationships at the widest possible level of generality. . . . Today, it would seem, we have them no longer. The tradition has been broken and our assumption is misplaced. . . . For the moment, anyway, political philosophy is dead.[1]

We are living in a period of rapid change, when moments are very momentary and the same commentator, Peter Laslett, who thus solemnized the demise of political philosophy in 1956, celebrated its revival a scant six years later.[2] But his earlier obsequy has elicited so much more response than the later revival, that anyone writing today on political philosophy can hardly avoid being mustered into the funeral procession.

Personally, I prefer autopsies to funerals. My autopsy of the tradition would deprive 1956 of its privilege as the *articulum mortis.* If we must select a moment, 1776 strikes me as somewhat more plausible. Or if it only serves to date the first symptoms that the health of the patient was in mortal danger, it at least allows time for that lingering death which is the fate of traditions.

Laslett has three explanations for the demise of political philosophy. One is, of course, the emergence of the social sciences. We have seen that the publication in 1776 of *The Wealth of Nations* marked the emergence of the first of the social sciences from the traditional British context for the treatment of political problems—a theory of human nature. It was this context that had previously enabled British philosophers "to concern themselves with political and social relationships at the widest possible level of generality."

Laslett's second explanation for the demise of political philosophy draws our attention to the extent that philosophy itself has today become analytic, and thus distrustful of the effort to handle relationships at the widest possible level of generality.[3] The analytic procedure of separating and distinguishing what had traditionally been related, we have seen, is at least as old as Locke. But Hume is often preferred today as the predecessor of contemporary British analysis. In 1776 he died, leaving behind him the Advertisement in which he repudiated his *Treatise Of Human Nature*. The relationships between the parts of this originally comprehensive theory of human nature we watched disintegrate, leaving in its place Hume's treatment, in his *Enquiries* and *Essays*, of more specific, separate, and distinct subject-matters.[4]

Bentham is sometimes preferred today to Hume (as he was by Mill) as the predecessor who extended the analytic procedure to political problems. In 1776 Bentham published his first and major political work, the *Fragment on Government*. This treatment of political problems is for Bentham only a fragmentary part of a general theory of legislation, and it happens that the philosophy of law is the only part of Anglo-American political philosophy (if it is a part of political philosophy) which still stirs with much vitality today, for it lends itself rather less readily to complete and final annexation by the social sciences and rather more readily to the analytic procedure of distinguishing the meanings of terms, constructing separate arguments, and citing specific cases.[5]

Laslett has a third and final explanation for the death of political philosophy: "Politics have become too serious to be left to philosophers."[6] It is not quite clear, however, as to what other form of thought can be taken to approach the seriousness of politics today. Indeed Laslett's pronouncement may seem so extravagantly platitudinous as to be susceptible of elucidation neither by philosophical analysis nor by any inquiry in the social sciences. But we need not allow it to fall entirely flat if we take it as supplementary to his other two explanations of the death of political philosophy. When it has been suggested that the problems of political philosophy have been dispersed among the social sciences, or dissolved by the chemistry of the analytic method, some acknowledgment is still needed of the formidable vitality of political problems today. If the philosopher or the social scientist no longer extends his grasp to include facts which are great, existing, and political, these facts nonetheless retain their scale in the realm of public concern. The formulation and treatment they receive there is, roughly speaking, journalistic.

Journalism may seem an informal, loose, and dissipating activity, patterned only by periodic deadlines. Indeed when the term "journalism" is used today of the intellectual effort of a philosopher or a social scientist, it is as a term of opprobrium, so that it may seem out of keeping for me to have assigned journalism in the last chapter methodolog ical footing in any sense comparable to that of a systematic political philosophy. But why should we continue to pay so solicitously our respects to the deceased? In Part I we did so because we did not fully realize that the deceased was deceased. We were trying to identify characteristics of liberal political thought. But in Part I we missed one crucial characteristic—liberalism's resort to what I am now proposing to identify as journalism. The identification can be established by reviewing Mill's three adjustments in relation to his predecessors.

Method and Opinions

The first adjustment which we examined was Mill's abandonment of his father's political philosophy "as a philosophy" or "as a scientific theory." (These two criteria we found he regarded as equivalent.)[7] Even if we did not realize it fully then, we were confronted with the demise of political philosophy in the answer which Mill sponsored to his own question: "If I am asked, what system of political philosophy I substituted for that which, as a philosophy, I had abandoned, I answer, no system."[8] Having in the meantime dealt with this utilitarian political philosophy, we can proceed to the further question of what was involved in Mill's abandoning it "as a philosophy."

A philosopher abandons a philosophy when it begins to fall apart. It begins to fall apart when he draws a distinction it cannot accommodate. During the period of his crisis, Mill abandons utilitarian political philosophy by drawing a distinction which seems to have taken shape in his mind as a result of Macaulay's attack on the *Essay on Government*. "It is utterly impossible," Macaulay protested, "to deduce the science of government from the principles of human nature."[9] James Mill, his son reports, dismissed this protest as "simply irrational, an attack upon the reasoning faculty, an example of the saying of Hobbes, that when reason is against a man, a man will be against reason."[10] This dismissal merely reasserted the role reason had played in the logical deduction. To an attack on the deductive method, Mill's father had no other retort available except the psychological justification provided by his rationalistic theory of human nature.

I have cited the son's report of his father's reaction because Mill's preoccupation with his relation to utilitarian political philosophy survived his abandonment of it "as a philosophy." Indeed his reaction to Macaulay's attack was more of a reaction to his father's reaction than a direct reaction.[11] His father's reaction, Mill admitted, "made me think that there was really something more fundamentally erroneous in my father's conception of philosophical method, as applicable to politics, than I had hitherto supposed there was." The process of locating this error, Mill explains, was the laying of a "foundation . . . for the 'Logic of the Moral Sciences', which rendered "my new position in respect to my old political creed . . . perfectly definite."[12]

The son's defining his new position in the context of a logic shifted from under the father the ground which the father had held under attack by reasserting his allegiance to his rationalistic theory of human nature. The problems posed for the son by the attack were not what they were for his father, indistinguishably methodological and psychological. They were, instead, to be distinguished as methodological problems, to be handled in a logic rather than in the context of a theory of human nature.

This distinction between *logic* and *psychology* is Mill's decisive contribution to the disintegration of the theory of human nature as a context, and thereby to the demise of British political philosophy. Bentham had not drawn this distinction, any more than James Mill.[13] Consider once again the application of the principle of utility that the youthful Mill found so impressive when he first read Bentham that he concluded "that all previous moralists were superseded, and that here indeed was the commencement of a new era in thought." What was superseded was "dogmatism in disguise, imposing its sentiments upon others under cover of sounding expressions which convey no reason for the sentiment, but set up the sentiment as its own reason."[14] The terms "reason" and "sentiment" here carried more than psychological implications. They gained their vigor from the fusion in Bentham's utilitarianism of psychological with methodological implications.

After his break with utilitarianism as a political philosophy, Mill may continue to commend Bentham for having "introduced into morals and politics those . . . modes of investigation which are essential to the idea of science." Yet this continuity is largely illusory. Mill is still able to commend Bentham because Mill has himself introduced into morals and politics a distinction between Bentham's substantive opinions in these subjects and Bentham's mode of investigation: "It was not his opinions . . . but his method that constituted the novelty and the value of what he did—a value beyond all price, even though we should reject the whole, as we unquestionably must a large part, of the opinions themselves."[15] When he rejects this large part, Mill is severing the method from the utilitarian theory of human nature which had been at once the result and the context of the method's application. The cleavage alters in retrospect the entire history of utilitarianism:

> In all ages of philosophy one of its schools has been utilitarian. . . . It was by *mere accident* that this opinion became connected in Bentham with his peculiar method. The utilitarian philosophers antecedent to him had no more claim to the method than their antagonists. To refer, for instance, to the Epicurean philosophy, according to the most complete view we have of the moral part of it by the most accomplished scholar of antiquity, Cicero: we ask anyone who has read his philosophical writings, . . . whether the arguments of the Epicureans do not, just as much of those of the Stoics or Platonists, consist of mere rhetorical appeals to common notions, . . . notions . . . never so looked into as to ascertain in what sense, and under what limitations, they are true. . . . Bentham certainly did not learn his sifting and anatomizing method from them. This method Bentham has finally installed in philosophy, has made it, henceforth, imperative on philosophers of all schools. . . . This is nothing less than a revolution in philosophy.[16]

In the last chapter we saw that Bentham's application of this method erected the principle of utility into a methodological principle and excluded the adoption of any other substantive psychological phenomenon (e.g., sympathy) as a methodological principle.[17] Bentham's method could not, in Bentham's own view, be severed from his utilitarian theory of human nature and put at the disposal of other schools of philosophy which are committed to an antagonistic theory. When Mill identifies utilitarianism as a perennial opinion which became by mere accident connected in Bentham with his scientific method, when Mill explains that utilitarian philosophers antecedent to Bentham had no more claim to the method than their antagonists and that Bentham has made it imperative on philosophers of all schools, whatever their theory of human nature, Mill is substituting for any theory of human nature a psychologically neutral logic as a context for the treatment of moral and political problems.[18]

Within this logical context, the utilitarian theory of human nature shrinks to a treatment of the subject-matter of psychology. As a subject-matter, psychology is not treated in the context of Mill's *Logic*, any more than the political problems which Mill's father treated by deduction from psychological premises. In fact the methodological problems raised by Macaulay's attack on this deduction can be settled by Mill in the context of this *Logic* without benefit of any treatment of psychological or political problems. In the *Logic* Mill is presenting "precepts of Method," which he admits are not "practically exemplified in the establishment of any body of doctrine."[19] This was a difficulty for us in Part I, when we tried to identify Mills' political thought. But his distinction between method and opinions (or a body of doctrine) at least serves to distinguish his political thought from that of his predecessors. Like them, Mill proposes to "remedy the backward state of the Moral Sciences, by applying the methods of Physical Science."[20] Unlike them, he does not actually construct these sciences.

Theory and Practice

It is at this juncture, where Mill carries through his first adjustment in relation to his predecessors, that we can mourn the demise of political philosophy. But we can find something else to do—which is perhaps more profitable. We have already tried to circumvent Mill's distinction between method and opinions. We have done so by seeking problems of philosophical method in the way political problems have actually been treated, rather than waiting on the solution to these problems which may supervene when philosophical method eventually becomes scientific. So far this treatment of political problems has taken the form of political philosophies. Mill may not have any political philosophy, but he does at least have political opinions which are available for comparison with his predecessors' political philosophy. It is true that in dealing with these opinions we face the disheartening verdict, so often passed on Mill today, "Rigour in argument is not among his accomplishments,"[21] so that it may seem that Mill cannot escape dissection by his own distinction between method and opinions: if he offers in his "Logic of the Moral Sciences" a method which is not exemplified in any body of doctrine, he offers in his actual political writings doctrines which do not exemplify any method. Emulation of the method of physical science is a recurrent adjustment in the development of political thought, and in this study I have tried to take it into account. Yet at least as characteristic of liberal political thought is readiness to acquiesce in the unsystematic, unscientific character of its actual political doctrines. Acquiescence may tempt philosophical attention less than aspiration, but at least the evidence of the liberal's acquiescence is more available than the outcome of his aspirations.

In Mill's case the evidence is not only available; in some sense it has already been examined. We do not need to compare his political opinions with the political philosophy of his predecessors, since his political opinions are the form in which their political philosophy survives after his abandoning it as a philosophy:

> In politics, [1] though I no longer accepted the doctrine, of the Essay on Government as a scientific theory, [2] though I ceased to consider representative democracy as an absolute principle, and regarded it as a question of time, place, and circumstance; [3] though I looked upon the choice of political institutions as a moral and educational question more than one of material interests . . .; nevertheless, this change in the premises of my political philosophy did not alter my practical political creed as to the requirements of my own time and country. I was as much as ever a radical and democrat for Europe, and especially for England.[22]

Mill may here be abandoning his father's political philosophy "as a philosophy" or "as a scientific theory." But he is coming to its rescue by conceiving it instead as "a practical political creed." He thought his father should have given a double reply to Macaulay: "I was not writing a scientific treatise on politics. I was writing an argument for parliamentary reform."[23] The son was keeping his thoughts to himself (for reasons we shall later examine); he was not in the habit anyway of suggesting what his father should have said. But James Mill had boasted that the deductive argument of the Essay was "close and strong,"[24] and it seems likely that he would have resented the consolation that it was not scientific as much as he did Macaulay's sneer that it was unscientific. However, to sense the impertinence, from James Mill's point of view, of his son's silently volunteered defense, is to face the question of its cogency for the son himself.

This question is not answered directly when Mill's *Logic* rendered his new position in respect to his old political creed perfectly definite. Since Mill is concerned in the *Logic* with the methodological requirements of a political philosophy "as a philosophy," he adopts a largely negative attitude toward the utilitarians. In constructing their political philosophy, they made a "mistake," which "consisted in presenting in a *systematic* shape, and as the *scientific* treatment of a great *philolosophical* question, what should have passed for that which it really was, the *mere polemics of the day*." Mill confesses his "regret that the small though highly important portion of the philosophy of government, which was wanted for the immediate purpose of serving the cause of parliamentary reform, should have been held forth by thinkers of such eminence as a complete theory."[25]

A change in the criteria to be satisfied by a scientific philosophy of government, as these are set forth in Mill's *Logic,* is only the first adjustment in Mill's relation to his predecessors. What to Mill's father was a scientific theory, what Mill himself rejects as not a scientific theory, he nonetheless retains as his practical political creed. The salvage operation, initiated by Mill's distinction between theory and practice, bypasses the negative verdict of the *Logic*. The "immediate purpose" of "parliamentary reform" acquires positive implications for Mill as one of "the requirements of my own time and country." The adjustment is not a matter (as it may have seemed in Part I) of James Mill's thought occupying one side of a distinction between "a scientific theory" and "a practical political creed," but turning up, in John Mill's reappraisal, as his own political thought, on the other side of the distinction. It is John Mill alone who is drawing the distinction between the methodological requirements of a scientific theory and the practical requirements of his own time and country. In the *Essay on Government,* his father was offering what was indistinguishably a systematic political philosophy and a practical argument for parliamentary reform. In contrast, John Mill's own political thought divides and turns up on both sides of the distinction. For his father's political philosophy, which Mill abandons as a philosophy, he substitutes, on the one hand, in his "Logic of the Moral Sciences," precepts of scientific method which are not exemplified in any body of doctrine; on the other hand, he salvages this political philosophy as body of less rigorous practical arguments conceived with reference to the immediate political requirements of his own time and country. Practical arguments so conceived can be identified as journalistic.

Journalism

Because Mill distinguishes the requirements of a scientific theory from the practical requirements to be met by journalism, and reserves the first set of requirements for treatment in a logic, he fails to bring out the differences between his conception of journalism and his father's, in the way he brings out the differences between his own and his father's conceptions of scientific method. We need not, however, resign ourselves to Mill's failure, for we have not equated the requirements of method as applied to politics with the requirements of scientific method.[26] We have recognized in Mill's own case that the requirements of scientific method are directly involved only in the first of his three adjustments. The requirements to be met by what I shall describe as Mill's journalistic method are in effect determined by his two remaining adjustments.

In interpreting Mill's adjustments again, we are not repeating the interpretation of Part I. There we first tried to identify *liberal* political thought. But then we were forced to consider as well the identification of the *political.* Thus Mill's first adjustment retained for us the priority it had for Mill himself.[27] As a commitment to the principle of "distinct and separate" sciences, it facilitated our locating the political in relation to "other studies," within the general structure of knowledge. But in taking up now Mill's "practical political creed," our attention finally shifts to liberal political *thought*. In other words, we are no longer dealing with knowledge which must be discriminated with respect to subject-matters; we are dealing with thinking which remains unconfined, and concerned with "political and social relationships at the widest possible level of generality." Philosophers are prone today to analyze competing conceptions of philosophy and of scientific method. Yet if the demise of political philosophy leaves journalism pretty much in charge of political thought so far as the wider, more serious problems of politics are concerned, it may be almost as worthwhile to analyze competing conceptions of journalism. But we are no longer dealing with a well-articulated structure of knowledge, and the vagaries of journalism may seem next to impossible to delineate. Is there any hope of discovering that the heir to political philosophy is not irremediably tainted with intellectual dissoluteness?

Since the time we first began our attempt to identify Mill's political thought, we have acquired some background in the history of political thought. Paradoxical as this may sound, this historical background enables us to examine with somewhat more confidence journalistic political thought in lieu of systematic political philosophy. For we have discovered that thought does not always go on at the same level. Problems which at one stage of their history were technical philosophical problems (e.g., the problem of recollection which Plato treated in the setting of his theory of ideas) can become more loosely treated at some later stage (e.g., the problem of recognition which Cicero treated in the setting of his esthetic exemplarism), and their earlier systematic treatment can then illuminate their later less formal treatment.[28] Furthermore, these loosely treated problems can become again at some later stage technical philosophical problems (e.g., when Cicero's problem of recognition becomes in effect an epistemological problem for Hobbes).[29] In tracing such continuities between more rigorous and less rigorous forms of thought, we have also become better acquainted with the relevance of "other studies" to the political. The epistemological problem of recognition which Hobbes solved with a political theory, Locke solved with an economic theory.[30] Such adjustments we have found are not always restricted to a study like economics whose political relevance would readily be admitted today. Cicero solved his problem of recognition esthetically by adopting a rhetorical method, and if his solution remained loose, it became more systematic in Hume's and Smith's theories of human nature.[31] Indeed, the attention that has been paid to the rhetorical and esthetic strand in the composition of the humanistic tradition has provided a measure of methodological continuity which would not have been found in the history of modern political thought if the only factor taken into account had been successive scientific adjustments. The utilitarians' journalistic attack on tradition may have been rigorously scientific in their view, but it is journalistic, not scientific, from Mill's mature point of view. From both points of view, however, what was at the focus of this attack was the rhetorical method of the traditionalists.[32] We shall see later that Mill identifies journalism as such as a rhetorical method.[33] But we shall also see that his conception of journalism will involve his rejection of the traditional definition of esthetic criteria in rhetorical terms.

A Great Existing Fact

First, however, we must reexamine Mill's second adjustment. Even though this *historicist* adjustment undermines utilitarian reliance on a theory of human nature, it enables Mill to rescue his father from the brunt of Macaulay's criticism. His father, Mill has explained, was not constructing a political philosophy or a scientific theory of politics, but was meeting the practical requirements of their own time and country. Mill's historicist adjustment, which we examined in Part I as an adjustment in Mill's conception of scientific method, has to be reexamined now as an adjustment in his conception of journalistic method. The pressing requirements of our own time and country we take so much for granted today that we have forgotten that journalism in our sense became conceivable as a legitimate undertaking only when these historical requirements came to be distinguished as pressing. If James Mill attacked periodical literature as such, it was because he refused to distinguish the requirements of his period from the requirements of his theory of human nature. To accept the distinction in the context of this theory would be itself to reject reform, by succumbing to an immediate purpose. The son may defend an "immediate purpose" as an immediate purpose of their "time and country," but "an immediate purpose" was discredited in the father's theory of human nature as characteristic of the kind of journalism which was "gratification administered to the mind in its present stage."[34] Such gratification was psychological pandering. Deduction from a theory of human nature was the only unflinchingly rational way in which a journalist could serve the cause of parliamentary reform. Thus the conception of journalism with which Mill defends his father is somewhat similar (if we overlook the difference of context—i.e., the difference between the historical and the psychological reference of "immediate purpose") to the conception of journalism that his father attacked.

Another dimension is added to our comparison as soon as we realize that Mill, like his father, is a journalist who attacks journalism. In *On Liberty,* Mill is committed to the liberty of the press. But he rapidly passes over "this aspect of the question,"[35] although for his father, and for the youthful propagandist which he himself had been, this was the pivotal form of liberty. In fact Mill no longer welcomes in *On Liberty* the prospect of the liberty of the press throwing (in Bentham's phrase) "all men into the public presence."[36] Or rather, this utopian prospect, to which he had looked forward when as a youthful propagandist he defended liberty of the press, now seems to have become the already existing fact which he identifies with democracy in America. In *On Liberty,* Mill complains that "public opinion *now* rules the world."[37]

Before concluding that history must have gotten ahead of itself, we should recall what we first learned in Part I—that existing facts can be difficult to pin down historically. In Part I we encountered democracy in America as the "great existing fact" to which Mill was drawing our attention in *On Liberty* and which he was construing as evidence of "the tendencies of modern commercial civilization."[38] However interested we may now be in determining the *articulum mortis* of political philosophy, we cannot pretend that journalism became its heir precisely in 1776—when Hume repudiated his comprehensive theory of human nature, when the first social science emerged, and the philosophy of law. Democracy in America became "a great existing fact" for Mill's political thought when he read Tocqueville's *Democracy in America.* In *On Liberty,* instead of imagining (as Mill had as a youthful propagandist) "the horrors of an oriental despotism" from which "we are protected only by the press,"[39] Mill follows Tocqueville in fearing "the American form of democracy," which he identifies with "the despotic yoke of public opinion," to which men are in danger of being handed over by the press, insofar as it represents their "thinking . . . done for them by men very much like themselves."[40]

Just as Mill defends his father with a conception of journalism which is somewhat similar to the conception of journalism which his father attacked, so there is a certain similarity between the kind of journalism that Mill is attacking and the kind of journalism which his father's writings and his own "Youthful Propagandism" exemplified. In both instances journalism is conceived as an instrument of exposure to public opinion.[41] In detecting this similarity we are again disregarding the difference of context: Mill has an historical conception of the kind of journalism he is attacking, whereas his youthful conception derived a psychological justification from his father's utilitarian theory of human nature.

The first step in the elucidation of the differences between these conceptions is to take into account the different relation each conception presupposes between the individual and other men. In the context of the utilitarian theory of human nature, the individual had emerged, as the methodological result of scientific analysis, uniform with all other individuals and thereby qualified to enter an impartial process of calculation in which any individual can be counted as one —that is, in the same way as any other individual.[42] This methodological result is somewhat similar to the historical result in *On Liberty* of the pressure of public opinion, "wearing down into uniformity all that is individual."[43] Such pressure is menacing because Mill is concerned that men's thinking not be "done for them" by other men —least of all by other men "very much like themselves."

Before we can appreciate Mill's concern, we have to reconnoiter the change of context itself. It illustrates, of course, the unstraightforward way such changes take place in the development of political thought, however blunt the existing facts may seem that push through these changes. Uniformity of individuals, which was the sought-for methodological result in the old *psychological* context, becomes re-identified in the new *historical* context as the result of historical changes. Two concomitant historical changes are involved. The first change undermines the utilitarian deduction: "As society proceeds in its development, its phenomena are determined more and more, not by the simple tendencies of human nature, but by the accumulated influence of past generations over the present."[44] But utilitarianism itself is now no longer simply a method of deduction from the simple tendencies of human nature; it has entered the historical context where it is to be reidentified as an influence of the last generation on the present. It is an influence which has been diffused as one of the characteristic manifestations of the "tendencies of modern commercial civilization," whereby "uniformity tends to become greater . . . as society advances," so that "the longer our species lasts and the more civilized it becomes, . . . the more . . . does the influence . . . of mankind *en masse* over every individual in it, predominate over other forces."[45] This tendency, however, is not merely something which has to be traced historically; at a higher level it also helps shape methodologically the historical context in which such tendencies are to be traced. In other words, if the tendency is the consolidation in *practice* of the pressure of public opinion on the individual, it is also the consolidation of a subject-matter for a scientific *theory* of social history:

> The increasing preponderance of the collective agency of the species . . . is constantly bringing the general evolution of the race into something which deviates less from a certain and preappointed track. Historical science, therefore is always becoming more possible; not solely because it is better studied, but because in every generation, it becomes better adapted for study.[46]

If the evolution of the race had actually become geared to a preappointed track, the unilinear history of political thought which I disavowed in Part I could be written, beginning perhaps with Mill's generation.[47] It would have been unnecessary and frivolous on my part to have detected various criteria lying behind Mill's three adjustments. The scientific criterion put forward by the first adjustment would coincide with the historicist criterion supplied by the second adjustment. It would have been equally pointless to have traced back to Antiquity the development of these criteria, for their variety could be seen to have been associated with earlier, now outmoded, deviations from history's preappointed track.

Unfortunately, however, Mill's own history of political and social thought is not unilinear, even at that juncture where the influence of mankind *en masse* over every individual in it is acknowledged to be predominating over other forces. This predominance takes the form of democracy in America as a preappointed *historical* track for mankind. But democracy in America is also a *moral* threat. In becoming better adapted for historical study, mankind is not thereby becoming better. Mill's historicist track is intersected by his *moralistic* track (i.e., by his third adjustment), so that the positive relevance which public opinion—and journalism as its instrument—enjoyed in the utilitarian theory of human nature is largely lost at the present stage of history. What is now needed is that "internal culture of the individual" which equips him to resist the pressure of public opinion.[48]

Morals and Politics

Mill's awareness of the limited *historical* relevance of utilitarianism was traced back in Part I to the Saint-Simonian theory of social history with which he became acquainted after Macaulay's attack in 1829.[49] Since Mill's awareness of these historical limitations did not take the scientific form of a theory of social history comparable to the Saint-Simonian, we have now reexamined this second adjustment as a break with the utilitarian conception of journalism which he had adopted as a youthful propagandist. Mill's awareness of the limited *moral* relevance of utilitarianism, was traced back in Part I to his initial crisis of 1826.[50] Since Mill's awareness of these moral limitations never took the scientific form of a theory of human nature comparable to his father's or Bentham's, we must also reexamine this third adjustment as a break with the utilitarian conception of journalism.

In fact Mill went so far as to break off the career as a journalist which he had begun as a youthful propagandist. The chapter in his *Autobiography,* "A Crisis in My Mental History," begins with this break: "for some years after this I wrote very little, and nothing regularly, for publication." (The "after this" refers to the last article which Mill wrote before the break, and which he has been describing at the end of the preceding chapter, "Youthful Propagandism—Westminster Review.") "Had I gone on writing," Mill explains, "it would have much disturbed the important transformation in my opinions and character, which took place during those years." He reminds us of why he had previously been writing:

> From the winter of 1821, when I first read Bentham, and especially from the commencement of the Westminster Review, I had what might truly be called an object in life; to be *a reformer of the world.* My conception of my own happiness was entirely identified with this object.[51]

It was his entire *moral* identification as an individual with this *political* object that was dislocated by the breakdown of 1826:

> It occurred to me to put the question directly to myself: "Suppose that all your objects in life were realized; that all the changes in institutions and opinions which you are looking forward to, could be completely effected at this very instant: would this be a great joy and happiness to you?" And an irrepressible self-consciousness distinctly answered, "No!" At this my heart sank within me: the whole foundation on which my life was constructed fell down.[52]

The youthful propagandist had been seeking to effect changes in opinions, and thereby in institutions. Thus his imaginative experiment with these changes can be compared with the imaginative experiment which he performed only a year before, with the changes in institutions that would be effected by liberating the journalist from legal restrictions:

> Convey . . . the imagination, not to any living example of prosperity and good government, but to the furthest limit of happiness which is compatible with human nature and behold that which may in time be attained if the restrictions under which the press still groans, merely for the security of the holders of mischievous power, be removed.[53]

In this 1825 experiment the consequences anticipated are those changes in institutions which are required by the utilitarian theory of human nature, and the decisive factor in obtaining these consequences is journalism as the instrument of public opinion. In the 1826 experiment, these political changes have become morally irrelevant because the decision is no longer left to *public opinion* but is claimed by an irrepressible *self-consciousness.* The compatibility of these changes with Mill's own nature as an individual is in question. He is coming to recognize that the youthful propagandist attached "almost exclusive importance to the ordering of outward circumstances," and neglected his own "internal culture" as an individual.[54]

This reflexive or *moralistic* adjustment carries implications for the structure of Mill's political thought. Some of these were anticipated in Part I when we identified the liberal as a self-conscious individual who puts questions directly to himself regarding changes in institutions and opinions, rather than simply succumbing to the external pressure of such changes as democracy in America.[55] We are now reexamining this third adjustment with respect to its implications for the structure of Mill's political thought as journalistic thought. For although we cannot trace the *moralistic* adjustment in the scientific form of the theory of human nature in which ethology was to be generalized as political ethology, we can try to trace it as an adjustment in Mill's conception of his role as a journalist.

In 1835, after the period of his crisis was over, Mill assumed the editorship of a new journal which was founded, he explains, "to take the place the Westminster Review had been intended to fill." Our topological method for exploring the structure of Mill's thought enables us to get behind this assertion of continuity, which is dictated by his desire to present himself "as much as ever a radical and democrat." New historical and moral criteria of relevance have been introduced by Mill's second and third adjustments and have altered his conception of journalism. That the new review does not take quite the same place as the old is suggested by the fact that Mill no longer has a single object, but "two principle objects . . . in the conduct of the Review."[56] He has again become concerned with political changes, though as a result of his second adjustment he has come to appreciate socio-historical limitations: the "world," which he had undertaken to reform as a youthful propagandist, is no longer, all of it, within his reach. His political purpose can now be pinpointed as an "immediate purpose" for his own time and country: he is "as much as ever a radical and democrat for Europe, and especially for England." He therefore hopes the new *Westminster* will "stir up the educated Radicals . . . and induce them to make themselves . . . a powerful party capable of taking the government of the country."[57] To this extent, the new *Westminster*, like the old, is an instrument of *political* changes. But Mill in the new *Westminster* is also concerned with the *moral* change that had taken place, during his period of crisis, in his attitude toward changes in political institutions and political opinions. His second principle object is "to free philosophical radicalism from the reproach of sectarian Benthamism," and this object has its personal aspect for Mill. The new *Westminster,* Mill explains, "answered my personal purpose as a vehicle for my opinions, . . . [enabling] me to express in print much of my altered mode of thought, and to separate myself in a marked manner from the narrower Benthamism of my early writings."[58] To this extent, the new *Westminster* is an instrument of Mill's new self-consciousness.

Self-Consciousness

If Mill was self-conscious, it was of course partly because he was conscious of the personal problem which he faced as an individual—the problem of separating himself from what he had been as his father's son. But a principle was also at stake: any individual is to be kept separate in certain respects from any other individual. The operation of this "principle of individuality" can be discerned in "one of the peculiarities" which distinguished the new review. Mill laid down the requirement "that every article should bear an initial, or some other signature, and be held to express the opinions *solely* of the individual writer."[59] When Mill decided that sectarian solidarity was a reproach to Benthamism he was awarding personal purposes and personal opinions a new legitimacy. The liberal journalist characteristically combines these two distinct objectives. He is concerned to stir up a constituency and induce them to make themselves a powerful party capable of taking the government of the country; he is also concerned to express his personal purposes and his personal opinions. He usually encounters considerable difficulty in combining these two objectives, and (like Mill) he usually fails to achieve the first objective while succeeding with the second.[60]

Mill's own personal purpose of separating himself in a marked manner in the new *Westminster* was achieved "by the general tone of all I wrote, including various purely literary articles, but especially by the two papers . . . which attempted a philosophical estimate of Bentham and of Coleridge."[61] A general tone might prove elusive, so let us respond first to Mill's "especially" and consider his philosophical estimate of Bentham, with which we already have a certain familiarity. Perhaps the most devastating verdict which Mill reaches on Bentham is the following: "Self-consciousness . . . was never awakened in him."[62] In Mill's own case, self-consciousness, once it was awakened, remained so "irrepressible" as to find expression, not only in his quasi-autobiographical procedure of "separating" himself in his journalistic writings from "the narrower Benthamism" of his "early writings," but also in the *Autobiography* itself. So far I have exploited the *Autobiography* for factual information regarding Mill's break with utilitarianism. But autobiography (like journalism) is a genre, a form of thought, and Mill's resort to this genre itself serves to distinguish him from his utilitarian predecessors.[63]

Bentham, it is true, had provided the autobiographical footnote I earlier quoted for its report of his conversion to utilitarianism on reading Hume.[64] But it was not self-consciousness which prompted either Bentham's conversion or this report of his conversion. "Perhaps a short sketch," Bentham indicated, "of the wanderings of a raw but well-intentioned mind [his own] in its researches after moral truth may on this occasion be not unuseful; for the history of one mind is the history of many."[65] Bentham was referring to himself in the third person. He was offering a short sketch, relegated to a footnote, in contrast with Mill's full length *Autobiography,* and the only justification for the footnote was that it was the history of many minds. No crisis of self-consciousness had made this history distinctively his own as an individual.

Mill's self-consciousness, his adoption of autobiography as a genre, as well as his quasi-autobiographical conception of his mature journalistic activity, is the outcome of his third adjustment. This adjustment we have so far traced as an adjustment in the relation between morals and politics and between the individual and other men. But it is also an adjustment in "the moral relations" of an action.[66] In appraising Bentham's adjustment of these relations, Mill complains that for Bentham "all our acts are determined by pains and pleasures in *prospect,* pains and pleasures to which we look forward as the *consequences* of our acts." But almost any action, Mill argues, is also likely to have a retroactive effect—"to fix and perpetuate the state or character of mind in which itself has originated." Mill further insists that an individual is not "really virtous" unless he "recoils from the very thought" of committing an immoral action, because "the idea of placing himself in such a situation" is itself "painful." In overlooking the occurrence of these reflexive experiments, Bentham was overlooking the fact that "the pain or pleasure which determines our conduct is as frequently one which precedes the moment of action as one which follows it."[67] Thus "man is never recognized by him [Bentham] as a being capable . . . of desiring for its own sake, the conformity of his own character to his standard of excellence, without hope of good or fear of evil from other sources than his own inward consciousness."[68]

Mill's moral crisis was itself a reflexive experiment. His self-consciousness short-circuited his entire identification with the changes in institutions and opinions to which he had looked forward as the consequences of his youthful propagandism. A fundamental change in opinion to which he had been dedicated as a youthful propagandist was the elimination of any such reflexive reference as he is now reinstituting. Journalism (as the scientific method of observation which he had then conceived it as being) depended for its effectiveness on its making actions available for control by their public consequences; it was by observing and publicizing these consequences that journalism alters them, and thereby the future expectations of agents and their future actions.[69]

Mill's adjustment in "the moral relations" of an action is illustrated by his protest against Bentham's adjustment. "There is no need," he explains in his estimate of Bentham, "to expatiate on the deficiencies of a system of ethics which does not pretend to aid individuals in the formation of their own character; which recognizes no such wish as that of self-culture, we may even say no such power, as existing in human nature; and if it did recognize, could furnish little assistance to that great duty, because it overlooks the existence of about half of the whole number of mental feelings of which human beings are capable of, including all those of which the direct objects are states of their own mind."[70]

Other Studies

Nevertheless Mill never constructed a system of ethics in which these deficiencies were corrected. So far as the *moral* relations of an action go, Mill in his estimate is still willing to commend Bentham "for fixing attention upon the consequences of actions" as "unquestionably the first and most important mode of looking at them."[71] Reference to the inner "qualities" of character of which an action is "evidence," Mill distinguishes as the "*esthetic* aspect" of an action, to which our "imagination" responds. He further distinguishes the "*sympathetic* aspect" to which our "fellow-feeling" responds. Instead of handling these two relations of an action as moral relations, Mill is accommodating them as non-moral "aspects" of an action.[72] He accordingly criticizes Bentham for treating the "moral view" of an action "as if it were the sole one." The "error, or rather one-sidedness" of neglecting the other two aspects, Mill attributes not just to Bentham but to moral philosophers "in general."[73]

When Mill sweeps all moral philosophy aside with this generalization, he is imposing a format which we shall see his estimates regularly impose on previous thinkers. When they come within his purview, they regularly become narrowly one-sided, and his own purview comprehensive. Mill's criticism, we recall, of his father's and Bentham's substantive treatment of political problems is not that it was simply erroneous, but that there were "many things" which "that doctrine, professing to be a theory of government in general, ought to have made room for, and did not."[74] Instead of undertaking himself a substantive treatment of problems, Mill regularly finds a place to put them by drawing distinctions; instead of quarreling with his predecessors' substantive treatment, Mill makes room with these distinctions for a separate and supplementary treatment. Thus an ethology is needed to supplement Mill's father's utilitarian psychology.[75] Similarly, in the present estimate of Bentham, the utilitarian "moral view" survives more or less intact as a moral view, but a supplementary reliance on "other studies" is required for the treatment of the esthetic and sympathetic aspects of an action.

At this point in Part I we were frustrated by the fact that Mill had "no system."[76] He offered "only a conviction that the true system was something more complex and many-sided" than anything he had envisaged so long as he remained a utilitarian.[77] All that was available for our examination were the distinctions that composed this largely empty structure which scientific knowledge should exhibit. Now, however, we are examining the structure exhibited in the journalistic form taken by his "practical political creed." The principle of individuality presides over his journalistic handling of the relation between morals and politics. This principle, we now recognize, is itself a principle of distinction and separation which imposes the same complex and many-sided structure on the relation between one individual and other men as the principle of distinct and separate sciences would impose on the relation between one subject-matter and "other studies." The full complexity of the relation between one individual and another must wait for our investigation in the next chapter of "the sympathetic aspect" of an action. But we have already seen the principle of individuality applied, as a principle of distinction and separation, by Mill's journalistic policy, whereby "every article" in the new *Westminster* was to "be held to express the opinions *solely* of the individual writer." We have also seen that one of the objectives of Mill's own articles was "to separate" himself "in a marked manner from the narrower Benthamism" of his "early writings." Both the policy and the extent to which Mill's objective is "personal" carry implications for "the moral relations" of an action, for the relation between morals and politics, and for the relation between one individual and other men. The structure of these different relations can be ferreted out of Mill's mature conception of journalism, even though he does not offer for our examination a science of ethology or a political ethology or a social theory, inasmuch as the construction of these moral sciences has to wait on the eventual extension and generalization of the methods of physical science.

Poetry and Rhetoric

In dealing with Mill's adjustment of "the moral relations" of an action, we have not yet examined the relation between its "esthetic aspect" and its distinctively "moral aspect"—"its foreseeable consequences," which are still for Mill, as for his utilitarian predecessors, "the first and most important mode of looking at them." Characteristically, Mill does not follow up this distinction between the two aspects with any substantive treatment of their relationship. But if there is any cogency to my topological interpretation of the relation between one subject-matter and "other studies," we ought to be able to find in Mill's esthetics itself relevant commentary on the "esthetic aspect" of his activity as a journalist.

Mill's effort to separate himself from the narrower Benthamism of his youthful propagandism itself took later the journalistic form, not only of a "philosophical estimate" of Bentham, but also (we have anticipated) of "various purely literary articles."[78] This distinction of the literary from the philosophical is a further illustration of the principle of separating one study from another. Literary articles in the old *Westminster* had not been purely literary. They were political philosophy as well, in that they had exposed the political interests of the literary writers being reviewed. As literary articles they had no distinctive significance but had been tolerated by Bentham only as "literary insignificancies."[79] It is this narrowness of Benthamism that Mill is separating himself from when he accords separate significance to literary articles.

The way this literary purity is achieved is a further illustration of the way one individual is to separate himself from another, in conformity with the principle of individuality. It was not moral philosophy which had opened up the route that Mill followed into his own inward consciousness. It was a literary route, along which he had been guided by Wordsworth's and Coleridge's Romantic poetry, and by the poetry and romance of Carlyle's writings, and by Mrs. Taylor, whom Carlyle described as "a living romance heroine,"[80] and whom Mill himself described as "more a poet" than Carlyle himself.[81]

We might not be inclined to think of either Carlyle or Mrs. Taylor as a poet. To get at the adjustment involved in Mill's thinking of them in this way, we should attend to the extended definition of poetry which Mill offers in a purely literary article. "Whosoever writes out truly any one human feeling," he generalizes, "writes poetry."[82] But the poet so defined can express his own feelings "exactly as he felt them" only to the extent of his "utter unconsciousness of a listener."[83] To distinguish anything exactly had been the aim of Bentham's analytic method. But Mill is, in effect, finding a place for the subject-matter of poetry by distinguishing the mental feelings which Bentham overlooked in his theory of human nature—the mental feelings whose "direct objects" are states of the individual's own mind.[84] The distinctiveness of this subject-matter is explicitly guaranteed by the purity of the poet's unconsciousness of other men. Even when a poem is in fact written for publication, "no trace of consciousness that any eyes are upon us must be visible in the work itself." Thus the characteristic procedure of the poet is reflexive withdrawal into his own inward consciousness. Poetry is not merely the description of a state of mind, of an inward feeling, but is also "feeling confessing itself to itself in moments of solitude."[85] As such it is to be distinguished from "eloquence," which is "feeling pouring itself out to other minds, . . . endeavoring to influence their beliefs."[86]

This distinction between poetry and rhetoric explains why Mill swept aside all previous moral philosophers with the generalization that they had neglected the esthetic and sympathetic aspects of an action. Mill may have seemed to forget that his father, and Bentham, and the youthful propagandist himself, had criticized moral philosophers for taking into account the esthetic and sympathetic aspects of an action.[87] Mill could forget, we now realize, because their account had not been poetic but rhetorical,[88] whereas Mill's own esthetic experience became distinctively poetic as soon as he discovered in Wordsworth's poems "a source of inward joy."[89]

Poetry and Painting

Mill has extended and generalized a distinction between poetry and rhetoric, so that it becomes involved in the adjustment of the relation between morals and politics. In the moral sphere Mill has attained individuality by his poetic preoccupation with his own "inward culture"; politics remains the sphere of rhetorical preoccupation with the changes in other men's opinions which are needed to effect changes in the institutional "ordering of outward circumstances." The extension and generalization can be more easily traced if we first watch the shorter step that Mill takes in extending the distinction so that it will "intersect the whole domain of art."[90] Here Mill comes up against the case of painting, not just because it seems less plausible for paintings to remain invisible than for poems not to be published,[91] but also because the traditional theory of literature had assimilated poetry to rhetoric,[92] and in the process of doing so had assimilated poetry to painting—*ut pictura poesis.* The process of assimilation had in fact gone even further. We can recall the scope the analogy to painting acquired in Hume when he used it in order to impress on us the moral role of the spectator and to assimilate to rhetoric the whole domain of art, including moral philosophy.[93] Even though Hume had taken into account other aspects of an action besides its consequences, he had nothing to contribute to the reflexive transformation which separated Mill from narrow utilitarianism. The esthetic aspect of a moral action Hume had treated from the rhetorical point of view of the spectator.

From Mill's point of view the visibility of a painting is no more warrant for taking the reactions of the spectator as such into account than the publication of a poem. A painting, Mill asserts, is poetry, "if the feeling declares itself by such signs as escape from us when we are unconscious of being seen," although it is "oratory, if the signs are those we use for the purpose of voluntary communication."[94] Thus Mill would approve the painting we see only insofar as what we see can be taken as poetic evidence that the painter was unconscious, when he painted the painting, of its ever being seen. But the criterion whereby a painting is approved of as poetry must be kept reflexive in its operation by our construing this poetic evidence as evidence that the painter's feeling declared itself to *him* by such signs as would escape from *us* when we ourselves are unconscious of being seen. Thus even while we are functioning as spectator-critics of another's painting, our own as well as his poetic solitude is protected against contamination. Furthermore, although this reflexive criterion of withdrawal into solitude may seem to determine only the external relations between the painter, his painting, and ourselves as critics who see the painting, the application of a reflexive criterion tends to internalize relations so that it can determine ultimately the relations within the pictorial composition itself. Thus Mill prefers the painting of a single figure to the painting of a group, where "the single figures . . . are rather the eloquence of painting than the poetry," since they "express the feelings of one person as modified by the presence of others."[95] As for those paintings where the style is that of "corrupted eloquence," the criterion of solitude is twice violated, by the painters as well as by their grouping of several figures together; the painters themselves are "attitudinizers," and "every figure seems to be showing itself off before spectators."[96]

I am not prepared to suggest that even a liberal could maintain in politics this poetic criterion in all its purity. But Mill's persistent extension of the reflexive criterion across the whole domain of art helps us to discern its operation in *On Liberty*. The Mill who no longer shares his father's and Bentham's regret "that a window has not been placed in the breast of every man," who no longer welcomes the prospect of the liberty of the press throwing "all men into the public presence" until finally "the whole world" becomes an "Inspection-House" or "gymnasium" where all socially relevant activities are nakedly exposed,[97] is the Mill who has defined poetry as "feeling confessing itself to itself in moments of solitude," who requires of the expression of this feeling that "no trace of consciousness that any eyes are upon us must be visible in the work itself." In *On Liberty*, actions, and the reactions of public opinion, are no longer the only relevant consideration: the moral character that lies behind these actions becomes relevant in politics, but as analogous to a work of art:

> It really is of importance, not only what men do, but also what manner of men they are that do it. Among the works of man, which human life is rightly employed in perfecting and beautifying, the first in importance surely is man himself.[98]

Liberty is no longer freedom of public inspection; exposure to the influence of the public has become the threat to freedom that it is in the Romantic theory of art as self-expression.[99]

Mill may have inherited from his predecessors the methodological conviction, which inspires his *Logic,* that "the backward state of the moral sciences can only be remedied by applying to them the methods of Physical Science, duly extended and generalized," but his liberalism is distinguishable from their utilitarianism by the fact that his conception of liberty is rather the result of his extending and generalizing what he himself analyzed as an esthetic procedure of the poet.[100] When Mill in *On Liberty* insists on "the importance of genius, and the necessity of allowing it to unfold itself freely both in thought and practice," he comments, "people think genius a fine thing if it enables a man to write an exciting poem or paint a picture." But Mill goes on to assert that genius "in its true sense" is not exclusively esthetic. It is "originality in thought and action." Mill is generalizing Romantic esthetic theory, and one mark of the generalization is his promotion of "individuality" as a synonym for "genius."[101]

Individuality

Mill's esthetic emphasis on originality and on self-isolation as a way of attaining it, has explained one methodological feature of his later conception of journalism—the requirement which he laid down for the new *Westminster* "that every article should bear an initial, or some other signature, and be held to express the opinions *solely* of the individual writer." But then the signature Mill himself adopted may seem a somewhat quixotic rendering of his own originality. The "A" with which he usually signed his articles was the initial of *Antiquus*, which had been his signature for the two articles of 1833 on poetry that we have just examined. Mill had employed this identification in an earlier article (October, 1832) which is usually regarded as a preliminary version of *On Liberty*, for it was a discussion of originality in thought and action, as well as in art, and as such was his first published step toward the generalization in *On Liberty* of the principle of individuality. With this step, moreover, Mill took his first stand as an individual thinker with original opinions—opinions which were not inherited from his father. What remains to be determined is the relevance he felt in identifying his first forward step as the backward step of an *Antiquus*.

To this article the publisher assigned the title "On Genius," since Mill had given it the form of a letter "Addressed to the Author of an Article, entitled 'Some Considerations respecting the Comparative Influence of Ancient and Modern Times on the Development of Genius.' " These considerations raise "a question," Mill urges, "with which, if we well consider its significance, none of the controversies which fill the present age with flame and fury is comparable in interest." He therefore commends the questioner for having "shown that, without being indifferent to politics, you can see a deeper problem in the existing aspect of human affairs, than the adjustment of a ten pound franchise."[102]

Even without its signature, the article would be a little difficult to place in Mill's development in relation to his predecessors, for although he sounds no longer as indifferent to politics as he was in 1826, he is disdaining the question of the franchise which was at issue in the Reform Bill of 1832, and we know that he will later endorse his father's *Essay on Government* as an argument for the passage of the bill as meeting a practical requirement of his own time and country.[103]

Nevertheless, we can face the deeper problem, which Mill formulates as follows: "What are really the intellectual characteristics of this age; whether our mental light—let us account for the fact as we may—has not lost in intensity, at least a part of what it has gained in diffusion?"[104] Mill is formulating the problem as a question. But the article to which he is responding was a plea "for the moderns against those who placed the ancients above them,"[105] so that Mill's signature would seem to imply an answer to his question which would place the ancients above the moderns. (I therefore converted Mill's question into an affirmation when I cited it as the epigraph for this chapter.) The phrasing of the question is, in any case, an endorsement of a reflexive criterion that Mill's father would repudiate: " 'The intense' was with him a bye-word of scornful disapprobation."[106] In fact Mill is pitting the Romantic and poetic criterion of inner "intensity" against his father's utilitarian and journalistic criterion of public "diffusion." That Mill has lost his youthful confidence in the progress attendant upon the diffusion of knowledge is even more evident from his next question: "Whether our 'march of intellect' be not rather a march towards doing without intellect and supplying our deficiency of giants by the united efforts of a constantly increasing multitude of dwarfs?"[107]

If Mill leaves us with questions in this letter, it is because "knowledge comes only from within," and "all that comes from without is but questioning."[108] (I was therefore risking an oversimplification when I converted Mill's first question into an affirmative epigraph for this chapter.) Thus he finds no incompatibility between his solicitude for originality and his resort to Antiquity: "I may be indebted to my predecessor for setting my own faculties to work—for hinting to me what questions to ask myself."[109] In fact, what Mill would revive from Antiquity is its questioning, reflexive procedure:

> Education *then* consisted not in giving what is called knowledge, that is, grinding down other men's ideas to a convenient size, and administering them in the form of *cram*—it was a series of exercises to form the thinking faculty itself. . . . Such was the education of Greece and Rome, especially Greece. Her philosophers . . . helped the disciple to form to himself an intellect fitted to seek truth for itself.[110]

But today the question has to be asked, "Is there anything a man can do, short of swindling or forgery (*à fortiori* a woman) which would so surely gain him the reputation of a dangerous, or, at least, an unaccountable person, as daring . . . to make a practice of forming his opinions for himself?"[111]

This daring practice Mill identifies with thought. Thus thought becomes identical with original thought:

> Is genius any distinct faculty? Is it not rather the very faculty of thought itself? . . . The capacity of extracting the knowledge of general truth from our own consciousness . . . is originality; and where truth is the result, whoever says Originality says Genius. The man of the greatest philosophic genius does no more than this, evinces no higher faculty; whoever thinks at all, thinks to that extent originally.[112]

Accordingly, the thought of a modern *Antiquus* need not be antiquated but can be original:

> Philosophic genius is said to be the discovery of new truth. But what is new truth. That which has been known a thousand years may be new truth to you or me. . . . The truths which we have inherited still remain traditional, and no one among us, except here and there a man of genius, has made them *truly his own*.[113]

Pictures of Socrates

"On Genius," I have said, is at once Mill's first original work and his first published defense of originality as a reflexive performance. As a preliminary version of *On Liberty,* it is also an intervening link with the earlier reflexive withdrawal of Mill's moral crisis. Long ago I anticipated the role Socrates would play in *On Liberty* as an exemplification of the principle of individuality.[114] The ancient route of reflexive withdrawal that Mill follows in "On Genius" is Socratic. In preparing "On Genius," Mill dug out some translations which he had made of Platonic dialogues. These are the only writings which can be dated as having been composed during the period of crisis itself. During that period Mill felt himself incapable of original work, but he retained a sort of intellectual momentum in that he could carry out "mechanically . . . a certain sort of mental exercise . . . when all the spirit had gone out of it."[115] These translations may have been the mechanical exercises of a young man who had begun to learn Greek at the age of three. If the moral crisis was the moment that Mill confessed to himself his indifference toward "all the changes in institutions and opinions which you are looking forward to," these translations represent the ensuing moment when all he could do was to look backward:

> In vain I sought relief from my favorite books; those memorials of past nobleness and greatness from which I had always hitherto drawn strength and animation. I read them now without feeling.[116]

For the first time—in the history of humanism we have traced—a classical revival has obviously failed to come off. *Antiquus fit animus* is no longer a reliable reprieve from the present.[117] Mill therefore sought animation from other sources, turning to the poetry of Wordsworth and of Coleridge.[118] But this poetic "cultivation" of his feelings merely continued (he claims, from the retrospective point of view of his *Autobiography*) an earlier poetic culture:

> Long before I had enlarged . . . the basis of my intellectual creed, I had obtained . . . poetic culture of the most valuable kind, by means of reverential admiration for the lives and characters of heroic persons; especially the heroes of philosophy. The same inspiring effect which so many of the benefactors of mankind have left on record that they had experienced from Plutarch's lives, was produced on me by Plato's pictures of Socrates, and by some modern biographies. . . . The heroic virtues of these glorious representatives of the opinions with which I sympathized, deeply affected me, and I perpetually recurred to them as others do to a favorite poet, when needing to be carried up into the more elevated regions of feeling and thought.[119]

The continuity asserted by Mill conceals certain adjustments in his handling of the humanistic tradition. Its fabric is being rewoven poetically so that it becomes a Romantic tradition. We may grant that once Mill faced the crisis of discovering "all feeling was dead within me"[120] it would be natural for him to attempt to revive his feelings in the fashion that they had already been cultivated earlier by his classical education. But Mill tells us that his education had in fact resulted in "an undervaluing of poetry," so that he was "*wholly blind* to its place in human culture, as a means of educating the feelings."[121] Rather than having earlier read Platonic dialogues in order to cultivate his feelings, it seems more probable that Mill would have read them in the way his father had. "There is no author," Mill recalls, "to whom my father thought himself more indebted for his own mental culture than Plato."[122] Mill bears "similar testimony" with regard to his own early reading:

> The Socratic method, of which the Platonic dialogues are the chief example, is unsurpassed as a discipline . . . The close, searching elenchus by which the man of vague generalities is constrained either to express his meaning to himself in definite terms, or to confess that he does not know what he is talking about . . . —all this, as an education for precise thinking, is inestimable, and all this . . . took such hold of me that it became part of my own mind.[123]

The key phrases in this testimony, "vague generalities" as opposed to "precise thinking," betray the fact that the Socratic method is being assimilated to the utilitarian method of analysis, which had been applied by Mill's father both in the *Analysis of the Phenomena of the Human Mind* and to the education of Mill's own mind.[124] Since Mill explains his moral crisis as due "to the habit of analysis" having "a tendency to wear away the feelings," his attempt to attain "relief" by rereading and translating Platonic dialogues would have remained "in vain" so long as it continued an exercise in analysis. But Mill is reading these dialogues in a different way from his father, when he finds in them "pictures of Socrates." His mentioning that his reading had "the same inspiring effect" as others derived from reading Plutarch identifies a tradition in which modern lives are led that parallel those of the ancients.[125] But Mill is readjusting the relationship. To find in Platonic dialogues inspiring "pictures of Socrates" is a Romantic revision of the humanistic procedure of adopting a predecessor as a model for imitation.[126] Not until after Mill began reading Romantic poetry would he have become conscious of reading Platonic dialogues for their pictorial effect. Mill's Romantic theory of poetry substitutes a relationship of inspiration for the humanistic relationship of imitation;[127] it supplies the reflexive criterion of what is "truly his own" with which the truly pictorial can be assimilated to the poetic, and it reverses the humanistic assimilation, *ut pictura poesis,* whereby poetry imitated painting, which Neoclassicism took to be the characteristically imitative genre.[128] Only as a result of these adjustments could the continuity of Mill's "poetic culture" supervene in retrospect—the continuity that is affirmed by his retaining the signature *Antiquus* for his articles on Romantic poetry.

For the rest of his career Mill's individualism will remain humanistic to the extent he will continue to draw on Antiquity for "memorials of past nobleness and greatness" as sources of Romantic inspiration.[129] Yet Mill's career as an *Antiquus* comes, in a sense, almost to an end (as well as our attempt to trace the continuity of the humanistic tradition) in a footnote which he adds to this signature after his second article on poetry:

> This signature is only used to identify the authorship of the present article with that of a paper headed "What is Poetry" . . . The writer had a reason for the title when he first adopted it; but he has discarded it in later articles, as giving a partial, and so far a false notion of the spirit by which he would wish his thoughts and writings to be characterized. As Wordsworth says,
>
> 'Past and future are the wings
> On whose support, harmoniously conjoined
> Moves the great spirit of human knowledge;'
>
> A title which points only one way is unsuitable to a writer who attempts to look both ways. In future, when a signature is employed it will be the single letter A.[130]

When Mill in 1835 resumes his historical responsibility toward the modern world by launching the new review which was to take the place of the old *Westminster,* his own individual contributions are usually signed with this noncommittal "A"; sometimes with "A.B.", perhaps to disavow the past implications of "A." Divorced from what it had initialed, "A" merely indicates the importance Mill attaches to the individualistic expression of different opinions, by himself as well as by other contributors. The quarrel of "On Genius" between the ancients and the moderns loses its centrality. From now on the differences between an ancient and a modern are only one of the cognitively significant differences between individuals which Mill wants to acknowledge: "Every inquirer is either young or old, rich or poor, sickly or healthy, married or unmarried, meditative or active, a poet or a logician, an ancient or a modern, a man or a woman."[131] A more modern inquirer than Mill might find the alternative "an ancient" a less relevant option than the others paired on this list. But in this instance, as in the others, Mill is introducing another criterion of relevance besides his reflexive principle of individuality. His pairing procedure is an effort "to look both ways" in a fashion which is consecrated by "the principle of antagonism."[132] Having examined the operation of the principle of individuality in this chapter, we shall have to examine this supplementary principle in the next chapter, for its operation ensures the relevance which we have watched other men's opinions lose, insofar as their opinions become homogeneous as public opinion.

In order, however, to complete Mill's history as an *Antiquus*, we can anticipate now one outcome of Mill's appeal to this principle of antagonism—when he attempts to meet the threat to individuality posed by the homogenizing and leveling tendencies of democracy in America, or more broadly of modern commercial civilization:

> We think M. de Tocqueville right in the great importance he attaches to the study of Greek and Roman literature, not as being without faults, but as having contrary faults to those of our own day. . . . Those literatures . . . exhibit precisely that order of virtues in which a commercial society is apt to be deficient; . . . if a lower average of virtue, more striking individual examples of it; fewer small goodnesses but more greatness; more which tends to exalt the imagination and inspire high conceptions of the capabilities of human nature. If, as everyone may see, the want of affinity of these studies to the modern mind is gradually lowering them in popular estimation, this is but a confirmation of the need of them, and renders it more incumbent upon those who have the power to do their utmost towards preventing their decline.[133]

"Le monde moderne avilit . . ." Or, as Mill puts it in his review of *Democracy in America,* "the spirit of a commercial people will be . . . essentially mean and slavish" unless counterbalanced by elevating tendencies.[134] Even though one recourse here is to classical studies, Mill's application of the principle of antagonism would provide society with a spiritual structure of "counterbalancing"[135] tendencies that is quite different from the balance sought by Neoclassicism. But we shall see in the next chapter that in Mill's case (as in the previous cases we have examined) the structure the thinker seeks for society is the same as the structure of his own arguments.[136]

Notes

1. Peter Laslett, ed., *Philosophy, Politics and Society* (New York: Macmillan, 1956), p. vii.

2. Peter Laslett and W. G. Runciman, eds., *Philosophy, Politics and Society,* 2nd series (New York: Barnes and Noble, 1962), p. vii. The editors comment: "The forthright statement made in the original collection—'For the moment, anyway, political philosophy is dead'—became the text most cited from the volume as a whole" *(ibid.).*

3. *Philosophy, Politics and Society* (1956), pp. ix–xi.

4. See p. 213, this vol.

5. Note the place that Laslett and Runciman assign to the philosophy of law: "In *The Concept of Law* (1961) Professor Hart has in fact fulfilled the prophecy made in 1956 that the philosophers of law would be the first to turn linguistic analysis to positive use. We believe that this is the most important work for the general sociology of law and politics as well as for their philosophy to have appeared since political philosophy was proclaimed to be dead six years ago" (*Philosophy, Politics and Society,* 2nd series, pp. vii–viii). Professor Hart himself adopts Bentham as a very recent predecessor. He explains that the selections from Bentham which were published by Ogden in 1933 "brought to the notice of philosophers . . . the fact that Bentham had anticipated by a century part of Bertrand Russell's doctrine on logical constructions and incomplete symbols. That doctrine, at the time of Mr. Ogden's publication, was looked upon by many English and American philosophers as the paradigm of philosophical method and the prime solvent of philosophical perplexities" (H. L. A. Hart, "Lecture on a Master Mind: Bentham," *Proceedings of the British Academy* [London: Oxford University Press, 1962], 48: 298). For Bentham's anticipation of propositions advanced in Wittgenstein's *Tractatus,* see Hart, p. 308; for the renewable relevance of Bentham's analyses to problems in political and legal philosophy, see esp. pp. 302–5. Hart himself has largely relinquished his own efforts in political and legal philosophy in order to supervise the reediting of Bentham's works.

6. *Philosophy, Politics and Society* (1956), p. vii.

7. See vol. 1, p. 12.

8. See vol. 1, p. 11.

9. Thomas Macaulay, *Critical and Miscellaneous Essays,* 5 vols. (Philadelphia: Carey and Hart, 1844), 5: 362. See my vol. 1, pp. 21–22.

10. *Autobiography* (New York: Columbia University Press, 1924), p. 111.

11. Mill's thought will accordingly take its place within a structure of relations where his father is to be identified as his predecessor rather than as his antagonist, in spite of all the differences between them. The philosophical indifference that prevails today regarding such a structure (see vol. 1, p. 7) is perhaps illustrated by Marshall Cohen's misinterpreting James Mill's dismissal of Macaulay as John Mill's dismissal of his father: "His father's reaction to Macaulay's review seemed to him to exemplify the dictum of Hobbes that when reason is against a man, a man will be against reason" (*The Philosophy of John Stuart Mill,* ed. Marshall Cohen [New York: Modern Library, 1961], p. xiv). This double misattribution deprives Mill's crisis of its philosophical significance as a reaction against his father's rationalistic psychology. Thus it may also illustrate the readiness of the philosopher today to disregard as dead issues the problems I am reconstructing regarding the relation between psychology and logic. Cohen is preoccupied instead with the relation between psychology and morals, for these issues, to which Mill himself was largely insensitive, have become crucial today.

12. See vol. 1, pp. 11, 14; vol. 2, p. 339.

13. See pp. 237–39, this vol.

14. *Autobiography,* p. 46; see p. 189, this vol.

15. See p. 153, this vol.

16. "Bentham," *Mill's Essays on Literature and Society,* ed. J. B. Schneewind (New York: Collier Books, 1965), pp. 252–53; italics added. Compare the retrospect Mill offers in *Utilitarianism:* "After more than two thousand years, the same discussions continue, philosophers are still ranged under the same contending banners, and neither thinkers nor mankind at large seem nearer to being unanimous on the subject than when the youth Socrates listened to the old Protagoras, and asserted . . . the theory of utilitarianism against the popular morality of the so-called Sophist" (*Mill's Ethical Writings,* ed. J. B. Schneewind [New York: Collier Books, 1965], p. 276).

17. See p. 243, this vol. For another example, see n. 84, below.

18. We have seen (p. 238, this vol.) that the opposition between the utilitarians and their antagonists was indistinguishably psychological and logical, and that the logical issue was over the applicability of an analytic method in psychology. The distinction that Mill draws in constructing his psychologically neutral logic is implicit in the following disclaimers: "I do not attempt to decompose . . . mental operations . . . into their ultimate elements. . . . Most of the conclusions arrived at in this work have no necessary connexion with any particular views respecting the ulterior analysis [i. e., the analysis which would be carried out in "the science which deals with the constitution of the human faculties"]. Logic is common ground on which the partisans of Hartley and of Reid, of Locke and of Kant may meet and join hands. . . . I can conscientiously affirm, that no one proposition laid down in this work has been adopted for the sake of establishing, or with any reference to its fitness for being employed in establishing, preconceived opinions in any department of knowledge or of inquiry on which the speculative world is still undecided" (*A System of Logic* [London: Longmans, Green, 1941], p. 8). Mill is affirming that his *Logic* is neutral with respect to the entire structure of knowledge, for the science which he envisages as dealing "with the constitution of the human faculties" embraces what we regard as metaphysics and epistemology as well as psychology. I am using the term *psychology* in this broad sense in which its scope is equivalent to that traditionally assigned a theory of human nature (see chap. 3, n. 52). Mill's own usage often illustrates this broad sense as well as the narrower sense in which psychology is a "distinct and separate" science (see p. 114, this vol.). Thus in stating the doctrine of circumstances which underpins his father's confidence in the applicability of an analytic method, Mill substitutes the term *psychology* for the term *philosophy* which he had originally used: "In philosophy his fundamental doctrine was the formation of all human character by circumstances, through the principle of association" (*The Early Draft of John Stuart Mill's Autobiography,* ed. Jack Stillinger [Urbana: University of Illinois Press, 1961], p. 100, n. 271). Compare vol. 1, p. 25.

19. *Logic,* p. 546.

20. See vol. 1, p. 12.

21. Isaiah Berlin, *John Stuart Mill and the Ends of Life* (London: Council of Christians and Jews, 1959), p. 18.

22. See vol. 1. p. 9. When Mill is concerned with practical political implications, his *Logic* turns out to be no longer a psychologically neutral analysis: "You have very rightly judged [Mill is writing the German translator of his *Logic*] that to give the cultivators of physical science the theory of their own operations was but a small part of the object of the book; and that any success in that attempt was chiefly valued by me as a necessary means towards placing metaphysical and moral science on a basis of analysed experience

in opposition to the theory of innate principles so unfortunately patronized by the philosophers of your country" (letter to Gomperz; I am citing from R. P. Anschutz, *The Philosophy of J. S. Mill* [Oxford: Clarendon Press, 1953], pp. 65–66). Contrast n. 18, above, where the analysis of experience was an "ulterior analysis." In his *Autobiography* Mill fits his *Logic* to the same structure of opposition between utilitarian analysis and the point of view of their antagonists: "The German, or *à priori* view of human knowledge, and of the knowing faculties, is likely for some time longer . . . to predominate among those who occupy themselves with such inquiries, both here and on the Continent. [Mill identifies British traditionalists with the continental *à priori* view, and they did of course borrow Kantian arguments.] But the 'System of Logic' supplies what was much wanted, a textbook of the opposite doctrine—that which derives all knowledge from experience, and all moral and intellectual qualities principally from the direction given to the associations. . . . The notion that truths external to the mind may be known by intuition or consciousness, independently of observation and experience, is, I am persuaded, in these times, the great intellectual support of false doctrines and bad institutions. By the aid of this theory, every inveterate belief and every intense feeling, of which the origin is not remembered, is enabled to dispense with the obligation of justifying itself by reason. . . . There never was such an instrument devised for consecrating all deep-seated prejudices" (*Autobiography,* pp. 157–58). Mill goes on to link his *Logic* with his father's analytic psychology: "The intuitive school, even after what my father had written in his Analysis of the Mind, had in appearance . . . on the whole the best of the argument" (*ibid.,* p. 158). Confronted with Mill's two inconsistent interpretations of the *Logic,* Anchutz argues that "the *Logic* reflects a way of thinking whose fundamental tenets have not been disclosed to us or even, perhaps, consciously realized by its author" (*The Philosophy of J. S. Mill,* p. 66). My concern is not with the *Logic* itself, since it provides no substantive political theory, but with Mill's "practical political creed." Yet here too we see that Mill draws the distinction between theory and practice in a fashion which enables him to criticize his father's theory of government (insofar as it is deduced from a faulty or incomplete psychological theory and neglects the political relevance of a theory of history), and yet to remain as much "a radical and democrat" as he had been as his father's son. See vol. 1, pp. 37–38, 56–57.

23. *Autobiography,* p. 111.

24. James Mill, *An Essay on Government* (New York: Liberal Arts, 1955), p. 59. Compare his later assertion: "The whole of this chain of reasoning is dependent . . . upon the principle that the acts of men will be conformable to their interests. Upon this principle we conceive that the chain is complete and irrefragable" (*ibid.,* p. 84).

25. *Logic,* pp. 582–83; italics added. Practical politics and the polemics of the day were perhaps more complicated than John Mill acknowledged. Consider Ricardo's appraisal of James Mill's *Essay on Government,* as reported by Joseph Hamburger: "Ricardo . . . immediately recognized its polemical purpose when he commended Mill for not revealing his favorable opinion on the secret ballot, saying that to raise the question 'would have given the article too much the appearance of an essay on Reform of Parliament which it was desirable to avoid' " (*Intellectuals in Politics: John Stuart Mill and the Philosophic Radicals* [New Haven: Yale University Press, 1965], p. 5).

26. See vol. 1, pp. 12–16 and accompanying n. 34.

27. See vol. 1, pp. 26–27, 46. So far in my interpretations I have usually respected the priority this first adjustment has for Mill (see, e.g., vol. 1, p. 94; chap. 4, n. 37; vol. 2, pp. 71, 156–57 and accompanying n. 22).

28. See vol. 1, pp. 190–91, 241, 264, 279; vol. 2, pp. 5, 18–23 and accompanying nn. 48, 60; p. 48.

29. See pp. 47–48, this vol., and accompanying n. 139.

30. See pp. 94, 124, this vol.

31. See pp. 211, 218, this vol.

32. See pp. 192, 239, this vol.

33. See pp. 297–98, this vol.

34. See p. 256, this vol.

35. "The time, it is to be hoped, is gone by when any defense would be necessary of the 'liberty of the press' as one of the securities against corrupt or tyrannical government. [For this appeal to "time" as rendering the arguments of his predecessors no longer relevant, see vol. 1, p. 30.] . . . This aspect of the question . . . has been so often and so triumphantly enforced by preceding writers that it need not be specially insisted on in this place" (*On Liberty* [New York: Liberal Arts, 1956], p. 19).

36. See p. 260, this vol.

37. *On Liberty*, p. 80; italics added.

38. See vol. 1, pp. 31, 32, 37, 39–40.

39. See p. 253, this vol.

40. Mill's review of vol. 1 of *Democracy in America*, reprinted in Schocken Books ed. of Tocqueville (New York, 1961), p. xxxix; *On Liberty*, p. 80. Note the distinction between knowledge and communication that Mill employs in this review: "For the first time, the power and the habit of reading begins to permeate the hitherto inert mass. Reading is power: not only because it is knowledge, but still more because it is a means of communication—because, by the aid of it, not only do opinions and feeling spread to the multitude, but every individual who holds them knows that they are held by the multitude; which of itself suffices, if they continue to be held, to ensure their speedy predominance" (p. vii). In his review of vol. 2 of *Democracy in America*, Mill returns to the same point: "The constituent elements of political importance are property, intelligence, and the power of combination . . . It is in this last element . . . that the progress of the Democracy has been the most gigantic. . . . Various associations are not the machinery of democratic combination, but the occasional weapons which that spirit forges as it needs them. The real political unions of England are the newspapers. It is these which tell every person what all the other persons are feeling, and in what manner they are ready to act. . . . The newspapers and the railroads are solving the problem of bringing the Democracy of England to vote, like that of Athens, simultaneously in one *agora*; and the same agencies . . . are making us more than ever (what is the first condition of a powerful public opinion) a homogeneous people" (*Mill's Ethical Writings*, ed. J. B. Schneewind, pp. 115, 117, 118). The distinction which Mill is drawing here between knowledge and journalism (as the communication or diffusion of knowledge) could not be so sharply drawn by a utilitarian for whom knowledge was intrinsically public (see p. 255, this vol.).

41. See p. 259, this vol.

42. See p. 243, this vol.

43. *On Liberty*, p. 76. Mill employs a comparable metaphor for the effect of his analytic education on his own mind—"the habit of analysis has a tendency to wear away the feelings" (*Autobiography*, p. 96). See also n. 55, below, and page 378, this vol.

44. See vol. 1, p. 22.

45. *Logic*, p. 615. For Mill's reidentification of utilitarianism as an historical phenomenon, see pp. 414, 429, this vol. For the relation between generations, see p. 430–31, this vol.

46. *Ibid.*

47. See vol. 1, p. 53. For another disavowal of unilinear history, see chap. 4, n. 7.

48. See vol. 1, p. 40.

49. See vol. 1, pp. 22–23.

50. See vol. 1, pp. 41–43.

51. *Autobiography*, p. 93; italics added.

52. See vol. 1, p. 42.

53. See p. 253, this vol.

54. See vol. 1, p. 40.

55. See vol. 1, pp. 43–45. Mill visualizes as external the pressures which wear down into uniformity all that is individual (see p. 287, this vol.) inasmuch as he identifies what is significantly individual as the outcome of reflexive withdrawal and meditation. Thus "the turmoil and bustle of a society in which every one is striving to get on, is . . . our author observes, not favorable to meditation. 'Il règne . . . un petit mouvement incommode, une sorte de roulement incessant des hommes les uns sur les autres, qui trouble et distrait l'esprit sans l'animer et l'élever.' Not to mention that the universal tendency to action, and to rapid action, directs the taste to applications rather than principles, and hasty approximations to truth rather than scientific accuracy in it" ("De Tocqueville on Democracy in America," pp. 135–36). For Mill's quietism, see n. 96, below.

56. *Autobiography,* pp. 139, 149. For Mill's recurrent assertions of continuity with his predecessors, see vol. 1, pp. 37, 38, 56.

57. *Ibid.,* p. 150. I shall not be concerned here with Mill's first objective, except in its relation to his second objective. For Mill's role in relation to the parliamentary Radicals, see Joseph Hamburger's *Intellectuals in Politics,* and my chap. 17, nn. 22, 77, 89.

58. *Autobiography,* p. 152.

59. *Ibid.,* p. 140: italics added.

60. Mill's specific difficulty was that "The Review was established to be the representative of the 'philosophic radicals,' with most of whom I was now at issue on many essential points" *(ibid.).* Of course the difficulty was somewhat eased by Mill's new focus on "immediate" political objectives. Consider Mill's two comments on his relation with Roebuck, who had been his closest ally so long as he remained a youthful propagandist: "Our differences of opinion on life & philosophy became so strongly pronounced that we ceased to consider ourselves as allies in opinion, further than as we were both of us radicals & democrats" and "Our differences of opinion on life & philosophy became so strongly pronounced that we ceased to be allies either in opinion or in action except as to the immediate objects of radicalism" (*The Early Draft,* p. 127). Mill's wife marked the first comment for revision, and Mill replaced it with the second. See pp. 325–26, this vol. for the history of Mill's relations with his future wife and with Roebuck.

61. *Autobiography,* p. 152.

62. "Bentham," p. 259.

63. For the relevance of Mill's resort to autobiography as a genre, see pp. 377–78, this vol.

64. See p. 241, this vol.

65. *A Fragment on Government,* ed. F. C. Montague (London: Oxford University Press, 1951), p. 153.

66. See p. 153, this vol; see also p. 240, this vol. and accompanying n. 27.

67. "Remarks on Bentham's Philosophy," *Mill's Ethical Writings,* pp. 50, 55. The at

once (1) uncalculating and (2) reflexive structure of this experience precludes its analysis in terms of utilitarian psychology. (1) Without calculating its consequences, the agent "recoils" from performing an action: "The fear of pain *consequent* upon the act, cannot arise, unless there be *deliberation;* and the man as well as 'the woman who deliberates' is in imminent danger of being lost." Indeed unless the agent recoils without deliberating, he is "not really virtuous" in Mill's view; but in his father's view, "Where there is no calculation . . . there is no morality; in fact, there is nothing rational, any more than moral" (see chap. 15. n. 36). (2) The reflexive structure of the experience Mill attributes to the "really virtuous" agent precludes the forward-looking analysis of utilitarian psychology (see p. 242, this vol.) which imposes a means-end sequence: "With what propriety shrinking from an action without deliberation can be called yielding to an *interest,* I cannot see. *Interest* surely conveys . . . the idea of an *end,* to which the conduct (whether it be act or forbearance) is designed as the *means.* Nothing of this sort takes place in the above example. It would be more correct to say that conduct is *sometimes* determined by an *interest,* that is, by a deliberate and conscious aim; and sometimes by an *impulse,* that is, by a feeling (call it an association if you think fit) which has no ulterior end, the act or forbearance becoming an end in itself" (*ibid.,* p. 55). Observe the disdain with which Mill in the last parenthesis shrinks from undertaking an analysis of the feeling. He is prepared to accept the feeling as a fact which is morally ultimate, even if not psychologically ultimate. Compare n. 18, and contrast his utilitarian refusal to accept such "ultimate facts" (p. 233, this vol.).

68. "Bentham," p. 262.

69. See pp. 254–60, this vol.

70. "Bentham," pp. 265–66.

71. *Ibid.,* pp. 282–83. The relevance Mill attaches here to the consequences of actions" is not inconsistent with his insistence on the reflexive structure of moral experience (see n. 67, above). Unlike Bentham, Mill envisages the consequences of an action for the agent's own character. "In estimating the consequences of actions, in order to obtain a measure of their morality, there are always two sets of considerations involved: the consequences to the outward interests of the parties concerned (including the agent himself), and the consequences to the characters of the same persons and to their outward interests so far as dependent on their characters. In the estimation of the first two classes of considerations, there is in general not much difficulty, nor much room for differences of opinion. . . . But it often happens that an essential part of the morality or immorality of an action consists, in its influence upon the agent's own mind" ("Professor Sedgwick's Discourse," *Mill's Ethical Writings,* pp. 84–85).

72. "Bentham," p. 283. Obviously Mill does not always use the term "moral" in this restricted sense. When he refers to "the moral relations" of an action (see p. 153, this vol.), he is including its "esthetic" and "sympathetic" aspects.

73. For the moral irrelevance of esthetic considerations in James Mill, see chap. 15, n. 29.

74. See vol. 1, p. 8.

75. For ethology as the gap in the structure of knowledge where Mill put his unsolved problems, see vol. 1, pp. 60–61.

76. *Autobiography,* p. 113; see vol. 1, p. 11.

77. *Autobiography,* p. 113.

78. See p. 292, this vol.

79. Bentham had planned to have "one-half" of the original *Westminster* "consecrated to politics and morals, the other half left to literary insignificancies" (*The Works*

of Jeremy Bentham, ed., John Bowring, 11 vols. [Edinburgh: William Tait, 1843], 10: 540).

80. I am citing Carlyle from F. A. Hayek, *John Stuart Mill and Harriet Taylor* (Chicago: University of Chicago Press, 1951), p. 80. Carlyle soon altered this appraisal.

81. *Autobiography,* p. 124.

82. "The Two Kinds of Poetry," *Mill's Essays on Literature and Society,* p. 118.

83. "What is Poetry?" *Mill's Essays on Literature and Society,* p. 109.

84. See my exposition of Bentham's criterion of precision, pp. 232–36, this vol. In proposing a place in psychology for these poetic feelings which Bentham overlooked, Mill is intruding his own distinction between subject-matter and method (see p. 280, this vol.). Bentham had not simply overlooked a portion of the *subject-matter* of psychology—"about half of the whole number of mental feelings"; poetic feelings posed a *methodological* issue for Bentham because "all poetry is misrepresentation" ("Bentham," p. 285)—the poet as defined by Mill would be incapable of representing anything exactly. In other words, the opposition, examined in chap. 14, between reason and sentiment, was an opposition between reason and poetry. Mill cites a notorious announcement in the first issue of the *Westminster*: " 'Mr. Moore *is* a poet and therefore *not* a reasoner' " (*Autobiography,* p. 78).

85. "What is Poetry?" p. 109. Thus "all poetry is of the nature of soliloquy" *(ibid.)*. This definition is a Romantic cliché. M. H. Abrams cites Keats—"I never wrote one single line of Poetry with the least Shadow of public thought" and Shelley—"A poet is a nightingale who sits in darkness and sings to cheer its own solitude" (*The Mirror and the Lamp: Romantic Theory and the Critical Tradition* [New York: W. W. Norton, 1958], p. 26).

86. Mill's distinction can be further illustrated: "Poetry and eloquence are both alike the expression or uttering forth of feeling. But if we may be excused the seeming affectation of the antithesis, we should say that eloquence is *heard,* poetry is *over*heard. Eloquence supposes an audience. . . . Poetry . . . is the natural fruit of solitude and meditation; eloquence, of intercourse with the world. The persons who have most feeling of their own, . . . have the highest faculty of poetry; those who best understand the feelings of others, are the most eloquent. The persons, and the nations, who commonly excel in poetry, are those whose character and tastes render them least dependent for their happiness upon the applause, or sympathy, or concurrence of the world in general" ("What is Poetry?" pp. 109–110).

87. See pp. 241–43, this vol., and accompanying n. 29.

88. I am not suggesting that Hume's account belongs on one side of Mill's distinction, Mill's own account on the other. Hume drew no fundamental distinction, and his theory of poetry was a rhetorical theory of poetry (see the citation from M. H. Abrams, n. 92, below.).

89. *Autobiography,* p. 104.

90. "What is Poetry?" p. 110. The extensive relevance of poetry is the fundamental assumption of Mill's answer to this question: "That . . . the word 'poetry' *does* import something quite peculiar in its nature, something which may exist in what is called prose as well as in verse, something which does not even require the instrument of words, but can speak through those other audible symbols called musical sounds, and even through the visible ones, which are the language of sculpture, painting, and architecture; all this, as we believe, is and must be felt, though perhaps indistinctly, by all upon whom poetry in any of its shapes produces any impression beyond that of tickling the ear. To the mind, poetry is either nothing [this would seem to be Mill's assessment of his father's and Bentham's utilitarian attitude], or it is the better part of all art whatever, and of

real life too" (*ibid.*, p. 103). As the succession of arts in this list suggests, Mill facilitates extending and generalizing his expressive theory of poetry "even" to the visual arts, by first extending it to music—i.e., to the art which is "so peculiarly the expression of passion" (*ibid.*, p. 110).

91. Mill handles the question of publication as follows: "A poet may write poetry with the intention of publishing it; he may write it even for the express purpose of being paid for it; that it should *be* poetry, being written under any such influences, is far less probable; not, however, impossible; but not otherwise possible than if he can succeed in excluding from his work every vestige of such *lookings-forth into the outward and everyday world,* and can express his feelings exactly as he has felt them in solitude, or as he feels that he should feel them, though they were to remain forever unuttered. But when he turns round and addresses himself to another person; when the act of utterance is not itself the end, but a *means* to an *end*—viz., by the feelings he himself expresses to work upon the feelings, or upon the belief, or the will of another,—when the expression of his emotions, or of his thoughts, tinged by his emotions, is tinged also by that purpose, by that desire of making an impression upon another mind, then it ceases to be poetry, and becomes eloquence" ("What is Poetry?" pp. 109–110; italics added). Observe that the poetic experience is comparable, with respect to its reflexive structure, to a moral experience as analyzed by Mill, and is opposed to the rhetorical act of utterance, which lends itself to the same sequential means-end analysis as a moral action receives when it is taken by utilitarianism to be a means for achieving certain social consequences (see n. 67, above; n. 92, below).

92. M. H. Abrams comments on the revolutionary character of Mill's definition of poetry: "The purpose of producing effects upon other men, which for centuries had been the defining character of the art of poetry, now serves precisely the opposite function: it disqualifies a poem by proving it to be rhetoric instead" (*The Mirror and the Lamp*, p. 25). Abrams' unrestricted "centuries" reminds us that classical rhetoric is often too exclusively identified with the function of moving the minds of an audience. I have tried to show that Cicero's rhetorical theory (like his political theory) is an ambivalent treatment of the individual's relation to other men. It is not merely a theory of persuasion but also a theory of expression see chap. 10, nn. 50, 60, 75, 111), in which the appropriateness of a speech to the mind and character of the orator is a crucial consideration. A sharp distinction between persuasiveness and expressiveness as criteria only develops with the Romantic reaction against Neoclassicism and with the elaboration of a Romantic theory of the history of esthetics in which the Romantic stage itself is viewed as a reaction against the centuries during which classicism prevailed.

93. See pp. 208–11, this vol. Recall, too, Hume's introduction of the spectator in a setting in which the orator himself is identified as a painter: "Attend to Palladio and Perrault, while they explain all the parts . . . of a pillar. . . . But should you ask the description . . . of its beauty, they would readily reply, that the beauty . . . results from the whole, when . . . presented to an intelligent mind. . . . 'Till such a spectator appear, there is nothing but a figure of such particular dimensions. . . . From his sentiments alone arise its elegance and beauty. . . . Attend to Cicero, while he paints the crimes of a Verres or a Catiline; you must acknowledge that the moral turpitude results, in the same manner, from the contemplation of the whole, when presented to a being whose organs have such a particular structure and formation" (see p. 209, this vol., for the complete citation). There are three fundamental differences between the way "sentiments" function in Hume's esthetics and the way "feelings" function in Mill's: (1) "sentiments" in Hume are the sentiments of a spectator-critic, whereas "feelings' in Mill are the feelings of the poet himself; (2) "sentiments" in Hume are aroused by the object observed by the spectator (or described for his benefit by the critic), whereas for Mill "the poetry is not in the object itself . . . but in the state of mind in which [it] may be contemplated" ("What is Poetry?" p. 107) by the poet, who "merely pours forth

the overflowing of his feelings" ("Two Kinds of Poetry," p. 121); (3) "sentiments" are therefore closely associated with the cognitive process of observation, description, and judgment (see chap. 14, n. 18), whereas "the poetry of a poet is Feeling itself, employing Thought only as the medium of its utterance" ("Two Kinds of Poetry," p. 121).

94. "What is Poetry?" p. 113.

95. *Ibid.*, pp. 113–14. Contrast the social analysis yielded by Adam Smith's rhetorical esthetics where "assembling and grouping" are artistic accomplishments (see chap. 14, n. 126).

96. "What is Poetry?" p. 114. Mill has in mind primarily the Neoclassical paintings of David, "the great corruptor of taste" (*ibid.*, p. 114). Along with the doctrine of imitation (see vol. 1, pp. 104–5), Mill is disparaging the French Neoclassicists who "fancy themselves imitators of the classics, yet . . . seem to have no understanding and no feeling of that *repose* which was the peculiar and pervading character of Grecian art, until it began to decline—a repose tenfold more indicative of strength than all their stretching and straining" ("What is Poetry?" p. 115). What is ostensibly an historical distinction between classical art as it originally was and its later corruption is also Mill's repudiation of the Benthamite forward-looking "logic of the will" (see p. 238, this vol. and accompanying n. 21), in favor of the "wise passiveness" of a Wordsworth who recollects in tranquillity. For a further illustration of Benthamite activism, see James Mill's endorsement of "a life of exertion in contradistinction to one of self indulgent indolence" (n. 122, below); for a further illustration of John Mill's repudiation of Benthamite activism, see chap. 17, n. 21.

97. See pp. 258, 260, this vol.

98. *On Liberty*, p. 72. For the sense in which all that counted for Bentham was "what men do," see chap. 15, n. 27.

99. The individual who can be "said to have a character" in the sense required by Mill's principle of individuality, is "a person whose desires and impulses are his own—are the expression of his nature, as it has been developed and modified by his own culture" (*On Liberty*, p. 73).

100. The process of extension has already reached this climactic result in Mill's treatment of poetry as "the better part of all art whatever, and of real life too" (see n. 90, above). This process of extension is a portion of the historical justification for the importance I attached to the liberal imagination in the Introduction and to esthetic analogies in chap. 4 and in the present volume.

101. "Persons of genius are . . . more individual than any other people" (*On Liberty*, p. 79).

102. "On Genius," *Mill's Essays on Literature and Society*, p. 87.

103. See p. 282, this vol. For the place of "On Genius" in Mill's development, see p. 419, this vol. Questions regarding the precise course of Mill's development I am postponing until chap. 18 and the Conclusion.

104. "On Genius," pp. 88–89.

105. *Ibid.*, p. 94.

106. *Autobiography*, p. 34.

107. "On Genius," p. 89. Traditionally, of course, modern "dwarfs" had been able to stand on the shoulders of ancient "giants," but we shall see that Mill's stress on originality renders this operation more difficult to perform.

108. *Ibid.*, p. 92.

109. *Ibid.*, pp. 91–92. When Mill is being intensely Romantic the only role a predecessor can assume in relation to him is that of hinting. Hence his sometimes cavalier interpretations of Bentham, which have not been easy for us to adapt to the purpose of tracing the actual development of utilitarianism. A characteristic fluctuation is Mill's double claim regarding the article on Sedgwick: "I . . . have represented the 'utilitarian theory of morals,' I think for the first time in its true colors. At all events, I have incidentally represented my own mode of looking at ethical questions, having never yet seen in print any statement of the principles on the subject to which I could subscribe" (letter to J. P. Nichol which I am citing from *Mill's Ethical Writings,* p. 78). In admitting his Romantic idiosyncrasy, Mill can go so far as to confess that he is not "a utilitarian at all, unless in quite another sense from what perhaps any one except myself understands by the word" (letter to Carlyle, *The Collected Works of John Stuart Mill* [Toronto: University of Toronto Press, 1963], 12: 207).

110. "On Genius," p. 96.

111. *Ibid.*, p. 99.

112. *Ibid.*, pp. 89, 92. The esthetic implications of this conception of originality were considered in vol. 1, pp. 104–5.

113. *Ibid.*, pp. 89, 96; italics added. One reason why Mill is prepared to accept the designation *Antiquus* is that the genius required to make one's own traditional truths belonging to other ages is in a sense even greater than the genius required to be original in the ordinary sense: "I have sometimes thought that *conceptive* genius is, in certain cases, even a higher faculty than *creative*. From the data afforded by a person's conversation and life, to frame a connected outline of the inward structure of that person's mind, so as to know and feel what the man is, . . . still more to decipher in that same manner the mind of an age or a nation, and gain from history or travelling a vivid conception of the mind of a Greek or Roman, a Spanish peasant, an American, or a Hindu [note the company we keep], is an effort of genius, superior, I must needs believe, to any which was ever shown in the creation of a fictitious character, inasmuch as the imagination is limited by a particular set of conditions, instead of ranging at pleasure within the bounds of human nature" (*ibid.*, p. 93). In the next chapter we shall be dealing with the superior effort required for the exercise of "conceptive genius" (see esp. p. 332).

114. See pp. 13–14, this vol.

115. *Autobiography,* p. 98.

116. *Ibid.*, p. 95. Insofar as Mill merely reread these books it would almost inevitably have been "in vain," since "feeling" had not been what he had originally read them for.

117. See vol. 1, p. 303.

118. See pp. 334, 382, this vol.

119. *Autobiography,* p. 79. Cf. chap. 17, n. 112.

120. *Ibid.*, p. 99.

121. *Ibid.*, pp. 78–79.; italics added.

122. *Autobiography,* p. 15. Except insofar as it bears on his son's education, I am not making any attempt to interpret the debt which James Mill acknowledged to classical philosophy—in such sharp contrast with Bentham's attitude.

123. *Ibid.* The original draft was more emphatic and personal: "Nothing in modern life & education, in the smallest degree supplies its place [the place of the Socratic method]. . . . I have ever felt myself, beyond any modern that I know of except my father & perhaps beyond even him, a pupil of Plato, & cast in the mould of his dialectics" (*Early Draft,* p. 48).

124. However analytic Mill's classical education may have been, Mill never succeeded in distinguishing and separating it from his father's *Analysis,* which provided the theory behind it (see p. 376, this vol.). Indeed Mill's classical education was so entangled with the personality of his father, who administered it, that Mill characterizes his father in its terms: "In his view of life he partook of the character of the Stoic, the Epicurean, and the Cynic, not in the modern but the ancient sense of the word. In his personal qualities the Stoic predominated. His standard of morals was Epicurean, inasmuch as it was utilitarian, taking as the exclusive test of right and wrong, the tendency of actions to produce pleasure or pain. But he had (and this was the Cynic element) scarcely any belief in pleasure. . . . Accordingly, temperance, in the large sense intended by the Greek philosophers [in dealing with these Greek philosophers I tried to preserve this large sense by translating the Greek term as "self-control" rather than "temperance"], . . . was with him, as with them, almost the central point of educational precept. His inculcations of this virtue fill a large place in my childish remembrances. . . 'The intense' was with him a bye-word of scornful disapprobation. He regarded as an aberration of the moral standard of modern times, compared with that of the ancients [observe that this comparison was no novelty for the Romantic Mill of "On Genius" but had been a piece of his intellectual equipment since childhood], the great stress laid upon feeling. Feelings, as such, he considered to be no proper subjects of praise or blame" (*Autobiography,* pp. 33–34). Nevertheless, this focus on character in Mill's portrayal of his father was itself no more characteristic of Mill's father than "pictures of Socrates" would have been. Mill is applying to his father his own Romantic distinction between "what men do" and "what manner of men they are that do it" (see p. 300, this vol.): "The effect my father produced on my character, did not depend solely on what he said or did with that direct object, but also, and still more, on what manner of man he was" (*Autobiography,* p. 33).

125. See chap. 4, n. 43.

126. For instances of the humanistic procedure, see vol. 1, pp. 102, 185, and 190–91 with accompanying nn. 26, 28, 29. Mill's revision of this procedure was probably prompted in part by some inkling of the distinction between the Hellenistic and the Classical (compare n. 96, above, and see vol. 1, p. 105)—that is, between the Hellenistic Socrates (who had been upheld as a model by Xenophon, Stoicism, and Cynicism and who was often confused in the humanistic tradition with the Platonic Socrates, as he still is by James Mill) and the Socrates whom Mill came to portray in the light of Romantic Platonism (especially Coleridge's). The distinction seems to be present in Mill's account of his relations to Socrates and Plato, although these are entangled (as already indicated in n. 124) with his relation to his father: "My father's moral convictions . . . were very much of the character of those of the Greek philosophers. . . . Even at the very early age at which I read with him the Memorabilia of Xenophon, I imbibed from that book & from his comments a deep respect for the character of Socrates; who stood in my mind as a model of ideal excellence [the entanglement is illustrated by Mill's having removed this last sentence from his account of his early education to his account of his father's character; see *Early Draft,* p. 48, n. 65]. . . . At a later period the lofty moral standard exhibited in the writings of Plato, took great effect on me. My father's moral inculcations were at all times mainly those of the 'Socratici viri': justice, temperance, veracity, perseverance; readiness to brave pain & especially labour; . . . a life of exertion, in contradistinction to one of self indulgent indolence." Mill seems to be conflating his father's Benthamite "logic of the will" (see n. 96, above) with the Stoic and Cynic tradition (*Early Draft,* p. 62). The entanglement is illustrated by the way the sentence referring to "a later period" interrupts the continuity of Mill's account of his father's Socratic moral convictions. It is not clear when this later period was, but "lofty" suggests the need, which is a distinctive trait of the Romantic Mill, "to be carried up into the more elevated regions of feeling and thought" (see p. 304, this vol.).

127. Mill disdains Sedgwick's "harping on the value of the writings of antiquity as 'patterns' and 'models'," and goes on to comment: "The study of the ancient writers has been of unspeakable benefit to the moderns; from which benefit, the attempts at *direct imitation* of these writers, have been no trifling drawback" ("Professor Sedgwick's Discourse," *Dissertations and Discussions,* 3 vols. [London: Longmans, Green, Reader, and Dyer, 1867], 1:110 [italics added]). For the way the doctrine of inspiration is posed in Mill's Romantic classicism against the Neoclassical doctrine of imitation, see vol. 1, pp. 104–5. In the present chapter I am merely reutilizing this earlier broad opposition. In chapter 18 I shall take up the chronology of Mill's development and locate more precisely his Romantic phase.

128. Mill's "pictures of Socrates" are not Neoclassical. He is quite capable of using the pictorial analogy in the reflexive sense that is a feature of his definition of poetry. Thus when Mill identifies Carlyle as the "poet" of the French Revolution (see p. 385, this vol.), it is by considering "the very process by which he [Carlyle] arrives at his own thoughts; he paints the thing *to himself*—he constructs a picture of it *in his own mind*" ("Carlyle's *French Revolution,*" *Mill's Essays on Literature and Society,* p. 195 [italics added]).

129. Thus Socrates will remain a source of inspiration that meets the requirements of Mill's own time and country—"a man unique in history, of a kind at all times needful, and seldom more needed than now" (*Dissertations and Discussions,* 2: 501).

130. This footnote is not reprinted by Schneewind. It is reprinted in *Early Essays by John Stuart Mill,* ed. J. W. M. Gibbs (London: George Bell, 1897), p. 236.

131. "Bentham," p. 257.

132. See vol. 1, pp. 48–51.

133. "De Tocqueville on Democracy in America," *Mill's Ethical Writings,* p. 153. For earlier versions of this distinction between ancient and modern, see chap. 11, n. 35.

134. "De Tocqueville on Democracy in America," p. 122. For the demeaning character of the American experience, see Mill's citation from Tocqueville (n. 54, above). But remember that Mill's appraisal is a *moralistic* analysis of society, not a *social* analysis in my sense of that term which involves distinguishing between social classes (see vol. 1, p. 2; vol. 2, p. 90). A social analysis in this sense has in Mill's view become irrelevant to democracy in America, inasmuch as "America is *all* middle class" ("De Tocqueville on Democracy in America," p. 119). Cf. way England is becoming homogeneous (n. 40, above).

135. *Ibid.,* p. 158.

136. For the balanced structure sought by Hume, see chap. 14, n. 31; chap. 15, n. 55; chap. 17, n. 85; conclusion, n. 145.

17

Light from Other Minds

À fortiori *a woman—Mill*

The Inner Fortress

Since the methodological program of Mill's "Logic of the Moral Sciences" remained largely unfulfilled, we turned to his practical opinions in the last chapter. Comparison with his immediate predecessors helped us circumvent his distinctions between method and opinions and between theory and practice—they did not draw these distinctions. Their theory of politics, which he disavowed "as a scientific theory," he retained as his own "practical political creed," and since this creed took journalistic form, it could be compared with his own "Youthful Propagandism," as illustrated by the way he (as well as his father) had attacked the journalism of their antagonists. This attack had methodological implications in the context of their utilitarian theory of human nature. In spite of the fact that the mature Mill had no comparable theory of his own, I tried to tease comparable methodological implications out of his resort to poetry, autobiography, and Antiquity.

Rather than pursuing these implications topologically into what may have seemed out of the way places of Mill's thought, wouldn't it have been more sensible to have accepted Isaiah Berlin's verdict, "Rigour in argument is not among his accomplishments"?[1] Since Mill's time, moreover, distinctions have hardened between methods and opinions and between theory and practice. Philosophical as well as scientific arguments have become more rigorous, so that it has become more difficult to rebuff such a verdict as Berlin's. But curiously enough, rigor in argument has itself become a less reliable and definitive accomplishment, as Berlin himself pleads in Mill's defense:

It was, I think, Bertrand Russell—Mill's godson—who remarked somewhere that the deepest convictions of philosophers are seldom contained in their formal arguments: fundamental beliefs, comprehensive views of life, are like citadels which must be guarded against the enemy. Although the reasons they find, and the logic that they use may be complex, ingenious and formidable, they are only defensive weapons; the inner fortress itself—the vision of life for the sake of which the war is being waged—will as a rule, turn out to be exceedingly simple and easily intelligible.[2]

Exceeding simplicity, easy intelligibility are tempting, especially since we reached at the end of the last chapter the point where Mill was sacrificing the analytic "rigidity" of his father's and Bentham's arguments to a poetic vision of life.[3]

Nevertheless, there *were* methodological implications to be found in Mill's poetic vision, even though they were not scientific. He was assigning the "proper place to the . . . internal culture of the individual," and thereby rectifying his predecessors' attachment of "almost exclusive importance to the ordering of outward circumstances."[4] This *moralistic* adjustment in the relation between morals and politics was at the same time an adjustment in Mill's method. The ordering of outward circumstances became a tissue of political metaphors for the moral fate of the soul itself. Thus democracy in America was no longer to be identified with political institutions, as Mill's predecessors had identified it, but with "the tyranny of the prevailing thought and feeling . . . enslaving the soul itself."[5] The soul was morally enslaved when it succumbed to the outward influence of public opinion, not only in America but also in the theory of human nature from which Mill's predecessors had deduced their theory of democracy.[6] Mill's "more fundamental" treatment of democracy was largely metaphorical, but insofar as it was metaphorical, the soul was liberating itself with these metaphors from outward circumstances.[7] It was assigning a proper place to its own internal culture, by transforming political references to outward circumstances into metaphorical references to its own inner predicament of being morally menaced by outward circumstances.[8]

When Berlin interprets Mill as the occupant of an "inner fortress," he is in effect offering an alternative metaphor to replace Mill's "the internal culture of the individual." My objection to Berlin's metaphor is that rigor in interpretation should require us to examine Mill's own metaphors. An "inner fortress" is not one of them. The rigid and simple structure of a fortress does not suggest the flexible and complex structure Mill's thought exhibits in its relation to other men's thinking. But before considering the different implications of Berlin's and Mill's metaphors, let us remind ourselves of what can be at stake when a philosopher prefers one metaphor to another. Berlin prefers his metaphor because the structure of a fortress renders easily intelligible the defensive character of a philosopher's position. Berlin's preference is itself an example of a recurrent process of philosophical construction which my topological method is designed to analyze for its effect on the development of political thought—the extending of the implications of some substantive position so that it becomes warrant for some methodological procedure. The "inner fortress," as Berlin is well aware, is a metaphorical rendering of the Stoic position in ethics, or rather of the moral posture of the great-souled individual himself.[9] In Berlin's extension of the implications of this position or posture, the metaphor is reconstructed to become a general methodological justification for conceding that any intellectual position is ultimately beyond the reach of argument, so that we have perhaps to accord it a certain deference that is usually reserved for a distinctively moral posture.

If we consider the structure of a fortress, we encounter the difficulty that Berlin's general metaphor allows little or no scope for the process of extension and reconstruction that has gone into its own generalization. Reconsider this process in the pertinent instance of the Stoics. In dealing earlier with the way in which Stoic ethics had become by extension humanistic political philosophy, I stressed the reflexive movement with which "outward" political arrangements (such as the ruler-ruled relationship, balanced government, government by *consensus*) were reconstructed as metaphors that lent structure to the "inner" moral realm; for the adoption of these metaphors in moral philosophy also facilitated later reversals in this movement of withdrawal from the "outward" to the "inner" realm. Successive crisscrossing movements of withdrawal and extension were successive renderings of the irrelevance to the moral of the political, and of the relevance of the moral to the political—of "inner culture" to the "ordering of outward circumstances." To the extent that Berlin's metaphor of the "inner fortress" protects and immobilizes "the deepest convictions of philosophers," it fails to do justice to the flexibility of these reversals. This failure is not philosophically accidental; British philosophers assume today, without further argument, that "political philosophy, is, or was, an extension of ethics."[10] Thus the process of extension itself is not examined, or the part that can be played in this process, for example, by poetic metaphors, which can lend ethical arguments the flexibility (or lack of rigor) needed for their extension to politics.

Insofar as Berlin's metaphor of the "inner fortress" immobilizes "the deepest convictions of philosophers," it fails to do justice in particular to the flexible and poetic way in which Mill reconstructed his deepest utilitarian convictions, when they came under attack, including his utilitarian conviction as to the relation between morals and politics, between "inner" and "outward." It even fails to do justice to the fact that the structure of Mill's philosophy is not in his view a construction, but a complete reconstruction, which began when, as he recalls, "My heart sank within me—the whole foundation on which my life was constructed fell down."[11]

The Collision of Opinions

The eventual outcome of this reconstruction might still have been a solid "inner fortress" in which the individual immures himself from the pressures of public opinion. If Mill never employs this or any similar metaphor for the inner realm, it is because he does not regard the individual's reflexive withdrawal as a finally consolidated withdrawal to a defensive position. The metaphors he does employ—the "inner culture of the individual," "the cultivation of the feelings," "poetic culture," etc., bring out the continuing activity of reconstruction to which he was dedicated. Furthermore, once Mill's fundamental position is metaphorically rendered as a defensive position, it becomes difficult to do justice to the stand he takes in *On Liberty* for freedom of discussion as the occasion for a struggle between opposing opinions during which they undergo reconstruction.

As a youthful propagandist, Mill had been a debater as well as a journalist. His reconstruction involves a return from poetry, from reflection on his inward consciousness, and from Antiquity, to the modern world, to journalism, and to public debate. To understand

Mill's return, we have to understand what was previously at stake in his departure.[12] He returns to the modern world, journalism, and public debate with an attitude towards the modern world, journalism, and public debate, which differs from the attitude he had upheld as a youthful propagandist; in each instance the change is fundamentally a change in his conception of his relation as an individual to other men; and this fundamental change had taken place during his period of poetic withdrawal and reflection. This fundamental change has already been illustrated by the difference between his youthful and his mature attitude towards journalism as an instrument of public opinion. A further illustration of the same change is provided by his different attitude towards public debate.

Shortly after his withdrawal "from attendance on the Debating Society," Mill explained, "I have a great dislike to controversy, and am persuaded that discussion, as discussion, seldom did any good."[13] Mill was reacting against what he described as "the dogmatic disputatiousness of my former narrow and mechanical state."[14] As a utilitarian debater, Mill had displayed his father's "almost unbounded confidence in the efficacy . . . of complete freedom of discussion" as a way of arriving at the truth.[15] But after his period of poetic withdrawal Mill no longer entertained "any great notion of the advantage of what the 'free discussion men call the 'collision of opinions,' it being my creed that Truth is *sown* and germinates in the mind itself, and is not to be struck *out* suddenly like fire from a flint by knocking another hard body against it."[16] Mill regained his confidence in journalism and public debate when he encountered, and dwelt upon, something softer.

But I'm getting ahead of the story. Mill's withdrawal from the Debating Society had been prompted by other changes besides his arrival at the conviction that truth could be attained by solitary insemination and "inner culture." Separating himself from his own former narrow and mechanical state of mind naturally involved separating himself from the more narrow-minded, more mechanically-minded utilitarians. But Mill was not merely avoiding further collisions with hard bodies; a certain softening also took place in Mill's conception of his *relation* to other individuals.

To this change, too, poetry made its contribution. Mill recalls that just before he left the Debating Society "the merits of Wordsworth were the occasion of my first public declaration of my new way of thinking and separation from those of my habitual companions who had not undergone a similar change."[17] What begins in the *Autobiography* as Mill's recollection of the part poetry played in transforming his own opinions and character reaches a climax as a contrast with the untransformable opinions and character of J. A. Roebuck, who had been the closest, as well as perhaps the narrowest, of Mill's utilitarian allies.[18] It was with Roebuck that Mill had been "most in the habit of comparing notes on every subject";[19] together they had kept the Debating Society going when the interest of other members had flagged;[20] but it was against Roebuck that Mill defended the merits of Wordsworth.[21] Although this debate was "the first debate on any weighty subject in which Roebuck and I had opposite sides, . . . the schism between us widened from this time more and more,"[22] and "I fell more and more into friendly intercourse with our Coleridgian adversaries."[23]

We might want to dismiss this episode in Mill's mental history as mere autobiography without philosophical implications. One reason for hesitating to do so, is that it may not be accurate autobiography. When Roebuck himself read Mill's *Autobiography*, he discounted as without any "basis of fact" the "whole of Mill's account of their schism as "originating with reference to poetry and to Wordsworth."[24] If the account has no basis of fact, surely then it must be philosophically significant.

A Really Soft Cushion

Roebuck himself traced the beginning of their schism to his later "remonstrating with Mill on the danger to his future prospects from his relation to Mrs. Taylor."[25] Roebuck must have approached Mill with this utilitarian argument without realizing that Mill was no longer quite a utilitarian and that actions for him now had two other "aspects" besides their future consequences."[26] In my own terminology, Roebuck did not realize that there lay behind Mill's "relation to Mrs. Taylor" a shift in his criteria of relevance. The utilitarian could take Bentham's notoriously lighthearted attitude that poetry was comparable to push-pin,[27] but for Mill, poetry had become a "weighty subject." Poetry was no longer a matter on which there could be a merely substantive "difference of opinion"; it had promoted the adjustment in "the moral relations" of an action which had rendered considerably less relevant the utilitarian criterion of "future prospects," and had assigned weight instead to the reflexive cultivation of the feelings. Poetry was also a subject which was not as readily distinguishable as Roebuck seems to have thought from the subject of Mill's relation with Mrs. Taylor. It was as "years of poetic culture," that he remembers "the first years of my friendship with her."[28] During this period Mill even redefined poetry, so that his definition no longer applied to his own favorite poet, Wordsworth, whom he had defended against Roebuck, but to Mrs. Taylor's favorite poet, Shelley, and thus by implication by reference to what she was herself, inasmuch as he identified her "with Shelley, in general spiritual characteristics as well as in temper and organization."[29]

I am getting into deep water, or worse. Mill in "On Genius" raised the question, "Is there anything a man can do, short of swindling or forgery," and interjected "(*à fortiori* a woman)," before continuing, "which would so surely gain him the reputation of a dangerous, or at least, an unaccountable person, as daring . . . to make a practice of forming his opinions for himself."[30] In raising this question, Mill was doubtless thinking of Mrs. Taylor's daring, and perhaps of her indifference to the opinions of others regarding their relationship. I should probably have left this reference to her in its original parentheses, for far more scholarly ink has been spilt over Mill's relationship with Mrs. Taylor than on any other factor in the transformation of his opinions and character.[31] Let it not be said that such scholarly concentration has netted no results. Scholarship has progressed from nineteenth-century speculation as to whether or not Mill had sexual relations with Mrs. Taylor while she was still married to Mr. Taylor, to the more refined twentieth-century suspicion that Mill never had sexual relations with her even after he married her himself. This issue I am willing to leave to subtler scholars. I am satisfied with the more tangible methodological issue posed by Mill's intellectual relation with her. This issue I cannot shirk, since Mill prostrates himself before her intellectual attainments in the dedication of that classic of liberalism *On Liberty*.[32] What is often taken to have been the preliminary version of *On Liberty*, "On Genius," was also inspired by her, more than a quarter of century before.[33] Thus she straddles Mill's development into a liberal.

At this late moment in my effort to single out factors in the development of liberalism, I do not propose to surrender to the love of a good woman, whatever may have been her temper and organization. But neither do I propose to stand Mill on his own feet again. His intellectual relation with Mrs. Taylor was not a matter of "comparing notes," as his relation with Roebuck had been. Mill was not "flint," any more than he was a "fortress," and there is something—as I have already hinted—to Laski's comment that "Mill, brought up to fight Austin, Praed, Macaulay, and Grote, had never met a really soft cushion before."[34] Laski is commenting on such stories as Bain's report that Mrs. Taylor "repeated to . . . Mill in the morning what he had said to her the night before and astounded him by the depth of her grasp." Whatever may or may not have happened during the night or in the morning, however skeptical we may be over his astonishment, we have to recognize how distinctive a feature of Mill's thought, in comparison with that of his predecessors, is his acknowledgment of intellectual debts. If any weight in interpreting Mill is to be assigned to his own criteria of relevance, we should not forget his admission at the beginning of his *Autobiography* that the motive for writing which "weighs more" than any other "is a desire to make acknowledgment of the debts which my intellectual and moral development owes to other persons; some of them of recognized eminence, others less known than they deserve to be, and the one to whom most of all is due, one whom the world had no opportunity of knowing."[35]

Sympathy

Since Mill's time, a parade of acknowledgments at the beginning of a book has become so taken for granted, that no one supposes it need have very much to do with the way the author actually thought.[36] But in Mill's case the acknowledgments exhibit the actual structure of his thought, and we have to try to explore this structure even though it may have been softened into a cushion in his relation to Mrs. Taylor.[37] This relation was not entirely idiosyncratic. Mill describes in less exaggerated, but in similarly submissive terms his relation to Carlyle, who succeeded in part (before finally being displaced by one "who was more a poet than he") to the intellectual role played by Mill's "Coleridgian adversaries" after the schism with Roebuck.[38] If what Mill had shared with Roebuck was the utilitarian philosophy, what he sought from Carlyle was not "philosophy to instruct, but poetry to animate."[39] In this regard, Mill admitted his own limitations as an individual, "I am not in the least a poet, in any sense; but I can do homage to poetry."[40] He therefore did homage to Carlyle,[41] and when he brought his essay on poetry to Carlyle's attention, confessed, "I have not got quite into the heart of that mystery, and I want you to show me how."[42]

Why Mill is in trouble and needs help is, in effect, explained by his interpretation of Bentham, which he brings more confidently to Carlyle's attention.[43] Mill, we have seen, criticizes Bentham for neglecting reflexive feelings—that is, those mental feelings of which the direct objects are states of the individual's own mind.[44] These mental feelings we traced in the previous chapter both to their esthetic source in the essay on poetry and to their political outcome in the principle of individuality.[45] But Mill also criticizes Bentham for neglecting mental feelings whose objects are states of *others'* minds—"the more complex forms of sympathy" such as "the love of loving, the need of sympathizing support, or of objects of admiration and reverence."[46] It was not merely the need of cushioning support that Mill's relation with Mrs. Taylor satisfied; other states of her mind were objects of Mill's feelings. And something besides a personal relationship to other individuals is emerging from Mill's criticism of Bentham—a methodological relationship, or, at any rate, methodological implications that attach to Mill's conception of personal relationships.

Let us pursue these methodological implications. Bentham's neglect demonstrates "the incompleteness of his own mind as a representative of universal human nature." This incompleteness might pass as a substantive psychological fact, but Bentham's neglect also demonstrates "his determination to create his philosophy wholly out of the materials furnished by his own mind and by minds like his own."[47] We are reminded of Mill's misgivings regarding journalism, as an instrument of uniformity of opinion, insofar as it represents men's "thinking done for them by men much *like* themselves."[48] The line of argument followed by Mill's criticism is also familiar: Mill is first criticizing Bentham for having neglected particular substantive psychological facts—complex forms of sympathy; but then Mill generalizes this neglect as methodological—as Bentham's having "failed in deriving light from other minds,"[49] and therefore from other philosophies of mind such as Coleridge's,[50] Mill himself is deriving this light when he completes his "philosophical estimate" of Bentham with his "philosophical estimate" of Coleridge.

Here too (as in such previous instances as democracy in America, and Mill's relations with Roebuck and Mrs. Taylor) the justification for my discerning methodological implications is that Mill's interpretation of Bentham goes further than any basis in existing fact would seem to explain. As an interpretation of Bentham's philosophy of mind in terms of Bentham's *particular* mind, Mill's interpretation is not psychologically plausible; for since Bentham, by Mill's own showing, lacked self-consciousness,[51] he must also have lacked a sense of the differences between his mind and other minds, so that there can hardly be ascribed to him a psychological "determination to create his philosophy wholly out of materials furnished by his own mind and by minds like his own." As a matter of fact, Bentham assumed that all minds were fundamentally alike, so that he would have thought of himself as taking, not his own mind, but any mind as "representative of universal human nature." This procedure had to be followed if the methodological requirement was to be satisfied of counting each individual as one when he reached his political conclusions by deduction from his psychological premises. And this methodological requirement could hardly be met without disregarding the more complex forms of sympathy, which Mill alleges to be psychological facts; if Bentham had tolerated the exercise of these complex forms of sympathy, they would have hopelessly complicated the counting process.[52]

Points of View

Methodological implications are equally present in Mill's concern to stress differences, instead of likenesses, between individuals:

> A thinking person has . . . the accidental peculiarities of his individual modes of thought. Every circumstance which gives a character to the life of a human being carries with it its peculiar biases—its peculiar facilities for perceiving some things and for missing or forgetting others. But, from points of view different from his, different things are perceptible; and none are more likely to have seen what he does not see than those who do not see what he sees.[53]

Thus it is not just Bentham's particular mind, but any individual's mind which must be regarded as "incomplete" as "a representative of universal human nature." But the limitations of Bentham's philosophy of human nature are not simply the accidental peculiarities of an individual's mind; they are the limitations of a philosophy (i.e., of an effort toward complete comprehensiveness) in which the particular limitations of any individual's mind are not taken into account. In the last chapter we recognized the relation between Bentham's method and his utilitarian philosophy of human nature. This relation Mill severed as "a mere accident." But the exigencies of Mill's own method (as instanced by this "philosophical estimate" of Bentham) are such that Bentham's taking his mind as "a representative of universal human nature" is not a merely accidental peculiarity of Bentham's mind, but exhibits a universal characteristic of human nature—the natural tendency of all men "to deny or disparage all feelings and mental states of which they have no consciousness in themselves."[54] Thus the reflexive criterion loses the comprehensive scope, which it traditionally supplied for the construction of a philosophy of universal human nature, and which we might have assumed in the last chapter it still had for Mill as an *Antiquus*.

Mill's complaint about the tradition is that philosophers, "while they have busied themselves for two thousand years, more or less, about the few *universal* laws of human nature, have strangely neglected the *diversities*."[55] Here we can intrude the example of Cicero, which goes back a little less than two thousand years. Cicero had not merely neglected the diversities; he had disposed of them as malignant:

> No individual thing is so like another individual thing, so comparable, as all of us are to each other. Indeed if bad habits and false beliefs did not distort weaker minds and bend them in different directions, no one would be so like himself as all men would be like all the others.[56]

For nearly two thousand years human nature and virtue had been uniform and individual differences had been vicious. Now with Mill's Romanticism conformity becomes a vice of weaker minds, and individuality becomes a virtue.

It is true that Cicero in the *De Officiis* insisted that not all individual differences were vicious,[57] and we were able to find in the *De Offi-*

ciis a source for the development of individualism in modern political theory. It is also true that Cicero drew on the Stoic tradition where the philosopher sometimes played the role of a Cynic individualist and made a moral virtue of his individuality and a vice of conformity.[58] Liberalism (or more precisely the *moralistic* adjustment that is one feature of liberalism) is the transformation of the antithesis between the individual and the state into an antithesis between individuality and conformity, and this transformation we have seen involves for Mill as an *Antiquus* renewed admiration for the individuality of the Socrates who belonged to the Stoic tradition.[59]

Nevertheless, there is a change of context which must be taken into account. Although the antithesis between individuality and conformity was Stoic (or Cynic) in origin, it was transcended in the Stoic and humanistic tradition by the individual's higher conformity to the universal requirements of human nature. In this sense the individual could take himself as "a representative of universal human nature." This prospect is no longer available when the "diversities" of human nature are stressed, along with the limitations of any particular individual's point of view.[60] Mill then faces the methodological problem of comprehensiveness, which the philosophy of a universal and uniform human nature had assured for nearly two thousand years, but which will now have to be achieved in a new philosophical way.

If Mill selects Bentham's particular mind as an illustration of the universal tendency of men "to deny or disparage all feelings of which they have no consciousness in themselves," it is because Bentham's creation of "a philosophy out of materials furnished by his own mind and minds like his own" gives "the sanction of philosophy" to this tendency.[61] Mill's own philosophy retracts this sanction.

The operation of sympathy, whereby an individual derives "light from others' minds" cannot pretend (any more than the individual's reflexive operation on his own mind) to the methodological dignity of derivation from the methods of physical science. Thus Mill has to smuggle both operations into philosophy by distinguishing between poetic procedures and generalizing the distinction. The reflexive operation, which we examined in the last chapter, is a distinguishing characteristic of the poet insofar as he is a lyric poet; the exercise of sympathy is a distinguishing characteristic of the poet insofar as he is something more than a lyric poet—that is, "insofar as he does anything but melodiously utter his own actual feelings."[62] What is distinctive of lyric poetry is not the outward metrical structure of the poem but the reflexive structure of the poet's mind, which enables him to "express his feelings exactly as he has felt them in solitude."[63] The reflexive criterion can then be generalized so that it applies to any individual.[64] What is similarly distinctive of the dramatist is not, for example, his division of the drama into five acts, but the dramatic procedure, which he, or any individual, must employ to surmount the differences between his mind and circumstances and those of other men. "One mind understands a mind different from itself, only when it "throws itself into the feelings of that other mind."[65]

This Romantic and poetic conception of sympathy is not to be confused with Hume's Neoclassical and rhetorical conception. We have seen that the operation of sympathy in Hume takes place in the context of a rhetorical version of the humanistic theory of universal human nature, and that it is triggered by the individual's consciousness of the likenesses between himself and other men.[66] The operation of sympathy in Mill presupposes the prior, poetically conceived reflexive operation, whereby the individual who has become self-conscious has also become conscious of the differences separating him from other men. These differences have to be surmounted. Sympathy in Mill is an active and voluntary performance. It is not the mechanism which in Hume operates on the passive mind of a spectator. The individual sympathizing in Mill is not a spectator who merely observes the actions of others; he has to take the initiative when his mind throws itself into the feelings of other minds.[67]

Mill is exercising sympathy, so conceived, when he becomes aware of the limitations, not only of his own mind, but also of a mind like his own (e.g., Roebuck's) and enters into "friendly intercourse" with their "Coleridgian adversaries." He is exercising sympathy at a higher, philosophical or methodological level when he supplements his "philosophical estimate" of Bentham with a "philosophical estimate" of Coleridge, and in this way separates himself in a marked manner from the narrower Benthamism of his earlier writings. In these two essays, "Bentham" and "Coleridge," Mill is attempting to create a philosophy out of materials furnished by a mind like his own mind and by a mind different from his own.

It is difficult to measure what Berlin refers to as "the deepest convictions of philosophers," but it is obvious by now that Mill's deepest convictions do not belong in a Stoic fortress. The inner realm entered by Stoic reflection was as broad and lofty as the universe.[68] It was not located in the depths of a soul where one individual plumbs the differences separating him from other individuals. The metaphor of a fortress fails, moreover, to do justice to Mill's profound conviction that sympathy has to be exercised toward minds different from one's own. If Mill never employs the metaphor of a fortress, it is because he is more belligerent in throwing himself into the feelings of other minds than he is in defending his own position.[69] It is true that Mill obtains his metaphorical description of this procedure by generalizing his distinction of what is dramatic in a poetic performance, so that we may wish to accept Berlin's verdict, "Rigour in argument is not one of his accomplishments." But if rigor in interpretation requires attention to Mill's own metaphors, we should pay the closest attention to the metaphor that discloses the relation he solicits between the individual and others as determining one of the procedures that Mill adopts in his arguments.

The metaphor of an "inner fortress," as used by Berlin, may be one way of rendering the principle of individuality, but it illustrates a later phase in the development of the principle (and in the disintegration of the philosophy of a universal and uniform human nature) than Mill's pluralistic liberalism—a later phase when the deepest convictions of different individuals have become largely defensive and largely immobile, and we have to resign ourselves to their mutual irreducibility and mutual irrelevance. What nineteenth-century performance then seems more outdated than the energetic optimism of Mill's behest that we throw ourselves into the feelings of other minds!

Modes of Thinking

This performance, I have anticipated, is illustrated by Mill's relation to Carlyle. As soon as his father's death "exempted" Mill from "restraints and reticences," he enlisted Carlyle as "a frequent writer" for the new *Westminster*, although in Carlyle's writings, Mill concedes, "for a long time I saw nothing (as my father saw nothing in them to the last), but insane rhapsody" in which "almost the only clear thing was a strong animosity to most of the opinions which were the basis of my mode of thought."[70] Mill may have accepted Carlyle's animosty as "poetry to animate," rather than as "philosophy to instruct," but he also boasts, "I did not seek and cultivate Carlyle less on account of the fundamental differences in our philosophy."[71]

Mill's sympathetic cultivation of Carlyle took the specific form of a rhapsodic review of Carlyle's *French Revolution*. Mill is being sympathetic toward the individuality of a poetic genius when he hails this history at once as "a poem" and as "one of those products of genius which are above all rules and a law to themselves."[72] A genius who is a law to himself may seem far afield from the sphere of politics, but Mill also raises a more humdrum consideration, "What are Mr. Carlyle's *opinions*?" Mill's reply toys with the question:

> If this means, whether is he Tory, Whig, or Democrat; is he for things as they are, or for things *nearly* as they are; or is he one who thinks that subverting things as they are, and setting up Democracy is the main thing needful? we answer, he is none of all these. We should say that he has appropriated and made part of his own frame of thought, nearly all that is good in these several modes of thinking.[73]

Mill has raised the question of Mr. Carlyle's opinions—perhaps a little disdainfully—on behalf of his fellow Benthamites, who are sensitive only to Carlyle's animosity to most of their opinions and do not feel the same need as Mill for animation.[74] In the setting of their philosophy of human nature, opinions obtain their relevance as substantive political commitments for or against outward institutional changes. So long as opinions are identified in this way, Tory and Democrat remain irreconciliably opposed: one cannot be both for things as they are and for subverting things as they are. (The way Benthamites deal with Whig compromisers will be taken up in the next section.) But insofar as a Tory or Democrat thinks primarily with reference to outward institutional changes, his thinking is misdirected. Although Mill himself, we remember, remains "as much as ever a radical and democrat" with respect to outward institutional changes, he can at the same time regard the differences between a Democrat and a Tory, between Bentham and Coleridge, between himself and Carlyle, less as substantive differences of opinion with respect to these outward institutional changes than as illustrating something much more relevant—different modes of thinking. These are more relevant because they reflect differences between individuals—

differences which in fact are not entirely due to their different outward circumstances but which to some extent emerge from their internal culture and self-questioning.[75] But once the relevance of different modes of thinking is recognized, the need must also be recognized for a sympathetic effort to appropriate and make part of one's own frame of thought nearly all that is good in these different modes of thinking. (It is easier, of course, to credit this effort to Mill than to Carlyle; Mill is trying to persuade himself, as well as Carlyle, that Carlyle is a liberal.)

Mill and his father, in their writings for the old *Westminster*, had been so restricted by their doctrine of circumstances that they could not draw any distinction between substantive political opinions and modes of thought. They respected only one mode, the method of linear deduction. Starting from a utilitarian philosophy of human nature, which was deduced from the doctrine of circumstances, they had continued the deduction until they arrived at the outward institutional changes which were required to secure "the furthest limit of happiness which is compatible with human nature."[76] En route, the deduction had disposed of opposing opinions (on virtually any philosophical subject) by exposing these opinions as covert political opposition to these institutional changes. The deduction exposed and explained this opposition as a psychological matter of "the partisan interests" of their opponents,[77] not only in maintaining their privileged circumstances, which would be leveled by these changes, but also in disguising these same partisan interests.

SEE-SAW

Although this deductive argument undermined the uncompromisingly Tory opinions of the *Quarterly Review*, the deductive structure of argument had itself to be asserted in dealing with the readiness of the Whig *Edinburgh Review* to conciliate opposing opinions. Its temporizing had been the target of Mill's father's attack in the article on "Periodical Literature" which Mill himself had helped his father prepare for the first issue of the old *Westminster:*

> Having spoken a while on the one side, they must speak a while on the other. . . . It matters not how much the one set of principles are really at variance with the other. . . . They do not allow that two contradictory opinions on one and the same point destroy one another, and should be

regarded as *no opinion at all.* They hold that two contradictory opinions are good for nothing, each of them by itself; but that, both together, they form another nice opinion, exactly in the middle way between both.[78]

Such "playing at see-saw" in disregard of the deductive criterion of non-contradiction, Mill's father would doubtless have detected in Mill's later procedure of combining "half-truths."[79] It is not surprising that Mill waited until his father's death had "exempted" him from "restraints and reticences" before employing this method[80]

The mature Mill, even when he is dealing with substantive commitments to political institutions, attempts to reconcile opposed political points of view. In Part I we saw what happens when Mill is confronted with the opposition between liberal and conservative. He at once rises above party and from this vantage point offers "a better doctrine," which is "not a mere compromise, by splitting the difference between the two." The "superior comprehensiveness" which Mill is reaching for, is something which "might be adopted by either Liberal or Conservative without renouncing anything which he really feels to be valuable in his own creed." Mill's reluctance to split the difference is not his father's respect for the deductive criterion of non-contradiction. It is sympathetic solicitude for what an individual "really feels" is at stake.[81]

Unlike individuality, sympathy never quite attains in Mill the full status of an avowed principle. This status is reserved for the "principle of antagonism," which in effect replaces his father's principle of non-contradiction.[82] The principle of antagonism justifies supplementing the reflexive operation of the mind, consecrated by the principle of individuality, with the sympathetic operation, but it presides over an adjustment which sympathy, as a faculty of a limited individual's mind, cannot always finally carry out:

> Truth in the great practical concerns of life, is so much a question of the reconciling and combining of opposites, that very few have minds sufficiently capacious and impartial to make an adjustment [e.g., in the fashion attempted by Mill's philosophical estimates of Bentham and Coleridge] and it has to be made by the rough process of struggle between combatants fighting under hostile banners.[83]

Mill's "better doctrine" does not discredit or supersede political partisanship. Philosophical estimates can do their work: the moral appeal of the estimate of Bentham to derive "light from other minds" can be supplemented with the moral appeal of the estimate of Coleridge, "Lord, enlighten thou our enemies."[84] But there are still political conflicts which moralizing and enlightenment cannot entirely cushion—a certain place left in practice for the collision of opinions. Politics is not poetry. It remains a distinct and separate arena where hard bodies must sometimes knock against each other.[85]

THE COMPOSITION OF FORCES

Mill seems to explicitly resign himself to a lack of rigor when he accepts a rough process of conflict and reconciliation as the way of attaining truth in the great practical concerns of life. Yet this process is not unprincipled or unstructured. It has a structure comparable to the structure that Mill envisages for a scientific system. We can at last complete our attempt to circumvent his distinction between method and opinions, between theory and practice.

In Part I we dealt with the way the principle of antagonism presided over Mill's procedure for adjustment. I made use of Mill's comparison of the operation of this principle with the check-and-balance system of mixed government.[86] The comparison illustrated the extent to which political arguments are not merely substantive arguments about the structure appropriate for political institutions. Political institutions, as well as political arguments, can embody a procedure for the resolution of differences of political opinion. The procedure followed by the theorist in his arguments is often identical in its structure with the way he conceives political institutions should operate. We have had frequent illustrations of this identity of structure.

Mill's procedure we have now contrasted with the rigorously deductive method which James Mill follows in repudiating, as see-saw deviations from the line of utility, the *Edinburgh's* procedure of mixing conservative arguments with democratic arguments. We shall next see that Bentham detects the same deviousness in the operations of the check-and-balance system. Thus the contrast that holds between the way a political argument proceeds in the *Edinburgh* (as its procedure is analyzed by James Mill) and the utilitarian procedure of linear deduction, will also hold between the operation of the check-and-balance system (as its operation is analyzed by Bentham) and the way government is required to operate by the utilitarian deduction. Let me spell this out. In the check-and-balance system, the monarch, the aristocratic class, and the people, are separately represented by different institutions of government, and these institutions are designed in turn to check and balance each other. Bentham presents this theory as a composition of forces which are antagonistic to each other:

> The constitution is composed of three forces, which, antagonizing each other, cause the business of government to be carried on in a course which is different from that in which it would be carried on if it were directed solely by any one. The course which results is the product of the joint influence of all three.[87]

If the utilitarian theory of human nature is a deduction which cannot tolerate any deviation from "the line of utility" in a political argument,[88] it is also a deduction which cannot allow the operations of government to be impelled in two or three different directions:

> In proportion as the business of government is well conducted, it is uniformly carried on in a direction tending toward a certain end: the greatest happiness of the greatest number. In proportion as they are well conducted, the operations of all the agents concerned will tend toward the same end.[89]

This conclusion regarding the structure of government is indistinguishably psychological and methodological—that is, it depends indistinguishably on Bentham's identification in his theory of human nature of a single end for the operations of government—the greatest happiness of the greatest number—and on his adoption, in reaching this conclusion, of the method of linear deduction.[90] Hobbes had followed a similar method and had also rejected mixed government.[91] Mill himself lumps the Benthamite deduction together with Hobbes' deduction when he criticizes the assumption that any political problem can be treated as if its occurrence were the result of "only one force, one simple property of human nature."[92] This was the "error" or "one-sidedness" which he detected, after Macaulay's attack, in the utilitarian conception of "philosophical method as applicable to politics." The "error" we recall, "flashed" upon Mill while he was "attempting to fathom the mode of tracing causes and effects in physical science." The principle which we have just watched Bentham discard as inapplicable to politics, is the principle which Mill now proposes to apply:

> I soon saw that in the more perfect of the sciences [viz., Newtonian mechanics], we ascend . . . to the tendencies of causes considered singly, and then reason downward from those separate tendencies to the effect of the same causes when combined. . . . My practice (learnt from Hobbes and my father) being to study abstract principles by means of the best concrete instances I could find, the Composition of Forces, in dynamics, occurred to me as the most complete example of the logical process I was investigating. On examining, accordingly, what the mind does when it applies the principle of the Composition of Forces, I found that it . . . adds the separate effect of the one force to the separate effect of the other, and puts down the sum of these separate effects as the joint effect.[93]

Then Mill hesitated:

> But is this a legitimate process? In dynamics . . . it is; but in some other cases, as in chemistry, it is not.

Next came the flash of insight:

> I then recollected that something not unlike this was one of the distinctions between chemical and mechanical phenomena. . . . This distinction at once made my mind clear as to what was perplexing me in respect to the philosophy of politics. . . . Both Macaulay and my father were wrong; the one in assimilating the method of philosophizing in politics to the purely experimental method of chemistry; while the other, though right in adopting a deductive method, had made a wrong selection of one, having taken as the type of deduction, not the appropriate process, that of the deductive branches of natural philosophy, but the inappropriate one of pure geometry.[94]

Finally there emerged from the application of the principle of the Composition of Forces the principle of "distinct and separate" sciences:

> My new position in respect to my old political creed, now became perfectly definite. If I am asked, what system of political philosophy I substituted for that which, as a philosophy, I had abandoned, I answer, no system: only a conviction that the true system was something much more complex and many-sided than I had previously had any idea of.[95]

All that concerned us here in Part I was Mill's resort to "other studies," in his effort to find a method for treating the subject-matter of politics. Now we are able to take into account the methodological perfection which he ascribes to one of these studies (Newtonian mechanics), the specific principle that he borrows from this science, and the way it structures the relations between the sciences. Mill, it should be noted, hesitates over the legitimacy of extending the principle of the Composition of Forces. Hobbes never hesitated over the principle that legitimated his linear deduction—the law of inertia held for all phenomena. But Mill is facing a methodological problem with respect to the differences between chemical and mechanical phenomena. Indeed the principle does not hold, strictly speaking, of the subject-matter of any science. It is a "logical process"—something that "the mind does." Mill is thereby committed to an investigation in a logic of the applicability of this principle, as a distinct and separate question from the actual treatment of the subject-matter of the sciences themselves.

Mill explains the methodological error of his predecessors by alleging their inadequate "scientific education" and their "insufficient consideration of the specific nature of the subject matter of politics."[96] But Bentham's scientific education (not to mention Hobbes') was not so inadequate that he was unaware of the principle of the Composition of Forces. After all, he explicitly discarded it as inapplicable to the operations of government. By now we are fully aware too of the extent to which the nature of the subject matter of politics is the result of the application of some method which determines its relaion to other subject matters. Take Mill's case—even though he does not actually apply the scientific method he proposes in the *Logic* and leaves us instead with the "conviction that the true system would be something much more complex and many-sided" than his predecessors' "system of political philosophy." This endorsement of "distinct and separate" sciences, in conformity with the principle of the Composition of Forces, sets up the same pluralistic structure as Mill's endorsement of distinct and separate individuals in conformity with his principle of individuality, and as his endorsement of distinct and separate political parties in conformity with the principle of antagonism. In view of this identity of structure, it is hard to believe that the first of these principles is uniquely scientific while the other two are reserved entirely for the "great practical concerns of life." This is one reason we may have been justified in refusing in the Introduction to accept Mill's reduction of the problems of "philosophical method as applicable to politics" to problems of scientific method.[97] Mill's "true system," even though it must wait upon some eventual extension and generalization of scientific method, already exhibits the same structure as his actual treatment of moral and political problems.

Indeed, the fact that Mill does not complete the construction of this scientific system might itself be taken as further illustrating the same structure that he imposes in practice on the individual's mind and on the relations between individuals. The structure in question can again be brought out by a contrast with Mill's predecessors. Their system was a single and final theory of human nature in which a single end supplies uniformity of direction as a criterion for the operation of political institutions as well as for the construction of a political theory. In lieu of a single and final theory of human nature, Mill as a liberal is concerned in practice with "the importance to *man* and *society* of a large variety in types of character, and of giving full freedom to human nature to expand itself in innumerable and conflicting directions."[98] Such freedom for expanding diversity is important to *man* as an individual in the fashion indicated by the principles of individuality and antagonism. On the one hand, "individuality is the same thing with development."[99] On the other hand, Mill had learned from his own development that training in deductive analysis "had consequences which required to be corrected, by joining other kinds of cultivation" (viz., "poetic culture"), in order to achieve "a due balance among the faculties."[100] There should be introduced within the mind of the individual, if he is to achieve his full development, the check-and-balance system which had traditionally presided over the operation of political institutions.[101]

These principles of individuality and antagonism must be extended and generalized, if *society* at large is to develop and progress: "The unlikeness of one person to another is not only a principle of improvement but would seem almost to be the only principle of improvement."[102] Expanding diversity is the structure of progress, not only for society but also for the *theory* of society.[103] This is why the "true system" can never be consolidated in some final form. Mill has to leave the question open as to what "distinct and separate" sciences may turn out to be relevant to society and to its improvement.[104] The "complex and many-sided" structure he assigns to the "true system," is the same structure of expanding diversity which he commends in practice for society and for the individual.[105]

The contrast between this methodological structure and that exhibited by Mill's predecessors' political theory is equally illustrated by the different conception of journalism which Mill adopts when he retains their theory as his "practical political creed." The contrast is implicit in Mill's detection of the threat to the progress of society that democracy in America is, as the tyranny of public opinion, and of the threat to intellectual progress that journalism is, insofar as it "wears down into uniformity all that is individual."[106] The individual for Mill is someone who should be different from other men, while journalism, when it is merely the instrument of public opinion, is "thinking" which is done for men "by men very much like themselves."[107]

The Two Schools

This developmental structure of expanding diversity is not, however, the sheer dispersal which Mill's endorsement of the "distinct and separate" might lead us to expect from our own experience today of the fragmentation of the social sciences into specialized research projects and of society into individual defenders of inner fortresses. In the Conclusion I shall try to sketch the different structure of our thought today, insofar as we have inherited Mill's liberalism and yet interpret it differently from the way he did. For the present, we can recognize that although Mill characteristically defends the moral and political relevance of "other studies" and of other individuals, he never risks alienation. His principle of antagonism does not condone uncontrollable otherness and diversity, but imposes a pairing procedure.

Consider first the place Mill assigns himself in relation to other philosophers. We have already considered the place he assigns the utilitarians:

> In all ages of philosophy, one of its schools has been utilitarian. . . . It was by mere accident that this opinion became connected in Bentham with his peculiar method. The utilitarian philosophers antecedent to him had no more claims to the method than their antagonists. To refer, for instance, to the Epicurian philosophy, according to the most accomplished

scholar of antiquity, Cicero: we ask anyone who has read his philosophical writings, . . . whether the arguments of the Epicureans do not, just as much of those of the Stoics or Platonists, consist of mere rhetorical appeals. . . . Bentham certainly did not learn his sifting and anatomizing method from them. This method Bentham has finally installed in philosophy; has made it, henceforth, imperative on philosophers of all schools.[108]

Mill is here separating, as we earlier observed, Bentham's method from his utilitarian theory of human nature. This separation illustrates Mill's distinction between logic and psychology, and his segregation as uniquely methodological any procedure which is an extension and generalization of scientific method. Mill is accordingly also distinguishing two periods in the history of philosophy: the first features opinions unsupported by any scientific method; during the second, which is dawning, all schools must rally to scientific method. This distinction assigns Bentham his revolutionary place in the history of philosophy.

What place then does Mill assign himself when he offers this "philosophical estimate" of Bentham and of Bentham's "revolution in philosophy"? We have seen that Mill reaches this "philosophical estimate" by pairing the essay on Bentham with an essay on Coleridge. In other words, he retains from the first period in the history of philosophy a distinction between "two schools"—the utilitarian and their antagonists. The distinction between these two schools emerged, we recall, from Cicero's revival and reconciliation of the Platonic with the Stoic school, for their reconciliation turned on their mutual antagonism to the utilitarianism of the Epicureans. Although Mill dismisses all the traditional schools for their lack of rigor in argument whenever he is concerned to advance a scientific conception of method, although he does not identify Cicero as a philosopher but merely as "the most accomplished scholar of antiquity,"[109] he is in effect bringing Cicero's philosophical interpretation of the history of philosophy down to his own day when he finds his own conciliatory task as a philosopher cut out for him by the contemporary version of this perennial antagonism—the "two schools" of Bentham and Coleridge.[110]

Such pairing of schools had been characteristic of histories of philosophy which were fitted to some philosophy of human nature. Whatever psychological distinction was drawn within the historian's own philosophy (e.g., between reason and the passions in Cicero's case, or between reason and sentiment in the cases of Hume and Bentham) found a methodological illustration as a distinction between his own and some antagonistic philosophy of human nature. Mill's justification for pairing has to take another form. We have seen that Cicero's and Hume's philosophies of human nature were based on likenesses between individuals and that Bentham's assumes that they can be treated as identical units. But Mill cannot pull together into a philosophy of human nature all the relevant differences that he is concerned to acknowledge between individuals and their points of view. The philosophy of human nature unravels instead into a series of oppositions:

> Every inquirer is either young or old, rich or poor, sickly or healthy, married or unmarried, meditative or active, a poet or logician, an ancient or a modern, a man or a woman.[111]

This pairing procedure may derive its most irresistible cogency from Mill's relation to a woman. But we have recognized that Mrs. Taylor was something more than womanly. She performed a poetic and philosophical function in relation to Mill that other individuals were also in some measure able to perform. What we have seen Mill identify as "poetic culture of the most valuable kind" was "reverential admiration for the lives and characters of heroic persons, especially the heroes of philosophy." Mill explained:

> The same inspiring effect which so many of the benefactors of mankind have left on record that they had experienced from Plutarch's lives, was produced on me by Plato's pictures of Socrates, and by some modern biographies. . . . The heroic virtues of these glorious representatives of the opinions with which I sympathized, deeply affected me, and I perpetually recurred to them as others do to a favorite poet, when needing to be carried up into the more elevated regions of feeling and thought.[112]

Mill is reminding us of the typological structure of the humanistic tradition in which men can lead parallel lives—can take other men's lives as models.

However Mill's adoption of the pairing procedure introduces a certain complication in his use of models. At one level, the other mind should be a different mind, if light is to be derived from it; at a higher level, the other mind should be itself a model of the pairing procedure.

Thus Mill pairs Bentham with Coleridge, but at the higher level he derives the pairing procedure itself from Coleridge. At this higher level, moreover, Coleridge was able to typify the synthetical comprehensiveness Mill seeks by this procedure: "In Coleridge, a poetic nature has been united with logical and scientific culture," so that "truth" is "arrived at by two processes, verifying and correcting each other," rather "than by one alone."[113] The same typological complication is found in the way Mill's relation to Mrs. Taylor is structured: "It was necessary that the object of my admiration should be [1] of a type very *different* from my own; should be a character preeminently of feeling, [2] *combined* however as I had not in any other instance known it to be, with a vigorous & bold speculative intellect."[114]

When we began exploring the structure of the humanistic tradition, we recognized the contrast between its typological use of authoritative predecessors as models and the use of models, which I interpreted topologically, in the tradition of Hobbes, Locke, and Mill where "the methods of physical science" are "the proper models for political [science]."[115] But we found that the two traditions could be brought within the scope of a single interpretation; the one procedure could be converted into the other in that the selection of a predecessor as typologically relevant also determines the relation between politics and "other studies", whereas the selection of some other study as topologically relevant also determines the relevance of predecessors.[116] In the last section we finally circumvented Mill's distinction between "the true system," which he envisages as the result of extending and generalizing from Newtonian mechanics the model of the Composition of Forces, and his practical political creed with respect to the individual's relation to himself and his relation to other men. Now that we have discovered that these relations are not sheer dispersal but are controlled by a pairing procedure, we are able to recognize that this procedure, even if it derives its most irresistible cogency from Mill's relation to Mrs. Taylor, extends all the way from the two political parties that Mill distinguishes to the structure of the sciences that surround his proposed treatment of political problems in the *Logic*, where ethology is paired with the psychology of his predecessors to compose a philosophy of human nature, and this philosophy of human nature is in turn paired with the continental philosophy of social history.[117]

Since Mill failed to construct his philosophy of human nature, we concentrated in the previous chapter on the reconstruction of the utilitarian philosophy of human nature that is implicit in his adoption of the principle of individuality, and in the present chapter on the reconstruction of the utilitarian philosophy of human nature that is implicit in his pairing the principle of individuality with the principle of antagonism. In the next chapter we shall similarly have to consider the form taken by his reconstruction of the antagonistic continental philosophy of social history, before we can consider in the Conclusion the way in which Mill reconciles this historical approach with the psychological approach of his predecessors.

Notes

1. See p. 281, this vol. Cf. John Plamenatz' appraisal of *On Liberty* (as well as of *Utilitarianism* and *Representative Government*) as "written by a sick man in his premature old age," and as exhibiting "all his defects as a thinker, his lack of clarity, his inconsistency, and his inability either to accept wholeheartedly or to reject the principles inherited from his father and from Bentham" (*The English Utilitarians* [Oxford: Basil Blackwell, 1966], p. 123). It should be remembered that I am not addressing myself in this study to the familiar question of the rigor or lack of rigor of the arguments that can be sorted out in *On Liberty* (see vol. 1, p. 66). I am only examining the respects in which Mill thinks of himself as both rejecting his father's and Bentham's political theory "as a scientific theory," and accepting it as a "practical political creed." To carry out this examination is to trace some of the implications of his arguments, but it is not to test their rigor.

2. *John Stuart Mill and the Ends of Life* (London: Council of Christians and Jews, 1959), p. 29.

3. See p. 240, this vol.

4. See vol. 1, p. 40; vol. 2, p. 290.

5. See vol. 1, p. 37.

6. For the sense in which the two forms of inner enslavement to the outward are comparable, see vol. 1, p. 44. Sometimes Mill equates democracy as such with "the government of public opinion" ("Civilization," *Mill's Essays on Literature and Society*, ed. J. B. Schneewind [New York: Collier Books, 1965, p. 157]), and "despotism" with the despotic yoke of public opinion" (see p. 287, this vol.) or with "whatever crushes individuality" (*On Liberty* [New York: Liberal Arts, 1956], p. 77). The first equation (as we saw in chap. 16) derives much of its plausibility from his predecessor' theory of democracy, in which public opinion was the agency of democratic control: this theory of democracy was based psychologically on the doctrine of circumstances, which provided an explanation of how men's opinions are formed; and it was this explanation which threatened to crush Mill's individuality. Mill recalls how the doctrine "weighed on my existence like an incubus," since it implied that "my character and that of all others had been formed for us by agencies beyond our control, and was wholly out of our own power" (see vol. 1, p. 42). Mill's persisting complaint against his father's psychology is "the almost total absence . . . of the recognition of any active element, or spontaneity, in

the mind itself" ("Bain's Psychology," *Dissertations and Discussions*, 3 vols. [London: Longmans, Green, Reader, and Dyer, 1867], 3: 119). See chap. 18, n. 103.

7. See vol. 1, p. 47.

8. The metaphor of "internal culture" is, of course, not original with Mill. For Cicero's use of the metaphor, see vol. 1, p. 272. But the crucial step in the literary enterprise of liberating the mind from literal references to outward circumstances was illustrated by Augustine's *peregrinatio animae* (see vol. 1, p. 308).

9. "Retreat to the Inner Citadel" is the title of section iii of Berlin's *Two Concepts of Liberty* (Oxford: Clarendon Press, 1950). In that section Berlin is describing the "traditional self-emancipation" of "stoics" and others who would escape "the yoke of society or public opinion, by some process of deliberate self-transformation that enables them . . . to remain, isolated and independent, . . . no longer vulnerable to its weapons" (p. 20).

10. *Philosophy, Politics and Society*, ed. Peter Laslett (New York: Macmillan, 1956), p. ix. Berlin makes the same assumption: "Political theory is a branch of moral philosophy, which starts from the discovery, or application, of moral notions in the sphere of political relations" (*Two Concepts of Liberty*, p. 5). This assumption can be reinforced, and placed almost beyond the reach of argument, by the principle of "distinct and separate" sciences: "Philosophy was once a name for all human knowledge. . . . With the growth of specialization and the perfection of scientific methods, various branches of knowledge developed their own technique and, one after the other, split off from philosophy. . . . Thus the problem now is . . . whether there is any place left for political philosophy when these sciences [the social sciences] have occupied their own fields" (J. D. Mabbott, *The State and the Citizen* [London: Hutchinson's University Library, 1947], pp. 171–72). Mabbott responds to this topological problem by assigning to political philosophy the place he regards political philosophy as having had from Hobbes on as a theory of political obligation. To phrase Mabbott's assumption in Berlin's terminology: the moral notion of obligation is applied to the sphere of political relations. The resulting truncation of the political is illustrated by Mabbott's "observations on theories which might be supposed to involve political philosophy." On the one hand, "totalitarianism is a political philosophy," since it is a theory of political obligation. On the other hand, "the essential difference between Nazism and communism is not one of political philosophy or of political institutions. It does not lie in the range of political authority or in the way in which it is exercised, but in the purposes for which political power and political machinery are used. . . . The only ideological element in it [Nazism] —the racial theory—is the concern not of philosophers but of ethnologists. In the U.S.S.R. a very similar machine was applied for the institution and maintenance of new economic arrangements for ownership and control of factories and land, in the interests of the workers. The ideological element here concerns the economist, not the philosopher. . . . Communism, like capitalism, is not a political philosophy" (pp. 172–73). Such shedding of political problems to the social sciences is too simplistic. See my topological argument in chap. 12 that the structure of political philosophy has itself been altered by the detachment of economic theory from political philosophy.

11. See p. 290, this vol.

12. I am renewing my argument of vol. 1 that "the way later 'returns' to society and politics are conducted" is "influenced by the way previous 'flights' were conducted" (chap. 9, n. 171).

13. Letter to Gustave d'Eichthal, February 9, 1830, I am citing from the *Collected Works of John Stuart Mill*, ed. Francis E. Mineka (Toronto: University of Toronto Press, 1963), 12:45. Mill is explaining why "I am not about to make this letter a controversial one," but his explanation would seem also to apply to his withdrawal from the Debating Society shortly before.

14. Letter to Thomas Carlyle, May 18, 1833 (*Collected Works,* 12: 153).

15. *Autobiography* (New York: Columbia University Press, 1924), p. 74.

16. Letter to Carlyle, May 18, 1833 (*Collected Works,* 12: 153).

17. *Autobiography,* p. 105.

18. "I suppose that of the set of young men with whom I had associated, Roebuck would have been & was generally regarded as the most complete type of what was considered narrow Benthamism" (*The Early Draft of John Stuart Mill's Autobiography,* ed. Jack Stillinger [Urbana: University of Illinois Press, 1961], p. 127. Mill goes on to qualify this judgment. He explains that "nine years of his [Roebuck's] boyhood & youth had been passed in the back woods of Canada," but though "his character had a great tinge of the backwoodsman," his mother "had cultivated in him a polish of manners not at all American which he always manifested towards friends, though not always towards opponents" (*ibid.,* p. 128). Mill of course also tends to regard himself as having been the most complete type of what was considered narrow Benthamism: "I conceive that the description so often given of a Benthamite, as a mere reasoning machine [*Early Draft*: "a dry, hard logical machine" (p. 101)] though extremely inapplicable to most of those who have been designated by that title, was during two or three years of my life not altogether untrue of me" (*Autobiography,* p. 76).

19. *Autobiography,* p. 105.

20. See p. 372, this vol.

21. Mill recalls how in 1829 Roebuck and I "agreed to have the fight out at our Debating Society, where we accordingly discussed for two evenings the comparative merits of Byron and Wordsworth, propounding and illustrating by long recitations our respective theories of poetry" (*Autobiography,* p. 105). The theory Mill propounded can be partly reconstructed from his *Autobiography.* Having reread his favorite authors "without feeling" (see p. 304, this vol.), Mill's next recourse was Byron: "I . . . read through the whole of Byron (then new to me), to try whether a poet, whose peculiar department was supposed to be that of the intenser feelings, could rouse any feeling in me" (ibid., p. 103). But Mill "got no good from this reading." It was so unsuccessful that when Mill first read a collection of Wordsworth's poems "in the autumn of 1828," it was "from curiosity, with no expectation of mental relief from it." What Mill unexpectedly came to feel was "that there was real, permanent happiness in tranquil contemplation" (*ibid.,* p. 104). Mill then faced three overlapping issues in the theory of poetry which he opposed to Roebuck's: (1) Mill was proposing to modify the Benthamite theory of knowledge, which he and Roebuck had both shared, in order to find a place for the arousal of poetic feelings: "He [Roebuck] wished that his feelings should be deadened rather than quickened. . . . He saw little good in any cultivation of the feelings, and none at all in cultivating them through the imagination, which he thought was only cultivating illusions. It was in vain I urged on him that the imaginative emotion which an idea, when vividly conceived, excites in us, is not an illusion but a fact, as real as any of the other qualities of objects" (*ibid.,* pp. 106–7). (2) The poetic feelings thus cultivated would participate in the extension and generalization (which I traced in chapter 16) of esthetic criteria to moral theory: "He [Roebuck] was a lover of poetry and of most of the fine arts. . . . But he never could be made to see that these things have any value as aids in the formation of character" (*ibid.,* p. 106). (3) As a result of this ethological extension and generalization, "tranquil contemplation" finds its place in Mill's moral theory, and he repudiates the outward orientation of Benthamite activism: "I, like most Wordsworthians, threw myself into strong antagonism to Byron, both as a poet and as to his influence on the character. Roebuck, all whose instincts were those of action and struggle, had, on the contrary, a strong relish and great admiration of Byron, whose writings he regarded as the poetry of human life, while Wordsworth's, according to him, was that of flowers and butterflies" (*ibid.,* p. 105).

Mill's rejection in this debate of Byron's poetry of "action and of struggle" in favor of Wordsworth's poetry of "tranquil contemplation," doubtless prefigures his giving up the action and the struggle by withdrawing "from attendance on the Debating Society" with the explanation, "I had had enough of speech-making, and was glad to carry on my private studies and meditations without any immediate call for *outward assertion of their results*" (*ibid.*, p. 110; italics added). For a further illustration of Mill's repudiation of Benthamite activism, see chap. 16, n. 96.

22. I am primarily concerned with the philosophical or methodological significance of Mill's personal break with Roebuck, just as I was primarily concerned in chap. 16 with the philosophical or methodological significance of his "personal purpose" in using the new *Westminster Review* "to separate myself in a marked manner from the narrower Benthamism of my early writings" (see p. 292, this vol.). But we saw in chap. 16 that Mill had a second and distinctively political purpose "in the conduct of the Review"—"to stir up the educated Radicals . . . and induce them to make themselves . . . a powerful party capable of taking the government of the country" (see p. 291, this vol.). That what I am now concerned with as philosophically significant was also politically significant has been demonstrated by Francis E. Hyde: "It is evident from information recently brought to light in documents among the Roebuck Papers that the friendship between John Stuart Mill and John Arthur Roebuck was of greater significance than has generally been believed. The course of this friendship and the consequences of its abrupt termination had repercussions on the fortunes of the radical party both before and after the passing of the Reform Bill. In this brief episode in the lives of these two men lies one explanation of the failure of the radicals to secure leadership and organization" ("Utility and Radicalism, 1825–1837: A Note on the Mill-Roebuck Friendship," *Economic History Review*, 16 [1946]: 38). The following details of this explanation might be cited: "Mill and Roebuck became prominent as the leaders of this little band of philosophical radicals [those who participated in the debating society], their skill in debate marking them out as active propagandists in the cause of radical reform. Among those who looked with favour on the Mill-Roebuck friendship were Jeremy Bentham and Francis Place. . . . Bentham and Place began to take an active interest in coaching Mill and Roebuck in the art of political leadership. The two young men were constant visitors to Bentham's house, and, under his tutelage the practical plans for future political activity were worked out. . . . The two men seemed to be complementary to each other. Acting together they had proved that they could command the respect of men of all shades of radical opinion; their record in the debating society had demonstrated how well they had performed the difficult task of checking the centrifugal tendencies of some of the other members. Mill's intellectual powers, coupled with Roebuck's dash and fire and ability to translate ideas into action [see my n. 21, above, for the way this contrast between their two characters emerged in their conflicting theories of poetry], had seemed to augur well for the leadership of this advanced group of thinkers. . . .The two men not only appeared to be essential to the radical plan of action, but the maintenance of their friendship seemed to be a point of major political strategy" (pp. 38, 39, 40). Hyde notes that "various memoranda in Roebuck's handwriting between 1826 and 1829 deal with plans for the ultimate victory of radical ideas in parliament," that "some are headed 'For discussion with J. S. M.,' " and that a letter to Roebuck in 1832 reports " 'Place . . . filled with anxiety lest a difference of opinion between you and Mill might compromise the fortunes of the good government party' " (p. 40). Hyde concludes: "The quarrel between Mill and Roebuck was something more than a personal affair. It destroyed the homogeneity of the group of advanced reformers who might well have given unity and leadership to the discordant ranks of the radicals in parliament. As it was, the annihilation of the radical party in the General Election of 1837 reflected the tragedy of this lost opportunity" (p. 44).

23. *Autobiography*, pp. 106, 107. The pivotal Coleridgian adversary was John Sterling (see vol. 1, p. 57). To his reference to the debate on Wordsworth, Mill attaches

his account of Roebuck, and of how "while my intimacy with Roebuck diminished, I fell more and more into friendly intercourse with our Coleridgian adversaries in the Society, Frederick Maurice and John Sterling." In this sequel Maurice is paired with Sterling much as Roebuck is implicitly paired with Mill himself. Sterling was the "impassioned expositor of thoughts which, at this period, were almost entirely formed for him by Maurice" (*Autobiography*, p. 107); at this period too Roebuck was the impassioned expositor of thoughts which had been almost entirely formed for him by Mill (as Roebuck indeed admitted). But Maurice retreated into clerical sectarianism, much as Roebuck remained a Benthamite sectarian; whereas Sterling's "mind was ever progressive" (as was Mill's mind; see p. 366, this vol.), so that although "he and I started from intellectual points almost as wide apart as the poles, . . . the distance between us was always diminishing" (*Autobiography*, p. 109). Mill dates the beginning of the diminishing of this distance from Sterling (as well as the beginning of his diminishing intimacy with Roebuck) from his defense of "the merits of Wordsworth"; he attributes to Sterling, listening to this defense, the discovery "that Wordsworth & all that is implied in Wordsworth 'belonged to' me as much as to him & his friends" (*Early Draft*, p. 132). But the initial distance between them was soon dramatized by a collision: "One vehment encounter between Sterling & me, he making what I thought a violent & unfair attack on the political philosophy I professed, to which I responded as sharply, fixed itself particularly in my memory because it was immediately followed by two things: one was, Sterling's withdrawing from the society; the other, that he & I sought one another privately much more than before, & became very intimate" (*Early Draft*, p. 133).

24. Alexander Bain, *John Stuart Mill* (London: Longmans, Green, 1882), p. 39.

25. *Ibid.* See n. 35, below.

26. See pp. 294–95, this vol. Compare Mill's contemptuously utilitarian comment on Roebuck's politics: "An ambitious young man with his fortune to make is naturally a Radical" (comment deleted from *The Early Draft*, p. 128).

27. "Bentham," *Mill's Essays on Literature and Society*, p. 285.

28. *Early Draft*, p. 154. Mill explains the phrase "poetic culture" in an expanded but deleted passage: "I am not now speaking of *written* poetry, either metrical or otherwise; though I did cultivate this taste as well as a taste for paintings & sculptures, & did read with enthusiasm her favorite poets, especially the one whom she placed far above all others, Shelley. But this was merely accessary. The real poetic culture was, that my faculties, such as they were, became more & more attuned to the beautiful & elevated, in all kinds, & especially in human feeling & character & more capable of vibrating in unison with it" (*Early Draft*, p. 199). This outward/inner distinction between "written" (or "metrical or otherwise") and "real" renders Mill's theory of poetry susceptible of the moralistic generalization whereby it acquires implications for the formation of character (see n. 21, above; chap. 16, n. 90; and chap. 18, n. 92). The implications of Mill's "real poetic culture" for his relations to those whose faculties were not so attuned, is illustrated by the sequel to this passage (see n. 35, below).

29. *Autobiography*, pp. 130–31. Thus the theory of poetry which Mill originally found implicit in his experience of reading Wordsworth in 1828 and opposed in 1829 to Roebuck's theory (see n. 21, above) is not identical with the theory which he published in 1833 and which we examined in the previous chapter. Mill's recollection of his original poetic experience in fact ends with a warning which could be taken as distinguishing between the two theories: "I long continued to value Wordsworth less according to his intrinsic merits, than by the measure of what he had done for me. Compared with the greatest poets, he may be said to be the poet of unpoetical natures. . . . But unpoetical natures are precisely those which require poetic cultivation. This cultivation Wordsworth is much more fitted to give, than poets who are intrinsically far more poets than he" (*Autobiography*, p. 105). In the published essays there is no reference

to Byron; he has been discarded as completely from Mill's theory as Roebuck has been discarded from his life. But Mill still opposes two kinds of poetry. Confronted with the evidence of Mrs. Taylor and Shelley, it now seems to Mill "undeniable in point of fact, and consistent with the principles of a sound metaphysics, that there are poetic natures" ("The Two Kinds of Poetry," *Mill's Essays on Literature and Society*, p. 118), as opposed to such "unpoetical natures" as his and Wordsworth's, which require "poetic culture." In order to give precedence to her favorite poet (the poet "whom she placed far above all others"; see n. 28, above) over his favorite poet Wordsworth, Mill turns Wordsworth's definition of poetry as "the spontaneous overflow of feeling" against Wordsworth's actual poetry, which "has little even of the appearance of spontaneousness: the well is never so full that it overflows. There is an air of deliberateness about all he writes, which is not characteristic of the poetic temperament; his poetry seems one thing, himself another; he seems to be poetical because he wills to be so, not because he cannot help it. . . . The genius of Wordsworth is essentially unlyrical" (*ibid.*, pp. 122–23). For Mill's maneuver, see M. H. Abrams, *The Mirror and the Lamp* (New York: W. W. Norton, 1958), p. 24.

30. See p. 302, this vol. The parenthetical interpolation "(*à fortiori* a woman)" we would have expected to come after "a man can do," but it is awkwardly delayed. Mill may be holding it back until what is at issue is independence of thought. If the parenthesis had been located at the grammatically normal place in the sentence, the ensuing reference to "swindling or forgery" might have suggested similarly dishonest or unfair dealings on Mrs. Taylor's part toward her husband. By the time Mill composed the parallel passage of *On Liberty*, Mr. Taylor was long since dead, Mill was married to Mrs. Taylor, and the grammar can be straightened out: "The man, and still more the woman, who can be accused either of doing 'what nobody does,' or of not doing 'what everybody does,'" is the subject of as much depreciatory remark as if he or she had committed some grave moral delinquency" (p. 83).

31. For a summary of the debate and one version of the argument that "Mill without Harriet would still have been Mill," see J. C. Rees' review of H. O Pappe's *John Stuart Mill and the Harriet Taylor Myth*, in *Political Studies*, 10 (1962), 198–202. There is also a brief sensible discussion of their relation in Stillinger's introduction to the *Early Draft* (pp. 22–28).

32. The dedication begins, "To the beloved and deplored memory of her who was the inspirer, and in part the author, of all that is best in my writings." It concludes: "Were I but capable of interpreting to the world one half the great thoughts and noble feelings which are buried in her grave, I should be the medium of a greater benefit to it, than is ever likely to arise from anything that I can write, unprompted and unassisted by her all but unrivaled wisdom."

33. Consider Michael St. John Packe's appraisal of the inspiration she had initially provided: "The article on Genius was quite unlike anything that Mill had thought before. It was, on the other hand, a lucid expansion of a principle stated by Harriet in a paper written at this time though never published. 'Whether it be religious conformity, Political conformity, moral conformity or Social conformity,' she said, 'no matter which the species, the spirit is the same: all kinds agree in this one point, of hostility to individual character.'" (*The Life of John Stuart Mill* [London: Secker and Warburg, 1954], pp. 133–34). Rees largely rejects this appraisal in the review cited in n. 31, above.

34. I am quoting Laski's letter to Justice Holmes from Stillinger's introduction to the *Early Draft* (pp. 24–25). The "cushion" is Laski's metaphor, but the opposition of hard and soft is a recurrent metaphor of Mill's own. It usually carries a reference to the antithesis between reason and sentiment, between intellect and feeling. We have seen (n. 18, above) Mill apply to himself the characterization of the narrow Benthamite as "a dry, *hard* logical machine" (italics added; for Mill's "exsiccation," see chap. 18, n. 90). He similarly refers to his having suffered "the *petrification* of a narrow philosophy" (let-

ter to Carlyle, October 5, 1833, *Collected Works,* 12: 181). Just before the dispute with Roebuck over Mrs. Taylor, Mill expressed the conviction that " 'the greatest happiness of mankind' could never be achieved by men calling themselves utilitarians as long as they despised and neglected every art that '*softened* manners and charmed the imagination' " (Hyde, "Utility and Radicalism," p. 41, italics added). The contrast with Roebuck, or with what Mill himself had been, or at any rate with the narrow Benthamite, is probably implicit in Mill's identifying Mrs. Taylor's "earnest protest against many things which are still part of the established constitution of society," as a protest resulting "not from the *hard* intellect, but from strength of noble and elevated feeling" (*Autobiography,* p. 130; italics added).

35. *Autobiography,* p. 1. The world had deprived itself of this opportunity. In the face of its pressure to conform and disapproval of their relation, Mill and Mrs. Taylor had withdrawn together from the world. Roebuck regarded the youthful Mill as unable to face the world: "He was utterly ignorant of what is called society; . . . of the world, as it worked around him, he knew nothing; and above all, of *woman* he was as a child. He had never played with boys. . . ." Roebuck's "remonstrating with Mill on the danger to his future prospects from his relation to Mrs. Taylor" was prompted by the scene he witnessed the next time he saw Mrs. Taylor after the original dinner party when Mill too first met her. Roebuck recalls watching "Mill enter the room with Mrs. Taylor hanging on his arm. The manner of the lady, the evident devotion of the gentleman, soon attracted universal attention, and a suppressed titter went round the room. My affection for Mill was so warm and sincere that I was hurt by anything which brought ridicule upon him. I saw, or thought I saw, how mischievous might be this affair, and as we had become in all things like brothers, I determined, most unwisely, to speak to him on the subject" (I am citing Roebuck's recollection from F. A. Hayek, *John Stuart Mill and Harriet Taylor* [Chicago: University of Chicago Press, 1951], pp. 79–80.) From Mill's own point of view, his withdrawal from the world was of course due, not to tittering, but more profoundly to his "real poetic culture." This is the explanation provided by the deleted passage I began citing in n. 28 above: "The first years of my friendship with her were, in respect of my own development, mainly years of poetic culture. . . . The real poetic culture was, that my faculties, . . . became more & more attuned to the beautiful & elevated, in all kinds, & especially in human feeling & character & more capable of vibrating in unison with it. *In the same proportion,* & *by a natural consequence,* I became less excitable by anything else. All society & personal intercourse became burthensome to me except with those in whom I recognized, along with more or less sympathy of opinion, at least a strong taste for elevated & poetic feeling, if not the feeling itself. I gradually withdrew myself from much of the society which I had frequented" (*Early Draft,* pp. 199–200; italics added).

36. If a contrast is desired, consider Hume's *Life* which is intended (like Mill's; see chap. 18, n. 76) to provide a kind of introduction to his writings. Hume acknowledges no intellectual debts; other men enter his *Life* not in any sense as predecessors but as an audience for his writings after they are written. They play the role of the spectator-critic (see chap. 16, n. 93).

37. In Mill's case the acknowledgments are not restricted to the beginning; the *Autobiography* is virtually a succession of acknowledgments—primarily of course to his father for the education Mill had received and to Mrs. Taylor for rescuing Mill from what he had been as a result of this education.

38. What Mill is reporting is not just a shift in friends and allies but a shift in which adversaries as such assume a relevance no ally had enjoyed. If Mill's erstwhile ally, Roebuck remained "the most complete type of . . . narrow Benthamism," it was largely in virtue of his attitude "towards opponents" (see n. 18, above). Roebuck, like Bentham, "failed in deriving light from other minds" (see pp. 328–29, this vol.): "He had a decided character of his own, & took only that portion of any creed which was in har-

mony with his character. Of this, pugnacity was one of the principal elements. . . . He arrived at his conclusions by deduction from the principles of his creed, never anxious to enlarge the basis of the creed itself. . . . This deficiency I used to account for to myself, by the deep rooted pugnacity of his character. When any proposition came before him as that of an opponent, he rushed eagerly to demonstrate its falsity, without taking any pains to discover & appropriate the portion of truth which there might be in it. This mental type, very natural to persons of impetuosity of character & which I saw in a less extreme degree in my father, became more & more alien to my tastes & feelings. I had now taken a most decided bent in the opposite direction, that of eclecticism" (*ibid.*, pp. 128–29). Consider Mill's similar reference to his father's "pugnacious & polemical intellect" (*ibid.*, p. 159) and the interpretation I offered in vol. 1, p. 8. Thus Mill could identify Roebuck as the sectarian Benthamite he himself would have remained, as his father's son, had he not taken this "most decided bent in the opposite direction." In this regard John Sterling's nature not only contrasts with Roebuck's but bears an astonishing resemblance to Mrs. Taylor's: "Il réunissait à l'un des plus nobles caractères qui puissent exister, une profondeur de sympathie qui tient de l'idéal féminin et qu'on ne trouve que fort rarement en angleterre si ce n'est dans les femmes et encore très exceptionnellement" (letter to Auguste Comte, October 5, 1844, *Collected Works*, 13: 637).

39. *Autobiography*, p. 123.

40. Letter to Carlyle, July 5, 1833, *Collected Works*, 12: 163.

41. Take, for example, the way Mill adjusts his relation to Carlyle: "My vocation . . . lies in a humbler sphere; I am rather fitted to be a logical expounder than an artist. You I look upon as an artist, and perhaps the only genuine one now living in this country: the highest destiny of all, lies in that direction; for it is the artist alone in whose hands Truth becomes impressive, and a living principle of action" (letter to Carlyle, July 17, 1832, *Collected Works*, 12: 133).

42. Letter to Carlyle, April 11, 12, 1833, *Collected Works*, 12: 149.

43. *Ibid.*, p. 152; letter to Carlyle, August 2, 1833, *Collected Works*, 12: 172. Mill is referring to his "Remarks on Bentham's Philosophy," which were published anonymously as an Appendix to E. L. Bulwer's *England and the English*.

44. See p. 294, this vol.

45. See pp. 297, 300, this vol.

46. "Bentham," *Mill's Essays on Literature and Society*, p. 263.

47. "Bentham," p. 258.

48. See p. 287, this vol.; italics added.

49. "Bentham," p. 256.

50. In *On Liberty* Mill recalls how Cicero "always studied his adversary's case with as great, if not still greater, intensity than even his own. What Cicero practiced as the means of forensic success requires to be imitated by all who study any subject in order to arrive at the truth" (pp. 44–45).

51. See p. 292, this vol.

52. See p. 243, this vol. For the methodological implications of Bentham's neglect of poetic feelings, see chap. 16, n. 84.

53. "Bentham," p. 257.

54. *Ibid.*, pp. 260–61. Hence "the tendency of all opinions to become sectarian" (*On Liberty*, p. 63).

55. "Two Kinds of Poetry," p. 120. To deal scientifically with "the *diversities*" would be to construct an ethology (see chap. 3, n. 23). Thus Mill's interpretation of Bentham (e.g., as "determined to create his philosophy out of materials furnished by his own mind and by minds like his own" is not, strictly speaking, a psychological but an ethological interpretation. In the context of the "true system" the methodological issue dividing Mill from utilitarianism is the need of an ethology to supplement and complete utilitarian psychology (see p. 345, this vol.).

56. *De Legibus* 1. 29.

57. See p. 18, this vol.

58. See pp. 14–17, this vol.

59. See pp. 13–14, this vol.

60. The individual in the Stoic and humanistic tradition who took himself as a representative of universal human nature was conforming ultimately to the universal nature of which he was a "part" (see chap. 11, n. 97). But this ultimate prospect is also unavailable in Mill. It is not the Stoic principle of universal sympathy (or the Newtonian principle of universal gravity—for the relation between these two principles, see p. 160, this vol.) that presides over Mill's understanding of nature, but the principle of the Composition of Forces, which justifies "distinct and separate" sciences (see p. 115, this vol.). Thus no particular science provides comprehensive understanding of universal nature; the "true system" must be "complex and many-sided" (see p. 340, this vol.).

61. "Bentham," p. 260.

62. "Bentham," p. 258. See n. 28, above, and chap. 18, n. 92.

63. See chap. 16, n. 91.

64. See p. 300, this vol.

65. "Bentham," p. 258. Cf. *On Liberty*, p. 45.

66. See chap. 15, n. 55, where I point out that Hume construes resemblance as a more fundamental relation than contrast or contrariety. Mill, in effect, takes contrast or contrariety to be more fundamental. See also chap. 14, n. 113.

67. Thus Mill criticizes Hume for failing to exercise sympathy (see chap. 18, n. 18).

68. See n. 60, above.

69. The sharp difference here is between Roebuck's "pugnacity" exercised "towards opponents" (see n. 38, above) (or Mill's father's "pugnacious & polemical intellect") and Mill's "decided bent in the opposite direction, that of eclecticism" (see n. 23, above).

70. *Autobiography*, pp. 144, 113, 123.

71. *Autobiography*, p. 123.

72. "Carlyle's *French Revolution*," *Mill's Essays on Literature and Society*, p. 184; *Autobiography*, p. 152. Remember that the poetry of the poetic genius is "above all rules" because it creates the rules by which it is to be evaluated.

73. "Carlyle's *French Revolution*," p. 194.

74. For Mill's need for animation, see pp. 380–82, this vol.

75. See vol. 1, pp. 43–45.

76. See p. 290, this vol.

77. See pp. 248–49, this vol.

78. *Westminster Review* 1 (Jan., 1824): 218, 220; italics added. Cf. the youthful John Stuart Mill's comments in the sequel: "What can be more immoral than the see-saw? a

practice . . . which habituates its votaries to play fast and loose with opinions—to lay down one, and take up another, with every change of audience? Can there be a spectacle more repugnant to the candour and sincerity which are so essential a part of morality, than a continual attempt to varnish over inconsistencies, and to reconcile in appearance doctrines which are really irreconcilable?" (*Ibid.*, 1 [April, 1824]: 527.) This elimination of the "middle way" was the elimination of the Whig party as such in favor of a simple opposition between Tories and Radicals. The youthful Mill dismissed the Whigs as "afraid of principles"— as "men of shifts and expedients." He admitted that it was possible to give "to Toryism (. . . though not to Whiggism) something like a philosophic basis." He defined Philosophical Radicalism simply as "enmity to the aristocratic principle," and looked forward to a realignment of parties which would reflect the "contest . . . between the two principles which divide the world, the aristocratic principle and the democratic" (I am citing Mill from Joseph Hamburger, *Intellectuals in Politics* [New Haven: Yale University Press, 1965], pp. 60–67, 68, 61). Roebuck likewise described the Whigs as in "a strange and anomalous position" and anticipated: "Parties will be divided by one broad line of distinction. Aristocracy and Democracy will be fairly arrayed against each other; no *middle* party will exist, and no *middle* course will be pursued" (I am citing from Hamburger, pp. 66, 60, and adding italics).

79. *Westminster Review*, 1 (Jan., 1824): 218. This procedure of combining "half-truths" Mill both derived from and applied to Coleridge (*Autobiography*, p. 114; see also "Coleridge," *Mill's Essays on Literature and Society*, p. 340).

80. See p. 333, this vol.

81. See vol. 1, pp. 48–49 and accompanying n. 26. A further difference can now be observed between James Mill's arithmetic and John Stuart Mill's. The father regards as units both each individual and each interest of the individual. The son not only multiplies the influence to be ascribed to "one individual with a belief, as compared with individuals "who have only interests," but he also divides the individual's beliefs, which become "half-truths" or "fractional truths" ("Bentham," p. 261).

82. For instances of Mill's application of the "principle of antagonism," see nn. 83, 101, 102, below.

83. *On Liberty* (New York: Liberal Arts, p. 58). In the preceding sentence, some of the "opposites" are listed: "Unless opinions favorable to democracy and to aristocracy, to property and to equality, to cooperation and to competition, to luxury and to abstinence, to sociality and individuality, to liberty and discipline, and all the other standing antagonisms of practical life, are expressed with equal freedom and enforced and defended with equal talent and energy, there is no chance of both elements obtaining their due; one scale is sure to go up, and the other down."

84. "Coleridge," *Mill's Essays on Literature and Society*, p. 345.

85. In the Neoclassical context of Hume's theory of human nature (as in Cicero's classical theory) politics is rhetoric and the likenesses between men (see n. 66, above) prevail in the process of persuasion. In this context, the philosophical mind of a Hume can easily become (in Mill's phrase) "capacious and impartial." There is no need for the process of "reconciling and combining of opposites" to take the "rough" form of a "struggle" between political parties. Indeed even this struggle can take the form of a "tendency to a coalition" (see chap. 15, n. 55). Thus Hume's analogous philosophical procedure is "to encourage moderate opinions, to find the proper medium in all disputes." (Observe his assumption that it can be found.) Such a procedure, if transferred to the context where Romantic "diversities" are to be respected, risks "a mere compromise, by splitting the difference between the two" (viz., Liberal and Conservative). What Mill reaches for as a philosophical "adjustment" is "something wider than either, which in virtue of its superior comprehensiveness, might be adopted by either Liberal or Con-

servative *without renouncing anything* which he really feels to be valuable in his own creed" (see vol. 1, p. 51; italics added).

86. See vol. 1, pp. 49–51.

87. *Handbook of Political Fallacies* (New York: Harper, 1962), pp. 164–65. Bentham has already disposed of the notion of a "balance" or "equipoise" (p. 164) and is now interpreting the check-and-balance system as operating with "the image of the composition and resolution of forces" (p. 165). In both cases he is exposing the latent fallacy by taking the mechanical analogy literally. He thus eliminates the moralistic implications of mixture and harmony which Cicero had introduced (see vol. 1. pp. 247–48). Moralistic and mechanistic implications lie side by side in Blackstone's version of the "constitutional government of this island" as "so admirably *tempered* and *compounded,* that nothing can endanger or hurt it, but destroying the equilibrium between one branch of the legislature and the rest" (I am citing Blackstone from Corinne Weston, *English Constitutional Theory and the House of Lords* [New York: Columbia University Press, 1965], pp. 127–28; italics added. She comments: "This description of the English government dominated for almost 100 years the thinking of the great majority of Englishmen who gave any thought at all to their government.") Blackstone's direct debt to Cicero is sometimes overlooked (see vol. 1, p. 110). Cicero's *temperantia* serves both to translate the moral virtue of self-control (σωφροσύνη) and to introduce the conception of a mixture (see chap. 7, n. 94).

88. James Mill, "Periodical Literature," *Westminster Review* 1 (Jan. 1824): 222.

89. *Handbook,* p. 165. The realignment anticipated in n. 78, above, was merely a necessary simplification of the struggle. In the long run there was no justification for any party as an instrument of partisan interests: "The object we have in view is to establish a National Government. . . . We seek to take away *all* power from every sect and party" (I am citing Roebuck from Hamburger, *Intellectuals in Politics,* p. 63).

90. The contrast could be renewed here between Bentham's reliance on the single principle of utility and Hume's adoption of the supplementary principle of sympathy (see p. 241, this vol.). Bentham has to reject mixed government because he accepts the principle of non-contradiction; Hume endorses mixed government because "the heart of man" in his theory of human nature "is made to reconcile contradictions" (see p. 248, this vol., and n. 85, above).

91. See, e.g., *Leviathan,* chap. 29.

92. *A System of Logic* (London: Longmans, Green, 1941), p. 579. Mill's interpretation distorts both Hobbes' and Bentham's procedures. My analysis of the operation of the "three principall causes of quarrell" in Hobbes (see pp. 125–26, this vol.) has suggested that he does not simply assume "that government is founded on fear—that the dread of each other is the one motive by which human beings were originally brought into a state of society, and are still held in it" (*Logic,* p. 580). Even though there is a sense in which fear is "the passion to be reckoned on" (see p. 95, this vol.), it is to be reckoned on in the context of an understanding of its place in relation to other passions in Hobbes' deduction. But when Mill assimilates the assumption that he attributes to Hobbes—"that government is founded on fear"—to the Benthamite procedure of founding "their general theory of government on one comprehensive premise, namely, that men's actions are always determined by their interests" (*Logic,* p. 580), Mill is overlooking the very great differences between Hobbes' psychology and the utilitarian psychology. He overlooks these differences because he envisages method as a "logical process" abstractable from the psychological subject-matter of any theory of human nature (see pp. 278–80, this vol.).

93. *Autobiography,* pp. 111–12; see vol. 1, pp. 14–16.

94. *Autobiography,* pp. 112–13.

95. *Ibid.*, p. 113.

96. *Logic*, p. 579.

97. See vol. 1, pp. 13, 15.

98. *Autobiography*, p. 177. See chap. 18, n. 76.

99. *On Liberty*, p. 77.

100. *Autobiography*, p. 101.

101. In "The Two Kinds of Poetry" Mill also raises the question, "When will education consist, not in repressing any mental faculty or power, from the uncontrolled action of which danger is apprehended, but in training up to its proper strength the *corrective* and *antagonist* power" (p. 126; italics added). Mill again generalizes from his own experience in "Professor Sedgwick's Discourse on the Studies of the University of Cambridge," where he explains "how . . . the *corrective* and *antagonist* principle to the pursuits which deal with objects only in the abstract, is to be sought in those which deal with them altogether in the concrete, clothed in properties and circumstances: real life in its most *varied* forms, poetry and art in all their branches" (*Dissertations and Discussions*, 1: 104–105; italics added).

102. "M. de Tocqueville on Democracy in America," *Mill's Ethical Writings*, ed. J. B. Schneewind (New York: Collier Books, 1965), p. 154. The principle which is applicable to the faculties of the individual's own mind is extended to the relation between his mind and other minds when Mill recommends "the steady habit of *correcting* and *completing* his own opinion by collating it with those of others" (*On Liberty*, p. 25; italics added), and then to democratic society generally: "When the opinions of masses of merely average men are everywhere become or becoming the dominant power, the *counterpoise* and *corrective* to that tendency would be the more and more pronounced individuality of those who stand on the higher eminences of thought" (*ibid.*, p. 81; italics added). Remember that the individual does not stand alone on these higher eminences. Mill needed the "steadying influence" of Mrs. Taylor (see the Conclusion, n. 144) and *On Liberty* itself is the product of "the conjunction of her mind with mine" (*Autobiography*, p. 177).

103. Cf. chap. 3, n. 4, where Comte's criticism of "a society which is animated by 'l'esprit d'individualisme et de spécialité' was shown to be structurally identical with his criticism of the "empirisme dispersif" of Mill's tradition in the theory of knowledge."

104. See p. 114, this vol.

105. I have insisted both on the particular importance to Mill of esthetic experience and on the part played generally by analogies and metaphors in sustaining the structure of a philosophy, so that it may be worth noting that Mill's esthetic experience and poetic metaphors alike illustrate his "concrete" feeling for an "abstract" (see n. 101, above) structure of expanding diversity. When Mill seeks for a more comprehensive political theory, it is because he has become aware of "the many things" which his father and Bentham "ought to have made room for" in their theory "and did not" (*Autobiography*, p. 110). The feeling of having been constricted by the limitations of narrow Benthamism finds analogous expression in Mill's personal brooding over the problem of artistic creativity: "The octave consists only of five tones and two semi-tones, which can be put together in only a limited number of ways, of which but a small proportion are beautiful: most of these, it seemed to me, must have been already discovered, and there could not be room for a long succession of Mozart and Webers, to strike out, . . . entirely new and surpassingly rich veins of musical beauty" (*ibid.*, p. 102). To convey his protest against constriction, and his feeling for expression and expansion, Mill often employs breathing metaphors. He borrows Coleridge's lines describing the "stifled . . . grief" the poet feels when his creativity as an artist fails him (see p. 380, this vol.). The borrowing is justified by the fact that "whosoever writes out truly any one human feeling, writes

poetry"—i.e., anyone whose "capacity of feeling . . . is not stifled" ("Two Kinds of Poetry," pp. 118, 126; cf. p. 297, this vol.). Spontaneous expression of feeling Mill finds in the lyrical poems of Shelley, which "are obviously written to exhale, perhaps to relieve, a state of feeling" ("Two Kinds of Poetry," p. 124). The spontaneous happiness Mill craves in his "stifled . . . grief" would not be a matter of Benthamite calculation: "You will inhale happiness with the air you breathe, without dwelling on it or thinking about it" (*Autobiography*, p. 100).

106. See p. 287, this vol.

107. See p. 287, this vol.

108. See p. 279, this vol.

109. See vol. 1, p. 193.

110. In *Utilitarianism* Mill carries the conflict between the two schools back to Socrates' debate with Protagoras. But however Plato's dialogue is interpreted, it has to be admitted that Socrates and Protagoras shift their positions in relation to each other. Mill's doctrine of two schools attributes to both schools fixed, perennial positions ("the same discussions continue . . . the same contending banners"—see chap. 16, n. 16), and this doctrine is Ciceronian, not Platonic.

111. See p. 306, this vol.

112. See p. 304, this vol. Cf. Mill's comment on Plato's *Gorgias:* "The love of virtue, and every other noble feeling, is not communicated by reasoning, but caught by inspiration or sympathy from those who already have it; and its nurse and foster-mother is Admiration. We acquire it from those we love and reverence, especially from those whom we earliest love and reverence; from our ideal of those, whether in past or in present times, whose lives and characters have been the mirrors of all noble qualities; and lastly, from those who, as poets or artists, can clothe those feelings in the most beautiful forms, and breathe them into us through our imagination and our sensations. It is thus that Plato has deserved the title of a great moral writer (*Mill's Ethical Writings*, pp. 76–77).

113. "The Two Kinds of Poetry," p. 129.

114. *Early Draft*, p. 199; italics added.

115. See vol. 1, p. 14.

116. See vol. 1, p. 191, for example.

117. For other instances of pairing, see nn. 23, 29, 83, 102, above.

18

Mental History

There may be somewhat both of interest and benefit in noting the successive phases of any mind that was always pressing forward.—Mill

The Weather-Cock

Confronted by the common verdict on Mill today, "Rigour in argument is not one of his accomplishments,"[1] we have observed that one of his efforts is to derive "light from other minds," for it is the result of this effort which is often construed as lack of rigor. Indeed the interpretation of Mill frequently follows out the various "strands of thought" in the nineteenth century that "converge on him and contribute to that unstable eclecticism which he fashioned out of 'the fabric of my old and taught opinions.' "[2] His deepest convictions are interpreted as so unfortified, the influences to which he responded as so diverse, his capitulations to them as so abject, that he becomes a weather-cock: "Somewhere or other in his writings you can discern traces of every wind that blew in the early nineteenth century."[3]

This appraisal does finally dismantle Berlin's "fortress," but it also raises a problem of interpretation that must be met: liberalism may be so eclectic a form of political thought as to defy any firm identification. Initially we could have hoped that our attempt to identify liberalism would be eased by picking a philosopher as its representative. But if the philosopher is prone to "unstable eclecticism"—only loosely structured by his pairing procedure—the attempt cannot be very rewarding. Mill as a weather-cock can only provide us with evidence of certain changes in the nineteenth- century climate of opinion.

Mill himself admits the flow of influences to which he succumbed during the period of his crisis:

The influences of . . . Continental thought . . . were now streaming in upon me. They came from various quarters: from the writings of Coleridge . . . from the Coleridgians with whom I was in personal intercourse; . . . from Carlyle's early articles.

But Mill also asserts his own unremitting effort to cope with these influences in a way that would clarify and stabilize his thinking:

I never, in the course of my transition, was content to remain for ever so short a time, confused and unsettled. When I had taken in any new idea, I could not rest till I had adjusted its relation to my old opinions, and ascertained exactly how far its effect ought to extend in modifying or superseding them.[4]

Mill may not be proposing to construct a fortress, yet he is claiming complete control over the process of adjustment.

Before we can continue our examination of the process of adjustment, we have to consider certain new ideas which Mill singles out as involved in this process:

From these sources [e.g., as we have just seen, from Coleridge, Coleridgians, Carlyle], and from the acquaintance I kept up with the French literature of the time, I derived, among other ideas which the general turning upside down of the opinions of European thinkers had brought uppermost, these in particular: that the human mind has a certain order of possible progress, in which some things must precede others . . . that all questions of political institutions are relative, not absolute, and that different stages of human progress not only will have, but ought to have, different institutions; that any general theory or philosophy of politics supposes a previous theory of human progress, and that this is the same thing with a *philosophy of history*.[5]

To this report Mill appends the qualification, "These opinions, true in the main, were held in an exaggerated and violent manner." It is here that we face the more specific problem of interpretation which is posed by Mill's eclecticism. We are prompted to ask: In what more sober, tamer, perhaps less upside-down manner, does Mill himself hold these opinions? Exactly how far does the effect of taking in each of them "extend in modifying and superseding" Mill's old opinions? What precisely is the "order of possible progress" which the human mind must follow for Mill? What are the "different stages" of this progress? What, in short, is Mill's "philosophy of history"? Consistent and final answers to these questions are difficult to find in Mill. Just as his *moralistic* adjustment does not come to fulfillment in a philosophy of human nature of his own comparable to his predecessors', so his *historicist* adjustment does not come to fulfillment in any philosophy of history of his own comparable to that constructed by their continental antagonists. Indeed, in spite of the importance Mill clearly is attaching to the historical approach, this most versatile writer never wrote a single historical work.

Mill does in his *Logic* commit himself to the prospect of a science of history, just as he commits himself to a science of human nature, and he does endorse Comte's contribution to this prospect, just as he endorses his father's *Analysis of the Phenomena of the Human Mind* as a contribution to the science of human nature.[6] It is also true that Mill accepted the Saint-Simonian philosophy of history in his "The Spirit of the Age." But one sense, perhaps, in which Mill "kept history in second place,"[7] was by leaving us less certain as to his final attitude toward the series of articles which he published under the title "The Spirit of the Age," than we can be of his final attitude toward the articles in which we were able to trace in the last chapter implicit modifications in the utilitarian philosophy of human nature. Mill seems to have more or less disavowed "The Spirit of the Age"; he left it unfinished, and he never republished any of its component articles in *Dissertations and Discussions,* as he did his articles on poetry, Bentham, and Coleridge.

The French Mind

What we do find canonized in *Dissertations and Discussions* are reviews which Mill had written of historical works. The fact that so much of his writing took the form of reviews may illustrate the extent to which his thinking involved taking in new ideas put forward by others. The illustration we have found most relevant to Mill's political thought as a liberal was his review of the second volume of *Democracy in America.*[8] So far we have regarded Mill as concerned in this review with "a great existing fact." But we should allow for his qualifications that "America needs very little government, . . . has no wars, no neighbors, no complicated international relations, . . . no half-fed and untaught millions in want of food and guidance," and that she is "intellectually speaking, a province of England."[9] At least as important to Mill, intellectually speaking, as democracy in America is a fact we have previously overlooked—*Democracy in America* was written by a Frenchman.[10]

It may be difficult to pin down the order of possible progress which the human mind must follow for Mill, but it is usually the French mind which is making progress.[11] And usually Mill conceives his own distinctive contribution as helping the English mind catch up. Thus Mill laments, in a footnote to his essay on Coleridge, "the Cimmerian darkness still prevailing in England . . . concerning the very existence of the views of general history which have been received throughout the Continent of Europe for the last twenty or thirty years."[12] Mill's reviews of Tocqueville are only two of a series of articles in which the other minds from which Mill would derive light to enlighten English darkness are French historians.[13]

Some of the enlightenment Mill himself had received can be ascertained from an article in which he traces the recent progress of the French mind:

> The period of six years [1824–30] . . . formed the culminating point of one of the most brilliant developments of the French national mind. . . . The national intellect seemed to make a sudden stride from the stage of adolescence to that of early maturity. It has reached the era corresponding to that in the history of an individual mind, when after having been taught to think (as every one is) by teachers of some particular school, and having for a time exercised the power only in the path shown to it by its first teachers, it begins, without abandoning that, to tread also in other paths; . . . and from being one-sided, becomes many-sided and of no school.[14]

This history of the French national mind has in effect been extended to become a kind of general history, as soon as Mill has interpolated that it is "everyone" who is "taught to think by teachers of some particular school" and must therefore start out his intellectual career one-sided and unsympathetic to other points of view. This generalization correlates the history of a national mind with the history of an individual mind. The correlation is supported by Mill's use of the terms "adolescence" and "maturity" with reference to the national mind, and by his tacit assumption that "the course of history" is "the education of the human race' "—"the progressive unfolding of the capacities of the human mind."[15] Actually the history Mill is presenting of a national mind can be correlated with the actual history of one individual mind. When Mill goes on to explain, "It was above all . . . in history and historical disquisition that the new tendencies of the French national mind made themselves way,"[16] we recall that it was French historical disquisition which emancipated Mill from the one-sided, anti-historical view of his first teachers—his father and Bentham.[17]

This correlation occurs as the result of Mill's resort to the sympathetic procedure of deriving light from other minds. In the previous chapter we examined this procedure for its psychological implications, and we traced its development into the methodological principle of antagonism.[18] Mill is paying his respects to this principle here, when he commends the dexterity of the mind that treads in other paths without abandoning the path shown to it by its first teachers. But the correlation is not merely the result of a procedure with *psychological* implications, and we must go beyond our last chapter's interpretation. The correlation is also *historical* in an obvious chronological sense: "this period of six years" in which the national intellect of France has made "a sudden stride from the stage of adolescence to that of early maturity" coincides with the period of six years in which Mill took his own stride from adolescence to early maturity: 1824 was the year when the *Westminster Review* was founded, when Mill (at the age of seventeen) began his journalistic career as a youthful propagandist, by aiding his father in the attack on "Periodical Literature"; 1830 was the year when Mill overcame his indifference to politics after his crisis, and resumed his journalistic career.

The reader may demur at regarding this chronological correlation as anything but a coincidence, especially if he already feels that I attached unwarranted significance in the last two chapters to the change in Mill's conception of journalism and therefore to these two different periods of his career as a journalist. Fair enough: this chronological correlation may be accidental; but I shall later probe similar chronological correlations which cannot be so easily discounted.

For the present, I am satisfied to work with Mill's correlation of the history of a national mind with the history of another individual mind besides Mill's. In the article we have been considering, Mill is presenting something as comprehensive in its scope as a history of the

French mind from 1824 to 1830 as background for a "memorial" to an individual historian, Armand Carrel, who became a journalist in 1830—the year Mill resumed his journalistic activity. This French historian became in 1830 "the editor of a republican newspaper," and his "glory," Mill announces, "consists precisely in this, that being that, and *by* being that, he was the greatest political leader of his time."[19] Mill's precision can be appreciated if we remember the extent to which he reduces political changes to changes in opinions, and therefore political leadership to the initiation of these changes in opinions. It is perhaps not entirely irrelevant to reflect that when he published this memorial (1837) Mill was himself the editor of the new *Westminster*.[20]

The Exemplary Mind

The history Mill has presented of "the French national mind" is not, however, sufficient in its scope to delineate the greatness of Carrel. His example elicits Mill's proclamation, "the mind needs such examples, to be reminded by . . . them that . . . man is still man" and that "a hero of Plutarch may exist amidst all the pettiness of modern civilization, and with all the analyzing and questioning spirit of the modern European mind."[21] This analyzing and questioning spirit is itself an extension and generalization of the methodological spirit exemplified by utilitarianism.[22] But Mill is proclaiming a performance which is more fundamental than any carried out by the utilitarian or by the French mind or by the modern European mind. He is assigning a role to be played by man as such. It is in the context of the humanistic philosophy of mind that a modern individual can become an ancient hero; it is in the context of the humanistic philosophy of mind that the human mind "needs" memorable "examples" of greatness in order to be "reminded" that the humanistic philosophy of mind is still valid for man in spite of changes in circumstances. Mill does not have to specify these changes historically, insofar as he is relying on the humanistic philosophy of mind. History, in this context (to cite the traditional humanistic definition of history) is merely "philosophy [sc. of mind] instructing by examples,"[23] and the most instructive example is the example of the great mind whose superiority to his circumstances demonstrates the pettiness of circumstances as such.

In "On Genius" Mill himself had taken on the color of an *An-*

tiquus.[24] But since writing "On Genius," Mill has returned to the modern world and become the editor of a journal. Although his procedure in "Armand Carrel" is still the humanistic procedure of writing *Memorabilia*,[25] he is not drawing directly from Antiquity "memorials of past nobleness and greatness," for what is demonstrated by the greatness of Carrel is that "man is still man," even in this petty modern world.[26]

"On Genius" enabled us to trace Mill's reflexive route of withdrawal from the modern world, and arrival at his first formulation of what will become the principle of individuality in *On Liberty*.[27] The "memorial" to Carrel enables us to trace the historical route Mill follows in returning to the modern world where the individual now plays a dual role. In one sense he still remains an *Antiquus*—he can still play an exemplary role as "a hero of Plutarch," demonstrating that man is still the man that he was in the humanistic tradition. But in the modern world the individual acquires another, quite different exemplary role—as a representative man. His individuality is not the sheer particularity which being an individual seemed to entail in the previous chapter, insofar as Mill discounted the legitimacy of an individual taking "his own mind as a representative of universal human nature," as individuals had in the humanistic tradition. The individual's individuality now acquires a certain general relevance insofar as he represents his particular period in history. In the "memorial" the recent history of the French mind has not been presented by Mill just as background for appreciating Carrel; it is also represented in some fashion by the history of Carrel's own mind.

One Stage Onward

We can now drop Mill's example of Carrel in favor of another example. The part played by the history of Carrel's mind in representing the recent progress of the French mind has made us aware of the breadth of typological implication the history of an individual's mind can have for Mill, so that we are prepared to recognize the relevance of the one exception to my initial generalization that Mill never wrote an historical work. Mill's *Autobiography* is the history of his own mind. It is a history which is structured in a particular way around a central episode—"A Crisis in My Mental History—One

Stage Onward." The individual may retain the responsibility of demonstrating that man is still the man he was in the humanistic tradition, and to this extent he may still take himself as "a representative of universal human nature." But he also has the responsibility of representing the forward movement of his particular period in history.

Acceptance of this responsibility is a feature of the justification Mill offers for publishing his *Autobiography:*

> It has . . . seemed to me that in an age of transition in opinions, there may be somewhat both of interest and of benefit in noting the successive phases of any mind which was always pressing forward, equally ready to learn and to unlearn either from its own thoughts or from those of others.[28]

We began interpreting Mill's *Autobiography* in chapter 16 by presuming that it takes some measure of self-consciousness on the part of an individual to write an autobiography,[29] and to this extent we were able to interpret Mill's work as an illustration of his commitment to the principle of individuality. But he warns us, "I do not for a moment imagine that any part of what I have to relate, can be interesting to the public . . . as being connected with myself."[30] Thus the emphasis of his justification shifts to the structure of "mental progress"[31] which his history exemplifies, and in particular to the readiness of his mind "to learn and to unlearn either from its own thoughts or from those of others." His acknowledgments of his debts to others we interpreted in chapter 17 as illustrating his commitment to the principle of antagonism.[32] As a result in part of this readiness, Mill's *Autobiography* takes the form of noting "the successive phases" of a mind that was "always pressing forward. "But this format assumes a further relevance from Mill's characterization of the age as "an age of transition in opinions." The implications of this characterization have to be postponed, for they were worked out by Mill in "The Spirit of the Age" without any explicit reference to himself; and the *Autobiography* belongs to a much later phase in Mill's "mental history"—a phase, indeed, when he decided not to republish "The Spirit of the Age."[33] Not until we have first sorted out Mill's "successive phases" will we be able to gauge the implications that carry over from "The Spirit of the Age" to Mill's *Autobiography*. What is already clear, however, is that some correlation is implied between the transitional character of Mill's age and the history of a mind that presses forward through successive phases. "Something both of interest and benefit" may be vague, but criteria of relevance are obviously entailed.

Historical Periods

Even before we try to distinguish any of these "successive phases" or to discover what is at stake for Mill as a liberal in his "pressing forward" from one to another, we can see that his breaking up his life into phases is itself a procedure which marks his abandonment of utilitarianism. I have already considered and reconsidered Bentham's autobiographical footnote where he recalls the influences which had "lifted his infant thoughts to the side of despotism" until he finally discovered, on reading Hume's *Treatise*, "that the foundation of all virtue is laid in utility."[34] Since the justification which Bentham alleges for this "short sketch" is that "the history of one mind is the history of many," he may seem to be assuming the kind of relevance that Mill assumes for his *Autobiography*. But if (as was indicated earlier) no crisis of self-consciousness had made the history of this one mind distinctively the history of Bentham's one mind, there was also no breaking of this history into "successive phases." Thus Mill can complain, in his "philosophical estimate" of Bentham:

> He knew no dejection, no heaviness of heart. . . . He was *a boy to the last*. . . . Self-consciousness, that daemon of the men of genius of our time, . . . never was awakened in him.[35]

The awakening of Mill's own self-consciousness, we shall see, initiated a period of dejection and melancholy in his life. The self-consciousness that was never awakened in Bentham, we have already seen, is the individual's consciousness of himself as different from other men.[36] But such self-consciousness, we now see, is further identified by Mill as the "daemon of the men of genius of our time." In other words, self-consciousness is not simply what it was in "On Genius"—the reflexive operation whereby the individual thinks for himself. It is also a distinguishing characteristic of men of genius of our time as different from other times. History obtains its significance as a subject-matter, when it acquires a periodic structure. It is broken up by Mill into phases or periods, with self-consciousness as a differentiating characteristic of men of genius in Mill's own period. But even the history of an individual's mind in this period obtains its full significance only insofar as it can in turn be broken up into different phases or periods. The history of Bentham's mind is not a history in this interesting and beneficial sense. It is—somehow regrettably, in Mill's view—not broken up into different periods by the disruption of continuity that ensues with the awakening of self-consciousness.

It was not a philosophical accident that the continuity of Bentham's life was uninterrupted. If Bentham remained "a boy to the last," if he took no "stride" from "adolescence" to "maturity," as Mill's mind did or the French mind did, it was because he adhered to the last to a deductive philosophy of human nature, one in which no relevance could be attached to the differences between "the successive phases" of a human life. In Mill's *Autobiography* his youthful opinions may *lose* their native relevance as deductions from Bentham's utilitarian philosophy of human nature, and his writings from this period can therefore be consigned to "oblivion."[37] Yet at the same time they can be reported in the *Autobiography*, where they *gain* a distinctively historical relevance as illustrating the phase in the history of his mind when he was a strict utilitarian—the period of his "narrower Benthamism." But Bentham's becoming a utilitarian was not a transition which allowed his earlier opinions to retain any relevance: on reading Hume, Bentham dismissed his "infant thoughts" as irrelevant "wanderings" which were over now that "the scales" had "fallen" from his eyes. In the systematic analysis which he then undertook of the process by which any mind's opinions are formed, transitions from one opinion to another are deductions from the principle of utility; they do not compose a sequence of historical phases.

When Mill, in contrast to Bentham, adjusts the relations between his old opinions and the new ideas that he took in during the course of his transition, it is by writing an *Autobiography* in which he distinguishes as historical phases three broad periods. The first of these, the phase when he was a strict utilitarian, is the period of "narrower Benthamism" which is covered by the chapter "Youthful Propagandism." The second phase is the period covered by the next chapter, "A Crisis in My Mental History—One Stage Onward," which reports how he became emancipated from strict utilitarianism and succumbed to the influences of poetry and the continent. The remaining phase Mill refers to as the "third period," and it is covered by the chapter "General View of The Remainder of My Life." It is distinguishable, he explains, as a period when "I have no further mental changes to tell of," except that "I had completely turned back from what there had been of excess in my reactions against Benthamism [sc., during the second period]."[38] Thus Mill's general way of distinguishing all three periods in his *Autobiography* is by reference to changes in his relation to his utilitarian predecessors.

Already in the Introduction we recognized that Mill's continuing preoccupation with his relation to his predecessors is one of the contrasts between Mill's thought and theirs.[39] What we failed to recognize was that this preoccupation is cast in the historical form of distinctions between periods. Thus the contrast between Mill and his predecessors becomes even sharper. When Bentham does make one of his infrequent references to his predecessors (such as the reference in his footnote to Hume), he never conceives the relation between his opinions and theirs as an historically changing relation, which could be sorted out into phases. He often conceives the relation instead as the result of his rational effort to apply the principle of utility without flinching or swerving—and more uniformly and systematically—where they had faltered in its application (as Hume had when he gave way to sentimentalism).[40]

Throughout our study of the development of political thought we have headed in the direction of liberal political thought by allowing ourselves to be guided by the distinctions which Mill draws in making two of his three adjustments—his *scientific* adjustment and his *moralistic* adjustment. We cannot now afford to neglect the distinctions between periods that he draws in making his *historicist* adjustment. It may be that there emerges from Mill's *historicist* adjustment some conception of historical development which is as characteristic of Mill, and perhaps of liberalism, as the *moralistic* adjustment we have dealt with in the last two chapters and which has netted the principles of individuality and of antagonism.

Mill is the first noteworthy political thinker in the British tradition to accord theoretical relevance to history as a progressive development.[41] We would expect him to write some work in political and social history, in view of his endorsement of the historicist convictions "that the human mind has a certain order of possible progress, . . . that all questions of political institutions are relative, . . . and that different stages of human progress . . . ought to have different institutions."[42] But we have had to recognize, in our search for a history to illustrate this order of possible progress for the human mind, that the only historical work we can find (aside from the more or less disavowed "The Spirit of the Age") is Mill's own "mental history." Yet since he does trace here the progressive development of his thought as a process of adjustment in relation to his predecessors, we can hope to get at some conception of history as a progressive development by considering the distinctions he draws between periods in his adjustment of this relationship. To this extent the historical structure of his thought can be illustrated by his *Autobiography.*

We must examine the *Autobiography* as history with the same attention to detail with which we examined Polybius' cyclical history, once we recognized that Polybius was the first political thinker to accord theoretical relevance to history. To examine the *Autobiography* as history is a quite different task from our previous quarrying here and there in the *Autobiography* for evidence of the modifications that the *moralistic* adjustment introduced in the utilitarian theory of human nature. We were then reading the *Autobiography* in the way we did Mill's other writings, which are not historical. In particular we were rather casual about the dates of these writings. But we must now pay close attention to dates; they become the essential facts of history, once history is conceived as a progressive development.

Dates

In examining the organization of Mill's *Autobiography* as history, we can concentrate on the framework of the chapter "A Crisis in My Mental History—One Stage Onward," for it is around this second period that the distinctions are drawn with which Mill's life breaks up into three periods. It is during this second period, moreover, that the psychological point of view of the utilitarians (defined by such psychological distinctions as that between reason and sentiment) and of Mill's first period is displaced by the historical point of view (implicit in his distinguishing this second period from the other two periods).

Furthermore, this second period is a period of considerable historical importance. F. R. Leavis stresses the place of Mill's crisis as a "*locus classicus*" which has "a direct bearing" on "what should be the central theme in any study of the Victorian Age."[43] It has some bearing too on our own age. At the beginning of our own study we saw how Lionel Trilling in his effort to foster *The Liberal Imagination,* seizes on "the classic instance of John Stuart Mill" as illustrating a recurring crisis in liberalism.[44]

Unfortunately, however, when we begin examining the distinctions Mill draws around the period of his crisis, it will turn out that this portion of Mill's history at least is unhistorical—or at any rate inaccurate and distorted history.[45] Begin with the title of the chapter covering this second period—"A Crisis in My Mental History." Ask the historical question, "What actually happened when?" The expression, "A Crisis" only occurs in the title. It is never used in the text. It has usually been taken to refer to the episode which Mill dates as having occurred "in the autumn of 1826," when "the whole foundation on which my life was constructed fell down."[46] Yet the expression "A Crisis" cannot be restricted as easily to a single episode as the singular might lead us to expect. It was only after first reading Wordsworth, "in the autumn of 1828," that Mill, as he recalls, "gradually but completely emerged from my habitual depression and was never again subject to it."[47] Then "Macaulay's famous attack," in the spring of 1829, gave Mill "much to think about"; it would seem also to have been some sort of a crisis in his mental history.[48]

A crisis might be prolonged, but there is a more serious difficulty with Mill's periodization itself. If we accept his dating of the period of crisis as having begun "in the autumn of 1826" and as having continued at least until "the autumn of 1828," the period would overlap the earlier period of Mill's "Youthful Propagandism," and the years belonging to both periods are differently described in the two chapters. Mill's description in the chapter on the crisis of "the dry heavy dejection of the melancholy winter of 1826–7," includes an account of his public activities:

> During this time I was not incapable of my usual occupations. I went on with them mechanically. . . . I even composed and spoke several speeches

at the debating society, how, or with what degree of success, I know not. Of four years continual speaking at that society, this is the only year of which I remember next to nothing.[49]

Mill's memory was better in "Youthful Propagandism." In this chapter he has given a vivid account of his participation in the debating society. He has recalled that the patience of the other founders of the society had become exhausted, but that "in 1826–7 things began to mend," and the society was successfully revived, to a considerable extent as the result of his and Roebuck's having taken the initiative in the debates.[50]

There are other inconsistencies between the descriptions in the two chapters of the years 1826–28. In the chapter on the crisis, Mill describes his "dejection" and "habitual depression" during these years, by borrowing lines from Coleridge's poems "Dejection" and "Work without Hope."[51] But in "Youthful Propagandism" Mill describes as "a labour of love" the months of work he put into preparing the longest article he had yet written.[52] This article was published in April, 1828, and it is obviously propagandistic, since it is "a defense of the early French Revolutionists against the Tory misrepresentations of Sir Walter Scott."[53] In the chapter on the crisis, Mill justifies citing the two poems by explaining that in Coleridge "alone of all writers I have found a true description of what I felt."[54] But since Mill added to the final draft of the chapter the admission that he had not at the time read the poem he is quoting, our misgivings over his periodization seem confirmed.[55]

The fact that the second period in Mill's mental history overlaps the first has perhaps gone unnoticed because it is concealed by Mill's beginning the chapter on "A Crisis" at the chronological point where he has just concluded his account of his "Youthful Propagandism." The chapter on "A Crisis" opens: "For some years after this I wrote very little, and nothing regularly, for publication."[56] The "after this" refers to the article of April, 1828, on the early French Revolutionists, and thus implies that the period about to be described began only in 1828. But if we were to accept this implication, and try to eliminate the overlap by disregarding Mill's references later in this chapter back to 1826 and 1827, we would run into other discrepancies in Mill's chronology. There is no difficulty in determining the *terminus ad quem* of the period when Mill "wrote very little, and nothing regularly, for publication." In 1830 Mill hailed another French Revolution:

> The French Revolution of July . . . aroused my utmost enthusiasm, and gave me, as it were, a new existence. . . . I entered warmly, as a writer, into the political discussion of the time. . . . For the next few years I wrote *copiously* in newspapers.[57]

That Mill regards 1830 as the *terminus ad quem* of his period of crisis is confirmed in the next chapter, "Commencement of the Most Valuable Friendship of My Life." Mill met Mrs. Taylor in 1830. And although he is carried away in this chapter by his fulsome gratitude for her elevating influence on his thought, he pauses long enough to comment "The only actual revolution which has ever taken place in my modes of thinking was *already complete*."[58]

It is precisely because the *terminus ad quem* is fixed with this definiteness that we would have difficulty in accepting as the *terminus a quo* the date 1828 with which the chapter began: the two years between 1828 and 1830 seem too brief to qualify as the "some years after this" which are anticipated at the beginning of the chapter.[59]

Mill's actual description of the years 1829–30 only compounds the difficulties we have already faced with regard to his description of the years 1826–28. At the beginning of the chapter Mill has explained his writing "very little and nothing regularly, for publication" after his "defense of the early French Revolutionists" in 1828. His explanation I have already cited as an explanation for his abandoning journalism:

> It was of no common importance to me, at this period, to be able to digest and mature my thoughts for my own mind only, without any immediate call for giving them out in print. Had I gone on writing, it would have much disturbed the important *transformation* in my opinions and character, which took place during those years.[60]

In the middle of the chapter Mill gives a similar explanation of his withdrawal from public debate:

> After 1829 I withdrew from attendance on the Debating Society. I had had enough of speech-making, and was glad to carry on my private studies and meditations without any immediate call for outward assertion of their results. I found the fabric of my old and taught opinions giving way in

many fresh places, and I never allowed it to fall to pieces, but was incessantly occupied in weaving it anew. I never, in the course of my *transition*, was content to remain, for ever so short a time, confused and unsettled.[61]

This insistence in the middle of the chapter on the continuity of his transition, and the way the explanation of his withdrawal from public debate seems to echo his explanation, at the beginning of the chapter, of his ceasing to publish regularly in order to carry out his self-transformation, leaves the reader with an overall impression of a single continuous period of reflective withdrawal. Yet if we allow Mill to extend this period back before his "defense of the early French Revolutionists" in 1828, so that it begins with the crisis of 1826, we are faced not only with the discrepancies which we have found by comparing his description of the years 1826–28 in this chapter with his description of these same years in the preceding chapter, but also with a further discrepancy between his two descriptions of the years 1826–30 in this chapter itself. What had begun as a "crisis" in 1826, followed by a period of "transformation" beginning in 1828, has by 1829 subsided into a "transition." I say "subsided" because the adjustment is considerably less drastic: in 1826 "the whole foundation" of Mill's life "fell down," but by 1829 he is claiming, "I never allowed" the "fabric of my old and taught opinions . . . to fall to pieces."

I am not examining Mill's mental history in order to demonstrate the obvious—that memory can play tricks, especially when abetted by the reading of poetry. I am not embracing the cliché that life is more complicated than art; I do not believe that it is. I am only concerned here with Mill as an historian and with his "mental history" as an illustration of his conception of historical development. I am therefore concerned less with the actual events than with his interpretation of these events. But to sharpen this contrast is to misread Mill's "mental history." In the first sentence of the *Autobiography*, Mill admits that his life was "uneventful."[62] The major events, in fact, of the years from 1826–30 were largely reinterpretations of his life. These reinterpretations compose portions of the fabric which Mill incessantly wove anew. I shall now unravel this fabric. In this chapter I shall disentangle (1) what happened in 1826 from (2) its reinterpretation in 1828 as a *crisis* which was the beginning of a *transformation*. I shall then in the Conclusion disentangle from this reinterpretation

(3) Mill's later reinterpretation in 1829–30 of his crisis and transformation as a period of *transition*. Disentanglement is feasible, because once the crisis and transformation subsided into a transition, Mill felt no need to cut all the threads of the earlier interpretations. The clues we need to trace these threads are the discrepancies we have observed in Mill's chronology and descriptions. These discrepancies betray discrepant interpretations which are associated with the adjustments that we are already familiar with, but which can also be pinned down historically, since we can date Mill's reading of the books which provided these interpretations. The *first* interpretation (i.e., the interpretation of Mill's life which was established before the process of adjustment began) was founded, of course, on the theory of human nature constructed in his father's *Analysis of the Mind*. The *second* interpretation was a reinterpretation of the breakdown of 1826 as a *crisis* which involved the breakdown of this theory of human nature and hence of the first interpretation. Thus the ensuing *transformation* involved the restructuring of Mill's father's theory of human nature as well as Mill's reinterpretation of his life. When this restructuring became extended to the treatment of political problems, it became what I have identified as the *moralistic* adjustment. The *third* interpretation (i.e., the reinterpretation of the crisis and transformation as belonging to a period of *transition*) is the *historicist* adjustment, and involved replacing the restructured theory of human nature of the second interpretation with a theory of history. The implications of these three interpretations can be followed out by referring to (1) Mill's footnotes to the second edition of the *Analysis of the Mind*, (2) his essay on poetry, which was largely inspired by his reading Wordsworth and Coleridge, and (3) his articles on "The Spirit of the Age," which were largely inspired by the Saint-Simonians.

The Crisis

With a view to extracting Mill's interpretation, consider once again his description of the crisis:

> It was in the autumn of 1826. I was in a dull state of nerves, such as everybody is occasionally liable to. . . . In this frame of mind it occurred to me to put the question directly to myself: "Suppose that all your objects in life were realized; that all changes in institutions and opinions which

you are looking forward to, could be completely effected at this very instant: would this be a great joy and happiness to you?" And an irrepressible self-consciousness distinctly answered, "No!" . . . The whole foundation on which my life was constructed fell down.[63]

This foundation, we have already recognized, was the utilitarian theory of the human mind which had become the foundation of Mill's life as a result of the education which he had received from his father. The final phase of this education had been "the higher branches of analytic psychology."[64] During this phase, Mill's father had "commenced writing his *Analysis of the Mind*, working on it "during several vacations, up to the year 1829, when it was published." His father had Mill "read the manuscript, portion by portion, as it advanced."[65] Thus Mill's father had been completing Mill's education and the *Analysis of the Mind* at the same time; Mill had been reading the *Analysis of the Mind* to complete his education, and it was itself a theory of education in that its "fundamental doctrine," as Mill points out, was "the formation of all human character by circumstances, through the universal Principle of Association, and the consequent unlimited possibility of improving the moral and intellectual conditions of mankind."[66] The crisis that Mill is recalling is the moment when he recognized that his indifference to this possibility was the enigmatical result of his education.

This indifference was the collapse of his father's theory of mind, as the theory which had been behind his education, which had been included in his education, and which should have helped him interpret its result. But his father, Mill recalls complaining, "had no knowledge of any such mental state as I was suffering from."[67] In fact, so long as Mill relied on his father's theory of mind, his mental state would have remained what it was initially, simply "a dull state of nerves, such as everybody is occasionally liable to," and to which no special significance could be attached.[68] For there was no place for an irrepressibly self-conscious state of mind in the *Analysis of the Mind*, where "being conscious of a feeling" was not distinguished from "merely having the feeling."[69]

I am now citing one of the critical notes that Mill appended to the second edition of the *Analysis of the Mind*, which he himself edited. In this note Mill proposes "a slight correction." He identifies "a mental process over and above the mere having of a feeling to which the word Consciousness . . . can hardly be said improperly applied, viz. the reference of the feeling to our self."[70] In detaching this critical note from Mill's edition of the *Analysis of the Mind,* and utilizing it to interpret Mill's *Autobiography,* as an expression of Mill's own self-consciousness, I am not assuming that psychological theories are only of autobiographical significance, disclosing the state of mind of the theorist. I am recognizing that Mill himself left such criticisms dangling in footnotes because he was reluctant to follow out their theoretical implications. His edition of the *Analysis of the Mind,* like the *Autobiography* itself, belongs to his "third period" when he had "completely turned back from what there had been of excess" in his "reaction against Benthamism."[71] He had again come to accept his father's analysis of mind into "a series of feelings," which are to be explained as the effects of "outward circumstances." The explanation precluded Mill's attaching any *theoretical* significance to the reference of feelings to a self. Mill is then faced with such mental phenomena as memory, which suggest "that something which *ex hypothesi* is but a series of feelings, can be aware of itself as a series."[72] However, he backs away from this "paradox" by locating "the real stumbling block" as "perhaps not in any theory of the fact, but in the fact itself." We are up against the "true incomprehensibility . . . that something which has ceased . . . can still be, in a manner present; that a series of feelings, the infinitely greater part of which is past, can be gathered up, as it were, into a single present conception. . . ."[73]

Autobiography itself may then seem an incomprehensible undertaking.[74] Nevertheless, Mill could undertake his *Autobiography,* because at this juncture he recommends that the theorist abdicate: "By far the wisest thing we can do is to accept the inexplicable fact, without any theory as to how it takes place; and when we are obliged to speak of it in terms which assume a theory, to use them with a reservation as to their meaning."[75] Mill did in a sense abdicate: his editing and republication of his father's psychological theory can be regarded as his final abandonment of his project of a psychological theory of his own—his long-cherished "Ethology." But Mill did not simply abdicate. If Mill's sexual frustration can be supposed to have found an outlet in a sexual relation as devious as his relationship with Mrs. Taylor, then it might be supposed that a theorist who accepts an inexplicable fact without any theory as to how it takes place was frustrated as a theorist, and became devious. How could Mill, once he accepted the momentous distinction between "merely having a feeling" and "being conscious of the feeling" as referable to a "self," remain satisfied with "a slight correction" in a footnote? Self-consciousness remained for him no less "irrepressible" a fact because it was theoretically inexplicable. Mill never carried through his *scientific* adjustment in relation to his father; he never reconstructed the foundation on which his life had been constructed in the way it had been constructed; he never found a place in a psychological theory for the state of mind his father had no knowledge of. Instead, he satisfied the claims of his self-consciousness by gathering up, in his memory and in his *Autobiography*, the series of feelings he had experienced when this foundation had fallen down.[76]

Dejection

The collapse became self-conscious as "the dry heavy dejection of the melancholy winter of 1826–7,"[77] which Mill describes by borrowing from "Dejection" and from "Work Without Hope." Mill's feelings, when gathered up in memory and in the *Autobiography*, are no longer merely a series. A change in orientation or in level has intervened, with the distinction between "merely having a feeling" and "being conscious of the feeling" as referable to a "self." The *moral* crisis of the autumn of 1826 Mill recalls as primarily a psychological change in his feelings about *political* changes. His dejection during the winter of 1826–27 he recalls as a self-conscious feeling about this *psychological* change: what he no longer hoped for in the autumn were the political changes for which he had been working as a youthful propagandist, but what became the more "hopeless" the more he thought about it during the winter was his own state of mind. Interpreting the crisis as the result of his education, he concluded, on the one hand, that the application of his father's *Analysis of the Mind* to the formation of his own mind had tended to "wear away" his feelings, and, on the other hand, that the "doctrine of circumstances," on which the *Analysis of the Mind* and his education were based, left him without any hope that he could "begin the formation of my character anew, and create in a mind now irretrievably analytic, fresh associations of pleasure with any of the objects of human desire."[78] He was a "mere reasoning machine," a "dry, hard logical machine," a "made or manufactured man, having had a certain impress of opinion stamped on me which I could only reproduce."[79] After the crisis, "the cloud seemed to grow thicker and thicker"; finally it solidified: "During the later returns of my dejection the doctrine of what is called Philosophical Necessity weighed on my existence like an incubus. I felt as if I was scientifically proved to be the helpless slave of antecedent circumstances."[80]

Since Mill is still struggling here with his father's psychological theory "as a scientific theory,"[81] we can suspect that the theory has not yet entirely collapsed. We know as a matter of historical fact (at least as the facts are presented in the chapter on his "Youthful Propagandism") that this theory has not entirely collapsed; up until the 1828 article defending the early French revolutionists, Mill continued to work hopefully as a propagandist for the political changes that were deducible from his father's psychological theory. It could be, of course, that this fact was obscured from him by his memory of a thickening cloud of poetic gloom. But since he did not read Coleridge's or Wordsworth's poetry before 1828, it seems historically more probable that his poetic description of his state of mind during the years 1826–28 is largely anachronistic.

At any rate, this poetic description is based on the distinction between "merely having a feeling" and "being conscious of the feeling." And this distinction is not found in the *Analysis of the Mind* but could have been derived from reading Wordsworth and Coleridge. When Mill first read Wordsworth "in the autumn of 1828," he discovered that Wordsworth "had had *similar* experience to mine, that he also had felt that the first freshness of youthful enjoyment of life was not lasting; but that he had sought for compensation, and found it, in the way in which he was now teaching me to find it."[82] The similarity between the first freshness of Wordsworth's youthful enjoyment and Mill's "Youthful Propagandism" may seem far-fetched to us, but it could hold for Mill as soon as he derived from Wordsworth the distinction between "merely having feeling" (a state of mind which could be referred for explanation to outward circumstances) and the reflexive phenomena of "being conscious of the feeling." The enjoyment which had not lasted in Mill's case was happiness as conceived in his father's utilitarian psychology, and it was similar to youthful enjoyment as conceived by Wordsworth in that it was "immersed in outward things."[83] The compensation which Wordsworth had found, and which, Mill explains, "made Wordsworth's poems a medicine for my state of mind, was that they expressed, not mere *outward* beauty, but states of feeling. . . . In them I seemed to draw from a source of *inward* joy."[84] What Mill read in Wordsworth's poems he read back into his own experience, perhaps all the more readily, inasmuch as it was only when gathered up in the retrospect of memory —"recollected in tranquillity"—that Wordsworth's own feelings had become these poems.

Coleridge had imposed a similar psychological sequence on the series of his feelings. We may suppose that the series of Mill's feelings became more clearly identified when located within this sequence, on his later reading in "Dejection" the lines which "exactly" described his own state of mind before he had read them. Perhaps Mill's "dull state of nerves" (the first interpretation of what happened in 1826) then became reinterpreted as "the dull pain" expressed in the lines which Mill quotes:

> A grief without a pang, void, dark and drear,
> A drowsy, stifled, unimpassioned grief,
> Which finds no natural outlet or relief
> In word, or sigh, or tear.[85]

Coleridge's "grief" was "stifled"; it had found no natural outlet or relief, but it did at last find poetic outlet and relief at the higher level of this poem, which is the renewed flow of "passion and of the life, whose fountains are within." Mill must in turn have obtained some measure of relief from an exact description of the state of mind which he could not find described in his father's psychological theory, where there was a place for the pain that is the effect of outward or physical circumstances, but no place for the self-conscious, poetic feeling of dejection.

The Transformation

I have already anticipated that by the time Mill writes the *Autobiography* he has arrived in his third period when he reacts against his earlier reaction against Benthamism. He has restored his allegiance to his father's psychology theory, so that self-consciousness has lost the *theoretical* implications it was accorded by Coleridge, retaining only poetic and autobiographical significance. Thus Mill in his *Autobiography* refers only to Coleridge's and Wordsworth's poetry. He does not refer to their psychological theories of poetry. But these references too have to be supplied, if we would understand Mill's transformation. Mill not only had been educated in the fashion required by the *Analysis of the Mind*, but he also had read this psychological theory, as the final phase of his education. To cope then with the state of mind that was the result of this education, Mill in fact read not only Coleridge's "Dejection" (and Wordsworth's "Intimations of Immortality"—the poem to which Coleridge himself was responding), but also their theories of poetry. Their two poems are descriptions of successive states of mind; their theories of poetry are theories of the psychological sequence involved. Mill's familiarity with their theories is demonstrated by his own essay on poetry.[86] Mill's commitment to theorizing was such that his father's psychological theory could only have finally collapsed before the challenge of an alternative psychological theory. Empiricism never tempted Mill. (Nor did any of the rawer forms of experience which some theorists may suppose are untainted by any theory.) If Coleridge's and Wordsworth's poems provided "medicine" for Mill's state of mind, it was because they provided a diagnosis.

It is possible to hazard a guess as to what Mill owed to Coleridge and Wordsworth respectively. Coleridge's version of the distinction between "merely having a feeling" and "being conscious of the feeling" enabled Mill to combine an interpretation of his mental *crisis*, as the result of the analytic formation of his mind, with an interpretation of his mind's *transformation* as the result of reading poetry. For Coleridge accepted analytic psychology as an account of the impressions which are the passive results of the mechanical process of association, but he also found room for the poetic imagination as a creative power that performs a reflexive operation transforming these impressions.[87] "Dejection" exhibits this distinction of level: on the one hand, it describes Coleridge's dejection over a crisis—the failure of his poetic imagination, which left him uncreative, at the mercy of his impressions;[88] on the other hand, it expresses the "self-activity," the creative "joy" of the renewed flow of his imagination.[89] It is the imagination conceived as a "transforming power" which had come to Coleridge's rescue with his writing of the poem "Dejection," and which came to Mill's rescue when his reading romantic poetry transformed the passive impressions stamped on his mind by his education. Thus Mill's dejected explanation, that his crisis was the result of the analytic formation of his mind, was (at the higher level which Coleridge helped Mill reach) a denial that this explanation was final. Or to use Mill's own phraseology: the Mill to whom it seemed (reportedly in 1826–27) that there was "no power in nature sufficient to begin the formation of my character anew, and create in a mind now irretrievably analytic, fresh associations of pleasure" is no longer a dispassionate adherent of "the doctrine of circumstances"; he is the Mill who in 1828 has become aware of the transforming power ascribed by Coleridge to the imagination (and to nature itself by Wordsworth), for the hopelessness of what is irretrievable and the joy of creation, of novelty, of freshness, are features, not of the *Analysis of the Mind*, but of Coleridge's theory of the poet's mind.[90]

While quoting Coleridge, Mill gives most of the credit for his transformation to Wordsworth. This is not a matter merely of differences between their poetry. A difference between their theories of poetry is also at stake. Mill might in fact have been discouraged from employing Coleridge's poetry to describe his own state of mind, inasmuch as the transforming power of the imagination is, in Coleridge's theory, peculiarly the endowment of the poet's mind. Coleridge's poetry, when read in the light of Coleridge's theory of poetry, might therefore only have added to Mill's hopelessness over his state of mind, had he not been aided by Wordsworth's *theory* as well as by Wordsworth's poetry. The feelings which Mill found in Wordsworth's poetry "could be shared by all human beings."[91] That Mill's feeling about his lack of feeling could be "similar" to the feelings of a poet, is of course implicit in Mill's quoting Coleridge to describe his own feelings. But the implication becomes explicit in Mill's theory of poetry, where he, in effect, sides with Wordsworth against Coleridge, by claiming "Whosoever writes out truly any one human feeling writes poetry."[92] In this Wordsworthian sense, Mill's writing out truly his own feelings in the chapter on the crisis is poetic.

Poetic Truth

The application of a reflexive criterion of poetic truth is illustrated not only by the sometimes poetic prose of this chapter but also by its framework. We remember that Mill argues that a man can be a poet—i.e., can express his own feelings "exactly as he felt them"—only to the extent of his "utter unconsciousness of a listener," so that even when a poem is written for publication, "no trace of consciousness that any eyes are upon us must be visible in the work itself." As "feeling confessing itself to itself in moments of solitude," poetry is to be distinguished from "eloquence," which is "feeling pouring itself out to other minds . . . endeavouring to influence their beliefs."[93] An inward psychological orientation must be enforced, if we are to become distinctly "conscious of a feeling," instead of merely "having" it. This inward orientation, which is eventually implemented by Mill's withdrawal from the Debating Society, is identical with the orientation which was initially embodied in his recognition that writing for publication would have much disturbed his transformation.[94] The impression left by this identity of orientation (we have noted) is that the chapter as a whole covers a continuous period of reflective withdrawal.

At the same time, this psychological orientation is a reorientation —a reorientation which serves to mark the discontinuity that distinguishes this period from the period of "Youthful Propagandism" covered in the previous chapter. If, in order to distinguish the period of crisis, Mill takes as its *terminus a quo* his recognition that continued writing for publication would have much disturbed his transformation, if he also gives this recognition pride of place at the beginning of the chapter on the crisis, it must be because he has become committed (as a matter of psychological theory—i.e., of the psychological theory he adopted to explain the operations of the poet's mind) to so sharp a psychological distinction between an inward and an outward orientation that this *psychological* distinction could become, though historically (sc., chronologically) unwarranted, an *historical* distinction between two periods in his mental history—between the period when he was endeavoring as a youthful propagandist to influence the beliefs of others and the period of self-transformation when he was poetically preoccupied with his own feelings. Although the psychological distinction is pivotal in his report of the crisis of 1826, it does not belong to the period that only ends in 1828, as this period is described in "Youthful Propagandism." In this previous chapter, Mill's psychological theory is still utilitarian, and an entirely different, more humdrum reason is given why his "defense of the early French Revolutionists" was "the last article" he wrote for the old *Westminster.* Mill was merely seconding his father's refusal to continue contributing when Bowring took over as editor. In the "Crisis" chapter, the fact that his father distrusted Bowring is not mentioned as an explanation for Mill's writing "very little, and nothing regularly, for publication." His father's attitude was a relevant psychological fact in the previous chapter, but it is no longer psychologically relevant in the poetic retrospect now provided for the years 1826–28, even though these years were already covered in "Youthful Propagandism." Conversely, since Mill's psychological theory for the period of his "Youthful Propagandism" was still his father's utilitarian theory, the report of the crisis, even though the crisis itself is dated as occurring in 1826, has to be deferred until the next chapter, where it becomes the explanation for Mill's writing "very little, and nothing regularly, for publication" after the article of April, 1828. Only when Mill had read Wordsworth "in the autumn of 1828" could a poetic distinction between the two periods be drawn at the expense of chronological accuracy.

Mill, I admit, was a theorist with scruples as well as frustrations. But the scruples, I shall argue, came later. If I seem too ready to assume that a feature of his transformation was his poetic stretching of the fabric of his history, permit me to cite a review he wrote that is closer in time to the period of his transformation than his *Autobiography.* This review has a further pertinence. Let me explain. We have been consulting Mill's *Autobiography* for his view of history since it is the only historical work which he ever wrote. But there was another historical work which Mill *almost* wrote. In the last sentence of the chapter on his "Youthful Propagandism," Mill offers an explanation of his readiness to put so much labor into his article of April, 1828, defending the early French Revolutionists: "I had at that time a half-formed intention of writing a History of the French Revolution; and though I never executed it, my collections afterwards were very useful to Carlyle for a similar purpose."[95] The next sentence

("For some years after this I wrote very little . . .") became the first sentence of "A Crisis in My Mental History," when Mill broke his narrative up into separate chapters. But in the *Autobiography* as first written,[96] this sentence might explain, not only in general why he discontinued writing for publication, but also in particular why he did not write an historical work on the French Revolution. Since the period "after this" was a period when he became indifferent to political changes and preoccupied instead with changes in himself, it would not be surprising if a long-range result of this reorientation was Mill's writing, in lieu of a *History of the French Revolution*, a history of these changes in himself. That this result was not a complete departure from the historical format of his original project is suggested by the fact that he can describe the period of crisis and transformation as a "revolution . . . in my modes of thinking."[97] I shall deal with Mill's affinity for French revolutions, when I return in the Conclusion to the question of the correlation between his mental history and the history of the French mind.

Poetry and History

For the present, I would only observe that some of the poetic criteria that we have watched Mill apply to his history of the revolution in his modes of thinking do emerge in the review he wrote of Carlyle's *History of the French Revolution*. Mill hails this history as "the truest of histories" because "it is the history of the French Revolution, and the poetry of it, both in one."[98] Mill is applying poetic criteria of historical truth when, in the course of the review, he discounts "the dry, mechanical facts which compose the story," in favor of the "feelings" aroused by the story. He concludes that the facts "must be presented" as they "can exist only in the mind of a great poet—of one gifted with creative imagination, which, from a chaos of scattered hints and confused testimonies, can summon up . . . a completed whole."[99]

When Mill writes his own mental history and recalls that before his feelings were aroused he could be regarded as "a mere reasoning-machine," a "dry, hard logical machine," that during the "dry heavy dejection of the melancholy winter of 1826–7" he went on "mechanically" with his "usual occupations" as a youthful propagandist, he is offering a description which we have seen is at variance with his earlier description of the same year in "Youthful Propagandism." The facts of that year were not described as "dry" and "mechanical," for Mill's psychological theory during that year was still utilitarian. The facts of that year acquire the attributes "dry" and "mechanical" when redescribed in the chapter on the crisis: his occupations in the previous chapter then become mechanical undertakings; what had been "a labor of love" becomes "Work Without Hope." Mill is now furnishing us in the chapter on the crisis with the truest of histories —the history and the poetry both in one. The dry, mechanical facts are not, strictly speaking, historical facts.[100] Rather, they are features of an organic theory of the poetic imagination; they are the "scattered hints and confused testimonies" which undergo reflexive transformation into the "completed whole" that a history should be. They undergo this transformation in the same psychological way in which scattered and confused impressions, which have been produced by the mechanism of association, undergo a reflexive transformation into the "completed whole" that a poem should be. Historically speaking the "completed whole" in Mill's case is the continuous period of reflection and transformation that he distinguishes from the period of his "Youthful Propagandism." To create this period of reflection, the overlap between it and the preceding period has to be eliminated; the snake must grasp its tail in its mouth.[101] However, the "completed whole" which was originally at stake for Mill in this reflexive movement was not an historical period; it was a psychological whole. In other words, the poetic transformation Mill was originally seeking during this period was not the poetic transformation of the impressions he was receiving so that they composed a completed period in his "mental history"; it was rather their poetic transformation so that the half-man he was coming to realize he had been[102] (during the period he will come to identify in retrospect as the period of his "Youthful Propagandism") would become a "completed whole"—a fully developed self.[103]

I am not claiming that Mill in carrying through his poetic transformation of himself was in fact "gifted" with the "creative imagination" which he regarded as requisite for completing a whole self or for composing a history as well as a poem. I am not quite claiming that his autobiographical report of his crisis is an *Anima Poetae* or even a

Biographia Literaria. I have already cited his disclaimer to Carlyle, "I am not in the least a poet," but he also pleaded, "I have not got quite into the heart of that mystery, and I want you to show me how."[104] In other words, I am only claiming that Mill had derived considerable light during the period of his transformation from the mind of Coleridge as well as from Carlyle's. In their theories of the mind's operations, the creative imagination plays the transformatory role which Mill credits to Carlyle's imagination in his appraisal of Carlyle's *History.* But our application to Mill of this theory, should be guided by Carlyle's appraisal of Mill's history. "It is wholly the life of a logic-chopping machine," Carlyle protested. It is "the *Autobiography* of a steam-engine.[105] The evidence of "logic-chopping" in the *Autobiography* should not be mistaken for the evidence of "scattered hints" and "confused testimonies." These had been poetically transformed. When this process of transformation was going on in Mill's life, he was not a logic-chopper but "a new Mystic."[106] For our purposes here, the logic-chopping that Carlyle detected can be taken as referring to Mill's procedure of scrupulously adjusting the relations between his old opinions and his new ideas. Strictly speaking, his procedure during his second period was not the process of *adjustment* that it became later in retrospect, but something more strenuous —a process of *transformation* in conformity with the theory of the creative imagination that Mill had borrowed at a time he was entertaining serious misgivings regarding his father's psychological theory. But this process of transformation is not fully reported as such in the *Autobiography,* where it has weakened into a process of adjustment. The weakening and the piecemeal report are not due to the defectiveness of Mill's memory so much as to his no longer accepting the psychological theory in which so creative a process as self-transformation was theoretically explicable. During his "third period" when he wrote the *Autobiography,* Mill became again committed instead to his father's psychological theory, in which the operations of the mind were analyzed as a mechanical and serial process of association. Even though the process of transformation is not fully reported in the *Autobiography,* the discrepancies both in Mill's periodization and in his historical descriptions can only be accounted for by taking into consideration the theory with which he was sympathizing at the time of his transformation, and this theory is fully illustrated by his own essay on poetry and by his review of Carlyle's *History of the French Revolution.*

These discrepancies cannot be accounted for by assuming that Mill's memory of the *history* of what had happened to him later became distorted by his reading of *poetry*. Matters are more complicated. We already have recognized a certain sense in which "the poetry of it" came before the "history": Mill started interpreting his life in terms of a theory of poetry before he adopted a theory of history. The fabric which he had woven around a poetic sequence, he later wove anew, so that this poetic sequence became an historical sequence. This historical reweaving is the reinterpretation of Mill's life we have still to examine before we can consider historically what our relation is to Mill, if we are still liberals.

Notes

1. See p. 281, this vol.

2. J. C. Rees, "A Phase in the Development of Mill's Ideas on Liberty," *Political Studies* 5 (Feb., 1957): 33.

3. R. P. Anschutz, *The Philosophy of J. S. Mill* (Oxford: Clarendon Press, 1953), p. 5.

4. *Autobiography* (New York: Columbia University Press, 1924), pp. 113, 110. See vol. 1, pp. 8, 16, for my initial argument (which will be assumed in the present chapter) that liberalism—at any rate, Mill's liberalism—is to be identified with the way this process of adjustment is carried through rather than simply with any set of specific doctrines associated with its outcome.

5. *Ibid.*, pp. 113–14; italics added. See vol. 1, pp. 26, 32, for the "turning upside down." The continental influences which streamed in on Mill directly were usually French. He was exposed to German influences largely through the interpretations of Coleridge, Coleridgians, Carlyle, and French writers. Mill accordingly contrasts the German influences on these writers with the French influences to which he was exposed: "Les anglais cherchent plus volontiers des idées nouvelles chez les allemands que chez les francais et bien du monde a lu non seulment Kant, mais encore, Schelling et Hegel sans même avoir lu Cousin, qui présente les mêmes idées ténébreuses avec une lucidité et un esprit de systématisation tout francais" (letter of March 22, 1842, to Auguste Comte, *Collected Works of John Stuart Mill* [Toronto: Toronto University Press, 1963], 13:509). "Je suis bien sensible à l'honneur que vous me faites en demandant mon avis sur votre project [*sic*] de prendre une connaissance spéciale de la philosophie allemande. Je ne suis pas peutêtre [*sic*] en droit de donner là-dessus une opinion très décidée, n'ayant moi-même lu ni Kant ni Hegel ni aucun autre des chefs de cette école, que je n'ai d'abord connue que par ses interprètes anglais et français. . . . Plus tard lorsque j'ai essayé de lire quelques ouvrages philosophiques allemands, il s'est trouvé que je possédais déjà tout ce qu'ils avaient d'utile pour moi, et le reste m'a été fastidieux au point de ne pouvoir pas en continuer la lecture" (letter of March 13, 1843, to Comte, *Collected Works,* 13: 576).

6. See vol. 1, p. 59. Henceforth I shall abbreviate this title to *Analysis of the Mind,* as J. S. Mill usually does.

7. See vol. 1, p. 60.

8. Recall that Mill will rely on Tocqueville's *Democracy in America* in initiating the *historicist* as well as the *moralistic* adjustment that he carries through in *On Liberty*, which was published nineteen years later than his review of the second volume (see vol. 1, pp. 31, 36, and vol. 2, pp. 286–87).

9. "M. de Tocqueville on Democracy in America," (*Mill's Ethical Writings*, ed. J. B. Schneewind [New York: Collier Books, 1965], pp. 129, 134).

10. So far I have tried to interpret (1) the place Mill assigns democracy in America as "a great existing fact" in social history that the political theorist must take into account and (2) the place Mill assigns *Democracy in America* as an illustration of the socio-historical approach that is needed in political theory if such facts are to be taken into account. In this chapter my topological interpretation of Mill is reoriented toward the facts of Mill's own "mental history." Here the crucial fact would be (3) the place Mill assigns his own review of *Democracy in America*. In his letter of Sept. 5, 1840, to Macvey Napier (the editor of the *Edinburgh*, which published this review), Mill anticipates reprinting "a collection of the few things I have written which either I or any one else thinks worth preserving," and explains that "I should like to include this [review] in it, as forming a sort of *completion & winding up* of the view which the publication will exhibit of my present opinions & modes of thinking" (*Collected Works*, 13: 433; italics added). Compare the general "conclusion" reached by Iris Mueller: "With the exception of the influence Mill felt under the tutelage of his father and Jeremy Bentham, Mill's study of French political movements and French thought had most to do with determining the nature of his final attitude toward government and individual liberty expressed in such culminating works as *On Liberty, Considerations on Representative Government* (*John Stuart Mill and French Thought* [Urbana: University of Illinois Press, 1956], p. vi).

11. At the beginning of his review of the second volume of *Democracy in America*, Mill complains: "The general movement of the European mind sweeps past us, without our being drawn into it, or even looking sufficiently at it to discover in what direction it is tending. . . . The revolution which has taken place in the tendencies of French thought, which has changed the character of the higher literature of France, and almost that of the French language, seems hitherto, as far as the English public are concerned, to have taken place in vain" ("M. de Tocqueville on Democracy in America," pp. 105–6). See p. 411, this vol., for another illustration of Mill's conception of his contribution as helping the English mind catch up.

12. *Mill's Essays on Literature and Society*, ed. J. B. Schneewind (New York: Collier Books, 1965, p. 316). The sentence to which this footnote is appended recalls "that series of great writers and thinkers, from Herder to Michelet, by whom history, which was till then 'a tale told by an idiot, full of sound and fury, signifying nothing,' has been made a science of causes and effects; who, by making the facts and events of the past have a meaning and an intelligible place in the gradual evolution of humanity, have at once given history, even to the imagination, an interest like romance, and afforded the only means of predicting and guiding the future, by unfolding the agencies which have produced, and still maintain, the present."

13. Mill's review of the first volume of *Democracy in America* appeared in 1835; his memorial to Armand Carrel (see n. 14, below), in 1837; his review of the second volume of *Democracy in America*, in 1840 (i.e., in the same year as "Coleridge"). Mill's main literary preoccupation then became the completion of his *Logic* (1843). His next article on French historians is a review of "Michelet's History of France" (1844), in which Mill continues his lament: "It has of late been a frequent remark among Continental thinkers,

that the tendencies of the age are set strongly in the direction of historical inquiry, and that history is destined to assume a new aspect from the genius and labours of the minds now devoted to its improvement. The anticipation must appear at least premature to an observer in England, confining his observation to his own country. . . . France has done more for even English history than England has" (*Dissertations and Discussions*, 3 vols. [London: Longmans, Green, Reader, and Dyer, 1867], 2:120, 122). The fourth article is a review of "Guizot's Essays and Lectures on History" (1845) (*ibid.*, pp. 218–82). For Mill's other articles on French subjects, see Iris Mueller's bibliography to *John Stuart Mill and French Thought.*

14. "Armand Carrel," *Dissertations and Discussions*, 3 vols. (London: Longmans, Green, Reader, and Dyer, 1867), 1:231, 232–33. I am beginning with this article as the earliest of Mill's articles on French historians which he felt worthy of republishing in *Dissertations and Discussions.* Mill's review of the first volume of *Democracy in America* was published before his father's death "exempted" him from "restraints and reticences" (see n. 20, below).

15. *Dissertations and Discussions*, 2: 221. Mill is citing Lessing. It should be kept in mind that I am making no attempt to interpret in this study the continental use of an analogy between the history of the individual's mind and the history of humanity; I am only concerned with Mill's own use of the analogy.

16. "Armand Carrel," p. 235. Mill finds "the whole spirit of the new historical school" (i.e., of the approach identified as "socio-historical" in vol. 1—see pp. 2, 23, 59) exhibited by two sentences from Carrel's *Histoire de la contre-revolution:* "Everywhere and at all times . . . it is the wants of the times which have created the conventions called political principles and those principles have always been pushed aside by those wants. '. . .' All questions as to forms of government . . . have their data in the conditions of society" ("Armand Carrel," pp. 237, 238–39).

17. When Mill identifies as "eclecticism" the "most decided bent" he took in this "direction" of deriving light from other minds (see chap. 17, n. 38), he considers the label primarily French. In "Armand Carrel" he traces the formation in France of "an eclectic philosophy," and he clearly has in mind a general tendency, not just the philosophy of Victor Cousin. Mill refers specifically to "the new political philosophy of the present generation in France" as "a philosophy rather scattered among many minds than concentrated in one" ("Armand Carrel," p. 234). In other words, Mill is an eclectic not only in that he derives light from other minds, but also in that he pulls together (in his series of articles on French historians) a new political philosophy which was itself scattered among many French minds, though he singles out *Democracy in America* as the most remarkable specimen.

18. The psychological analysis of the previous chapter has to be presupposed, for the procedure of the historian himself is an instance of the sympathetic procedure, inasmuch as Mill assimilates differences between historical periods to differences between minds. The "faculty" of imaginative sympathy "by which one understands a mind different from itself, and throws itself into the feelings of that other mind, . . . constitutes the dramatist entirely," as we saw (p. 332, this vol.). But this faculty is also "one of the constituents of the historian: by it we understand other times; by it Guizot interprets to us the Middle Ages; Nisard . . . places us in the Rome of the Caesars: Michelet disengages the distinctive characters of the different races and generations of mankind" ("Bentham," p. 259). Conversely, Hume's *History of England* can be discounted as unhistorical, because it fails to meet the challenge: "Does Hume throw his own mind into the mind of an Anglo-Saxon or an Anglo-Norman?" ("Carlyle's *French Revolution,*" *Mill's Essays on Literature and Society*, p. 187).

19. "Armand Carrel," p. 212.

20. Mill himself compares Carrel's "political position" in France with that in England of Fonblanque (letter of Nov. 25, 1833, to Thomas Carlyle, *Collected Works,* 12: 195), who was the editor of the *Monthly Repository* in which Mill's article "On Genius" (1832) and his two articles on poetry (1833) had been published. By 1837, however, Mill has become most conscious of his own role as an editor. In 1834 he had made arrangements for the new radical review which was "to take the place the *Westminster Review* had been intended to fill" (see p. 291, this vol.). He had agreed "to be the real, if not the nominal editor" (*The Early Draft of John Stuart Mill's Autobiography*, ed. Jack Stillinger [Urbana: University of Illinois Press, 1961], p. 157). But this new review was "established to be the representative of the 'philosophical radicals,' with most of whom," Mill admits, "I was now at issue on many essential points, and among whom I could not even claim to be the most important individual," inasmuch as "my father's co-operation as a writer we all deemed indispensable" (*Autobiography*, p. 140). Mill was only "exempted" from "restraints and reticences" (see p. 333, this vol.) by his father's death in 1836. He then "resolved henceforth to give full scope to my own opinions and modes of thought" (*Autobiography*, p. 144). The results of this resolution are manifest in three articles which he wrote after his father's death. The first was "Aphorisms: A Fragment" (January 1837). The title and subtitle are alike significant. Mill is drawing a distinction between "two kinds of wisdom." The first is "properly philosophy," and "depends on long chains of reasoning, a comprehensive survey of the whole of a great subject at once [a description which coincides with Mill's appraisal of Bentham's philosophy—see "Bentham," *Mill's Essays on Literature and Society*, pp. 254–55], or complicated and subtle processes of metaphysical speculation [a description which coincides with Mill's appraisal of his father's *Analysis of the Mind*]." The other kind is the "unsystematic wisdom" which "has oftenest assumed" the form of aphorisms and which Mill takes to be "at once the materials and the tests of philosophy itself" (*Dissertations and Discussions*, 1: 206–7). According aphorisms this place subverts the opposition, fundamental for Bentham and James Mill, between their systematic and precise analysis, on the one hand, and traditional prejudices, on the other (see pp. 232–34, this vol., with accompanying n. 6). Mill is accepting the traditionalist protest against Bentham's dismissing as " 'vague generalities, . . . the whole unanalyzed experience of the human race" ("Bentham," p. 256). The other two unrestrained and unreticent articles rehabilitate this experience in historical form. "Carlyle's *French Revolution*" (July 1837) I am postponing, since Mill did not see fit to republish it in *Dissertations and Discussions,* any more than "The Spirit of the Age." Thus I have begun with the third article, "Armand Carrel" (October, 1837).

21. "Armand Carrel," p. 283.

22. In presenting his discussion of Bentham's method of analysis, Mill endorses the suggestion of a contemporary "that to Bentham more than any other source might be traced the *questioning spirit* which was producing such important consequences in these times" ("Bentham," p. 243). Mill learned from the Saint-Simonians and Carlyle to regard utilitarian analysis as a manifestation of the spirit of the age (see p. 429, this vol.).

23. See vol. 1, p. 239, and accompanying n. 9.

24. See p. 301, this vol. We began this volume with Mill's finding his principle of individuality illustrated by "the whole stream of Greek history" as a "series of examples of how often events on which the whole destiny of subsequent civilization turned were dependent on the personal character for good or evil of some one individual" (see p. 3, this vol.). In modern times there are fewer examples: "He [Carrel] lived long enough to show that he was one of the few, never so few as in these later times, who seem raised up to turn the balance of events at some trying moment in the history of nations, and to have or to want whom, at critical periods, is the salvation or the destruction of an era" ("Armand Carrel," p. 211). Eleven years later Mill will reflect on the Revolution of 1848: "In my meditations and feelings on the whole matter, every second thought has

been of Carrel—he who perhaps alone in Europe was qualified to direct such a movement. . . . Without Carrel, or, I fear, any one comparable to him, the futurity of France and of Europe is most doubtful" (letter of February 29, 1848, to Henry S. Chapman, *Collected Works,* 13:731–32).

25. See pp. 13–15, this vol. Mill asserts in effect the continuity of his procedure with the humanistic procedure by concluding his memorial with the passage from Tacitus' memorial to a great mind: " 'Si quis piorum manibus locus; si, ut sapientibus placet, non cum corpore extinguuntur magnae animae; placide quiescas, nosque ab infirmo desiderio et muliebribus lamentis ad contemplationem virtutum tuarum voces, quae neque lugeri, neque plangi fas est: admiratione te potius, et immortalibus laudibus, et si natura suppeditet, similitudine decorabimus' " ("Armand Carrel," p. 283; *Agricola* 46.1–2). The appeal of these last two words is the leitmotiv of the humanistic tradition as a tradition of moral imitation (see vol. 1, p. 190), which Mill transforms into a tradition of Romantic admiration (see p. 304, this vol., and chap. 17, n. 112). It is the procedure itself, not the example of Agricola, which is relevant. Agricola was a quietist whose *sapientia* was *inertia* (*Agr.* 6. 3); confronted by tyranny, he did not indulge in a provocative exhibition of liberty (*Agr.* 42. 4), in contrast with Thrasea (see chap. 11, nn. 36, 42, 47).

26. Mill had probably picked up Carlyle's refrain from *Sartor Resartus:* "When the Saint-Simonian Society transmitted its Propositions hither, and the whole *Gans* was one vast cackle of laughter, lamentation, and astonishment, our Sage sat mute; and at the end of the third evening said merely: 'Here also are men who have discovered, not without amazement, that Man is still Man" (*Sartor Resartus* [New York: Doubleday, Doran, 1837], p. 296). Mill considered *Sartor Resartus* Carlyle's "best and greatest work"; he "read it with enthusiastic admiration and the keenest delight" (*Autobiography*, p. 123) when it was published in *Frazer's Magazine* (1833–34). Conversely it had been Mill's Saint-Simonian "The Spirit of the Age" which had induced Carlyle to seek the acquaintance of Mill, whom he hailed as "a new Mystic" (*Autobiography*, p. 122).

27. See pp. 302–3, this vol.

28. *Autobiography*, p. 1.

29. See p. 293, this vol.

30. *Autobiography*, p. 1.

31. See pp. 341–42, this vol.

32. See p. 327, this vol.

33. Mill revised the early draft of the *Autobiography* in 1861 and completed the *Autobiography* in 1869–71. The first edition of *Dissertations and Discussions* was published in 1859, and the second edition in 1867. For other writings of the third period, see n. 76, below.

34. See pp. 154, 203, 241, this vol.

35. "Bentham," p. 259; italics added. The four "men of genius" that Mill lists are Wordsworth, Byron, Goethe, Chateaubriand—all of whom were autobiographical writers.

36. See p. 329, this vol.

37. See p. 252, this vol.

38. *Autobiography*, pp. 155, 161.

39. See vol. 1, p. 6.

40. See pp. 197, 241, this vol.

41. See pp. 287–88, this vol. For Mill's conception of history as a progressive development, see vol. 1, p. 99, and accompanying n. 27.

42. See p. 360, this vol.

43. *Mill on Bentham and Coleridge* (London: Chatto & Windus, 1959), p. 12. See p. 403, this vol.

44. See vol. 1. p. 1, and p. 45 with accompanying n. 22.

45. Historians have failed to interpret the inaccuracies. They have challenged Mill's *Autobiography* mainly where he is reporting on Mrs. Taylor. The challenge has come here, not because the historical facts to discredit this report are more easily ascertainable, but because there have been more decisive changes in our criteria of sexual relevance since Mill wrote than in our criteria of historical relevance. The latter, we shall see in the Conclusion, have hardly changed in certain important respects. When criteria of historical relevance do change, it becomes obvious that an historian is unhistorical. Thus it was altogether obvious to us that Polybius was not simply writing a history of Rome and that Machiavelli was not simply commenting on the history of Rome. Their cyclical theory became obviously a distortion of history, once history came to be conceived as a progressive development. The historian is then no longer disposed to interpret their histories in terms of their own cyclical theory of history. He is tempted instead to find distortions and to explain these by resorting to his own progressive conception of history, as I showed in the case of Walbank's "second draft" interpretation of the development of Polybius' theory of history (see vol. 1, pp. 166–67).

46. *Autobiography*, p. 94.

47. *Ibid.*, p. 105

48. *Ibid.*, p. 110; see vol. 1, pp. 11, 21, 24.

49. *Autobiography*, p. 98.

50. *Ibid.*, p. 89

51. *Ibid.*, pp. 94, 98. For the lines borrowed from "Dejection," see p. 380, this vol.

52. *Autobiography*, p. 92.

53. *Ibid.* Scott's *Life of Napoleon*, which Mill was reviewing in this article, was published in 1827.

54. *Ibid.*, p. 98.

55. The admission, "I was not then acquainted with them," is added with respect to the lines borrowed from "Dejection" (*Autobiography*, p. 94; compare *Early Draft*, p. 118). With respect to the lines from "Work without Hope," Mill explains both in the early draft and in the final version that he read these lines "in a later period of the same mental malady" (*Autobiography*, p. 98).

56. *Autobiography*, p. 93.

57. *Ibid.*, p. 121; italics added.

58. *Ibid.*, p. 133; italics added.

59. That Mill found his own chronology embarrassing is suggested by the *Early Draft* (p. 122). He scratched the phrase "during the next few years [sc. after 1827] I had several relapses," and wrote instead "before the gloom entirely passed away I had several relapses."

60. *Autobiography*, p. 93; italics added.

61. *Autobiography*, p. 110; italics added.

62. *Ibid.*, p. 1. See n. 100, below.

63. *Ibid.*, p. 94.

64. *Ibid.*, pp. 48, 49.

65. *Ibid.*, p. 49; cf. p. 86.

66. *Ibid.*, p. 75.

67. *Ibid.*, p. 95.

68. This initial interpretation remained the orthodox associationist interpretation of Mill's crisis. Alexander Bain, whom Mill accepted as his father's successor in analytic psychology, retrieves Mill's merely passing reference to his "dull state of nerves." Mill's dejection, according to Bain, was "due to physical causes." It was the result of "overworking the brain" (*John Stuart Mill* [London: Longmans, 1882], p. 38). In other words, it was not a question of Mill's working without hope. Coleridge's poem was irrelevant.

69. *Analysis of the Phenomena of the Human Mind*, 2 vols. (London: Longmans, Green, Reader and Dyer, 1869), 1: 229.

70. *Ibid.*, p. 230.

71. During the period of excessive reaction, Mill's appraisal of the *Analysis* had not been restricted to slight corrections. He wrote John Sterling, "I am very far from agreeing, in all things with the "Analysis," even on its own ground" (letter of September 28, 1839, *Collected Works*, 13: 406).

72. *An Examination of Sir William Hamilton's Philosophy*, 2 vols. (Boston: W. V. Spencer, 1865), 1: 261–62. Mill is equally perplexed by the phenomenon of expectation (see p. 431, this vol.)

73. *Ibid.*, p. 262. I have omitted from Mill's sentence the final clause ("accompanied by a belief of reality"), since we are not concerned here with the strictly epistemological issue (see chap. 12, n. 22). This examination of Hamilton Mill links with "my father's Analysis of the Mind" and "my own Logic" as attempts to "re-introduce a better mode of philosophizing" than that of their intuitionist and traditionalist opponents (*Autobiography*, pp. 192–93; see chap. 16, n. 22).

74. My extrapolation from Mill's psychological theory to his *Autobiography* will have to be qualified later (p. 406, this vol.); we shall have to recognize that Mill does not in fact present in his *Autobiography* "a single present conception" of himself but a "mental history"—i.e., a conception of himself as "pressing forward" through "successive phases." Other qualifications hedge my present interpretation. I am not coping with the problem which Mill is raising as a matter of psychological (and epistemological) theory, or even with the further problem raised by my interpretation of the relation between a literary product and the psychological operations that have gone into its production. (I have tried to formulate this further problem elsewhere, but in an entirely different setting—see my "The Literature of Extreme Situations," in *Aesthetics Today*, ed. Morris Philipson [New York: Meridian Books, 1961]. pp. 377–412.) Here I am only making the general assumption that an autobiography is the product of memory and the specific assumption that the way Mill remembered in his particular *Autobiography* was entangled with theoretical issues. The evidence the *Autobiography* and Mill's other writings provide for this specific assumption is evidence for more detailed conclusions: (1) that he adopted a Romantic version of the humanistic conception of what is memorable about an individual (whether Armand Carrel or Mill himself); (2) that he also adopted a Romantic theory of self-consciousness in the light of which the "series of feelings" he is now remembering in the *Autobiography* had become interpretable as episodes in a poetic crisis and transformation; (3) that he has repudiated this Romantic theory as a theory by the time he wrote the *Autobiography*.

75. My interpretation of Mill's report in the *Autobiography* of his crisis and transformation can be phrased as an adaptation of the final sentence: Mill is obliged to speak

of himself (as he was at the time when his "series of feelings" became episodes in a poetic crisis and transformation) in terms which assume the Romantic theory he then adopted, but he now uses the term self-consciousness with a reservation as to its meaning for a scientific psychological theory.

76. I am revising here R. P. Anschutz' interpretation of Mill in his relation to his predecessors: "He was an *inveterate systematizer* and, search as he might, he never succeeded in finding a system which had anything like the appeal of the one he had been brought up in. Thus . . . it is of the first importance in trying to understand him that we should understand Bentham and James Mill, since it was *within the framework* provided by them that he tried to organize the new truths that he discovered for himself" (*The Philosophy of J. S. Mill* Oxford: Clarendon Press, 1953, pp. 5–6; italics added). In my interpretation there remains, outside the framework of Mill's systematic theories, a series of feelings which he considered ethological in their implications and which he planned to treat systematically but had eventually to gather up in other ways. I have already interpreted as ethological Mill's preoccupation with the formation of character and with individuality and diversity of character (as illustrated by his treatment of poetic feelings—see p. 330, this vol., and accompanying n. 55). Although Mill relinquished the attempt, proposed in his *Logic*, to construct a systematic political ethology in favor of the *Political Economy* (see vol. 1, p. 60), he continued to cherish the project of an ethology, at least in a less systematic form. In a letter of January 29, 1854, to Harriet, Mill recalls his systematic theories—the *System of Logic* and the *Political Economy*—and considers what still has to be written: "I see one large or two small posthumous volumes of Essays, with the Life at their head" (I am citing from F. A. Hayek, *John Stuart Mill and Harriet Taylor* [Chicago: University of Chicago Press, 1951], p. 191). In his next letter (February 7, 1854), Mill lists eleven possible subjects for these essays. The first on the list, and the subject which Mill suggests he may do first since it is "the one I could do most to by myself," is "Differences of character (nation, race, age, sex, temperament)" (Hayek, p. 192). In his letter to Harriet on February 20, 1854, Mill reports that he has "been revising & correcting" the "Life" (Hayek, p. 197). Stillinger considers that the early draft was probably completed in 1854 (*Early Draft*, pp. 7–10). In his letter to Harriet of December 31, 1854, Mill confesses, "I cannot make up my mind what to write" (Hayek, p. 214), but in his letter of January 15, 1855, he reports that while sight-seeing in Rome (see p. 60, this vol.) his mind became made up "that the best thing to write & publish at present would be a volume on Liberty" (Hayek, p. 216). After Harriet's death in 1858, Mill completed *On Liberty*, which we have seen is ethological in its theoretical implications, insofar as it is "a kind of philosophic text-book of a single truth . . . : the importance, to man and society, of a large variety in types of character, and of giving fully freedom to human nature to expand itself in innumerable and conflicting directions" (see p. 341, this vol.). After the publication of *On Liberty* in 1859, Mill wrote Alexander Bain: "I may hereafter write on Ethology—a subject I have long wished to take up, at least in the form of Essays, but have never yet felt myself sufficiently prepared" (letter of Nov. 14, 1859, cited from *Letters of John Stuart Mill*, ed. Hugh Elliot, 2 vols. [London: Longmans, Green, 1910], 1: 226). I am not aware of any later reference to the project of an ethology. Mill revised the early draft of the *Autobiography* in 1861. He next reentered the systematic framework provided by his father: from 1863 to 1865 he worked on the *Examination of Sir William Hamilton's Philosophy;* from 1867–69, on his edition of his father's *Analysis of the Mind*. But then "in the winter of 1869–70" (*Early Draft*, p. 11) Mill finally revised and completed the *Autobiography*, which I have been arguing cannot be placed "within the framework" provided by his predecessors and yet yields implications for the structure of his thought. See Conclusion, n. 141.

77. See p. 371, this vol.

78. *Autobiography*, p. 98.

79. *Ibid.*, p. 76; *Early Draft*, p. 101.

80. *Autobiography,* pp. 94, 118.

81. This is one of the criteria which Mill applied to his father's political theory (*Autobiography,* p. 120; see vol. 1, p. 9), but it is clearly also applicable to the psychological theory from which the political theory was deduced.

82. *Autobiography,* p. 105; italics added.

83. See n. 100, below.

84. *Autobiography,* p. 104; italics added.

85. *Ibid.,* p. 94.

86. See also Mill's letter of October 20, 1831, to John Sterling: "When you get Wordsworth on the subjects which are peculiarly his, such as the theory of his own art . . . , no one can converse with him without feeling that he has advanced that great subject beyond any other man, being probably the first person who ever combined, with such eminent success in the practice of the art, such high power of generalization & habits of meditation on its principles" (*Collected Works,* 12: 81–82). Mill had had breakfast with Wordsworth on February 27, and he may have met Wordsworth even earlier.

87. See M. H. Abrams, *The Mirror and the Lamp* (New York: W. W. Norton, 1958), pp. 168–69. See p. 181, for Coleridge's criticism of Wordsworth for failing to distinguish the two levels. See also René Wellek's generalization, "The break with the Lockean tradition is precisely a crucial test of romantic aesthetics" (*Concepts of Criticism* [New Haven: Yale University Press, 1963], p. 201).

88. See Abrams' appraisal, "Two of the greatest and most representative poems of the early nineteenth century, Wordsworth's 'Intimations of Immortality' and Coleridge's 'Dejection,' turn on the distinction between data and addenda in sense experience" (p. 66). The failure of the poetic imagination in Coleridge's "Dejection" not only left Coleridge at the mercy of that faculty whose operation could be explained by the associationist theory of analytic psychology but was also due to the tendency of "abstruse research to steal / From my own nature all the natural man." In Mill's case, unlike Coleridge's, the "abstruse research" could be equated directly with his education in analytic psychology, so that the experience of dejection is much tighter in its theoretical implications for Mill than for Coleridge.

89. The Coleridgian criterion of "joy," as well as the utilitarian criterion of "happiness," was reportedly applied in Mill's 1826 experiment: "Would this be a great joy and happiness to you?" (See p. 290, this vol.)

90. Thus the intrusions in Mill's *Autobiography* from Coleridge's poetry are not restricted to the actual lines Mill cites. When Mill identifies "the dry heavy dejection of the melancholy winter of 1826–7," the metaphors of dryness and of the heaviness, as well as the theme of dejection are taken from a poet he had not read in 1826–27. Compare Coleridge's account of his dejection in his letter to William Godwin of March 25, 1801: "I have been undergoing a process of intellectual *exsiccation.* . . . "The Poet is dead in me. . . . I have beaten myself back into weight and density" (*Collected Letters of Samuel Taylor Coleridge,* ed. E. L. Griggs, 4 vols. [Oxford: Clarendon Press: 1965–59], 2: 713–14). Needless to say, Mill's "cloud" is standard Coleridgian and Romantic equipment.

91. *Autobiography,* p. 104.

92. See p. 297, this vol. Mill's claim disposes of that "wretched mockery of a definition" of poetry—"the vulgarist" definition of all—"the one with which no person possessed of the faculties to which Poetry addresses itself can ever have been satisfied— . . . that which confounds poetry with metrical composition" ("What is Poetry?" *Mill's Essays on Literature and Society,* p. 102; see chap. 17, n. 28). Coleridge assumed meter to be essential to poetry, whereas Wordsworth assumed it to be "but adventitious." For the arguments, see M. H. Abrams, pp. 116–17.

93. See pp. 297–98, this vol.

94. The literary character of this orientation is suggested by a passage Mill eliminated from *The Early Draft* (p. 116), where Mill refers to "a passage of Herder on this subject quoted in Coleridge's *Biographia Literaria,* though Mill presumably had not read the *Biographia Literaria* at the time he arrived at this recognition. The passage concludes Coleridge's "An affectionate exhortation to those who in early life feel themselves disposed to become authors" and itself begins, "Am sorgfältigsten meiden sie die Autorschaft" (*Biographia Literaria,* 2 vols. [London: Pickering, 1847], 1: 240).

95. *Autobiography,* p. 92.

96. The early draft was a continuous manuscript.

97. See p. 373, this vol.

98. "Carlyle's *French Revolution,*" *Mill's Essays on Literature and Society,* p. 184. This review is crucial for tracing Mill's development, since it was Mill's first ambitious effort after his father's death had "exempted" him from "restraints and reticences" (see n. 20, above). At the same time Mill enlisted Carlyle himself as "a frequent writer in the Review" (see p. 333, this vol.).

99. "Carlyle's *French Revolution,*" p. 190. Repudiation of the "mechanical" was, of course, as characteristic of Carlyle as it was of Coleridge.

100. Remember that Mill's life was "uneventful," so that he has to admit at the beginning of the *Autobiography,* "I do not for a moment imagine that any part of what I have to relate can be interesting to the public as narrative" (p. 1; cf. p. 374, this vol.). Mill's employment of poetic citations and metaphors to describe his crisis and transformation suggest that the description cannot be construed merely "as narrative," for Mill draws a firm distinction in his theory of poetry between poetry and narrative: in the one the interest "is derived from incident;" in "the other from the representation of feeling." Furthermore, poems which are "essentially stories" are of "the lowest and most elementary kind" of poetry: "The feelings depicted, or rather indicated, are . . . such joys and griefs as the immediate pressure of some outward event excites in rude minds, which live wholly immersed in outward things, and have never . . . turned themselves to the contemplation of the world within" ("What is Poetry?" pp. 104–5).

101. "The common end of all *narrative*, nay, of *all*, Poems is to convert a *series* into a *Whole*: to make those events, which in real or imagined History move on in a *strait* line, assume to our Understandings a circular motion—the snake with it's Tail in it's mouth" (*Collected Letters of Samuel Taylor Coleridge*, 4: 545). I feel free to cite for purposes of illustration statements of Coleridge which were not published in Mill's time, especially since Mill's Coleridgian friends (and Mill himself on at least one occasion) sat at the master's feet.

102. For the notion of the "half-man," see p. 402, this vol.

103. The relevance of this autobiographical rendering of the structure of a self to the structure of Mill's political thought should not be lost sight of. Just as the threat of tyranny which Mill felt in the conformist pressures of public opinion could only be understood fully by taking into account (1) the function of public opinion in his predecessors' utilitarian political theory, (2) the uniformitarian theory of human nature from which they deduced this political theory, and (3) the weight of an "incubus" which Mill felt in "the doctrine of circumstances," from which they deduced their theory of human nature itself, so the individuality which Mill upholds against conformity (see p. 287, this vol.) can only be understood fully, if we take into account (1) the sense in which "individuality is the same thing with development" (see p. 341, this vol.), (2) the sense in which the requisite development involves self-transformation, and (3) Mill's relinquishment of his predecessors' deductive procedure in favor of poetry in order to credit creativity to the process of self-transformation.

104. See p. 328, this vol.

105. J. A. Froude, *Thomas Carlyle. A History of his Life in London,* 2 vols. (New York: Scribner's, 1898), 2: 359. Sterling offered a kindlier application of this metaphor when he described Mill as "uniting a warm, upright and really lofty soul with a still and even cold appearance, and with a head that reasons as a great Steam Engine works" (I am citing from Michael St. John Packe, *The Life of John Stuart mill* [London: Secker and Warburg, 1954], p. 86. During the period of his transformation from a reasoning-machine, Mill himself adopted Carlyle's practice of using the terms "mechanical" and "logical" interchangeably.

106. See n. 26, above.

Conclusion

Tradition and Transition

Whatever we may think or affect to think of the present age, we cannot get out of it.—Mill

The Necessity of a Philosophy

For the purpose of tracing the development of liberal political thought, Mill has been selected as the representative of traditional liberalism. This selection was not dictated merely by the continued influence today of *On Liberty* as the classic of liberalism. Circumstances have changed since the time Mill wrote, and other influences have intervened, modifying the character of liberalism. But we have not been pursuing influences in the manner of the historian of ideas. In Part I we became concerned less with Mill's specific ideas or doctrines and their specific influences than with the criteria of relevance determining the structure of his thought.[1]

These criteria determine the influences Mill himself finds relevant, and his conception of the way an influence is exerted:

There are two men, recently deceased, to whom their country is indebted not only for the greater part of the important ideas which have been thrown into circulation among its thinking men in their time, but for a revolution in its general modes of thought and investigation. These men, dissimilar in almost all else, agreed in being closet-students—secluded . . . from the business and intercourse of the world. . . . But they were destined to renew a lesson given to mankind by every age, and always disregarded—to show that speculative philosophy, which to the superficial appears a thing so remote from the business of life and the outward interests of men, is in reality the thing on earth which most influences them.

The name of Coleridge is one of the few English names of our time which are likely to be oftener pronounced, and to become symbolical of more important things, in proportion as the inward workings of the age manifest themselves more and more in outward facts. . . . It is hardly possible to speak of Coleridge . . . without reverting to Bentham. . . . It would be difficult to find two persons of philosophic eminence more exactly the contrary of one another.[2]

By analyzing Mill's criteria, we have discovered why "ideas" and their "circulation" are a less relevant form of influence than "modes of thought." The ideas with which any mind is furnished could in principle be explained, in the setting of Mill's father's *Analysis of the Mind,* by the mechanically operating influences of "outward circumstances" upon that mind. "Modes of thought" incorporate differences between individuals which emerge, at a remove from these "outward circumstances," out of their "internal culture" and self-questioning.[3] Although Mill's principle of individuality solicits this "internal culture," and hence the individual's seclusion from "the business and intercourse of the world," Mill yet assumes that the philosophical reflection of a Bentham or a Coleridge exercises a decisive influence on "the business and intercourse of the world." Indeed the fact of its decisiveness is itself a "lesson" which is more relevant for Mill than any specific ideas that may in the process happen to become influential. What Bentham and Coleridge have most significantly in common, permitting their comparison, is their renewal of this lesson: "They agreed in being the men who, in their age and country, did most to enforce, by precept and example, the necessity of a philosophy."[4] This lesson is "always disregarded" because men are "superficial"—immersed in "the business and intercourse of the world." Thus the "lesson" needs to be renewed "in every age." The human "mind needs such examples . . . to be reminded" of its superiority to "outward circumstances."[5]

Mill would seem himself to have renewed this lesson during the course of his own "mental history." Its central period was demarcated at its beginning by his withdrawal from public activity as a journalist, and at its end by his return to public activity as a journalist.[6] During this period he came to view the previous period of his "Youthful Propagandism" with the same disdain with which he came to view his father's psychological theory that had provided his "Youthful Propagandism" with its justification. His father's theory, applied to Mill's own mind, had produced "a dry, hard logical machine;"[7] applied to the way Mill had been oriented as a propagandistic journalist towards "other minds, . . . endeavoring to influence their beliefs," his father's theory had justified "the collision of opinions"—the "knocking" of one "hard body" against another.[8] Mill now preferred the role of an *Antiquus* and to read poetry, and in the process he became distrustful of influences that were mechanically exercised. The relation he sought between minds softened; it did not remain an external relation between hard bodies, but became a matter of sympathetic participation.[9]

The Representative Mind

This transformation in Mill's conception of the relation between minds did not itself yield the impetus for his returning to the modern world and to journalism. Also involved was an enlargement of the area of relevant relations. Mill returns with (1) the conviction that an individual can take "his own mind as a representative of universal human nature," that "man is still man," that "a hero of Plutarch" can still "exist," exemplary in his superiority to "all the pettiness of modern civilization," even when he is a journalist.[10] This *classical* conception of the individual as a representative figure[11] we encountered in chapter 16. But it undergoes two adaptations. In chapter 17 we encountered Mill's *psychological* conception of the individual as one-sided, so that unaided he can see only half a truth.[12] When Mill returns to the modern world and to journalism it is with (2) the conviction that universality can only be sought by combining half-truths. He therefore selects Bentham and Coleridge as two representative figures who are "the contrary of one another." In chapter 18 we discovered that when Mill returns he is able to do so because he has reached (3) the *historical* conviction that the individual can become a figure who represents his period.[13] But the significant influences that the individual then exercises do not stem from what he is as a particular individual with "modes of thought" specific to him as an individual. What is more significantly influential are "the inward workings of the age" insofar as they compose "a revolution in its general modes of thought." The individual's thinking attains a larger relevance, becomes increasingly representative, as these inward workings "manifest themselves more and more in outward facts."[14] Yet since it takes time for the inward to manifest itself outwardly, there is a certain historical justification for Mill's intervening during the "transition" and expounding the thought of philosophers who belong to the immediately preceding generation, so that his own generation may catch up with what has already happened inwardly.[15] This historical justification for Mill's intervention has to be taken into account along with the psychological justification, if we would appreciate the format of his exposition of Bentham and Coleridge. What has to be worked out is some reconciliation which is at once historical and psychological—that is, some reconciliation which will supervene at a *later* period, as well as at a *higher* level than the psychologically one-sided points of view which are still upheld by Mill's contemporaries as antagonistic. Mill's exposition accordingly brings Bentham and Coleridge together with philosophical confidence in their implicit representative relevance to his own age:

> Whosoever could master the premises and combine the methods of both, would possess the *entire* English philosophy of his age. . . . *Every* Englishman of the present day is by implication either a Benthamite or a Coleridgian; holds views of human affairs which can only be proved true on the principles either of Bentham or of Coleridge.[16]

The antagonistic roles Mill is assigning to Bentham and Coleridge in the nineteenth century, he has borrowed from Carlyle's eighteenth-century application of the principle:

> In a world which exists by the balance of Antagonisms, the respective merit of the Conservator and the Innovator must ever remain debatable. . . . In our little British Isle, the two grand Antagonisms of Europe . . . have stood embodied, under their very highest concentration, in two men produced simultaneously among ourselves. Samuel Johnson and David Hume . . . were children nearly of the same year. . . . Greater contrast, in all things, between two great men, could not be. . . . In spiritual stature they were almost equal; both great, among the greatest, but how unlike in likeness! . . . They were the two half-men of their time.[17]

Carlyle may himself have adapted this contrast from Sallust's confrontation of Cato and Caesar as representative types of *greatness of mind*.[18] But now that Mill is no longer posing as an *Antiquus,* we are more interested in his own role as a representative figure who can be assigned to a period which enjoys a certain relevance as immediately preceding our own twentieth century.[19] Mill's qualification for this representative role has been endorsed by many historians of ideas. In his edition of *Mill on Bentham and Coleridge,* F. R. Leavis would make these two "classical" essays available to those "committed to a pretty general study of the Victorian background" and to "some sort of charting of the main currents."[20] Leavis, however, is concerned not only with Bentham and Coleridge as "the key and complementary powers by reference to which we can organize into significance so much of the field to be charted,"[21] but also with "a mind different from either—the mind that appreciates both," who "is a great representative figure in Victorian intellectual history."[22] We should accordingly turn from Mill on Bentham and Coleridge to Mill's *Autobiography* as "an immediately relevant piece of Victorian history" which "lends itself peculiarly to the business of educing significant organization in the whole complex field."[23] We should turn in particular to the account of Mill's education and "the consequent spiritual crisis"—"a *locus classicus* of great significance."[24]

Emory Neff too is concerned "to make clearer and more vivid the relationship of the thought of the twentieth century to that of the nineteenth," but he finds his "clue for guidance through the multitudinous and complex details involved in this undertaking . . . in a consideration of the relations of Thomas Carlyle and John Stuart Mill, whose representative character was abundantly recognized by their contemporaries." Thus Neff (like Carlyle and Mill) presents us with "Two Representative Men" in his *Carlyle and Mill: An Introduction to Victorian Thought.*[25] Leslie Stephen selects Mill and Newman as antagonistic figures;[26] Edward Alexander selects Arnold and Mill as "Representative Men."[27] The grounds of qualification for a representative role doubtless vary when different figures are selected.[28] I am only drawing attention to two considerations: Mill is almost invariably selected for this role, and assigning such a role is a standard typological procedure (in Leavis' phrase) for "charting" the "main currents" or (in Neff's phrase) for making "clearer and more vivid the relationship of the thought of the twentieth century to that of the nineteenth."

What historians of ideas have failed to examine is Mill's own conception of the representative role, even though they have been enticed (I suspect) into selecting Mill for this role by his own sense of qualification, as well as by his contribution to the development of this typological conception itself, not only in his essays on Bentham and Coleridge, but also in his *Autobiography*. Indeed if the *Autobiography* "lends itself peculiarly to the business of educing significant organization in the whole complex field," it is because it presents Mill as a significantly representative figure, both in the *psychological* sense that he attempted during his period of transition to transcend the one-sidedness of his thinking during his first period, and in the *historical* sense that his "pressing forward" in this way from one period in his thinking to another satisfies the requirements of "an age of transition in opinions."[29]

The Gap

The problem of the relation between Mill's *psychological* adaptation and his *historical* adaptation of the *classical* role of the representative figure, is a final version of the problem that has dogged our interpretation of liberalism from the beginning of *Human Nature and History*. In this final version the problem has become the problem of the role which Mill assigned himself in the development of liberal political thought and which later liberals have often accorded him. But it is still our initial problem in that it cannot be settled by reference to Mill's theory of human nature or to his theory of history, since he has no theory of human nature of his own and no theory of history of his own.

Mill's "Logic of the Moral Sciences" is a scientific program for adjusting and reconciling the differences of method and subject-matter that separate the psychological approach of his predecessors from the historical approach of their antagonists. But there is a discrepancy between this program as proposed in the *Logic* and as reported in the *Autobiography*. In the *Logic* the gap is to be bridged by an ethology and its generalization by a political ethology.[30] Mill never built this bridge, and in our study of the development of liberal political thought, we have been guided by the presence of this gap in his thinking. By the time Mill came to write the *Autobiography,* he must have realized that he was unable to build this bridge in the fashion proposed in the *Logic;* in the report of the *Logic* he gives in the *Autobiography,* there is no mention of ethology or political ethology. Mill can no longer envisage this scientific adjustment as a solution to the problem of reconciling his father's *Analysis of the Mind* with continental theories of social history.

I would now suggest in conclusion that there are certain respects in which Mill's *Autobiography* is the alternative solution to this problem that Mill came eventually to accept. We are already aware of the fact that the *Autobiography* is not merely a report of Mill's actual "mental history." At any rate, we are already aware that the chapter "A Crisis in My Mental History—One Stage Onward" is not an accurate report of Mill's second period. During this period the "foundation" may have been "laid," as Mill claims, for the scientific adjustment he later proposed in the *Logic*.[31] But the *Autobiography* itself represents a later stage in the process of adjustment than the *Logic*. If it is inaccurate as a report of the adjustments of the second period, it is partly because the problem of adjusting the relation between his predecessors' theory of human nature and an antagonistic theory of history was not finally resolved by Mill during his second period or even in his *Logic*, but remained a methodological problem for him during his third period. In other words, some of the inaccuracies and distortions in the *Autobiography* can be accounted for by recognizing that Mill was still attempting to resolve his methodological problem during his third period by imposing in retrospect on his thinking a format which differed from that which he had started to work out in the second period and continued to work on in his *Logic*. What we must try to fathom is the intellectual satisfaction this format could have afforded Mill as a theorist who was frustrated because he could not carry his unremitting process of adjustment through in the scientific form of the "true system" proposed in the *Logic*.

Earlier I suggested that when Mill finally resigns himself to reaccepting his father's psychological theory, there still remains a place in his thinking for the psychology implicit in his *Autobiography*—that is, for "the inexplicable fact, without any theory as to how it takes place, that a series of feelings . . . can be gathered up, as it were, into a single present conception."[32] This gathering up is an operation of self-conscious recollection with which Mill became familiar from reading Romantic poetry and Romantic theories of the way the poet's mind operates. We have seen that these theories have left their mark on Mill's organization of the chapter, "A Crisis in My Mental History." But if the psychology implicit in the *Autobiography* is not

Mill's father's *Analysis of the Mind,* it is also not the Romantic organic theory of the poet's mind. The series of feelings Mill recollects in his *Autobiography* are not gathered up into "a single present conception." The *Autobiography* may wax poetic in its description of his crisis, but it is not poetry as Mill defines poetry. It is not "a completed whole" comparable to "Dejection" or to "Intimations of Immortality" or perhaps even to Carlyle's *History of the French Revolution.*[33] The structure is looser. It is a "mental history"; the series of Mill's feelings are sorted out and assigned to successive periods in this history.

We have already watched Mill arrive at a distinction between the period of his "Youthful Propagandism" and the period of his crisis, transformation, and transition. To distinguish this second period itself, Mill would also have had to become somehow convinced of the continuity of his thinking during this period. It is this conviction which is the particular distortion that should now puzzle us, for this period obviously lacks continuity. "After 1829" Mill withdrew from the Debating Society on the grounds, "I was glad to carry on my private studies and meditations without any immediate call for the outward assertion of their results."[34] This explanation of his withdrawal is consonant with his preceding account of the theory of poetry and inward transformation with which (before finally withdrawing) he defended Wordsworth against Roebuck, who was entirely committed to the outward assertion of results.[35] But it then turns out (in the next paragraph) that what Mill had been meditating (before finally withdrawing) was not poetry but political philosophy. He had found "much to think about" in "the famous attack" which Macaulay had launched in March, 1829, on James Mill's *Essay on Government.*[36] Macaulay had attacked this political philosophy as unhistorical, and Mill recalls (later in the *Autobiography*) the "change" that took place "in 1829 and 1830" in "the premises of my political philosophy" (i.e., the change from psychological to historical premises), but he recalls it as a change which "did not alter my practical political creed." He asserts, "I was *as much as ever* a radical and a democrat."[37] Thus we are given the impression that he is responding to practical political changes which he had always supported, when he responds to the Revolution of 1830 with such "utmost enthusiasm" that he "entered warmly, as a writer, into the political discussions of the time."[38] In returning to journalism, how was Mill able to forget so soon his crisis—his dejected indifference to political changes?

Because we have become sensitive in this study to the differences of subject-matter that separated the psychological point of view of Mill's predecessors from the historical point of view of their continental antagonists, we are prepared to recognize the extent to which Mill's history of his crisis and its aftermath is not organized in a strictly chronological fashion but with some attention to his fundamental methodological distinction between theories of human nature (whether utilitarian psychology or Romantic psychology) and theories of history. We have already recognized that Mill's distinction between the chapter "Youthful Propagandism—The Westminster Review" and the first part of the chapter on the crisis is chronologically unwarranted,[39] but is adopted because it is more fundamentally a distinction between the outwardly oriented utilitarian psychology (which Mill himself accepted as a youthful propagandist, at least until he had defended "the early French Revolutionists" in April, 1828) and the Romantic psychology, which prompted his misgivings over utilitarian psychology and infiltrated his poetic account of his crisis and transformation. We should now recognize that just as the first part of the chapter on the crisis is devoted to these Romantic misgivings over utilitarian psychology, so the second part of the chapter takes up quite separately Mill's arrival at an historical point of view. Thus even though the chapter begins chronologically with his abandonment of journalistic activity after defending "early French Revolutionists" in April, 1828, it goes back to the crisis of 1826 as the psychological beginning of these misgivings. Similarly, even though the second part of the chapter begins with Mill's withdrawal "after 1829" from the Debating Society, it goes back to Macaulay's attack in March, 1829, which is handled almost as if it were a second distinct crisis.[40] Thus one reason why Mill forgets his crisis so soon is that his return to politics (at least as it is reported in the *Autobiography*) was the brusque displacement of the psychological point of view he had taken toward his crisis by the historical point of view which he acquired "in 1829 and 1830" when he "became acquainted with some of their [the Saint-Simonians'] writings," and which he then took toward the Revolution of 1830."[41]

The displacement is brusque in that there is no explanation discernible in the *Autobiography* of why Mill's withdrawal and poetic transformation (with attendant misgivings over the *Analysis of the Mind*) should suddenly have turned out to have been preoccupation with the historical treatment of political problems (with attendant misgivings over the *Essay on Government*).[42] Why didn't Mill go on reading poetry and moralizing about its value as an aid in the formation of a character as unlike his father's or Roebuck's as possible?[43] Why didn't he remain permanently indifferent to history, politics, and journalism? Why did he instead enter "warmly, as a writer, into the political discussions of the time," becoming again the radical and the democrat that he now pretends to have always remained? Why did the Revolution of 1830 change his mind so promptly and so completely—a mind which so recently had been indifferent to political changes?

A New Existence

We have been misled. Since Mill has just given us a psychological explanation of his withdrawal and poetic transformation, we have been looking for a comparable psychological explanation of his journalistic return to modern history and politics. But remember what the outcome was of Mill's arrival at the psychological explanation of his withdrawal; the chronological overlap between the previous period of propagandism and the period of crisis was eliminated for him, in retrospect, as soon as he explained what happened between 1826 and 1828 in terms of poetry and psychological theories of poetry which he had not read before the "autumn of 1828."[44] Is it not possible that the gap in continuity between this dejected psychological explanation (which he reached in 1828–29) and his renewed enthusiasm for political changes in 1830, was bridged, similarly in retrospect, not by a further psychological explanation but from the side of his later theory of history?

In considering this possibility, recall first the fact that reading Romantic poetry was not Mill's complete transformation; it has only given him "relief" from his dejection.[45] The Revolution of 1830 gives him considerably more—"a new existence."[46] But this "new existence" is not just an historical moment—the beginning of a new period in Mill's public career as a journalist. It is also in some sense the "self," the "completed whole"—the completion of the psychological transformation he was seeking poetically.[47] But it has emerged as the product, not of the poetic imagination which had initiated the process of transformation, but of a French Revolution.

Mill's review of Carlyle's *French Revolution* yielded evidence that for Mill a poetic imagination was needed to recreate the first French Revolution.[48] But a new French Revolution is not the whole story of Mill's "new existence." Just as the theoretical implications of Mill's poetic transformation are not followed out in the *Autobiography,* because Mill when he wrote it no longer accepted the Romantic Coleridgian psychological theory of his essay on poetry and his review of Carlyle's *History*, so Mill's "utmost enthusiasm" for the Revolution of 1830 had certain theoretical implications which are not followed out in the *Autobiography* because Mill when he wrote it no longer accepted the Romantic Saint-Simonian theory of history. His exposition of the Saint-Simonian theory in the *Autobiography* ends by merely suggesting its relevance to the "frame of mind" in which "the French Revolution of July found me."[49] If the procedure is valid which I employed in reconstructing the theoretical implications of Mill's dejection and poetic transformation, we must again pick up the chips of theorizing that are still available in the *Autobiography* and retrieve their original implications by consulting what Mill wrote when he resumed publication after the Revolution of 1830.

So long as Mill remained a youthful propagandist, his "premises" were supplied by his father's utilitarian psychology. But starting with these premises, where had he gone? By answering this question, we can discover a certain continuity at least in the period that finally came to an end with his last piece of propaganda, before he gave up publishing—his 1828 "defense of the early French Revolutionists." This defense, we remember, was "a labour of love."[50] In fact the enthusiasm with which Mill in his youth had looked forward to political changes, he in fact traces back to the first time he read a history of the French Revolution of 1789: "From this time . . . the subject took an immense hold of my feelings. It allied itself with all my juvenile aspirations to the character of a democratic champion."[51] This alliance was Mill's deduction of the political program of "the early French Revolutionists" from the premises supplied by his father's utilitarian psychology.[52]

This deductive procedure, as exhibited by Mill's father's *Essay on Government,* was what Macaulay attacked in March, 1829; "It is utterly impossible," the historian protested, "to deduce the science of government from the principles of human nature."[53] A "change" ensued, Mill admits, "in the premises of my political philosophy," when he then became acquainted "in 1829 and 1830" with the Saint-Simonian theory of history.[54] This change to historical premises brings with it a change in Mill's interpretation of the French Revolution of 1789. He can no longer abstract "the early French Revolutionists" from the later dismaying, most unutilitarian history of the Revolution, by defending their political principles in terms of a *psychological* theory. The course *history* actually took has to be respected. Thus Mill now reinterprets the first French Revolution as "one turbulent passage in a progressive transformation embracing the whole human race."[55] Mill is still engaged in the pursuit of comprehensive wholes. But the vantage point for his sweeping reinterpretation is not psychological but historical.[56] It is the French Revolution of 1830 as the culminating moment in this all-embracing progressive transformation.[57] It is not his father's utilitarian theory of the human mind, but "the spirit of the modern world" that is "triumphant in July 1830."[58]

Originally Mill's sense of the personal irrelevance of the political changes to which he had looked forward with youthful enthusiasm had retained these changes in a psychological context. His crisis was his carrying out the quite unhistorical experiment of imagining these political changes "completely effected at this very instant" in order to ask himself the question, "Would this be a great joy and happiness to you?"[59] The fact that his "self-consciousness" had been "irrepressible" had staked out its claim to explore this psychological context with the Romantic theory of poetry. Now the inescapable fact is that "whatever we may think or affect to think of the present age, we cannot get out of it."[60] Mill can no longer withdraw from the historical context: "Il faut être de son temps."[61] The revolutionary "new existence" conferred on Mill in July, 1830, is a new consciousness of his existence as historical. Mill's "utmost enthusiasm" for this revolution is, of course, a psychological change, but a psychological change which is no longer restricted to a psychological context. It is relocated in the broader historical context of the spirit of an age that stretches from the first to the second French Revolution and beyond.[62]

This broader historical context is the "frame of mind" in which the July Revolution reportedly "found" Mill when it triggered his "utmost enthusiasm" and conferred on him "a new existence." Mill's "new existence" was as inextricably theoretical as his old existence had been. It derived from the "new ideas" which he had taken in, mainly from the Saint-Simonians. It was not simply dictated by practical political changes, even though he "entered warmly, as a writer, into the political discussions of the time, which soon became still more exciting" with "the proposing of the Reform Bill."[63] The distinction I am introducing is Mill's own. Despite the fact that the articles with which Mill in 1831 expounded the Saint-Simonian philosophy of history were expositions of "The Spirit of the Age," they were, he admits in the *Autobiography*, "ill-timed and missed fire altogether," precisely because "great political changes [those to be enacted in the Reform Bill] were impending and engrossing all minds."[64] Mill's own mind was an exception to the English rule. And at the time he was less indulgent ethologically than he has become in the *Autobiography* toward the English lack of craving for generality:

> The very idea of beginning a reformation in men's minds by preaching to them a comprehensive doctrine is a notion which would never enter into the head of any person who has lived long enough in England to know the people. Englishmen habitually distrust the most obvious truths, if the person who advances them is suspected of having any general views.[65]

Mill turned to France, not only because of the July Revolution but also in pursuit of theoretical comprehensiveness.[66] In France "the supremacy of a general theory" was acknowledged. "In political philosophy," Mill commented, "the initiative belongs to France at this moment, not so much from the number of truths which have yet been practically arrived at, but rather from the far more elevated terrain on which the discussion is engaged; a terrain from which England is still separated by the whole interval which lies between 1789 and 1832."[67] The reformation in men's minds that Mill preached in "The Spirit of the Age" was a transformation with which England would catch up with the spirit of the age—would move on, as France has already moved, from the Revolution of 1789 to the Revolution of 1830. This movement transcended impending political changes by raising political discussion of these changes to the more elevated terrain of a general theory of political change.[68]

One Stage Onward

The continuity we have been seeking for this crucial period in Mill's "mental history" is the movement of his own mind to successively higher levels of reinterpretation. Let us retrace this movement in order to appreciate its continuity. It began when his no longer looking forward to political changes could no longer be interpreted as simply a "dull state of nerves," but became first "a crisis," and then a dejected recognition of the psychological implications of the change which had taken place in his state of mind when he no longer looked forward to political changes. Mill was reinterpreting this state of mind as the result of an analytic education which had been based on the utilitarian theory in which the human mind was merely an associative mechanism. Mill reached this reinterpretation by arriving at the more elevated terrain of the Coleridgian theory of the poet's mind in which associations, formed mechanically at a lower level, can be transformed by the creative imagination.[69] In tracing this upward movement earlier, we assumed that the change in Mill's state of mind was simply a psychological change; up until "1829 and 1830," when Mill first "became acquainted" with Saint-Simonian writings, he himself seems to have assumed that this change was a psychological change, in the sense that the series of feelings involved could be interpreted in terms of the Coleridgian theory of the poetic mind which provided him with a distinction between "merely having a feeling" and "being conscious of the feeling."[70] This distinction of level is no longer simply a psychological sequence, but becomes historical after Mill becomes acquainted with the Saint-Simonian theory of history.

Mill admits in the *Autobiography* that "a new mode of political thinking" had been "brought home" to him by the Saint-Simonians.[71] This would be an innocent idiom were we not faced with the exegetical problem that he has been describing himself, not as thinking about political changes, but as preoccupied with the change that had taken place in himself. The Saint-Simonian mode of political thinking embraced the whole history of the whole human race, but it may have been "brought home" to Mill by its applicability in retrospect to his own "mental history." In other words, it may have offered a reinterpretation, at a still higher, more comprehensive level than the Coleridgian theory of poetry, of the series of changes in his personal feelings about political changes.[72] Consider the autobiographical report which Mill gives of the initial impression made on him by the Saint-Simonian theory of history:

> I was greatly struck with the connected view which they for the first time presented to me, of the natural order of human progress; and especially with their division of all history into organic periods and critical periods: During the organic periods (they said) mankind accept with firm conviction some positive creed. . . . A period follows of criticism and negation, in which mankind lose their old convictions. . . . These ideas, I knew, were not peculiar to the St. Simonians . . . but they had never, to my knowledge been so completely systematized as by these writers, nor the distinguishing characteristics of a critical period so powerfully set forth.[73]

One reason Mill would have felt the power of these distinguishing characteristics was that he could recognize that he was already distinguishing them poetically as characteristics of his own state of mind. It is true that our problem of interpretation has been his failure to make any explicit reference in this report to his poetic state of mind, so that a gap seems to be left in the continuity of his series of feelings. But this may be because his preoccupation with his own state of mind had been superseded as soon as this state of mind had acquired comprehensive significance from the Saint-Simonian general view of history. Remember that his self-conscious dejection had been not only a sense of the personal irrelevance to himself of outward changes affecting the rest of mankind, but also a self-isolating sense of the irrelevance to the rest of mankind of his own personal state of mind.[74] He had moaned (reportedly in 1826–27) that "mine was not an interesting, or in any way respectable distress."[75] If his reading romantic poetry in 1828 brought "relief" from his dejection, it was partly because he discovered that Wordsworth "had had *similar* experience to mine."[76] But his inability to look forward to changes affecting the rest of mankind, was not supplanted by his "utmost enthusiasm" for the July Revolution until this inability no longer seemed the result, which it was "hardly possible for time to remove,"[77] of a utilitarian education that had worn away his feelings and convictions. It was not supplanted until time itself no longer seemed simply the mere passage of time but became "the natural order" (i.e., the Saint-Simonian order) of the progress of the human mind, in which the weakening of feelings and the loss of old convictions are "distinguishing characteristics of a critical period." In the Saint-Simonian theory of history, the final phase of a critical period is marked by such *crises* as the French Revolution of 1789.[78] In Mill's reweaving of the fabric of his recollections, the term "crisis" can function as a *Stichwort,* because it belongs to both the sequence of the poet's experience (as psychologically interpreted, for example, by Coleridge's "Dejection") and to the sequence of mankind's experience (as historically interpreted by the Saint-Simonians.) Thus the "dull state of nerves" of 1826, which Mill had reinterpreted poetically in 1828 as a *mental* crisis, became in 1829 and 1830 an *historical* crisis. It had perhaps undergone an historical reinterpretation comparable to Mill's Saint-Simonian reinterpretation of the original French Revolution; it had perhaps also become "one turbulent passage in a progressive transformation embracing the whole human race."[79] The process of extension and generalization involved in this pursuit of a comprehensive whole would help explain why what happened in 1826 did not remain in retrospect merely a particular, brief episode of that autumn but acquired general significance as beginning an extended period of progressive transformation in Mill's mental history, despite the chronological evidence to the contrary.

This *historicist* adjustment, whereby the previously inward and upward movement of Mill's *moralistic* adjustment becomes an historical forward movement, is probably dramatized by the double title of the chapter we are considering: "A Crisis in My Mental History—One Stage Onward." Just as Mill's *historical* consciousness of crisis succeeds to the role of elucidating what had happened to him in 1826, which had previously been played in 1828 by his poetic *self-consciousness,* so the ensuing process of poetic transformation becomes a stage in an historical process of progressive transformation. When Mill discovers that whatever he "may think or affect to think of the present age" he "cannot get out of it," he is thinking of the present age as the Saint-Simonians thought of it, as the final stage of "transition" in a "critical" period. He is unable to get out of it any longer, because he has been thinking of himself, in terms of a Romantic theory of poetry, as a mind that was "irretrievably" analytic and critical.[80] For although this theory previously helped him withdraw inwardly from the present age, the conception of his mind that it perpetrated now coalesces in his thinking with the supervening Saint-Simonian conception of what inevitably happens to the human mind during a "transition." This coalescence establishes in retrospect a continuity between Mill's poetic "internal culture" and the "inward workings of the age," and this continuity transcends the distinction between the two parts of the chapter on the crisis—the distinction that reproduces Mill's separation of the subject matter of psychology from the subject-matter of history.

We can now see how this continuity was established in retrospect. Having obtained from the Saint-Simonians "a clearer conception . . . of the peculiarities of an era of transition in opinion," Mill explains, "I looked forward, through the present age of loud disputes but generally weak convictions. . . ."[81] This Saint-Simonian antithesis characterizing the present age could have supplied the impetus for Mill to withdraw from the loud disputes of the Debating Society "after 1829," in order to cope inwardly with the weakening of his old convictions. We therefore find separately indicated in the *Autobiography* this second withdrawal, lasting for some five or six months until the July Revolution. It is a withdrawal separable from the first insofar as it was prompted by a different theory—an historical theory of "transition" as distinguished from the psychological theory of inward "transformation" which had prompted Mill's first withdrawal. But we are also given an overall impression of a continuous period of withdrawal, going back to Mill's abandonment of "Youthful Propagandism." This impression of continuity prevails because the Saint-Simonian antithesis would have supplied additional impetus to the movement of withdrawal that had been initiated by the psychological antithesis between propagandistic rhetoric and poetic reflection with which Mill was interpreting his having abandoned his "Youthful Propagandism."[82]

When Mill returns to journalism with the Revolution of 1830, it is not simply because "the revolution" in his "modes of thinking" was "already complete." Its completion was its coalescence with "the revolution which had already taken place in the human mind" (according to the Saint-Simonians) and "is rapidly shaping external things."[83] Mill has received from the Revolution of 1830 a positive answer to the question to which his irrepressible self-consciousness had originally answered "No" in 1826. The "enthusiasm," as well as the "No," may have been a debt to the Saint-Simonian theory of history, for *enthousiasme* is the positive characteristic they attributed to the way convictions are held during an organic period, as distinguished from their weakening during a critical period of negation and loud disputes.[84]

Journalism

There is, of course, something questionably anachronistic about my reconstruction of Mill's successive interpretations of his crisis, transformation, and transition. In reconstructing his series of feelings between 1826 and 1830, I have consulted his writings between 1830 and 1840, in order to retrieve the original implications of the pieces of theory which still survive in the *Autobiography*. The question that has then to be faced is itself a problem of periodization. If the *terminus ad quem* of Mill's second period is the July Revolution of 1830, the *terminus a quo* of his "third period" is 1840. We can perhaps allow that a transition would be more gradual than a crisis and transformation.[85] We are also presumably intended to attach to the preceding period what Mill published between 1830 and 1840 as exhibiting the changes which had taken place in his thinking when he found publishing uncongenial. In other words, before 1830 Mill separated himself inwardly from the utilitarian "outwardness" of his youthful propagandism by disengaging himself from journalism; after the July Revolution his journalism demonstrated publicly and "in a marked manner" that he had separated himself inwardly.[86]

We have seen that Mill seems to be indebted to Saint-Simonian theory, as well as to the Revolution of 1830, for his return to journalism.[87] The debt is illustrated by his first major journalistic undertaking "The Spirit of the Age." But Mill's account of his debt to the Saint-Simonians concludes with the following qualification: "In giving an account of this period of my life, I have only specified such of my new impressions as appeared to me, both at the time and since, to be a kind of turning points, marking a definite progress in my mode of thought."[88] The periodization of *social* history to which Mill became temporarily committed in "The Spirit of the Age," he later largely discarded. But I shall argue he retained it in some measure for his own "mental history" when he came to specify as an autobiographer the "turning points" which marked "a definite progress" in his own "mode of thought." A first step toward this argument can be taken now. When we began our final interpretation of the structure of Mill's thought, we discovered the quasi-autobiographical relevance of his mature journalism as a self-conscious undertaking.[89] Now that we are dealing with the *Autobiography* itself as the outcome of his self-consciousness having become historical consciousness, we can see that the quasi-autobiographical relevance his journalism acquired is borne out by the rest of his historical periodization. Since the second period in his mental history was distinguished as ending in 1830 with Mill's return to journalism, since it was distinguished as having begun with his temporarily ceasing to write for the old *Westminster,* it is worth noting that the third period is distinguished as beginning in 1840 with Mill's relinquishment of the new *Westminster*. Mill's exercise of sympathy towards his Coleridgian adversaries having reached its climax in the article on Coleridge in March, 1840, he must have felt that he had achieved his self-conscious journalistic objective of separating himself "in a marked manner" from the "narrower Benthamism" of his "Youthful Propagandism." He had vindicated in the pages of an ostensibly radical journal the conservative opinions of their antagonists.

In his *Autobiography* Mill specifies this turning point by drawing attention to the fact that "the number of the *Review* which contained the paper on Coleridge, was the last which was published during his proprietorship." From now on Mill usually found the *Edinburgh Review* "a suitable vehicle" for his writings.[90] Among these, the most important were the articles on French historians, beginning with the review (October, 1840) of the second volume of *Democracy in America.* Inasmuch as Mill identifies Tocqueville's historical approach as "almost the reverse" of James Mill's "purely ratiocinative approach,"[91] we might add that the *Edinburgh* was a uniquely suitable vehicle, for Macaulay's attack in 1829 on this ratiocinative approach as unhistorical had been the Edinburgh's counterattack to the original attack in

"Periodical Literature" with which James Mill had launched the old *Westminster,* and with which his son had originally launched his own career as a journalist.[92] Thus any skepticism that may be entertained regarding Mill's periodization in the *Autobiography* only brings us back to the following consideration: even if his distinctions between periods are chronologically inconsistent with each other, they are consistently drawn, not simply by reference (as we earlier observed) to changes in his attitude toward utilitarianism, but more definitely by reference to changes in his attitude towards journalism, as changes in his attitude toward utilitarianism.[93]

Recurrence

We have already examined several articles from the period between 1830 and 1840 as marking changes in his attitude toward utilitarian *psychology*. But since we are now concerned with this period as an historical period, we should both place these articles in their historical sequence and consider any changes they may also mark in his attitude toward *history*. The series of articles on "The Spirit of the Age" (January 9 to May 29, 1831) is unfinished, but the last article ends with Mill's crediting himself with one accomplishment: "That we are in a state of transition is a point which needs no further illustration." The "sequel" he anticipates writing will be "a careful survey of the properties of the English national mind in the present age," in order to determine "the future fate of our country." Mill is looking forward, as he has been since the July Revolution. But he "postpones" the "sequel" until "after the present bustle and tumult," when "the interests of the day and of the hour naturally and properly engross every mind." He promises to "resume my subject as early as possible after the passing of the Reform Bill."[94] However in 1832 something goes wrong. Mill discontinues the newspaper reports on France which he began after the July Revolution. He explains, "All that has been doing in that country is so paltry, so devoid of any importance in the immediate result, and of any indication with respect to the future, that we felt no inducement to record . . . in addition to the trivialities of our own country, the still smaller trivialities of another country."[95] Mill has lost his Saint-Simonian *enthousiasme;* the spirit of the age has lost its scope and triumphant momentum. In "The Spirit of the Age"

Mill looked forward to the "transformation" through which every man will "achieve his destiny"; this prospect was "the conclusion of every man who can *feel the wants of his own age* without hankering after past ages." Mill warned, we remember, "whatever we may think or affect to think of the present age, we cannot get out of it."[96] "On Genius" (October, 1832) is an unexpected sequel to *The Spirit of the Age*. When Mill raises again the question he had not finally answered in 1830, "What are really the intellectual characteristics of this age?" he hankers after a past age; he can no longer abide the trivialities of the present age and attempts to get out of it by becoming an *Antiquus* who recognizes "that the truths which we have inherited still remain traditional, and no one among us, except here and there a man of genius, has made them truly his own."[97]

This attempt in 1832 is the recurrence of Mill's initial *psychological* attempt to cope with his crisis of 1826, and the recurrence may have reinforced in retrospect Mill's interpretation of this initial attempt: "I sought relief from my favourite books—those memorials of past nobleness and greatness from which I had always hitherto drawn strength and animation."[98] This initial attempt, we recall, eventually took the mechanical form of translating and abstracting Socratic dialogues—or what seemed in retrospect to have been a mechanical form,[99] as soon as Mill's psychological attempt to cope with his crisis took the further form in 1828 of reading Wordsworth and finding "relief" from the feeling that he was a "reasoning machine."[100] The psychological attempt also recurs in this further form when Mill engages in "poetic culture" (this time under the tutelage of Mrs. Taylor) and writes his articles on poetry (January and November, 1833; April, 1835).[101] By signing these articles *Antiquus,* and by publishing in 1834 the abstracts of the Platonic dialogues which he had put to one side, Mill asserts the psychological continuity of his poetic revival with his classical revival.[102] Next there recurs the *historicist* adjustment of "1829 and 1830" which had culminated in "The Spirit of the Age," as Mill interests himself again in theories of history: in October, 1835, he reviews the first volume of *Democracy in America;* in 1836 he publishes an article on "Civilization," strongly influenced by the Saint-Simonians and by Tocqueville; in 1837 he is "exempted" from "restraints and reticences," reviews Carlyle's *History of the French Revolution,* memorializes Armand Carrel, and begins reading Auguste

Comte. Finally he launches in 1840 his series on French historians for the *Edinburgh Review* by publishing his review of the second volume of *Democracy in America*.

This switch in his journalistic allegiance begins, however, another "period of withdrawal for Mill."[103] Outward changes only enlist Mill's utmost enthusiasm again with the French Revolution of 1848.[104] For the third time in his career as a journalist, Mill defends French revolutionists against Tory misrepresentations,[105] and then, for a third time, disillusionment intervenes, and it is during this stage of disillusionment that Mill again withdraws. Only this time his withdrawal to reflect on his own "mental history" as an individual now takes a literary form; he writes the first draft of his *Autobiography*. He also reflects on history as a struggle for individuality and writes the first draft of *On Liberty*.[106]

Thus we have to recognize that the successive stages of Mill's thought follow a sequence which is neither strictly chronological nor entirely irreversible. Mill may not retain the Saint-Simonian cyclical theory of history, except for the expression "turning upside down," which he employs for the nineteenth-century displacement of eighteenth-century theories of mind by theories of history,[107] but his own mental history manifests almost cyclical recurrences.

Mental Progress

The process of recurrence itself was already familiar to us from earlier withdrawals from and returns to politics—especially those which reinforced the role, in the development of the humanistic individualistic tradition, of the *Antiquus*—of the thinker whose "mind becomes ancient" when he draws strength and animation from memorials of past nobleness and greatness.[108] Anachronistic indifference to historical facts was characteristic of the *moralistic* adjustment that constituted this tradition; these outward historical facts were recurrently drawn within the context of the humanistic theory of the human mind, in order to provide a figurative rendering of what did make a difference inwardly to the individual. Since Mill's time, moreover, returns, withdrawals, and returns again, have continued to punctuate the development of liberalism. "Utmost enthusiasm" for a revolution, more discriminating "defense" of "early" revolutionists, are succeeded by disillusion with the actual historical prospects of revolution, and by withdrawal and literary criticism, as the *moralistic* adjustment supervenes on the *historicist* adjustment.

In the case of the liberal tradition, as in the case of the humanistic tradition, recurrences tend to reinforce the role of the individual (at least in his own mind), but they also tend to blur any strictly chronological distinction of stages. Why then does not Mill's liberalism likewise become, as these readjustments recur, a diffuse blur? The distinct stages do not in fact disappear in Mill's remembering, as they largely did in the *Memorabilia* of the humanistic tradition;[109] the distinction of stages still remains relevant to Mill. The same year in his *third* period in which he published *On Liberty,* he revived his *second* period by republishing (in the first volume of *Dissertations and Discussions*) articles he had written during this second period—his period of transition. He has selected (he explains in the Preface) those articles which "he considers . . . in any way desirable to preserve." He admits, "Everyone whose mind is progressive, or even whose opinions keep up with the changing facts that surround him, must necessarily, in looking back to his own writings, . . . find many things which, if they were to be written again, he would write differently, and some, even, which he has altogether ceased to think true."[110] Where Mill has altogether ceased to think an article to be true, he excludes or revises it. The most obvious exclusion is the longest—the article which has been most useful to us in tracing the development of the theory of history which survives only piecemeal in his *Autobiography*. It is this exclusion of "The Spirit of the Age" which is posing the problem of what survives in Mill in the way of a theory of history.

One thing that does survive is an historicist criterion of relevance. That "he would write differently" (i.e., now in his third period from the way in which he had written in his second period) is not sufficient, Mill emphasizes, to justify exclusion or even revision:

> I have not attempted to render papers written at so many different, and some of them at such distant, times, a faithful representation of my present stage of opinion and feeling. I leave them in all their imperfection, as memorials of the states of mind in which they were written, in the hope that they may possibly be useful to such readers as are in a corresponding stage of their own mental progress.[111]

Distinguishing periods was irrelevant to the memorials of past nobleness and greatness that composed the *Memorabilia* of the humanistic tradition. But distinguishing periods is necessary if Mill is to preserve memorials of his states of mind at earlier stages. These earlier stages, we have seen, tend to recur in Mill's own mental history. His hope that these memorials may be useful to his readers assumes that these stages could recur later in *their* mental history. Mill has in fact allowed for the difference between a mind that is "progressive" and a mind whose "opinions" merely "keep up with the changing facts." This difference is one surviving version of the gap we originally encountered as a gap between his poetic arrangement of the series of his feelings in a psychological sequence and their rearrangement in an historical sequence in response to the July Revolution and to the prospect of the Reform Bill. The survival of the gap in this version helps account for the looseness of the correlation with which Mill justifies his functioning as a representative figure in his *Autobiography:* "In an age of transition in opinions, there may be somewhat both of interest and of benefit in noting the successive phases of any mind which was always pressing forward."[112]

Two different processes of adjustment are visualized here; the second is loosely correlated with the first but not actually synchronized with it. The looseness of this correlation is perhaps characteristic of liberalism. The liberal is able to get a little way out of his age. This is the leeway which Mill had himself exploited as an *Antiquus,* and for his later, less drastic withdrawals. It provides the scope which in *On Liberty* enables him to marshal moral pressure from within and uphold the principle of individuality over against the increasing pressures to conformity which are the tendencies of democracy in America and of "modern commercial civilization."[113] This loose correlation gives the liberal leeway for making a *moralistic* as well as an *historicist* adjustment and for adjusting the relations between these two adjustments, as the one supervenes upon the other. The liberal is someone who is conscious of living in an age of transition, but he does not simply "keep up with the changing facts that surround him." He is an individual who is "always pressing forward," because some of the pressure for change comes from his own initiative, from his own conception of himself, and dedication to his "individuality" as "the same thing with development."[114] In the way that he presses forward, there is not only self-questioning, but also a certain fidelity to the moral requirement that he make "mental progress." This fidelity cannot be reduced entirely to the demands for adjustment laid upon him by historical changes in the facts that surround him.

At the same time, however, Mill's adjustment of the relation between his *moralistic* adjustment and his *historicist* adjustment helps explain the inaccuracies and distortions of his *Autobiography*. I have not been attempting to determine the exact chronology of Mill's actual "mental history" except insofar as discrepancies point up the format imposed on it by his *Autobiography*. But such an attempt would show that Mill regularly predated episodes (or his interpretation of their implications), beginning with his "crisis" and "transformation." Since his "transition" is a distinctively historical conception, the most pertinent illustration of Mill's predating is his report to the effect that the "frame of mind" in which "the French Revolution of July found me" was a Saint-Simonian theory of history. Mill's interpretation of this revolution in fact only became Saint-Simonian in retrospect.[115] Mill's predating is too regular and too extravagant to be dismissed as the retrospective illusion of ordinary humans. What seem to be later recurrences, merely reinforcing earlier interpretations, were in fact decisive for the development of the format of the *Autobiography*. The predating indicates that this format imposes, on what his "mental history" actually was, the moral requirement of making "mental progress." His "mental history" has been accelerated in order to demonstrate that his mind "was always pressing forward."

The History of Ideas

Mill's own anachronisms may not be those of an *Antiquus*—of a thinker whose "mind becomes ancient" because he draws strength and animation from "memorials of past nobleness and greatness." But his forward looking orientation does take the form of the "hope" that "memorials" of his "states of mind" would be "useful to such readers as are in a corresponding stage of their own mental progress." This hope may be justified by the continued vogue of his writings today. Indeed they may have earned their continued vogue partly by catering to a feeling for mental progress of a kind which is not rigidly synchronized with successive historical changes—including those that have taken place since Mill's time in the facts surrounding his readers.

Yet in spite of the continued vogue of Mill's writings, a certain change has taken place in the way he is read and interpreted, and this change can provide a rough indication of some differences between his liberalism and ours. Mill thinks of himself as refusing to remain confused and unsettled during the course of his transition; today his interpreters often welcome the evidence that he did remain confused and unsettled:

> What makes Mill one of the most interesting figures of the nineteenth century is that a number of the main strands, of thought converge on him and contribute to that unstable eclecticism which he fashioned out of "the fabric of my old and taught opinions."[116]

Uninteresting as a philosopher, because of his unstable eclecticism, Mill becomes instead one of the most interesting figures of the nineteenth century. But he then is of still further interest to the extent that there emerges from what he fashioned a configuration of thought which satisfies a criterion of interestingness that is different from that of a philosophy. This configuration can be identified; there is a sense in which Mill himself almost becomes in his *Autobiography* an historian of his ideas. No previous philosopher we have encountered would employ in the interpretation of his thought so loose an expression as "when I had taken in any new idea."[117] The expression itself is new in its sweeping casualness. An idea is loosened from its relations to other ideas—the relations which would traditionally have constituted a subject-matter and determined the place of this subject-matter in the structure of knowledge.

We have already seen that the demise of political philosophy can be traced to analytic procedures which distinguish and separate what traditionally was related, to the encroachment of economic and legal considerations in the treatment of political problems, to the emergence of social science, and to the fragmentation of what for Mill was still "the social science" into research projects. But this accounting for the demise of political philosophy has failed to corner the guiltiest of its heirs—the heir who would disfigure the corpse. There is no structure of knowledge left when the historian of ideas finds any thinker relevant insofar as his thinking was transitional—that is, insofar as it was composed simply of adjustments between the new ideas he took in and the old opinions he inherited.

This configuration is not a context in the philosophical sense I have employed this term. The history of ideas is rather the final disintegration of a philosophical context. No set of relations between ideas is accepted as constituting a subject-matter or as determining the relation between this subject-matter and "other studies" in the fashion in which the utilitarians accepted a philosophy of human nature as a context for the treatment of political problems or the Saint-Simonians accepted a philosophy of history.[118] Thought comes instead in "strands" which the historian finds the thinker weaving out of new and old ideas. The adjustments between the new and the old necessarily remain confused and unsettled. For it is not even the thinker's own adjustments which are at the focus of a history of ideas, but the ideas themselves. His thinking is merely the result of the way different intellectual influences "converge on him." Some measure of convergence is assured by these influences all belonging to the same period. But this period itself is not a distinct and separate stage in history whose "inward workings" can be given a coherent interpretation as the spirit of the age, as they were in a philosophy of history such as the Saint-Simonian. All periods, insofar as they are of historical interest, are periods of transition.[119] Thus the thought of any period, as well as of any thinker, ultimately disintegrates into confused and unsettled adjustments between the new and the old. It is this process of disintegration which is the emergence of the history of ideas from the kind of *Geistesgeschichte* which the Saint-Simonians practiced.

The emergence of the history of ideas as a scholarly discipline lies quite outside the scope of this book. Here I have only singled out Mill as the typical representative of liberalism and traced the development of the conception of a representative figure back to an ancient typological tradition in which "the mind needs such examples." But I therefore have to admit in conclusion that the history of ideas is a discipline which ultimately undermines the ability of any individual to function as a representative figure, and thus the selection of Mill to represent liberalism.[120] The historian of ideas would identify and interpret liberalism very differently—in terms of some unstable and unsettled configuration of transitory influences. In this setting, Mill could be watched making his adjustments, but only as a weather-cock fluctuating with changes in the climate of opinion.

This contemporary interpretation of liberalism can be dealt with here only as a disfigurement of political philosophy. My autopsy has been a philosophical interpretation in that I have tried to interpret political philosophies as structures of knowledge, in order to show topologically where and how liberalism emerges as the final and fatal weakening of a particular kind of intellectual undertaking. Since it is not a matter of life or death, I have not bothered to examine Mill's arguments in order to show whether he did or did not remain confused and unsettled as a philosopher. Previous interpreters have done this. Such interpretations usually assume that political philosophy can be resurrected as an intellectual undertaking by reidentifying it with the piecemeal examination of specific political arguments.[121] Piecemeal undertakings of course survive the disintegration of traditional political philosophy. But more relevant to the intellectual character of liberalism today is the fact that Mill's effort not to remain confused and unsettled as a philosopher produced a sequence of adjustments which lends itself today to interpretation by the historian of ideas, whose stock in trade is confusion and unsettlement.

This sequence we have watched Mill derive from the philosophies to which he was more or less committed during his period of transition—from the Romantic philosophy of mind and the Saint-Simonian philosophy of history. But what Mill finally leaves us with is the way in which, during his third period, he adjusts his thought in "an age of transition in opinions" that encompasses all three periods in his thinking. It is this final process of adjustment which still enjoys some lingering vitality for liberalism today, rather than the traditional philosophies to which Mill succumbed during his second period. This final adjustment can be most easily identified as relocating the traditional problems of political philosophy in the new setting of a history of ideas. Since it is fatal both to political philosophy and to my philosophical interpretation of political philosophies, let me conclude with this final adjustment. I shall start with the history of ideas, insofar as it is a procedure illustrated by the *Autobiography* with which Mill in his third period reports his "mental history." I shall then retrace his process of adjustment during his second period—his period of transition. In this way I shall reach the final adjustment as marking both Mill's arrival at his concluding, third period, and the end of the tradition of political philosophy in England.

New Ideas

History would be for us today a dull proceeding, if the historian were not equipped to pick out crises and turning points, and to trace transformations and transitions. If the events in question then seem particularly eventful, what event in the history of ideas could be more eventful than the crisis which the ideas of "crisis," "turning point," "transformation," "transition," were first deployed to describe! So far as the history of ideas in England is concerned, there would be little doubt that this is the crisis which we have seen Mill date in his *Autobiography* as having taken place in 1826—if we could accept his dating. Some of these historicist ideas had been employed long before by Polybius, but he had applied them only to political history. It is Mill's application of this entire constellation of historicist ideas to the history of his own thought that I am interpreting as the passage of these historicist ideas from their originally philosophical context into a setting which approximates a history of ideas.

Among the new ideas that Mill took in during his period of transition, none were more significant than these historicist ideas, since they enabled him to adjust the relationship between other new ideas and his old opinions. The idea of "a period of transition," which we have watched him take from the Saint-Simonians, conferred such systematic significance on the discrimination of the new from the old that they could sometimes be identified succinctly as "partisans des idées nouvelles."[122] It must be conceded, however, that when Mill himself employs these historicist ideas in his *Autobiography,* they do not retain the systematic significance which they enjoyed in the context of the Saint-Simonian philosophy of history. In Mill's *Autobiography,* they seem almost as commonplace and as theoretically unpretentious as they have become today, when they are used by historians of ideas without commitment to any philosophy of history. The first draft of Mill's *Autobiography* was not written until almost thirty years after the crisis of 1826. Mill may insist that he is reporting "such of my new impressions as appeared to me, both at the time and since, to be a kind of turning points, marking a definite progress in my thought,"[123] and "at the time" may be Mill's commitment to an accurate report. Yet the discrepancies in the *Autobiography* have suggested that it is not entirely an entirely accurate report of what happened to him between 1826 and 1830. He has imposed on his "mental history" a conception of "mental progress" in which successive periods can be demarcated. He is committed to presenting a report of how he was "always pressing forward" in a way that exemplifies "a certain order of possible progress" for "the human mind"—the historical sequence in fact that the Saint-Simonians had delineated. But the reference of Mill's "since" presumably brings us down to Mill's third period. We have therefore to recognize that the evidence which has enabled us to go behind the *Autobiography*—the evidence of such writings of the second period as his articles on "The Spirit of the Age"—indicates that the new historicist ideas that Mill took in "at the time" of his exposure to the Saint-Simonians had much more definite and systematic relevance for social history than they retained when he wrote the *Autobiography* during his third period. The *Autobiography* is the final adjustment that remains to be traced as illustrating both a slackening of the systematic significance of these ideas, and their passage from their original context in a philosophy of history into the weaker setting which approximates a history of ideas.

During Mill's transition itself, it was less the Saint-Simonian ideas that impressed him than their systematization—the structure they lent his thought. The ideas themselves, he admits, were not "peculiar to the St. Simonians," but were rather "the general property of Europe," as befitted (we may add) manifestations of the spirit of the age.[124] What Mill stresses, in a letter of February 9, 1830, is the part played by the Saint-Simonians in systematizing ideas which he already had: "I had much changed from what I was before I read any of their publications; but it was their works which gave *order* and *system* to the ideas which I had already imbibed from intercourse with others, and derived from my own reflexions."[125] We have already traced the sequence of changes involved: (1) Mill had imbibed the poetical ideas of *crisis* and *transformation* from his reading and from his sympathetic intercourse with the Coleridgians, and he had applied these poetic ideas to the *psychological* movement of his own "reflexions"; (2) he had superimposed on this movement the Saint-Simonian idea of an *historical transition,* so that his poetic crisis and transformation took their place in a "connected view" which swept up "all history" in its scope.[126]

This view, we now have to recognize, had further provided him with a theoretical connection which he was looking for. The problem of finding a connection was posed by the way Mill's thinking had moved to a higher level of theorizing about his thinking. We must remind ourselves, once again, that Mill's crisis and transformation had been a change in his philosophy of mind as well as in his state of mind: he had interpreted his negative state of mind in 1826 as the result of an education based on the utilitarian philosophy of mind; he had interpreted his "relief" from his dejection in 1826–27 over this negative state of mind as a result of reading Romantic poetry in 1828, and in reaching this interpretation he had borrowed from the organic philosophy which in Coleridge had explained the operations of the poet's mind. Similarly, Mill's utmost enthusiasm for the Revolution of 1830 was eventually the result of interpreting it in terms of the Saint-Simonian philosophy of the history of the human mind, with which he had become acquainted "in 1829 and 1830." But the full cogency of this philosophy for Mill is felt only when we realize that the Saint-Simonian conception of the final phase of a critical period as transitional to an organic period was a conception which could be applied in interpreting, not only the changes in Mill's mind which had taken place during his crisis and transformation, but also to the higher-level change from an analytic philosophy of mind to an organic philosophy of mind. Insofar as the Saint-Simonian philosophy of history enabled Mill to assign analytic and organic philosophies of the mind to different periods in this history, his restless need for an adjustment was satisfied in a way that exempted him from achieving the adjustment in the form of a systematic philosophy of the mind comparable to his father's.

The Remainder of a Life

When we go on from the period of transition to the third period of Mill's mental history, we discover that the perspectives of Mill's philosophy of history undergo the same foreshortening that we originally traced in the view of history adopted at the beginning of *On Liberty*. The first stage in the struggle for liberty Mill surveyed as having gone on "almost from the remotest ages," but the second stage that he distinguishes is a swift transition from the "mode of thought, or rather perhaps of feeling," which "was common among the last generation of European liberalism" to the liberalism with which Mill would send his own generation forth.[127] Critical and organic ages were recurrent in the cyclical theory of the Saint-Simonians, who divided "all history into organic periods and critical periods."[128] The modern critical period had begun for them with the Reformation and the invention of printing.[129] But the critical age in Mill is usually abbreviated to the eighteenth century, with its critical analysis of traditional opinions, so that the Saint-Simonian distinction is brought to bear on the transition from the utilitarian analysis of mind, as an eighteenth-century philosophy, to the Coleridgian organic philosophy, as "a reaction" that "expresses the revolt of the human mind against the philosophy of the eighteenth century."[130] This foreshortening is illustrated by Mill's preference for the term "transitional," which the Saint-Simonians themselves reserved for the final stage of a critical period.[131]

The universal scope of the Saint-Simonian philosophy of history thus shrinks to the immediate problem of adjustment between generations, as this problem is posed within the lifetime of an individual thinker who is unable to get out of his age—that is, to the problem of adjustment between the opinions Mill inherited from his father so long as he remained a youthful propagandist, and the new ideas he took in as he approached maturity. In commenting on "the marked opposition between James Mill's spirit and that of the present time," Mill recalls the ancient prototype of those who were out of alignment with their time: "As Brutus was called the last of the Romans, so was he the last of the eighteenth century: he continued its tone of thought and sentiment into the nineteenth."[132]

With this reduction of its scope to the differences between generations as they emerge within the lifetime of an individual, Mill's *historicist* adjustment comes to approximate the perspective of our own historical experience today. No one today can doubt (unless he is able to get a long way out of our present age) that it was consoling to Mill to be able to leave his father behind in the eighteenth century.[133] The comparison with the last of the Romans may suggest to us an even more drastic effort at relegation. But continuing to be a figure representative of the eighteenth century in the nineteenth century involved for Mill more feeling for the role of a representative figure than we can still share today and probably carried some reference to the almost Stoic integrity with which Mill's father resisted historical changes, and in particular the change to the historical point of view that Mill finds distinguishes the nineteenth century from the eighteenth.[134] Today our fathers merely belong to a preceding generation.

When the third period of Mill's mental history began, the *historicist* adjustment of the period of transition was jeopardized in two ways: on the one hand, Mill renewed his adherence to his father's analytic psychology by republishing the *Analysis of the Mind;* on the other hand, Mill discounted "The Spirit of the Age," by deciding not to republish it in *Dissertations and Discussions.* We have seen that his father's analysis of the mind into "a series of feelings" which were explained as the effects of outward circumstances left Mill with the "inexplicable fact" of self consciousness on his hands in the footnotes. He could not explain its role, instanced by memory and expectation, of gathering up a series of feelings into a single present conception. I suggested originally that the place which Mill could not find for this fact, once so "irrepressible," in a systematic philosophy of mind, he finally found in his *Autobiography*.[135] But we have since observed that the series of feelings Mill reports in his *Autobiography* are not gathered up into a single present conception. His *Autobiography* is a "mental history," and the series of feelings are sorted out and assigned to distinct periods.[136] We have also observed that the historicist criteria involved are not irrelevant to his other writings: when Mill in this third period republished (in the first volume of *Dissertations and Discussions*) articles from the period of transition, he leaves them relatively unaltered as "memorials of the states of mind in which they were written."[137] The individual's thinking can gain historical significance only insofar as it has developed by going through stages. To have changed one's mind, then, is evidence not of confusion and instability, but of adjustability, of moral progressiveness, and of one's ability to represent an age of transition.[138]

To my previous interpretation that the *Autobiography* takes over at the juncture in Mill's thinking where Mill no longer envisages a philosophy of mind of his own which would revise his father's *Analysis of the Mind,* I now add the suggestion that this is also the juncture where Mill no longer envisages a philosophy of history which would exempt him from that revision, by enabling him to assign *The Analy-*

sis of the Mind as a whole to the "critical" period of the eighteenth century, where such analyses were relegated in the Saint-Simonian philosophy of history. Indeed Mill no longer even envisages filling out the largely empty methodological framework of "The Logic of the Moral Sciences" where an ethology and a political ethology were to have supplemented his father's *Analysis of the Mind,* providing a connecting bridge between it and continental philosophies of history.[139] We can then conclude that Mill's final reconciliation of the philosophy of mind with the philosophy of history is the blend which we have been examining—a "mental history" in which "new impressions" are "specified" as "turning-points, marking a definite progress" in Mill's "mode of thought." Autobiography, like journalism, is a genre which is slacker than philosophy. But there are reasons why a philosopher turns to autobiography, as there are reasons why he turns to journalism—or away from journalism, as Mill did temporarily when he became preoccupied with himself. And there are also reasons why Mill returned to journalism, assigning to it a quasi-autobiographical function. Even so, journalism had to remain primarily an effort to "keep up with changes in the facts surrounding him." Autobiography took on another and different primary function—that of tracing the progress of a "mind which was always pressing forward."

Mill's *Autobiography* illustrates the slackening of his earlier philosophical aspirations. Yet the survival of these philosophical aspirations in a slackened form were reasons for his turning to autobiography as a final adjustment which he did not achieve as a philosopher. The *Autobiography* is, on the one hand, a slacker dealing with self-consciousness, memory, and expectation than the psychological (or ethological) explanation would have been which Mill had projected earlier in his career and which would have revised (or supplemented) his father's philosophy of mind; it is, on the other hand, a slacker treatment of history than the Saint-Simonian philosophy, which had enabled him to distinguish so confidently (e.g., in "The Spirit of the Age") between successive periods in the history of the human mind, and in effect to explain away his father's philosophy of mind by assigning it to a period in this history.[140] At the same time, the process of adjusting the relation between his father's philosophy of mind and the philosophy of history has itself slackened to become a mental history in which Mill's dealings with self-consciousness, memory, and expectation take the historical form of his acquiring for himself a representative role in an age of transition, by remembering the successive periods in his mental progress, and the expectancy with which he had pressed forward one stage onward.[141] This slacker adjustment is the way Mill thinks about himself when he writes his *Autobiography*.

When I characterize Mill's *Autobiography* as at once the survival of Mill's philosophical aspirations and their slackening, I may seem to be discerning in the *Autobiography* a structure which I am also ready to admit is not quite there, as soon as I am confronted with a discrepancy or a distortion. But I am only discerning an effort towards structure that continues Mill's earlier process of adjustment. And this effort would gain credibility in Mill's own view to the extent that no outcome is achieved which smoothes away discrepancies and distortions, exempting him from further effort. For I have taken to heart what can be construed as Mill's own warning against regarding any of his writings as perfectly structured. Commenting on "the grand effort" of another writer "to make himself a Greek," Mill emphasizes the strenuous problem of being modern:

> With all this he never could succeed in putting symmetry into any of his own writings, . . . showing the utter impossibility for a modern with all the good will in the world, to tightlace himself into the dimensions of an ancient. Every modern thinker has so much wider a horizon, & there is so much deeper a soil accumulated on the surface of human nature . . . —in short the moderns have vastly more material to reduce to order than the ancients dreamt of & the secret of harmonizing has not yet been discovered —it is too soon by a century or two to attempt either symmetrical productions in art or symmetrical characters. We all need to be blacksmiths or ballet dancers with good stout arms or legs, useful to do what we have got to do, and useful to fight with at times—we cannot be Apollos and Venuses just yet.[142]

In the meantime we are left with the *Autobiography* as an adjustment Mill sought in the final period of his life. Strenuous adjustment was more characteristic of his second period, whereas the final period, covering "The Remainder of My Life," is distinguished as "the third period . . . of my mental progress," when "I . . . had completely turned back from what there had been of excess in my reaction against Benthamism."[143] This turning back is not an adjustment that entails Mill's losing ground. In fact it provides some clue as to how he expects order eventually to be achieved and the secret of harmony to be discovered. The final period begins with his having reached in "Bentham" and "Coleridge" that higher level for which the political operation of the check-and-balance mechanism provides an analogy.[144] But it is the force of this classical analogy which weakens when Mill turns back during this final period.[145] Oppositions which he had felt so sharply during the second period (including the opposition between the Benthamite philosophy of mind and the Saint-Simonian philosophy of history) have themselves become slacker than we would have anticipated from his adoption of the principle of antagonism to supplement the operation of the principle of individuality. Adjustment is no longer the reconciliation of opposed philosophies; it is now largely a matter of his having adjusted the relations to his old opinions of the new ideas that he had taken in. What Mill is giving us in his *Autobiography* approximates a history of his ideas.

There is now less at stake even in the operation of the principle of individuality itself, as exhibited in the initiative he had taken, during his period of transition, when he refused to remain confused and unsettled in his adjustments. There is now less at stake too in the principle of antagonism, for Mill is finally reacting against his excessive reaction against Benthamism, confident that "Every excess . . . determines a corresponding reaction–improvement consisting only in this, that the oscillation, each time departs rather less widely from the centre, and an ever-increasing tendency is manifested to settle finally in it."[146] As Mill comes to rely on this tendency, he feels less need "to enforce by precept," or at any rate by his own "example," the "necessity of a philosophy."[147] Instead of having to specify where and how some final settlement will be reached, the liberal is able to accept, for the remainder of his life, an autobiography which is a more complacent process of adjustment than his crisis, transformation, transition, and traditional philosophy had been.

Notes

1. See vol. 1, p. 53.

2. "Bentham," *Mill's Essays on Literature and Society,* ed. J. B. Schneewind (New York, Collier Books, 1965), pp. 240–41; "Coleridge," *Mill's Essays on Literature and Society,* pp. 290, 292. See vol. 1, p. 117.

3. See p. 335, this vol.

4. "Coleridge," pp. 292–93.

5. See p. 364, this vol.

6. See pp. 372–73, this vol.

7. See p. 379, this vol.

8. See p. 324, this vol.

9. See pp. 327–29, this vol.

10. See p. 364, this vol. For the demonstration that "virtue still exists" as a classical typological procedure, see p. 67, this vol., and accompanying n. 31.

11. See chap. 7, nn. 23, 28, 65, for the individual as a *figura* (τύπος).

12. See p. 329, this vol.

13. See p. 365, this vol.

14. Cf. n. 58, below.

15. For this effort to catch up, see pp. 362, 411, this vol., and n. 94, below.

16. "Coleridge," p. 293; italics added. Further scope is given to the antithesis by Mill's explaining that Bentham missed "the truth which is in the traditional opinions, and Coleridge that which is out of them" (p. 292).

17. "Boswell's Life of Johnson," *Critical and Miscellaneous Essays,* 4 vols. (Boston: Brown and Taggard, 1861), 3:130, 142–43. Although Johnson and Hume as half-men must be combined, "both realized the highest task of Manhood, that of living like men" (p. 143). Thus they played the same dual role of representing both their time and universal human nature that an individual can play in Mill.

18. See p. 68, this vol, and accompanying n. 35, where I anticipated Hume's own use of Sallust's confrontation. Carlyle's direct debt to Sallust seems probable inasmuch as he identifies both Johnson and Hume "by principle and habit" as "Stoics" (p. 143).

19. I am not denying that Mill can also be assigned a role as a representative of universal human nature: "The truest word about Mill has been spoken . . . by the most loved of all his disciples. 'Respect for him,' says Lord Morley, 'became an element of men's own self-respect.' No one, on any final estimate, can doubt that Mill, as no other figure of his time, raised the moral stature of his generation" (H. J. Laski, in his preface to Mill's *Autobiography* London: Oxford University Press, 1924, p. xx).

20. *Mill On Bentham and Coleridge* (London: Chatto & Windus, 1959), pp. 1, 5. Leavis' introduction begins: "John Stuart Mill's essays on Bentham and Coleridge, may, I suppose, properly be described as classical. Yet are they, for the literary students at any rate, in real and active recognition classical?" I am hinting that they might be recognized to be "classical" in the stronger sense that confronting "great opposing types of mind" (see n. 21, below) was an ancient procedure. We have already encountered other instances of Mill's use of this typological procedure. "The Two Kinds of Poetry" opens with the announcement, "*Nascitur poëta* is a maxim of classical antiquity." The traditional contrast between natural and artificial poetry then becomes "a parallel between the two English authors of our own day, who have produced the greatest quantity of true and enduring poetry, Wordsworth and Shelley." Mill explains, "The one might be cited as the type, the exemplar, of what the poetry of culture may accomplish, the other is perhaps the most striking example ever known of the poetic temperament" (*Mill's Essays on Literature and Society,* pp. 117, 121). For the contrast between Wordsworth and Shelley, see chap. 17, n. 29. Remember too that Mill identifies Mrs. Taylor with Shelley (see p. 326, this vol.) and as "a living type of the most admirable kind of human being" (*The Early Draft of John Stuart Mill's Autobiography,* ed. Jack Stillinger

[Urbana: University of Illinois Press, 1961], p. 199), just as Mill was for her "the type of the possible elevation of humanity" (letter to W. J. Fox and Eliza Flower—I am citing from F. A. Hayek, *John Stuart Mill and Harriet Taylor* [Chicago: University of Chicago Press, 1951], p. 54). Narrowness is almost identically typified by Roebuck, Mill's father, Bentham, and by the youthful propagandist Mill himself had been (see chap. 17, nn. 18, 38), and Mill imposes almost the same typological procedure of confrontation on his relations to Carlyle, Coleridge, the Coleridgians, and Mrs. Taylor.

21. Leavis, p. 7. Leavis admits, "Even if they [Bentham and Coleridge] had had no great influence they would still have been the classical examples they are of two great opposing types of mind." He then goes on to cite Mill's interpretation in evidence, without realizing that he has introduced a distinction which is not Mill's. In Mill's view Bentham and Coleridge are great influences primarily *as* classical examples of two great opposing types of mind. Even the further sense in which they are historically influential is largely a matter of typological representation. Thus Mill finds "the name of Coleridge . . . likely to become symbolical of more important things, in proportion as the inward workings of the age manifest themselves more and more in outward facts." This symbolical role is not an influence in the strictly causal sense Leavis would seem to be distinguishing.

22. Leavis, pp. 8. 12.

23. *Ibid.,* p. 12. Since Leavis is concerned to educe significant organization as background for the Victorian novel, he ties Mill to George Eliot. So far as I am aware, Mill never mentions George Eliot's novels. Indeed if something is to be made of Mill in this connection, it should have been interesting to note that Mill's comments on novels are nearly all on French novels. With Leavis' great respect for Mill's "very distinguished mind," it is still more surprising that Leavis pays no attention to the way Mill attempted to do what Leavis himself is doing—write literary history with reference to the main currents of the nineteenth century. Mill makes this attempt in his review, "Writings of Alfred de Vigny," where he deals with the main currents of thought in nineteenth century France. In this review, moreover, Mill first worked out the opposition between the Conservative and the Liberal or Radical which he superimposes on Coleridge and Bentham. Although Mill singles this review out among his literary essays as "the one which contained the most thought" (*The Early Draft of Mill's Autobiography,* ed. Jack Stillinger [Urbana: The University of Illinois Press, 1961], p. 165) and published it in *Dissertations and Discussions,* it has never been republished in England. In order to refer to its literary history, Leavis would have had to overcome the "Cimmerian darkness still prevailing in England" (see p. 362, this vol.).

24. For the role of a *figura* in organizing classical history, see, e.g., vol. 1, p. 307.

25. *Carlyle and Mill* (New York: Columbia University Press, 1926), p. vii. "Two Representative Men" is the title of Neff's first chapter.

26. *An Agnostic's Apology* (London: Smith, Elder, 1893), pp. 168–69.

27. *Matthew Arnold and John Stuart Mill* (New York: Columbia University Press, 1964). "Representative Men" is the title of Alexander's first chapter.

28. On the one hand, Stephen has in effect lost confidence in Mill's typological framework: "Some persons, it is said, still cherish the pleasant illusion that to write a history of thought is not, on the face of it, a chimerical undertaking. Their opinion implies the assumption that all contemporary thought has certain common characteristics, and that the various prophets, inspired by the spirit of this or any other age, utter complementary rather than contradictory doctrines. . . . And yet . . . it is difficult to see how two of the most conspicuous teachers of modern Englishmen [Mill and Newman] are to be forced into neighboring compartments of the same logical framework" (p. 168; for this loss of confidence in the spirit of an age, see vol. 1, p. 108, and vol. 2, p. 425). But Alexander

neglects the lower level (where Mill was located by Stephen and Newman's doctrines found hopelessly contradictory) and revives the upper level, where he accepts the place Mill implicitly preempts for himself in relation to Bentham and Coleridge and other antagonisms: "Matthew Arnold and John Stuart Mill are the representative figures of the Victorian age because in them the conflicting forces of the age came closest to attaining a kind of equilibrium. In their attempts to reconcile the ancient and the modern, literature and science, above all culture and democracy, Arnold and Mill were trying to synthesize the partial and diverse elements of their age into a unified whole which would survive into the next." (p. 1).

29. See p. 366, this vol.

30. See vol. 1, pp. 58–60.

31. See n. 66, below, for the full citation.

32. See p. 377, this vol.

33. See p. 385, this vol.

34. See p. 373, this vol.

35. See chap. 17, n. 21.

36. *Autobiography* (New York: Columbia University Press, 1924), p. 110; see p. 371, this vol.; vol. 1, p. 21.

37. *Autobiography,* p. 120; italics added; see p. 281, this vol. The two senses in which Mill's assertion of continuity is false have already been explored: (1) Mill's youthful "philosophical radicalism" was a refusal to distinguish between the requirements of philosophical theory and political practice, whereas the mature Mill draws this distinction (see p. 282, this vol.); (2) the youthful Mill was "a reformer of the world" (see p. 290, this vol.), because his political radicalism implemented a philosophy of human nature, whereas the mature Mill is "as much as ever a radical and a democrat for Europe, and especially for England," because theories of social history enable him to distinguish between societies and between periods in their development.

38. For the full citation, see p. 373, this vol.

39. See pp. 372–84, this vol.

40. Michael St. John Packe (whose *Life of John Stuart Mill* [London: Secker and Warburg, 1954] is regarded as the definitive biography) is insensitive to the distinction of subject matter around which Mill's report of his crisis is organized, and therefore goes along with the report as if it were chronological. Thus having given an account of Mill's crisis, of his reading Wordsworth and withdrawal from the Debating Society, of his relation with the Coleridgians and his reading Carlyle, Packe makes a dramatic, if facetious, one sentence paragraph transition to Macaulay's attack: "From these dangerous migrations he [Mill] was *soon* diverted by a real emergency" (p. 86; italics added). But Mill did not leave the Debating Society until some time after Macaulay's attack. And there is considerable evidence that Mill's "migrations" did not become particularly "dangerous" in 1829 or perhaps even in 1830 (see n. 115, below).

41. *Autobiography,* p. 114; see vol. 1, p. 22. The displacement is perhaps alluded to in a general way in the first of the three sentences intervening between ". . . outward assertion of results" and the next paragraph, which recalls Macaulay's attack: "I found the fabric of my old and taught opinions giving way in many fresh places, and I never allowed it to fall to pieces, but was incessantly occupied in weaving it anew. I never, in the course of my transition, was content to remain, for ever so short a time, confused and unsettled. When I had taken in any new idea, I could not rest till I had adjusted its relation to my old opinions, and ascertained exactly how far its effect ought to extend in

modifying or superseding them" (p. 110). Impressed by such incessant intellectual responsibility, we are pushing behind these generalizations to the topological problem of the relations between the different "places" where the old fabric gave way, and attempting to discover how exactly these relations were adjusted as Mill wove the fabric anew.

42. A specific illustration of this displacement is the fact that there is no mention of the publication in 1829 of James Mill's major work, *The Analysis of the Mind* (see chap. 18, n. 71), although this was "the great event" of the year (Alexander Bain, *James Mill* [London: Longmans, Green, 1882], p. 330), especially, one must add, from the point of view of utilitarian psychology.

43. See chap. 17, nn. 21, 38. The account Mill has just given of Roebuck, Maurice, and Sterling is ethological, and generalized in Roebuck's case into rudimentary political etholology: "Like most Englishment . . . he found his feelings stand very much in his way. . . . And, in truth, the English character, and English social circumstances, make it so seldom possible to derive happiness from the exercise of the sympathies" (*Autobiography,* p. 106). Thus ethological material helps paper over the gap in the *Autobiography* between Mill's report of his misgivings over his father's psychological theory and his report of his own eventual resort, after Macaulay's attack, to socio-historical theory. Compare the way ethology, in the program proposed by the *Logic,* is to bridge the gap between psychological theory and socio-historical theory.

44. See p. 371, this vol.

45. *Autobiography,* p. 103.

46. See p. 373, this vol. Novelty was already a criterion for Mill's self-transformation as a result of his adoption of the Coleridgian conception of the creative imagination (see p. 382, this vol.).

47. See p. 386, this vol.

48. See p. 385, this vol.

49. *Autobiography,* p. 121.

50. See p. 372, this vol.

51. *Autobiography,* pp. 44–45.

52. The alliance is illustrated by Mill's going on in the next paragraph to report how his first reading Bentham, "as interpreted to the Continent . . . by Dumont, in the Traité de Législation . . . was one of the turning points in my mental history" (see p. 151, this vol.).

53. Thomas Macaulay, *Critical and Miscellaneous Essays,* 5 vols. (Philadelphia: Carey, 1844), 5:362. See my vol. 1, pp. 21–22.

54. *Autobiography,* p. 120. See vol. 1, p. 22.

55. "A Few Observations on the French Revolution," *Dissertations and Discussions,* 3 vols. (London: Longmans, Green, Reader, and Dyer, 1867), 1:56.

56. The historical frame of mind of the July revolutionists Mill describes as "a reaction against the premises rather than against the conclusions" of the revolutionists of 1789 ("Armand Carrel," *Dissertations and Discussions,* 1:234). Thus Mill attributes to the July revolutionists the same "change" in "premises" that he credits to himself, along with the same continuity in political conclusions (see p. 406, this vol.).

57. Cf. the Saint-Simonian pronouncement: 'Messieurs, nous sommes en révolution; la révolution francaise dure encore, car son but n'est pas atteint" (*Le Globe,* July 14, 1831).

58. "Writings of Alfred de Vigny," p. 209. The Revolution of 1830 was the manifestation in "outward facts" of "the inward workings of the age" (see pp. 399–400, this vol.). The "utmost enthusiasm" with which Mill "went at once to Paris" and returned to politics and journalism was his being caught up in the momentum of this movement outward from within: "A few months before the first of these papers was written [the first of the six articles composing "The Spirit of the Age" appeared January 9, 1831, so "a few months before" is presumably intended to take us back to the July Revolution], it would have seemed a paradox to assert that the present era is one of moral and social transition [this assertion is the theme of "The Spirit of the Age"]. The same proposition now seems almost the tritest of truisms. The revolution which had already taken place in the human mind, is rapidly shaping external things to its own form and proportions" ("The Spirit of the Age," p. 78). Mill's being caught up is his recognition of a correlation between the revolution which had already begun to take place in his own mind, and the Revolution of 1830, historically interpreted. His recognition of this correlation involves at a higher level his equating "the spirit of the age" with "the whole spirit of the new historical school" (see chap. 18, n. 16). Thus Mill begins "The Spirit of the Age" by noting the novelty of the "expression" itself, inasmuch as the "idea of comparing one's own age with former ages, or with our notion of those which are yet to come . . . never before was itself the dominant idea of any age (see vol. 1, p. 104, where I show that this comparative procedure is the crux of the historical approach as Mill and Comte conceive it).

59. See p. 376, this vol.

60. "The Spirit of the Age," p. 29.

61. For the conviction of the 1820's, "Il faut être de son temps," see the article with this title by George Boas, *Journal of Aesthetics,* 1 (1941): 52–56.

62. This relocation brings with it a reorientation. Mill may be "as much as ever a radical and democrat" in the sense that he may now be looking forward to the same political changes as he did before he discovered, at the moment of his crisis, that he was no longer "looking forward" to "changes in institutions and opinions." But his "looking forward" during the period of his "Youthful Propagandism" was fitted to the structure of utilitarian psychology, where the individual is oriented towards the future consequences of his actions (see p. 243, this vol., and accompanying n. 36). His looking forward" is now fitted to the structure of the Saint-Simonian theory of history where the individual is oriented, "One Stage Onward," toward the next period of history, when the "outward facts" will manifest more fully present "inward workings."

63. *Autobiography,* p. 121.

64. *Autobiography,* p. 122.

65. Letter of February 9, 1830, to Gustave d'Eichthal (*Collected Works* [Toronto: University of Toronto Press, 1963], 12:48), who was contemplating converting England to Saint-Simonianism.

66. The relevance of the Saint-Simonian theory of history for Mill's renewed enthusiasm for political changes is concealed in the final version of the *Autobiography* where the "Logic of the Moral Sciences" is anticipated as the outcome of Macaulay's attack and as presiding not only over Mill's break with his father's political theory but also over his reception of historicist political theory: "A foundation was thus laid in my thoughts for the principal chapters of what I afterwards published on the Logic of the Moral Sciences; and my new position in respect to my old political creed, now became perfectly definite. If I am asked, what system of political philosophy I substituted for that which, as a philosophy, I had abandoned, I answer, no system: only a conviction that the true system was something much more complex and many-sided than I had previously had any idea of, and that its office was to supply, not a set of model institu-

tions, but principles from which institutions suitable to any given circumstances might be deduced. The influences of European, that is to say, Continental, thought, and especially those of the reaction of the nineteenth century against the eighteenth, were now streaming in upon me" (p. 113; for the continuation, see p. 360, this vol.) This version of Mill's "mental history" we followed out in our preliminary interpretation of Mill in chap. 3. But having since discovered that even "the true system" of the *Logic* would compose a developmental structure (see p. 341, this vol.), we are going behind this version and sorting out "the successive phases of a mind which was always pressing forward" (*Early Draft,* p. 35). In the original version of the early draft, Mill arranges these phases rather differently: "A foundation was thus laid in my thoughts for the principal chapters of what I afterwards published on the "Logic of the Moral Sciences"; & my position in respect to my old political creed was now to my own mind quite cleared up. I did not at this time push my logical speculations any further. This was not the only modification which was taking place in my old opinions in the political department of things. The early writings of the St. Simonian school, with which I had now become acquainted, were gradually opening my eyes to the very limited & temporary value of the old political economy, which assumes individual hereditary property as a necessary fact . . ." (p. 136). The original second sentence here would cut short the relevance of the *Logic,* which is asserted in the second sentence that replaces it by the reference to "the true system." In this original version Mill next goes on to deal with Saint-Simonian socialism, but then checks himself in two deleted sentences: "This however is anticipating; for at the time of which I am now writing the St. Simonians had not yet developed the practical parts of their system. The effect they had on me at this time was solely by their *philosophy of history*" (p. 140; italics added). "The Spirit of the Age" would seem evidence that "the effect" the Saint-Simonian philosophy of history had on Mill "at this time" was not confined, within the context of the *Logic,* to determining historically what the "given circumstances were," so that history would be "kept in second place" (see vol. 1, p. 60). Rather, history took first place in that the "principles" which had previously been psychological "premises" became historical (see p. 000, this vol.). In other words, Mill seems to have originally adopted the Saint-Simonian philosophy of history as a context replacing his old utilitarian philosophy of human nature, before he took the further step of attempting to reconcile the two contexts within the more comprehensive context of his *Logic.* For a listing of the "successive phases" through which Mill's mind seems to have "pressed forward" here, see, n. 140, below.

67. I am citing Mill's "Comparison of the Tendencies of the French and English Intellect" (*Monthly Repository,* 1833) from Richard Pankhurst, *The Saint-Simonians Mill and Carlyle* (London: Sidgwick & Jackson, 1957), pp. 74–75. English distrust of this ascent to a "more elevated terrain" is perhaps illustrated by the orthodox utilitarian reaction in the *Westminster Review* (32 [April, 1832]: 280–81) to the *Doctrine de Saint-Simon.* The reviewer compares this doctrine to "a plan for cleaving the air with artificial wings" or for an "air-balloon," pointing out that "no man should be blamed abstractedly, for wanting to escape in an air-balloon, but that attachment to the air-balloon distracts him from combining in more feasible operations"—e.g., the passage of the Reform Bill.

68. To raise political discussion to this theoretical level is for the Saint-Simonian to arrive at the *"état organique,* où tous les faits de l'activité humaine sont classes, prévus, ordonnés par une théorie générale" (*Doctrine de Saint-Simon, Exposition, Première année, 1829,* ed. C. Bouglé and Elie Halévy [Paris: Rivière, 1924], p. 127). Compare the citations illustrating Comte's conception of the organic relation between an organic theory and an organic society (chap. 3, n. 4).

69. See p. 381, this vol.

70. See p. 379, this vol.

71. *Autobiography,* p. 115.

72. When Mill resumes his thinking about political changes, he will draw a distinction of level similar to the distinction of level in Coleridge's description of the operations of the poet's mind (see p. 386, this vol.). Consider, for example, Mill's comment on recruitment for the American government: "In a settled state of things, the commanding intellects will always prefer to govern mankind from their closets, by means of literature and science (compare the role of Bentham and Coleridge as "closet-students" [see p. 399, this vol.]), leaving the mechanical details of government to mechanical minds. In national emergencies, which call out the men of first-rate talents, such men always step into their proper place" (review of first volume of *Democracy in America,* reprinted as an introduction to the volume [New York: Schocken Books, 1961], pp. xxxiv–xxxv). The mechanical level is similarly the level occupied by England (as compared perhaps with the more elevated terrain preempted by the organic thinkers of France): "The celebrity of England, in the present day, rests upon her docks, her canals, her railroads. In intellect she is distinguished . . . for doing all those things which are best done where man most resembles a machine, with the precision of machines" ("Professor Sedgwick's Discourse," *Dissertations and Discussions,* 1:96). Compare Mill's contempt for the railroad mania: "Politics are for the present very much out of vogue: nor do I know what is *in* vogue, except railroads" (letter of November 25, 1833, to Thomas Carlyle, *Collected Works,* 12:193). For this period of disillusionment, see n. 101, below.

73. *Autobiography,* p. 115. In chap. 3 I was focusing on the structure of Mill's "true system" in the *Logic,* and therefore stressed Mill's later debt to Comte (see also chap. 1, n. 3). But with respect to Mill's conception of the stages in his own mental history, it was the Saint-Simonian distinction between "critical" and "organic" periods that was influential, not Comte's "law of three stages." Regarding the applicability of this law even to social history, Mill had considerable doubts, prompted by both his ethological pluralism and his classicism: "There is according to M. Comte only one law of the development of human civilisation . . . Is it not clear that these two nations, England & France, are examples of the *advance of civilisation* by two different roads. . . . It is melancholy to observe how a man like M. Comte has had all his view of history warped & distorted by the necessity of proving that civilisation has but one law, & that a law of progressive advancement; how it blinds him to all the merits of the Greeks & Romans (letter of October 8, 1829, to Gustave d'Eichthal, *Collected Works,* 12:37).

74. Richard Wollheim seems a little puzzled, in his review of *The Earlier Letters of John Stuart Mill* (*Collected Works,* vols. 12, 13) that "the one event of any significance in this period on which these new volumes throw no light is the famous mental crisis, 'the dry heavy dejection,' which Mill according to his own account passed through in the melancholy winter of 1826–7!" (*New Statesman,* 13 December, 1963, p. 878). But quite aside from the historical question I have raised regarding what actually happened that winter, there has to be taken into account not only Mill's psychological commitment to poetic solitude (see p. 297, this vol.) but also his psychological reluctance to communicate, as the original version of the early draft makes particularly clear: "I said *in my own mind* that my love of mankind & of excellence for their own sake, had worn itself out. I sought no relief by speaking to others of what I felt" (*Early Draft,* p. 118; italics added). In the later version the first phrase is replaced with the more conventional, "I became persuaded." The only reference, in fact, to Mill's mental crisis in these letters is in the letter of April 15, 1829, in which Mill reaches out to John Sterling, confessing: "Among the various states of mind, some of them extremely painful ones, through which I have passed during the last three years, something distantly approximating to misanthropy was *one*. . . . There is now no human being (with whom I can associate on terms of equality) who acknowledges a common object with me, or with whom I can cooperate even in any practical undertaking without the feeling, that I am only using a man whose purposes are different, as an instrument for the furtherance of

my own. *Idem sentire de republica,* was thought by one of the best men who ever lived to be the strongest bond of friendship: for *republica* I would read "all the great objects of life" (*Collected Works,* 12:30). The authority cited as one of the best men who ever lived is probably Cicero, though he never used precisely this phraseology. The citation suggests that Mill is still trying to draw "strength and animation" from "memorials of past nobleness and greatness" (see p. 304, this vol.).

75. *Autobiography,* p. 95.

76. Italics added. See p. 379, this vol.

77. *Autobiography,* p. 99.

78. Thus Mill refers, for example, to writing "two letters to Adolphe d'Eichthal during our *crise politique*" (letter of May 30, 1832, to Gustav d'Eichthal and Charles Duveyrier, *Collected Works,* 12: 109). More fundamental for the Saint-Simonians than any specific *crise politique* was "la crise qui nous agite depuis trois siècles" (*Doctrine de Saint-Simon,* p. 127). Cf. n. 129, below.

79. See p. 410, this vol. But see also chap. 18, n. 15.

80. See p. 382, this vol.; see also *Autobiography,* p. 96. Romantic poetry, as well as analysis, the Saint-Simonians relegated to a critical period: "Le cachet des époques *critiques,* c'est l'*egoïsme.* . . . Le poète n'est plus le chantre divin, placé en tête de la société pour servir d'interprète à l'homme, pour lui donner des lois, pour réprimer ses penchans rétrogrades, pour lui révéler les joies de l'avenir, et soutenir, exciter sa marche progressive: non, . . . il lui chante en vers élégiaques les charmes de la solitude, il s'abandonne au vague des rêveries, il lui peint le bonheur dans l'*isolement*" (*Doctrine de Saint-Simon,* p. 146). There is thus a third Saint-Simonian reorientation (besides Mill's being caught up historically in a forward-looking movement [see n. 62, above] and in a movement outward from within [see n. 58, above]) which might be distinguished as an ingredient in the "utmost enthusiasm" with which Mill "went at once to Paris." In the Saint-Simonian theory, "Le fait le plus général dans la marche des sociétés, celui qui renferme implicitement tous les autres, est le progrès de la conception MORALE par laquelle l'homme se sent une *destination sociale*" (*Doctrine de Saint-Simon,* p. 161). Mill's moral and poetic individualism will, however, recover from this social orientation, and he will eventually reject "the heresy of the poetical critics of the present day in France who hold that poetry is above all & preeminently a *social* thing" (letter of May 6, 1841, to Robert Barclay Fox, *Collected Works,* 13:473). For Mill's withdrawal in 1841, see n. 103, below.

81. *Autobiography,* p. 116. The Saint-Simonians identified "les époques critiques" as "momens de débats" (*Doctrine de Saint-Simon,* p. 195). In his letter of February 9, 1830, to d'Eichthal (cited p. 324, this vol., in connection with Mill's withdrawal from the Debating Society) Mill accepts the Saint-Simonian view that debate is characteristic of the spirit of a critical period: "I have a great dislike to controversy, and am persuaded that discussion, as discussion, seldom did any good. This may show you how completely I am cured of . . . *habitudes critiques.* . . . The *esprit critique* is almost the only one which prevails among the best and most instructed men of this country, . . . and it will be one of the objects of my philosophical and practical labours . . . to contribute to the formation of a better spirit." (*Collected Works,* 12:45).

82. See pp. 297–98, this vol. This antithesis Mill was prepared to salvage from his two essays on poetry: "The only valuable thing in these two is I think the distinction between poetry and oratory" (letter written probably late 1840 to George Henry Lewes, *Collected Works:* 13:449). See also chap. 16, n. 91.

83. "The Spirit of the Age," p. 78; see n. 52, above.

84. Thus the Saint-Simonians attacked "les dogmes d'une politique dissolvante . . .

dont la puissance purement négative ne saurait commander l'enthousiasme et le dévoûement" (*Doctrine de Saint-Simon,* p. 90). Mill sometimes uses the French term "dévoûement." His "enthusiasm" similarly retains some of the theoretical implications of Saint-Simonian usage.

85. See p. 375, this vol.

86. See p. 292, this vol.

87. In the context of the Saint-Simonian theory Mill could not return to journalism in the manner of the old *Westminister:* "Les publicistes de notre époque sont restés les échos des philosophes du xviiie siècle, sans s'apercevoir qu'ils avaient une mission INVERSE à remplir. Ils ont continué l'attaque avec la même chaleur que si l'ennemi avait été encore en présence, et ils s'épuisent à combattre un fantôme (*Doctrine de Saint-Simon,* p. 151).

88. *Autobiography,* p. 118. This qualification originally followed the deleted qualification, "This however is anticipating" (see n. 66, above), which was a franker admission that he was violating chronology. In the later version Mill goes on in the next sentence to a further qualification: "But these few selected points give a very insufficient idea of the quantity of thinking which I carried on respecting a host of subjects during these years of transition." This further qualification suggests the extent to which Mill's report of his transition is both selective and organized by subjects rather than merely chronologically. Mill's ensuing sampling of the subjects he has not yet mentioned can be regarded as the third part of the chapter (see p. 407, this vol.).

89. See p. 293, this vol. For the historical significance of journalism, in so far as it is tied in with Saint-Simonian periodization, see n. 131, below.

90. *Autobiography,* pp. 153, 174.

91. *Ibid.,* p. 141; see chap. 18, n. 10.

92. See pp. 256, 335, this vol. In his letter of April 27, 1840, to Macvey Napier (the editor of the *Edinburgh Review*) in which Mill agrees to do the Tocqueville review, the opposition of the utilitarian towards the temporizing of the *Edinburg* (see pp. 335–36, this vol.) has disappeared: "I am myself under an impression that there is very little of what I should now be inclined to say to the public in a review, which would be at all in contradiction to the established character & purposes of the Edinburgh" (*Collected Works,* 13:431). In his letter of September 21, 1840, to Macvey Napier Mill admits, "My adhesion to the Edinburgh is in a certain sense political as well as literary" (*Collected Works,* 13, 445).

93. This periodization is also respected by Mill's *Dissertations and Discussions,* as Mill implies in the final sentence of chap. 6 of the *Autobiography:* "I inaugurated myself as a contributor to the Edinburgh, by the article on that work [*Democracy in America*], which heads the second volume of the 'Dissertations'" (p. 154). Chapter 7 ("General View of the Remainder of My Life") then begins, "From this time, what is worth relating of my life will come into a very small compass; for I have no further mental changes to tell of, but only, as I hope, a continued mental progress" (p. 155). Mill then goes on to explain how "the first use I made of the leisure which I gained by disconnecting myself from the Review, was to finish the Logic."

The early draft of the *Autobiography* is somewhat differently organized. It is broken into two parts. Part I originally ended with Mill's launching what became the *London and Westminster Review:* "From this time to 1840, first in association with Molesworth, afterwards by myself, I was the conductor of a political review. But this new phasis in my literary existence belongs to a different period in my personal history, for which all that preceded was of no value except as a preparation—that in which I enjoyed the friendship & was under the ennobling influence of one to whom I owe all that is best, either in me or in what I have written, & compared with whom I am in myself scarcely worthy of a passing thought" (*Early Draft,* p. 190). The *Logic* Mill originally assigned to "what may be termed the second period of my writings, reckoning the old Westminster Review period as the first" (*Early Draft,* p. 169); whereas "the 'Principles of Political Economy' & all subsequent writings belong to a third & different stage of my mental progress, which was essentially characterized by the predominating influence of my wife's intellect & character" (*Early Draft,* p. 169). In contrast with this original version, Mill's final version adopts a periodization by reference to his journalistic activity.

94. "The Spirit of the Age," p. 78. Observe that the survey Mill is promising is ethological. But the function of the survey is Saint-Simonian—to supply the historical consciousness of "what is the stage through which, in the progress of civilization, our country has next to pass, and to endeavor to facilitate the transition & render its safe & healthy" (letter of February 9, 1830, to Gustave d'Eichthal, *Collected Works,* 12:48).

95. *Examiner,* March 31, 1833, p. 201.

96. "The Spirit of the Age," p. 45. Cf. Mill's comment on Carrel, cited chap. 18, n. 16.

97. See p. 303, this vol. A "modern" is someone who cannot "get out of" his age; an *Antiquus* is someone who cannot "leave the Romans behind" (see vol. 1, p. 112); Mill becomes "a writer who attempts to look both ways" (see n. 73, above and p. 306 this vol.).

98. See p. 304, this vol.

99. See pp. 303–304, 386, this vol.

100. See p. 408, this vol.

101. Iris Mueller thinks that "Mill's disillusionment with the aftermath of the Revolution . . . may have heightened the interest he took in the theoretical schemes of the Saint-Simonians and Auguste Comte" (p. 47). Though this interest is illustrated by "The Spirit of the Age," the obvious effect of Mill's full disillusionment seems to have been his retreat from the modern world as an *Antiquus* and absorption in his poetic culture with Mrs. Taylor.

102. See p. 306, this vol.

103. J. H. Burns identifies "the first half of the decade after 1840" as a "period of withdrawal for Mill" ("J. S. Mill and Democracy, 1829–61," *Political Studies,* 5 [1957]: 281). In his letter of September 9, 1842, to Robert Barclay Fox, Mill writes: "I have scarcely been thinking at all except on . . . Logic & the Romans. As for politics I have almost given up thinking on the subject. Passing events suggest no thoughts but what they have been suggesting for many years past" (*Collected Works,* 13:543–44).

104. In his letter of February 29, 1848, to Henry S. Chapman, Mill recites "the extraordinary events of the last week at Paris, a second 'three days' ending in the proclamation of a French Republic." He exclaims: "I am hardly yet out of breath from reading and thinking about it. Nothing can possibly exceed the importance of it to the world or the immensity of the interests which are at stake on its success" (*Collected Works,* 13:731). In his letter of May 28, 1849, to Chapman, he proclaims that "the whole problem of modern society . . . will be worked out, as I have long thought it would, in France and nowhere else" (I am citing from Iris Mueller, p. 175). Compare Auguste Comte's location of "la France comme le siège necessaire de la principale élaboration sociale (*Cours de philosophie positive,* 4th ed., 6 vols. [Paris: J.-B. Baillière et Fils, 1877], 6:529).

105. See "Vindication of the French Revolution of February 1848, in reply to Lord Brougham and Others," *Dissertations and Discussions,* 2:335–410.

106. See chap. 18, n. 76.

107. Mill's earliest use of this conception is with reference to social history: "We must

leave to history to unfold the gradual rise of the trading and manufacturing classes, the gradual emancipation of the agricultural, the tumults and *bouleversements* which accompanied these changes in their course" ("Civilization," *Mill's Essays on Literature and Society,* p. 151).

108. See p. 304, this vol.

109. See vol. 1, pp. 197, 201.

110. *Dissertations and Discussions,* Preface.

111. *Ibid.* Mill is capable of regarding an article, even when he has just completed it, as belonging to a stage in his mental progress (see chap. 18, n. 10).

112. See p. 366, this vol. Mill's distinction between a mind which is "progressive" and a mind whose "opinions" merely "keep up with the changing facts" is both psychological and historical in its implications. We have already seen (p. 334, this vol.) the psychological relevance Mill attributes to the individual's "mode of thought" which emerges, at some remove from his "outward circumstances," out of his "internal culture" and "self-questioning." But Mill also remains committed historically to the conviction that mental progress is incumbent on the individual, even though he does not remain committed to the conviction that social progress necessarily involves progress in the sense of "improvement" (see n. 73, above, and chap. 4, n. 27).

113. See vol. 1, p. 32, vol. 2, p. 307.

114. See p. 341, this vol.

115. Consider Iris Mueller's drastic correction of Mill's chronology: "It would seem from the account in the *Autobiography* that he learned little that was new to him from the upheavals of 1830 and 1848, and that the ideas of such French thinkers as the Saint-Simonians, Comte, and de Tocqueville . . . had been judged by him prior to 1830. That such was the case is more than doubtful. . . . The enthusiasm with which Mill rushed to France in August, 1830, was not precipitated by his conviction that these new un-Benthamite impressions were about to be realized. . . . From other sources it appears that if Mill had thought at all about the ideas of Coleridge and of the Saint-Simonians before 1830, which he had, he nevertheless went to France expecting and hoping to see the *political implementation of English radical thought*" (*John Stuart Mill and French Thought* [Urbana: University of Illinois Press, 1956], pp. 17, 18; italics added). The Revolution had been precipitated on July 26 by an ordinance suppressing the liberty of the press, which Mill had fought for as a youthful propagandist (see p. 253, this vol.). Mill went to Paris with Roebuck early in August, and the attitudes expressed in the letters he wrote for the *Examiner* are largely indistinguishable from Roebuck's. For Mill's predating his break with Roebuck, see p. 325, this vol.

116. See p. 359, this vol.

117. See n. 41, above, for the full citation.

118. A context, in the sense I have used the term, is a structure of knowledge which determines a philosopher's relation to other philosophers, as predecessors or antagonists, as well as the location of the political in relation to "other studies" (see vol. 1, pp. 7, 24–26, 191). The historian of ideas recognizes that "ideas are the most migratory things in the world" (Arthur O. Lovejoy, "Reflections on the History of Ideas," *Journal of the History of Ideas* 1 [1940]: 3). And he encounters no topological problems in adjusting their relations because his discipline embodies the conviction that ideas can be treated in isolation. Their relations then become merely a matter to be determined by historical investigation.

119. See, for example, chap. 4, n. 58.

120. Leavis, Neff, and Alexander (see pp. 403–404, this vol.) may re-utilize the typological approach of Mill's essays on Bentham and Coleridge, in order to arrive on the threshold of the twentieth century. But what twentieth-century thinkers can be paired with the same philosophical confidence in their comprehensive representativeness that Mill displayed in selecting Bentham and Coleridge (see p. 402, this vol.)? It is true that we still frequently encounter references to Mill as the typical liberal, and I took advantage of some of these references in the introduction. But such references are not followed out as a reliable set of clues to the character of liberalism. Thus Minogue points out in *The Liberal Mind:* "In dealing with such a tradition of thought, we are dealing with an abstraction; there is no single person of whom it can be said he was a liberal pure and simple, though perhaps John Stuart Mill would be a guide to what such a person might be like" (see my Introduction, n. 14). But Minogue does not in fact employ Mill as a guide, and a type is not a mere "abstraction" for Mill.

121. I have been using the term "political philosophy" throughout in Mill's sense of systematic political philosophy. The fact that the term has been applied since Mill's time to other intellectual undertakings is not pertinent here, and an appraisal of these undertakings is no part of my effort to analyse the structure of Mill's thought. But it should not be supposed that my acceptance of Mill's usage betrays a predisposition on my part to favor systematic rather than piecemeal undertakings today (see p. 114, this vol.). Indeed the reader will have noticed how often I have been concerned to interpret apparently unsystematic stretches of the history of political thought, long before we reached Mill (see p. 284, this vol.). To be "suspected of having any general views" is to invite "distrust" (see p. 411, this vol.).

122. See *Doctrine de Saint-Simon,* p. 15, where this identification is repudiated. Compare Mill's usage, chap. 18, n. 5.

123. See pp. 416–17, this vol.

124. *Autobiography,* p. 115.

125. Letter of February 9, 1830, to Gustave d'Eichthal, *Collected Works,* 12:45; italics added.

126. See p. 413, this vol.

127. "On Liberty," (New York: Liberal Arts Press, 1956), pp. 3, 5; see vol. 1, p. 30.

128. See p. 413, this vol.

129. Mill had earlier adopted this Saint-Simonian periodization himself: "The political revolutions of the last three centuries were but a few outward manifestations of a moral revolution which dates from the great breaking loose of the human faculties commonly described as the 'revival of letters,' and of which the main instrument was the invention of printing" ("A Few Observations on the French Revolution," p. 57.)

130. "Coleridge," *Mill's Essays on Literature and Society,* p. 298: cf. *Autobiography,* p. 153.

131. The foreshortening is further illustrated by Mill's viewing journalism rather than simply printing as "the instrument" for the diffusion of knowledge. The "revolt" of his mind against utilitarianism thus takes the form of a revolt against journalism and the utilitarian philosophy of journalism, as I explained in chap. 16. And since utilitarianism was locked into opposition to traditionalism (see p. 234, this vol.), the Saint-Simonian distinction between organic and critical periods tends to take with Mill the form of a distinction between traditional and transitional periods.

132. *Autobiography,* p. 143.

133. The first time after his crisis that Mill's feelings were aroused was on reading Marm ntel's account of "his father's death" (*Autobiography,* p. 99; for a Freudian inter-

pretation, see Albert W. Levi, "The Mental Crisis of John Stuart Mill," *Psychoanalytic Review,* 32 [January 1945]: 86–101).

134. Cf. Mill's earlier characterization of his father: "In his personal qualities the Stoic predominated" (*Autobiography,* p. 33; see also chap. 16, n. 124).

135. See p. 378, this vol.

136. See pp. 368, 405, this vol.

137. See p. 421, this vol.

138. All interpreters of Mill recognize, of course, that the conception of self-development is crucial to his liberalism. Iris Mueller, for example, comments: "The standard by which he tried to justify personal freedom itself was its tendency to foster self-development. It was this process of growth, undefined and obscure in his writings, that Mill came to view as the absolute good and the absolute end of life" (*John Stuart Mill and French Thought,* p. 229). I am trying to show that in one of his writings, which reports Mill's own self-development, this process is not entirely undefined and obscure.

139. See vol. 1, p. 59.

140. Four successive adjustments seem distinguishable: (1) At the time Mill succumbed to Romantic theories, he was prepared to revise his father's *Analysis of the Mind*; (2) at the time he succumbed to Saint-Simonian theories, he discounted his father's *Analysis of the Mind* as belonging to a "critical period" in the history of the human mind (see nn. 66, 81, above); (3) at the time Mill wrote the *Logic* he presented it as psychologically neutral with respect to the differences between the *Analysis of the Mind* and the antagonistic philosophy of the mind; (4) at the time he republished the *Analysis of the Mind,* he regarded the *Logic* as no longer neutral but as identical in its aspirations with the *Analysis of the Mind* (see chap. 16, n. 18). In each instance of adjustment I have said "at the time," but there is a vacillation in Mill's periodization: the *Logic* is assigned to the second period in the early draft of the *Autobiography* and to the third period in the later version (see n. 93, above). Jack Stillinger has observed that "the later draft comes considerably closer than the earlier to being, in the passages describing him, a eulogy of his father" (*Early Draft,* p. 13). Stillinger conjectures an "access of charity," but I would add that the change may reflect Mill's further reaction against his excessive reaction against his father's philosophy of mind.

141. My interpretation of Mill's thought as a developmental structure might be further clarified by comparison with other interpretations besides Mueller's (see n. 137, above). My interpretation can be regarded as steering between the two extreme interpretations proposed by R. P. Anschutz: "For all his father's careful schooling there was never anybody less buttoned up against alien influences than Mill. Somewhere or other in his writings you can discern traces of every wind that blew in the early nineteenth century. On the other hand there was another strain in Mill which was perpetually at war with this. He was an inveterate systematizer and, search as he might, he never succeeded in finding a system which had anything like the appeal of the one he had been brought up in" (*The Philosophy of J. S. Mill* [Oxford: Clarendon Press, 1953], pp. 5–6). In chap. 17, I tried to rescue Mill from the first of these interpretations by examining the structure of adjustment which he imposes on his reception of influences from "other minds." This structure became historical when Mill discovered the place of the nineteenth century in the history of the human mind, and in chap. 18 I discerned traces of the influences on Mill of French historicism. In the present chapter I am suggesting that Mill's inveterate efforts at systematization, along lines in which he had been schooled by his father, failed in respects which can only be understood if we take into account the way the historicist system of the Saint-Simonians continued to exercise its appeal for Mill in a fashion illustrated by his own "mental history."

Because of the "Cimmerian darkness still prevailing in England" (see p. 362, this vol.), the interpretation has become well-established that whatever structure Mill's thought may exhibit is inherited from his father: "If he had been free from the jealous supervision of his father and the stricter members of the sect . . . , the revision of his philosophical principles might have been so thorough that he would have realized that 'higher unity' of Bentham and Coleridge to which he pointed as the complete philosophy. But, as it was, his method of incessantly weaving the new into the fabric of the old, and thus maintaining a semblance of continuity and consistency, made such a thorough revision impossible. The old groundwork remained, and the new elements appeared as *incongruous patches*. . . . His father's systematic training had in fact done its work more thoroughly than he was aware of (A. Seth Pringle-Pattison, *The Philosophical Radicals* [Edinburgh: William Blackwell, 1907], pp. 31, 32; italics added; cf. chap. 18, n. 76). Thus Pringle-Pattison, like Anschutz, has a double interpretation of Mill: "He must always remain one of the most interesting figures of the nineteenth century in the region of pure intellect, but the interest will be *more and more* that of a *transitional figure* in whose inconsistencies we can trace the gradual break-up of the robust and self-sufficient creed of his youth, and the sympathetic anticipation of larger truths" (*ibid.*, p. 4; italics added). This interpretation neglects the extent to which Mill himself utilized continental theories of history in legitimating his role as a transitional figure. But the prognostication ("more and more") has been fulfilled by the shift in the focus of interest, dislodging Mill from the region of pure intellect, so that "what makes Mill one of the most interesting figures of the nineteenth century" for a more recent interpreter "is that a number of the main strands of thought converge on him" (see p. 359, this vol.). It is this fulfillment of Pringle-Pattison's prognostication that I am associating with the emergence of the history of ideas.

142. The writer Mill is commenting on is Goethe whose "idol was symmetry" so that he could not accept "anything in outward objects or characters which was great & incomplete." Both this citation and the citation in the text are from Mill's letter of February 24, 1855 to Mrs. Mill (F. A. Hayek, *John Stuart Mill and Harriet Taylor,* p. 255). I have already discussed the sense in which Mill's "true system" is to remain incomplete (see p. 341, this vol.). The citations also indicate, I trust, that it is not my interpretation which is strained; I have been reproducing Mill's strenuous effort to weave incessantly his thought anew—his never resting when he had taken in any new idea, until he had adjusted its relation to his old opinions (see n. 41, above). But if Mill would display the strenuousness of a blacksmith or a ballet-dancer, he also looked forward (with the qualification not "just yet") to the outcome of modern effort—its eventually complete reduction of the material of human nature to classical order and harmony.

143. See p. 369, this vol.

144. See p. 341, this vol. and vol. 1, pp. 49–51. Of course Mill does not achieve this balance unaided: "My great readiness and eagerness to learn from everybody, and to make room in my opinions for every new acquisition by adjusting the old and the new to one another, might, but for her *steadying* influence, have *seduced* me into modifying my early opinions too much. She was in nothing more valuable to my mental development than by her just measure of the relative importance of different considerations, which often protected me from allowing to truths I had only recently learnt to see, a more important place in my thoughts than was properly their due" (*Autobiography,* p. 177; italics added). Through exercising this protective topological control, Harriet's "influence" became "the presiding principle" of Mill's "mental progress," which during his third period "went hand in hand with hers" (*ibid.*, pp. 133, 161). Like Mill's third period, Harriet herself was at a higher level and represented a more comprehensive synthesis than, e.g., Carlyle and his influence: "I never presumed to judge him, until he was interpreted to me by one greatly the superior of us both—who was more a poet than he, and more a thinker than I—whose own mind and nature included his, and infinitely

more" (*ibid.*, p. 124). Mill then did presume to judge Carlyle, and recognized that Carlyle's influence had seduced him into modifying his earlier opinions too much.

145. The force of the classical analogy is weakened not only by Mill's turning back but also by his looking forward to an order and harmony which are not achievable "just yet" (see n. 142, above). Contrast the Neoclassical structure of Hume's philosophy *within* which is achieved a balanced adjustment and reconciliation (see chap. 14, n. 31; chap. 15, n. 55). My employing an esthetic analogy to "outward objects" (see n. 142) is designed here as elsewhere to bring out the structure of a thinker's thought (cf. chap. 4, n. 60).

146. "Coleridge," p. 298. Compare Comte's formulation of this law, which assumes the process of adjustment is predictable: "La marche de la civilisation ne s'exécute pas, à proprement parler, suivant une ligne droite, mais selon une série d'oscillations, inégales et variables, . . . autour d'un mouvement moyen, qui tend toujours à prédominer, et dont l'exacte connaissance permet de régulariser d'avance la prépondérance naturelle, en diminuant ces oscillations et les tâtonnements plus ou moins funestes qui leur correspondent" (*Cours*, 4:292). Compare the way the history of civilization now "deviates less from a certain and preappointed track (p. 288, this vol.) and also the sympathetic way the "distance . . . was always diminishing" between Mill and Sterling (chap. 17, n. 23). "Coleridge" is not only the culmination of Mill's effort to derive "light from other minds" (see p. 332, this vol.) but it is also the end of Mill's second period of excessive reaction against Benthamism. As Mill became conscious during the third period of having reacted excessively, he must have also become conscious of his *oscillations* and *tâtonnements*. When at the outset of this study (vol. 1, p. 1) we viewed the liberal in his historical setting as "fumbling" with social history, we assumed that his *oscillations* and *tâtonnements* were just attempts to "keep up with the changing facts surrounding him" (see p. 421, this vol.). We now see that they also implement some conception of his own "mental progress" as "la marche de la civilization."

147. See p. 400, this vol.

Index